W9-AZG-036

VICTORIA AND THE VICTORIANS

VICTORIA AND THE VICTORIANS

HERBERT TINGSTEN

Translated and adapted by
David Grey and Eva Leckström Grey

London
GEORGE ALLEN & UNWIN LTD
RUSKIN HOUSE MUSEUM STREET

First published in 1972

ISBN 0 04 942086 0

Translated from the Swedish
Viktoria Och Viktorianerna

Printed in Great Britain
in Plantin type
by W & J Mackay Limited
Chatham

History is the essence of innumerable biographies.
Thomas Carlyle

Read no history: nothing but biography, for that is life without theory.
Benjamin Disraeli

History never repeats itself: historians repeat one another.
Arthur James Balfour

ACKNOWLEDGEMENTS

The author, translators and publishers would like to acknowledge the gracious permission of Her Majesty the Queen for allowing them to reprint extracts from the published writings of Queen Victoria which are still subject to copyright, namely: the Letters and Journals of Queen Victoria; *Leaves from a Journal*, 1856; *Leaves from a Journal of our Life in the Highlands; More Leaves from a Journal of our Life in the Highlands;* Letters between Queen Victoria and the Princess Royal, Crown Princess of Prussia, 1858–64.

They would also like to extend their sincere thanks to Prince Philip, Landgrave of Hesse, who is the owner of Queen Victoria's letters to the Empress Frederick, to the editor of the letters, Mr Roger Fulford, and to Evans Brothers Ltd., the publishers of *Dearest Child* and *Dearest Mama*, in which a selection of these letters is printed, for permission to quote extensive passages. Extracts from the letters of the Empress Frederick in reply to those of Queen Victoria, published in the two above-mentioned books, are republished here by gracious permission of Her Majesty the Queen, owner of the copyright. Thanks are also due to the editor and publishers of the two books for permission to quote extracts from those letters.

The author, translators and publishers would like to acknowledge the kind permission of the Beaconsfield Trustees and the National Trust to reproduce extracts from Disraeli's letters quoted in *The Young Disraeli* by B. R. Jerman, published by the Princeton University Press © 1960, and in *Disraeli* by Robert Blake, published by Messrs Eyre and Spottiswoode, as also to the authors and publishers of those two books for permission to do so. They would also like to express their gratitude to Sir Francis Sykes Bart for permitting them to quote extracts from the letters of Lady Henrietta Sykes, and to the Trustees of the British Museum for permission to quote from the letters of Benjamin Austin, and also to the respective authors and publishers for permission to quote from the books. They are also grateful to Sir John Murray K.C.V.O. for permitting them to quote from Monypenny and Buckle's *Life of Disraeli*, and to John Murray Ltd for permission to quote from Morley's *Life of Gladstone* and *Edward VII* by Sir Philip Magnus. They would like to thank Jonathan Cape Ltd for granting permission to quote extracts from Joanna Richardson's book *The Pre-eminent Victorian: a Study of Tennyson*, and Weidenfeld and Nicolson Ltd for permission to quote extracts from *Victoria R.I.* by Elizabeth Longford, *Lord Randolph Churchill* by J. R. Rhodes and *Jameson's Raid* by E. Pakenham.

The authors, translators and publishers are grateful to Macmillan and Co Ltd for permission to quote extracts from *Henry Ponsonby*, and from Rudyard Kipling's *Collected Works*, they would like to thank

Mrs George Bambridge for granting permission to quote from Kipling's poems 'White Man's Burden', 'The Absent Minded Beggar' and 'Loot', and the novel 'Stalky and Co'. Grateful thanks are also extended to the Clarendon Press, Oxford, for allowing the inclusion of 'The Latest Decalogue' by Arthur Hugh Clough.

The author, translators and publishers are grateful to all the authors, editors and publishers who have given permission to quote from their books, too numerous to acknowledge separately here. All such works, listed in the selected bibliography, are marked with an asterisk.

Every effort has been made to contact copyright owners of works cited, but should omissions be found, the publishers will be very pleased to rectify these at the earliest possible opportunity.

CONTENTS

ILLUSTRATIONS

For the use of these illustrations we are gratefully indebted to the following: The National Portrait Gallery (for No. 1); The Radio Times Hulton Picture Library (for Nos 2, 4, 5, 6, 7, 9, 12, 13, 14, 16, 17, 18, 26); The Mansell Collection (for Nos 3, 8, 10, 11, 15, 19, 20, 21, 22, 23, 24, 27).

TRANSLATOR'S NOTE

The original text of *Viktoria och viktorianerna* has undergone some adaptation in the course of translation into English: the adaptation has been made by the omission of certain comparisons intended for Swedish readers and drawn from Swedish history or literature; by the expansion of Parts I and III through the addition, with the author's approval, of background information to briefly summarized passages thought to be of interest in more detail to the English-speaking general reader; and, lastly, by the amplification of a number of quotations from the works or utterances of the statesmen and writers and men of action discussed in the various sections of the book. The wording of quoted passages, after translation, has been verified from the original sources. Footnotes indicating source references, usually placed at the foot of a page, have been omitted in favour of more generalized indications in the selected bibliography, in which all works from which quotations have been made are marked with an asterisk. The information contained in the author's original footnotes, few in number, has been incorporated in the text.

PART ONE

VICTORIA AND HER TIMES

I

VICTORIANISM

Who were the Victorians

'Victorianism' and 'The Victorian Age' are terms which are often intended to mean simply a span of time, June 1837 to January 1901, and in so describing the sixty-four years of Queen Victoria's reign one is apt to think of them in much the same way as one thinks of other great periods in history—the Augustan Age, for example, or the Elizabethan Age. There can be no doubt that the great significance of the term 'Victorianism' for historians lies in the extreme length of the Queen's reign, which was longer than that of any monarch of modern times, with the exception of the Emperor Franz-Josef of Austria (1848–1916). The term is significant, too, because during this period Great Britain took the lead in practically every field, notably in territorial expansion, technology, power as a nation, prosperity, political systems and poetry.

Nevertheless, 'Victorianism' is also taken to mean something quite different from a mere span of time. It is supposed to be a unity, an era defined to some degree by certain distinctive qualities common to ideas, outlook, customs and general culture. All Victorians are assumed to have possessed unmistakable characteristics, and terms like 'Victorian man' or 'the Victorian outlook' are frequently employed, so that in the course of time the Victorians have come to be regarded as a sort of race or nation, such as the Negroes for example, or the Swedes.

The validity of this concept, however, has not been upheld with any consistency. Statements about the typicalness of Victorian characteristics are often to be found virtually side by side with emphatic denials that any such uniformity existed—and it has even been claimed that the distinguishing peculiarity of Victorians was the noticeable dissimilarity of one to another.

The simplest argument against the usual concept of Victorianism as a time-span is that a period comprising sixty-four years and determined by factors as accidental as the accession and death of a queen could not possibly have given rise to any manifestation of ideological or psychological uniformity. Significative of this is the fact that many writers have maintained that Victorianism should never be strictly related to the actual span of Victoria's reign. G. M. Trevelyan emphasized that any study of the Victorians must go as far back as the close of the

Napoleonic Wars. G. M. Young, in his distinguished book *Victorian England: Portrait of an Age*, considered that the years 1845–60 were the true Victorian span, after which ideas and attitudes which could properly be called Victorian gradually died out. Walter E. Houghton, in an equally important treatise *The Victorian Frame of Mind*, believes that the years 1830–70 represented true Victorianism; yet he considers a statement made in 1896 to be equally 'Victorian', although in fact it was uttered so late as to fall outside the period he indicates. D. C. Somervell, in *English Thought in the Nineteenth Century*, mindful that the years between the death of Queen Victoria and the outbreak of World War I have been called 'the death-agony of the nineteenth century', thought they might equally well have been called 'the birth-pangs of the twentieth', but that in any case (at least for the purposes of his book) 'in general 1789–1901 may be taken as the nineteenth century . . .'. Neither Oscar Wilde (1854–1900), nor George Bernard Shaw (1856–1950) can properly be classed as Victorians, yet G. M. Trevelyan called Shaw 'the grand old Victorian'. Professor Kitson Clark regarded the years 1850–75 as 'the High Noon of Victorianism'. Sir Charles Petrie considered the Victorian Age to have begun only with the Crimean War and to have lasted right until World War I. It would be easy to add to this list of writers and their varying views, but it will suffice to say that the Victorian Age can be placed virtually anywhere between some twenty years before Queen Victoria's accession to the throne and several years after her death.

Another method which writers have used to reach the desired uniformity of character is to divide the Victorian Age into an early, a late and a middle period, and the question of when these began or ended has in turn become the subject of further controversy.

But let us assume the existence of Victorianism in the proper sense of the word, that is to say: a nucleus of ideas and circumstances which have given to some at least of the sixty-four years of Victoria's reign a uniquely distinctive character. How, then, can this essential quality be recognized?

A great many serious and intelligent works have been written, especially in recent years, about the Victorian era. Much research has gone into the attempt to arrive at some sort of reasonably acceptable generalization. But the difficulties are so great and the subject so vast that results have been only partially successful. Statistics which would cast light on such matters as, for example, church attendance, migration or prostitution, are not forthcoming. Records of what people read or thought are limited to a relatively small and scattered range of subjects; but the wealth of material within this range makes it essential to select with care and judgement.

As a rule one has to rely mainly or entirely on the ideas and opinions of well-known writers, preachers and statesmen; and for the purpose a number of eminent Victorians such as Carlyle, John Stuart Mill, Ruskin, Herbert Spencer and Tennyson, Wilberforce and Newman, Disraeli and Gladstone, have been pressed into service, on not entirely convincing grounds, as 'representative' interpreters of the Victorian way of life. It would seem that the social group which best represented the age was the middle class—however vague and elastic such a term may be, since it can include only about one third of the population. It is hard to imagine what thoughts, if any, were held generally by the masses, who either could not or did not read, were not given to letter-writing even when literate, and took no part in 'movements'. There are, in fact, great gaps in this field of research. No serious attempts have been made to study school books, collections of sermons, electioneering speeches or periodicals.

Writers working on studies of this nature have been only too eager to make some kind of discovery, and seeking (with biblically-inspired zeal), they have generally managed to find; it is a striking fact that even in the most reputable works one often finds generalizations based on, say, five or six examples which are assumed to be typical, while two or three contradictory examples are dismissed as exceptions. (As Professor Kitson Clark has indicated, even those remarkable sociological investigators J. L. and Barbara Hammond did not avoid this pitfall.) In works of this kind, explanations of cause and effect, definitions of concepts, all too easily lapse into vagueness and obscurity. Assertions are made that this or that way of thinking was typical of the middle class, or was conditioned by industrialization or the spread of democracy or by economic progress. There is mention of the 'Victorian compromise' between belief and doubt; of optimism and pessimism as impersonal forces of some kind; of religion as a drive, but also, in the form of exaggerated piety, as the external expression of subconscious motives (such as anxiety in the face of change, or the desire to be an arbiter of morality); of puritanism in its strict sense or as a cloak for vice. Marx and Freud are pressed into service and their ideas, watered-down and misapplied, help to underpin explanations and interpretations. Psycho-analysis in particular is made use of to turn conventional reasoning inside out, so that Victorian authoritarianism is interpreted as a manifestation of insecurity; Victorian prudery as evidence of powerful, though repressed, sexual impulses.

In addition to all this, writers who have tried to explain Victorianism, either in relation to a particular phase or to a specialized field, have often arrived at contradictory conclusions—due less to their use of different sources of information, it would seem, than to their personal beliefs. It is often possible to judge from a writer's statements, however objective in intention they may be, whether his political bias is conservative, liberal or socialist; whether he holds religious beliefs of some kind, or is an agnostic. It seems clear, however, even from the works of the most reputable of these writers, that not only were ideas and opinions constantly changing throughout Victoria's reign, but that even during the various phases of the period there was a vast conflict of such ideas and opinions.

In the face of this accumulation of interpretations and contradictory views, it would be tempting to topple down the card-castle and come to grips with the investigators, rather than join in the quest for the essence of Victorianism. Nevertheless, it does seem possible in certain instances to discover some sort of uniformity inherent in the period—at least in the works of the more eminent scholars who have addressed themselves to the problem. Their ideas, and the myths which have evolved, can therefore be regarded as acceptable current concepts of Victorianism. It is even justifiable to go a step further and consider these myths as an echo of what Max Weber called 'ideal types' of opinion and behaviour: that is, exaggerated but nevertheless essentially realistic manifestations of traits that were predominant throughout the various phases of the Victorian age. What follows will be limited to such facts, in an attempt to avoid sweeping generalizations and to stress the evolutionary process which gradually changed the English scene.

A detail of great interest, which unfortunately cannot be investigated properly owing to scanty and unreliable documentation, is the comparison of Victorian England with other countries—and even here writers have failed to agree. Some of them say that Victorianism had a lasting effect on all Christian nations of the West; others insist that it should be regarded as a specifically English phenomenon: no serious attempts have so far been made to prove the accuracy of either view.

Random reading on the subject nevertheless invites a few such comparisons. Conditions in America during the period were similar to those in England. Before the Civil War the southern states displayed, period for period, a more intensified version of English Victorianism, mainly in what concerned matters of religion, morality and the attitude to sex. Developments in Sweden during the Age of the Oskars (1844–1907) would seem to have run parallel with those in England under Queen Victoria.

No complete general history of ideas concerning Victorianism and the Victorians appears to exist, though numerous books have discussed one or other aspect of the subject. But there has been an undeniable change in the conventional English view of the Victorians. Lytton Strachey was the forerunner of a school which observed the age with a blend of condescension, irony and affection. Strachey's Victorians were at once ridiculous and touching in their innocence and sublime self-confidence.

But after Strachey reaction set in. Many people nowadays praise the stability and security of Victorian times and long for the return of similar conditions in much the same way as those who speak in romantic terms of 'the noble savage' and of the peace and stability to be found in genuine religious belief and in traditional order accepted by all. But it must be added that the general attitude to Victorianism, whether critical or sympathetic, is based not only on conflicting theories, but on contradictory opinions as to its true nature, so that the definition of what Victorianism really was springs from a series of myths. Strachey, for example, regarded the age he described as something in the nature of an absurd idyll. Others have seen in the conventional image of the period qualities which they look upon either with affection or extreme aversion. Still others have exposed or debunked the Victorians very differently from Strachey—unearthing secrets and peculiarities, either fascinating or distressing, from behind the façade.

The Path of Progress

Victorianism and the Victorians were discussed in a lengthy series of talks broadcast in 1948 by the BBC and published in the following year under the title of *Ideas and Beliefs of the Victorians.* The series of programmes, eighty-three in all, comprising talks, readings and a terminal discussion, was introduced by two of England's outstanding humanists, men old enough to have been in their young manhood while Queen Victoria still reigned. They were the historian G. M. Trevelyan and the philosopher and mathematician Bertrand Russell. Both of them, in their introductions, spoke in tones of obvious pleasure and pride, though with no trace of sentimentality, of the period they were attempting to describe. They regarded it as an age of progress, improvement and moral and intellectual evolution.

G. M. Trevelyan dwelt on the improvements and reforms which had reshaped England. He called the period 'The Age of Railways', for the spread of communications, more than anything else, was in his view the basic cause of all the other advances. The Crimean War and the various colonial wars were interludes which hardly affected the majority of the population. Political and social reforms had been brought about, admittedly amid great tension, but without barricades or bloodshed. England espoused such policies and causes as parliamentary government, franchise reform, free trade, freedom of the press, slavery abolition, trade unions and social reforms; she stood for rapidly increasing wealth which, though all too unevenly distributed, nevertheless led to a considerable increase in the wages of the working man; she stood, too, for an empire which prided itself on the responsible government of her dominions colonized by whites; and for increasing intellectual activity, exemplified mainly by her great writers. G. M. Trevelyan ended his talk by referring to 'the very great advance in the sentiment and practice of humanity—to the old and weak, to the poor and unfortunate, to women and children . . .' and concluded by saying: 'Our English love of liberty, of justice and humanity, for which we have just fought two world wars, came to us direct from the Victorian Age, though the roots lie in centuries further back.'

It is not surprising that Professor Trevelyan should have expressed himself with such authority. He was a great historian, author of works on Garibaldi and the Italian liberation movement, on parliamentary tendencies in England under Queen Anne, on the social development of the English people; but his temperament disposed him to hail the triumph of good in every event, not because he saw the hand of God or of History in them, but because he was a man of exceptionally happy and harmonious disposition. Bertrand Russell, on the other hand—and surprisingly, for he was a radical and a critic of society—described the Victorian Age almost as emphatically as a change for the better. He laid greater stress than Trevelyan on social justice and the class struggle, but his comparison of the Victorian Age with our own was virtually a hymn of praise to 'the good old days'.

> 'The daily life of our own time is so filled with uncertainties and haunted by dread of disasters, that the period when Victoria was on the Throne has already acquired all the character of a golden age. . . . In such a world the perception of present evil was bearable, since men felt that they knew what to do about it, and that it would soon be lessened. . . . The Victorian Age tackled its own problems with vigour and success. . . . They found a country deeply divided against itself—"the two nations" as Disraeli called it—a country full of brutality, misery, and ignorance. At the end the country was closely integrated; all the worst horrors of early industrialism had been mitigated; universal compulsory education had been in operation for thirty years; and democracy had been achieved except for the exclusion of women. All this without any violent upheaval. It is a good record; I wish it could be hoped that the present age could have one as good.'

For Trevelyan and Russell, as well as for most other historians of the period, it was the Victorians' faith in their progress that was so remarkable—perhaps the most remarkable aspect of the age. This faith was not particularly English—the idea of progress, during the nineteenth century, began to permeate the whole of Western civilization. But it seems likely that in England, in several respects, this idea was of a somewhat different nature, being extremely practical, even tinged with pragmatism. For a few decades at least, on either side of the mid-century, belief in progress was particularly strong, spontaneous and unassailed by any doubts. It was tinged with the nationalistic and patriotic feeling that England was the standard-bearer of progress.

One way of looking at the Victorian idea of progress is to see it as the inevitable consequence of a particular concept of the course of history—a course which the Victorians believed they could survey, whatever they might regard as the key factor in the process: whether God, intellect, the *Zeitgeist*, or the labour force. Their systematic belief in progress, which sprang from waning religious conviction mingled with metaphysics, was by its nature directed towards the universal. They divided up the history of mankind into definite periods, which of necessity succeeded each other, and they then thought they were able to isolate the decisive factors of the process and thus predict the future. These dogmatic exponents of progress pictured it as a flight of stairs in which each historical period represented a further step upwards; and they believed themselves to all intents and purposes to be standing before the next step, a new period, which, seen from their own central vantage point, seemed to be the final stage of the ascent, a transition from the stairway to level ground, along which humanity would thenceforward continue its march. Fourier, Saint-Simon and Comte, Hegel and Marx, are typical system-builders of this kind.

Very little of such grandiose and impassioned thinking was evident in England, although it could be detected here and there in amateur philosophers like Buckle and Spencer. The English belief in progress, constantly expressed by statesmen, professional philosophers and economists, men of letters and journalists, was more one of general optimism—things had turned out well up to now and would continue to do so. This meant that everything was considered to be improving day by day and that the future would see the fulfilment of all hopes. It implied faith in the possibilities open to the man of action rather than in the realization of some plan, doctrine, or process, formulated through philosophical speculation. The soundness of this belief in progress was proved by a comparison of the present with the past and the realization of day to day achievements. No other proofs were demanded, and this one was felt to be overwhelming.

This faith in progress, at once vague, intense and confident—in a word, this optimism—was directly related to England's successes, reforms and improvements, in such a way as to appear more like faith in England than in mankind, or at least as a conviction that England was the pioneer and leader in the affairs of all mankind. Two such opinions, incontestably typical of early Victorians, were voiced on the one hand by Lord Macaulay, one of the most widely read historians and essayists of his time, and on the other by Lord Palmerston, England's most popular and influential statesman during the last two decades before his death in 1865. Macaulay, who said more or less the same thing over and over again in his speeches and essays, wrote in one of his *Critical and Historical Essays* (1835) that the English had become

> 'the greatest and most highly-civilized people that ever the world saw, have spread their dominion over every quarter of the globe . . . have created a maritime power which would annihilate in a quarter of an hour the navies of Tyre, Athens, Carthage, Venice and Genoa together, have carried the science of healing, the means of locomotion and correspondence, every mechanical art, every manufacture, every thing that promotes the convenience of life, to a perfection which our ancestors would have thought magical . . . the history of England is emphatically the history of progress'.

Palmerston expressed the typical early Victorian view during one of the most remarkable debates in English parliamentary history, which took place in June 1850. A Portuguese Jew, Don David Pacifico, formerly a resident of Gibraltar and claiming British citizenship on the strength of it, had been unsuccessful, in Athens, in getting compensation from the Greek government for loss of property. When Britain failed, through diplomatic channels, to obtain satisfaction from the Greeks, her Foreign Minister, Lord Palmerston, in spite of disputes with several of his colleagues, and with the Queen and the Prince Consort, succeeded in persuading the government to blockade Greece, in the face of protests from Russia and France and with the threat of a possible war. At the end of a four-day debate (24–28 June), Palmerston was successful in getting a majority vote in the Commons, although men like Peel, Disraeli, Gladstone and Cobden, who led various parties and factions, were among his opponents. His celebrated four-and-a-half-hour speech, on the second night of the debate, which went on into the small hours, was a combination of nationalism and liberalism. England, he argued, as the champion of liberty unrivalled among the nations of Europe, must use her authority to protect not only her interests but her citizens, wheresoever they might be. He wound up by saying:

> 'I therefore fearlessly challenge the verdict which this House, as representing a political, a commercial, a constitutional country, is to give on the question now brought before it; whether the principles on which the foreign policy of Her Majesty's Government has been conducted, and the sense of duty which has led us to think ourselves bound to afford protection to our fellow-subjects abroad, are proper and fitting guides for those who are charged with the government of England; and whether, as the Roman in days of old, held himself

free from indignity, when he could say *Civis Romanus Sum;* so also a British subject, in whatever land he may be, shall feel confident that the wakeful eye and the strong arm of England, will protect him against injustice and wrong.'

Palmerston's speech was chiefly a glorification of England:

'We have shown that liberty is compatible with order; that individual freedom is reconcilable with obedience to the law. We have shown the example of a nation, in which every class of society accepts with cheerfulness the lot which Providence has assigned to it; while at the same time every individual of each class is constantly striving to raise himself in the social scale—not by injustice and wrong, not by violence and illegality, but by persevering good conduct, and by the steady and energetic exertion of the moral and intellectual faculties with which his Creator has endowed him.'

Such presumption in the name of progress was for a long time justified, especially in matters of national importance. In respect of political power, civil liberties and material expansion, England held a unique position among the nations for several decades. It is hardly necessary in this context to give statistics on trade, industry or the development of communications, which can easily be found in any book of reference: they give an overwhelming impression of Great Britain's advancement and of progress in England.

Two well-known facts about the changing international situation are not always given due recognition and deserve to be stressed: they have to do with the population explosion and the expansion of trade and industry. The period between 1815 and 1914 was on the whole a peaceful one for Europe and exceptionally so for England, involved as she was in only a single European war, the Crimean War, and otherwise merely with various colonial expeditions which were for the most part rapid victories with relatively little bloodshed. War casualties were insignificant factors in checking the growth of population, nor could they be compared with disease as a source of sorrow, suffering and misfortune—a major colonial engagement was less costly in human lives and hardship than a cholera epidemic in Manchester.

France had for centuries been England's greatest adversary in Europe and even in Victoria's times was still called 'the French menace'. But in comparison with England, France was progressively weakening because her birth-rate had been falling for years, whereas in England it was not until 1870 that any appreciable drop in the birth-rate could be observed. At the beginning of the nineteenth century the population of Great Britain was less than half that of France (12 million in 1811), but by the end of Victoria's reign it was about equal (37 million in 1901), and in addition there was the growing British population of the nation's dominions.

Britain's leadership in trade and industry remained unchallenged until America, after the Civil War, and Germany following unification, became powerful rivals. During the last decades of the nineteenth century, when other nations were beginning to catch up with Britain, boastful pronouncements about her progress were toned down and imperious utterances like those of Macaulay and Palmerston, quoted earlier, became rare, even though national self-confidence was never greater than at this time—greater, for example, than it was to be after the First World War and even more so than after World War II.

The year 1851 saw the opening in London of the world's first international exhibition, 'The Great Exhibition of the Works of Industry of all Nations', an apotheosis of English industry and technology. It is in this year, according to Professor Asa Briggs, that the first use of the word 'Victorian' can be established. He traces the expression to a chapter, 'The Victorian Commonwealth', in *The Age and its Architects* (1850), by Edwin Paxton Hood, who said:

> 'The Victorian Commonwealth is the most wonderful picture on the face of the earth, perhaps on no other spot of ground has Heaven ever grouped so bright a constellation of its best mercies.'

Hood went on to quote the Bible: 'He hath not done so with any people' and added:

> 'It is not self-adulation, it is not the outpouring of patriotism, it is the simple statement of fact, and there is no reason why, for ages hence, as surely as in the ages past, England may not be the workshop of the world, the brain and thinker of the race, the mighty necessity of civilization.'

In the same year, too, George Richardson Porter wrote, in his preface to *The Progress of the Nation*, a periodical compilation of statistics:

> 'It must at all times be a matter of great interest and utility to ascertain the means by which any community has attained to eminence among nations. To inquire into the progress of circumstances which has given pre-eminence to one's own nation would almost seem to be a duty!'

The obvious answer, self-evident to Victorian writers, was that God or History had placed the English in a position of privilege because they alone were worthy of it. The ability and strength of character of the Englishman was the reason for his success. And so the idea behind the Victorian self-portrait became clear: past and present events in England were not just the result of a combination of fortunate coincidence, favourable conditions and matchless geographical position, but were the consequences of qualities inherent in and peculiar to the British. The models for the portrayal of the national character were power and progress.

As a nation the British were remarkable for their technical and administrative abilities, for their initiative and energy and their spirit of independence; and if proofs were wanted, their discoveries and inventions and the uses they put them to, their successes in private enterprise, navigation and colonization, were plain for all to see. By nature they were thorough, cautious, conservative in moderation; all this was the result of a stable system of government and social order, and although there was change, it was an unhurried, unsubversive revolution, brought about by wise and timely measures which averted violent class conflict and political upheaval. In the seventeenth century it was usual to regard Englishmen as thorough-going renovators; the Victorians were just the reverse—conservative to the verge of complacency.

Another characteristic of the British was their philanthropy, and in the Victorian age this was demonstrated at home in the political activities of the nobility and abroad in the development of the dominions peopled by white colonists, as well as in the government of subject races overseas.

Any portrait of the typical Victorian must include, as a final touch, a tendency to anti-intellectualism, and this might lead some people to regard the Victorians as mere Philistines. It would, however, be fairer to call them pragmatists with a sound respect for common sense. In contrast to the theories and speculations upon which other nations acted, the English used their own practical judgement and this, coupled with their adaptability and diplomacy, enabled them to deal empirically but effectively with contingencies as they arose.

Other more imaginative races might be shrewder and possess keener insight, but the English preferred to rely on fact; they were typified by the 'strong, silent Englishman', a being who was earnest, matter-of-fact, sparing of speech, scornful of theory, unemotional, manly and athletic. Thomas Carlyle, though a dour Scot and yet given to verbose rhetoric, was nevertheless true to type in his repeated praise of silence—'Silence is deep as Eternity; Speech is shallow as Time'—and in *Past and Present* (1843) he dismissed Latins as a lot of chattering apes. In his paradoxical saying that the English had achieved so much because of their unusual stupidity, Carlyle stood the typical figure of the Englishman on its head. On closer examination, however, this 'stupidity' turns out to be a combination of horse sense, a disinclination to speculate and an ability to make the best of any given situation. The English have always been able to 'muddle through'.

This national self-portrait is in many respects a speaking likeness of the successful middle-class businessman whose advance was so typical of early Victorianism. This sort of man was sensible, prudent and circumspect; he did business with an eye to quick returns, kept his own counsel and was not inclined to give himself airs. His ideal was to hoist himself up and to adapt himself to the class which had already 'arrived'. The portrayal of national character is often a mixture of what it appears to be and what it is thought it ought to be; and even the most clear-sighted of the great Victorians constantly mingled glowing pronouncements with their more analytical judgements. Very probably the Victorians' conventional idea of themselves was not without its influence on the British character, or at any rate had some influence on habits of speech and ways of thinking. It is not unusual even nowadays among the English to come across the belief that intuition or common sense are the best guides to action; and the view dies hard that theorizing or even the use of logic is rash and un-English.

Before discussing the trend and development of nationalistic ideas about progress, it would be as well to mention two problems and the way in which the Victorians handled them—since their solutions to these problems were continually put forward in their day as proof both of the progress and the superiority of the English.

The ideas of what is now called the old-liberal economy, embodied in the policy of *laissez-faire*, were generally prevalent when Queen Victoria came to the throne. The fact that people were free to produce and consume, to buy and sell (even labour), was supposed to result in maximum prosperity for all. This freedom according to Adam Smith, was an 'invisible hand' which would order everything for the best.

But the effect of these principles was limited by the State safeguarding of the *status quo* in what concerned the unequal distribution of wealth: the rich remained rich or got richer, the poor were still desperately poor. Another obstacle to the greatest happiness of the greatest number was the increasing difficulty of the trader or craftsman to find the best markets for his products or his skill. But the early Victorians ignored such inconvenient details and were blind to the inconsistency of an economic free-for-all accompanied by tariffs which openly favoured particular groups.

The theories of Malthus and Ricardo—who held, respectively, that overpopulation causes constantly increasing poverty, and that the so-called 'iron law' of wages inevitably forces these down to a bare subsistence level—strengthened the belief that the State should not meddle in the economy, but should merely act as a watch-dog.

Even before Victoria's day, such 'early-Victorian' opinions had come under fire from writers and thinkers who were later on to be given the name of 'socialists'. The theories of some of them—such as John

F. Bray, John Gray, William Thompson and Robert Owen—even anticipated those of Karl Marx. The arguments of the supporters of *laissez-faire* were also attacked, or at least the flaws in their arguments were pointed out, by thinkers having no political views, with Carlyle and Dickens in the lead.

But at the time when Victoria came to the throne hardly anything had been done to improve social conditions. The indigent poor were relegated to the workhouse, frightful barracks or 'bastilles' (as the poor-houses were called), where husbands and wives were separated and families broken up; there were no factory laws to regulate working hours, no sanitary conditions, nor was there any state aid for the destitute.

Historians of economics have differed as to whether industrialism increased or decreased the misery of the working classes; the growth of population has been advanced as proof that in the early 1800s the standard of living rose in spite of every adverse circumstance. But there was still a vast gulf between rich and poor and the majority of the working classes lived for the most part in deplorable conditions of want such as are found today only in a few undeveloped countries. It is also true to say that the distribution of wealth was, to put it mildly, unequal: there was a minority which owned almost everything, while the masses owned nothing.

To take a few examples: in the mid-nineteenth century the death-rate in English towns was two to three times higher among the working classes than among the rich. A new-born child in a Manchester working-class family could be expected to live to the age of seventeen, a child in a 'better class' family to thirty-eight. Corresponding figures for Liverpool were fifteen and thirty-five; and for the fashionable city of Bath, twenty-five and fifty-five. It must be emphasized that urbanization and industrialization were still limited at the time. In 1851 a bare fifty per cent of the combined population of England and Wales lived in the towns; by 1901, seventy-three per cent were town dwellers. In 1851, 1·8 million were employed in agriculture, 1·1 million were in domestic service, as opposed to just over a million in the various combined branches of the textile industry and 220,000 in coal-mining. In 1873, one-sixth of the nation's land was owned by some 400 families of the aristocracy; 1,288 middle-class landowners accounted for another quarter; while more than 700,000 smallholders owned little more than one-half per cent of the land.

Many people, both in England and abroad, believed that England was ripe for revolution. The French historian Charles Seignobos wrote somewhat contemptuously that with one revolt in Paris the French could achieve more than the English had done in decades of political struggle. But it came to be considered more and more to the credit of the English that they chose to be slow but sure. Revolutions might threaten, as they had done before the Reform Bill of 1832 and during the Chartist agitation and riots of the 1840s, but there had been no single instance of clashes with any great loss of life. The Factory Acts ensured shorter hours and improved conditions for industrial workers. Basic wages rose steadily. Socialism made little headway until as late as the end of Victoria's reign. England was entering into a period unprecedented in the nation's history: a combination of progress with stability; and this, moreover, was beginning to be taken for granted.

One can do little more than speculate on the reasons for this combination of circumstances. Two factors are frequently overlooked: the farmers were relatively united in their attitude, smallholders and farm labourers often voting with the landlords—for the hatred of landowners which swept France after 1789 would seem to have been almost unknown in England. For a long time there were fewer factory workers than the continual discussion about the early days of industrialism would seem to suggest. Timely and skilful political measures must also be taken into account: free trade was introduced before unrest reached a dangerous peak and basic wages rose fairly rapidly. Social improvements were carried out before conditions became any more unbearable for the poor. It may be, too, that in England religion served as a preventive of some kind against bitterness and hatred. Enfranchisement and representative government possibly had a similar effect. One is inclined to believe, especially in the light of later experience, that ideas of patriotism, loyalty, respect for authority and the upper classes, either separately or combined (T. H. Green called it 'the flunkeyism pervading English society') were deeply ingrained in those Englishmen—the vast majority—who were not eligible to be classed as 'the gentlemen of England'.

In spite of the country's extraordinary industrial development, it should be emphasized that even at the time of Queen Victoria's death England was still lagging behind in social reform. Her legislation in this respect was unquestionably inferior to Germany's. Campbell-Bannerman's Liberal government of 1905–8 prided itself on being in the vanguard of social reform, but it was really not until many years later, under the 1940 Labour government, that a point was reached where it was no longer true to say, as Disraeli had done, that 'the Privileged and the People formed Two Nations'.

Parliamentary and political developments went hand in hand during Victoria's reign. Civil rights, representative government and the parliamentary system had achieved general acceptance when the Queen came to the throne, but the country was still far from being a democracy. The distribution of power altered slowly, without serious upheaval, so that when the disfranchised in their bitter discontent demanded a voice in the government, there were some groups among the holders of power who were on their side. After the Reform Bill of 1832 one English male in twenty-four had the vote; after 1867, one in twelve; after 1884, one in seven—which meant that the majority of adult males could now vote. It must be stressed, however, that although these reforms brought about one great change after another in the composition of the Commons, the privileged classes continued to dominate and the old political parties—Whigs and Tories—still took it in turns to rule the country.

In 1865, out of 650 members of the House of Commons, 37 were lords (but not peers of the realm, therefore not entitled to sit in the House of Lords), including eldest sons of lords; 64 were younger sons and 15 were grandsons of lords; 71 were baronets (hereditary noblemen but not peers); 11 were eldest sons, 19 younger sons, and 8 grandsons of baronets; add to these a hundred members who were close relatives of noblemen. It can be seen from all this that roughly half the members of the House of Commons could be regarded as members of the upper class in the strictest meaning of the term. Twenty years later, in the Commons of 1885, composed of 670 members (calculated on a different basis of division), the seats were held by 78 landowners and rentiers, 58 who were retired army and navy officers, 154 members of the learned professions, mostly lawyers; and 186 active in business and industry, most of them in high positions. In its effect on the social composition of the Commons, democracy was advancing at a snail's pace.

Even in politics the Victorian Age could be said to have ended in a compromise. Universal manhood suffrage had not yet been achieved; women, of course, as elsewhere in Europe, were not even considered. The Lords continued to hold the lion's share of power and had become more solidly conservative, although numerous Liberal governments had obtained peerages mainly for their own outstanding party men. On 23 August 1881 Gladstone wrote to the Queen!

> '. . . it is remarkable that while the very large majority of the Peerages granted since 1846 . . . have been granted on the advice of Liberal Ministers, yet such is the influence of wealth and privileged station on the human mind, that the Liberal minority in the House of Lords cannot be said to have increased . . .'

Even on points like these it was left to the Liberals and 'labourites' of the early twentieth century to carry out the reforms necessary for complete democracy.

Because change in Victorian England was gradual, there was in English politics throughout the whole period a significant absence of any extremist movement which advocated a total transformation of the system of government. There were, of course, writers like Carlyle,

Ruskin, W. H. Mallock, or Rudyard Kipling, and others, whose glorification of power and force, coupled with a belief in the right of an *élite* to protect, control and dominate, instantly call to mind France's absolute monarchy and Prussia's Junker cult, as well as appearing to foreshadow Fascism and Nazism. There were also one or two lesser-known writers who advocated far-fetched socialist theories. But it was not only among politicians that successive reforms gained acceptance, they also made headway among the aristocracy, the middle class and the trade unions. Indeed, such changes were regarded as links in a process of organic development—once a reform became law it seldom, if ever, had to be repealed.

During the long years of Victoria's reign the English political *élite* of party leaders and their adherents seems to have presented a united front; the aristocracy retreated, lawyers and business men came more and more to the fore; representatives of the Free Churches mingled with leaders of the Anglican Church. Now and again some man from the working class managed to get a seat in the Commons, but it was 'the gentlemen of England'—in the somewhat vague meaning of that phrase—who were the prominent statesmen and cabinet ministers, and the parliaments of Gladstone and Salisbury could be regarded as the heirs of a continuity springing from the parliaments of Grey and Peel.

This situation had no counterpart in the Europe of the day, and it is hardly surprising that the Victorians felt that stability and an unbroken tradition were the essentials that guided their progress.

Religion and Belief

> 'It is not too much to say that, more than any other single factor, the Evangelical Movement in the Church of England transformed the whole character of English society and imparted to the Victorian Age that moral earnestness which was its distinguishing characteristic: a moral earnestness which was perhaps especially conspicuous in the Victorian agnostics of the 1880s who inherited it from the Evangelical tradition itself against which they were in rebellion. The high seriousness of the Victorians may be traced back to the publication in 1797 of Wilberforce's best-seller: *A Practical View of the Prevailing Religious System of Professed Christians in the Higher and Middle Classes in this Country contrasted with Real Christianity*.'

Canon Charles Smyth made this observation in the BBC symposium *Ideas and Beliefs of the Victorians* broadcast in 1948. Similar views, though none as forthright or extreme, have been expressed by a number of other writers. Professor Kitson Clark, in one of his 1962 Ford Lectures, published as *The Making of Victorian England*, said:

> 'In fact it might not be too extravagant to say of the nineteenth century that probably in no other century, except the seventeenth and perhaps the twelfth, did the claims of religion occupy so large a part in the nation's life, or did men, speaking in the name of religion, contrive to exercise so much power.'

Professor Clark said elsewhere in his lecture that the Victorian religious revival was one of the great dynamic forces in all sections of the community, and he singled out the Evangelical movement in the Church of England from the late eighteenth century onward, the Oxford Movement which was started a few decades later and the revival of Roman Catholicism, mainly personified by such outstanding converts as Cardinals Newman and Manning. Critical observers like the sociologists J. L. and Barbara Hammond have drawn attention to the conservative effects of Victorian piety and its opiate effect on the masses during the schisms of the 1830s and 1840s.

These opinions are far too sweeping to be accepted without question and are really hypotheses which cannot be proved one way or another. Were Victorians really as pious and serious-minded as people of twenty or fifty years earlier? If so, was this due to the influence of evangelism and the other revivalist movements already mentioned? How much did religion affect the Victorians' attitude to their political and social problems? Such matters have not been investigated: nobody, for example, seems to have examined collections of sermons, nor has any enquiry been made into the political activities of the clergy, though this would not have been difficult, since there was no lack of Victorian bishops sitting in the House of Lords.

The paucity of evidence notwithstanding, one or two facts are reasonably clear. Complete religious freedom was achieved during Victoria's reign. Laws which discriminated against Roman Catholics and sectarians such as Methodists and Baptists were nearly all abolished. At the same time, piety, often tinged with puritanism, was manifested as a matter of course in all social and political relations. Biographies of the period show that the majority of adherents to parties and movements considered themselves to be good Christians, although as a rule they had no clear notion of what they meant by this.

Professed unbelievers were practically non-existent among leading Victorian intellectuals and statesmen. It is typical that Thomas Huxley had to coin a word to avoid calling himself an atheist. 'I took thought', he said, 'and invented what I conceived to be the appropriate title of "agnostic".' The sermons preached by the clergy would seem to have been conventional stereotypes full of references to the worthlessness of life on earth and to the heavenly Utopia of the Beyond; while bishops who sat in the House of Lords were little more than appendages to the Conservative party. From the eighteenth century onwards, nevertheless, there had been a growing tendency among the clergy in Parliament to demand social improvements, and even to believe that this earth could indeed eventually be transformed into some sort of temporary heaven—a line of thinking which caused some of them to become crusaders in various radical movements, notably William Wilberforce in the fight to abolish slavery, and Charles Kingsley, the apostle of 'muscular Christianity', in his efforts for Christian Socialism and the improvement of the working classes. The Church of England and other religious bodies displayed considerable activity in their attempts to reach the ever-increasing working classes.

Recent studies, notably that of C. K. Inglis, *Churches and the Working Classes in Victorian England* (1963), reveal the state of decay in the Established Church at the beginning of the nineteenth century. The persistence of ancient abuses such as clerical absenteeism and the holding of livings in plurality was such that at this time (1827) almost half of the clergy drew stipends for which they performed no duties. The great majority of the working classes in the towns had no contact with any denomination; they rarely, if ever, went to church and were for the most part totally ignorant of the rudiments of the Christian faith. Later in the period the Anglican Church joined up with other denominations in an effort to bring religion to the people.

The church-going sector of the population, which included practically the whole of the landed gentry, belonged to the Established Church. This was more conservative than the Roman Catholic Church (with a membership swelled in the 1840s by the influx of half a million destitute Irish immigrants), and decidedly more so than the Free Churches, whose members often supported the Liberal party and sometimes belonged to its Radical wing.

Since interpreters of Victorianism are at variance in their opinions on Victorian religion and morality, it is difficult to reach any definite conclusions. Myth and fact are inextricably mingled, and any discussion of the subject must always bear this uncertainty in mind.

Now that Victorians and Victorianism are distant enough to be seen in more simplified perspective, many people have been drawn to the rosy legend of 'the good old days', a time when belief was steadfast and minds untroubled, for the Victorians would seem to have accepted institutions and ideas unquestioningly and without any misgivings—an attitude which embraced the Constitution, the Empire and Christendom alike. Contrasting the Victorians with people of the mid-twentieth century, Professor Basil Willey, in his *Nineteenth Century Studies*

(1949), expressed a somewhat far-fatched conception of this impulse to hark back to the happier times of an idealized past:

> 'In our own unpleasant century we are mostly displaced persons, and many feel tempted to take flight into the nineteenth as into a promised land, and settle there like illegal immigrants for the rest of their lives. In that distant mountain country, all that we now lack seems present in abundance; not only peace, prosperity, plenty and freedom, but faith, purpose and buoyancy.'

This panegyric, which turns a blind eye on nineteenth-century want and misery, would seem—having been written in 1949—to have been prompted by the discomforts and privations of post-war conditions, but its mood, especially with regard to faith and purpose, is fairly typical of many utterances on the subject.

Victorian official documents frequently display this sort of unquestioning acceptance of the established order and that serene conviction of living in the best of all possible worlds which Professor Willey and others have considered to be the hall-mark of the age. Yet opposition and tension were not absent in Victorian times and other writers have demonstrated, in the Victorians' own words, that precisely with regard to religious belief the Victorian age was an age beset by perplexity, uneasiness and doubt.

The 'ideal type' of the middle-class Victorian was both enterprising and successful. He believed in progress on earth, approved of the Ten Commandments and regarded heaven as a haven of rest after death. People who held such views were in all likelihood more numerous than they are today. They fitted easily into Max Weber's definition of the Christian-capitalistic society, according to which the successful business life of the capitalistic entrepreneur was the expression of a 'calling' to which he had been summoned by Providence, a predestination which was a sign of God's grace—or at least an intimation that successful business men were deserving of it. Yet, parallel with this belief, was the consciousness of a contradiction between Christian doctrine and the active, competitive pursuit of self-interest, the problem of serving both God and Mammon.

The well-adapted Victorian surmounted this difficulty by being a good business man all the week and going to church on Sundays, perhaps even assembling his family (and the servants) for Bible reading and evening prayers. But it is evident from statements of biographers and from the observations of great writers of the period, that many Victorians were aware of their duplicity and suffered from uneasy consciences. Dickens, Thackeray and Trollope have given satirical and bitter descriptions of the effort to have the best of both worlds; yet even these writers seem to veer between veneration of unrestricted private enterprise under a liberal economy and horror at the scoundrels who were its representatives.

The Latest Decalogue, Arthur Hugh Clough's sarcastic parody of the Ten Commandments, written in about 1850, is an apt illustration of how Victorians reconciled Christian piety with profitable business:

Thou shalt have one God only; who
Would be at the expense of two?
No graven images may be
Worshipped, except the currency:
Swear not at all; for, for thy curse
Thine enemy is none the worse:
At church on Sunday to attend
Will serve to keep the world thy friend:
Honour they parents; that is, all
From whom advancement may befall:
Thou shalt not kill; but needst not strive
Officiously to keep alive:
Do not adultery commit;
Advantage rarely comes of it:
Thou shalt not steal; an empty feat
When it's so lucrative to cheat:
Bear not false witness; let the lie
Have time on its own wings to fly:
Thou shalt not covet; but tradition
Approves all forms of competition.
The sum of all is, thou shalt love,
If any body, God above:
At any rate shall never labour
More than thyself to love thy neighbour.

It is said—and this is as true for Victorians as for people today—that religious belief brings happiness and gives a sense of assurance and peace such as no one who doubts or denies the existence of a God can ever attain. This was doubtless true of many Victorians; they lived contented lives according to the Christian code and were simultaneously pious, happy and righteous, but they were also self-righteous. Among the statesmen Gladstone stands out as typical of this attitude. It must be emphasized, however, that even though parallels can be found in other periods, there is overwhelming evidence that the examination of conscience was a perpetual thorn in the flesh of the deeply devout Victorian, who was a constant prey to self-reproach and doubt about his salvation.

Even children were subjected to this soul-searching. Victorian methods of bringing up the young—which demanded of even the smallest children constant self-sacrifice, self-denial and implicit obedience to strict rules of conduct, all under threat of hell-fire—must have been totally bewildering to a sensitive child. Charles Kingsley, in his novel *Alton Locke* (1850), described this terrifying world of Victorian childhood:

> 'Now and then, believing in obedience to my mother's assurances, and the solemn prayers of the ministers about me, that I was a child of hell, and a lost and miserable sinner, I used to have accesses of terror, and fancy that I should surely wake next morning in everlasting flames.'

John Addington Symonds, from listening to 'dismal sermons', developed by the age of seven 'a morbid sense of sin and screamed at night about imaginary acts of disobedience'. On visits to his maternal grandmother, a rigidly devout and irritable insomniac, he used to dread the nights spent in the vast, dark loneliness of the old lady's house, empty it seemed to him but for the maids upstairs and the cat and cockroaches below, when he would lie awake listening in terror to the deep, sonorous voice of his sleepless grandmother chanting in tones which started with a groan and rose to a quaver: 'Thus saith the Lord: Woe, woe to the ungodly'.

Pious Victorians instilled obedience and self-sacrifice into their children in ways that must seem to us heartless, if not savage. John Addington Symonds's biographer relates that he kept collections of all sorts of curiosities and was particularly attached to a stuffed kingfisher, which he even took to bed with him. One day, on a visit, his aunt met a small French boy who shared Symonds's interests. On her return home she harangued her nephew until she had compelled him to wrap up his treasured kingfisher and send it to the other boy, whom he did not know and had never even seen. Many years later Symonds still remembered the incident as one of the most painful of his entire life.

Augustus Hare related in his autobiography that when he was barely six his mother repeatedly made him do without some childish pleasure or part with treasured possessions so that he should learn to be unselfish.

> 'I was not six years old before my mother . . . began to follow a code of penance with regard to me which was worthy of the ascetics of the desert. Hitherto I had never been allowed anything but roast mutton and rice pudding for dinner. Now the most delicious puddings were talked of—*dilated* on. . . . At length they were put on the table before me and then, just as I was about to eat some of them they were snatched away, and I was told to get up and carry them off to some poor person in the village.'

Hare recalled that

> 'in the most literal sense, and in every other I was "brought up at the point of the rod". My dearest mother was so afraid of over-indulgence that she always went to the opposite extreme: and her constant habits of self-examination made her detect the slightest act of especial kindness into which she had been betrayed, and instantly determine not to repeat it.'

At four years old the child's playthings were all banished to the loft, 'and as I had no companions, I never recollect a game of any kind or ever having played at anything'. The boy made a couple of attempts to play with children of his own age, 'but the mere request was not only refused, but so punished that I never dared to express a wish to play with any child again'.

When he was 'naughty' his uncle, the Revd. Julius Maurice was sent for to whip him.

> 'These executions generally took place with a riding whip, and looking back dispassionately through the distance of years, I am conscious that, for a delicate child, they were a great deal too severe. I always screamed dreadfully in the anticipation of them, but bore them without a sound or a tear.'

Hare's mother was greatly influenced by Julius Maurice and his wife—Aunt Esther—in the harsh disciplines devised for the child's upbringing. 'The winter of 1844–45 was the first of many which were made unutterably wretched by Aunt Esther.' A series of humiliations and punishments instigated by this aunt, whose puritanism was unmistakably sadistic, led to a crucial episode:

> 'Open war was declared at length between Aunt Esther and myself. I had a favourite cat called Selma, which I adored, and which followed me about wherever I went. Aunt Esther saw this, and at once insisted that the cat must be given up to her. I wept over it in agonies of grief: but Aunt Esther insisted. My mother was relentless in saying that I must be taught to give up my own way and pleasure to others; and forced to give it up if I would not do so willingly, and with many tears I took Selma in a basket to the Rectory. For some days it almost comforted me for going to the Rectory, for then I possibly saw my adored Selma. But soon there came a day when Selma was missing. Aunt Esther had ordered her to be—hung!'

Sir Edmund Gosse, in *Father and Son* (1907), told how he suffered under his father's puritanical severity—his mother, equally severe, had died when he was seven. Gosse, an only child, started reading at four, but story books of every description were strictly excluded. His mother believed that to compose fictitious narrative of any kind was a sin. He read whatever he could find in the house—books on natural history, the travels of scientists, geography, astronomy and theology, with little understanding of what he was reading. Without companions, story books or outdoor amusements, not knowing the existence of such things, he played with dolls. His dreams were entirely occupied with grown-ups and animals. At six he played by himself in an attic. During his mother's last illness he was left more than ever alone—he used to take refuge in the attic or in his tiny, cold bedroom. He had never spoken to another child until after his mother's death. He was 'pale and nervous and slept badly, with visions and loud screams' during his sleep.

In *Something of Myself* (1937), Rudyard Kipling gave a horrifying description of spite and malice operating under the guise of Christian conduct to the accompaniment of interrogations and beatings. As a small boy he was boarded for six years in Southsea with a woman who took in the children of parents who were on service in India.

> 'It was an establishment run with the full vigour of the Evangelical as revealed to the woman. I had never heard of Hell, so I was introduced to it in all its terrors—I and whatever luckless little slavey might be in the house, whom severe rationing had led to steal food. . . . I was regularly beaten. The woman had an only son of twelve or thirteen, as religious as she. I was a real joy to him, for when his mother had finished with me for the day he took me on (we slept in the same room) and roasted the other side.'

The woman's husband, who died soon after Kipling was sent to board, 'was the only person in that house, as far as I can remember, who ever threw me a kind word'.

'No day without a good deed' was a precept which very often meant to Victorians 'No day without denying yourself something you like and persuading others to do likewise'.

A Gallup poll, conducted a hundred years ago, to inquire into belief in a God, eternal life, heaven and hell, and other Christian dogmas, would undoubtedly have yielded more positive results than a similar poll today, even allowing for the conventionalism and social conformity of the Victorian age, which would have made it difficult for agnostics and those with any doubts to give an honest answer.

But many leaders of society—statesmen and intellectuals—who are always regarded as typical Victorians, would seem never to have accepted the Christian faith in its entirety, and indeed appear even to have rejected some of its principal tenets. Many were believers on principle without ever having given any thought to the matter.

Numerous biographers of Victorian statesmen refer to them as either practising Christians or sceptics, without vouchsafing any further explanation—a reticence that is also extended to their financial affairs, love-lives and general way of living.

Benjamin Jowett contributed to a symposium *Essays and Reviews* (1860), in which distinguished Anglican scholars examined critically the key points of Christian dogma: belief in the supernatural, the doctrine of redemption, the literal inspiration of the scriptures, the historical accuracy of the Pentateuch and so forth. Despite the controversial storm which the book aroused, the attempt of the Church to take disciplinary action against the scholars involved came to naught, although several of them were clergymen. This indicates that although the Christian faith was more defined and detailed in socially influential circles than it is today, deviations from the Church's official formulations of belief, and vague or symbolical interpretations of these, were quite common among laymen and not uncommon even among the clergy. Such eclecticism bred tolerance: dogma was felt to be no longer worth fighting over.

The twilight zone between belief that was both vague and insecure on the one hand, and uncompromising belief on the other, was wide. It is all the more difficult, therefore, to establish who did and who did not believe, because open rejection of religious belief was too compromising for leaders of society.

In 1847 Thackeray wrote a letter to his mother in which he discussed the 'odious people' he was creating in *Vanity Fair*, 'behind whom all there lies a dark moral I hope. What I want is to make a set of people living without God in the world (only this is a cant phrase) greedy and pompous men perfectly self-satisfied for the most part and at ease about their superior virtue.' Thackeray did not mean by 'people living without God' that either himself or the characters he was creating were freethinkers, but rather that God was remote, absent or of no significance in the life of *Vanity Fair*.

The American scholar Joseph Hillis Miller, in *The Disappearance of God: a study of five Victorian writers* (1963), has tried to show that writers like Matthew Arnold, Browning and Tennyson, having lost the more spontaneous, childlike belief in a Deity, were trying to find some sort of God-substitute in nature, or the brotherhood of man, or progress. Victorians often clung to religion as a safeguard against a nihilism that would have made life unbearable. Kingsley wrote that he would kill himself if ever he came to disbelieve in the existence of God. Tennyson confessed that if he ceased to believe in the prospect of an after-life and an all-powerful Being somewhere in the universe, he 'should not care a pin for anything'. Many passages in his poems bear witness to this groping, tenuous faith:

Behold, we know not anything;
I can but trust that good shall fall
At last—far off—at last, to all,
And every winter change to spring.

I falter where I firmly trod,
And falling with my weight of cares
Upon the great world's altar-stairs
That slope through darkness up to God,

I stretch lame hands of faith, and grope,
And gather dust and chaff, and call
To what I feel is Lord of all,
And faintly trust the larger hope.

These sentiments are vividly expressed in the celebrated prayer of an anonymous common soldier before the battle of Blenheim, which an ironic critic of the Victorians has ascribed to them for its fittingness: 'O God, if there be a God, save my soul, if I have a soul.'

The need of a personal faith was accompanied by the belief that a loss of faith must lead to moral degradation, that virtue and honour were impossible without the sanction of religion. Victorian literature is full of situations which illustrate this attitude, one which was typified in Sweden by the jesting remark of a professor of theology about one of his colleagues: 'So-and-so is an unmitigated unbeliever, but believe it or not he's a model husband and father.' Confronted by the tendency to regard belief in a God as essential to morality, the handful of openly-avowed Victorian free-thinkers parried by leading spectacularly blameless lives.

Walter E. Houghton has written, in *The Victorian Frame of Mind*, that of all the criticisms levelled at them by people of our own day, true Victorians would have rejected all but one. 'They would have defended or excused their optimism, their dogmatism, their appeal to force, their strait-laced morality, but they would have confessed to an unfortunate strain of hypocrisy.' Indeed, a great deal of Victorian literature does give the impression that Victorians were aware of the hypocrisy of their age. This awareness took either the form of ironical characterizations or reflections like those of Dickens, Thackeray, Trollope, Samuel Butler, Wilde and Shaw, or of the direct, hard-hitting attacks of Carlyle, Ruskin, John Stuart Mill, Sir Leslie Stephen and Matthew Arnold.

Hypocrisy, 'the homage paid by vice to virtue', is not considered here only as the pretence of Victorian men and women of being better than they were while condemning in others the sins they themselves were prone to; but as a general tendency to falsehood, self-deception and evasiveness under the sanction of convention and conformity.

Some of the features of this hypocrisy require discussion, especially its religious aspect. Victorian hypocrisy was, of course, not exclusively linked with piety, although its most obvious manifestations were connected with religion.

Those who did not believe in the fundamental points of doctrine taught (with certain significant variations) by various Christian bodies, were debarred both in law and in practice from certain professions and activities, became objects of suspicion, and were socially ostracized.

When Charles Bradlaugh, a professed atheist, was elected to Parliament in 1880 and claimed to make affirmation of allegiance instead of taking the customary parliamentary oath, the House refused to allow him either to make the oath or affirm, and though he was re-elected three times, it was not until 1886 that he was allowed to take his seat—after having at last taken the oath. Many of those who voted against his admission to Parliament were beyond a doubt irreligious men, but all of them acted as if they believed that the Christian formula of the traditional oath was all-important.

The universities were definitely Anglican, and Dissenters were virtually excluded from them, for at Cambridge a man could not graduate, nor could he matriculate at Oxford, without signing the Thirty-nine Articles. A great many university posts were for years reserved for Anglican teachers who were willing to subscribe to the Thirty-nine Articles; and several scholars have testified that they were torn between a desire to remain at the university and a reluctance to pay lip-service to ritualistic observances that were completely opposed to their own beliefs.

But the two cases, of Bradlaugh and the universities, have been given here merely as examples of a pervading tendency: legislation, bureaucracy, the social hierarchy, occupational life, were all riddled with regulations, conventions, habits and practices which upheld religious and moral conformity.

The historian J. A. Froude, a Christian, though hardly an orthodox Victorian, wrote of 'that utter divorce between practice and profession which has made the entire life of modern England a frightful lie'.

Charles Kingsley echoed these sentiments in a sermon he preached on 'God and Mammon':

> 'It is most sad, but most certain, that we are like those Pharisees of old in this . . . that we too have made up our mind that we can serve God and Mammon at once; that the very classes among us who are most utterly given up to money-making, are the very classes which, in all denominations, make the loudest religious profession; that our churches and chapels are crowded on Sundays by people whose souls are set, the whole week through, upon gain and nothing but gain.'

This way of behaving was not wholly hypocritical in the strict sense of the word: that of denying one's convictions, professing insincere convictions, acting in contradiction to one's real convictions—all to achieve selfish ends or to avoid censure and to save face. The motives of such people were usually more complex; consequently, any belief or attitude which was, or *might be*, of use to them, was given the traditional 'benefit of the doubt'. Not less important was their idea that faith and tradition were valuable in others, especially in the lower classes. They shied away from all self-examination, dreading the unpalatable truths they might unearth. Pious Victorians of this sort were not unaware of the rift between their competitive, mercenary weekday and the prayer-filled Sabbath, but they hoped to be perfected and purified in some degree by their piety. Religious doubt was regarded as something abnormal, even unmentionable, which might nevertheless be overcome by conformity of behaviour. What is more, they felt it wrong to voice any such doubts, for this would endanger the peace of mind of others.

This sort of double life was often lived out in almost complete innocence. In her autobiography *My Apprenticeship* (1926), Beatrice Webb related that her father, a railway magnate, always began his bedtime prayers with the words of Charles Wesley's well-known hymn:

> Gentle Jesus, meek and mild,
> Look upon a little child,
> Pity my simplicity . . .

Similar recources to self-deception, escapism, averting the gaze, wilfully forgetting, hushing things up, thinking on two planes, were also characteristic of much Victorian literature and were perpetuated as well by the biographers of the time, so that these thought-processes became decisive elements in subsequent conventional accounts of the period.

Such manifestations of human nature at its most pitiable must, of course, be counted among the failings common to mankind in general, but on the strength of the evidence they would seem to have been unusually prevalent in Victorian England.

Purity and Prudery

In their use of the terms 'Victorian' and 'Victorianism' people usually have in mind something more than the meanings so far discussed. The two words would seem to be even more readily used in connection with sex—as applied to Victorian morals, conventions in the relationship of the sexes and the relative positions of men and women in the family and the community. They refer more particularly to the Victorian attitude toward writing and talking (or rather, *not* writing and *not* talking) about sex, either in public or in private. The connotations of 'Victorian', in short, have to do with prudery, the pattern of virtue, conventional morality and respectability. In our day the word has become a disparaging synonym for that old-fashioned, exaggerated aversion to talk about sexual matters which has made the chief connotation of the word one of prudishness.

Taboos which today are all regarded as typically Victorian resulted in such refinements as bowdlerized Shakespeare, the concealment of legs (whether of females, pianos or chairs) beneath skirts and pantalettes, and the avoidance of such words as leg, breast, bottom, drawers, petticoat—to say nothing of such absolute unmentionables as belly, menstruation, or copulation.

A discussion of Victorian sexual *mores* which stops short at prudery is hardly complete; sexual morality and conventions in general must be considered—there is, for instance, an obviously close connection between the prudery of Victorians and their attitude to chastity. Any such discussion entails the definition of a concept which can be considered as the 'ideal type' of at least one particular class and period—the well-to-do middle class, say, from 1850 to 1880. Nor does this conflict with the fact that 'Victorian' ideas were equally strongly held, not only by other social groups, but also during earlier or later periods than the one singled out; even in our own day 'Victorian' notions about sex still die hard.

As a background to Victorian sex life it will be helpful to summarize point by point the relative positions of men and women in nineteenth-century England.

The legal position of women was inferior to men's in every respect. They were classed as infants in financial matters. They were debarred from colleges and universities, from the learned professions and from government posts. They were denied suffrage and were ineligible for service on municipal and parish councils; and although, by a sixteenth-century law of inheritance, a woman might occupy the throne, no woman could become a civil servant, a mayor, a doctor or a lawyer. A woman's place was in the home, and more precisely, in a home of her own. This principle naturally held good only for women of the well-to-do middle class. As for other women—according to the census of 1851, 900,000 were employed in domestic service, half a million in the textile industry, 370,000 were sempstresses or worked in shoe factories, and 145,000 were washerwomen. There was only one respectable way for a poor 'better-class' mid-Victorian girl to earn a living: she could become a governess or a lady's companion in a 'better-class' household.

The position changed in some respects towards the end of the century. Colleges for women were instituted, and women no longer had to defy convention if they wished to become hospital nurses, especially after the example of Florence Nightingale. In 1876 women were allowed to enter the medical profession. The development of three new-fangled devices—the telegraph, the telephone and the typewriter—came to the rescue of better-class English girls without means. By 1901 forty per cent of all those employed in the telegraph and telephone services were women. The number of female office workers had jumped from 18,000 in 1891 to 56,000 in 1900, enabling G. K. Chesterton, looking back, to make a typical quip about the emancipated woman: 'Twenty million young women rose to their feet with the cry *We will not be dictated to*, and promptly became stenographers.'

In spite of all this there was little general change in women's position of marked inferiority or in the middle-class woman's bondage to the home. Female emancipation made little headway with regard to legal and money matters. Woman had few champions in their demand for equality with men. Their most eminent spokesman was John Stuart Mill, whose book *The Subjection of Women* proved both a sensation and a great source of vexation to most Victorian ladies and gentlemen when it appeared in 1869. In that year it was only women radicals like Mrs Thomas Huxley, Mrs Leslie Stephen and Miss Beatrice Potter (later Mrs Sidney Webb) who signed a petition for 'Women's Rights'.

The reason given by men for the inequality of the sexes was that women were physically, intellectually and morally quite different from themselves. This dogmatic opinion crops up again and again in the writings of the period; and women, too, as we shall see, tended to echo such sentiments in their literary, political and social activities.

The textbook of physiology most in use among early-Victorian medical students was written by Dr John Elliotson, doyen of the London medical faculty. In this book, *Human Physiology*, published in 1840, he said that

> 'woman is greatly inferior to man in reasoning powers, extent of views, originality and grandeur of conception, as well as in corporeal strength. Woman possesses . . . a smaller range of intelligence and less permanence of impression . . . less consistency, impetuosity, courage, firmness of character, except where affection subsists. She is more disposed to believe all things and to confide in all persons; to adopt the opinions and habits of others; has no originality, but follows and imitates men . . .'

Dr Elliotson went on to say that 'woman is remarkable for the delicacy of her taste, her quickness of apprehension of things within her reach of intellect, her insight into character, and tact', adding in a footnote:

'Thus, though few women can take grand political views and be political philosophers, they are probably more fitted for the business of government than men . . . What man accomplishes by force, woman effects by stratagem or management. Being timid, credulous and deferential, she is the slave of fashion and custom, and of those habits and opinions in which she has been brought up, or which she hears most praised by those around her . . . her emotions, like those of children, are rapid, and from slight causes; and like them she passes in a moment from gaiety to grief, and in her distress she sheds tears, which are extracted from men only in the deepest sorrow. Man is proud of his force, intellectual, corporeal and even sensual; woman is retiring, unambitious of power, but vain of beauty and little acquirements. Her love of offspring is far stronger, and her sexual desire far less: she is also far more modest in sexual points . . .'

Such assumptions are more or less typical of all Victorian writing on the subject and the reasoning is like that which Victorians brought to bear on races or classes which they regarded as inferior. The conditions of dependency, ignorance and poverty in which such people lived were considered to be due to racial or inborn characteristics. Women's lot was what it was because women were what they were. Victorians occasionally backed up their belief in women's inferiority by references to the Bible: Woman was fashioned out of Adam's rib, and she it was who tempted Adam to sin in the Garden of Eden.

It should be emphasized that delineations of the male and female character were naturally not exclusive to the Victorian Age. It is abundantly clear from an extensive literature on the subject that the same stereotyped estimation of male and female qualities has been parroted for hundreds, perhaps thousands, of years. As late as the twenties of our own era the Encyclopaedia Britannica was defining female characteristics in terms hardly different from the notions of Dr Elliotson, with quotations to prove the point, culled from all that had been said about the subject down the ages. This article, moreover, advanced the sensible thought that the differentiation of the sexes can be increased by education and that those charged with bringing up the young go too far in educating them along such lines.

The Liverpool University sociologists, Joseph A. and Olive Banks, in their book *Feminism and Family Planning in Victorian England* (1964), have quoted the views of a number of early-Victorian and mid-Victorian writers on what was considered to be the proper relationship between the sexes. These views were expressed mainly in manuals of instruction, many of them written by women.

Theophilus Moore Esq., writing in 1820 on *Marriage Customs and Modes of Courtship*, set forth the character of a good wife as 'one who, ever mindful of the solemn contract which she hath entered into, is strictly and conscientiously virtuous, constant, and faithful to her husband: chaste, pure, and unblemished, in every thought, word, and deed: she is humble and modest from reason and conviction, submissive from choice, and obedient from inclination: what she acquires by love and tenderness, she preserves by prudence and discretion: she makes it her business to serve, and her pleasure to oblige her husband: conscious that every thing that promotes his happiness must in the end contribute to her own: her tenderness relieves his cares, her affection softens his distress, her good humour and complacency lessen and subdue his afflictions.'

The good husband, in his turn,

'treats his wife with delicacy as woman, with tenderness as friend: he attributes her follies to her weakness, her imprudence to her inadvertency: he passes them over, therefore, with good nature, and pardons them with indulgence: all his care and industry are employed for her welfare; and all his strength and power are exerted for her support and protection; he is more anxious to preserve his own character and reputation because her's is blended with it; lastly the good husband is pious and religious, that he may animate her faith by his practice, and enforce the precepts of Christianity by his example . . .'

A. Walker, the author of *Woman Psychologically Considered as to Mind, Morals, Marriage, Matrimonial Slavery, Infidelity and Divorce* (1840), declared:

'It is evident that man, possessing reasoning faculties, muscular power, and courage to employ it, is qualified for being a protector: the woman, being little capable of reasoning, feeble, timid, requires protection. Under such circumstances, the man naturally governs: the woman as naturally obeys.'

Ruskin wrote in a similar vein in *Sesame and Lilies* (1895):

'the man . . . must encounter all peril and trial; to him, therefore, must be the failure, the offence, the inevitable error; often he must be wounded, or subdued; often misled, and *always* hardened. But he guards the woman from all this; within his house, as ruled by her, unless she herself has sought it, need enter no danger, no temptation, no cause of error or offence. This is the true nature of home—it is the place of Peace; the shelter, not only from injury, but from all terror, doubt, and division.'

In the same year, 1869, in which John Stuart Mill published *The Subjection of Women*, Mrs Sarah Ann Sewell, in her book *Woman and the Times we Live in*, declared that 'it is man's place to rule, and a woman's to yield. He must be held up as the head of the house, and it is her duty to bend so unmurmuringly to his wishes, that the rest of the household will follow her example, and treat him with the due respect his sex demands'. For, she added, 'man is the head of all created things in our world—no sane person would for a moment dispute that palpable fact . . .'.

It was a husband's duty—as all these writers agreed—to give his wife a good home, to keep her in comfort while he lived and to provide for her future in the event of his dying first. His reward for all his endeavours was 'to take pleasure in her tranquil happiness'. Husbands were pictured as family warriors who went out daily to toil at the office and to do constant battle against enemies and business competitors. While a husband was away from home, wives were urged (in 1841, by the Religious Tract Society) 'to think on him for one moment labouring with busy hand, with anxious eye and thoughtful brow, for your support and comfort, and say, "Does he not deserve a happy home?" '

Wives were similarly exhorted by another writer, Mrs Sarah Ellis, in *The Daughters of England* (1845), to make the home a refuge from 'those eager pecuniary speculations . . . and . . . that fierce conflict of worldly interests, by which men are so deeply occupied as to be in a manner compelled to stifle their best feelings'. Mrs Sewell, in a similar vein, reminded wives that a husband

> 'is he who goes out day by day in all weathers to toil with business and endure its cares . . . showing such loving care and faith in her, that the wife should strain every nerve to be worthy of that care, without taking into consideration the real gratitude she ought to feel for him who has chosen her from amongst all others, and placed her in that position which will enable her to fulfil the holy and beautiful task that her Creator assigned to her, to be the helpmeet of man, the highest, the most loving, and the most responsible of positions that all nature contains . . .'

In the last chapter of her book Mrs Sewell thought that: 'Having pointed out the numerous failings of the softer sex, it would hardly be just to close this little volume without touching upon the failings of the "higher and nobler sex".' However, before discussing the imperfections of young men, husbands and old bachelors, and advising men on how to treat women, she deemed it prudent to add:

> 'The equalizing, strong-minded woman, who walks the public

platform with unblushing effrontery, and cavils with men upon political subjects, and argues upon the treacherous bubble they have falsely named "Woman's Rights", no doubt will dispute the title of nobler sex; but the writer maintains most stoutly, and in despite of the strong-minded ravings, that man is the noblest being in creation; placed by the Creator himself at the head of our known world; who walks erect, with his face turned heavenward; who was made strong and muscular, that woman might glory in his might and rely upon his protection; given an impulsive temper, that his warmth and ardour might win our love; and stronger passions, that we, the weaker sex, may feel the policy of submission to his sterner will; therefore does the writer stoutly maintain her assertion with pride, and which every genuine Englishwoman who rightly acknowledges her own position, as a woman, will echo from the deepest recesses of her heart.'

The position of women—in the middle class to which these Victorian writers were referring—changed to some extent after the mid-century. Mr and Mrs Banks have explained that a woman was urged to be 'the perfect wife' who would take care of the home and bear children. This womanly ideal gradually merged into that of 'the perfect lady', who represented the home and, through her behaviour, dress and manners, demonstrated the degree of her husband's social position. Her role was to be man's most cherished ornament, more a status symbol than a housekeeper and childbearer. Three housemaids became the minimum requirement for a 'better-class' family; a manservant, preferably several headed by a butler, was an indication that a man had really 'arrived'. Mr and Mrs Banks have connected this shift in the requisites of the ideal woman with the voluntary limitation of families which, as shown by statistics, began to be practised by the upper classes in about 1870.

It was argued—at least by the well-to-do—that men and women differed widely in character and were equipped for different functions. It followed, therefore, that the education of the sexes should be entirely different. It was obvious, indeed, that by differing the education of the sexes the Victorians wished not only to obey the laws of nature but to improve on Nature herself. Their aim was to make men as 'manly' and women as 'womanly' as possible.

This meant that woman should be educated in the home. She should learn the social graces, a little singing, a little piano playing, a smattering of languages, all under the guidance of governesses. If the family could not afford a governess, a young lady should be taught by a female teacher in company with other young ladies. Girls' schools were another possibility, and families began increasingly to take advantage of them.

Instruction in domestic matters, at least in prosperous families, was of minor importance. How children were begotten, how they developed, how their physical and moral education should be undertaken, were all subjects that appear to have been ignored in the upbringing of girls of 'better-class' families.

In contrast with girls, education away from the home was more or less obligatory for boys. The ideal of manliness, in combination with snobbery and the tremendous expansion of the middle class in mid-Victorian times, led to a great resurgence of the public schools. Indeed, this is one of the most typical features of Victorianism. Some boarding schools, such as Eton, Harrow and Westminster, had been founded in the Middle Ages or the sixteenth century and had long enjoyed great prestige as schools for the nobility and gentry—Waterloo, as we well know, was won on the playing fields of Eton. But the great flowering of the public school system took place in the nineteenth century, especially in the latter half of the century. Between 1850 and 1870, three times as many public schools were opened as in the whole of the previous century.

Public schools were exclusive and expensive, or less exclusive and less expensive; but to have gone to a public school of some sort was a badge of class that wealthy parents felt obliged to provide for their sons. The advantage of such a class distinction was the possibility of making connections with people higher up in the social scale. Apart from this, status was acquired by the mere fact of having been to a public school. The teaching in these schools was often mediocre and inadequate. The essential aim, as headmasters were fond of proclaiming, was to turn out manly, courageous, fair-minded, patriotic and God-fearing English gentlemen.

In *Tom Brown's Schooldays* (1856), Thomas Hughes gave a first-hand account of life at one of these schools, Rugby, which was founded in the sixteenth century and reached the peak of its fame in the 1830s under the regenerating influence of the renowned Dr Thomas Arnold. Rugby ranked among the top public schools, next to Eton and Harrow.

The chief interests of the boys in Tom Brown's day seem to have been football, cricket and fighting. According to Hughes, when Dr Arnold arrived at Rugby in 1828 he had 'found School, and School-House, in a state of monstrous licence and misrule, and was still employed in the necessary but unpopular work of setting up order with a strong hand'. It was Arnold's aim to turn out boys who should be 'in the highest and truest sense of the words, Christian gentlemen'.

Hughes highlighted the lofty moral tone of Rugby by stressing Tom Brown's nobleness of character—Tom only fights bullies, boys stronger or at least older than himself, in defence of some small, downtrodden fag, and is usually the winner.

> 'After all, what would life be without fighting, I should like to know? From the cradle to the grave, fighting, rightly understood, is the business, the real, highest, honestest business of every son of man. . . . It is no good for Quakers, or any other body of men, to uplift their voices against fighting. Human nature is too strong for them, and they don't follow their own precepts. Every soul of them is doing his own piece of fighting, somehow and somewhere.'

This sums up Tom's moral belief, given deeper meaning for him by one of Dr Arnold's Sunday-afternoon sermons, which

> 'brought home to the young boy for the first time the meaning of his life: that it was no fool's or sluggard's paradise into which he had wandered by chance, but a battlefield ordained from of old, where there were no spectators, but the youngest must take his side, and the stakes are life and death.'

Rudyard Kipling, in his novel *Stalky and Co.* (1899), gave a similar description of his own schooldays towards the end of 1870, at one of the less exclusive boarding schools, the United Services College at Bideford in Devon. There was more brutality at Kipling's school than at Tom Brown's. Toughened by their apprenticeship as the prey of bullies, the three schoolboy friends of Kipling's book, Stalky, M'Turk and Beetle, band together to waylay a pair of hulking bullies who have been torturing small boys, and inflict on them the same tortures. In his chapter 'The Moral Reformers' Kipling explains the methods of torture, commenting on their painfulness and their effects on the victims.

> 'When a little chap is whimpering in a corner and wears his clothes like rags, and never does any work, and is notoriously the dirtiest little "corridor-caution" in the Coll., something's wrong somewhere.' . . . 'We all caught it in our time,' says M'Turk. Beetle answers: 'But I got it worse than any one. . . . If you want an authority on bullyin' . . . come to me. Corkscrews—brush-drill—keys—head knucklin'—arm-twistin'—rockin'—Ag-Ags—and all the rest of it.'

The code of manliness at the United Services College was similar to the schoolboy code of the crack public schools—a stoic endurance of bullying and brutality, and the lusty enjoyment of a good fight, coupled with a horror of tale-bearing and pride in a boy's ability to look after himself without having to appeal to masters or parents.

Kipling revealed his admiration for this manly ideal in his poem *If*, a subtler, more complex inventory of the qualities he believed essential to the character of a real man. It is significant that both in *Tom Brown's*

Schooldays and *Stalky and Co.*, although the heroes are comparatively decent youngsters who never ill-treat boys smaller or weaker than themselves, these schools seem to have had a sizeable contingent of bullies and blackguards—which leads one to wonder about the fate of the decent boys who were less fortunate than the heroes in being unable to defend themselves with their fists.

The success of the public schools in turning out English gentlemen won them resounding praise. Many a distinguished ex-public-schoolboy in high office expressed his gratitude for all that his old school had done for him. Some distinguished 'old boys', nevertheless, detested their school days and did not hesitate to say so. Lord Salisbury, an old Etonian and three times Prime Minister, was a notable example. Several eminent men of letters were severely critical of the public schools they had gone to, as hotbeds of snobbery, spite, harshness and homosexuality.

Memoirs and biographies of Victorians, on the whole, are remarkably reticent about such aspects of public school life. In recent years, however, two scholars, an American and a Canadian, have unearthed and published frank and detailed accounts of appalling personal experiences at two public schools. Waldo H. Dunn, the most recent biographer (1961) of the historian James Anthony Froude, has reproduced Froude's gruesome accounts of his life at Westminster School in the early 1830s; while Phyllis Grosskurth, in the first really penetrating biography of John Addington Symonds (1964), has given facts from his unpublished *Memoirs*, to which she was permitted access, in which Symonds wrote about Harrow as he knew it in the late 1850s.

Froude, the youngest son of the Archdeacon of Totnes, was sent to Westminster when he was eleven. In fragments of autobiography he tells of his systematic bullying by older boys who beat him, pressed lighted cigars against his face, set his legs on fire to make him dance and forced him to swallow brandy punch to make him drunk. His clothes were ripped, his books taken from him or torn up, and when food was set on the table at mealtimes, the boys snatched it for themselves and flung him scraped mutton bones and refuse fat for his share, so that he was half-starved.

The boy was small and feeble for his age and could not fight because of an unhealed hernia. He was unable to sleep from the pain of his burns and he went about for weeks on end with a scarred and blistered face. Masters asked no questions and he said nothing about his ordeals. He realized the hopelessness of making any complaint—he would have been branded a cowardly milksop and the bullies would have persecuted him even more mercilessly.

When his health broke down he had to be removed to one of the outside boarding houses to recuperate. But

'. . . this did me little good as I was paid off at odd hours for what was called skulking. When I was sent back to College it all began again. My only peaceful moments were in the early summer dawn when I could steal out unperceived and wander up and down on the Millbank embankment by the river, speculating for what extraordinary reasons I had been condemned to such a fate.'

Foude's ordeal lasted for more than three years. It seriously impaired his health and arrested his education.

'Of course during all this I learned nothing, could learn nothing. Indeed I forgot most of what I brought with me. What study was possible for me in such a den of wild animals? My mind, if I could call it a mind, was incessantly occupied with reflections on my unfortunate condition. The Head Master who had formed expectations for me, was first disappointed, then irritated, then came I think positively to dislike me. The reports he sent home were more and more unfavourable.'

Froude's father, who had always treated him with great severity, was bitterly disappointed. He removed the boy from Westminster, gave him a severe beating, and kept him at home in idleness for two years.

All that John Addington Symonds learnt at Harrow, he wrote in his *Memoirs*, was moral corruption. The headmaster, Dr J. C. Vaughan, was renowned for his religious and moral teachings and his sermons. Since arriving at Harrow in 1844 he had set out to reform the school along the lines of Arnold's reforms at Rugby, instituting the monitorial and fagging systems as aids to character building. Under Vaughan's headmastership Harrow prospered: there were 60 boys when he arrived and more than 460 when he retired fifteen years later.

Symonds, who went to Harrow in 1854, was a sickly, sensitive and scholarly boy and the scenes of brutality and homosexuality he witnessed among his schoolfellows revolted him. In 1859 he learnt from a school friend of a love affair between this boy and the headmaster. Symonds, shocked and troubled, nevertheless kept silence about what he had been told, though the knowledge of it caused him mental conflict. A year later, having left Harrow prematurely for reasons of health, he went up to Oxford. At a seaside reading party, on impulse, he spoke to a friendly tutor about Vaughan's infatuation. He was advised, on grounds of morality, to tell his father, Dr J. A. Symonds, and eventually did so. Dr Symonds threatened Vaughan with public exposure unless he resigned and withdrew immediately from Harrow. Vaughan agreed to retire, and shortly afterwards left to become vicar of Doncaster—having also given his promise never to accept any important ecclesiastical post in the future. In 1863, however, doubtless believing that the affair had blown over, he accepted an offer to become Bishop of Rochester. He was again compelled by threats of exposure to withdraw, and it was not until eight years after the death of the elder Symonds that he was able, in 1871, to accept an appointment as Dean of Llandaff, a post he held until his death in 1897.

Froude's and Symonds's recollections of their schooldays cannot be regarded as typical of Victorian boarding schools, whether public schools or not. Conditions must have varied widely in different schools and at different periods. But the cult of manliness undoubtedly prevailed in all of them, while bullying, intimidation, obscenity and homosexual seduction were rife in many.

The Victorian ideal of a healthy-minded Christian love-life is best expressed in Tennyson's *Idylls of the King*, in the vow taken by the Knights of the Round Table:

> To lead sweet lives in purest chastity,
> To love one maiden only, cleave to her . . .

Under the laws of the period a marriage could be dissolved only in exceptional cases, and divorce among the middle classes was considered scandalous. It was naturally out of the question for the poor to get a divorce because of the high cost of the legal proceedings. Pre-marital or extra-marital sexual intercourse was mercilessly condemned until the late nineteenth century, when society, mainly in some circles of the aristocracy and the upper middle classes, began to take a more tolerant view. A girl who lost her virginity had little or no chance of getting a husband in the better-class marriage market. A double standard of morality did exist, of course, inasmuch as any slip of the husband's was regarded with more indulgence than a woman's 'fall from virtue'. But in theory and in fact, chastity was demanded of both sexes. All discussion of sex was taboo, and no enlightenment on the subject was given to the young, either in the home or at school. It was taken for granted that up to their wedding night most women were totally ignorant of the physical side of marriage, and that no intimate or sensual embraces were indulged in during an engagement. Novels and memoirs of the period imply that it was usual for the bridal night to be a complete fiasco or at least a distressing experience for the bride. Doctors said more plainly what novels only hinted:

> 'A first sexual intercourse is, even when sanctioned by marriage and with the most perfect mutual affection, the cause of considerable physical suffering to the female, not infrequently requiring medical attendance and the cessation of all sexual activities for some time.'

The distribution or advertisement of contraceptives was illegal, and it is probable that the very existence of such procedures or devices was unknown to many. The police and the medical profession took swift action in the few cases where the use of contraceptive measures was advocated by crusading reformers, Malthusians or neo-Malthusians, like Francis Place, John Stuart Mill (who was arrested in 1824 for helping to distribute birth-control literature to the London poor), Dr George Drysdale, Charles Bradlaugh and Mrs Annie Besant. When, in 1877, Bradlaugh and Mrs Besant published a forty-year-old American medical pamphlet, *Fruits of Philosophy; or, The Private Companion of Young Married Couples*, by Charles Knowlton (for which Dr Drysdale wrote notes), they were prosecuted for publishing 'a certain lewd, filthy, bawdy and obscene book', and were also subjected to violent public abuse. Mrs Besant, the wife of the Revd. Frank Besant from whom she had separated in 1873, lost many of her friends because of the prosecution, as well as being socially ostracized. Worse still, she was deprived of the custody of her three-year-old daughter, on the grounds that the child was in moral danger, through association with a woman who was not only an atheist, but, as the Lord Chief Justice put it, had violated 'morality, decency and womanly propriety', in her writings, and in publishing a work 'so repugnant, so abhorrent to the feeling of the majority of decent Englishmen and Englishwomen'.

Books, plays and publications of any kind considered to be immoral were liable to prosecution, but there were few cases where such action was taken. One of them, which became a *cause célèbre*, was the prosecution, in 1889, of Henry Vizetelly, the translator and publisher of Zola's novels in English. Although the novels were much bowdlerized in translation, Vizetelly was convicted of publishing corrupting literature, fined £300 and given a three-months prison sentence.

Nothing of all this was specifically Victorian. There were 'Victorians' before Victoria, and their sexual puritanism can be traced back to the late eighteenth century, with the rise of Evangelicalism and similar revivalist movements. Outstanding events and personalities of the Victorian Age undoubtedly had their earlier counterparts. Dr Thomas Bowdler's complete edition of Shakespeare, 'bowdlerized' for family use, appeared in 1818, a year before Victoria was born. Mrs Grundy, who was to become the well-known Victorian symbol of exaggerated concern for decency and decorum, first made her presence felt ('What will Mrs Grundy say?') in Thomas Morton's comedy *Speed the Plough*, long before Victoria's day—in fact, in Georgian England, a decade or more before the licentious days of the Regency.

Queen Victoria's virtuous rectitude, her dislike of licentiousness and disapproval of libertines, and her refusal to receive divorced persons at court, have either been condemned as narrow-minded or else praised as considerable contributions to Victorianism. The Queen's attitude was naturally of some influence in making chastity a requisite of social standing, but it is evident that her efforts in this respect were only a minor detail in the supposed, and probably frequently exaggerated, change in the Victorian social pattern. Sexual irregularity, as H. L. Beales has pointed out, was one of the great Victorian sins. 'Yet all through Victorian society sexual irregularity was prevalent—at the top, at the bottom and in the middle.'

Puritanism in its extreme form is manifestly hostile to every kind of sexual activity and indeed fundamentally hostile to life itself. Puritans held that man began his earthly existence with a fatal false step, under the apple tree in the Garden of Eden: there, in disobedience to God's command, the woman gave him of the tree and he did eat, and this was how sin came into the world. More of these Adam-and-Eve false steps had to be made by the couple's descendants, for Earth to be populated and Heaven supplied with angels—but however necessary, the steps were still false steps. Even the most passionate puritans confronted sin with mixed feelings: they realized that the battle could never be wholly won, for they saw that sex could only be pruned and tidied up, never rooted out. This belief explains why morality for most Victorians meant sexual morality and why, compared with sexual sinning, all other sins were mere peccadillos.

A pronounced dichotomy had become apparent in the Victorian manner of writing or talking about sex and love. The sexual act was regarded as something unclean, shameful, though necessary for the continuation of the species. 'Love' was a sacred thing, having the power to render sex almost respectable, even pure, while at the same time being something which could become a protection against sensuality. To love a pure woman, even merely to associate with virtuous women, was supposed to make chastity endurable and natural for men. It was even claimed that tenderness and chivalry to women could be traced to 'suppressed and therefore sacred and exalted passion . . . Is it not clear to us all that a young man can have no greater protection against sensuality and evil associates than an early, virtuous and warm affection?' A similar instance of Victorian 'double-think' about sex is apparent in the conventional notion about men's and women's erotic feelings. It was usual to regard men as lustful voluptuaries, or at any rate as not averse to sexual gratification; whereas 'good', that is 'better-class', women were considered as a matter of course to be so tranquil in their chastity that their very presence could quell a man's sexual urges. Even a married woman was supposed to be so pure that she was incapable of experiencing any enjoyment in sexual intercourse and merely yielded to a husband's male lust. Simultaneously with this belief, however, Victorians cherished the old biblical concept of woman as a temptress, an impure creature who entices men to sin. In practice this meant the prostitute, or at any rate women of the lower classes.

Strict sexual morality and prudery permeate almost the whole of Victorian literature, especially fiction—in marked contrast to books written by the uninhibited French, which were regarded as sensational and always branded as immoral. There is hardly even a suggestion of sexual intimacy or sensual feelings between the sexes in the great English novels and in the biographies of the period. Mention of illicit love-affairs is extremely rare, and in such cases the information is always conveyed obliquely and vaguely. Even such *fin de siècle* rebels against Victorianism as Oscar Wilde and Walter Pater express themselves with similar delicacy. Thomas Hardy caused a sensation and stirred up public indignation in 1891 with his 'immoral' book *Tess of the D'Urbervilles*, in which he dared to take for his theme the tragedy of an unmarried mother.

The Victorians were adept in dealing with scandals, and whenever there was one they quickly hushed it up, or if this were not possible they referred to it in conversation and in print vaguely, indirectly or swathed in euphemisms. Such things as venereal diseases, contraceptives and pre-marital or extra-marital sexual relations were never so much as mentioned in decent society or in respectable publications. Kipling gives a fantastic instance of this sort of squeamishness in *Something of Myself*, where he describes the plight of an annual five per cent of the men of Britain's army in India in the 1880s:

> 'I came to realize the bare horrors of a private's life and the unnecessary torments he endured on account of the Christian doctrine which lays down that "the wages of sin is death". It was counted impious that bazaar prostitutes should be inspected; or that men should be taught elementary precautions in their dealings with them. This official virtue cost our Army in India nine thousand expensive white men a year always laid up from venereal disease. Visits to Lock Hospitals made me desire . . . that I might have six hundred priests—Bishops of the Establishment for choice—to handle for six months precisely as the soldiers of my youth were handled.'

In the study of the sexual habits of the Victorians, researchers seem to have made little use of medical books and reviews. The work of the sociologists Joseph and Olive Banks is a notable exception. They have tapped these sources for their survey of *Feminism and Family Planning in Victorian England*.

Since material of this nature must be fairly true to type, such an examination of the writings of Victorian medical men proves highly revealing. Two striking facts are immediately apparent: few of these medical books or the articles in medical journals and reviews discuss sexual matters at all, and, with the exception of textbooks of anatomy and physiology, even doctors treat the subject with the utmost circumspection.

The three leading medical journals of the time—*The Lancet*, *The British Medical Journal* and *The British and Foreign Medico-Chirurgical Review*—in issues covering the forty years between 1848 and 1889 contain among them barely a score of articles which mention or discuss such problems as sexual education, sterility, neurasthenia from sexual causes, masturbation or illicit sexual intercourse. Books dealing with these and similar subjects are exceedingly scarce and most of the few that were published date from the 1890s.

Writers in these medical journals, when discussing sexual subjects, were morbidly shy of calling a spade a spade. One article which is obviously discussing masturbation refers to it throughout as 'impurity'. Venereal disease is tiptoed away from in such euphemisms as 'the frightful illness of which we are all aware'. Preventive measures are never mentioned or are only hinted at. One exception to this conspiracy of silence was Dr George Drysdale's *Elements of Social Science or, Physical, Sexual and Natural Religion*, published in 1854, and then only under a pseudonym, 'George Rex'. This work was either repudiated or ignored by the more reputable or 'respectable' doctors. When mention of strictly taboo words or acts—the genital organs or sexual intercourse, for example—was unavoidable, it was not unusual for Victorian medical writers to add that 'for natural reasons it is not seemly to pursue such matters in detail'.

A wider public was reached by instructional books of the kind written by British-born Dr Elizabeth Blackwell (1821–1910), the first woman to graduate as a doctor in the United States. She came to Europe in 1849 and after much difficulty was admitted to the Maternité in Paris and later to St Bartholomew's Hospital in London. She finally settled in England and practised there until her death in 1910. Her books, *The Moral Education of the Young in Relation to Sex* (1878) and *The Human Element in Sex* (1884), are a mixture of moral precepts and factual observations for which she claimed scientific proof: 'The principles laid down are true. They rest upon the firm foundation of physiological law and are confirmed by facts of universal experience.' It is interesting to note that the facts of universal experience, in every case, obligingly conformed to the Victorian moral code.

'Morality in sex,' said Dr Blackwell, 'will be found to be the essence of all morality, securing principles of justice, honour, and uprightness in the most influential of all human relations, and as it is all-important in life, so it is all-important in the education which prepares for life.' Sexual morality, as Dr Blackwell saw it, meant 'unblemished chastity', total sexual abstinence of the unmarried. She observed that physical sexual maturity in human beings is manifested earlier than mental maturity, which is not apparent until twenty-three to twenty-five years in the male and somewhat earlier in the female.

'Nubility . . . is that period of life when marriage may take place, without disadvantage to the individual and to the race. . . . About the age of twenty-five commences that period of perfect manly vigour, that union of freshness and strength, which enables the individual to become the progenitor of vigorous offspring. The strong constitution transmitted by healthy parents, between the ages of twenty-five and thirty-five, indicates the order of Nature, in the growth of the human race.'

Before this age sexual activity and all excesses (among which Dr Blackwell apparently included any sexual intercourse of the unmarried), were dangerous because they 'diminish the vital forces' and 'weaken and undermine the organs of procreation'.

She held up Antiquity and Orientals as awful examples.

'The records of History, confirm the teaching of Physiology and Observation, in relation to the fundamental character, of sexual virtue, as the secret of durable national greatness. The decline of all the great nations of Antiquity, is marked by the prevalence of gross social corruption. The complex effects of the same cause are strikingly observed in the condition of the Mahommedan and other eastern races; and in all the tribes subject to them . . .'

In support of her thesis she quoted

'the celebrated surgeon Lallemand, who says: "The contrast between the polygamous and sensual East, and the monogamous and intellectual West, displays on a large scale, the different results produced by the different exercise of the sexual powers. On one side, polygamy, harems, seraglios; the source of venereal diseases, barbarous mutilations, revolting and unnatural vice; with the population scanty, inactive, indolent, sunk in ignorance and consequently the victim of misery, and every kind of despotism. On the other side, monogamy, Christian austerity, more equal distribution of domestic happiness, increase of intelligence, liberty and general well-being; rapid increase of an active, laborious, and enterprising population, necessarily spreading, and dominating." '

Dr Blackwell went on to comment that 'No reference to the lessons of history, however brief, should omit the effect produced by religious teaching. The influence exercised by the Christian religion in relation to sex, is of the most striking character.'

According to Dr Blackwell:

> 'the harmful consequences of onanism are equal to those of other sexual vices. The aim therefore of all wise parents, should be to secure those influences which will preserve the chastity of their sons until the age of twenty-five; when marriage, as a rule, should be made possible, and encouraged.'

But though marriage between twenty-five and thirty years of age was to be recommended, chastity, she asserted, was never harmful. In support of this she pointed to the longevity of monks and priests:

> 'Strong testimony as to the compatibility of chastity and health is furnished by the Catholic priesthood. . . . who, by avoidance of temptation, by direction of the mind to intellectual pursuits, and devotion to great humanitary objects, pass long lives in health and vigour. The effect on the world of enforced celibacy is, of course, disastrous; but the power that has been gained by the institution of the priesthood, is indubitable; and the one object here insisted on, viz: the compatibility of physical health, with the observance of chastity, is proved by it, on a large scale.'

The enforced celibacy of prison life was another proof, according to Dr Blackwell, of the beneficial effect of chastity.

> 'The health of prisoners in a well-ordered prison, improves instead of deteriorating, the mortality being smaller than amongst a similar class of the civil population . . . The foregoing facts distinctly prove, that the exercise of the sexual powers, is not indispensable to the health of human beings; that men of all ages can live in full vigorous health, without such exercise, and that to the young, it is an immense physical advantage that they should so live.'

'Chastity is health' was the golden rule in bringing up the young. Suggestive literature was of course to be avoided. Fresh air and plenty of exercise were excellent safeguards against temptation.

A series of similar books of roughly the same period, written by doctors, gave more or less the same advice as Dr Blackwell. Such works as Dr Thomas Low Nichols's *Human Physiology* (1872) and *Esoteric Anthropology* (1873); Sir James Matthews Duncan's *Fecundity, Fertility, Sterility and allied topics* (1871); or *The Evolution of Sex* (1889), by Sir Patrick Geddes and Sir John Arthur Thomson, also advocated chaste monogamy but supported it by reasons that differed from those of Dr Blackwell. Dr Nichols stressed that if men and women married at the right age it became natural for them to abstain from sexual intercourse once a woman had passed the age of child-bearing. He claimed that copulation was an extremely hazardous activity for men of over fifty and that it was usually only the chaste who lived to a ripe old age. He explained, too, that many women were devoid of any interest in sex.

It was Sir James Duncan's opinion that sexual excesses led to sterility. Other writers thought that contraceptive measures were physically and mentally harmful and that sexual abstinence was the only sure protection against the over-production of offspring. A normal-sized family, according to Sir James, was one of ten children. He was writing at a time when married couples were increasingly inclined to practise the voluntary limitation of offspring.

In the medical reviews expert opinion presented the same picture. During the 1880s the burning question of whether sexual abstinence was beneficial or harmful was broached several times in *The Lancet* and *The British Medical Journal*. These two reviews reminded readers again and again in editorials and reports of lectures, that all extra-marital sexual activity—masturbation no less than fornication—was harmful or dangerous, either because of the risk of disease, or because it contributed to the moral and physical decline of the wrong-doer. Because of this, doctors should never under any circumstances advise young men tormented by sexual desire (women were not even considered) to yield to temptation. *The Lancet* of May 1889, in an editorial, emphasized the fact that:

> 'Ours is a very responsible profession. Young men are looking to us as men looked to the old type of priests who combined moral and medical functions. If clerical teachers are for the moment less in authority, we are in more, and it is of enormous moment that we realize the weight of our words, especially when they seem to be thrown into the already heavily weighted scale of human passion and inclination. Men are apt enough to err without giving them the push of medical encouragement. . . . Let no physician prostitute his profession or his authority even by his silence, to sanction a vice which is appallingly common.'

The editorial also commented, in similar terms, on one of the *Lettsonian Lectures* given by Dr W. R. Gowers, which was reported in full in the same issue:

> 'I must ask a question—said Dr Gowers—and give a warning that I would fain have left unasked, unsaid. But I cannot, I dare not, pass them by. Do we do all we can—and our profession gives us that power that no other has—do we do all we can to promote that perfect chastity which alone can save us [from moral and physical decline]? . . . With all the force that any knowledge I possess can give, and with any authority I may have, I assert . . . that no man

ever yet was in the slightest degree or way the better for incontinence; that for it every man must be worse morally, and that most are worse physically . . . And I am sure, further, that no man was ever anything yet but the better for perfect continence. My warning is—let us beware lest we give even upon the lowest grounds that we can take, advice against which we should resolutely set our face and raise our voice.'

Sir James Paget, another much-quoted authority, expressed himself even more strongly to his medical students in his *Clinical Lectures and Essays*, published in *The Lancet:*

'Many of your patients will ask you about sexual intercourse, and expect you to prescribe, fornication. I would as soon prescribe theft and lying, or any thing else that God has forbidden. Chastity does no harm to mind or body; its discipline is excellent; marriage can be safely waited for; and amongst the many nervous and hypochondriacal patients who have talked to me about fornication, I have never heard one say that he was the better or happier after it; several have said they were worse; and many, having failed, have been made much worse.'

The Lancet's editorial commented: 'Such is the sum of professional experience and observation. We shall not reduce its effect by multiplying words.' Writing on the same subject in *The British Medical Journal*, one doctor ended his article with the observation: 'We are not entitled to say in the privacy of our consulting rooms anything that we should not dare to say before a group of colleagues.'

Discussions of this kind were sometimes centred on the problem of promoting 'purity' and eradicating 'impurity', without any indication being given by so much as a word as to what was really meant by 'purity' or 'impurity'.

The Lancet of 10 May 1884, in an editorial on 'The Purity Question', said:

'Impurity may be considered as originating from a naturally inferior, if not actually diseased, nervous organization in which the inhibitory or controlling powers are diminished, so that the individual acts only in obedience to the promptings of his own passions and desires. By yielding to this self-indulgence, the will becomes further weakened, and the body itself becomes exposed to many disorders and diseases.'

'Disease'—a euphemism for the original euphemism 'impurity'—must be checked at the outset. 'What is really wanted', the writer went on to say, 'is that the disease be treated as an undoubtedly moral and social evil. It is not merely to inculcate the sentiment of purity, but to strike at the root of all impurity. Moral lessons of restraint should be impressed early in life.' Not only should fathers speak to their sons of the dangers of school life, but masters at schools 'should be vigilantly alert to the necessity of promptly dealing with such offenders . . .' and in boarding schools: 'Publicity is the only method of checking this evil, which is totally fostered by the system of cubicles, private studies, and small sitting-rooms; whilst all offenders should be removed. It is astonishing how quickly this vice will spread merely from the example of a small vicious circle.'

An article in *The Lancet* in August 1885 wondered if the young were not left too much in the dark about sex. A great many youths, the writer said, became adult and married 'in total ignorance of sexual matters', and this was the usual state of the majority of women—it goes without saying that this meant only women of the middle class. Such a situation was likely to be the cause of involuntary wrong-doing and consequently of disease and misfortune. Girls, for instance, were often seduced without their realizing what was happening to them. Elementary anatomical and physical knowledge might be of some value, it was thought, if it could be imparted gradually, starting with the skeleton and leading discreetly by way of the heart, lungs, stomach, and so forth, to the sexual organs and their functions. This proposal was attacked in several subsequent articles and in letters from readers. The objections were that sexual instruction would excite youthful minds as readily as dirty books. Purity could only be encouraged by firmly implanting the habit of self-restraint and exercising the most strict control over all reading of a disturbing nature. 'True innocence is virtually inconceivable without ignorance' wrote one fearless correspondent.

A dire warning was uttered by Dr Nichols against the temptations of body and mind. The passions are stimulated, he said, by

> 'idleness, luxury and every form of voluptuousness. Where it is desirable to avoid such excitement, all these must be guarded against. Passionate poetry and romances, warm pictures, dancing, especially the dancing of the stage, the fashionable display of female arms and bosoms, all fond toyings, and personal freedoms between the sexes, must be avoided by those with whom chastity is a necessity of age and circumstances. The lips are supplied with nerves of sensation from the cerebellum, and the kisses of the lips are sacred to love. The bosom is also supplied with nerves from the same source, and it is in the most direct and intimate sympathy with the female generative organs. A woman of sensibility, who would preserve her chastity, must guard her bosom well.'

The most commonly prescribed safeguards against sexual excitation, however, were mainly of a physical nature. *The British and Foreign Medico-Chirurgical Review* for January–April 1848 summed it all up in the words of Dr M. Lallemand, who recommended

> 'whatever discourages indolence, whether of body or mind, . . . active bodily exercise, carried to the verge of fatigue. . . . For all, early rising, hard beds, cold bathing or ablution: active exercise, the occasional use of aperients, spare diet, and the free enjoyment of respectable society, especially when females form part of this, are of great importance.'

Was there any consistency between Victorian theory and practice? Several writers have denied that there was. They maintain that the Victorians were in no way different from English men and women of earlier or later centuries. They frequently explain, employing the terminology of depth psychology, that the strict views and conventional prudery of the Victorians indicate that they were unusually licentious.

The available facts give no certain guidance on the matter. They have often been treated with considerable carelessness: no attempts have been made to clarify the differences between various periods or social groups; and conflicting inferences have been drawn from the evidence.

A good example of this source of confusion is the way in which modern historians have dealt with Victorian scandals. One school of thought has explained them as the result of Victorian official morality, that façade of respectability behind which Victorians led the double lives of those who omit to practise what they preach. The opposite school believes that scandals arose, or certain actions and events were considered scandalous, precisely because the majority of Victorians lived in strict conformance to the laws of their conventional morality.

Two of the most resounding Victorian scandals involving politicians were those in which Dilke and Parnell were implicated. Sir Charles Wentworth Dilke (1843–1911), while Under Secretary for Foreign Affairs in the second Gladstone government, was the co-respondent in a particularly damaging divorce suit. Convicted of adultery, he was dismissed, regardless of his undoubted ability, and spent the next six years in retirement from public life. Some years later, Charles Stewart Parnell lost the leadership of the Irish parliamentary party through his association with Mrs Katherine O'Shea, whose husband sued for divorce in 1890, citing Parnell as co-respondent. The decree was granted, with costs against Parnell, and the Gladstone party demanded his retirement.

What seems the most sensational feature of these two cases is not the fact of the divorces but the vehemence of public opinion. With the majority of people this was undoubtedly quite sincere, even though a few, the political adversaries of the two men, were hypocrites who for tactical reasons naturally professed to agree with the accusing puritans.

The Oscar Wilde case has often been claimed as evidence of widespread homosexuality, chiefly because Wilde's trial and conviction made it seem advisable for numerous celebrities and persons of rank to place themselves out of harm's way on the Continent (either from fright or, as some hinted of a few actors, out of bravado); but it hardly seems possible to draw any general conclusions from one isolated and unparalleled case.

It can be taken for granted that morals were loose in some circles of Victorian high society, whereas in others no laxity of morals was tolerated in any one who, through ill-luck or bad management, broke the eleventh commandment: 'Thou shalt not be found out'. Edward Prince of Wales and many of his companions were among Europe's most notorious libertines—a fact that not even modern biographers often care to admit in so many words. The Prince's affairs with married women were usually known to the whole circle of their friends and were fully accepted as long as appearances were kept up and decorum maintained. Lord Palmerston was known, even in his old age, for his embarrassing advances to women. Lord Hartington, later the eighth Duke of Devonshire, with his melancholy dignity and air of nonchalant authority, seemed the epitome of aristocratic virtue, yet he carried on a long and widely-known affair with the beautiful German-born Duchess of Manchester for many years before their marriage on her first husband's death. At country house parties the host was often hard put to it to know how to allot the bedrooms so that the guests who were not married to each other could keep their nightly assignations discreetly.

Modern scholarship has discovered that a number of Victorian statesmen and men of letters whose morals were thought during their lifetimes to be beyond reproach, or whose sex-lives were apparently normal, either led active extra-marital sex-lives or were sexually abnormal in some way or other. We now know about Dickens's unhappy love affair. Balfour's renowned chastity has been found to be a myth. Carlyle's and Ruskin's harsh puritanical upbringing has been shown to have rendered them impotent, and in other cases there have been indications of definite or probable homosexuality. In the light of modern psychology and psychoanalysis, such knowledge has ceased to cause surprise. The matter is now a commonplace, only mentioned here because books about the Victorians still frequently present these discoveries as astonishing and remarkable revelations.

Contrary to the opinion of some writers, reports on campaigns to improve morals conducted by notable social reformers of the period throw little fresh light on Victorian morality. One such campaign had as its aim the introduction of medical inspection of prostitutes in major cities and garrison towns. The physician William Acton, a pioneer in the agitation for the reform, made a detailed investigation of prostitution, and in 1857 published a report on his findings, *Prostitution, considered in its Moral, Social, and Sanitary Aspects, in London and other Large Cities and Garrison Towns, with Proposals for the Control and Prevention of its Attendant Evils.* Acton's report was instrumental in securing the passage of the three Contagious Diseases Acts of 1864–9. In 1870 he published a second edition of his book, enlarged and revised to include his observations of the workings of the new law.

Other social reformers, notably Mrs Josephine Butler, an active pioneer for social purity, regarded any form of legalized prostitution as State-sponsored immorality, and campaigned against the Contagious Diseases Acts. The slow, tenacious fight of Mrs Butler, the Moral Reform Union and other supporters during the 1870s, eventually led to the repeal of the acts.

Mrs Butler was instrumental in starting a similar campaign, which was conducted in 1884–5 and brought to public notice in the columns of the influential *Pall Mall Gazette* by the journalist and propagandist W. T. Stead, who had written for the paper from 1880 and was its editor from 1883. After lengthy investigations in the underworld of London, Stead published, in July 1885, a series of articles which he called *The Maiden Tribute of Modern Babylon.* The articles, advertised beforehand by an announcement which warned the squeamish and the prudish not to read them, were sensational exposures of the organized prostitution in London of young girls for sale at home and abroad. Stead's revelations caused great public excitement; the *Gazette* ran out of news-print and the editorial offices had to be placed under police protection. Stead's life was threatened by irate brothel-keepers and the powerful vested interests behind the traffic in prostitution.

Stead's articles revealed, among other things, that in ten days he had been able to buy nine young girls for less than thirty pounds. To demonstrate how easily the two-way traffic between England and the Continent could be carried on, he had bought from her parents for five pounds a thirteen-year-old girl, Eliza Armstrong, and had arranged for her to be taken (suitably chaperoned) to France and kept there for a time before being brought back to London—where she was medically examined to prove that she had not been violated.

Stead's revelations of the organized traffic in teenage girls were successful in forcing the Government to pass the Age of Consent Bill (which had been before them since 1881), altering the criminal law under which the traffic in vice flourished. But his underworld and political enemies were out to get him and used a technical loophole in the case of Eliza Armstrong to secure a prosecution for abduction. Stead's efforts to provide evidence for his exposures earned for him a three-months prison sentence for technical infringements of the new Criminal Law Amendment Act, which had thus involved him in the very traffic he was fighting to stamp out. One of his associates and helpers in his fact-finding had been Bramwell Booth (son of the founder of the Salvation Army), who stood trial with Stead but was acquitted. Though Stead was found guilty, the jury added a rider recommending mercy and putting on record 'their high appreciation of the services he had rendered the nation in securing passage of a much-needed law for the protection of young girls'.

All these and other similar reform activities are not particularly revealing about the state of Victorian morals, except as an illustration of the prudery and Podsnappery which hampered discussion of sexual problems and caused widespread outcry when they were brought into the open. Even statistics have been pressed into service to determine the situation concerning the state of morals, especially as an indication of the prevalence of immorality—as shown in the following much-quoted figures.

Forty-two thousand children were born out of wedlock in 1851. This figure is mentioned with horror; yet compared with 700,000 births in the same year the percentage does not seem high. The estimates show that in the same year one in every twelve girls over the age of puberty had 'strayed from the path of virtue'. This figure, too, was assumed to indicate wide-spread immorality, but in reality it can be considered very low. The Metropolitan Police report for 1857 gave the number of known London prostitutes as 8,600. Henry Mayhew queried this figure in his famous inquiry *London's Labour and the London Poor* (1851–62), and wondered whether 80,000 would not be nearer the mark. He added that 'large as this total may appear, it is not improbable that it is below the reality rather than above it'. Even this evidence of moral degradation seems highly questionable. The fact that Mayhew's and the police figures contradicted each other with so wide a divergence casts doubt on the reliability of both: the lower figure would appear to be an extremely moderate estimate for a city as big as London, which had a population of two million and was the market-place for the whole of south-east England. Acton, writing in 1870, agreed with Mayhew:

> 'The police have not attempted to include—in fact, could not have justly included—the unnumbered prostitutes who are not seen on the streets . . . I must observe that these returns give but a faint idea of the grand total of prostitution by which we are oppressed. Were there any possibility of reckoning all those in London who would come within the definition of prostitutes, I am inclined to think that the estimate of the boldest who have preceded me would be thrown into the shade.'

These reformers, who drew attention with obvious relish to statistics on prostitution as proof of moral decay, seem to have imagined that in the course of time Victorian puritanism would bring about the total triumph of virtue over vice.

It is highly probable that the lives of the social groups which primarily supported the doctrine proclaimed by politicians, journalists, clergymen and doctors, were considerably influenced (though how far it is difficult to estimate) by this moral code. Since chastity was generally approved, it should have been easy for the less passionately inclined to practise it; it was as difficult for middle-class women to flout the conventions as it was destructive in its consequences if they did. The somewhat naive saying that forbidden fruits are sweetest is only a half-truth: to suppose that prohibition and censure are greater incentives to wrongdoing, than are sanction and approval to doing what is right, is palpably absurd. Another factor which influenced support of the moral code was the sharp split between theory and practice in the lives of many Victorians, so that there was considerable scope for hypocrisy among the ambitious or the timid.

Two essays in *Ideas and Beliefs of the Victorians*, which discuss Victorian notions about sex, deserve mention as examples of contradictory interpretations of identical facts, combined with conflicting opinions as to their causes. In the one, H. L. Beales the economist, patently Marxist in outlook, believes (and supports his argument with numerous references) that the contradiction between official morality and general practice was unusually pronounced during the Victorian age. He believes that increased licentiousness was the result of urbanization and industrialization and that it was a stimulus to aggressive puritanism. He suggests that this situation would have been different in a socialistic society.

Edward Glover, in the second of the two essays, makes use of psychoanalysis to support the contrary view: that Victorian ideas and patterns of behaviour were much the same as those of earlier periods and of other countries. He appears to think, however, that Victorian prudery either originated in, or led to, a general exaggeration of sexuality of the kind that made piano legs seem suggestive and improper to some Victorians.

The two specialists have obviously made use of the ideological clichés peculiar to their own branches of science, not only to define the Victorian attitude to sex, but to explain why it took the form it did. Their conclusions have been arrived at by a series of intellectual somersaults: for H. L. Beales, immorality was the cause of the strict Victorian moral code; whereas Edward Glover believes that the prudery of the Victorians was the outward sign of their intense preoccupation with sex.

II

VICTORIA

The Legend

Queen Victoria celebrated two jubilees, one in June 1887 and another in June 1897. These were her Golden and Diamond Jubilees, the fiftieth and sixtieth anniversaries, respectively, of her accession to the throne. England continued to exist in 'splendid isolation', free of alliances, periodically at odds with one nation or another, in particular France and Russia. The network of treaties and alliances embracing Japan and Britain's age-old enemies France and Russia—with now the swordpoint, now the shield warding off Germany—was not yet as much as a gleam in the eyes of statesmen.

Imperialism and the consciousness of a united 'white' Empire were at their height. The dominions had grown, as one dark-skinned race after another was conquered at no great cost to Britain. A hint of unrest in South Africa was a mere presage of the bloody and humiliating Boer War, which now, in 1887, it seemed possible to avert. A Conservative government headed by Lord Salisbury led the country in both Jubilee years and saw to it that these anniversaries were occasions for displays of national grandeur.

State institutions, the army and the navy were mobilized to make of this homage to a queen a demonstration of the nation's unity and might. The elaborate pageant deployed a cast of thousands: Parliament, the Church, princes of the realm, foreign crowned heads, delegations from overseas in exotic national dress. The massed fleet, recalled from the Four Seas, was drawn up at Spithead in an endless line, with officers and ratings to the number of 20,000 saluting from the decks of every imaginable kind of naval craft—from battleships to training brigs. On land 'red jackets' paraded alongside troops from possessions in every corner of the globe. The great show was enlivened by thanksgiving services, processions, military parades, naval reviews, official receptions and banquets—each of them planned with the Queen as its focal point.

The hordes of foreign royalty and dignitaries were duly impressed: Lord Salisbury wrote to the Queen a couple of days after her Golden Jubilee:

'Lord Salisbury with his humble duty . . . congratulates your Majesty very cordially and respectfully on the wonderful scenes of the rejoicings of the last few days. He hears on all sides of the impression it has made on our foreign visitors . . .'

Nothing like this, people said, echoing the newspapers, had ever happened before in the whole of history. By the time of the Diamond Jubilee there was a new Poet Laureate, Rudyard Kipling, to add his voice to the paeans. When the festivities were over he wrote, in *Recessional*, of the responsibility that went with power. He urged a chosen people to be worthy of its destiny:

God of our fathers, known of old,
Lord of our far-flung battle-line
Beneath whose awful Hand we hold
Dominion over palm and pine—
Lord God of Hosts, be with us yet,
Lest we forget—lest we forget!

Far-called, our navies melt away;
On dune and headland sinks the fire;
Lo, all our pomp of yesterday,
Is one with Niniveh and Tyre!
Judge of the nations, spare us yet,
Lest we forget—lest we forget!

The Queen gave a detailed description of both the jubilees. After the Golden Jubilee she wrote:

'The morning was beautiful and bright with a fresh air. Troops began passing early with bands playing and one heard constant cheering. . . . The scene outside was most animated and reminded me of the opening of the Great Exhibition, which also took place on a fine day. Received many beautiful nosegays and presents . . .'

As she drove to Westminster Abbey for the Thanksgiving Service:

'The crowds from the Palace gates up to the Abbey were enormous, and there was such an extraordinary burst of enthusiasm, as I had hardly ever seen in London before; all the people seemed to be in such good humour. The old Chelsea Pensioners were in a stand near the Arch. The decorations along Piccadilly were quite beautiful, and there were most touching inscriptions. Seats and platforms were arranged up to the tops of the houses, and such waving of hands. Piccadilly, Regent Street, and Pall Mall were all alike most festively decorated. Many schools out, and many well-known faces were seen.'

Mingled with pride and satisfaction was her sense of loneliness and the melancholy thought that Albert was not there to share it all with her. During the Abbey service, she was conscious that: 'I sat *alone* (oh! without my beloved husband, for whom this would have been such a proud day!).'

Describing the official festivities, with whom she sat and how she was dressed, the Queen dwelt particularly on the joy, enthusiasm and affection displayed by the crowds in the streets. All over London, even in the back streets (the procession had passed along the Borough Road) the poor had decorated their houses, hung out garlands and slung across the streets banners which said 'Welcome' and 'God Bless Our Queen'.

In her Journal entry for the following day the Queen wrote:

> 'Thousands thronged the streets but there was no disorder . . . They shouted and sang till quite late, and passed the Palace singing "God Save the Queen" and "Rule Britannia" . . . These two days will remain ever indelibly impressed on my mind, with the gratitude to that all-merciful Providence, who has protected me so long, and to my devoted and loyal people. But how painfully do I miss the dear ones I have lost.'

The Diamond Jubilee though less spectacular than that of 1887 called forth even more lavish expressions of loyalty and affection. The Queen 'greatly touched and gratified' wrote in her Journal:

> 'No one ever, I believe, has met with such an ovation as was given to me, passing through those six miles of streets . . . the crowds were quite indescribable, and their enthusiasm truly marvellous and deeply touching. The cheering was quite deafening and every face seemed to be filled with real joy . . .' (22 June 1897.)

The same day Lord Salisbury wrote a letter of congratulation on

> 'the brilliant success that the Jubilee has been. It will live in history as a unique and incomparable expression of the increasingly warm affection that has grown up between the sovereign of a mighty dominion and her subjects from every part of the world.'

Judging by numerous other accounts Lord Salisbury's words were not at all exaggerated. But though the jubilees were a spectacular advertisement of England and her Empire, most of the Queen's loyal subjects regarded them as her own personal triumph. Her popularity and the affection in which she was held by the nation, rich and poor, silenced criticism of her long withdrawal from public life after the death of the Prince Consort. The fact that she rarely came to London or attended ceremonial functions lent to her two jubilee appearances the added value of rarity.

The theme of the nation's homage to its Queen was, first and foremost, her great age and long reign. There were few among the thousands sharing in the rejoicings of 1897 who had not not beheld the Queen for the better part of their lives as an enduring symbol of Empire, indeed, most of them had been born during her reign. Other public figures had shone for a while and then vanished, but the Queen lived on, the object from year to year of constant publicity, with the Court Circular and the newspapers announcing daily what she did and whom she received. The long period of her reign had been a fortunate one. There had been progress in every field, democratic government had increased, there had been peace almost unbroken during which, nevertheless, overseas possessions and the nation's might had grown continually. Even the insecure and overworked poor, whose miserable existences were momentarily enlivened by the processions and the pageantry, could share in the feeling that they were citizens of a master race, the most outstanding race of rulers since the Romans. Under the circumstances it was not difficult to make speeches and write articles full of national pride without exaggerating either the gains made during the Queen's reign or Britain's present greatness.

The personal devotion inspired by Queen Victoria in her subjects can be more fully understood by comparing it with the similar, though less fervently expressed popularity of her successors to the throne. As if some of the Queen's own popularity had rubbed off on her descendants, those of them who have reigned in the twentieth century have been accorded their own share of loyal admiration and homage at their accessions, coronations and jubilees.

This reflection of Victoria's popularity was enjoyed as much by her son Edward VII as by her grandson George V, though their natures were greatly dissimilar. These two sovereigns have been regarded as the essence of all that is British, though in aspects diametrically opposed: Edward, the pleasure-loving, party-going voluptuary: George, the more commonplace, respectable, stamp-collecting, devoted family man. Their two natures have also been examined in the more complicated terms of depth-psychology. According to these theories, Edward was the personification of the *id*, the subconscious, nocturnal, sleeping Englishman, dreaming voluptuous dreams; while George corresponded to the super-ego, the daytime Englishman concentrated on work and duty. The three later successors to the throne have been analysed on similar lines: Edward VIII, the playful, sportive Prince Charming, still boyish at forty; George VI, whose determination and devotion to duty following his brother's abdication, whose victory over the draw-back of a speech impediment, and whose diffidence and modest simplicity touched and won the hearts of the nation; similarly, his daughter Elizabeth, called as a very young woman to be the mother of her country, appealed because of her sex to men's sense of chivalry and to women's claim to equality with men; she seemed a sort of reincarnation of her great-grandmother as a young woman and a reminder that the figure of Queen Victoria is still at the heart of the persisting English liking for royalty.

When Queen Victoria drove through the streets of London in 1897, the combination of qualities which appealed to the onlookers was vastly different from those of her successors to the throne. In common with George V and VI she represented virtue, but in contrast to all of her descendants she was the embodiment of old age, sorrow and human destiny. Every onlooker must have been struck by the paradox inherent in the fact that this dumpy, anxious-looking old woman, with tired, purblind eyes (dulled by incipient cataracts) in the lined and jowly face, should be the symbol of a paramount world power. And then, everyone knew why the Queen invariably wore black and for whom it was that she had mourned for the past forty years, for she had spoken of her bereavement in her published Journals and it was well known that she shrank from appearing publicly as the sorrowing widow whose loneliness was a constant source of depression to her after Albert's death.

Only a few short years after her Diamond Jubilee the Queen herself was to die, thus bringing to an end the age already called 'Victorian'. On that second jubilee drive through London's streets many, including the Queen and her Prime Minister Lord Salisbury, must have realized that they were writing one more page into history.

By her jubilees, the Queen reaffirmed the monarchy and the meaning of monarchy in England—so much was clear to any one with the slightest knowledge of history. Victoria's actions and her fame have helped her descendants. They too, without being in any way remarkable, have had certain qualities useful to the professional monarch. With few exceptions, her predecessors since the reign of Queen Elizabeth had been bad rulers, shifty, deceitful, exceptionally stupid or exceptionally licentious, and all of them with a taint of general moral squalor.

The official biographer of both Queen Victoria and Edward VII, Sir Sydney Lee, though too deferential and often too lavish with the whitewash, did say, nevertheless, that before Victoria the throne of England had been successively occupied by 'an imbecile, a profligate and a buffoon'. Her grandfather, George III (1760–1820) was, when younger, notorious for his lack of intellect, narrowness of outlook and despotic nature. In later life he became mentally unbalanced and in 1810 went totally insane. His son, George IV, Victoria's uncle, Prince

Regent from 1810, King from 1820 to 1830, was notorious for his extravagance and profligacy. His scandalous divorce proceedings against Queen Caroline made him detested by the whole nation. When he died *The Times* summed up: 'Never has a person been less mourned by anybody than the late King. . . . If George IV ever had a friend, a real friend, in any social group—we can assure you that his or her name has never come to our ears.' Victoria's uncle, William IV (1830–37), was a blustering sailor-man, coarse and rowdy in his cups after his midday dinner. When he died, at twelve minutes past two a.m. on 20 June 1837, *The Spectator* for that week wrote:

> 'Notwithstanding his feebleness of purpose and littleness of mind, his ignorance and his prejudices, William the Fourth was to the last a popular sovereign; but his very popularity was acquired at the price of something like public contempt. . . . There might be a kind of fondness, but no real respect for such a person.'

The King was dead. Long live the Queen! She was barely eighteen. A short account of Victoria's life is appropriate, at this stage, as a background to the discussion of her complex and fascinating personality.

Victoria's father, the Duke of Kent, died when she was a year old. She was brought up in comparative simplicity by her mother, who was born a princess of Saxe-Coburg. Her two uncles, who became king in succession, took little interest in the girl who was to succeed them. Her ability in languages was good and she spoke fluent French and German. She learnt the customary social graces and acquired some knowledge of history, geography and politics. Her childhood was overshadowed by disagreements with her mother, whose friendship—or, as some thought, intimate relationship—with her Comptroller of the Household, Sir John Conroy, an unscrupulous, self-seeking intriguer, made the girl jealous and embittered. Victoria's despair at her mother's death, decades later, was perhaps caused by the remorse she felt because of her earlier estrangement from her mother and by disquieting memories of those unhappy experiences of her childhood.

When she was sixteen the young princess started a diary, though it was not till later that she wrote in it with any regularity. 'I *love* to be employed; I *hate* to be *idle* . . .' she wrote in one of her earlier entries (Tuesday, 27 January 1835).

These words could have been a motto for her life; she hastened from one duty to another, from letter to letter, and even her pleasures were managed with orderliness and energy—she was an ambitious wayfarer through life, each of her days filled with a sequence of big and small events.

A few months after her eighteenth birthday Victoria became Queen of England. From the start she displayed great self-assurance and a spirit of independence. As one of the first declarations of her emancipation she refused to sleep any longer in the same room with her mother. She also revealed a tendency to look for support toward some man—easily explainable without delving too deeply in depth-psychology: as a search for a father-figure. The first such figure was Leopold I of Belgium, her maternal uncle, with whom she carried on a regular correspondence until his death in 1865; she asked his advice constantly, especially before her marriage. The next paternal friend and mentor was her Prime Minister, Lord Melbourne, fifty-eight years old when she came to the throne in 1837; he was leader, at least in name, of the Liberal cabinet, and had been Lord Grey's great reform minister in earlier cabinets—worldly, conventional, a sceptic, possessing considerable literary culture, wit and with a broken heart to boot, or at any rate an attractive air of melancholy as a result of his wife's love affair with the great Lord Byron. Victoria very soon had complete confidence in Lord Melbourne. She became devoted to him and even slightly infatuated. They talked and wrote to each other, about politics, people, events and etiquette: on his side their discourse was a mixture of information and gossip, bantering and slightly didactic; on hers, it was coquettish, childishly inconsequent and scatterbrained, with even a touch of romantic flirtatiousness. She asked him about her looks, hinted that she was jealous of his other women friends. When Melbourne was forced out of office in 1839 the Queen was in despair and she prevented the leader of the Tories, Sir Robert Peel, from forming a government, by refusing, in her first political act, to bow to tradition, dismiss her Ladies of the Bedchamber and accept those appointed by the new cabinet. And Lord Melbourne came back with all his Whigs. But sixty years later, she admitted that because of her youth she had made a big mistake with her handling of the Ladies of the Bedchamber crisis—one which she would never have repeated.

In February 1840, the Queen, now turned twenty, married her cousin (on her mother's side) Prince Albert of Saxe-Coburg-Gotha, who was also twenty. The two of them—and especially Victoria—were in love before their marriage and their almost twenty-one years together became one of history's most celebrated examples of happy married life. Albert, as Victoria never tired of pointing out, was a man with a handsome face and a good figure; he was attentive, kind, cultured, earnest—not for nothing has he been called Albert the Good; his marital fidelity was assured through his lukewarm interest in other women and possibly because he was not of a very sensual nature—though this was something the Queen never noticed. Because of his knowledge and an almost idealistic sense of duty—which made some people feel that he was a bit priggish—he was also a suitable father substitute and Melbourne in this role soon faded to a shadow in the Queen's mind. As time went on Victoria, who bore nine children in eighteen years, gave Albert more and more say in political affairs; and it came to be said in later years that he was both king and prime minister—a highly exaggerated conception which, however, does give an idea of the kind of role he played. Even in their private life Albert was the stronger, the leader, and Victoria, with an almost aggressive tenderness, the clinging vine. Albert, according to Victoria's own expression was 'my father, my protector, my guide and adviser in all and everything, my mother (I might almost say) as well as my husband'. (9 June 1858.)

On 14 December 1861, the Prince Consort died at Windsor Castle, of typhoid fever and for the next forty years—half her lifetime—the Queen was alone, in the sense of not having a permanent adviser or collaborator. The indolence and profligacy of her eldest son, Edward, Prince of Wales, had estranged him from his mother, who neglected him in the domestic life of the royal family and systematically excluded him from any part in her political duties. Her eldest daughter (and her first-born) Princess Victoria, who was greatly attached to her, had married Prince Frederick of Prussia a few years before Albert's death and was to become the future German Empress. Victoria's official advisers, her Prime Ministers, came and went, sometimes detested, sometimes highly trusted. One of them, Disraeli, became a friend and served as an ageing, pallid version of the father-husband. In her widowhood the Queen lived for many years, usually at Balmoral, in lengthy isolation, which kept her away from London. Even when this extreme isolation was at last broken, she seldom attended official functions or went about in society. But during these decades of retirement she became a legend, world-famous as a symbol of England and England's immense power, and at the same time a symbol of devotion to duty, of mastery over sorrow, of womanly wisdom and goodness. With the passing of the years she became the world's oldest Queen, with children, grandchildren and great-grandchildren scattered throughout Europe's royal houses. A great myth grew up around her, the creation of fellow monarchs and statesmen and the features of this myth were added to and embellished by biographers and historians until, at her death, the real Victoria was hidden under a thicket of fact and fiction, distortion and idealization, so that even today, more than sixty years later, the search for the 'real' Victoria still goes on.

Meanwhile, we have her correspondence, in which the Queen reveals her own conception of the 'real' Victoria.

The most recent collections of Queen Victoria's letters to be published, *Dearest Child* and *Dearest Mama*, selected and edited with great skill by Roger Fulford, appeared in 1964 and 1968 respectively. The first of these comprises about a third of the letters written by the

Queen to her eldest daughter Victoria, the Princess Royal, between January 1858 (when the Princess married Prince William of Prussia) and December 1861. *Dearest Mama* continues the correspondence up to 1864. The collections include a number of letters from the Princess in reply to her mother, and their correspondence occupies more than 350 closely-printed pages, totalling some 100,000 words, in each book. Roger Fulford relates that this exchange of letters continued with almost the same intensity up to the time of the deaths of both mother and daughter in 1901—forty-three years all told. The Queen wrote at least twice a week; this means that her letters to her daughter comprised 250 to 300 printed pages a year, amounting to at least 10,000 pages. Her total output of letters was beyond any doubt many times greater than this. As one of the most prolific letter-writers on record Queen Victoria must have written at least a thousand pages a year and many tens of thousands throughout her lifetime. There can be few similar parallels of such epistolary industry; in fact the Queen's chief private occupation was letter-writing, partly because she had hordes of friends and relatives living abroad, and partly because she lived for long periods outside London—at Windsor or even farther away, generally at Osborne and Balmoral. But the principal reason for this overwhelming production was that the Queen had an irresistable urge to communicate and to do so in correspondence. She had a marked and progressive difficulty in expressing herself in speech. She detested casual conversation and small-talk and frequently gave orders to secretaries and courtiers in her entourage by means of little notes. Much of her correspondence has never been published and her Journal was piously transcribed, altered, abridged and the originals destroyed after her death by her youngest daughter, Princess Beatrice—an incalculable loss to posterity.

The most important collection of the Queen's letters is the official one, published between 1907 and 1932 in nine volumes comprising some 7,000 pages. A number of entries from the Queen's Journal are included, as well as letters from her private secretary, Sir Henry Ponsonby, conveying her orders, and letters from other persons to the Queen and Ponsonby.

A number of letters concerning the Queen have also been published in special collections and biographies. The Queen herself published two volumes of her Journals, reminiscences of happy holidays in Scotland: *Leaves from a Journal of Our Life in the Highlands* in 1865 and *More Leaves* in 1884.

The correspondence between Victoria and Albert is comparatively scanty—after their marriage they were never separated except for very short periods. The two largest single series of letters are contained in the Queen's correspondence with her uncle King Leopold of Belgium, from 1828 to 1865, and with the Princess Royal from 1858 to 1901. There are a great number of letters to relatives and also, of course, in a very great range, to leading statesmen.

The Queen wrote swiftly, without corrections or crossings-out, though she underlined copiously, with one, two or sometimes even three lines. Her handwriting, though graceful and decisive and full of character, is not easy to read. She used frequent abbreviations and contractions and almost invariably, instead of spelling out 'and' she used the ampersand. Her impetuousness is frequently apparent in the somewhat clumsy structure of her sentences, which are linked together by quantities of dashes and phrases in brackets. The underscorings have been omitted in some collections of letters and in letters quoted in biographies, but they are usually indicated by italicizing the underscored words—the procedure adopted here. The underscorings undoubtedly contributed to the Queen's peculiarly personal style and in some cases they were necessary to the general sense of what she was saying. According to Dormer Creston, however, in *The Youthful Queen Victoria* (1952), the Queen's often frenzied underlining was merely a bad habit which she had caught from her Uncle Leopold in their long correspondence of her youth, and if the letters are read 'ignoring these passionate italics' all her wisdom and shrewdness show through.

The Queen's character and actions, with their extraordinary mixture of contradictions, have continued to fascinate succeeding generations. The official biography, by Sir Sidney Lee, appeared in 1902. Today the biographies of Queen Victoria are legion. Perhaps the most famous of them all is Lytton Strachey's *Queen Victoria*, published in 1921. His book is a work of masterly precision and subtlety, in which irony and tenderness mingle but are accompanied by a 'dead-pan' matter-of-factness and mock solemnity, not to mention a patronizing air of superiority that can be extremely irritating. Strachey's 'pervasive mockery' has been the cause of much hostile criticism of the book and its author in recent years.

The latest biography, *Victoria R.I.* (1964), by Lady Longford (author, as Elizabeth Pakenham, of *Jameson's Raid*, 1960, and a distinguished biographer and researcher into aspects of the Victorian Age), is rich in factual detail and though occasionally somewhat too benevolent in argument and analysis, is on the whole wisely balanced in attitude and full of sympathetic understanding of the Queen. Other biographies are doubtless in preparation and will surely continue to appear for a long time to come, as further facts about Queen Victoria's life and fascinating personality are observed, explored or discovered.

The Woman

I

Victoria proposed to Albert on 15 October 1839 and they were married on 10 January of the following year. Their correspondence during the period of their courtship and their correspondence with King Leopold of Belgium—Victoria's maternal and Albert's paternal uncle—is of great interest, especially as it shows clearly the difference between the Queen's feelings for Albert, and her attitude to him, before and after their marriage.

Victoria, as a newly-engaged young woman, was head-over-heels in love and full of praises of her betrothed's physical, moral and intellectual qualities. But there was a note of self-assertiveness and superiority in her letters which indicated that she intended to remain the sovereign Queen in her relationship with Albert—of whose 'sacrifice', she said, she was well aware. By this she meant that Albert would be a mere husband, with none of the rights or duties of a monarch.

When Albert, on Uncle Leopold's advice, said that he would like to have a peerage after they were married, Victoria wrote (on 27 November 1839) that this would not be possible, because:

> '*The English are very jealous of any foreigner interfering in the government of this country, and already in some of the papers (which are friendly to me and you) expressed a hope that you would not interfere. And, though I know you never would, still, if you were a Peer, they would all say, the Prince meant to play a political part.*'

When the Prince asked to have a say in choosing his gentlemen in waiting, Victoria firmly refused his request.

> 'As to your wish about your gentlemen, my dear Albert, I must tell you quite honestly that it will not do. You may entirely rely upon me that the people who will be about you will be absolutely pleasant people, of high standing and good character.' (8 December 1839.)

She emphasized that these appointments could not be postponed until the Prince's arrival in England. '*It will also not do to wait till you come to appoint all your own people. I am distressed to tell you what I fear you do not like,* but it is necessary, my dearest, most excellent Albert.' (23 December 1839.)

When Albert wanted to alter the wedding arrangements to enable them to have a longer honeymoon—they only spent a couple of days at Windsor, and then not entirely alone—he was given a fresh rebuke:

> '. . . you have written to me in one of your letters about our stay in Windsor, but my dear Albert you have not at all understood the

> matter. *You forget, my dearest Love, that I am the sovereign, and that business can stop and wait for nothing. Parliament is sitting, and something occurs almost every day, for which I may be required, and it is impossible for me to be absent from London;* therefore two or three days is already a long time to be absent. I am never easy a moment, if I am not on the spot, and see and hear what is going on, and everybody, including all my Aunts (who are very knowing in all these things), says I must come out after the second day, for as I must be surrounded by my Court, I cannot keep alone. This is also my own wish in every way.' (31 January 1840.)

Victoria surely displayed her innocence, if not her ignorance, in believing that two or three days was too long for her to be away from the business of ruling. She herself had admitted that she 'knew nothing about anything'. When she came to the throne she wrote in her Journal: 'I felt how unfitted I was for my station'; and she recorded her confession to Lord Melbourne that: 'I often felt so conscious of saying stupid things in conversation, and that I thought I was often very childish'. Besides, she left politics so entirely to Melbourne that she could not have discussed them even if she had wished.

Immediately after the wedding Victoria's tone to Albert changed. The girlish infatuation became, almost overnight, all that was considered truly womanly by Victorian standards—she was now a loving wife, self-sacrificingly and devotedly intent on making her husband happy. In her usual prompt, frank and efficient way, Victoria wrote to Uncle Leopold, the very day after her wedding, to tell him all about her happiness.

> 'My dearest Uncle—I write to you from here [Windsor Castle], the happiest Being that ever existed. Really I do not think it *possible* for anyone in the world to be *happier*, or AS happy as I am. He is an Angel, and his kindness and affection for me is really touching. To look into those dear eyes, and that dear sunny face, is enough to make me adore him. What I can do to make him happy will be my greatest delight.' (11 February 1840.)

There is something oddly and touchingly artless about this letter, something which, considering that it was her wedding-night (and that she was later to emphasize often enough her distaste for matters of sex), might almost make one wonder if the marriage had really been consummated. As the years went by, this loving tone became typical of all her letters to or about Albert. She called him 'an angel', 'my beloved', 'the best man in the world', 'my lord and master'.

But it was some time before Victoria thought of Albert as her lord or master, or at any rate before she took to calling him that. Her change of attitude was slow to develop. After they had been married for more than a year there were letters in which Albert was praised to the skies as husband and lover, but there was never a hint of his being regarded as unofficial royal consort or regent.

'My dearest Angel is indeed a great comfort to me', she wrote to Uncle Leopold (18 May 1841). 'He takes the greatest interest in what goes on, feeling with and for me, and yet abstaining as he ought from biassing me either way, though we talk much on the subject, and his judgment is, as you say, good and mild . . .'

By degrees Albert became the dominating partner and quite obviously the one who made the decisions, with the Queen acting more or less as his secretary and, when necessary, as his deputy in dealings with ministers. Some years before Albert's death it had come to seem a matter of course that their eldest daughter, Princess Victoria, now the Crown Princess of Prussia, should write to her mother about personal matters, but discuss political affairs with her father—who did not always show these letters to his wife.

It is almost impossible to follow closely this change in Victoria. It took place so gradually, almost imperceptibly—as the Queen discovered her husband's superiority in knowledge and judgement, through his discussions with her about political affairs; as she became aware of his deductive and analytical gifts; as she pondered his criticism of her. In the end he was advising her on policy and even ordering her about. The change in Victoria was then so marked that some of her courtiers could not resist making unkind fun of her as 'Queen Albertine'.

Even the Queen's behaviour, in public and in private, altered under the Prince's influence and direction. She became more serious, more dignified, less impulsive and impetuous, less given to teasing and bursts of high-spirited laughter or fits of mere silliness. She once said to Albert: 'It is you who have entirely formed me.'

Victoria's relationship with Albert can be seen in some of the letters she wrote about him at various times. On 9 February 1857, four years before his death, she wrote to Uncle Leopold:

> 'Tomorrow is the eighteenth anniversary of my blessed marriage, which has brought such universal blessings on this country and Europe! For *What* has not my beloved and perfect Albert done? Raised monarchy to the *highest* pinnacle of *respect*, and rendered it *popular* beyond what it *ever* was in this country!'

She wrote to her daughter (on 25 January 1858), 'I have ever looked on the blessed day which united me to your beloved and perfect Papa—as the cause not only of my own happiness (a happiness few if any enjoy) but as the one which brought happiness and blessings on this country!'

When Albert died she gave vent to her despair in a series of letters in which she declared repeatedly that she intended to act in every way as Albert would have wished. She wrote to Uncle Leopold on 20 December 1861:

'. . . My *life* as a *happy* one is *ended*! the world is gone for *me*! If I *must* live on (and I will do nothing to make me worse than I am), it is henceforth for our poor fatherless children—for my unhappy country, which has lost *all* in losing him—and in *only* doing what I know and *feel* he would wish, for he *is* near me—his spirit will guide and inspire me! But oh! To be cut off in the prime of life—. . . is too awful, too cruel! And yet it *must* be for *his* good, his happiness! His purity was too great, his aspiration *too high* for this poor, miserable world! His great soul is now only enjoying *that* for which it *was* worthy!'

Some days later she wrote (24 December 1861):

'I am also anxious to repeat *one* thing, and *that one* is *my firm* resolve, my *irrevocable decision*, viz. that *his* wishes—*his* plans—about everything, *his* views about *every* thing are to be *my law!* And *no human power* will make me swerve from *what he* decided and wished . . . I am *also determined* that *no one* person, may *he* be ever so good, ever so devoted among my servants—is to lead or guide or dictate *to me*. I know *how he* would disapprove of it. And I live *on* with him, for him; in fact I am only *outwardly* separated from him, and only for a *time*.'

The Queen gave expression to her loss in a way that was strange even then and nowadays seems grotesque. Albert's bedroom at Windsor was kept exactly as it had been in his lifetime. His sheets and towels were changed regularly, as before. Hot water was brought to the room each evening. Everything that reminded Victoria of her husband was left untouched—pictures, clothing, furniture, knick-knacks. Her letters were written (then and as long as she lived) on notepaper with black borders more than half an inch wide, and she never left off her deep mourning attire or her widow's cap.

As her sorrow decreased with the years the Queen was sometimes a prey to feelings of guilt because her grief was less intense, but in all other respects she appeared to have no difficulty in being able to live up to her ideal conception of a sorrowing widow.

Victoria's letters to the Princess Royal display with unusual clarity the endearing qualities that are generally considered characteristic of her as a letter writer: vivacity, spontaneity, naturalness. 'Vicky' wrote to her mother (18 April 1859) from Berlin:

'Indeed it is as you suppose my greatest delight to write to you which I do whenever I have a spare moment and you are so easy to please, dear Mama, you allow me to write short or long ones just as I like. I never had a correspondence that I enjoyed so much because it is so natural and like thinking aloud.'

The Princess also wrote: 'It seems to me as if we have never understood each other so well and never enjoyed exchanging every passing feeling and thought so much and with so little restraint . . .'

The intensity of the Queen's interest is best illustrated by her barrage of questions and her advice to her daughter about every conceivable detail of her life, important or trifling. On 6 February 1858 (twelve days after the Princess Royal's marriage, four days after she had left for Germany with her husband), the Queen wrote from Buckingham Palace:

'Don't trouble yourself with descriptions of great things, leave that to Jane C. and Lord Sydney and the papers, but give me your feelings—and your impressions about people and things, and little interior details.

1. What dress and bonnet did you wear on landing? And what bonnet the 2 next days?

2. What sort of rooms had you at Cologne and Magdeburg?

3. Did you dine with your people at Cologne and did you sup at Magdeburg at 12?

4. What cloak did you wear on the road, and have you been drawing?

5. How do you like the German diet—and how do your poor maids bear this hurry scurry?'

(The two courtiers to whom descriptions of all the more important events were to be left were Lady Churchill—Jane C.—Lady of the Bedchamber, and Lord Sydney, Groom of the Bedchamber, who accompanied Princess Victoria to Germany.)

On 7 February 1858, the Queen wrote:

'Now that you are established at your new home, you must try and answer my questions and enter into some of the subjects I mention else we can never replace conversation. You remember how vexed you always were when you did not get answers to your letters. . . . but I can't tell you how trying, how almost unbearable it is to know so little of real details which alas! no one will tell us. . . . Get Jane C. to tell me all about your rooms—the railways, carriages etc. Has the railway carriage got a small room to it? And (you will think me as bad as Leopold B.) were your rooms on the journey and at Potsdam arranged according to English fashion? [Leopold B. was the Belgian Crown Prince, Leopold of Brabant (1835–1901), afterwards King Leopold II of the Belgians. His inquisitiveness—especially on domestic trifles—irritated the Queen. She was asking about the arrangements for retiring on the journey.] Then I see by the papers you wore a green dress at the Cologne concert. Was that the one with the black lace? You must not be impatient about all these details which I am so anxious to know, for I am anxious to know how all my toilettes succeeded? The pink ball dress at Brussels was so much admired.'

And so in this vein the questioning continued, page after page, letter after letter; the Princess was to give an account of the arrangement of her furniture, the names of her maids, what food she had been served at parties, when she got up and when she went to bed. Advice alternated with the questions. The Princess was to eat in moderation, not drink too much wine—which would make her fat and red-faced. She was to go to the dentist regularly, not slump down when she was reading or sewing, above all she was to see that there was plenty of fresh air in her rooms and that they were reasonably warmed.

The letters did not touch solely on such details. They contained the Queen's thoughts and accounts of her life, the family, education, marital experiences; they also touched on current politics either as topics for discussion, or perhaps as an outlet for her own feelings. Running through it all was the enthusiasm, the spontaneity and artlessness. The uninhibited flow of the Queen's thoughts avoided nothing, concealed nothing.

The underlying element of Victoria's personality, Lytton Strachey wrote,

'was a peculiar sincerity. Her truthfulness, her single-mindedness, the vividness of her emotions and her unrestrained expression of them, were the varied forms which this central characteristic assumed. It was her sincerity which gave her at once her impressiveness, her charm and her absurdity. She moved through life with the imposing certitude of one to whom concealment was impossible—either towards her surroundings or towards herself.'

Perhaps it should be added that honesty in this sense presupposes a certain insensitivity, even a touch of the superficial. The Queen never pondered or thought out what she was going to say or write, but dashed it off in a spontaneous expression of her immediate moods and feelings which, however intense, were not of long duration. But though she yielded to the mood of the moment, this of course did not rule out her ability to have feelings that were deep and lasting. With age and the added dignity of prestige—and after her husband's death when there was no longer anyone to criticize her to her face—this honesty of hers sometimes became wayward and capricious; her position made it possible for her to be blunt to the point of rudeness.

The best introduction to the Queen's personality is, in many ways, her letters to the Princess Royal and this is especially true in what concerns her intimate feelings about matters of love and sex, which are closely related to but still distinguishable from, her moral and political ideas on those subjects in their respective spheres of personal relationships and dynastic matchmaking.

Her love for her husband during the last years of her marriage—twenty years after her wedding—gives an air of blitheness and joy to most of her letters of this period. When her daughter praised her own husband, Victoria replied in a mood of slightly jealous monopoly that this was exactly what she felt for her own husband, whom, possibly, no other husband could ever surpass.

> 15 February 1858. 'You know, my dearest, that I never can admit any other wife can be as happy as I am—so I can admit no comparison for I maintain Papa is unlike anyone who lives or ever lived and will live.'

> 9 June 1858: '. . . I must also repeat that what you say about your feelings towards your husband are only those which I have ever felt and shall ever feel! But I cannot ever think or admit that anyone can be as blessed as I am with such a husband and such a perfection as a husband; for Papa has been and is everything to me. I had led a very unhappy life as a child—had no scope for my very violent feelings of affection—had no brothers and sisters to live with—never had a father—from my unfortunate circumstances was not on a comfortable or at all intimate or confidential footing with my mother (so different from you to me)—much as I love her now—and did not know what a happy domestic life was! All this is the complete contrast to your happy childhood and home. Consequently I owe everything to dearest Papa. He was my father, my protector, my guide and adviser in all and everything, my mother (I might almost say) as well as my husband. I suppose no-one ever was so completely altered and changed in every way as I was by dearest Papa's influence. Papa's position towards me is therefore of a very peculiar character and when he is away I feel quite paralysed.'

Victoria's close attachment to her husband did not prevent her from criticizing him sometimes to her daughter. A hint of jealousy is apparent even here, since the Queen seems to have been slightly irritated whenever the Princess praised her father too highly. All intelligent men, Victoria said, have a certain contempt for women. 'That despising our poor degraded sex—(for what else is it as we poor creatures are born for man's pleasure and amusement, and destined to go through endless sufferings and trials?) is a little in all clever men's natures.' Not even perfect Albert was without this failing.

'. . . dear Papa even is not quite exempt though he would not admit it—but he laughs and sneers constantly at many of them, and at our unavoidable inconveniences, etc. though he hates the want of affection, of due attention to and protection of them, says that men who leave their home affairs—and the education of their children to their wives—forget their first duties.' (10 August 1859.)

'You say no one is perfect but Papa. But he has his faults too. He is often very trying—in his hastiness and love of business—and I think you would find it very trying if Fritz was as hasty and harsh (momentarily and unintentionally as it is) as he is!' (1 October 1861.)

Victoria also wrote with considerable frankness about marriage. It seems clear that the nuptial night had been a shock to her, ignorant as she was in matters of sex, and that she considered her continual pregnancies a burden; she expressed herself in such a way as to indicate that she regarded pregnancy as the inevitable consequence of sexual intercourse and that because of this she could not properly distinguish between the unpleasantness of pregnancy and the enjoyment of sex—if, indeed, she did enjoy it. On the eve of 17-year-old Vicky's wedding and departure for Germany, Victoria exclaimed to Albert that it was like sacrificing a lamb. She discussed this later with her daughter. On 20 April 1859 she wrote to Vicky:

'Yes dearest, it is an awful moment to have to give up one's innocent child to a man, be he ever so kind and good—and to think of all she must go through! I can't say what I suffered, what I felt—what struggles I had to go through—(indeed I have not quite got over it yet) and that last night when we took you to your room, and you cried so much, I said to Papa as we came back "after all it is like taking a poor lamb to be sacrificed". You know now—what I meant, dear. I know God has willed it so and that these are the trials which we poor women must go through; no father, no man can feel this! Papa never would enter into it all! As in fact he seldom can in my very violent feelings.'

Again and again the Queen came back to the thought that it would have been wonderful if she could have had a year or two of married life with her husband without the presence of children to disturb them. '. . . you will now understand why I often grudged you children being always there, when I longed to be alone with dearest Papa! Those are always my happiest moments!', she wrote on 2 March 1858; and again, on 14 April: 'If I had had a year of happy enjoyment with dear Papa to myself—how thankful I should have been!'

Having heard rumours (which proved unfounded) that the Princess Royal was pregnant she wrote (21 April 1858) 'I cannot tell you how happy I am that you are not in an unenviable position. I never can rejoice by hearing that a poor young thing is pulled down by this trial.'

> 'Though I quite admit the comfort and blessing good and amiable children are—though they are an awful plague and anxiety for which they show one so little gratitude very often! What made me so miserable was—to have the two first years of my married life utterly spoilt by this occupation! I could enjoy nothing—not travel about or go about with dear Papa and if I had waited a year, as I hope you will, it would have been very different.'

In subsequent letters she went over all the details connected with her own pregnancies—the morning sickness, the feelings of shame, of being hampered and incapacitated. Having the first child, the Queen said, was a tremendous shock, for it so completely outraged the feelings of propriety of any young woman—feelings to which, Heaven alone knew! the marital act itself was quite shock enough to begin with. (12 April 1858.)

When the Princess Royal's husband wrote (26 May 1858) to say that she really was pregnant, the Queen replied to her daughter that 'the horrid news contained in Fritz's letter to Papa upset us dreadfully'.

Victoria harped continually on the difference between the states of the married and the unmarried woman—the one continually pregnant, the other free and untrammelled. 'I think people really marry far too much; it is such a lottery after all, and for a poor woman a doubtful happiness,' she wrote (3 May 1858); and two years later she repeated (16 May 1860):

> 'all marriage is such a lottery—the happiness is always an exchange —though it may be a very happy one—still the poor woman is bodily and morally the husband's slave. That always sticks in my throat. When I think of a merry, happy, free young girl—and look at the ailing, aching state a young wife generally is doomed to—which you can't deny is the penalty of marriage . . . I hope Fritz is duly shocked at your sufferings, for those very selfish men would not bear for a minute what we poor slaves have to endure.'

During the Princess Royal's convalescence from the birth of her first child—the future Kaiser Wilhelm II, who was born on 27 January

1859, little more than a year after the Princess's marriage—Victoria wrote to her full of immense pity. (The birth had been a difficult one and both the lives of mother and child had been in some danger.) '. . . it is a pleasure,' she said,

> 'to see how you feel like me even on all those distressing subjects so painful to a woman's feelings and especially to a young child as you are! I pitied you so! It is indeed too hard and dreadful what we have to go through and men ought to have an adoration for one, and indeed to do every thing to make up, for what after all they alone are the cause of! I must say it is a bad arrangement, but we must calmly, patiently bear it, and feel that we can't help it and therefore we must forget it, and the more we retain our pure, modest feelings, the easier it is to get over it all afterwards. I am very much like a girl in all these feelings, but since I have had a grown-up married daughter, and young married relations I have been obliged to hear and talk of things and details which I hate—but which are unavoidable.' (9 March 1859).

The Queen returned to this theme once more, in July 1860, when the Princess Royal wrote to tell her mother of her arrangements for the birth of her second child. She would, she said, arrange her rooms and make all final preparations 'the same as a person does that is going to have her head cut off'. The Queen replied (11 July 1860), in sympathetic agreement, that such arrangements were quite too horrid, and were indeed in the nature of an execution.

> 'Oh! if these selfish men—who are the cause of all one's misery, only knew what their poor slaves go through! What suffering—what humiliation to the delicate feelings of a poor woman, above all a young one—especially with those nasty doctors.'

The nastiness of doctors brought to the Queen's mind a book which she had recommended (unread) to her daughter some time previously, with the suggestion that it should be translated into German. Having now dipped into the book, *The Physiological and Moral Management of Infancy* by Dr Andrew Combe, an Edinburgh physiologist much in favour with the Royal Family (Dr James Paget the Court Physician had written the introduction), the Queen found it so 'horridly disgusting' on all subjects that she closed it, as she told her daughter, with indignation and 'shut it up in the press'. She took particular exception, she said, to 'the horrors about that peculiarly indelicate nursing', which she found far worse than all the other parts that had so disgusted her.

Victoria never ceased to complain about women's 'unenviable lot'. Her general remarks on the subject of sex, marriage and childbirth could be used to draw up a whole bill of indictment of men and nature—or of God, whom, nevertheless, she never mentioned without respect for his loving and guiding hand.

All this was perfectly in keeping with Victorian attitudes. The question of the Queen's erotic experience is quite another matter and it would seem opportune at this stage to discuss it in more general terms.

The subject is not so much as hinted at in the earlier biographies. And not even Lytton Strachey mentions it. The impression given by the body of writing about Victoria up to about 1930 is that she was a true Victorian woman, in other words, frigid. A totally different picture emerged later, especially through personal views expressed in private conversation. This altered view presented Victoria as concupiscent to the point of nymphomania. It has even been claimed that she hastened Albert's end by her sexual demands, which so debilitated him that his health was undermined. Lady Longford, Victoria's latest biographer, expresses this with more delicacy when she refers to 'those who argue that Queen Victoria, with her erotic Hanoverian inheritance, wore out Prince Albert by sheer greediness'.

This proliferation of rumour and conjecture, which almost succeeds in turning Victoria into some sort of Ninon de l'Enclos or Catherine the Great, can be attributed to a change in standards of what it is permissible to say as well as to the discovery of fresh material for study. The process of interpreting the Queen's sex life has been conditioned by a desire to extract from behind the Victorian façade a realistic conception more in keeping with modern beliefs about human behaviour. Biographers have seized upon Victoria's verbal preoccupation with chastity to suspect an overwhelming sensuality in her erotic make-up, and because of the Queen's general intensity of feeling, a corresponding sexual vitality has been taken for granted. Accounts of her relationship, in her widowhood, with the Highland gillie John Brown, have provided a supposedly firm basis on which to construct these fresh hypotheses.

Conversely, equally serious biographers have advanced the theory, through covert criticism of the more sensational assumptions, that the Queen, if not actually frigid, was only mildly interested in sex. Lady Longford, in her biography, has commented on Victoria's acknowledgement of her own 'passionate' nature in her frequent confession that 'my nature is too passionate, my emotions are too fervent'. But, as this biographer points out, by 'passionate' Victoria hardly meant 'hot blooded' in any erotic sense, only 'hot-tempered'; and in any case, unlike her ancestor King George IV, whichever of the seven deadly sins the Queen may have been beset by, lust was not one of them.

No definite verdict can be pronounced for the present. The facts as far as they are known support the hypothesis that the Queen's personal life was of a kind which even Victorians—those of them who were not exaggeratedly strict—regarded as decent: in other words, she lived in erotically satisfied monogamy. The fact that her wedding night was distressing and her continual pregnancies irksome naturally does not make this hypothesis any the less plausible. On the contrary, the ardour evident in Victoria's feeling for her husband would be incomprehensible in the absence of any erotic satisfaction.

Albert himself was possibly less sensual than the Queen. It seems certain that he was indifferent to other women and not especially ardent in his relationship with the Queen—the stories of Victoria having to coax her husband to bed might well have been based on old court rumours.

The 'Victorianism' of the Queen's speech and manners, and the attitude underlying them was undeniable. A wealth of information about this can be gleaned from her letters to the Princess Royal. The Queen was possibly more Victorian than the most perfect of Victorian ladies in her disgust of the physical side of sex. There was a lack of warmth in her attitude to small children, especially to tiny babies, whom she tended to regard as repulsive little animals. She wrote (4 May 1859) that she was not fond of babies,

> 'but I like them better than I did, if they are nice and pretty . . . Abstractedly, I have no *tendre* for them till they have become a little human; an ugly baby is a nasty object—and the prettiest is frightful when undressed—till about four months; in short, as long as they have their big body and little limbs and that terrible frog-like action.'

When there was no doubt about the Princess Royal's pregnancy the Queen wrote to her:

> 'What you say of the pride of giving life to an immortal soul is very fine, dear, but I own I cannot enter into that; I think much more of our being like a cow or a dog at such moments; when our poor nature becomes so very animal and unecstatic—but for you dear, if you are sensible and reasonable not in ecstasy nor spending your day with nurses and wet nurses, which is the ruin of many a refined and intellectual young lady, without adding to her real maternal duties, a child will be a great resource. Above all, my dear, do remember never to lose the modesty of a young girl towards others (without being prude); though you are married don't become a matron at once to whom everything can be said, and who minds saying nothing herself—I remained particular to a degree (indeed feel so now) and often feel shocked at the confidences of other married ladies.' (15 June 1858.)

And a year later, referring to a niece who was pregnant for the third time, she wrote:

> 'How can anyone, who has not been married above two years and three quarters (like Ada) rejoice at being a third time in that condition? I positively think those ladies who are always *enceinte* quite disgusting; it is more like a rabbit or a guinea-pig than anything else and really it is not very nice.' (15 June 1860.)

During the Princess Royal's first pregnancy the Queen was shocked by the uninhibited conversation of her cousin, Princess Mary of Cambridge (a plump young woman still not married-off at twenty-five), during a visit to Windsor of the young, newly-married Princess of Leiningen, who had captivated the Queen by her looks and charm.

> 'Marie looked lovely and is so ladylike and gentle and quiet, and such a contrast to poor Mary, who is so big now again—much worse than she was—and whose manners and I grieve to say conversation too, now—are not refined. Fancy . . . her asking *Papa*—if you had been very sick!!! A thing I now should not ask hardly any gentleman!!! and then very doubtful talk about wet nurses. I fear there is no hope for a husband. All this with her figure is too much. Her manners shocked our sweet modest rose—Marie.' (10 November 1858.)

Victoria's attitude often seems to be one of disgust at life—usually disgust with 'the facts of life', but even with things having nothing to do with sex. This trait can also be found in a few other Victorian figures. Possibly this peculiarity was intensified after Albert's death and, in conjunction with her grief and loneliness, may have formed the background to the emptiness and severity that can be glimpsed in her character. But she was unable to give intellectual or literary expression to such feelings: all she could do was to utter inarticulate cries of distress, the almost animal moans and wails with which she confronted crises.

A recurrent theme in her letters to the Princess Royal is criticism of her eldest son, Edward, Prince of Wales: 'I am in utter despair! The systematic idleness, laziness—disregard of everything is enough to break one's heart, and fills me with indignation . . to you I own, I am wretched about it. But don't mention this to a human being!' (8 March 1858.)

On her thirty-ninth birthday, teenage Bertie distressed her again. Describing the occasion and what the children did to celebrate it, she wrote: 'The only one of the children who neither drew, wrote, played or did anything to show his affection—beyond buying for me a table in Ireland—was Bertie. Oh! Bertie alas! alas! That is too sad a subject to enter on.' (28 May 1858.)

And again, in November:

> 'Poor Bertie! He vexes us so much. There is not a particle of reflection, or even attention to anything but dress! Nor the slightest desire to learn, on the contrary, *il se bouche les oreilles*, the moment anything of interest is being talked of. I only hope he will meet with some severe lesson to shame him out of his ignorance and dullness.' (17 November 1858.)

Poor Bertie, turned seventeen, was what we nowadays call 'a problem child'.

> 'Bertie continues such an anxiety, I tremble at the thought of only three years and a half being before us—when he will be of age and we can't hold him except by moral power! I shut my eyes to that terrible moment! He is improving very decidedly—but oh! it is the improvement of such a poor and still more idle intellect . . . But the greatest improvement I fear, will never make him fit for his position.' (9 April 1859.)

'Poor Bertie, I pity him; but I blame him too, for that idleness is really sinful.' (18 April 1860.)

Occasionally the Queen's accounts of her son's development were friendlier and more optimistic, but as a rule she only complained about his indolence, ignorance and lack of interest in anything serious. She also recorded her distaste of his appearance and looks—perhaps because his features were too like her own.

> 'Bertie is improved. . . . He is a little grown . . . but his nose and mouth are much grown also; the nose is becoming the true Coburg nose and begins to hang a little; but there remains unfortunately the want of chin which with that large nose and very large lips is not so well in profile . . .' (29 June 1859.)

And again, some months later:

> 'Bertie . . . is not at all in good looks; his nose and mouth are too enormous and as he pastes his hair down to his head and wears his clothes frightfully—he is really anything but good-looking. That coiffure is really too hideous with his small head and enormous features.' (7 April 1860.)

Victoria's image of her son almost gives the impression that she positively disliked him, although her evident bitterness was tempered by a semblance of compassion. To what extent she was justified by facts is something which cannot be gone into in detail at this juncture; but her comments on 'poor Bertie' would almost seem to bear out what Greville had written in his diary when the Prince was only seven: 'The hereditary and unfailing antipathy of our Sovereigns to their Heirs Apparent seems early to be taking root, and the Q. does not much like the child.'

Several writers, including Sir Philip Magnus, the latest biographer of Edward VII, believe that the strict upbringing mapped out for his son by Prince Albert and his adviser Baron Stockmar stunted the Prince of Wales's development and served to make his failings deeper-rooted. Others have pointed out that he possessed valuable qualities—an interest in people, an ability to get on with them and skill as a negotiator, qualities which his parents could not appreciate. Lord Ponsonby of Shulbrede, in his biography of his father Sir Henry Ponsonby, the Queen's Private Secretary from 1870–95, came to the same conclusions about the Prince of Wales as the Queen and Prince Albert. Sir Henry, too, believed that the Queen was undoubtedly justified in excluding her son from the reading of confidential papers and responsible official work: 'She had measured his capacities and inclinations and knew that nothing could be expected from him in that direction.'

On the other hand, Sir Henry said of the Prince of Wales's famous charm of manner that it would be quite impossible to overestimate what amounted to genius.

> 'It is not too much to say that in spite of drawbacks, faults and failures, it *made* him . . . foreign Ambassadors, Ministers of the Crown, representatives of the services and eminent men in all walks of life regarded him as the best-informed monarch that ever reigned. But it was all façade, the most engaging, decorative but quite misleading façade. There was practically nothing behind.'

At Edward's death, after his nine-year reign as Edward VII, those who had been deluded by his charm into overestimating his talents, Ponsonby wrote, tended to criticize Queen Victoria for not having made more use of them. 'But in her day Queen Victoria knew better.'

So much for poor Bertie—but there were signs of annoyance even with her beloved daughter, especially in retrospect. The Queen wrote to her that she had been a troublesome child because of her wilfulness and excessive high spirits, which her parents were forced to curb.

> 'I have no doubt dearest child that you can now much better appreciate Mama's love and affection and understand how all what you grumbled and struggled and kicked against was for your good, and meant in love!—your love and affection you know, dearest child, I never doubted, I was only often grieved and hurt at your manner, your temper.' (26 May 1858.)

And again:

> 'Doubt your real affection and your love, I did not, dearest child—but you did all you could to make me doubt it; for a more insubordinate and unequal-tempered child and girl I think I never saw! I must say so, honestly, now, dear. The tone you used to me, you know, shocked all who heard you, and if we had not made you feel that—you might have been very unhappy and made your husband very unhappy. The trouble you gave us all was indeed very great . . . you and Bertie (in very different ways) were indeed great difficulties . . . I am very curious to know whether I shall find some of the old tricks of former times in you? The standing on one leg, the violent laughing—the cramming in eating, the waddling in walking.' (28 July 1858.)

The Queen herself pointed out more than once that she did not care for small babies. Did she, in fact like children or the society of children, at all? The letters often give signs of an irritation which made it difficult for her to be indulgent towards the faults and awkwardnesses of her children. Her intimacy with her husband seems to have been so close that during his lifetime the children were more or less a matter of indifference to her. There is evidence of this in a letter to Queen Augusta of Prussia written a few years before the Princess Royal's marriage.

> 'I see the children much less and even here [at Balmoral], where Albert is often away all day long, I find no especial pleasure or compensation in the company of the elder children . . . And only very exceptionally do I find the rather intimate intercourse with them either agreeable or easy. You will not easily understand this, but it is caused by various factors, Firstly, I only feel properly *à mon aise* and quite happy when Albert is with me; secondly, I am used to carrying on my many affairs quite alone; and then I have grown up all alone, accustomed to the society of adult (and never with younger) people—lastly, I still cannot get used to the fact that Vicky is almost grown up. To me she still seems the same child, who had to be kept in order and therefore must not become too intimate. Here are my sincere feelings in contrast to yours.' (6 October 1856.)

After Albert's death the Queen undoubtedly came to need the children more, yet there do not appear to have been any noticeable demonstrations of affection in her daily sessions with them—such things were easier to express in letters.

Victoria's extravagant expressions of sorrow and despair at deaths and accidents are well-known and there are telling examples among her letters to the Princess Royal. When the Queen's mother, the Duchess of Kent, with whom she had previously been estranged for many years, died in 1861, at the age of seventy-five, she wrote:

> '. . . when I think that she can never speak to me again, that that dear loving voice is forever still that her love and affection can no longer cast a sunbeam over us—then I feel as if my heart would break! . . . You may imagine what it is—when it is the dearest object (but one) you possess! What the loss is to me—no one can tell! For forty-one years never parted for more than three months!' (16 March 1861.)

Three weeks later she still feels 'stupified—stunned—can't think how I lived through these three weeks . . . Lovely as the spring is here—I hardly can look at anything . . . I eat but little—and can't bear many faces' (6 April 1861).

When King Pedro V of Portugal, a distant relative by marriage, died of typhoid fever a few months later, within a week of his brother Ferdinand, the Queen was equally distraught at news of his death: 'We are in great sorrow and quite stunned and bewildered at the awful suddenness of this blow . . . Oh is it not shocking, too incredible that he should be gone! . . . It has been a terrible blow to us . . . we have been much crushed . . .' The words tumbled out—dreadfully shocked, awful misfortune, fearful loss, great sorrow, stunned and bewildered, shocking, too incredible, awful, dreadful, much shaken—the spate of emotional phrases filled a long letter.

It has been said, probably with some justification, that the Queen's manner of expressing sorrow when deaths occurred followed the conventional pattern of the period—when 'indulgence of woe was the measure of love for the departed'—but such was Victoria's intensity of utterance that it would seem also to have sprung from deep and sincere (though as a rule not lasting) feeling. Her formula for letters of condolence was similar to that employed by Henry James: the first part served to point out and emphasize the unique excellence of the departed; the second hinted that all was for the best and that the loved one's appointed time had come. The writer's sorrow was then converted into resignation or into comfort in the thought that the departed had gone to his or her rest, so to become a beautiful and restorative memory. By means of such a formula the earthly and the heavenly were united and human despair was merged into confidence in the hereafter.

The Queen, of course, added her personal touch to the formula. Arthur Ponsonby made the observation that

> 'Deaths and anniversaries of deaths drew from her repeated expressions of grief and sometimes in rather exaggerated terms, as if to

make up for not having paid much attention to the deceased when they were alive. Mixed with her genuine sorrow one cannot help detecting on occasions a note of resentment if not anger at the loss, so that one almost expects to find some direction in her best style of political indignation instructing her Private Secretary to address some remonstrance to the Almighty.'

2

'I will be good.' Victoria uttered these famous words when she was a child of eleven at the start of a history lesson with her governess, Fräulein Lehzen (created a German Baroness in 1827.) The girl was thinking primarily of being good at history and Latin and English grammar, but this not highly original resolve to be good at her lessons has been regarded as a key to her character and indeed there is some truth in the assumption. Victoria not only adjusted herself to moral behaviour, to following rules of conduct implanted in her, but also to being kind and good—that is, friendly, tolerant, considerate, and self sacrificing in the interests of others. Throughout her whole life she seems to have had moments of introspection—admittedly not profound—which filled her with dissatisfaction with herself and made her resolve to become a better person. In the recollections of her childhood which she wrote in 1872 she recorded her frequent bouts of bad temper and her subsequent regret.

'I was taught from the first to beg my maid's pardon for any naughtiness or rudeness towards her; a feeling I have ever retained, and think everyone should own their fault in a kind way to any one, be he or she the lowest—if one has been rude to or injured them by word or deed, especially those below you.' (Journal, 1872.)

When she was over sixty, in her Journal entry for New Year's Day 1881, she made one of her most revealing confessions:

'I feel how sadly deficient I am, and how over-sensitive and irritable, and how uncontrollable my temper is, when annoyed and hurt. But I am so overdone, so vexed, and in such distress about my country, that that must be my excuse. I will daily pray for God's help to improve.'

This propensity to self-examination, this spiritual concern, is unusual for one in the Queen's position. One looks in vain for a similar trait in the character of contemporary monarchs or heads of state. It is not unreasonable to suppose, as Lady Longford does, that the wish to be good was 'the guiding thread in Queen Victoria's life'. On 24 May 1837, she wrote in her diary: 'To-day is my 18th birthday. How old!

1. Queen Victoria, 1841. (By A. Penley)

2. Queen Victoria and Prince Albert at Buckingham Palace. (Photography by Roger Fenton, June 1854)

and yet how far am I from being what I should be.' And the following month, on her accession to the throne: 'I am very young, and perhaps in many, though not in all things, inexperienced, but I am sure, that very few have more real good will and more real desire to do what is fit and right than I have' (20 June 1837). Right through to her old age there is a note of dissatisfaction and longing in her letters and journal entries which indicate a spiritual yearning to be good. But this attitude was associated and indissolubly bound up with traits and ideas which were in direct contrast and tended to give a quite different and indeed a negative picture of the Queen. She was not unkind in the sense of taking pleasure in hurting or humiliating people, but she was often ruthless, brusque and indomitably self-willed. Her obstinacy, her unwillingness to alter her plans, her inability to put up with contradictions or disappointments increased with the years. This is most clearly noticeable in political matters but many examples of a similar nature among her personal relationships have been given by people of her entourage. Whenever the Queen had cause to be remorseful it was generally highly justified; but it is typical of her that although she was able to record her feelings of remorse she was never able to give concrete examples of the behaviour she regretted. On the whole she must have considered that her attempts to be good were successful—but this striving for perfection was not carried out with any saintly determination.

This aspect of her character must also include her great and increasing self-righteousness, also best illustrated in her political acts, of which more will be said later. She was rightly convinced of her good intentions and in consequence concluded quite naturally that what she wanted was for the best.

She spoke of herself as patriotic and also as liberal (though in a general, not a political sense). She had feelings of benevolence towards all races, loved peace and in her own clashes with monarchs and ministers was fortified by her conviction that people of the opposite opinion were unpatriotic, liberals, radicals and so forth—in short, that they were full of ill-will, were prompted by greed for power and party spirit or in the last resort were totally deranged. Heading the list of madmen was her arch-enemy Gladstone, whose behaviour and ideas she considered monstrous, wicked and socialistic. Not only were his motives actuated by vanity, ambition and malice, but he showed signs of madness. Over the decades she saw him variously as 'not quite sane', 'a half-mad fire-brand', a 'wild, fanatical old man', 'a half-crazy and in many ways ridiculous old man'. By 1892 he had become worse than a bad joke: 'a dangerous old fanatic . . . a deluded, excited old man of eighty-two trying to govern England & her vast Empire with the miserable democrats under him . . .'. Bad joke or no, he filled her with foreboding: '. . . the G.O.M. at eighty-two is a very *alarming look-out*'.

The respect accorded to her arguments and attacks bolstered Victoria's self-confidence, so that in many disputes she displayed an almost unbearable intolerance and lack of understanding in her unwillingness to enter into other people's motives and ways of thinking. The candour of her feelings and her awareness of this candour made her fanatically single-minded in any controversy over a practical matter—she could hardly be fanatical on any higher plane of ideas because of her lack of imagination and her inadequate education.

In the matter of 'goodness' and other nuances of the Queen's character, it has been said that because of her complicated and contradictory nature it is difficult to fit her into any definite or conventional category and that this is precisely what makes her unique. This not unusual way of sidestepping the problems of defining the character of a person seems particularly unconvincing in the case of Queen Victoria. One cannot read her letters without being struck by the simplicity and uniformity of the nature they express.

When Victoria made her first appearance as Queen in Privy Council before the dignitaries of the realm, many of those present testified that the eighteen-year-old girl had behaved with a natural and charming assurance. Somewhat later, Princess Lieven, who was used to mixing with royalty, was not overawed, and consequently had no reason for making an impression or flattering, said that 'she has an ease, a bearing of superiority and dignity which, combined with her childish face, her small stature and her charming smile, is the most remarkable thing one could imagine'. Similar testimonials were given throughout the Queen's reign, though as time went on, perhaps with less emphasis on the charm and more on the dignity. Further claims have often been brought forward that she impressed everybody with whom she came in contact—through sheer force of personality.

'Although she was so little', writes Roger Fulford in his *Queen Victoria* (1951), 'she was always the centre of whatever gathering in which she happened to be. When the Queen was present no one had eyes for anybody else.' And Ponsonby wrote:

> 'In spite of the smallness of her stature and absence of beauty, she managed always by her wonderful carriage and deportment which had characterized her from her early youth, to present unaccountably a figure of such dignity and distinction as to arrest the attention of the most unobservant spectator who at once decided that no one else in the assembly mattered.'

These accounts are seemingly contradicted by others which say that the Queen suffered from shyness and diffidence. Victoria herself wrote more than once that she felt uneasy and timid in large gatherings and that she was especially nervous at the prospect of conversations with learned men and intellectuals.

According to Lord Melbourne, Albert would have liked to invite literary celebrities and scholars to the Court. In a memorandum the Prince's Private Secretary, George Anson, reported that Melbourne had said:

> 'that the Prince would like to bring literary and scientific people about the Court, vary the society, and infuse a more useful tendency into it. The Queen, however, has no fancy to encourage such people. This arises from a feeling on her part that her education has not fitted her to take part in such conversation; she would not like conversation to be going on in which she could not take her fair share, and she is far too open and candid in her nature to pretend to one atom more knowledge than she really possesses on such subjects.'

In one of her letters to the Princess Royal she expressed her admiration of her daughter's knowledge of books and her ability to follow complicated arguments: 'You are so learned and so fond of deep, philosphical books, that you are quite beyond me, and certainly have not inherited that taste from me; for to say the honest truth, the sight of a professor or learned man alarms me, and is not *sympathique* to me' (27 April 1859).

In later life the Queen shunned society but everyone testified to her complete self-assurance on the rare occasions when she did meet people.

There is no difficulty in reconciling the two aspects, of dignity and diffidence. To some, the Queen's impressive dignity and her unquestioning ascendency over others were doubtless only the result of her exalted social position; this position, as Roger Fulford writes, was sufficient to make her the central figure everywhere. But the Queen's naturalness, her incapability of pretending or dissembling increased the dignity of this position. And doubtless a certain degree of timidity and anxiety contributed towards a reserve which had the same effect.

A glum or sombre expression and a stiffness of bearing and conversation can be caused by a sense of inner insecurity but can make a frightening impression on inferiors. And by taking advantage of her position, the Queen became accustomed to dominate by indicating her displeasure in few words—'we are not amused'—or by a glacial stare to reprimand breaches of etiquette; to take the lead either with a brief observation or by remaining silent. When Disraeli quizzed her at the wedding of the Prince of Wales to Princess Alexandra of Denmark, Victoria gave him such a 'look' that he quickly put away his glass. Because she functioned with self-control at ceremonies, as a symbol or as the focal point of a social gathering, it is pointless to try to distinguish between the shyness and the regal self-assurance or arrogance which accompanied and concealed it.

The Queen was not vivacious or witty and was not talkative except among the closest members of her own family. In spite of attempts to find qualities to admire in her, she never earned the reputation of being a charmer in the manner of her grandson the Kaiser or of the Swedish Oskar II. In this respect she resembled, if anybody, the Emperor Franz-Josef of Austro-Hungary, who was a notorious bore. But the abiding melancholy of her old age contributed even more to her dignity. To be amusing or amused was regarded by people of rank as beneath them, almost vulgar: as one of them, Victoria was 'not amused'. The Queen, as with so many who have little or no talent for small talk or the social graces, doubtless had moments during her forty years of mourning when she longed for some gaiety and wit in the people by whom she was surrounded, but any such longing was seldom gratified. The only person who responded in some degree to this need was Disraeli.

The Queen is usually regarded as lacking in a sense of humour or irony and it may be imagined that these gifts are hardly consistent with impeccable dignity. She is recorded as sometimes having had a good laugh; but the causes of her mirth were usually of a rudimentary or 'banana-skin' nature—as, for example, when the visiting Emperor Napoleon III upset his coffee over his cocked hat (causing 'great amusement') just as they were starting out for the Opera; when the Duke of Argyll dropped the crown and brought it into the Robing Room looking like a collapsed pudding; or when Lord Kinnoul, showing Victoria and Albert round his garden, tumbled headlong down a bank:

> [We] 'lunched at Dupplin, Lord Kinnoul's, a pretty place with quite a new house, and which Lord Kinnoul displayed so well as to fall head over heels down a steep bank, and was proceeding down another, if Albert had not caught him; I did not see it, but Albert and I have nearly died with laughing at the *relation* of it.' (8 September 1842.)

Similar stimulating events were staged by the Prince of Wales, who was fond of playing crude practical jokes. Lord Granville once said that wit was wasted on a family that could be convulsed by merely hearing about somebody's finger being caught in a door.

Nevertheless the Queen was not entirely devoid of an appreciation of more subtle humour. She enjoyed Disraeli's jokes—as for example when he called her 'mistress', perhaps hardly with any conscious realization of his possibly intentional double meaning—though in fact she did underline the word in her Journal. She wrote with astonishing irony about herself that though Vicky was like Albert—'You are quite your dear, beloved Papa's child'—Edward, with his arrogance and aversion to cultural matters, was her own image, though a distorted one. 'Bertie is my caricature, that is the misfortune, and in a man—this is so much worse.' She said that people who always went about with solemn expressions had on a 'Sunday face'. However in a collection of letters of thousands of pages such gems are few and far between.

Like numerous other monarchs—among whom can be mentioned Franz-Josef of Austria and Gustavus VI of Sweden—Queen Victoria mastered the art of speaking to people for a few moments by putting questions to them. This is an obvious solution: to say something personal and original to fifty persons in turn at some ceremony or function must be a taxing duty for the royal personage to whom such people are presented. The most frequently quoted of her interrogation-conversations took place between Victoria as a youthful Queen and the diarist Charles Greville, recorder of court and society gossip.

The Queen: Have you been riding today, Mr Greville?
Greville: No, Madam, I have not.
The Queen: It was a fine day.
Greville: Yes, Ma'am, a very fine day.
The Queen: It was rather cold, though.
Greville: It *was* rather cold, Madam.
The Queen: Your sister, Lady Francis Egerton, rides I think, does not she?
Greville: She does ride sometimes, Madame.

(A pause when—said Greville—I took the lead though adhering to the same topic.)

Greville: Has your Majesty been riding today?
The Queen: (*with animation*) O yes, a very long ride.
Greville: Has your Majesty got a nice horse?
The Queen: O, a very nice horse.

Greville's claim that he interrupted this ordeal by taking the liberty of asking the Queen about her own riding activities should possibly be taken with a pinch of salt. He was probably exaggerating, for the convention that it was the Queen who should lead the conversation was too firmly established for anybody to think of committing such an audacious breach of etiquette.

It goes without saying that the Queen must have had more natural and informal conversations with the ladies and gentlemen in waiting and other courtiers surrounding her and with statesmen about practical matters. But talks of this nature became less frequent as time went on. Instead the Queen wrote notes—fortunately for posterity, which has thus been enabled to learn more about her than if she had merely conversed or given her orders verbally.

The Queen's timidity before scholars and scientists was the outcome of her deficient education. She seems never to have studied any works dealing with history, politics or the sciences with the exception—if they can be called that—of a few theological works which she read during the period of one of the wars. Of the famous contributions to natural science and philosophy which were made during her lifetime, by Darwin, Mill, Spencer, there is not a hint in her correspondence. It is more than likely, of course, that the Queen shared this ignorance of the current literature of ideas with practically the whole of the aristocracy and the middle class. She is often described as not very well read. Her letters, however, indicate that, apart from the favourite novels of her youth, she did occasionally read a few 'good' books. Among the authors she mentions are Walter Scott, Jane Austen, Tennyson, Trollope, George Sand, Charlotte Brontë and George Eliot. She was fond of the theatre and before Albert's death she went quite frequently to the play. Some well-known authors were practically unknown to her, although a number of celebrated poets were invited to tea a few times. Accounts of some conversations with Alfred, Lord Tennyson show that these two respectable Victorians could profitably exchange ideas about the life hereafter. In comparison with Tennyson the Queen was ignorant, but she was not totally illiterate and unintellectual like 'poor Bertie'.

An exchange of letters in which the Queen and the Princess Royal aired their views on play-going and Shakespeare, gives an illuminating example of the struggle between the Queen's hankering for literary culture and her prudish ideas and, indeed, of her attitude to literature in general.

An English company had been giving a series of Shakespeare's plays in Berlin and the Princess Royal had been to see some of them. News of these outings reached the Queen.

> 'By the by you went to see the "Merry Wives"; you must have found it very coarse; even I have never had the courage to go and see it—having always been told how very coarse it was—for your adored Shakespeare is dreadful in that respect and many things have to be left out in many of his plays.' (16 April 1859.)

The Princess Royal replied that she had gone out of a longing to hear a play in English but that she had not stayed till the end. She had, indeed, seen part of *The Merry Wives of Windsor* she told her mother, but 'everything improper was left out'. She confessed that she hated the subject and had never read the play. Shakespeare's coarseness, she felt, was not suited to the times nor to the German court ladies. She found that 'he gives the worst names to the worst things and makes every improper thing revolting'. On the other hand, she thought the French a thousand times worse because 'they make improper things interesting and gloss the wickedness over'. She tried to avoid seeing French plays. As for German plays, she had never had the courage to see *Faust*, she said, and although her husband had read it aloud to her and she found it magnificent, 'I should feel rather ashamed to see it' (18 April 1859).

To all this the Queen replied:

> 'With regard to what you say about Shakespeare, I quite agree. You need not be afraid of seeing *Faust;* I am as bad and shy as anyone, matron as I am, about these things—and it is so beautiful that really one does not feel put out by it. I advise you to see it, dear. Also as regards the French plays—you should go; there are many—indeed quantities of charming little plays—and dear Papa—who you know is any thing but favourable to the French—used to delight in going to the French play—more than to any other, and we used for many years—when we had a good company (we have had none since 54) to go continually and enjoyed it excessively. It is such good practice for the language. So, I hope, dear, you will go. One's dislike to a nation need not prevent one's admiring and being amused by what is good, clever and amusing in it.' (20 April 1859.)

With regard to certain traits for which the names are vague and shifting, the Queen's character has been interpreted in different ways. For instance, was she vain? Her habit of describing in detail how she was dressed on ceremonial or festive occasions and her questions about the Princess Royal's own attire, indicate that she was not entirely devoid of that traditionally feminine attribute, vanity. She wrote to Vicky: 'I hear from all sides how much your dresses and toilettes are admired, so I take a good deal for myself as I took such great pains with your dresses' (18 February 1858). But she had relatively little inclination to ostentatious finery, at least for herself. Even on great occasions such as her two jubilees, she insisted on wearing her usual bonnet—with some splendid trimmings on it, to be sure, but none the less a bonnet.

In 1866, on the occasion of the official opening of the exhibition connected with the recently erected Imperial Institute, the Prime Minister, Lord Rosebery, was anxious that the Queen should come in full state robes and crown 'to impress the imagination of the Colonial representatives who would be present'. Lord Rosebery in his letter to Sir Henry Ponsonby, the Queen's private secretary, added, 'The symbol that unites this vast Empire is a Crown not a bonnet'—an opinion which the Queen chose to regard with supreme indifference.

This, of course, does not indicate any modesty on her part, as has sometimes been suggested. Victoria was perfectly aware that she was a symbol and the focus of attention, regardless of crowns or bonnets. Indeed, it can be assumed that it was precisely her awareness of this which led her to prefer a bonnet; possibly, too, she may have thought it somewhat ludicrous for an elderly woman with a worn and wrinkled face to deck herself out in the glittering Imperial regalia. Nevertheless, her sense of occasion was as unerring then, and her bonnet as regal, as it was for her Golden Jubilee drive in 1897, for which she wore 'a dress and bonnet trimmed with white *point d'Alençon*, diamond ornaments in my bonnet, and pearls round my neck, with all my orders'.

When it came to holding her own with equals, that is with other royalty, she was more particular in asserting herself in matters of prestige, precedence and protocol. On one occasion she had cause to instruct the Princess Royal in the high position held by the British royal house. Vicky had written that the Crown Princess of Württemberg (the former Grand Duchess Olga of Russia) had been very cold and uncivil to her 'almost rude; when I went to see her she never asked me to sit down but sat at the table with her back turned to me, and condescended to ask me when I went away, whether I was sixteen'. 'Of course', Vicky added, 'I kept my reflections to myself and only tell you and Papa on paper what I think' (22 September 1858).

The Queen was incensed. 'What could she have meant by being so rude to you? You ought not to keep your feelings to yourself, for you owe it to your own position—to the country you come from, not to allow yourself to be treated with rudeness.' And certainly, the Queen implied, not by a mere member of

> 'the Russian family who have never been considered as better or as high as our family. . . . She is the second daughter of the Emperor of Russia, married to the son and Heir-Prince of Würtemberg consequently less in rank than her husband; you are the eldest daughter of the Queen of England, with a title and rights of your own, fifth in succession and married to a nephew of the King, therefore decidedly higher in rank than your husband . . . our princes never admitted the Grand Dukes of Russia having precedence over them; Romanoffs are not to be compared to the houses of Brunswick, Saxony and Hohenzollern . . . These are things which may appear trifles, but which the honour and dignity of one's country do not allow to be overlooked.' (27 September 1858.)

The Queen, in 1873, eagerly welcomed the idea of becoming Empress of India and it was she, as Disraeli frequently maintained, who was most in favour of this promotion. She was not unmindful of the King of Prussia who had recently become Emperor of Germany and of the prospect of his daughter-in-law—her own Vicky—eventually becoming an Empress. By dint of prodding Disraeli the Queen got her way, and three years later, after a stormy passage through Parliament, the Royal Titles Bill was passed. Victoria was declared Queen-Empress of India on May Day 1876 and henceforth could sign herself Victoria Regina et Imperatrix.

Was Queen Victoria haughty—'high', as she called it—to the courtiers and officials in her entourage or to people from different social strata? These questions are often answered in various ways, in spite of the Queen's unvarying behaviour to others. Her kindness has been praised, partly because of the special value set on common politeness from people of high degree to those around them. It is true that she displayed unusual sympathy toward, and was more deeply moved by, the unhappiness and misfortune of others.

She has been accused of arrogance and doubtless with good reason, since, used as she was to take the initiative and lead conversation, she resolutely rebuffed anything that she considered impertinent and when in possible doubt about how to deal with specific contingencies could be unnecessarily curt and abrupt in the face of unexpected and what she considered intrusive approaches.

She has been admired nevertheless for her 'democratic' behaviour, and by this was meant that she did not too obviously mete out her benevolence according to rank.

To royalty and exalted personages looking down from the lofty eminence of rank the lowly usually appear to exist on a single plane of deservingness and so can all be treated alike. Queen Victoria possessed to a high degree this sense of *noblesse oblige* towards common folk, a graciousness which depended to some extent on the fact that she had nothing to fear from them on the score of culture or intellect; but no one could have been more convinced than she was that society was properly a hierarchy of classes, functions and occupations and that the British brand of this hierarchy was unrivalled.

This opinion of hers also held good for relations between the sexes, indeed, her conventionality and prejudices were particularly marked and unreasoning on this point, which is well illustrated in several letters to Gladstone quoted by Frank Hardie. The growing agitation for 'Women's Rights' which made considerable strides during Victoria's reign seemed to her 'dangerous and unchristian and unnatural' and she wrote to Gladstone concerning female medical students:

> 'The Queen is a woman herself—& knows what an anomaly her *own* position is . . . But to tear away all the barriers which surround a woman, to propose that they should study with *men*—things which could not be named before them—certainly not *in a mixed*

audience—would be to introduce a total disregard of what must be considered as belonging to the rules and principles of morality. . . . Let woman be what God intended; a helpmeet for man—but with totally different duties and vocations.' (6 May 1870.)

Women's rights was a subject which 'makes the Queen so furious that she cannot contain herself', she told Sir Theodore Martin. 'God created men and women different—then let them remain each in their own position.' She declared that she was 'most anxious to enlist every one who can speak or write to join in checking this mad, wicked folly of "Women's Rights", with all its attendant horrors, on which her poor feeble sex is bent, forgetting every sense of womanly feeling and propriety'. And she thought that Lady So-and-so, who was involved in the movement 'ought to get a good whipping'. It was the Queen's opinion that 'Woman would become the most hateful, heathen and disgusting of human beings were she allowed to unsex herself; and where would be the protection which man was intended to give the weaker sex?' (29 May 1870).

The Queen's letters on this subject display some rather muddled thinking, and it would be easy to draw the conclusion from them that she was exceptionally simple-minded were it not for the fact that many other prominent men and women of the period held the same views and wrote in a similar vein of outraged hostility. Those who thought as the Queen did held that God and nature had ordained women's status, but at the same time they accepted the idea that it could be altered and they justified woman's dependency on man by the claim that if she were independent men would have nobody to protect. The Queen was obviously thinking only of upper-class and middle-class women; to judge by her letters she was unaware that hundreds of thousands of women worked side by side with men in the heavy industries and were forced to lead existences that were humiliating and debased.

The Queen's fury at all demands for the emancipation of women was possibly exacerbated by the thought that her own position was in such contrast to her declarations. Nevertheless, she was more or less consistent on this point. She was conscious, as we have seen in the letter quoted above, of the 'anomaly' of her position and in another letter, to King Leopold of the Belgians, she said: 'We women are not *made* for governing—and if we are good women, we must *dislike* these masculine occupations; but these are times which force one to take *interest* in them *mal gré bon gré*, and I do of course, intensely' (3 February 1852). But as a rule Victoria cannot have felt the contradiction between the woman and the sovereign too strongly or she would never have been able to carry out her royal task so resolutely and with such self-confidence. Subconsciously she must have considered herself an exception, a sort of super-woman, and her deficiencies in powers of reasoning and logic facilitated her muddled thinking on this question.

On Women's Rights, then, the Queen was a typical example of the true Victorian. It has been emphasized earlier here that in her reactions to husband and children and to personal sexual conventions she was also true to type. It remains to be added that in court policy and other personal relations she imposed puritanism with full rigour. She insisted that not only the court but all those who associated with and were received by the royal couple should present an unblemished conduct sheet. On the whole, the women were hardest hit—as usual—and the most strictly observed of the Queen's rules was the one which rigidly excluded divorced women from court. But she approved highly of Lord Salisbury's suggestion that

> 'with respect to men who have been divorced for their own adultery, Lord Salisbury would be very glad if your Majesty should decide to give them no social recognition of any kind. It would have a very valuable effect on public morality. But this would be a very considerable change.' (23 March 1887.)

The Queen eagerly agreed to the proposal and wrote next day to Sir Henry Ponsonby:

> 'The Queen sent all the papers about the ladies to Lord Salisbury and sends his decision which she thinks excellent. Let it be copied and sent to Lord Lathom and be adhered to. She entirely agrees about the gentlemen. It would have the best effect. Society is too bad *now;* some stop should be put to it.'

It has been suggested that the Queen's aggressive virtue, like that of other women of this type, was connected with a lack of sex appeal. Apart from the Brown myth (which we shall come to later) and apart from the admiration of a youthful riding companion, Lord Alfred Paget, one of the Queen's Gentlemen, for his young Sovereign, not to mention a couple of minor instances of infatuated admiration or devotion from the lowly, which are quite negligible in this context, there is little or no reason to suppose that any man other than Albert ever made romantic overtures to Victoria or was strongly attracted to her, whether as a young girl, unmarried Queen, wife or widow.

There are a few descriptions of her appearance as a young woman which point to her girlishness, her beautiful complexion, (which, however, flushed too easily), her lively gestures and captivating smile. Official portraits make her look pleasant in a general and conventional way. Descriptions of her in later life stress her good carriage, her dignified yet imperious expression. But the Queen's physical shortcomings were evident and she seems to have been conscious of them, at least when she was younger. She constantly deplored her lack of inches: 'I am rather short for a Queen' she once said, and on another occasion protested that she was 'not a dwarf'—she was something under five feet as a young woman, looked short and stout as a matron, and small and shrunken in her old age. When she was nineteen she became alarmed about her weight. She wrote in her Journal: 'was weighed and to my horror weigh 8 stone 13!!' (13 December 1838). By present day standards she was at least twelve pounds overweight for her age and height.

In spite of intermittent attempts at dieting (with only relative success because she did not persevere) she grew stouter as the years went by. To judge by her portraits she must have been quite dumpy at the age of forty; a few years later she was stout to the point of no recall and must have weighed between eleven and twelve stone.

Her features had defects which she herself sometimes noticed—defects which became more pronounced with the years: the prominent eyes with their fixed and vacant stare, the small receding chin (inherited by Edward VII who, however, could conceal it with his beard), the slightly projecting teeth, the puffy cheeks and hanging jowls of her middle and old age. Her hands and voice have been praised—the hands tiny and the voice silvery—as if under the circumstances they were some sort of consolation prize. And doubtless, as many have testified, people forgot that she was not beautiful whenever she smiled her radiant smile. Alas! she seldom does this in her portraits and even less so in photographs, in which she looks as if she were apprehensive of what the camera might reveal. From widowhood to old age it revealed the 'mournful face, fixed stare and drooping mouth' with which she faced the world.

The first volume of Victoria's *Leaves from a Journal of Our Life in the Scottish Highlands*, which she published in 1865, is dedicated to the memory of Albert: 'To the dear memory of him who made the life of the writer bright and happy, these simple records are lovingly and gratefully inscribed.'

The second volume *More Leaves from a Journal of Our Life in the Highlands*, published in 1884, bears the following dedication: 'To my loyal Highlanders and especially to the memory of my devoted personal attendant and faithful friend John Brown these records of my widowed life in Scotland are gratefully dedicated. Victoria R. I.'

John Brown is mentioned several times in the official collection of the Queen's letters. In September 1859 she spoke of 'Johnny Brown (who is our factotum and really the perfection of a servant for he thinks of everything)'. On 24 February 1865 she wrote to King Leopold: 'I have now appointed that excellent Highland servant of mine to attend me ALWAYS and everywhere out of doors, whether riding or driving or on foot; and it is a *real* comfort, for he is *so* devoted to me—so simple, so intelligent, so unlike an *ordinary* servant and so cheerful and attentive.'

She told the Princess Royal about this in October 1858: 'He is now my special servant; and there can't be a nicer, better or handier one. Really there is nothing like these Highlanders for handiness.' Because the Balmoral gillie MacDonald had been incapacitated, 'Brown has had to do everything for me, indeed had charge of me and all, on all those expeditions and therefore I settled that he should be specially appointed to attend on me (without any other title) and have a full dress suit' (18 October 1868).

On 26 June 1867 she complained to her equerry, Lord Charles FitzRoy, that as she had taken Brown as an upper servant attending her carriage

> 'everywhere *with her* for *two years* on public as well as on private occasions, she is much astonished and shocked at an attempt being made by some people to prevent her faithful servant going with her to the *Review* in Hyde Park . . . thereby making the poor, nervous, shaken Queen, who is so accustomed to his watchful care and intelligence, terribly nervous and uncomfortable . . .'

She went on to say that something should be done in future 'to prevent her being plagued with the interference of others' and she wanted moreover 'to make it *completely understood* once and *for all* that her Upper *Highland* servant . . . belongs to her outdoor attendants on State as well as on private occasions. The Queen will not be dictated to, or *made* to *alter* what she has found to answer for her comfort . . .'

On a later occasion (29 February 1872) John Brown was praised for 'his wonderful presence of mind' when he seized a half-witted youth, Arthur O'Connor, who had pointed an unloaded pistol at the Queen in order to try to frighten her into releasing imprisoned Fenian agitators for Home Rule. 'It is to good Brown and to his wonderful presence of mind that I greatly owe my safety, for he alone saw the boy rush round and followed him.'

John Brown's name is often mentioned in other collections of letters and in biographies and memoirs. He even got a memoir all to himself (unfinished and unpublished, however) from his royal admirer. When Brown died, at Windsor on 29 March 1883, from complications following a chill, the Queen herself was laid up with a rheumatic attack. She was told of Brown's death by Prince Leopold and wrote in her Journal:

'Leopold came to my dressing-room, and broke the dreadful news to me that my good, faithful Brown had passed away early this morning. Am terribly upset by this loss, which removes one who was so devoted and attached to my service and who did so much for my personal comfort. It is the loss not only of a servant, but of a real friend.'

She wrote the same day to one of her grandsons, Prince George of Wales (later King George V): 'I have lost my *dearest best* friend who no-one in *this World* can *ever* replace . . . *never forget* your poor sorrowing old Grandmama's *best* & *truest* friend . . .' (27 March 1883). Tennyson was asked to write an inscription for a statue of Brown erected at Balmoral. The couplet was more well-intentioned than lyrical:

'Friend more than servant, loyal, truthful, brave:
Self less than duty even to the grave.'

Brown's position was the object of considerable discussion during his lifetime but after his death historians shrouded him in veils of silence. Queen Victoria's own memoir of him never saw the light of day—she was discreetly dissuaded from publishing it—and he was soon forgotten. Interest in Brown has revived in recent years. There is considerable information about him in Lord Ponsonby's life of his father; and in Lady Longford's remarkable biography of Queen Victoria there are numerous references to him in sixty pages, which include a whole chapter on Brown's strange story, in which the problem of his relationship to Queen Victoria is discussed. It is mainly from Lady Longford's and Lord Ponsonby's books that the facts given here have been drawn.

That Brown should have become once more the subject of discussion is due to the greater frankness that is the fashion nowadays and to persistent and intriguing rumours, current even in Victoria's own day, that Brown was her lover or was even secretly married to her. A prominent historian of the present writer's acquaintance is firmly convinced of the truth of this and maintains that a near relative, forty years ago, had seen the marriage certificate—which, however, has never since come to light.

Brown's relationship with the Queen has naturally been found unusual enough to invite investigation. A few essential facts are all that need detain us at this point. The Queen constantly proclaimed her affection for Brown, whom she called 'her best friend' and who, as time went on, became her constant companion wherever she went in England or Scotland, as well as on visits to the Continent. Brown behaved with great familiarity to the Queen and talked about her and to her with outspoken naturalness. He sat down in her presence (something only Prime Ministers were allowed to do, and then only seldom), entered her room without knocking, sometimes called her simply 'wumman' in the rough usage of his own Scottish folk, spoke brusquely to her—'What's this ye've got on to-day?', if he did not like what she was wearing. 'Hoots, then, wumman, can ye no hold yerr head up?' when he pricked her chin while pinning her cape. The two of them went for solitary picnics together. 'The Queen has gone out for the day with her luncheon in a basket—so I'm off also', said her Private Secretary on one occasion; and on another, one of the Maids of Honour, hearing that the Queen was going out and seeing Brown carrying a basket, asked if he was taking tea out. Brown replied: 'Well, no, she don't much like tea—we tak oot biscuits & sperruts.'

Even on more ceremonious occasions when Brown, as the Queen's servant, sat up beside the coachman he often took command, which proved an embarrassment to the Queen's closer entourage, especially on visits abroad. The Queen often gave orders about household arrangements at Balmoral or Osborne—at what time smoking rooms were to be closed, when fishing or hunting or riding were allowed—orders which obviously emanated from Brown and were palpably intended to suit his convenience. The Queen's family and Household detested Brown's influence and found him personally unbearable. They regarded him as 'simple' in a much more elementary meaning of the word than the Queen's use of it. They considered him uncouth, untutored, tactless and too fond of the bottle, whereas to the Queen he was a simple soul whose devotion and care for her outweighed his rustic forthrightness and lack of social graces. It was admitted that his looks were manly and quite handsome but that this good impression was outweighed by his rough and rustic manners. Victoria's demands that he should be treated with special politeness and consideration were a source of irritation to the aristocratic members of her Household. He was given the title of 'The Queen's Highland Servant', and took orders only from her. Later she made him an Esquire, and his salary was raised several times at short intervals. Court and family tried in vain to get rid of this servant elevated to a courtier of sorts. Rumours concerning the odd relationship spread once or twice through the British and foreign press; on one occasion a British diplomat, in his tactless concern for the Queen's good name, sued a Swiss newspaper, only to make matters worse.

It is not surprising that so many believed that there was an erotic relationship between Queen Victoria and Brown. Undeniably there was something provocative in the idea of this chink in the armour of Victorian respectability, the titillating thought of the Queen, a sorrowing widow, the personification of virtue and fidelity, actually carousing and going to bed with a servant and after such a fall from grace perhaps being made an honest woman of by becoming Mrs Brown.

However, in the opinion of the present writer, this theory—even though there is no proof to the contrary—simply does not hold water. But not because of the chief reason given by Lady Longford for not believing it—that it was not in the Queen's character: 'Her passionate nature . . . did not require physical ardours so much as intense, undivided affection producing a sense of safety and comfort'.

The present writer is inclined to believe, as he has stated earlier, that Lady Longford's theory of the Queen's lack of sensuality is not wholly convincing, and moreover it seems unreasonable to assume that Victoria—however much or little her sensuality—could never under any circumstances have allowed herself to fall into the arms of her servant without feeling that she would have to marry him afterwards.

Just as doubtful, and somewhat 'Victorian', is the assumption that if the Queen had felt constrained to marry again 'a sense of propriety would have ruled out Brown. It would *never* do'. On the contrary, following this argument, if an erotic relationship had been established between herself and Brown, propriety would all the more have demanded marriage with him.

The strongest grounds for repudiating not only the imputation of a marriage but also of sexual intimacy, seem to be quite simply that if either of these things were true, then all Victoria's letters, diaries and statements would have been a tissue of lies and deceptions. This, more than anything else, was not in her nature, which was 'extraordinarily straightforward, truthful and direct: she was not subtle, for she always wrote and said exactly what was in her mind'. The most conclusive evidence against either sexual intimacy or marriage is the passage quoted by Lady Longford from Queen Victoria's Journal for 24 May 1871, written at a time when Brown's ascendancy was at its zenith and her relationship with him at its closest—yet her thoughts were with Albert: 'My poor old birthday, my 51st! Alone, alone, as it will ever be! But surely, my dearest one blesses me.'

The Queen's devotion to Brown, as her Private Secretary realized, 'dated back to the happy days before her widowhood and had from that an almost sacred foundation'. Her relationship with Brown can be regarded as unusual but not in any way inexplicable. Sheer loneliness, her difficulties of communication with people of her own station and even with her family, were the chief sources of her dependence on her Highland Servant. Both she and Albert had always got on better with the servants. Like Brown, Victoria had a 'simple' nature, and in small talk with him she felt uninhibited and entertained.

It is of course not impossible that sensuality may have played a subconscious role in her feelings towards Brown and that she felt stirrings of attraction to the 'rough, handsome, intelligent Scot . . . with a strong arm . . . long legs, curly hair and beard, blue eyes and firm chin' when, at Balmoral or Osborne, he flung her cape round her, lifted her from her carriage and carried her indoors.

3

Time and again in her letters the Queen either longed for solitude or was in despair over her loneliness. In some respects this was connected with normal human changes of mood; but these cries from the heart were related for the most part to different phases of Victoria's life. It was only after Albert's death that she came to lament continually the loneliness of being alone—and by this she meant the loneliness of life without Albert.

As princess and young unmarried Queen, Victoria seems to have found social life normally enjoyable, whether it was conversation with Lord Melbourne and her ladies in waiting, or ceremonial occasions, parties, balls and visits to the theatre. After her marriage this official and superficial existence became increasingly irksome to her; she felt tired and depressed during and after her numerous pregnancies; she longed for a tranquil *solitude à deux* with Albert, or for family life with husband and children. The Prince Consort became both a bulwark sheltering her from statesmen and other dignitaries, and at the same time a go-between in her business with them. Her happiest moments were spent on the Isle of Wight or in the Scottish Highlands, at Osborne and Balmoral respectively. Windsor Castle she disliked, but it was still preferable to Buckingham Palace. It goes without saying that the royal family lived in constant contact with other people even in the country—ladies and gentlemen in waiting, visiting royalty and ministers making their reports. But occasionally, especially on picnics or excursions, it did so happen that Victoria and Albert could sit down to a meal with just a couple of ladies and gentlemen in waiting as guests or that they were able to have a few hours of the day entirely to themselves.

This longing for isolation—inevitably highly relative—was conditioned by the intimate relationship of the couple and especially by Victoria's constant desire to have Albert to herself. But it must also be seen against the background of the Queen's limited interests and education and the difficulty (resulting from these handicaps) of finding enjoyment in the society of others. Through her concentration, first and foremost, on Albert and her merely secondary interest in her family, she prepared the ground for the intense feeling of loneliness which was a consequence of her husband's death and her increasing severance from her children.

The forty years of her widowhood, and especially the first fifteen or twenty years, became a constant escape from people, state duties and ceremonies. During the whole of this period Victoria spent just twenty nights at Buckingham Palace and attended the opening of Parliament only seven times. She took refuge at Windsor, Osborne and above all at Balmoral.

The monotony and boredom of life at Balmoral have been described by her secretaries and visitors. During dinners all political or serious conversation was banned, every topic had to be opened by the Queen, only small talk was allowed, and that preferably laced with innocuous and mildly amusing anecdotes. The Queen's dislike of stuffy rooms and open fires and her faith in the virtues of fresh air was an ordeal to her Household and guests. As has been mentioned earlier, she usually avoided giving verbal instructions about any matters which could be dealt with in writing. She sent little notes by the footmen and received the answers in the same way. Both the Queen's Private Secretary, Sir Henry Ponsonby, and her Keeper of the Privy Purse, Sir Thomas Biddulph, bemoaned the state of affairs at Balmoral because 'we think she is getting to like to be still more alone and to see no one at all, governing the country by means of messages through footmen to us'.

She turned a deaf ear to the entreaties of her ministers that she should come more often to London and take part in state ceremonies, and she ignored press criticism of her continued retirement—criticism which for some years threatened to undermine her popularity. The Queen answered every appeal to emerge from her retirement with the excuse that her nerves could not stand official appearances; and her doctors backed her up.

In a letter to the Prime Minister, Lord John Russell, on 22 January 1866, Victoria described what she felt about her promised opening of Parliament—it would be for the first time since Albert's death five years previously. There had been some preliminary discussion about the date on which Parliament was to open and Lord Russell wished the Queen to come from Osborne a couple of days beforehand, in readiness.

> 'The Queen can assure Lord Russell that he need be under no apprehension of her not arriving in time for the opening of Parliament. If she has the whole Monday open she can go when she likes, and with the Alberta [one of the royal yachts] she has no longer cause to fear a bad passage.'
>
> 'To enable the Queen to go through what SHE *can* only compare to an execution, it is of importance to keep the *thought* of it as much from her mind as possible, and therefore the going to Windsor *to wait* two *whole* days for this dreadful ordeal would do her positive harm.

'The Queen has never till now mentioned this painful subject to Lord Russell, but she wishes once for all to just express her own feelings. She must, however, premise her observations by saying that she entirely absolves Lord Russell and his colleagues from *any* attempt to *press* upon her what is so very painful an effort. The Queen *must say* that she does feel *very bitterly* the want of feeling of those who ask the Queen to go to open Parliament. That the public should wish to see her she fully understands, and has no wish to prevent—quite the contrary; but why this wish should be of so unreasonable and unfeeling a nature, as to *long* to *witness* the spectacle of a poor, broken-hearted widow, nervous and shrinking, dragged in *deep mourning*, ALONE, in STATE as a SHOW, where she used to go supported by her husband, to be gazed at, without delicacy of feeling, is a thing *she cannot* understand, and she never could wish her bitterest foe to be exposed to!

'She *will* do it *this time*—as she promised it, but she owns she resents the unfeelingness of those who have *clamoured* for it. Of the suffering which it will cause her—nervous as she now is—she can give no idea, but she owns she hardly knows *how* she will go through it. Were the Queen a woman possessed of strong nerves, she would not mind going through this painful exhibition, but her nerves—from the amount of anxiety, and constant and unceasing work, which is quite over-whelming her, as well as from her deep sorrow—are terrible and *increasingly* shaken, and she will suffer much for some time after, from the shock to her nervous system which this *ordeal* will occasion. It is hard when she works and slaves away all day and till late at night, not to be spared at least such trials.'

After the opening of Parliament the Queen wrote in her Journal:

'A fine morning. Terribly nervous and agitated. At ½ past 10 left Windsor for London, with the children, ladies, and gentlemen. Great crowds out, and so I had (for the first time since my great misfortune) an escort. Dressing after luncheon which I could hardly touch. Wore my ordinary evening dress, only trimmed with minniver, and my cap with a long flowing tulle veil, a small diamond and sapphire coronet rather at the back, and diamonds outlining the front of my cap.

'It was a fearful moment for me when I entered the carriage *alone*, and the band played; also when all the crowds cheered, and I had great difficulty in repressing my tears. But our affectionate girls [her daughters Princesses Helena and Louise, who sat facing her in the carriage] were a true help and support to me, and they so thoroughly realised all I was going through. The crowds were most enthusiastic, and the people seemed to look at me with

sympathy. We had both windows open, in spite of a very high wind.
'When I entered the House, which was very full, I felt as if I should faint. All was silent and all eyes fixed upon me, and there I sat alone.'

Afterwards the Queen wrote:

'I was greatly relieved when all was over, and I stepped down from the throne.

'So thankful that the great ordeal of to-day was well over, and that I was enabled to get through it.'

Queen Victoria's feelings about such 'ordeals' have been regarded with some irony and with the suggestion that she played up her anxieties out of attention-getting coquetry. Her reflexions in the letters quoted above, similar to many others she made, would seem to show that her anxieties were genuine rather than feigned and that she really did feel these public appearances to be distasteful and humiliating. Her reaction to them seems more natural and does her more credit than her critics have considered to be the case, because the public appearances of royalty are by their very nature spectacles which fall into the category of 'bread and circuses'. As such they were repugnant to the Queen because of the crowds grinning and gaping at her and chattering to each other about the sorrowing widow and what she looked like and how she behaved. The Queen herself was the only one to sense the humiliation of this spectacle which had as its protagonist a grieving and lonely human being.

Countless passages in her Letters and Journals indicate that the principal factor in her feeling of intense loneliness was the loss of her husband. A typical example can be found in *More Leaves from a Journal of Our Life in the Highlands*, in which she records visits made to castles in Scotland: 'For the first time in my life I was alone in a strange house, without either mother or husband, and the thought overwhelmed and distressed me deeply' (19 September 1865).

Again, as guest of the Duke of Roxburghe she stayed at Floors with the children in 1867 and wrote:

'Breakfast over, the Duchess showed us to our rooms upstairs. I had three that were very comfortable, opening one into the other; a sitting room, dressing-room, and the largest of the three, the bedroom, simple, with pretty chintz, but very elegant, nice and comfortable. The children were close at hand. But the feeling of loneliness when I saw no room for my darling, and felt I was indeed alone and a widow, overcame me very sadly! It was the first time I had gone in this way on a visit (like as in former times), and I thought so much of all dearest Albert would have done and said and how he would have wandered about everywhere, admired everything, looked at everything—and now! Oh! must it ever, ever be so?' (21 August 1867.)

In her Journals and Letters Victoria touches frequently on religious matters. As a rule the language is conventional and trivial and her tone optimistic and reassured. Her observations give the picture of a woman who believes dutifully and unquestioningly what she has been taught, who seeks no deeper implications and is content to rely for consolation upon a few generalizations based on watered-down Christian beliefs. Two views dominate her thoughts on the subject: (a) The Lord's ways are inscrutable but in the end everything is for the best; and (b) after our existence on earth we shall be reunited with our loved ones in an everlasting life of joy and goodness.

A good example of her belief in these things is a letter she wrote in the happy period of her early married life, to Uncle Leopold, condoling with him on the death of Duke Ernst of Saxe-Coburg-Gotha —her father-in-law and Uncle Leopold's brother. First came the usual exaggerated expressions of sorrow and sympathy—the Duke, it must be remembered, had been a notorious old libertine, as insufferable as he was licentious and often tiresome as a father-in-law:

'My dearly beloved Uncle,—*You* must now be the father to us poor bereaved, heart-broken children. To describe to you *all* that we *have* suffered, all that we *do* suffer, would be difficult; God has heavily afflicted us; we feel crushed, overwhelmed, bowed down by the loss of one who was so deservedly loved, I may say adored, by his children and family; I loved him and looked on him as my own father; his like we shall not *see again* . . . The violence of our grief may be over, but the desolate feeling which succeeds it is worse, and tears are a relief. I have never known real *grief* till now, and it has made a lasting impression on me. A father is *such* a *near* relation, you are a *piece* of him in fact—and all (as my poor deeply afflicted Angel says) the earliest pleasures of your life were given you by a dear father; that can *never be replaced* though time may soften the pang. And indeed one loves to *cling* to one's grief . . .' (6 February 1844.)

After this the 25-year-old Queen tried to console her uncle Leopold, thirty years her senior, with a little sermon, naively sententious, yet not devoid of earnest sincerity:

'God knows, poor dear Uncle, you have suffered enough in your life, but you should think, dearest Uncle, of *that blessed* assurance of eternity where we shall all meet again never to part: you should think (as we constantly do now) that those whom we have lost are far happier than we are, and *love us* still, and in a far more perfect way than *we can* do in this world! When the first moments and days of overwhelming grief are over these reflections are the greatest balm, the greatest consolation to the bleeding heart.' (13 February 1844.)

The same faith in God's guidance and in a life after death appears—with variations—in the Queen's letters and journals as she advanced from maturity to old age, although during the latter part of her life these ideas were expressed less naively and rhetorically and with less complacency than in her comforting letter to King Leopold. At times her faith almost seemed to make her resigned to the loss of Albert. In 1869, on the anniversary of her accession to the throne she wrote in her Journal:

'My Accession Day, already thirty-two years ago. May God help me in my solitary path, for the good of my dear people, and the world at large. He has given me a very difficult task, one for which I feel myself in many ways unfit, from inclination and want of power. He gave me great happiness and He took it away, no doubt for a wise purpose and for the happiness of my beloved one, leaving me alone to bear the heavy burden in trying and troubled times. Help I have been given, and for this I humbly thank Him; but the trials are great and many.' (20 June 1869.)

But during the years of her maturity and especially after the Prince Consort's death, the Queen's piety appeared more alert, restless and reflective—tinged with brooding, questioning, mysticism—even doubt. After her mother's death in March 1861, she and Albert held long discussions about life after death. And at Balmoral, after a sermon on the text 'Prepare to meet thy God', which gave a cheering picture of the Duchess of Kent in a better world, the Queen wrote to Vicky: 'It was fine! Those things affect me now so much! I feel now to be so acquainted with death—and to be so much nearer that unseen world' (7 October 1861).

After Albert's death in December of the same year, the problem of immortality became even more urgent. The Queen read a number of popular theological works and when a new edition of Bishop Butler's *Analogy of Religion*, his famous proof of life everlasting in the beyond, came out in 1865, she wrote to the Princess Royal that she was convinced by the Bishop's arguments. This quest for certainty shows that she was often beset by doubts—indeed, on one occasion she asked her chaplain Randall Davidson (Dean of Windsor 1883–91, later a bishop and finally Archbishop of Canterbury) if he really believed some of the Christian doctrines or were they just 'pious opinions'? Years later she confided to him that she had 'waves or flashes of doubtfulness whether, after all, it might be all untrue' that there was a future life. This may have been only a brief and passing crisis, when her misery at her husband's death had made her whole world totter. At one time she even felt suicidal, but was prevented by a mysterious inner 'voice', as she told the Princess Royal years later:

'I too wanted once to put an end to my life here, but a voice told me for His sake—no, "Still Endure".' This psychic experience was so intense, Lady Longford observes, that the Queen adopted the talismanic words 'Still Endure' as her motto.

The Queen's statements, allusions and intimations give the general impression that she had firm religious convictions which she carried into her old age as untarnished and steadfast as they had been in her youth. Influenced by opinions widespread among social leaders her personal assurance was fortified in the belief that religion was necessary to the authority of government and the obedience and contentment of the masses. In a letter to the Princess Royal (17 June 1878), summarized by Lady Longford in her biography, Victoria observed that 'Disbelief in God leads to lack of reverence for those in authority, including parents'. Belief, she thought, was more important than knowledge. 'Shake this in the masses & you shake the foundations of every thing. An Empire without religion is like a house built upon sand.' She added that she thought education could be overdone, making people selfish. As a result the working-classes were becoming discontented with 'the simple & necessary occupations in life' (notably with domestic service). Some years later she expressed in identical terms to Mr Gladstone these linking ideas about disbelief, education and the servant problem.

What the Queen said about these and other matters was at times marked by an intense faith and a passionate will to goodness. During the Schleswig-Holstein crisis of 1864 she wrote to King Leopold that for the first time she understood the meaning of prayer.

> 'I *never* really realised the *power* of prayer till *now*! When in an agony of loneliness, grief, and despair I kneel by that bed where *he* left us, decked with flowers, and pray earnestly to be enabled to be courageous, patient, and calm, and to be guided by my darling to *do what* HE would wish; then, a calm seems to come over me, a certainty my anguish is seen and heard *not* in vain, and I feel *lifted* ABOVE this miserable earth of sorrows! It is *only* when *one* feels as though *all* were gone, all had deserted you, as I feel so often and so *much during* this *terrible crisis*, that one can *truly* appreciate the power and strength of prayer, and that one's *faith rises* with one's *utter* prostration of woe! But it is cruel, hard and fearful, to live in such constant sorrow and anxiety!' (25 February 1864.)

She wrote in her Journal on 29 April 1865 that she was convinced of

> 'the utter vanity of all earthly greatness. . . . I would as soon clasp the poorest widow in the land to my heart, if she had truly loved her husband and felt for me, as I would a Queen or any other in high position. . . . Such a feeling of humility comes over me, such a wish to forgive any wrong, and to try to make all good!'

The only question of religious belief that Victoria pursued in any detail was the question of eternal life. She thought of it in some such terms as: 'There is a life after this one and in that life we shall meet our loved ones again, I shall meet Albert again'—this was the tenor of her faith.

In her Journal for 7 August 1883 she recorded a conversation with Tennyson, now an old man.

> 'He spoke of the many friends he had lost, and what it would be if he did not feel and know that there was another world where there would be no partings, of his horror of unbelievers and philosophers, who would try to make one believe there was no other world, no immortality, who tried to explain everything away in a miserable manner. We agreed that were such a thing possible, God, Who is Love, would be far more cruel than a human being.'

With Randall Davidson, now Bishop of Rochester, she

> 'agreed entirely about what he calls the "absurd" notion that our dear departed ones are "sleeping" till the day of judgment, which so many hymns express and people think. He agrees that it is impossible. The spirit cannot be asleep for a moment, but there must be a progression, and the means and power of redeeming the past.' (7 February 1892.)

To believe this it was essential that there should be a Heaven but not a Hell. Victoria time and again expressed her contempt and disgust of doctrines of hell and damnation which she found 'unutterably horrible and revolting'. The clergy who taught such 'absurd and monstrous doctrines' as that of Hell ought to be improved, she thought, not ridiculed. It is possible that she received guidance in all this from her spiritual advisers, but her willingness to believe in Heaven though not in Hell seems characteristic of her; she thought of reunion but not of judgement.

It was rumoured, though without any convincing evidence, that Queen Victoria dabbled in spiritualism—nothing strange in late nineteenth-century England, where it was all the rage. Lady Longford, who has been at pains to sift a great deal of rumour and purported evidence, is highly sceptical and demolishes the claims one by one.

If, as seems extremely doubtful, the Queen did at any time try to communicate with the spirit world it could only have been in the hope of reaching Albert.

Four years before she died the Queen made her will

> 'earnestly trusting to be reunited to my beloved Husband, my dearest Mother, my loved children and 3 dear sons-in-law—And all who have been very near & dear to me on earth. Also I hope to meet those who have so faithfully and devotedly served me especially good John Brown and good Annie Macdonald [her wardrobe maid for thirty-one years] . . . who I hoped would help to lay my remains in my coffin & to see me placed next to my dearly loved Husband in the mausoleum at Frogmore.'

As Queen Victoria lay on her death-bed two clergymen—Randall Davidson, who was now Bishop of Winchester, and the local vicar—prayed at intervals. Victoria, gradually sinking, lay motionless, giving no sign that she heard them. But as Davidson recited the last lines of her favourite hymn, Newman's *Lead Kindly Light*, she seemed to be listening:

> 'And with the morn those angel faces smile
> Which we have loved long since and lost awhile.'

Whether she heard or not the poignant moment was central to the Queen's belief. She mingled heavenly with earthly love, God and Albert, the good life that had been with the good life that was to come. Browning's vision, in *Pospice*, of husband and wife meeting after the final struggle with Death, could have been written for Victoria and Albert:

> For sudden the worst turns the best to the brave,
> The black minute's at end,
> And the elements' rage, the fiend-voices that rave,
> Shall dwindle, shall blend,
> Shall change, shall become first a peace, then a joy,
> Then a light, then thy breast,
> O thou soul of my soul! I shall clasp thee again,
> And with God be the rest!

The Monarch

I

During Queen Victoria's reign and the early decades of the reign which followed she was usually described as a perfect constitutional or parliamentary monarch—both attributes were frequently used as synonyms. This meant, first and foremost, that the formation of a government depended upon the political composition of Parliament or, more precisely, of the Commons, and not on the sovereign. It also meant that the government in reality exercised the powers which had formerly belonged to the Crown and that even within these established limits the influence of the monarch was negligible. The classical definition of this ideal parliamentary system was given by Walter Bagehot in *The English Constitution* (1867). According to him the monarchy was a splendid and popular institution, but the power lay with parliament and successive ministers and that 'to state the matter shortly, the sovereign has, under a constitutional monarchy such as ours, three rights—the right to be consulted, the right to encourage, the right to warn. And a king of great sense and sagacity would want no others'.

Later political historians, both in England and abroad, thought much the same as Bagehot, and Victorian order under the system was regarded as a model by continental advocates of parliamentary democracy.

A different picture gradually emerged, especially after the publication of Queen Victoria's letters had thrown light upon her political opinions and interventions. It became apparent that the Queen had not been a strictly parliamentary or even a strictly constitutional monarch: her power had been far from negligible. Earlier writers were misled by the official declarations which statesmen had felt more or less in duty bound to make concerning the Queen's adaptability to a system which had been developed before she came to the throne. Formerly there had been a much greater insistence on strict adherence to parliamentary rules than during Victoria's reign. Nowadays many historians maintain—and they are surely right—that the sovereigns who succeeded her were considerably more passive and more strictly constitutional than Victoria was. This complex matter has been referred to here only very briefly and for the purpose of stressing one or two points which have hitherto been underestimated, at least in discussions of a purely political nature.

When Victoria came to the throne it was commonly agreed (as it is today) that there was in existence a parliamentary system having an unwritten constitution based on tradition, practice or custom, whichever term is most appropriate—a system which functioned by a whole set of rules outside 'the law' commonly referred to nowadays as 'constitutional conventions'. But it is practically impossible to say what 'constitutionality' was considered to be. Historians and politicians differ, one side claiming, for example, that the right to dissolve the Commons still rested with the sovereign and the other denying that this was so. To attempt to establish the views of informed opinion in

1837, 1867 or 1897 concerning the English parliamentary system would be a task of scholarship beyond the scope of the present study. The important fact that must be borne in mind is that later generations have based the discussion on a fixed conception of the meanings of 'rule' and 'convention', a distinction which had not arisen in Victoria's day and therefore could not be the determining factor in her thinking and actions or in those of her ministers.

Moreover, the distinction is not always made between authorized powers and the actual capacity for influence which operated to one side of them. The Queen is considered to have exercised power incompatible with constitutionality—even though this power merely consisted in coaxing or bullying her ministers into following her suggestions, so that she got her own way by hook or by crook.

The Queen undoubtedly acted in ways which must seem dubious for any system of government in which a cabinet is responsible for government measures—any system, that is, except a despotic monarchy, a dictatorship or a presidency of the American type. It was doubtful, for example, whether the Queen was behaving in a constitutional manner when she intrigued with the opposition against ministers of the party in power or even incited minor officials to adopt obstructive tactics. But her influence, which has slowly become more apparent with the increasing publication of private papers and from the Queen's own writings, is seen to have been greatly facilitated by the deference of her ministers and their willingness to comply with her wishes.

Finally, if the concept of 'constitutionality' was not clear to statesmen or political theorists, it was even less clear to Queen Victoria. She had been taught a little history and politics but she would never have been able to give coherent answers to any questions on the principles of government. It is typical of her in this respect that seven years after her accession she could still complain that 'she could hardly avoid feeling guilty of dishonesty in giving her confidence suddenly to persons who had been acting in opposition to those to whom she had hitherto given it'.

Her intellectual and moral innocence were apparently such that she was unable to understand the typical situation of the parliamentary system in which a change of government reverses the opposition in the Commons—a situation which seemed to her both unnecessary and somewhat indecent: she was inclined to take the fiction of the royal prerogative at its face value.

Throughout the sixty years following her accession, her letters, hastily written and unreflecting as they often are, give the most varied opinions about the monarchy, government and parliament. Sometimes the letters very significantly reveal that the Queen really considered herself properly the one to choose her ministers as she wished and to have a personal right to make decisions, at least in matters of moment. Yet she sometimes seemed to be aware of the limitations of the sovereign's power. In any case it all worked quite well. The Queen obstinately used to stick to her guns, but hesitated or backed down at the decisive moment and this provided a balance which in addition to the ministers' fear of friction and their willingness to humour her—a desire that at times surely encompassed both the woman and the sovereign—led to a state of affairs in which matters were conducted with reasonably unshaken constitutional procedure. As a proof of which, there was no constitutional crisis worth considering during the whole of Victoria's reign of nearly sixty-four years.

Without going into detail, what now follows is based on the fact that the main principles of a constitutional parliamentary system are the following:

1. The formation of a government depends on Parliament.
2. The sovereign must approve the government's suggestions.
3. The dissolution of Parliament (the Commons) is really decided by the government, even though as a matter of form and in a fictitious sense the right to do so is accorded to the sovereign.

How did these rules work in Victoria's day? The party composition of the Commons was unquestionably the determining factor in a choice of government. All changes of government necessitated a fresh election, which altered the composition of the Commons, or a vote of confidence which, if it was a no-confidence resolution, obliged the Government to resign or gave it an excuse to do so.

On several occasions the Queen was in despair over one of these changes, as in 1841 when Lord Melbourne was succeeded by Peel or when the Liberals came to power in 1880 and she had to lose her beloved Disraeli, or again in 1886 and 1892 when she had to accept the detested Gladstone; but she did not hesitate to recognize the changes as inevitable. There were times when she must have longed to dismiss a Prime Minister she disliked (Russell and Gladstone), but she knew that this was not possible. She can be accused of intriguing and wilfulness in the autumn of 1885 when she tried to effect a coalition between the Moderate Liberals and the Conservatives; but there was no refusal to abide by the results of the elections. Once or twice the Queen influenced or tried to influence the choice of a Prime Minister, but she did so in cases where there was no definite candidate, so her actions in these situations cannot be criticized. In 1859 the post went to Lord Palmerston after considerable indecision and difficulties in forming a Government. In 1868 the Queen decided on Disraeli from a choice of three possible candidates, and in 1894 she chose Lord Rosebery out of the four or five who aspired to succeed Gladstone. After the general election of 1880 she tried to get some Liberal—anyone rather than Gladstone—but after sounding out Lord Granville and Lord Hartington without results she was forced to send for Gladstone, whom she disliked and distrusted. That she had not done so immediately was probably because he had officially resigned from the party leadership. In all these cases she can be accused of bad judgment or a certain capriciousness but not of unconstitutional behaviour.

Much the same can be said of the Queen's attitude to proposed Bills. She often tried to bring her influence to bear on the drafting of a measure and was sometimes successful in doing so. The final shaping of Gladstone's Bill to disestablish the Irish Protestant Church during his first government was a case in point. Another was Disraeli's Royal Titles Bill which made her Queen Empress in 1876. But when, in spite of her opinions, or wishes, the Cabinet persisted in the course they had agreed to take, she eventually gave way. This made it possible to introduce with her consent many measures with which she personally strongly disagreed. This was also the case with numerous other measures, including a great number of Irish reforms and in particular the Home Rule Bill of the third and fourth Gladstone governments. It is evident from some of her letters that the Queen apparently held the preposterous notion that the speech from the throne was not a government declaration but her personal statement, and indeed there were occasions when parts of the speech were altered by her wishes. But on the whole she insisted that the wording of the speech should be the concern of the Cabinet.

The prerogative of dissolution is a third vital point in the parliamentary system. If a sovereign believes that he or she can refuse a dissolution there is a risk of conflict with the Cabinet, and in such cases sovereign and cabinet are publicly exposed as being in opposition. The Cabinet is thus forced to resign and the succeeding Cabinet becomes a 'Crown Cabinet'. This is even more obviously the case when it is the sovereign who demands a dissolution, on the grounds that a proposed measure cannot be accepted before its discussion and approval by vote. Both of these situations actually arose during Queen Victoria's reign.

In May 1858, Lord Derby who, as leader of the Conservatives, had been Prime Minister since February, requested permission to dissolve if the Government were defeated on the issue of the Indian question (reorganization of the Government of India following the suppression of the Indian Mutiny, and transfer of India to the Crown) which was then under debate. Derby expected to be defeated by 15 to 35 votes, but still thought he could be saved if it were known that the Queen would not refuse a dissolution. He also asked for permission to make known beforehand that the Queen was willing to give her consent to a dissolution.

The Queen, on the Prince Consort's advice, refused either to authorize a Dissolution or to permit Lord Derby to say that she would consent to one, and to guard herself against any supposition that she had made up her mind beforehand to refuse her consent, she told Lord Derby that she could make no prospective decision then on the matter.

The Queen was in fact disinclined to authorize a Dissolution, but she refused to allow Lord Derby to make in advance the announcement he requested because she considered that it would be 'a very unconstitutional threat for him to hold over the head of the Parliament, with her authority, by way of biassing their decision'.

In doubt about what to do next, the Queen and Prince Albert sent Sir Charles Phipps, (George Anson's successor as the Prince's Private Secretary) to seek counsel from Lord Aberdeen, a former Prime Minister and a man noted for his caution and integrity. According to Phipps's undated memorandum of May 1858 he first of all gave Lord Aberdeen, in the strictest confidence, the Queen's account of the dilemma and the explanation of her action. Lord Aberdeen told him that the Queen had done right, and said that he had never heard of such a request being made, or authority for such an announcement being sought.

> 'He knew the Government had threatened a Dissolution, that he thought they had a perfect right to do so, but that they would have been quite wrong in joining the Queen's name with it. He said that he had never entertained the slightest doubt that if the Minister advised the Queen to dissolve, she would as a matter of course do so . . . There was no doubt—he said—of the power and prerogative of the Sovereign to refuse a Dissolution—it was one of the very few acts which the Queen of England could do without responsible advice at the moment; but even in this case whoever was sent for to succeed, must, with his appointment, assume the responsibility of this act, and be prepared to defend it in Parliament.'

Lord Aberdeen added that

> 'he could not remember a single instance in which the undoubted power of the Sovereign had been exercised upon this point, and the advice of the Minister to dissolve Parliament had been rejected—for it was to be remembered that Lord Derby would be still at this time her Minister.'

It was Lord Aberdeen's opinion that 'the result of such refusal would be that the Queen would take upon herself the act of dismissing Lord Derby from office, instead of his resigning from being no longer able to carry on the Government.'

At a second audience with the Queen and the Prince Consort Lord

Derby again asked for the Queen's consent to a Dissolution and permission to announce it since—he said—Lord Palmerston's supporters were saying that she had refused. The Queen insisted that it would be quite unconstitutional to threaten Parliament, and to use her name for that purpose. Lord Derby disclaimed any such intention and said there were ways of letting the fact be known without any risk. The Queen and the Prince refused to discuss this, but the Queen hinted to Lord Derby that a Dissolution would not be refused to him, and trusted that her honour would be safe in his hands as to the use he made of that knowledge. 'He seemed greatly relieved, and stated that had he had to resign, he would have withdrawn from public business, and the Conservative Party would have been entirely, and he feared for ever, broken up' (16 May 1858).

Lord Derby accordingly allowed a *démenti* to leak out to the effect that the Queen had no intention of refusing a Dissolution. In fact, there was no Dissolution because the Government was not defeated—perhaps precisely because the threat of dissolution had thus been unofficially conveyed to the Opposition. The disputed measure was eventually passed and the government of India was transferred to the Crown. Whether the decision to leak the Queen's willingness to sanction a Dissolution was justified or not must remain a matter for controversy, though nowadays there is every reason to believe that it was.

During the Liberal administrations of 1892–95 (under the leadership of Gladstone, then Rosebery), the Queen's prerogative of Dissolution was discussed on two occasions. The arguments were both involved and vague; the underlying situation was the conflict over Home Rule, with the Queen, the Lords and the Conservative Party on one side and the Government, and a small majority of the Commons which supported it, on the other. Lord Salisbury, the leader of the Conservatives, who had been corresponding with the Queen behind the backs of the Cabinet, agreed that she could ask for a Dissolution but he emphasized simultaneously in a memorandum that the constitutionality of the whole thing was doubtful.

> 'A committee of leading Unionists has met weekly, during this session, to watch the progress of the Home Rule Bill. Among other subjects of discussion has been the question whether, after the rejection of the Bill in the Lords, the Queen should be approached, either by way of petition, signed on a large scale, or by Address from the House of Lords, praying her to exercise her prerogative of Dissolution. I have advised her against any such step for the present, for the following reasons.
>
> 'A Dissolution by the Queen, against the advice of her Ministers, would, of course, involve their resignation. Their party could hardly

help going to the country as the opponents of the royal authority; or at least, as the severe critics of the mode in which it had been exerted. No one can foresee what the upshot of such a state of things would be! It might be good; or it might be bad! But there must be *some* hazard that, in the end, such a step would injure the authority of the Queen'.

The Queen did not dissolve Parliament. It was obvious that such an action, as Lord Salisbury had intimated, would have been tantamount to a dismissal of the Cabinet and therefore a breach of parliamentary rules.

On the determining issues of appointment and dismissal of the Cabinet, objections to cabinet proposals and the use of the prerogative of Dissolution the Queen did indeed always act in a constitutional manner, even if on several occasions she does seem to have deliberated on a different course of action and considered that she would be within her rights in acting differently.

A popular monarch's strongest weapon is the threat of abdication. The Queen had recourse to this expedient to an extent which is undoubtedly unique in history. It is hardly possible to say how many times the Queen threatened to abdicate if she did not get her own way, or to estimate the effect of these threats on the government; it is difficult to distinguish between her hints of a wish to abdicate and her more direct threats.

It is also difficult to decide if and how much the Ministers were impressed by the Queen's threats or if indeed they took them seriously. One instance of an outright threat to abdicate occurred in 1871, when Gladstone pressed the Queen to come out of her Highland seclusion, spend more time in London and take a greater part in state functions. The Queen wrote to Lord Hatherley, the Lord Chancellor, one of her resounding moans about ill-health, overwork and worry:

> 'What killed her beloved Husband? Overwork & worry—what killed Lord Clarendon? The same. What has broken down Mr Bright and Mr Childers & made them retire, but the same; & the Queen, a woman, no longer young is supposed to be proof against all & to be driven and abused till her nerves & health will give way with this worry & agitation and interference in her private life. She must solemnly repeat that unless her ministers support her & state the whole truth she cannot go on & must give her heavy burden up to younger hands. Perhaps then those discontented people may regret that they broke her down when she might still have been of use' (10 August 1871).

A series of such threats, in varying degrees of vehemence, made

3. Victoria and her children, in mourning for Prince Albert. (Photography by W. Bainbridge, March 1862)

ueen Victoria with John
wn at Balmoral.
otograph by G. W. Wilson,
3)

5. Official Diamond Jubilee Portrait of Victoria, 1897

between 1877 and 1878 are good examples of her tactics. At a time when the Queen was urging a still more aggressive policy towards Russia than the one Disraeli and especially his Foreign Minister, Lord Derby, favoured and were carrying out, she made four statements in the course of six months in which she intimated that she might have to consider abdicating.

In April 1877 she wrote to Disraeli to tell him that the Queen

> 'wishes no general war—God knows! for no one abhors it more than she does: but then there ought to be an understanding that we cannot allow the Russians to occupy Constantinople, and that we must see that this is promised or the consequences may be serious. To let it be thought that we shall never fight and that England will submit to Egypt being under Russia would be to abdicate the position of Great Britain as one of the Great Powers—to which she will never submit, and another must wear the crown if this is intended.' (25 April 1877.)

In June 1877 she complained, again to Disraeli, of

> 'this delay—this uncertainty, by which, abroad, we are losing our prestige and our position, while Russia is advancing—and will be before Constantinople in no time. Then the Government will be fearfully blamed and the Queen so humiliated that she thinks she would abdicate at once.' (27 June 1877.)

In July she threw up her hands in horror, incensed at 'the language—the insulting language—used by the Russians against us! It makes the Queen's blood boil! What has become of the feeling of many in this country?' (20 July 1877).

By January 1878 the Queen, at Osborne, felt that she could not

> 'as she before said, remain the sovereign of a country that is letting itself down to kiss the feet of the great barbarians, the retarders of all liberty and civilization that exists . . . Oh if the Queen were a man, she would like to go and give those Russians, whose word one cannot believe, such a beating! We shall never be friends again till we have it out. This the Queen feels sure of.' (10 January 1878.)

And in February:

> '. . . she feels deeply humiliated and must say that she thinks we deserve great censure for the way in which we have abandoned our standpoint; her own first impulse would be to throw everything up, and to lay down the thorny crown, which she feels little satisfaction in retaining if the position of this country is to remain as it is now.' (9 February 1878.)

But there was no war, and in July Disraeli returned from the Berlin Congress having given back to the Russians all that they had lost in the Crimean War, but bringing back his 'Peace with Honour'.

It is clear from all this that the Queen was able to contemplate the possibility of abdication even when she was in general agreement with a government, but of course she tended to make such threats only when she regarded her Prime Minister—in this case Gladstone—as a personal enemy. Victoria was not alone in employing such tactics: just as Bismark blackmailed the nonogenarian Emperor Willhelm of Germany with threats of resignation, so the Queen used threats of abdication to try to bring her Ministers to heel.

Lord Ponsonby quotes his father's observations on one of the Queen's threats to abdicate—when she lost Disraeli in 1880:

> 'The change from this to Gladstone would be most trying to her and in fact she says she will not have him. What this fully means one cannot say, but she has declared she would abdicate rather than submit to dictation. Gladstone once told me that this threat of abdication was the greatest power the Sovereign possessed—nothing would stand against it, for the position of a Minister who forced it on would be untenable.'

The Private Secretary added: 'True. But on the other hand what a terrible victory it would be for her. It would almost be ruin. And I earnestly hope these mutterings may not go beyond me.'

These conflicting statements of the Queen's give a good picture of the situation. A threat of abdication by a popular parliamentary monarch on the grounds of antagonism to the prime minister can be compared to an invitation to join in a suicide pact. If the prime minister refuses to give way and the monarch as a result abdicates a severe blow is dealt to the government and its party. But it also means that the institution of the monarchy is endangered because a strong reaction against this form of pressure will in time become inevitable. To use abdication in the same way that a Prime Minister can use resignation is obviously not possible. It has been debated (both in England and Sweden) whether a monarch has any right at all to abdicate—a futile discussion, since no one can prevent a head of state from stepping down if he wants to.

What enabled the Queen to exercise her influence was that, by tradition and through her own and Prince Albert's initiative, she took a considerable share in State affairs and that she frequently expressed a personal opinion—whether it was really her own or Prince Albert's. When she lived away from London, which she did as a rule after she became a widow—she was always accompanied by a minister in attendance. The Prime Minister sent her his own handwritten despatches after each cabinet meeting and he or some other minister gave similar reports on parliamentary debates. A great many higher appointments in the Administration, the Army and the Church—exactly how many cannot be ascertained—were submitted to the Queen and her opinions and preferences frequently decided such appointments, especially those of the Church and the Diplomatic Corps. Theoretically, she was supposed to see all incoming and outgoing diplomatic dispatches. Instructions to ambassadors and envoys had to be approved by her. According to Lord Palmerston as many as 28,000 incoming and outgoing dispatches were attended to by the Queen during 1880, a particularly heavy working year. For reasons of his own Palmerston was often remiss in this respect and used to delay sending drafts until the dispatches had been sent off. At one time there was a long correspondence between himself and the Queen in which she took him to task over this habit of his. In addition to the work required by the dispatch boxes, she carried on a vigorous correspondence about Foreign Affairs with her relatives and acquaintances throughout all the courts of Europe.

This involved a labour for the Queen, and perhaps most of all for Albert during his lifetime, which it is not possible to calculate in hours but which undoubtedly must have occupied the greater part of her life. As regards her prime ministers, their rendering of accounts to the Queen was both time-consuming and tiring, even more so when she was living at Balmoral (seven years all told) or at Osborne, which made daily letter-writing a necessity.

Several of these statesmen complained bitterly (though privately) of the trouble she caused them. Disraeli wrote from Balmoral: 'Carrying on the Government of a country six hundred miles from the Metropolis doubles the Labour'; while Gladstone gloomily told Lord Rosebery: 'The Queen alone is enough to kill any man!' Even Lord Salisbury, whose dealings with the Queen were much less exasperating than Gladstone's, admitted 'I could do very well with two departments: in fact I have four—the Prime Ministership, the Foreign Office, the Queen, and Randolph Churchill—and the burden of them increases in that order!'

The extent of the Queen's influence also depended on the fact that her ministers, as subjects before their Sovereign—perhaps also as men before a woman and especially an ageing woman—found it difficult to assert themselves, obliged, as they were, always to be respectful, polite, and to tread warily for fear of a set-to with her, either in person or in writing. Because the Queen was self-willed, unreasonable and irritable, they found it less troublesome to give in to her, or at least to appear to do so in the face of her obstinacy and nagging. The letters of some of them reveal the irritation they felt at never being able to speak their minds, at always having to couch their replies in beseeching, appealing and apologetic terms, at having to show humility and admiration to the point of servility and only as a last resort to use the harsh weapon of logic.

This is especially true for the period following the death of the Prince Consort, for in his lifetime he often acted as the Queen's spokesman or deputy. He talked to ministers, whereas the Queen preferred to write to them, and in their dealings with him an attitude of exaggerated respect was not necessary.

Mention must be made of several cases in which the Queen influenced or was considered to have influenced decisions in government affairs. On several occasions she is believed to have persuaded the Prime Minister to alter the composition of his cabinet. She once intervened to prevent Gladstone from including Sir Charles Dilke in the Cabinet—a man who had several times given voice to his Republican sympathies; and in 1895 Lord Salisbury chose his Home Secretary at the Queen's suggestion. In these and similar cases it is nevertheless still difficult to gauge the extent of the Queen's intervention. The Prime Minister himself may have been undecided and it is not beyond the bounds of possibility that to follow the Queen's wishes was an easy way out and a welcome opportunity to have his mind up for him—in cases where the party situation seemed to indicate an appointment which was unwelcome to a Prime Minister called upon to form a new cabinet. Several times the Queen's decided preference seems to have been the determining factor in appointments of the clergy. In 1888 she obliged Disraeli to make the Bishop of London, Archibald Campbell Tait, Primate of all England, and she usually insisted on deciding who should be Dean of Windsor—and her court chaplain. She wrote to Sir Frederick Ponsonby: 'For obvious reasons and after much reflection on the subject the Queen thinks that it would be best to associate the office of Domestic Chaplain with that of Dean of Windsor' (26 September 1882). Ponsonby observed: 'She came to regard the position of Dean of Windsor as her own nomination, a view not entirely shared by the ecclesiastical and political authorities.'

The Queen also seems to have been responsible for the dismissal and appointment of some envoys—in particular when she intervened in the appointment of ambassadors to Berlin in 1864 and again in 1870 at the instigation of the Princess Royal and of her husband, who was then Crown Prince of Prussia. In the first case it was suggested that Sir A. Buchanan was not fit for his post and he was removed. In the second, Lord A. Loftus was considered inadequate by the Crown Princess (not without justification) and was substituted by Mr Odo Russell.

In what concerns general policy, cases have already been mentioned here in which the sovereign made contributions of importance. But it is most difficult to determine to what extent the Queen's and Prince Albert's often very decided opinions on foreign policy influenced her ministers. The probability is that the Prince played a considerable role, through constant discussions with cabinet ministers, although this cannot be verified from accessible documents. A remarkable and much-quoted instance of this was when Prince Albert, shortly before his death, was able to induce the Government to tone down the severity of a note to Washington concerning the *Trent* affair, which occurred during the eighth month of the American Civil War.

An English vessel, the *Trent*, bound for England with two Confederate envoys on board, was chased by Federalists, boarded, and the envoys kidnapped with all the male passengers. Lord Russell drafted a harsh ultimatum to the Federal Government, demanding the release of the envoys, with the threat of the recall of the British Ambassador from Washington and a declaration of war if the men were not released. Albert, who disagreed with this line of procedure, rewrote Russell's draft, leaving a loophole for negotiation. The Cabinet accepted the toned-down draft—it was Albert's last political act: he was so ill that he could hardly hold his pen, and he died a fortnight later. The note was dispatched, the Federalists eventually negotiated and the affair blew over. It has been claimed that it was Albert's intervention which thus prevented war between England and America, but this is a theory which not only cannot be proved, but seems debatable.

The Queen's letters indicate that she—or she and Albert—always tried to influence the Cabinet in a crisis, often with great insistence; more will be said further on about the Queen's general attitude to foreign policy and some of her actions concerning it.

It can be assumed that Queen Victoria's influence was generally greater than that of her successors and for the most part much more than could be expected of a constitutional monarch. But there is no doubt that it was the successive governments and not the sovereign who played the leading role in all the essentials of British policy. The frequently suggested idea that it was really Victoria who made the decisions, especially on the main trends of foreign policy during crises, is based on a legend just as absurd as the one which makes her son Edward VII the architect of Britain's early-twentieth-century policy of alliances. In her dealings with her prime ministers Victoria was not so much a great force as a great nuisance.

2

Ten prime ministers served the Queen during her reign. Her first, Lord Melbourne, who headed a government which lasted seven years, had been in office for two years when Victoria came to the throne in

1837. Four of her premiers served a single term, three of them were twice in office, Lord Salisbury three times and Gladstone four. It is significant that seven out of the ten, whether they sat in the House of Lords or not, belonged to old families of the aristocracy. The exceptions were Peel and Gladstone, who came from rich upper-middle-class families, and Disraeli, who was brought up in a wealthy intellectual Jewish family but adopted the Christian faith as a boy of twelve.

Victoria's prime ministers and their terms of office were: Lord Melbourne (1835–41), Sir Robert Peel (1841–46), Lord John Russell (1846–52 and 1865–66), Lord Derby (1852, 1858–59, 1866–68), Lord Aberdeen (1852–55), Lord Palmerston (1855–58, 1859–65), Benjamin Disraeli, later Lord Beaconsfield (1868, 1874–80), Gladstone (1868–74, 1880–85, 1886, 1892–94), Lord Salisbury (1885–86, 1886–92, 1895–1902) and Lord Rosebery (1894–95).

The Queen's relationships with all these statesmen differed greatly. She was beside herself when Melbourne, whom she adored, was forced to make way for Peel, whom she disliked. But she soon grew to like and respect him and to place her confidence in him, especially as he and Albert—both of them so thorough, so conscientious and earnest—got on very well together. The Queen detested Lord John Russell, a Whig and a party man, because he was somewhat pompous, dogmatic and opinionated, a 'little man' both intellectually and physically—according to Greville 'a very clever man whose mind was nevertheless "little" '. Palmerston never won her confidence. She had numerous clashes with him and distrusted him to the end. In her letters she generally called him 'Pilgerstein', a Teutonic pun on the words palmer (or pilgrim) and stone, devised by Albert and Uncle Leopold. Nevertheless she was frequently in sympathy with his nonchalantly forceful foreign policy. Her relationship with Lord Derby was good and she had a special esteem for Lord Aberdeen. Her weakness for Disraeli is as well known as her detestation of Gladstone. There was comparatively little friction in her dealings with Lord Salisbury though a trifle more with Lord Rosebery.

The Letters give revealing impressions of the attitude of these statesmen towards the Queen as well as of their personalities in general. It would appear that their tendency to be compliant and servile is most apparent in the two most famous of the statesmen towards whom the Queen's feelings touched the poles of extreme liking and dislike. Disraeli bent over backwards in his servility and exaggerated respect, but there was a touch of good-humoured banter and irony in his manner which it was not in Gladstone's nature to achieve. In many of the prime ministers a touch of conceit, of pride and even a feeling of equality can often be glimpsed through their invariably impeccable courtesy. This would seem to apply especially to Russell, Aberdeen,

Palmerston and Salisbury. Palmerston, who still retained at the age of eighty something of the dandified elegance of a Regency buck, could sometimes permit himself to be satirical or to give her a mildly ironic reproof. A few examples go to show that the premiers could at times and to some degree display determination and stubbornness, or even put an authoritative foot down.

At the turn of the years 1853–54 the Queen wrote to Lord Aberdeen to complain about certain newspaper attacks on Prince Albert and his influence. In this letter, which has apparently never been published, the Queen seems to have made some exaggerated statements about the Prince's position and importance. Lord Aberdeen, dissociating himself from the press criticism of the Prince replied:

> 'Lord Aberdeen presents his humble duty to your Majesty. He cannot wonder at the indignation expressed by your Majesty, at the base and infamous attacks made upon the Prince during the last two or three weeks in some of the daily papers. It cannot be denied that the position of the Prince is somewhat anomalous, and has not been specially provided for by the Constitution; but the ties of Nature, and the dictates of common-sense are more powerful than constitutional fictions; and Lord Aberdeen can only say that he has always considered it an inestimable blessing that your Majesty should possess so able, so zealous, and so disinterested an adviser.'

Lord Aberdeen then went on to stress the power and independence of the Government:

> 'It is true that your Ministers are alone responsible for the conduct of public affairs, and although there is no man in England whose opinion Lord Aberdeen would more highly respect and value, still if he had the misfortune to be differing from his Royal Highness, he would not hesitate to act according to his own convictions, and a sense of what was due to your Majesty's service.' (6 January 1854.)

During the Italian crisis of 1859–60 the Queen was critical of the Palmerston government's benevolent, pro-Italy and anti-Austria attitude towards the attempt to liberate Italy from Austria under Habsburg rule and to secure complete Italian unification. She expressed her disapproval in a letter to Lord John Russell, the Foreign Secretary, who answered with a pointed rebuff.

> 'Lord John Russell presents his humble duty to your Majesty; he has just had the honour to receive your Majesty's letter of this date.
>
> 'Lord John Russell has sent to Lord Palmerston the proposal he humbly submits to your Majesty.
>
> 'He will therefore only venture to say that the doctrines of the

Revolution of 1688, doctrines which were supported by Mr Fox, Mr Pitt, the Duke of Wellington, Lord Castlereagh, Mr Canning and Lord Grey, can hardly be abandoned in these days by your Majesty's present advisers. According to these doctrines, all power held by Sovereigns may be forfeited by misconduct and each nation is the judge of its own internal government.

'Lord John Russell can hardly be expected to abjure those opinions, or to act in opposition to them.' (11 January 1860.)

The Queen replied with some asperity:

'The Queen has received Lord John Russell's note of this day, in which she is not able to find any answer to her letter, or even allusion to what she had written, viz. that Austria & France being asked to abstain from interference, such an arrangement would be partial and incomplete unless Sardinia was pledged also to non-interference.

'The Queen cannot make out what the doctrines of the Revolution of 1688 can have to do with this, or how it would necessitate Lord John Russell to abjure them.' (11 January 1860.)

Russell's reply to this is not included in the published correspondence. Even during the period which followed, the sharp wording of Russell's letter continued to rankle and the Queen complained to Lord Palmerston. The Prime Minister and his Foreign Secretary gave her lukewarm apologies and some sort of half-hearted explanation, but they naturally refused to be deflected from their course.

In the Schleswig-Holstein crisis of 1864 involving Denmark and Germany, the Queen was whole-heartedly pro-German. When one of the daily papers printed an article commenting on this, Lord Palmerston gave her a scolding. He told her that:

'. . . this paper, and others which have been mentioned to Viscount Palmerston, tend to show, that an impression is beginning to be created that your Majesty has expressed personal opinions on the affairs of Denmark and Germany which have embarrassed the course of the Government. Nothing can be further from the truth, for in all that has been done, or abstained from being done, the views and policy of the Government have been suggested by their own sense of public duty and have met with the sanction and approval of your Majesty, in the most constitutional manner. But it would be a great evil if public opinion were to divest your Majesty of that proper and essential protection which the Constitution secures for all that is done or not done; and if your Majesty's personal opinions and views were to become the objects of criticism or attack. Your Majesty has no doubt been duly careful as to the degree and manner in which your Majesty's opinion and views have been expressed, but it might be well that no indiscreet expressions from persons about your Majesty should give any countenance to such remarks as those in this newspaper.'

The Queen could not fail to understand Palmerston's meaning—that she should keep her personal opinions to herself and see to it that her gentlemen and ladies did likewise. She was vexed and complained in a letter to Uncle Leopold '. . . Pilgerstein is gouty, and extremely impertinent in his communications of different kinds to me' (10 May 1864). All the same, and on the advice of Sir Charles Phipps, she had written Palmerston a polite answer the previous day.

The Queen's treatment of Gladstone in the last years of the 1870s stands in a class by itself. When he first took office, in November 1868, his relations with her were passable, even promising, although during his first Ministry (1868–74) there were several clashes in which the Queen protested against reforms he pushed through. She was incensed by his efforts in 1871 to detach her from Balmoral and persuade her to make more frequent appearances in London. Their relations deteriorated progressively through Disraeli's second Ministry (1874–80) until her hostility became the obsessive animosity to Gladstone and his policies which was so fatefully to characterize all her dealings with him until his death.

The reasons are debatable. The clash of dissimilar personalities no doubt had much to do with it. When Victoria grew to like Disraeli in the 1870s Gladstone, his rival, became the object of her dislike. Disraeli is supposed to have fanned this by speaking about Gladstone with spiteful sarcasm. It would seem, too, that Victoria's dislike was not helped by Gladstone's manner which, apart from his policies, which she detested, made her feel uncomfortable. She was both put off and put out by his solemn pomposity, which became more pronounced with the years, his humourlessness and lack of tact, the 'terrible earnestness', dreary and boring, with which he harangued her—'he talks so very much', she said.

Her discomfort at Gladstone's perfect and unvaried respect was matched by her pleasure in Disraeli's graceful and playfully flirtatious intimacies. Gladstone bore the Queen's dislike with grieved dignity, but if he had once given her a piece of his mind and countered her animosity with a firm critical stand, perhaps Victoria, whose spoilt-child behaviour became more wilful under his kid-glove handling, would have realized that she was going too far and would have become less insolent to him, at least in the presence of others.

But a change in the political climate was very likely the greatest deciding factor in the Queen's dislike and distrust of Gladstone. During the decade 1870–80 the contrast between the two parties continually sharpened. Gladstone's reforms during his first Administration were one of the reasons, others were his opposition to Disraeli's Russian policy during 1877–78, especially his Midlothian campaign of 1879 with its vehement attack on Turkey's 'Bulgarian Atrocities', as well as the Franchise Reforms which made political agitation more widespread and vociferous, and republican tendencies in the radical wing of the Liberals with attacks on the monarchy by Joseph Chamberlain and Charles Dilke. The split in the party reached a climax with the conflict over the Irish question and especially with Gladstone's proposals for land reforms and later with Home Rule for Ireland. The Conservatives and Liberals had formerly shown themselves to be fighting teams inside the same social class; but now the aristocracy and the middle-class became staunchly Conservative while the Liberals were regarded in some social circles as exploiters of working-class discontent and therefore as traitors to their class—though hardly by political leaders and the politically active—so that now it was no longer a matter of course to invite the gentlemen of England to the same social gatherings with Radicals and the revolutionary minded with Liberal tendencies. In this state of affairs the Queen became a sound, if not extreme, Conservative. She was an imperialist who feared democracy and she looked upon demands for Home Rule for Ireland as threats to the Empire. She was contented when the Tories were in power and in this respect she was fortunate, since the Liberals were only in power for three out of the last sixteen years of her reign.

Gladstone saw the situation clearly. In a memorandum to the Queen on 28 October 1892 (of course she never answered it properly) he emphasized the difference in the attitude of the upper class before and after the battle for Home Rule.

> 'Mr Gladstone presents his humble duty to your Majesty, and offers his apologies for troubling your Majesty with any remarks on what is commonly termed the political situation.
>
> 'The leading fact to which he would point is a very painful one: it is the widening of that gap, or chasm, in opinion, which more largely than heretofore separates the upper and more powerful from the more numerous classes of the community. Such an estrangement he regards as a very serious mischief. This evil has been aggravated largely by the prolongation and intensity of the Irish controversy.
>
> 'But it began to operate years before the present Irish controversy began in 1885–86. There were at least six ducal houses of great wealth and influence, which Mr Gladstone had known to be reckoned in the Liberal Party at former times, and which had completely severed themselves from it before Irish Home Rule had

come to be in any way associated with the popular conception of Liberalism.'

Since Home Rule had become an issue, the social split had widened. In the Lords the Liberal minority had dwindled to a tenth or a twelfth. The Home Rule Bill of 1893 was defeated by 419 votes to 41. Mr Gladstone went on:

> 'Such was the character of this movement of Liberal dissent, that the supporters of the present Government in the House of Lords cannot be estimated at more than one-tenth or one-twelfth of that assembly. As regards landed property, Mr Gladstone doubts whether Liberals now hold more than one acre in fifty, taking the three kingdoms together. In the upper and propertied classes generally, the majority against them, though not so enormous, is still manifold. Yet, for the first time in our history, we have seen in the recent election a majority of the House of Commons, not indeed very large, but also not a very small one, returned against the sense of nearly the entire peerage and the landed gentry, and of the vast majority of the upper and leisured classes.'

It is not too much to say that Victoria and Gladstone were the protagonists in a class struggle which reached its fiercest eruption in the twentieth century, with the Liberal government of 1905, the restriction of the power of the House of Lords and social reform from Lloyd George to Clement Attlee.

The relationship between the Queen and Gladstone has been much discussed and apart from the official biography by Lord Morley (1903) there are two books of major importance, Sir Philip Guedalla's *The Queen and Mr Gladstone* and Frank Hardie's *The Political Influence of Queen Victoria*. But up to the present, as far as is known, their clashes and struggles have never been recounted systematically in more popular biographies about them. When Lord Morley wrote his massive biography of Gladstone the letters and memoranda had not been published and were not available for study. Sir Philip Magnus in his biography of Gladstone does not dwell in detail on this aspect of their relations nor do biographers of Queen Victoria. In the present book the treatment of these episodes is limited mainly to Gladstone's second administration and is much condensed. It is intended chiefly to give a picture of the Queen's behaviour and methods. The picture shows Victoria at her worst. But this view, though one-sided, is an indispensable part of the whole.

During the Eastern Question of 1875–78 Victoria continually made explicit her sympathies towards Disraeli's policy and expressed her exasperation with the Opposition. She wrote to Ponsonby:

> 'The Queen must say that she does consider the conduct of the Opposition on the Eastern Question . . . for the last two years most *unpatriotic* . . . and since she pinned her faith to the Government's policy she deplored the action of the Liberals at a moment when the honour and dignity of her great Empire are at stake—to *condemn* the policy of the Government which *their* former conduct has rendered necessary—is a cause of deep annoyance, pain & *anxiety for the future* to the Queen.'

She ended on a sublimely egocentric note: 'As the Queen can't separate herself from those interests she *does* consider it *very wanting* in *regard* for *her comfort, peace of mind & well being* to act as they are doing & the sooner they are undeceived about *her feelings* the better.'

She was beside herself with fury and despair when she was frustrated in her hopes of a victory for Disraeli in the general election of 1880. She wrote to Ponsonby (himself a Liberal with leanings towards the Radicals, but generally in favour of the Government's policy):

> 'The Queen sends the letter from Lord Beaconsfield . . . The great alarm in the country is Mr Gladstone, the Queen perceives, & she will sooner *abdicate* than send for or have any *communication* with that half-mad firebrand who would soon ruin everything & be a *Dictator*. Others but herself *may submit* to his democratic rule, but *not the Queen*. She thinks he himself don't wish for or expect it.'

She wrote more or less the same thing to Disraeli, hoped he would make a speedy return to power and asked him to write to her 'in confidence', on public matters even after his departure from office. After the change of government she boasted to Disraeli: 'I *never* write except on formal *official* matters to the Prime Minister'.

When there was no help for it but to form a Liberal government, she summoned two of Gladstone's closest colleagues, Lord Hartington (at the time party leader of the Commons) and Lord Granville, Liberal leader of the House of Lords. Neither of them felt that a government headed by them would succeed without Gladstone and doubted that he would accept a subordinate position. The Queen mentioned to them 'one great difficulty', her lack of confidence in Gladstone, so Hartington went off to see if Gladstone would serve under him. Gladstone gave an emphatic No! and the Queen had no alternative but to send for him.

The formation of a Cabinet met with difficulties, not least because of the Queen's dislike of those of the Radicals who had voiced republican sympathies; her attitude was responsible for the exclusion of Sir Charles Dilke from the Cabinet at this time, but she made no objection later to his becoming Under Secretary for Foreign Affairs—beyond insisting on a repudiation of his Republican tendencies in a written declaration of loyalty. After the Cabinet had been formed the Queen put off as long as possible a meeting with Gladstone and frequently by-passed him to confide her opinions to Hartington or Granville.

In numerous entries in her Journal and in letters to Prince Albert's Private Secretary, George Anson, as well as to Liberal statesmen and members of the Tory opposition, the mistrust and disagreement with which the Queen followed the actions of Gladstone's government show up clearly. Odd beyond belief are her underhand—'confidential'—overtures to statesmen of moderate leanings to persuade them to resist the Radicals in the Cabinet—among whose number she was inclined to count Gladstone. In August 1880 she wrote a long letter of warning to the Foreign Secretary, Lord Granville—which she urged him to show to Cabinet members. She said she was

> '*seriously* alarmed at the *extreme Radicals* being at all cajoled by the present Government, and she must tell Lord Granville that she thinks the moderate Members of the Government *ought* to do *all* to obtain the *support* of their *moderate Whig* supporters *instead* of courting the support of the extreme Party. She knows that the Opposition would give them *every support*, in resisting any policy which strikes at the *root and existence* of the Constitution and the Monarchy. The Queen herself can *never* have *any confidence* in the men who encourage reform for the sake of alteration and pulling down what exists and what is essential to the stability of a Constitutional Monarchy. A *Democratic Monarchy* . . . she will not *consent to belong to*. *Others* must be found *if* that is to be, and she *thinks* we are on a dangerous and doubtful slope, which may become too rapid for us to stop, when it is too late. The Queen is all for *improvement* and *moderate reform* of *abuses*, but not merely for *alterations' and reform's sake* . . . The Queen thinks, from what Mr Gladstone and *his* private Secretaries write, that *Mr G.* will require *very long rest*.' (8 August 1880.)

The confused thinking of the whole letter, like that of so many others of her letters, gives the impression that the Queen regarded many members of the Government as either inept or ill-willed.

She wrote a similar letter in December to W. E. Forster, Secretary for Ireland and a member of the Cabinet who was an advocate of firm measures for the Irish and was a strong opponent of Home Rule.

> 'The Queen is as sincerely liberal in her views for the improvement of her Empire as anyone can be, but she is as *sincerely* and *determinedly* opposed to those advanced, and what she must call destructive, views entertained by so many who unfortunately are in the

Government. If *these* prevail instead of the moderate, far-seeing and loyal ones, the Queen will not remain where she is; she *cannot* and will not be the Queen of a *democratic monarchy*; and those who have spoken and agitated for the sake of party, and to injure their opponents, in a very radical sense must look for *another monarch*; and she doubts if they will find one. The Queen has spoken *very strongly*, but she thinks the present Government are running a very dangerous course, and she knows that Mr. Forster would not wish to see this country follow the dreadful example of France!' (25 December 1880.)

The Queen even had a series of personal set-tos with Gladstone. In September 1883 he went on a holiday cruise as guest of the shipowner Sir Donald Currie. Other guests included some of Gladstone's friends, among whom were the Home Secretary, Sir William Harcourt, and Alfred Tennyson, the Poet Laureate. Instead of the original plan to sail round the British Isles, an impromptu visit to Norway and Denmark was decided on, and Gladstone accompanied his fellow-guests. They were fêted in Copenhagen and invited by the King and Queen of Denmark to a dinner at which the Tsar of Russia and the King of Greece were present. Gladstone, by his visit, had broken the rule that a Prime Minister may not set foot in a foreign country without permission from the Sovereign, and Queen Victoria was highly indignant. She wrote to her Private Secretary:

'The Queen is a good deal surprised & she must say annoyed at Mr Gladstone's "Progress" . . . The Queen thinks it most unusual & not she thinks respectful towards herself that the Prime Minister should go to a foreign country without mentioning it to the Sovereign. And she thinks considering the extraordinary & tactless publicity given to every single movement & trifling act of his, his presence in Norway when affairs are very critical seems indiscreet & ill-judged.'

And to Lord Granville she wrote: 'The Prime Minister—and especially one not gifted with prudence in speech—is not a person who can go about *where* he likes with impunity.'

On Gladstone's return the Queen gave him a sharp reprimand in which she stressed the presence of the Russian Tsar among the Copenhagen dinner guests, which, she thought, made Gladstone's presence imprudent and politically embarrassing. Gladstone, full of apologies, assured her that he had not discussed politics and reiterated that the outing to Scandinavia had been Tennyson's idea and was decided on the spur of the moment. Privately he told Sir Edward Hamilton that the Queen was jealous of the deference paid to an old man of whom she strongly disapproved.

In July 1884 the Queen attacked Gladstone in a letter for allowing certain statements to be made by Joseph Chamberlain. She wrote:

> 'The Queen had not intended replying to Mr Gladstone's letter . . . but she feels bound to observe upon the language of *defiance* in the speech of one of the Cabinet Ministers, one whom she has long considered as most dangerous in the Cabinet and one to whom she fears Mr Gladstone is inclined to listen far more than to those who hold moderate opinions. His speech, which Mr Gladstone *should read*, is most dangerous and tending to stir up class against class in a very reckless manner.'

She rejected with particular indignation any thought of the reforms in the House of Lords advocated by Chamberlain.

> '. . . The Monarchy would be utterly untenable were there *no balance* of power left, *no restraining* power! The Queen will yield to no one in TRUE LIBERAL FEELING, but not to destructive, and she calls upon Mr Gladstone *to restrain, as he can,* some of his wild colleagues and followers.' (25 July 1884).

When withdrawal from the Sudan, the matter of the relief of Khartoum, besieged by the Mahdi, and the rescue of General Gordon became a burning controversy the Queen's antagonism towards Gladstone came to a head. She really wished the Sudan to be defended and felt that this should be the aim of the expedition which set out, following Gladstone's fateful delay in deciding to send one. She went so far as to write to Lady Wolseley telling her how furious she was with the Government and urging Wolseley to take a firm stand.

> 'In strict confidence I must tell you I think the Government are more incorrigible than ever, and I do think your husband should hold strong language to them, and even THREATEN to resign if he does not receive strong support and liberty of action.
>
> 'I have written very strongly to the Prime Minister and others, and I tell you this; but it must never appear, or Lord Wolseley ever let out the hint I give you. But I really think they must be frightened. . . . Pray either destroy this, or lock it up, but I cannot rest without asking you to tell Lord Wolseley.' (3 March 1885.)

At the end of the month she wrote another 'top secret' letter—this time to Wolseley himself.

> 'Whatever happens, the Queen hopes and trusts Lord Wolseley will *resist* and strongly oppose all *idea* of retreat! His words on that subject, both in one of his telegrams when asked whether he could

do so, and also in his dispatch of the 1st of March, have *plainly* spoken out on this point. But she *fears some* of the Government are very unpatriotic, and do *not* feel what is a *necessity*. This and the absolute necessity of having a *good Government* at Khartoum [i.e. the Sudan should remain in Anglo-Egyptian hands] the Queen trusts Lord Wolseley *will insist on*. But then comes the health of the troops . . . Altogether the Queen's heart is sorely troubled for her brave soldiers . . . our soldiers fight and have on every single occasion in this exceptionally trying campaign fought like heroes individually, and she hopes he will tell them so from the highest to the lowest from her.

'The Queen would ask Lord Wolseley to destroy this letter as it is so very confidential, though it contains nothing which she has not said to her Ministers and over and over again . . . if he fears it might get into wrong hands, pray destroy it at once.' (31 March 1885.)

Her attempts to incite an army chief to insubordination against the Government fell on fruitful ground. Wolseley replying from Camp Korti in Egypt, had thanked the Queen for her appreciation of the army's vain efforts to save General Gordon, and permitted himself to observe:

'It is very disheartening to the soldiers of the army to find Mr Gladstone and all his colleagues have ignored all the toil they endured without a murmur on the river, all the fatiguing marches under a burning sun in the desert, and all the severe fighting they have had. It is very ungracious on Mr Gladstone's part, seeing that it is his fault that all these trials have been endured in vain, and all our dead comrades killed to no purpose.'

Wolseley thought that a few well-deserved cheering words would have cost Gladstone nothing and would have been appreciated by the soldiers, unpopular though he was in the army. 'However, if the Queen is satisfied with the conduct of her troops I don't think our men care very much what Mr Gladstone may think of them: they certainly don't think much of him' (22 March 1885.)

When news of Gordon's death (on 26 January 1885) reached England the Queen telegraphed Gladstone from Osborne. 'These news from Khartoum are frightful, and to think that all this might have been prevented and many precious lives saved by earlier action is too frightful' (5 February 1885). She insisted that the message be sent *en clair* and caused identical messages, also uncoded, to be sent to Granville and Hartington. The contents naturally became known and Gladstone, filled with furious indignation at what he considered an undeserved rebuke made publicly, half-contemplated sending in his resignation. Nevertheless, his reply to the Queen was respectful, as always, though he rejected any implication of blame in the affair. Ponsonby's efforts to make her take it all back were fruitless. She refused to make any sort of apology for this blow below the belt and continued her anti-Gladstone campaign.

The Queen's relationship with Gladstone during the period which followed—June 1885 to July 1886—does not need to be gone into in any detail. It was a twelve-month in which one eventful upheaval followed on the heels of another—Gladstone's departure in June 1885 because of a trivial defeat in the Commons; the formation of the Salisbury government; the elections in the late autumn which gave a majority to the Liberals and Irish Nationalists; Salisbury's overthrow in January 1886 and the return of Gladstone to form his third cabinet; their involvement in the agitation for Home Rule and the split within the Liberal Party; fresh elections held in July, with a victory for the Conservatives and Liberal Unionists; finally, the formation of Salisbury's second cabinet.

It must be borne in mind, nevertheless, that all this time the Queen was unsparing of her criticism and intrigues against Gladstone. After the election of 1885 she tried to get moderate Liberals to break with him. She wrote to George Goschen:

> 'I appeal to *you* and to all moderate, loyal, and *really patriotic* men, who have the safety and well-being of the Empire and the Throne at heart, and who wish to save them from destruction; with which, if the Government again fall into the reckless hands of Mr Gladstone, they would be threatened, to rise above party and to be true patriots! You must convince Lord Hartington of what is at last *his duty* and of which he owes to his Queen and country, which really goes before allegiance to Mr Gladstone, who can persuade himself that *everything* he takes up is right, even though it be calling black, white, and wrong, right. . . . Let me urge and implore you . . . to do all you can to gather around you all the moderate Liberals, who indeed ought to be called "Constitutionalists", to prevent Mr Gladstone recklessly upsetting the Government without being able to form a Government himself, which should stand . . . I am sure that you with Lord Hartington and many other moderate Liberals would save the country by standing aloof from Mr Gladstone, who is utterly reckless and whose conduct at this moment, in proposing what would be *Home Rule*, is most mischievous and uncomprehensible . . . I do not speak of *myself*, but I may say I think a Queen, and one well on in years and who has gone through terrible anxieties and sorrows, ought not to appeal in vain to British gentlemen, who have known and served her long!' (20 December 1885.)

During the spring of 1886 she worked in a similar way to bring about a split among the Liberals and to secure a coalition between Conservatives and Moderate Liberals. She sent Salisbury copies of Gladstone's most important letters to her and was delighted by his failure to get Liberal lords and ladies to enter the royal household or to prevent others from resigning from it—this, though inconvenient, she found 'patriotic'. Her treatment of Gladstone was no different when he formed his fourth and last government in 1892.

It can be seen, therefore, that the Queen made grave mistakes in her dealings with Gladstone—mistakes which must be regarded as unpardonable in a parliamentary or more-or-less constitutional monarch. She conspired with the Opposition against the party leader and head of the Government, and with his own colleagues. She encouraged subordinate officials (Wolesley's is the most flagrant of such cases) to forget their loyalty to the Government. These and other dubious political actions of Victoria's were practically unknown to her contemporaries and were seldom regarded with any critical eye, even for many years afterwards. Statesmen behaved with the utmost correctness, considering it their duty, perhaps even on tactical grounds, to praise the Queen for her constitutional behaviour and to keep silent about their differences with her. Even nowadays, when the publication of state papers, letters and biographies has made it possible to examine the Queen's behaviour and procedure in detail, there seems still to be a tendency to omit and gloss over, and a lingering reluctance to take an unabashed look behind the arras. Most people like to see the English Parliament as a smooth and orderly system devoid of cracks or blemishes; they also like to see Queen Victoria as a great and untarnished figure, and this is understandable because, despite all her faults, hers was an impressive and fascinating personality; but this desire for perfection can easily lead to the rctouching of awkward facts or a general sweeping under the carpet of clay from the feet of the idol.

It has been emphasized earlier here that during the latter decades of her reign the Queen was a staunch Conservative. This coincides in the first place with the fact that the two parties during this period were in clearer and stronger opposition than they had been earlier. If the term Conservative is used in a more general sense as a desire to maintain the *status quo*, then the Queen was a Conservative her whole life long. She clung to the Monarchy and the House of Lords, to the Established Church—not only for England but for the whole of Great Britain—and to the traditional caste system. She was almost always hesitant or critical in the face of drastic or far-reaching reforms, but none of this led in the early decades of her reign to any party-political attitude of significance, since the differences between Whigs and Tories were negligible then. She was against the limitation of working hours in the 1850s and abolition of the tax on newsprint in 1860; in the 1890s she was similarly opposed to death duties and increased taxes on beer. No great interest in social problems is discernible in the Queen—apart from the mobs who cheered her during her drives through London she hardly ever saw any of the poor—even though, of course, she spoke with benevolence about factory-hands and farm-labourers and occasionally supported measures to improve their lot. Her conservative prejudice against the emancipation of women was strong, although it was probably no more than typical of the attitude of middle-class women and possibly of women in general. On one issue she can perhaps be regarded as relatively broad-minded—she held some vague notions about the superiority of the Anglo-Saxon race but, at the same time she expressed in her letters her disapproval of racial oppression and the harsh treatment of the 'natives' in India and other British possessions. An essential feature of the Queen's political thinking is that she made up her mind about each problem as it arose, impulsively and without forming any considered opinion or drawing reasoned conclusions; and the background to this thinking was a tangle of obscure notions which, however, seemed perfectly obvious to her—indeed, she was hardly conscious of them.

When Victoria died, Lord Salisbury told the House of Lords that she had possessed a remarkable knowledge of what the people wanted, all the more striking because it was intuitive and could not have been reached by any personal contact. He said, in his eulogy of the Queen:

> 'She had an extraordinary knowledge of what her people would think—extraordinary because it could not have come from any personal intercourse. I have said for years that I always thought that when I knew what the Queen thought I knew pretty certainly what view her subjects would take and especially the middle classes of her subjects. Such was the extraordinary penetration of her mind.'

Several writers have fastened on this saying of Lord Salisbury's and Frank Hardie in particular has regarded the Queen as a typical representative of the middle class, 'the middle-class monarch *par excellence*.' There is something to be said for this view: she had an ever increasing mistrust of high society—she identified it with the Prince of Wales's profligacy and idleness—and in many respects she was the epitome of what used to be called the bourgeois virtues—diligence, clean living, thrift, orderliness. But Lord Salisbury's eulogy probably expressed more than just the obvious and meant that she reacted to events just as most ordinary people do, that she was not particularly original or 'different', and that at the end of her life she was, in terms of party and politics a Conservative—in short, that she thought very much the same as Lord Salisbury.

The Queen's opinions on foreign policy were decided mainly by her patriotism or—for those who prefer to call it that—her nationalism or jingoism. England was always right, the nation, like the Queen, was a peace-loving one but ready to go to war if it was in a worthy cause—England's cause—'We don't want to fight, but by jingo! if we do! . . .'

In almost every critical situation the Queen's attitude was one of readiness to arm, aggressive and bellicose to the verge of war, whether the crisis concerned Afghanistan, South Africa and the Boers, Egypt or any other state or people suitable for colonization; and this attitude held good for conflicts with European rivals, Russia first and foremost, but even France and occasionally Germany. Her attitude was tied up with and influenced by a number of ideas, often so rigid and irrational as to be little more than prejudices. Russians were barbaric, even though visiting Russian princes turned out to be both civilized and agreeable. Republican nations were suspect, a view which held good for America and France alike—though for good measure she had an added belief in the depravity of the French. In 1870, after the defeat of the French in the Franco-Prussian war (1870–71), when she heard a sermon on the text 'God, saith the prophet, punisheth wickedness, vanity and fornication', she observed that it was remarkable how appropriate these words were to the French. (Journal, 2 October 1870); but for some years the charm of Napoleon III tipped the scales of her prejudices in favour of France. For many years she was favourably disposed towards Prussia and Germany, especially after the Princess Royal's marriage to Prince Frederick of Prussia, and she favoured Prussia during the crises of 1863 (the Polish national uprising, ruthlessly crushed by the Russians) and 1864 (the invasion and occupation of Schleswig-Holstein by the Prussian armies) when she was strongly opposed to intervention. But later, also surely under her daughter's influence, she came to hate Bismarck and was extremely critical of her grandson Wilhelm II. In her emotional way she tended to identify foreign nations with persons, exasperating or praiseworthy as the case might be.

At times the Queen's patriotic feelings could impel her to say things that were positively grotesque. After the fall of Sebastopol to the French in 1855 and the failure of the British attack on the Redan, with the prospect of an armistice with Russia, she told the Foreign Secretary, Lord Clarendon, that she was not in favour of an armistice at that time because the English had been ignominiously repulsed in the final action of the Redan.

'The Queen cannot conceal from Lord Clarendon what her own feelings and wishes at this moment are. They *cannot* be for peace *now*, for she is convinced that this country would *not* stand in the eyes of Europe as she *ought*, and as the Queen is convinced she *would* after *this* year's campaign. The honour and glory of her dear Army is as near her heart as almost anything, and she cannot *bear* the thought that "the failure of the Redan" should be our *last fait d'Armes*, and it would cost her more than words can express to conclude a peace with *this* as the end. However, what is best and wisest must be done.' (15 January 1856.)

(Did the Prince Consort read this letter, one wonders ?) Lord Palmerston answered on Clarendon's behalf that one could not very well postpone an armistice on such grounds: '. . . if peace can now be concluded on conditions honourable and secure, it would, as your Majesty justly observes, not be right to continue the war for the mere purpose of prospective victories' (January 17 1856).

Whether the Queen was more often 'right' and her ministers 'wrong' or vice versa on questions of foreign policy has been the subject of debate, but such questions seem of little interest in view of the fact that they issue from the (provisional) opinion of posterity on the subject. The Queen has sometimes had the gift of prophecy conferred on her, as for example in assertions that her statements about friendly relations with Russia and France foretold the *Triple Entente* alliance. This is unconvincing, because she also made innumerable contradictory statements and predictions that were wide of the mark—just like any other statesman—and out of these, the number which, by any laws of probability or chance, have proved to be correct, can be counted on the fingers of one hand. The obvious fallacies in her thinking about foreign policy, such as her nationalistic and other prejudices and her emotionally-coloured opinions, must not lead one to ignore the fact that she read innumerable dispatches and followed the daily news closely and that she undoubtedly and quite frequently formed her opinions with as much knowledge of the situation as her ministers. To offset this, it is apparent from her correspondence that the Queen's knowledge of history was sketchy and that she appears to have made as superficial a study of that subject as she had of practically any other.

Her ignorance of wider causal relationships was often staggering. Her Journal entry for 2 October 1896, when she was seventy-seven, is a touching example of this. She had questioned the young Tsar Nicholas II about the reason for Russia's friendship with France. His answer was over-simplified, not even wholly accurate, but she accepted in all seriousness the elementary, misleading facts he gave her.

Where did the Queen's talents lie? More important—was she really gifted as a statesman? Opinions have been and still continue to be divided on this score. Lord Granville's opinion of 1882 took an effective middle way. 'It was impossible', he said, 'to treat the Queen as a great statesman because she was such a child, but it was equally impossible to treat her as a child because she had the *aperçus* of a great statesman in some things.'

By now, and in the light of her own words and those of her contemporaries which have been quoted and referred to here, the reader has doubtless formed some opinion of what Queen Victoria was like. Here, briefly, is the author's own view. The Queen's strong points were her vitality, her sincerity, her eagerness and her impulsiveness; her way of making up her mind and of expressing herself were alert and energetic and must be considered intellectual assets. Almost everything she wrote can be read with interest and must of it with fascinated pleasure, but in the matter of sharply defined ideas and the ability to carry on a rational and coherent argument the Queen was certainly not greatly endowed, and her obstinacy and prejudice made her judgement highly unreliable. Despite all this she would have played a valued and respected rôle in any ordinary walk of life; but she would surely never have occupied any significant place in history had she not been born to become Queen of England.

PART TWO

THE TREND OF IDEAS

I
THE BASIS OF UTILITARIANISM

Bentham's Doctrine

Jeremy Bentham's life-work, the ethical and political writings concerned with human welfare from which sprang the doctrine of utilitarianism, was an endeavour to replace the fundamentals of morals and legislation, in which religion and the law of nature were regarded as ordained by a power above and beyond human society, with another set of fundamentals. These, though lacking any metaphysical validity, claimed to be justified by the need for human coexistence. It was an attempt which helped to undermine the already severely affected social systems governed by theology and natural law. However, just as the concept of human rights, which implied an emancipation from theology, was strongly coloured by theological concepts, so utilitarianism, which was averse to accepting the idea of natural law, was at the same time full of ideas which arose from the very concept it rejected. Even the sources from which utilitarianism sprang, its ideas concerning general welfare, social utility and so forth, could be seen on closer scrutiny to be merely a dissociation from metaphysics and not a tenable starting point for a new social system. The permanent value of the contribution made by utilitarian theory is that it was essentially a liberation from all forms of dogma. In a narrower sense its real value was that in some fashion it complemented the liberal economy of the time. Bentham's philosophy pointed the way to Liberalism and Radicalism.

In his *Anarchical Fallacies* (1843) Bentham picked the French *Declaration of the Rights of Man* to pieces, article by article, subjecting to caustic critical examination the various statements concerning the rights of man, natural law, freedom, equality and so on, set out in the famous document. He decided that natural law was utter nonsense and the articles of the *Declaration* a mixture of the unintelligible, the false and a combination of the two.

He attacked, for example, the statement in Article I on the rights of man, which said:

> 'The end in view of every political association is the preservation of the natural and imprescriptible rights of man. These rights are liberty, property, security and resistance to oppression.'

This statement, said Bentham, springs from the assumption that such things as rights exist 'anterior to the establishment of governments: for natural, as applied to rights (if it mean anything), is meant to stand in opposition to *legal*—to such rights as are acknowledged to owe their existence to governments, and are consequently posterior in date to the establishment of government'. He went on to ask:

> 'Whence is it, but from government, that contracts receive their binding force? Contracts come from government, not government from contracts. It is from the habit of enforcing contracts, and seeing them enforced, that governments are chiefly indebted for whatever disposition they have to observe them.'

He then tackled the proposition in Article II, that existing governments 'derive their origin from formal associations entered into by partnership contract, with all the members for partners . . .'. 'More confusion, more nonsense, and the nonsense, as usual, dangerous nonsense', he commented and went on to say that

> 'All governments that we have any account of have been gradually established by habit, after having been formed by force . . . . The organization of governments from a contract is pure fiction, or in other words, a falsehood. It never has been known to be true in any instance; the allegation . . . is neither necessary nor useful to any good purpose.'

His comments on the rights of man were scathing. 'Natural rights', he said, 'is simple nonsense: natural and imprescriptible rights, rhetorical nonsense—nonsense upon stilts.'

Having demolished the notions implied in the first part of the article, Bentham asked:

> 'How stands the truth of things? That there are no such things as natural rights—no such things as rights anterior to the establishment of government—no such things as natural rights opposed to and in contradistinction to, legal: that the expression is purely figurative; that when used, in the moment you attempt to give it a literal meaning it leads to error, and to that sort of error that leads to mischief—to the extremity of mischief.'

He pointed out that 'the word "right" is the name of a fictitious entity: one of those objects, the existence of which is feigned for the purpose of discourse, by a fiction so necessary, that without it human discourse could not be carried on'. When men talk of rights—natural, moral and political rights—the only instance, Bentham believed, in which a right can be said to have any determinate and intelligible meaning is when it is a political right and that when any one has a political right, what this really means is merely 'the disposition on the part of those by whom the powers of government are exercised, to cause him to possess and so far as depends upon them to have the faculty, of enjoying, the benefit to which he has a right'.

The *Declaration* states elsewhere in Article I that: 'Men (all men) are born and remain free, and equal in respect of rights. Social distinctions cannot be founded but upon common utility.' This statement, Bentham commented, contains four propositions, all of them false. 'All men, on the contrary, are born in subjection, and the most absolute subjection—the subjection of a helpless child to the parents on whom he depends every moment for his existence . . . for a great number of years—and the existence of the individual and of the species depends on his so doing.'

One man is born rich, another poor; there is no such thing as equality, Bentham said, as he disposed of the *Declaration of Human Rights* point by point with his fascinatingly pedantic methods of demolition—methods which frequently ignored the most obvious meaning—to show that the whole thing was a tissue of absurdities.

Having worked his way through the *Declaration* in this fashion, he tossed it out as a practical basis for a political philosophy. That religion cannot fill the bill was a fact which, to judge by his constant intimations was so self-evident that it was not worth discussing. On the contrary, he found his appropriate foundation for a political system partly in an axiom drawn from experience—that every man aspires to the highest possible degree of happiness and that as a rule men generally act in accordance with this aspiration; and partly on a basis of his postulate, largely dictated by his own natural benevolence, that 'The right and proper end of government in every political community, is the greatest happiness of all the individuals of which it is composed, say, in other words, the greatest happiness of the greatest number'.

Concerning this axiom, postulated among the 'First Principles' of his *Constitutional Code* (1841), Bentham emphasized that it enclosed not so much a truth as an evaluation.

> 'When I say, the greatest happiness of the whole community ought to be the end or object of every pursuit, in every branch of the law—and of political rule of action, and of the constitutional branch in particular, what is it that I express?—this and no more, namely, that it is my wish, my desire, to see it taken for such, by those who, in the community in question, are actually in possession of the powers of government . . .!'

Those who did not entertain this desire would gain nothing from Bentham's *Constitutional Code*. He evidently supposed, however, that his ideas about the aims of a community would be shared by all.

By means of these principles Bentham believed that he would be able to settle in every detail how a government ought to be organized and how legislation could be constituted. It was only necessary to apply his 'First Principles' in any given field or to any circumstance. Nevertheless, he believed it to be impossible to measure degrees of happiness or unhappiness. In his *Principles of the Civil Code* (1838), discussing the 'Propositions of Pathology upon which the advantage of Equality is founded', he concluded that

> '. . . moral pathology would consist in the knowledge of the feelings, affections and passions, and their effects upon happiness. Legislation, which has hitherto been founded principally upon the quicksands of instinct and prejudice, ought at length to be placed upon the immoveable base of feelings and experience: a moral thermometer is required, which should exhibit every degree of happiness and suffering. The possession of such an instrument is a point of unattainable perfection; but it is right to contemplate it.'

Nevertheless Bentham did start out from the proposition that a definition having some degree of accuracy was possible. Consequently it was axiomatic for him that all human beings should be considered equally valuable, in the sense that one person's happiness is equal in importance with that of any other person. Here Bentham virtually allied this concept with the ideas concerning the law of nature and the concept that all men are born equal which he had already subjected to critical examination.

The happiness of the most helpless pauper, he believed, constitutes as much of the general happiness as the happiness of any one of the most powerful and wealthy members of the community. 'Why have my wants been so long neglected, while those of my neighbour have been so long satisfied?' asks Bentham's beggar, who plies before the rich man's door. 'Am I less a citizen than he? is my happiness less a part of the happiness of the community than this?'

Bentham employed similar reasoning on the subject of men versus women, arguing that there was no reason to suppose that one sex should possess a greater right to happiness than the other. To those who asked, with derisive intent, why women should not have votes as well as men, Bentham promptly countered with the question: And why not? From this standpoint he arrived at certain claims of equality between the sexes which will be discussed later in another connection.

One of the problems which gave him cause for the greatest preoccupation was whether this equality, in its relation to the importance of happiness ought, as a consequence, to include economic equality. It was perfectly clear to Bentham that such equality would in itself result in a maximum amount of happiness. He thought he could prove this with mathematical certainty and expressed his belief in the following maxims:

1. Each portion of wealth is connected with a corresponding portion of happiness.
2. Of two individuals, possessed of unequal fortunes, he who possess the greatest wealth will possess the greatest happiness.
3. The excess of happiness in the part of the most wealthy will not be so great as the excess of his wealth.
4. For the same reason, the greater the disproportion between the two masses of wealth, the less the probability that there exists an equally great disproportion between the masses of happiness.
5. The more nearly the actual proportion approaches to equality, the greater will be the total mass of happiness.

To demonstrate the truth of these axioms Bentham gave examples. A person, he said, with an income of £10,000 a year is usually happier than one with only £10, but he is not a hundred times as happy and at the utmost probably not even twice as happy. For the first man an increase in £10 of income does not mean an appreciable increase of happiness while for the second the same increase is a source of the greatest happiness. The essence of Bentham's doctrines in this respect. therefore, is this: that any given sum from the point of view of happiness will have the greatest effect when it alters the mutual position of two persons in the direction of equality.

In spite of his views on the value of equality as a principle, Bentham dissociated himself most emphatically from any sort of legislation that would work directly to bring about greater equality. Against this theory of equality he set a theory of security and believed that security should always come first. By security he simply meant the preservation of existing economic conditions and distribution of property. He was fervently opposed to slavery but he insisted that it should be maintained in the interests of security, unless slave-owners received indemnities which fully compensated them for the loss of their property. On the same grounds he opposed all legal regulation of revenue. Bentham's motive in giving primary importance to security is best explained by his statement that the loss of, or fear of losing, what one already possesses or with reasonable certainty can expect to possess, implies suffering of a different kind from that which could arise from the lack of equality. But he employed what is essentially a different argument to prove that security must be protected in all circumstances. In his general exposition of the importance of security he used the word to mean, first and foremost, the ordered life of a community; he contrasted the power of security with the dreadful conditions which he supposed existed among barbaric and lawless savages. From this aspect he could rightly assert that security is the primary requirement of life and happiness, while equality only brings with it a certain quantity of happiness. Subsequently, however, as has been stated earlier, he equated security with the existing order; as a result, all the arguments he employed to show the superiority of civilization over savagery became arguments for a given distribution of property. This shift of meaning made it superfluous for him to discuss whether *certain* measures taken in the interests of equality at the expense of security would increase the total sum of happiness. The value of security became absolute because it was mainly identified with society and especially with law and order. Bentham's fervent espousal of the case for security was pursued by means of justifications of the right of property, the institution whose inviolability follows mainly from the principle of security. Property is not a natural right, but is the most important right instituted by society. Property and law are born together and must die together. Before the laws, there was no property: take away the laws, all property ceases. Because property brings with it happiness, so the desire to own urges men to work and thus it has been an incentive to progress.

Now it could be said of this, Bentham wrote, that the regulation of the right of property is desirable for those who own but not for those who own nothing. In reality, however, ownership is still to the benefit of all. The poor in a social organization are no worse off than they were before society was constituted or property existed. On the contrary, security is valuable to those who own little or nothing; in any case, and in various respects, they enjoy the protection of society's laws. The right of property, it is true, has often been abused, but as an institution in itself it has been a source of much happiness.

Bentham concluded, in effect, that it is the right of property

> 'which has overcome the natural aversion to labour—which has bestowed on men the empire of the earth—which has led nations to give up their wandering habits—which has created a love of country and of posterity. To enjoy quickly—to enjoy without punishment,—this is the natural desire of man; this is the desire which is terrible, since it arms all those who possess nothing, against those who possess any thing. But the law, which restrains this desire, is the most splendid triumph of humanity over itself'.

In 'The Levelling System', an appendix to his *Civil Code*, Bentham dealt with the impossibility of making an equal distribution of property. As he had already discussed the principal reasons which had led him to give priority to security in preference to equality, this section is of relatively minor interest. It may be emphasized, however, that he used every argument generally accepted at the time. An equal distribution of property, he found, could not be permanent, but would continually have to be adjusted. This would lead to a situation in which the labour and the savings demanded by the increased exploitation of the means of production would decrease. Large enterprises, such as defence, for example, would be rendered impossible because there would be no great source of wealth available to draw upon. 'The establishment of equality is a chimera: the only thing which can be done is to diminish inequality.' Having arrived at these conclusions, Bentham proceeded to attack the desire for equality, a procedure not exactly consistent with his theoretical evaluation of the principle of equality:

> 'The passion for equality has no root in the benevolent affections: its root is either simply in the selfish affections, or in the selfish, combined with the malevolent. You being superior to me in wealth or power; my wish is that we may be equal. What is the object of that wish? in what possible way can it have its gratification? In one or other, and only in one or other of two ways: either by raising myself to your level, or by pulling you down to mine. If it be the first only that is in my thoughts, self-interest and that only, is my ruling motive: if the first and the second, envy conjoined with selfishness are the passions that govern me. The man of benevolence is the man to whom the spectacle of another's happiness is delightful. The lover of equality, in its most refined form, is the man to whose eyes the spectacle of another's prosperity is intolerable. What is the envious man but the same? What then is the so much boasted passion for equality? It is a propensity which begins in vice and leads to ruin. In the scale of merit, it is as much below selfishness as selfishness is below the virtue of benevolence.'

> He clinched his attack on the levelling system by saying:

> 'Equalization laws, made at the expense of existing rights and expectations, are alike destructive to present security in respect to property, and to permanent security in respect of subsistence. The desire to establish such laws, or to cause them to be established—the love, the passion for equality—has its root, not in virtue but in vice, not in benevolence, but in malevolence. A law of this complexion is a mere act of robbery—but of robbery on a large scale.'

He concluded by stressing once more that there is no such thing as equality.

> 'Inequality is the natural condition of mankind. Subjection is the natural state of man. It is the state into which he is born: it is the state in which he always has been born, and always will be, so long as man is man: it is the state in which he must continue for some of

the first years of his life, on pain of perishing. Absolute equality is absolutely impossible. Absolute liberty is directly repugnant to the existence of every kind of government.'

Bentham thought, nevertheless, that society itself would develop towards a greater equality, if only one particular reform were to be carried out in the interests of freedom of industry and commerce, namely the abolition of the institution of entail. Under the feudal system which not so long ago was abolished throughout the greater part of Europe, he wrote, all property was in the hands of a minority, in spite of which there was subsequently an extremely wide distribution of wealth. This was because the rich are accustomed to squander money without working for it while the poor have become accustomed to working and saving. If all monopolies and restrictions on commerce were to be done away with, the great fortunes would soon be split up and a more equal and general welfare would be achieved. The ideal would have been reached when all economic differences were relatively slight and a great number of small fortunes had replaced the few large ones. It can therefore be assumed that '*Security*, in maintaining its position as the highest principle, leads indirectly to the preservation of equality, while the last-named principle, if it were to be used as a basis for social order, would destroy security . . .'.

It is clear from the foregoing that in the matter of commerce and industry Bentham's whole position is based on the theories of economic liberalism. In his *Manual of Political Economy* (1843), he expounded Adam Smith's doctrines even more systematically and dogmatically than the Master himself. When it came to increasing the national wealth and general welfare, the general rule, he believed, was that 'nothing ought to be done or attempted by government. The motto, or watchword of government, on these occasions, ought to be—*Be quiet*'. He emphasized two main reasons for this.

'1. Generally speaking, any interference for this purpose on the part of government is needless. The wealth of the whole community is composed of the wealth of the several individuals belonging to it taken together. But to increase his particular portion is, generally speaking, among the constant objects of each individual's exertions and care. Generally speaking there is no one who knows what is for your interest, so well as yourself—no one who is disposed with so much ardour and constancy to pursue it.'

'2. Generally speaking, it is moreover likely to be pernicious, viz. by being unconducive, or even obstructive, with reference to the attainment of the end in view. Each individual bestowing more time and attention upon the means of preserving and increasing his portion of wealth, than is or can be bestowed by government, is likely to take a more effectual course than what, in his instance, and on his behalf, would be taken by government.'

From this it followed, said Bentham, that government intervention must always imply compulsion in some form or other, which in itself leads to suffering. '*Security* and *freedom* are all that industry requires. The request which agriculture, manufactures, and commerce present to governments, is modest and reasonable as that which Diogenes made to Alexander: "*Stand out of my sunshine*".'

Having set forth this general theory, Bentham embarked on a detailed inquiry into what a government ought to do to promote particular industries. His deep-rooted conviction was that it ought to *Keep quiet*—that the best results were reached through a policy of *laissez-faire*. In the section of his *Manual* which deals with industry and in particular with wages, he summarized his point of view in characteristic fashion:

'The natural course of things gives a bounty upon the application of industry to the most advantageous branches—a bounty of which the division will always be made in the most equitable manner. If artificial bounties take the same course as the natural, they are superfluous—if they take a different course, they are injurious.'

In the matter of education, on the other hand, Bentham went farther than many other liberal economists in demanding state intervention. He thought, especially as the neglect of education leads to crime, that the state should care for the education of the poor. On these, as on so many other points, Bentham made suggestions for reform which were to be of invaluable practical importance for the future.

Bentham Criticized

It has been pointed out frequently and in considerable detail that Bentham's principal postulate for government action, that it should aim to achieve 'the greatest happiness of the greatest number' is, strictly speaking, meaningless. In the first place because this formula 'has the mathematical peculiarity that it postulates the simultaneous maximization of two magnitudes which are not independent of each other', as both Henry Sidgwick and Gunnar Myrdal have indicated. If, for example, one were to agree with Bentham's axiom that happiness increases with wealth, even though not in proportion to it, and were to attempt to distribute it according to his theory, the absurdity of the statement would be seen to be obvious; one could just as well give the wealth either to a few or to a single person—in which event the operative words would be 'greatest possible happiness'; or one could distribute it evenly to give some happiness to 'the greatest possible number'. It would then be plain that Bentham envisaged an ideal *average* happiness for the greatest number; this is clear from his reasoning on the value of equality. But even from this aspect the problem is insoluble unless it is taken to apply to a population which neither increases nor decreases. The question as to whether a population ought to increase even if this would decrease its average happiness, is an issue which Bentham did not raise; if happiness is considered to be a measurable quantity, it would nevertheless be possible in such a situation for the total given amount of happiness to increase.

More important still is the fact that when a short-term application of Bentham's theory is attempted, the very idea of measuring happiness will not hold water. It is simply not possible to apply methods of addition and subtraction to the emotion of 'happiness' which is the sum of the various forms of the need for contentment or enjoyment. It would be still more inconceivable to refer in mathematical terms to the feelings of individual persons. When the utilitarians attempted to construct a scale of happiness, that is, to calculate the value of various phenomena in terms of happiness, the result was entirely arbitrary, and in reality only a collection of suppositions conditioned by moral concepts; spiritual enjoyment, and specifically a single well-regarded action, was considered to be the means of affording a quantitatively large, or in some way special, kind of happiness.

Bentham got over this difficulty to some extent by supposing that all men act in their own interest, and partly by assuming that the sum total of actions of 'self-preference' is equivalent to an action in the common interest. If his suppositions can be considered acceptable then a scale of happiness is unnecessary, since the desired maximum happiness is reached automatically.

When Bentham maintained that all men act in their own interest, he generally appeared to mean that as a rule every person acts in a manner that is to his advantage, in other words, to increase his happiness. This idea, which he put forward with certain reservations at times, is the basic condition of his whole system, and was arrived at by a series of shifts in the meaning of the word 'interest'. He started out from the view that a definite and more or less conscious motive prompts every action. When he explained with more elaboration the meaning of the concept 'interest', he described it as some logically necessary appendage to the motive; this entailed, therefore, no special explanation of the action. But as a rule he gave another definition of 'interest', as a tendency to aim for advantages which would lead to a lasting increase of happiness. Interest became synonymous with self-interest and self-interest was assumed to be self-evident, that is, stemming from the rational conviction of an individual that any given action of his would lead to or be favourable to his happiness. Precisely in those cases where the concept of 'interest' was important in the formation of a conclusive argument, Bentham did not believe it possible that a person could act without wishing to increase his happiness, that he could mistake the effectiveness of his action to bring about the desired result or that he could choose an immediate advantage which would act to the detriment of his chances of future happiness. All this is too absurd to require further analysis. What Bentham really meant was that every individual, with rare exceptions, acts to further his own best and lasting interest; he was, in other words, imagining a kind of individualistic teleology.

But Bentham also believed that to act in one's own interest leads to social harmony and that as a rule no conflict will arise between the interests of individuals. As an exception, an individual can doubtless act against the common good; but this he believed to be due partly to a lack of judgement of the individual in question with regard to his own interest—a matter of insufficient insight. On the other hand he considered such cases a matter for social intervention or punishment to bring about an act in a broader sense, that would be more decisively in the general interest, socially fitting and rational. The special group of actions mentioned in this connection can be ignored since they are unimportant to Bentham's basic political system. Central to this thesis is the idea of harmony; that to act in one's own interest is to act in the interest of the community or for the best of all its members.

How then did Bentham arrive at this idea—that to act in one's own interest would lead to social harmony: that to act in one's own interest would be to act in everybody's interest? His assumptions sometimes give one the impression that they have been arrived at by a simple deductive error of the sort mentioned earlier. The general interest, or everybody's interest is considered to be the sum or result of individual interests; freely effective self-interest must therefore promote the general interest; or, expressed in another way, if every one had complete freedom to increase his own happiness the total of happiness must increase. Here, then, Bentham took for granted what remained to be proved. The question, however, is whether one man's interest cannot conflict with another man's and therefore, whether some people because of wealth, talent, ruthlessness and so forth, might not increase their happiness at the expense of others.

Another, more promising train of thought appears in Bentham's arguments as well as in those of other utilitarians. By shifting the meaning of 'interest', Bentham spoke in some connections—as has already been pointed out—of interest which embraces every motive—even, for instance, a desire to further the good of others. He saw even this as a kind of egoism, although of a different nature from the interest which, in his main thesis, is supposed to be the deciding factor in human actions. In this respect Bentham's opinion of himself was typical. 'I am a selfish person,' he said, 'as selfish as any man can be. But in me, somehow or other, so it happens, selfishness has taken the form of benevolence.' Bentham thought that with higher education this unselfish form of egoism would increase. Although he said he only expressed a quite subjective opinion when he sought to achieve the greatest happiness of the greatest number he evidently considered this attitude morally superior to the more limited kind of egoism and that 'altruistic' egoism would predominate in the future. By shifting from one to another meaning of the word 'interest' he made it easier for himself to cling to the supposition, essential to his doctrine, that there could be harmony between self-interest and the general interest. He believed in a balance between self-interest and altruism. The utilitarian optimum, as Gunnar Myrdal has pointed out in *The Political Element in the Development of Economic Theory* (1953), lay in the naïvely optimistic assumption 'that the point at which egoistic impulses become harmful to society coincides with the point at which they become harmful to the individual'. No attempt has been made to prove the accuracy of this opinion, all that can be said for it is that it is quite arbitrary and smacks of mysticism. With regard to Bentham's general tendency to say that there would be a fusion of interests with everybody acting not in their own but in the general interest, it is obvious that this statement completely breaks down his more fundamental line of thought which was quoted earlier. This would, of course, mean that self-interest would be the norm and that such a course of action would lead automatically to the maximum happiness for all. If, on the other hand, it is supposed that all men wish to ensure 'the greatest happiness of the greatest number', one is faced with the difficulties contained in this proposition which have been mentioned earlier.

Perhaps the most decisive idea in Bentham's concept of harmony between different interests was the *laissez-faire* theory of economic liberalism. It is clear from Bentham's *Manual of Political Economy* that he accepted the idea that if all who worked were motivated by self-interest it would lead to the greatest prosperity: this fundamental principle was ready to hand to be extended to all human activity, whether economic or not. However, Bentham expressed more definitely than the liberal economists the idea that the advantages which it was considered would follow from economic freedom would lead to political stability by being accepted even by the poorer classes. This optimistic concept of Bentham's owed much to the belief that the principle of liberty would automatically bring about equality and would work towards economic levelling. It is strange, nevertheless, that Bentham with his individualistic outlook should imagine that an insight into how progress happened on the whole to operate for the best would prevent all conflict of interests in the present. Why should not the poor, even if they believed in the ultimate value of economic liberalism, wish to improve their lot immediately and for that reason covet the wealth of the rich? It would seem by this that although Bentham did not mention class and class-interest he supposed a sort of group-feeling actually to exist among the poor, which would cause them patiently to endure injustices at the thought of improvement in the future. He obviously meant something of this kind when he spoke of 'humanity's most glorious triumph over itself'. This idea, however, does not fit in very well with his predominantly individualistic theory of interest.

Critical observations of yet another kind have been directed against Bentham's doctrine and against utilitarianism as a whole. It has been emphasized, with some hint of moral judgement, that the utilitarians stressed the material aspect of the demand for happiness and did not pay sufficient attention to the value to mankind of faith, ideas and dreams. The very doctrine of happiness has been branded as crass and vulgar; in contrast to happiness or utility, other aims have seemed more worth while and more splendid. The contradiction between the teachings and personal lives of the leading utilitarians has been the target of considerable irony. There is surely something tragi-comic in the fact that three such dismal puritans as Bentham, James Mill and John Stuart Mill, should have spent their lives talking and writing of happiness and joy. John Stuart Mill in his *Autobiography* (1873) has described the resigned and gloomy atmosphere in which his father and he used to work. After his mental crisis, 'the dry, heavy dejection of the winter of 1826–7', he realized that to achieve some sort of happiness, 'The only chance is to treat, not happiness but some end external to it, as the purpose of life . . .'. To win back some peace of mind, he made this theory the basis of his philosophy of life. By his own admission his future work in the service of the happiness of others was a personal anodyne.

The Importance of Utilitarianism

In attempting to construct a political system, utilitarianism ended up with a few general, supposedly empirical principles which were inevitably arbitrary and contradictory. The essential contribution of the doctrine was to systematize the revolutionary theory that the aim of government should be the happiness of the people. The attempt entailed a disengagement from or a rejection of other, cruder mystical or metaphysical theories. Prominence was given not to eternal bliss but to temporal welfare. Plans were to be made for people living a communal life that was not determined by ideas of natural rights which had been developed or established by a higher power before the existence of society. Utilitarianism looked askance at collectivist theories of independent values and aims—whether of governments or people—which were taking shape on the Continent. The lack of a sense of historical relativity became a defence against the historical school which flourished under the wing of the prevailing idea of progress. Romantic anti-intellectualism which, at this period, just as a hundred years later, fostered a spirit of political and social reaction, was met by an unreflecting but unshakeable belief in reason. By and large, utilitarianism was a success. The worldly, individualistic faith in progress round which its principles centred, has probably played a greater role in Western politics during the past century than any other doctrine. Such notions as 'social benefits', 'general welfare', 'the happiness of the individual', have become terms of common usage which, despite their familiarity, have lost none of their magic.

In England utilitarianism exercised an extreme though more limited influence on legislation. Bentham's disciples emerged as leaders of various reform movements; they worked for universal suffrage, secret ballots, repeal of the Corn Laws, reforms of the administrative and judicial systems. Albert Venn Dicey, perhaps the foremost writer on the later development of English law, spoke of the period between 1825 and 1870 as 'the period of Benthamism or individualism'. What this primarily aimed at was not the victory of the principles of *laissez-faire* but the spirit of rationalism and scientific method in which legislation was to be effected whenever it should be necessary for the state to intervene. Above all, in what concerned the judicial system, which was Bentham's chief interest, his ideas were in the main decisive, even if the principle of codification for which he fought with such energy was never adopted by English courts. Many of the leading nineteenth-century statesmen, Liberals especially, were deeply inspired not only by the general utilitarian position but by particular lines of utilitarian thinking as well.

However, the guiding principles formulated by Bentham could be applied in ways entirely unfamiliar to the older utilitarians. The principle of utility could be used to justify socio-political and economic levelling, but it could equally well be applied to *laissez-faire* and absolute ownership; the democratically elected form of government demanded by Bentham to replace the existing parliamentary organization was in reality determined by other views than his. Sir Henry Maine, the great authority on the origin and growth of legal and social institutions, could say in 1885 that Bentham's ideas on democracy had been successfully adopted but with consequences which were quite the opposite of what the utilitarians had expected. Later, utilitarianism became the watchword for the growing socialist movements, especially the Fabians, who were its leading intellectual group. English socialism, it has been said, learnt more from Bentham than from Marx. Bentham's insistence on economic equality as a condition of maximum happiness, and especially his idea that the increase in individual welfare is in direct proportion to the wealth possessed previously, was adopted by socialists as an essential argument for heavy taxation in the interests of the poor.

The very feeling that the system would work, which buoyed up the utilitarians, was important to a movement which was striving to promote the communal planning of production. Bentham is not very much read nowadays; his pedantic perfectionism is somewhat forbidding to the lay reader. Nevertheless, his ideas, more than those of any other nineteenth-century social philosopher, are still a force in the English social structure and way of life.

II
QUESTIONS OF GOVERNMENT

The Great Reform Bill of 1832

For a hundred years after the close of the seventeenth century, the English government was the most 'liberal' in the world and a shining example to Continental devotees of progress. During that century there had been hardly any constitutional conflict in England, nor had any movement of importance arisen to cry out for drastic alterations in the established order. The situation changed towards the end of the eighteenth century, and when the twenty years of the Napoleonic Wars were over, the demand for parliamentary reform once more began to exercise the minds of the voteless. It could not be denied that during its long period of constitutional calm, the English parliamentary system had sunk into a torpor of reaction. The mentally deranged King George III, in intervals of lucidity between his bouts of madness, played an independent and at times a leading political role and thus to a certain extent restored the principle of monarchy: it has been made abundantly clear to what degree even the resolute William Pitt, during his first term of office as Prime Minister (1783–1801), was dependent on the King's will. The House of Lords, mainly owing to Pitt's diligence in raising Conservative landowners and capitalists to the peerage, became more and more an appendage to the Tories in the Commons. The very lack of change in the existing composition of Parliament implied in itself, and in one particular, the need for a very real and far-reaching change; for while industrialization had resulted in an increase in the urban, at the expense of the rural population, the distribution of seats in the Commons had remained unaltered. This had led to a situation in which rural areas with a handful of inhabitants subservient to the local landowners could return a member to Parliament, while rapidly growing industrial towns like Birmingham and Manchester were devoid of any form of representation. The number of qualified voters in England and Wales in 1831 was only 435,000, or less than ten per cent of the adult male population. But this figure is of little interest in itself; the essential point is that the towns were less than adequately represented and that in a great many constituencies—the so-called close or pocket boroughs, owned or controlled by a single person or a family—no really democratic election was possible because the candidates, the landowners or rich men who had bought the borough, were virtually appointed by the government.

In the main, however, this government possessed such authority that no demand for a total renovation was voiced from any quarter worth taking seriously. The general opinion, during the period of agitation for reform which followed, was that the existing institutions should be preserved, though with certain modifications and improvements. The transformation took place gradually, during the course of nearly a century. Some decisive changes were effected without legislation. Slowly, by imperceptible degrees, the king, from wielding independent power, became merely a symbol of power. The ideological breach was reflected most strongly in the various debates over the reforms of the voting process. This was particularly noticeable in the reform of 1832, which can be said to have marked the complete breakthrough of liberal ideas in English politics.

There was no clear dividing line between the two loose-knit groups which, under the old party names of Whigs and Tories, ruled the English parliament at the beginning of the nineteenth century. By and large, however, they represented tendencies which by mid-century had come to be known as Conservatism and Liberalism. Tories clung more tenaciously than Whigs to existing situations and institutions; with the monarch still to a certain extent acting independently, the Commons (except in the formation of a government and in budgetary matters) was, broadly speaking on an equal footing with the Lords, the Church, local government (which was more or less in the hands of the landowning aristocracy), and with agriculture. The Tories represented the landowners in particular, though the social borderline was far less sharply defined than the political one. The Whigs, who had held a position of permanent though slender minority for decades after the French Revolution had already made demands before the revolution for a reform of the composition of the Commons, and in the 1830s vigorously renewed this demand. They strove to secure religious tolerance and were effective in getting the Tory government to abolish laws dictated by religious prejudice—emancipation of Nonconformists in 1828 and Catholics in 1829. Most of those who supported reforms in administration, the judicial system, public assistance and local government were Whigs. The principles of economic liberalism were for the most part accepted by both of the major parties, but the Whigs, who were beginning increasingly to represent a growing well-to-do middle class—merchants, businessmen, employers—espoused these principles with greater vigour than the Tories, who regarded the progress of industry and commerce with aversion. It must be remembered, however, that up to the parliamentary reform of 1867 both parties appealed primarily to relatively small social groups—since only these had the vote. For the most part they were and remained voting parties, adapting their programmes to the political situation and what the voters wanted, as well as to a number of important reforms—such as for example the abolition of slavery, Factory Acts to restrict and establish hours of work, free trade—all of which were first agitated for by organizations which, like American 'pressure groups', were in principle independent of the parties and only used them as a last resort to attain their particular aims. The realization of this circumstance is essential to an understanding of English politics throughout the whole of the nineteenth century.

When the Whigs, early in 1830, reached the position of power which—save for only two major breaks, in 1841–45 and 1874–80—they were to hold for more than half a century, the party comprised politicians and statesmen of varying interests and opinions. A number of the oldest and richest families of the English nobility were traditionally Whigs, and it was mainly from these dyed-in-the-wool Whigs that cabinet ministers and the actual leading statesmen were drawn. A typical instance of this was the 1832 Reform Government of Earl Grey, which was one of the most aristocratic governments in the history of modern England; on the other hand, when parliamentary reform was put to the vote in the Lords in 1831–32, most of the peers of old families voted for reform while the new peers voted against it. In time the Whigs as a group melted away; some of them joined the Tories, others retired from politics and at length the term Whig came to represent the Liberal party's right-wing minority and the Lords became solidly Conservative. In the 1830s the core of the Whig party was a small group of theorists and reformers who made use of the political quarterly the *Edinburgh Review* as a mouthpiece from which to air their views and disseminate their ideas. They could be, and indeed were, called the *Edinburgh Review* group, and they included men like Lord Brougham, Lord Chancellor in 1830 and one of the founders of the quarterly; Lord Macaulay, who more than any other personified the earliest phase of English liberalism; and Sydney Smith, 'The Smith of Smiths' in Macaulay's phrase, another of the *Edinburgh Review* founders, a courageous reformer and brilliant talker. Unlike Brougham and Macaulay, Sydney Smith, a country rector and eventually a Canon of St Paul's, was never a member of Parliament, but exercised great influence through his ready polemical wit. A third group, only sparsely represented in Parliament, were the Radicals, influenced by utilitarianism and, in contrast to the other two groups, holding chiefly democratic views. These Radicals, through the action of men like Francis Place and William Cobbett, mediated between the Whig House of Lords and the great mass of the English people. Though lacking the vote, this mass frequently and effectively expressed its opinions, by means of strikes, demonstrations, and violence with looting and was at critical moments the most vociferous goad and ally of the Whigs. By yielding to its threatening attitudes at the right times and to a reasonable and sufficient degree, giving a say in government step by step to fresh groups of the population, Parliament, and primarily its Liberals, was successful in putting through reforms without unleashing revolution and, ultimately, in combining traditionalism with a democratic form of government.

During parliamentary debates before the Reform of 1832, the Tories adhered to an extreme conservative party line. The Duke of Wellington, leader of the House of Lords, made his famous rebuff to the Radicals and Whigs during the debate to introduce the Reform Bill. Replying to Grey's quite moderate proposal, the Duke said he thought that the present House of Commons was as complete a one as could be formed, and one which had shown itself to be the most efficient legislative body in thc world without any exception. 'I am fully convinced', he said, 'that the country possesses at the present moment a Legislature which answers all the good purposes of legislation, and this to a greater degree than any Legislature ever has answered in any country whatsoever.' He claimed that the Government deservedly enjoyed the full and entire confidence of the country, and exercised great influence over public opinion.

> 'I will go still further, and say, that if at the present moment I had imposed on me the duty of forming a Legislature for any country, and particularly for a country like this, in possession of great prosperity of various descriptions,—I do not mean to assert that I could form such a Legislature as we possess now, for the nature of man is incapable of reaching such excellence at once,—but my great endeavour would be, to form some description of legislature which would produce the same results. The representation of the people at present contains a large body of the property of the country, and in which the landed interest has a preponderating influence. Under these circumstances . . . I am not only not prepared to bring forward any measure of this nature, but I will at once declare that, as far as I am concerned, as long as I hold any station in the government of the country, I shall always feel it my duty to resist such measures.'

The Whig proposals, he declared, were full of revolutionary intention; if they were carried out they would lead to the breakdown and dissolution of the English social structure.

The *Quarterly Review*, the leading Tory periodical, which summarized most lucidly the Conservative position, said that after the initial reform new reforms would follow until universal franchise had been achieved. It was really a question of a struggle between those without property and the landed gentry; if the vote were to be extended, the majority of the poorer classes would seize power, abolish the right of property and oppress the former ruling classes. Politically speaking it would result either in anarchy or in dictatorship by adventurers supported by the poor, or at the very worst, after a period of chaos, a restoration of absolute monarchy. The Whigs, said the *Quarterly Review*, were surely actuated in their demands for reform by fear of the masses; the proper way to deal with mob violence would be to meet it with repression, not concession.

The motives behind the demand for reform must be seen against the background of these opinions. The proposals were extremely moderate; they entailed on one hand a partial extension of suffrage and primarily, on the other, a distribution of parliamentary seats more in keeping with the density of population in various urban districts. Above all, the reform measures were designed to do away with the 'rotten' boroughs, that is, parliamentary boroughs no longer having real constituency, which from time immemorial had been represented in Parliament, although they contained only a tiny handful of eligible voters and were therefore virtually under the complete control of the nobility and rich landowners.

The Whigs said, borrowing Burke's phrase, that they wanted 'to correct in order to conserve'. It was frequently said that because of changes in the population of the electoral districts during the past century the character of the Commons had completely altered and that parliamentary reform meant restoration rather than renovation. In another sense, too, reform would be justified precisely from a conservative point of view. By means of relatively small alterations it would be possible to appease the restless masses and allow a share in government to prospering economic and social groups of growing wealth and status, hitherto excluded from the franchise.

If this were not done there would be a violent upheaval. Most Whigs were as much afraid of universal franchise as the Tories. A number of reasons, however open to question, contributed to their fear. On the one hand they believed that democracy would involve a threat to property and to the whole existing order, and on the other they feared that democracy, as recent events in France had shown, would lead to despotism.

For aristocratic Whig leaders like Grey, Melbourne and Russell, moderation was the only conceivable course. Grey wrote, in agreement with Locke, that the aim of government was 'protection and security of rights', that citizens were entitled to the form of government which best suited this aim and that for this purpose a limited franchise was indicated.

Lord John Russell explained in a subsequently much-quoted statement that the proposed reform was definitive and that therefore any further extension of the suffrage was out of the question. But fear of democracy was also felt by the middle-class nucleus who wrote for the *Edinburgh Review*, as well as by their representatives in Parliament and the cabinet. One article which appeared in the periodical said that the franchise would lead to class-rule (that is, lower-class rule) and end in dictatorship.

> 'A demagogue will seize the despotic power which he has long exercised in the name of his party. The fickle masses will eventually follow the leader to the throne of dictatorship with the same enthusiasm as when he led them in the struggle against existing institutions.'

If any single class was to rule, it should be the middle class 'because it possesses the greatest share of common sense and public spirit and because it has the strongest ties with the other classes of society'. In a speech on the Reform, made in the Commons, Lord Brougham said that the Government's proposal aimed directly at preventing a revolution and that the Opposition were in fact the revolutionaries since they wished to cling to antiquated laws in circumstances which were entirely changed.

Lord Macaulay expressed fully and lucidly the prevailing Whig opinion. During one of the Commons debates he said that he regarded all general theories of suffrage and the constitution with suspicion. In some countries it might be possible to give the vote to all but not in England. If the workers were continually in employment and earned good wages, it was conceivable that they could be given political power. Nevertheless, in time of crisis or distress the temptation to abuse this power would be too great, for:

> 'There is no quackery in medicine, religion, or in politics, which may not impose even on a powerful mind, when that mind has been disordered by pain or fear. . . . But, Sir, every argument which would induce me to oppose Universal Suffrage, induces me to support the plan which is now before us. I am opposed to Universal Suffrage because I think it would produce a destructive revolution. I support this plan because I am sure that it is the best security against revolution.'

There was, said Macaulay, a class and party which stood firmly behind the proposal of reform:

> 'I speak of that great party which zealously and steadily supported the first Reform Bill, and which will, I have no doubt, support the

second Reform Bill with equal steadiness and equal zeal. That party is the middle class of England, with the flower of the aristocracy at its head, and the flower of the working class bringing up its rear. That great party has taken its immovable stand between the enemies of all order and the enemies of all liberty.'

Ten years later, in May 1842, replying to a petition to pass into law the People's Charter, Macaulay put forward the very same opinions and emphasized them even more dogmatically. Universal suffrage was not only incompatible with the government of England, but with any other form of government. It signified a threat to property and consequently to the culture which depended on the security of property.

'If it be admitted that on the institution of property the well-being of society depends, it follows surely that it would be madness to give supreme power in the state to a class which would not be likely to respect that institution. And if this be conceded, it seems to me to follow that it would be madness to grant the prayer of this petition. I entertain no hope that, if we place the government of the kingdom in the hands of the majority of the males of one and twenty told by the head, the institution of property will be respected . . . because the hundreds of thousands of males of twenty-one who have signed this petition tell me to entertain no such hope; because they tell me that, if I trust them with power, the first use which they will make of it will be to plunder every man who has a good roof over his head . . . The inequality with which wealth is distributed forces itself on everybody's notice. It is at once perceived by the eye. The reasons which irrefragibly prove the inequality to be necessary to the well-being of all classes are not equally obvious. Our honest working man has not received such an education as enables him to understand that the utmost distress that he has ever known is prosperity when compared with the distress which he would have to endure if there were a single month of general anarchy and plunder.'

The Reverend Sydney Smith, discussing whether the masses should have the ballot, believed that parliamentary reform would be of service to all classes, since it would lead to economy in government spending and to lower tariffs; the poor would get lighter taxation and cheaper bread. Above all, the rich would be obliged to consider the wishes of the poor more than in the past. But to give the vote to any but the landed gentry would be absurd. If power were put in the hands of the great unpropertied masses, said Sydney Smith, it would be tantamount to 'shaking those laws of property which it has taken ages to extort from the wretchedness and rapacity of mankind'. He agreed that: 'The people have a right to ballot or to anything else which will make them happy; and they have a right to nothing which will make them unhappy. They are the best judges of their immediate gratification, and the worst judges of what would best conduce to their interests for a series of years.' So, he advised, no ballot. In the future, as in the past, parliamentary seats should go to 'men of rank or men of fortune known in the neighbourhood: they have property and character to lose'. The great masses should influence government only indirectly.

The very word 'democracy' was hateful to the great majority of both Whigs and Tories. They saw in democracy, declared an outstanding writer on the pre-history of parliamentary reform, much more than a mere degree of government reform; to them it was 'a threatening domination of evil . . . a catastrophe which would engulf everything'. A different view was held by the Radical movement, only weakly represented in Parliament, and even the opinions of this group were by no means unanimous. George Grote, the banker-historian and philosophical Radical, one of the most influential writers of propaganda for reform, advocated the immediate expansion of the electorate to include all men with an income of at least £100 a year; the electorate which would evolve in consequence, estimated at some million persons, could not, he emphasized, be expected to constitute a threat to property.

> 'It cannot with any pretence of reason be maintained that a man of £100 annual income has not enjoyed the full faculties for instructing himself up to the requisite pitch. A pecuniary qualification, therefore, if fixed at £100 annual income, would embrace no one, as far as could be reasonably presumed, unworthy of the trust. . . . Nor could any reasonable alarmist anticipate either hostility to property, or general unsoundness of views, from the richest million in the country. They might as soon be imagined to surrender England to a foreign enemy, or to plant in it the seeds of an epidemic disease, as to invade or unsettle the sanctity of property.'

General education of the masses would train and prepare them for political maturity so that ultimately and gradually they would gain admission to the polls. The utilitarian line, however, was to demand an immediate general vote for all males, on grounds which will be discussed further on. The urban and rural artisans with no parliamentary representation, whose threatening demonstrations and violence had induced the Whigs to act energetically and had caused certain Tory groups to yield, had no unified political or social programme. Among their leaders, for example, was Francis Place the London tailor and economist, a utilitarian and a Radical who also worked primarily to further the organization of skilled artisans and the education of the working man;

while William Cobbett, fiercely Radical reformer, journalist and champion of country life and traditions, with his diffuse agitation in Parliament and through his *Weekly Political Register*, made demands which included the annulment of government loans, and measures to create a system of small independent farms.

The parliamentary reform which was carried in 1832 after fierce disputes and clashes between the two Houses, to the accompaniment of demonstrations and rioting in the big industrial towns, and after the king had agreed to break the resistance of the Lords with the threat of mass elevations to the peerage, at last made its way through the reluctant Lords and was given equally reluctant royal assent. The Bill was completely attuned to the view which advocated moderation. It increased the total electorate by just under fifty per cent, to just over 650,000, which meant that about one Englishman in twenty-four was now entitled to the vote. What was more important was the fact that the redistribution of seats, though still favouring the rural boroughs and proportionally far from uniform, had greatly increased the ability of the Commons to constitute a real representation for the electorate. It is usually claimed that the middle class acquired a decisive influence as a result of the reform. This statement must not be taken too literally. If by middle class is meant wealthy industrialists and business-men then it is true that the influence of this class was greatly reinforced and as a rule gained supremacy among the urban electorate; but even after the Reform, the Commons consisted of about seventy per cent of landowners, and it was not until thirty years later that the interests of trade, industry and finance were able to achieve a stronger position than that of agriculture.

Bentham's Political Doctrine

In his early writings Bentham paid little attention to government. His interest was chiefly centred on reform of the penal laws and his cherished 'Panopticon' prison system, and it would seem as though he felt confident that he would be able to see his ideas realized through the channels of existing governments or even through the intervention of an absolute monarch.

When his proposals met with resistance or indifference Bentham was seized with the conviction that monarchy and aristocracy were systems which were inevitably obstacles to the general welfare. He became a convinced democrat and in the 1820s wrote *The Constitutional Code*, in which he developed with extreme clarity and in voluminous detail his ideas about constitutional policy. His theories of government, however, were presented as the inevitable consequences of his basic principles: that all men act in their own interest and that the ultimate aim of society is to promote 'the greatest happiness of the greatest number'.

In accordance with the first of these principles Bentham asserted that a governing individual or group uses the power of government for personal aims. Thus, while he rules, the aim of an absolute monarch becomes 'the greatest possible happiness' for himself and as far as he is able he will 'accumulate under his own grasp all the external instruments of felicity, all the objects of general desire, in the greatest quantity possible: all at the expense of, and by the sacrifice of, the felicity of other members of the community'. The natural tendency of a monarchy, therefore was 'at all times and in all places to produce the greatest infelicity of the greatest number'. A monarch inevitably became an

> 'arch-forciant, arch-terrorist, arch-corruptor, arch-deluder. . . . His instruments real and corporeal are three: the soldier, the lawyer and the priest: his fictitious and incorporeal are four: force, fear, corruption, and delusion: with these incorporeal instruments he by the hands of his corporeal instruments works.'

Whether in a limited monarchy, or an aristocracy or any form of government 'in which the possessors of the supreme power have not the great body of the people for their constituents, the situation of every possessor of a share in the supreme operative power is that of an enemy of the people . . . a people governed in any one of these three ways is a people governed by its enemies'.

The 'sinister interest', as Bentham called the selfish interest of the individual, inevitably becomes dominant in such cases. If all govern or—the only alternative in a big state—if representatives govern on behalf of all, then full justice can be done to the interest of all. The only possible form of government which has or can have as its aim and end 'the greatest happiness of the greatest number', is a democracy.

The assembly elected by the people should exercise the sovereign power. Bentham rejected Montesquieu's theory of the division of power; if a state organ because of its composition works for the general welfare, another organ constituted according to different bases must work for different aims and has no useful function. Every dual system, whether in the form of a two-chamber system or of an independent governing body hand-in-hand with a parallel body of representatives, is therefore to be rejected. The routine executive work which, for technical reasons, a legislature composed of numerous members cannot carry out, should be delegated to agents chosen by the legislators. On similar grounds Bentham rejected charters, bills of rights and similar special restrictions of rights which would limit the freedom of action of representatives. Under a monarchy or an aristocratic system such laws would have their value; under a system which guaranteed the working of the State for the general welfare, restrictions of this kind would be meaningless.

Bentham demanded unlimited power for representative government; at the same time he demanded the strongest guarantees that a government should reflect the will of the people and not wield power in the selfish interest of their representatives. Election of representatives should be for the shortest possible term, preferably a year, and the possibility of re-election to office should be strongly discouraged. A rotation system of some such kind would ensure against corruption and oppression. Special measures of control would have to be introduced so that the representatives should become the people's delegates, not independent wielders of power. Elections should be conducted by means of secret balloting. This method—which was regarded at that time as utterly radical—would guarantee that the electors voted without coercion, in their own interests.

Universal manhood suffrage—with the exclusion of illiterates—followed the principle that the happiness of each and every individual is of equal importance. Bentham believed, on the same grounds, that women were also entitled to the vote, especially as he saw no reason to believe that they were intellectually inferior to men. Nevertheless, he thought that the vote for women was not feasible on account of the 'reciprocal seduction' which would ensue if the two sexes were to meet in the legislature or the executive. He thought it better for the time being not to demand the vote for women because the resistance which such a proposal would arouse would be an obstacle to the realization of democracy for a long time to come.

Bentham's leading disciple, James Mill, expanded the Master's ideas concerning government in a famous article on Government, one of several written for the *Encyclopedia Britannica* (1816–23). Those in power would act only in their own interest if this were not prevented by special guarantees. In an absolute monarchy there is this natural tendency which leads those in power to organize affairs 'not only to that degree of plunder which leaves the members (excepting always the recipients and instruments of the plunder) the bare means of subsistence, but to that degree of cruelty which is necessary to keep in existence the most intense terror'. The only rational government therefore is a representative democracy. The right to vote must belong to all men; suffrage for women is unnecessary because women's interests coincide with those of their fathers and husbands. However, James Mill, in contrast to Bentham, pointed out that agreement between the actions of a government and the actions of the governed is not synonymous, even in a democracy, with strong public means of control:

'The whole chain of this deduction is dependent on the principle that the acts of men will be conformable to their interests. Upon this principle, we conceive that the chain is complete and irrefragible. The principle, also, appears to stand upon a strong foundation. It is indisputable that the acts of men follow their will; their will follows their desires; and that their desires are generated by their apprehensions of good or evil; in other words, by their interests. . . . The apprehensions of the people respecting good and evil may be just or they may be erroneous. If just, their actions will be agreeable to their real interests. If erroneous, they will not be agreeable to their real interests, but to a false supposition of interest.'

James Mill believed, nevertheless, that this difficulty did not alter his main argument. If a few governed, their actions as a rule would be contrary to the interests of society; if many governed there would be the kind of government which is conducive to real misunderstanding. However, it would be possible through education to instil gradually in the members of a society the insight which would enable them to understand their true, objective interest. Mill also thought that in all circumstances the middle class, whose interests he equated more or less with those of the community, would exercise a decisive influence over the greater part of the population; this mass, which in itself could be considered to lack insight about its true interests, would as a result, act in accordance with the influence of the middle class.

The difference between the victorious Whig-programme of 1832 and the utilitarian programme on the constitutional question was, as has been shown, quite considerable. With regard to the aims which it was desired to achieve by reform there was unity, nevertheless, on essential points. The principle of universal suffrage, formulated and expounded by Bentham and James Mill, and promoted by their supporters in Parliament, was not intended as a means of reshaping society. On the contrary, the utilitarians, like most so-called radicals, clung like the leading Whig groups to *laissez-faire*, the inviolability of property and the value of the predominant influence of a wealthy middle class. Bentham stressed that radicalism was not 'dangerous', that is to say, it was not directed against the economic order, and James Mill believed that with universal suffrage the enlightened middle class would become leaders of the great unpropertied masses.

'The opinions of that class of people who are below the middle rank are formed, and their minds directed, by that intelligent and virtuous rank who come the most immediately in contact with them . . . There can be no doubt that the middle rank, which gives to science, to art, and to legislation itself their most distinguished ornaments, the chief source of all that has exalted and refined human nature, is that portion of the community of which, if the basis of representation were ever so far extended, the opinion would be sure to be guided by their advice and example.'

In a review in the '*Edinburgh*' of Mill's article in the *Encyclopedia Britannica*, Macaulay turned Mill's own argument against him; if the middle class were to represent the interests of the whole community and in every circumstance remain the actual governing class, it would be simplest to guarantee this position through suitable conditions of suffrage. 'The system of universal suffrage, therefore, according to Mr Mill's own account, is only a device for doing circuitously, what a representative system, with a pretty high qualification, could do directly.' If everybody had an equal right to vote, there would be a risk that the poor would use their power to plunder the rich, in similar fashion to Mill's absolute monarchy or aristocracy, which exploited their position to subdue and impoverish the masses of the people.

John Stuart Mill on Government

In discussing government, or indeed any other subject, John Stuart Mill followed the tradition of utilitarianism. His essay on *Representative Government* (1861), has probably been the most influential of all explanations or justifications of democracy by an English writer. Mill's method, his manner of reasoning and arguing is, however, quite different from that of the earlier utilitarians. Whereas Bentham and James Mill evolved their dogmas by deduction from schematic, often ambiguous statements, John Stuart Mill employed a vague common-sense reasoning which he expressed in carefully worded statements shrouded and disguised in all kinds of reservations.

Democracy or representative government, Mill wrote, is obviously the 'ideally best polity', that is, the polity that is best if the necessary conditions for its introduction and preservation are present. In respect of the immediate results on human welfare, he based its superiority on two axiomatic principles.

'The first is, that the rights and interests of every or any person are only secure from being disregarded, when the person interested is himself able, and habitually disposed, to stand up for them. The second is, that the general prosperity attains a greater height, and is more widely diffused, in proportion to the amount and variety of the personal energies enlisted in promoting it.'

Both these conditions, he believed, are met by a democracy, in which each citizen has the same possibility of influencing government and all cooperate in general affairs. The superiority of a democracy is even more obvious when the future effects of government are considered. The development of the character of citizens is promoted by a democratic government because only through democracy are active personalities formed, such as will become accustomed to responsibility and will work with energy towards proposed aims. On this point Mill deviated from the pioneer utilitarians in comparing active and discontented, or 'uncontented' persons with passive, contented ones, by which he arrived at the obvious conclusion that the former accomplish more and therefore are of greater value from a social point of view. '. . . nothing is more certain, than that improvement in human affairs is wholly the work of the uncontented characters; and, moreover, that it is much easier for an active mind to acquire the virtues of patience, than for a passive one to assume those of energy.' Oddly enough, he thus implied indirectly that a democracy would produce a greater number of discontented persons and thus contradicted his earlier statements to the effect that the value of a democracy consists in its regard for the interests and welfare, and hence the contentment, of the individual. This is typical of Mill's tendency to use words ambiguously. The idea behind this particular statement is obvious, that a democracy should protect rather than promote the interests of individuals, because their true interest lies in their acting outside the framework of the State; when Mill equated activity with discontent and expressed his approval of them, he was not thinking in terms of politics.

Democracy is not suitable under all conditions, Mill believed. There are cases in which individuals do not want democracy or are either unable or unwilling to fulfil the obligations which a democratic system entails. The nature of human beings is such that all or most of them will work only for private or local interests and thus no opinions about large general interests ever arise. In this instance Mill's ideas are allied to Rousseau's theory of a 'General Will', that a certain homogeneity of feeling or pervading communal sense of particular values is the necessary condition conducive to democracy; his conclusions emanate, with some inconsistency, from his view, referred to above, that democracy demands of the individual aims and actions directed toward the general welfare. Other phenomena, besides, can make the people of a nation incapable of, or at least less suitable for self-government. A nation can be too headstrong and turbulent to be able to submit to a democratic form of government or it may be too passive and resigned to be able to fulfil the duties and discharge the functions which a government of this kind imposes on them; such a mentality—one which Mill believed characteristic of the French—would lead to an exaggerated concentration of power by the State and consequently to oppression of the minority, as in the dictatorship of

Napoleon III. The character of the English people, Mill thought, was distinguished by quite contrary features and was therefore especially suited to democracy. The English only wished to be successful in the pursuit of their private affairs and did not wish to wield power over others through the State; they were therefore opposed to public force, government coercion and expansion of government bureaucracy. Bentham and John Stuart Mill arrived by different reasoning at the same conclusion: a combination of democracy with *laissez-faire*—although Mill did not pursue the principle of *laissez-faire* with anything like Bentham's energy and determination.

Mill's view seems still more clear in Chapter VI of his *Representative Government*, in which he discussed 'the infirmities and dangers' to which representative government is liable:

> 'One of the greatest dangers, therefore, of democracy, as of all other forms of government lies in the sinister interest of the holders of power; it is the danger of class legislation: of government intended for (whether really effecting it or not) the immediate benefit of the dominant class, to the lasting detriment of the whole.'

In the first place, Mill feared that the selfish and short-sighted 'sinister' interest would assert itself in political disputes between rich and poor, between employers and labourers. He feared especially that the workers would impose legislation which would be contrary to his ideas of the requirements of the general interest in a policy of economic liberalism.

> 'We all know what specious fallacies may be urged in defence of every act of injustice yet proposed for the imaginary benefit of the nation. We know how many, not otherwise fools or bad men, have thought it justifiable to repudiate the national debt! We know how many, not destitute of ability, and of considerable popular influence, think it fair to throw the whole burden of taxation upon savings under the name of unrealized property, allowing those whose progenitors and themselves have always spent all they received, to remain, as a reward for such exemplary conduct, wholly untaxed. We know what powerful arguments, the more dangerous because there is a portion of truth in them, against the power of bequest, against every advantage which one person seems to have over another.'

How, then, should such class legislation be prevented? The ideal, Mill said, would be a representative system in which the two chief classes, corresponding to two divergent directions of apparent interest—on the one hand, the employers of labour and those allied with them, 'retired capitalists and possessors of inherited wealth and the highly-paid description of labourers (such as the professional), whose education and way of life assimilate them with the rich and whose prospect and ambition it is to raise themselves into that class'; and on the other hand, the labourers and with them 'the smaller employers of labour who by interests, habits and educational impressions are assimilated in wishes, tastes, and objects to the labouring classes: comprehending a large proportion of petty tradesmen'—would each have more or less an equal mandate. In such a situation most of them would strive exclusively for class interests but one could count on an enlightened minority in each class which would be concerned for the general welfare and this minority would maintain a balance and would, in each particular issue, be the determining influence. Mill did not demand that parliamentary seats should be equally divided between employers and labourers, but hoped for a sort of balance between the selfish class interests of either side which would lead to the furtherance of the general interest. The reasoning he pursued as the crux of his argument is strange in the extreme:

> 'The reason why, in any tolerably constituted society, justice and the general interest mostly in the end carry their point, is that the separate and selfish interests of mankind are almost always divided; some are interested in what is wrong, but some, also, have their private interest on the side of what is right: and those who are governed by higher considerations, though too few and weak to prevail against the whole of the others, usually after sufficient discussion and agitation become strong enough to turn the balance in favour of the body of private interest which is on the same side with them.'

This principle, which contains no trace of real justification or proof, but only expresses expectation or hope in the form of a statement, is in itself the corner-stone of Mill's theory of constitutional policy. It only needs to be added at this point, that he recommended a form of proportional representation, which he called 'representation of minorities', to insure that no class should be dominant in representation, and that therefore the enlightened judgement which coincides with the common interest would become the decisive factor in government.

> 'In a really equal democracy, every or any section would be represented, not disproportionately, but proportionately . . . It is an essential part of a democracy that minorities should be adequately represented. No real democracy, nothing but a false show of democracy, is possible without it.'

From Mill's private statements it is abundantly clear that proportionalism was intended to be a guarantee against the dominance of the labouring class, in other words, it was to be essentially a safeguard against too far-reaching State intervention. His aim was realized in so far as a very imperfect form of proportionalism was introduced in some urban constituencies as a result of the franchise reform of 1865; but by 1885 it had been abolished.

In his eighth chapter, 'On the extension of the Suffrage', Mill repeated the arguments in favour of democracy quoted above. But now his defence of universal suffrage was based on two differing points of view. On the one hand, in conjunction with his basic principles, he declared that active participation in government implied intellectually and morally educated citizens. 'Among the foremost benefits of free government is that education of the intelligence and the sentiments which is carried down to the very lowest ranks of the people when they are called to take a part in acts which directly affect the great interests of their country.' On the other hand, he thought that it was

> 'a personal injustice to withhold from any one, unless for the prevention of greater evils, the ordinary privilege of having his voice reckoned in the disposal of affairs in which he has the same interest as other people. If he is compelled to pay, if he may be compelled to fight, if he is required implicitly to obey, he should be legally entitled to know what for; to have his consent asked, and his opinion counted at its worth, though not at more than its worth.'

On this point, then, in relation to his previous principal postulate Mill gave a new justification for democracy, tinged, nevertheless, with the faint hue of natural rights. Only the illiterate, in which he included those unable 'to perform the common operations of arithmetic'; those who paid no taxes, thus 'disposing by their votes of other people's money', and who would supposedly 'have every motive to be lavish, and none to economize' the nation's wealth; and those on poor relief, 'people who have not acquired the commonest and most essential requisites for taking care of themselves; for pursuing intelligently their own interests and those of the persons most nearly allied to them', should be excluded from the right to vote.

In contrast to the majority of liberals and radicals of his time, Mill was emphatic in his opinion that women deserved the vote. Sex made no difference, he said:

> 'I consider it to be as entirely irrelevant to political rights, as difference in height, or in the colour of the hair. All human beings have the same interest in good government; the welfare of all is alike affected by it, and they have equal need of a voice in it to secure

their share of its benefits. If there be any difference, women require it more than men, since, being physically weaker, they are more dependent on law and society for protection . . . Nobody pretends to think that women would make a bad use of the suffrage. The worst that is said is, that they would vote as mere dependants, at the bidding of their male relations. If it be so, so let it be. If they think for themselves, great good will be done, and if they do not, no harm. . . . Let us hope that . . . before the lapse of another generation, the accident of sex, no more than the accident of skin, will be deemed a sufficient justification for depriving its possessor of the equal protection and just privileges of a citizen.'

However, on one point Mill made a not insubstantial departure from his democratic principles. He imagined a situation in which, possibly, persons with special intellectual qualifications—employers of labour for cxample, or members of the learned professions—were given more than one vote. The right to this multiple vote, he said, would be justified by the assumption that the educated ought to be able to prevent class legislation to the detriment of their interests, but the right should not have such scope as to enable these persons to impose class legislation to the disadvantage of others. Well-developed local self-government can be singled out among the other guarantees which Mill considered desirable.

Mill's justification for a democracy, therefore, was a mixture of various, partly contradictory theories. In conjunction with Bentham and the elder Mill he expounded his principle of interest as the mainstay of democracy, but he did not argue it with the same consistency and single-mindedness as his predecessors. His defence of democracy also included ideas about the rights of man and general discussions of the educational value of democratic government. Perhaps because of their very eclecticism Mill's views acquired an importance out of the ordinary; even so, his ideas about the educative value of democracy did make a certain original contribution to the debate on government.

The Franchise Reforms of 1867 and 1884

The demand for universal suffrage was brought to the fore in the 1830s and 1840s, primarily by Chartism, with its socialistic leanings. The movement was sparked off by William Lovett and Francis Place, aided by a number of English and Anglo-Irish demagogues and extremists, and supported chiefly by disillusioned trades unionists, radical artisans and a handful of weavers and similar craftsmen whose traditional livelihood was jeopardized by the new industrial methods—all of them disappointed in the limitations of hard-won parliamentary reform, such as it was at the time. The Chartists, in their six-point People's Charter, demanded universal suffrage, equal electoral districts, the secret ballot, abolition of property qualifications for M.P.s, payment for M.P.s and annual parliaments. After the repeal of the Corn Laws, however, and as a result of the rapid increase of prosperity which accompanied the repeal, this spearhead of agitation for suffrage was weakened. Internal dissension and rivalry, misguided tactics, the resort to violence, all helped to discredit the Chartists. They presented three, ever longer petitions to Parliament, in 1839, 1842 and 1847, all of which were rejected. When the third petition, said to contain some six million signatures, was found to be padded out with multiple and ludicrous forgeries including the Queen's name, inserted several times, the Chartists became a laughing stock. All this, coupled with stern government repression, hastened the decline and disintegration of the movement, which faded into insignificance until finally, in the 1860s, it was dissolved.

During the period in which Chartism was active, and until about 1865, the representative Liberals of the time not only rejected outright any thought of universal suffrage, but turned a deaf ear to all demands for further extension of the franchise. As in the past, they maintained that the middle class should govern and that universal suffrage was a danger to the two central tenets of liberalism: security of property and liberty of the individual.

The examples of the United States and France, the only big nations in which democracy had been tried out, influenced the debate to a not inconsiderable degree. The events of 1848–51 in France provided telling arguments for the opponents of an extended suffrage: the revolution of June 1848 highlighted the danger to property; the Napoleonic *coup d'état* of 1851, the danger to liberty. In the matter of evaluating the American constitution, the position was less well-defined and more complex. During the struggle for the Great Reform Bill, the United States had been held up both as a shining example and as a timely warning. After 1832, when leading opinion in England rejected demands for further democratization, the attitude towards the functioning of the American constitution was fairly critical, the more so as at this time the suffrage had been extended in the majority of states of the Union. The American Civil War of 1861–65 was regarded in England, much more than in the United States, as a test of democracy and was judged accordingly. The sympathies of both the upper and middle classes seem to have been overwhelmingly on the side of the South; at all events, it was believed or at any rate hoped, that the eleven seceding southern states would eventually unite in a federation of their own. It was frequently claimed that the Civil War was a proof of the failure of democracy. The concentration of power in Lincoln, as earlier in Napoleon III after his *coup d'état*, was believed to make abundantly clear that a democracy must inevitably result in despotism. English radicals and the working classes all wanted the North to win the Civil War and when this actually happened they regarded the victory as a vindication of democracy.

After about 1840, a radical wing of the Liberals led by Richard Cobden and John Bright worked systematically for an expansion of the suffrage. The reasons they gave were for the most part similar to those given by the advocates of reform in the 1830s. Groups of citizens whose low earning level and deficient education had been the pretext for their exclusion from participation in politics, had now reached a position such that it was imperative to heed their demand for a share in government. Reform would not endanger the existing order but, on the contrary, would serve to reinforce it. The middle classes, as before, would set the tone of leadership. These radicals occasionally referred to artisans and better-paid factory operatives as a new middle class, and it was sometimes stressed that the middle class in the hitherto accepted meaning of the term would still hold supremacy in Parliament, although, after an extension of the franchise the interests of a new, increased electorate would have to be considered much more attentively than in the past. The idea that the suffrage ever could be exploited to bring about sweeping social reforms was something that never entered the heads of Cobden and Bright, who were fervent supporters of *laissez-faire*.

In the mid-1860s the question of suffrage became a burning question once more, partly because of the victory of the Unionists in the American Civil War, and in 1867 the second great Reform Bill was carried, officially by the Tories, but in reality by the radical Liberals and above all as a result of pressure brought to bear by the excluded sector of the community. The most significant result of the reform was that a considerable portion of a hitherto excluded class, the urban working man, was now enabled to vote; the qualified electorate in England and Wales rose from some 1,057,000 to nearly two million. The Reform Bill of 1832 had increased the electorate by almost fifty per cent, from about 435,000 to some 655,000; but whereas formerly it had been mixed, the electorate now came from a more clearly defined stratum, the industrial middle class. With the passing of the Reform Bill of 1832 one person in twenty-four had received the vote: the Second Reform Bill gave the vote to one in twelve. Nevertheless, factory operatives, mill-hands, the working man in general, were still without a vote.

The conflict of opinion among the Liberals in 1866, during the debates on the proposal for further parliamentary reform, throws considerable light on the liberal attitude. Though far less sweeping than the Bill introduced and carried the following year by Disraeli, as Chancellor of the Exchequer in the third Derby administration, the second Bill was rejected by a combination of Tories and the disgruntled element of the Liberals, the 'Adullamites' as they were called; and these were divided in their views about the results of the Bill but united in their general attitude to the problems of constitutional policy. In the speech with which Gladstone, then Chancellor of the Exchequer and Leader of the Commons, introduced the rejected Bill, a very moderate proposal to enlarge the franchise in boroughs and counties, he attempted to show that, far from opening doors which they would be unable to close, in other words, instead of starting a process which would eventually lead to a democracy, the Bill was merely adding a few final touches to perfect a constitution which had been left incomplete after the reform of 1832. All that was needed, in order to achieve the political emancipation of the middle class, was an adjustment of the electorate to conform with the altered social situation. It was true that a considerable proportion of the working class had now got the vote, but this class would never become a majority. Besides, more often than not the poor were conservative in habits and outlook. Gladstone commented:

> 'We cannot consent to look upon this proposed addition, considerable although it may be, to the political power of the working classes of this country, as if it were an addition fraught with mischief and with danger. We cannot look, and we hope no man will look, upon it as some Trojan horse, approaching the walls of the sacred city, and filled with armed men, bent upon ruin, plunder and conflagration. . . . Consider what you can safely and justly afford to do in admitting new subjects and citizens within the pale of the Parliamentary Constitution, and, having so considered it, do not I beseech you, perform the act as if you were compounding with danger and misfortune. Do it as if you were conferring a boon, that will be felt and reciprocated in grateful attachment. Give to these persons new interests in the Constitution; new interests which by the beneficent processes of the law of nature and of Providence, shall beget in them new attachment; for the attachment of the people to the Throne, the institutions and the laws under which they live, is, after all, more than gold and silver, and more than fleets and armies, at once the strength, the glory, and the safety of the land.'

Other Liberal leaders expressed themselves in more or less the same vein. They did not insist that the reform would either be a cause of, or a step in the direction of democracy; on the contrary, they emphasized its limiting nature and its close link with the established order of things. It was now argued, just as it had been from 1830–32, that under existing conditions the dissatisfied masses would be content with a moderate extension of the franchise but were bound to demand more drastic reforms if the decision on the matter were put off any longer. Only a couple of Liberals, John Bright and John Stuart Mill, who were in sympathy with reform and were regarded as belonging to the radical minority, declared that the reform was a step farther on the road to universal suffrage.

The sharpest criticism of the government, however, came from a splinter of the Liberal Party, nicknamed the 'Adullamites' and led by Robert Lowe, a fierce opponent of reform who, two years later, was to be Chancellor of the Exchequer in Gladstone's first ministry. Lowe's opponents had gleefully seized on the nickname after a speech by Bright in the Commons in March 1860, during which he raised a laugh by his sarcastic reference to Lowe and his clique: 'The right honourable gentleman . . . has retired into what may be called his political Cave of Adullam—and he has called about him everyone that was in distress and everyone that was discontented.' Bright's allusion was to the cave where all who were distressed, in debt or discontented flocked to join David in his flight from Saul; and the nickname stuck.

Lowe and his Adullamites declared that in view of rising wages franchise reform would soon lead to total democracy. What was more, reform would be only a first step towards universal suffrage. If the working classes were given the vote, the first result would be that parliamentary elections would be plagued with coercion, corruption and disorder. Later on the working classes would become aware of their opportunities as a result of which they would proceed to the overthrow of the social structure. Property would be abolished, capital shared out equally; commerce and industry as a consequence, would fall to pieces. Democracy, Lowe felt, would be especially dangerous in England, where the executive and the legislative powers formed a unity and where, as a result, no guarantee against unchecked domination by force existed. A concentration of power followed in the wake of democracy. 'Under such a system the private individual is small and the government big. . . . This must become the character of a government which represents the majority of the people and which ruthlessly tramples down and levels all things except itself.' The dictatorship in France under Napoleon III showed just what democracy led to. Only in America had democracy been without disastrous consequences and this was due partly to the fact that democracy there was combined with a constitutional system of balances, and partly to the tremendous resources offered by the vast American continent, a condition which tended to reduce discord between individuals and groups.

The effects of the reform of 1867 were calculated to reassure the

Tory and Liberal groups who, like Carlyle, were filled with apprehension at this 'leap in the dark'. Contrary to what had been expected, however, the working classes displayed no marked tendency to any unanimity at the polls, but continued to vote for the big traditional parties. It was often said, though it is surely open to question, that Disraeli's victory of 1874 was due to the fact that the trades unions had voted mostly for Tory candidates. The decisive change in the attitude of leading social groups occurred probably after 1867.

Government in England began to be spoken of as a democracy without the word being used in a derogatory or critical sense; and the repudiation of democracy as a matter of principle at length disappeared from politics; no anti-democratic propaganda has since been observed in England save from a few extremists with no political influence.

When the second Gladstone administration (1880–85), in fulfilment of the election promises of 1884, presented a proposal for further extension of the franchise, it was possible, because of the changed attitude to the idea of democracy, to carry the bill without great opposition. All that needs to be pointed out concerning this debate is that the liberal leaders in general produced the same arguments as those they had put forward in 1867. They argued that the earlier reforms had proved not to be a danger to the community, that great numbers of the working classes had voted Tory and that the groups to whom it was now proposed to give the vote could be considered to be as well qualified to vote as those who had been included in the electorate in the previous reforms. Those who were now about to be admitted to the electorate could hardly be described as a sector of the middle class but speakers in the debates conferred on them the same qualities or virtues as those traditionally ascribed to the middle class: responsibility, sound common sense, conservatism, thrift, and loyalty to the country.

The idea that reform could take a radical or revolutionary turn was thought to be quite out of the question. On the contrary, said Gladstone, speaking in the Commons in February 1885, 'the broad scope and general effect of the measure' would serve to strengthen and unite the nation.

> 'Let us hold firmly together and success will crown our effort. You will, as much as any Parliament that has conferred great legislative benefits on the nation, have your reward, and . . . you will have deserved it by the benefits you will have conferred. You will have made this strong nation stronger still, stronger by its closer union without; stronger within by union between class with class, and by arraying all classes and all portions of the community in one solid, compacted mass round the ancient throne which it has loved so well, and round a Constitution now to be more than ever powerful, and more than ever free.'

Matters of principle were hardly touched upon during the debate. At all stages of the Bill the proceedings were conducted as if the measure were a completion of earlier reforms, of a process hallowed by British tradition. Several statements, nevertheless, show how far, in reality, the attitude to democracy had actually advanced from the Liberal standpoint of fifty years earlier. Gladstone declared, in reference to the American experience of democracy, that the constitution had grown stronger through the extension of its popular basis and he added that belief in the people was an essential element in a Liberal philosophy.

The parliamentary reforms of 1884–85 enfranchised the majority of England's adult males. With this step, the battle to achieve democracy could be considered virtually won.

Civil Rights

In the early nineteenth century, England enjoyed a wider range of civil rights than any other European country, despite the considerable restrictions which had been imposed in horror of the French Revolution and its aftermath. First and foremost there was a free press: there was no censorship and press lawsuits were tried before juries. There was considerable freedom in other fields too: political and religious freedom were well developed. The attacks on government and church which were made in public discussion during the critical years of the early 1830s were made without any interference by the government, which show how strongly rooted was the principle of liberty. During the whole of the nineteenth century basic concepts long sanctioned by tradition were confirmed and expanded. Legislation against trade unions introduced at the turn of the century was abolished in 1825. Catholics were allowed to hold office in 1829 and religious freedom was extended step by step, through the abolition of such laws as those which discriminated against catholics and nonconformists; laws to supress freedom of the press, of speech, of trade unions and the right of free congress were all adjusted or their non-observance accepted in practice. The driving force behind all this was primarily the Liberal party, although the Tories increasingly came to accept Liberal principles, frequently acted in cooperation with the Liberals and seldom offered any very energetic resistance to reforms.

The concept which lay at the root of these ideas of freedom and tolerance corresponded to the policy of *laissez-faire* in its application to the economy and to commercial and industrial life. Through free competition, conditional on a necessary minimum of common sense and education, the 'right' opinions would prevail; moreover, right thinking was advantageous just as much to the individual as to the community. Because democracy was feared in the leading spheres of influence, it was believed that only people with a higher level of education and economic status were capable of acting with good sense, restraint and rational deliberation, qualities hardly to be expected from any but those with a higher level of education and income. The optimistic view on freedom of discussion depended on the conviction that the right sort of public opinion had been found and was about to demonstrate the beneficial results which were expected of it. For the first time in the nation's history, independent thinking, freed from the trammels of theology, had dictated laws which were to regulate human existence. It had been proved that common sense could provide a basis for life in an organized society, stronger and of more lasting practical value than that of religion or metaphysics. Economic liberalism had no need of witch-hunts or inquisitorial pyres as a safeguard against heretics. In what concerned differences of opinion in religious matters, these were of little or no consequence, since politics directed by rationalism and liberalism was a matter which concerned this world, not the next. The primary religious concept of the guidance of the human race by the Almighty was considered proven precisely because of the discovery heralded by economic liberalism that the welfare of society was dependent on due respect for law and order. The Whigs, who were terrified of democracy, expressed themselves as trenchantly on these matters as utilitarians and radicals. As Macaulay wrote:

> 'The people never have so great an opportunity of settling a question in the right way as when they can discuss it freely. The Government as such never can support its opinion other than through the influence exercised by hope and fear. Its contribution to an argument consists not of concrete reasons but of threats and force. In this way, therefore, we do not get a struggle between two sides of an argument, but a struggle between argument on one side and force on the other. Instead of a struggle in which truth, by reason of the natural character of human reason has a clear preference over error, we get a struggle in which truth can win only by chance.'

For public discussion to give the best possible result, it would be necessary to provide education which would give sufficient understanding and adequate intellectual training. According to the older Liberal influential opinion, education should be voluntarily regulated, otherwise it could become an instrument of propaganda in the hands of government, and civil rights would in reality be undermined. Education, properly regulated, would reinforce existing institutions and the dominant trend of ideas, and would not, as was earlier believed and still assumed by the Tories, undermine the notions necessary to the maintenance of established social order.

The Revd Sydney Smith preached a sermon in St Paul's in 1837, on the accession of Queen Victoria, in which he outlined the duties of the young Queen. One of the most important of these duties said the Dean, was the education of the masses.

> 'First and foremost, I think the new Queen should bend her mind to the very serious consideration of educating the people. . . . When I see the village school, and the tattered scholars, and the aged master or mistress teaching the mechanical art of reading or writing, and thinking that they are teaching that alone, I feel that the aged instructor is protecting life, insuring property, fencing the altar, guarding the throne, giving looseness and liberty to all the fine powers of man, and lifting him up to his own place in the order of Creation.'

In the same spirit, Lord Brougham, who worked more tirelessly than any other leading Liberal for the spread of education, demanded that the State should in every way support, though on no account direct, the educational system. By means of education every citizen would learn to understand the significance of the truths of economic liberalism; the workers would cease to struggle against the application of the law of supply and demand. General education would also do away with wars. In a speech of 1828, Brougham said:

> 'Let the soldier be abroad if he will, he can do nothing in this age. There is another personage, a personage less imposing in the eyes of some, perhaps insignificant. The schoolmaster is abroad, and I trust him, armed with his primer, against the soldier in full military array.'

Equal in importance with education, the press was the great medium for the enlightenment of mankind and through this it helped to secure the right of property, and to further progress and peace.

Bentham, though proclaiming the natural tendency of the individual to act in his own interest, that is to his own enduring advantage, strongly emphasized the value of discussion and consequently the value of civil rights. He believed, in reality, that public discussion would really help individuals to realize their true interests, thus enabling them to make decisions which would accord with the general interest. Public censorship, he believed, would hinder progress by the suppression of new ideas; 'A true censorship', he said, 'is one that is practised by an enlightened public, that denounces dangerous and false opinions and rewards useful discoveries'. Above all, however, and as a consequence of his distrust of all government on principle, he regarded unlimited freedom of discussion as an opportunity for the people to keep a check on their representatives and to pave the way for changes in government. A free press signified for Bentham 'a bridle on the activity of government', and was therefore considered by him 'absolutely necessary for good government'. Freedom of the press, of trade unions and of the right of congress was, on the whole, necessary, Bentham thought, not only to make the spread of knowledge and understanding easier, but to render possible agitation against those in power, when they abused their power. Even hostile and intemperate comment directed against civil servants and delegates should be exempt from punishment, he thought, because the risks involved in this behaviour must be regarded as negligible in contrast to the danger of any restriction of the right to citicize. As an example of this—as of so many other matters concerning democracy—Bentham pointed to the United States, where public discussion at that time enjoyed an even greater freedom than in England. James Mill further strengthened Bentham's defence in his *Liberty of the Press* (1828) one of his *Encyclopedia Britannica* Supplement articles, in which he combined Bentham's ideas with belief in the infallibility of enlightened public opinion:

> 'Every man, possessed of reason, is accustomed to weigh evidence, and to be guided and determined by its preponderance. When various conclusions are, with their evidence, presented with equal skill, there is a moral certainty, though some few may be misguided, that the greater number will judge right, and that the greatest force of evidence, wherever it is, will produce the greatest impression.'

Bentham, in a typical passage, defended even freedom of worship and in conjunction with this attacked the principle of an established church. Every man could be considered to be interested in religious questions and anxious to prove the truth of religious beliefs, he said. If a religion was true, then it was unnecessary to proclaim it at the expense of the State. To pay people for disseminating religious propaganda implied, moreover, a systematical encouragement of falsehood and deception, since some people did not regard religion as true, however true it might be for others. A state-supported church, Bentham thought, had in reality always been a medium which enabled rulers to get power over the ruled by means of deceit and dread.

In his celebrated essay *On Liberty* (1859), John Stuart Mill advanced detailed and more varied reasons for tolerance, civil liberties and the right of individual self-determination. He started out from the theories of utilitarianism: the matter was not one of asserting an abstract right, but of promoting the 'lasting interest' of the individual. The theory he attempted to prove was that

> 'the sole end for which mankind are warranted, individually or collectively, in interfering with the liberty of action of any of their

number, is self-protection. That the only purpose for which power can be rightfully exercised over any member of a civilized community, against his will, is to prevent harm to others. He cannot rightfully be compelled to do or forbear because it will be better for him to do so, because it will make him happier, because, in the opinion of others, to do so would be wise, or right. . . . The only part of the conduct of anyone, for which he is amenable to society, is that which concerns others. In the part which merely concerns himself, his independence is, of right, absolute.'

To substantiate his statement Mill divided freedom into several categories. He discussed, first of all, freedom of conscience and freedom of speech, which are the basic essentials of civil rights. He summarized his argument on four grounds:

'First, an opinion which it is attempted to suppress by authority may possibly be true. To refuse a hearing to an opinion on the grounds that it is false is to decide the question for all mankind, and exclude every other person from the means of judging. All silencing of discussion is an assumption of infallibility. . . . The peculiar evil of silencing the expression of an opinion is, that it is robbing the human race: posterity as well as the existing generation; those who dissent from the opinion still more than those who hold it.'

In this context Mill criticized the usual view that true and useful ideas—which he assumed to be identical—cannot be suppressed, that truth will out:

'the dictum that truth always triumphs over persecution is one of those pleasant falsehoods which men repeat after one another till they pass into commonplaces, but which all experience refutes. History teems with instances of truth put down by persecution. If not suppressed forever it may be thrown back for centuries.'

This is all very possible, but it is irrelevant, because though truth may be extinguished once, twice, or many times, one of its appearances will fall on a time which will favour its escape from persecution 'until it has made such head that it will withstand all subsequent attempts to suppress it'.

Mill then proceeded to the next division of his argument:

'Secondly, though the silenced opinion be an error, it may, and very commonly does, contain a portion of the truth; and since the general or prevailing opinion on any subject is rarely or never the whole truth, it is only by the collision of adverse opinions that the remainder of the truth has any chance of being supplied.

> 'Thirdly, even if the received opinion be not only true, but the whole truth; unless it is suffered to be, and actually is, vigorously and earnestly contested, it will, by most of those who receive it, be held in the manner of a prejudice, with little comprehension or feeling of its rational grounds.'

Fourthly, 'the meaning of the doctrine itself will be in danger of being lost, or enfeebled, and deprived of its vital effect on the character and conduct'.

Finally, concerning freedom of opinion, Mill maintained that allowance must be made for the propagation of error; just as a clever and able man maintains his vigour and activity by contending with his fellow men, so truth flourishes and prevails in constant battle with falsehood.

Mill then passed to the question of personal liberty, the freedom of the individual to act in accordance with his inclinations or convictions. Here he pointed out an involuntary limitation: society can prohibit actions which are harmful to others as well as the individual who commits the actions. With this exception liberty of action should be absolute. 'The mental and moral, like the muscular powers', said Mill, 'are improved only by being used'. Only by cultivating freely his gifts and aptitudes will the individual become a well-developed, mature human being.

> 'Among the works of man which human life is rightly employed in perfecting and beautifying, the first in importance surely is man himself. . . . Human nature . . . requires to grow and develop itself on all sides, according to the tendency of the inward forces which make it a living thing.'

With regard to society, freedom to develop is necessary because variations in character and activity are a condition both of culture and progress.

> 'Free scope should be given to varieties of character short of injury to others . . . and . . . in things which primarily do not concern others, individuality should assert itself, for individuality of character . . . is one of the principal ingredients of human happiness, and quite the chief ingredient of individual and social progress.'

Even when individuals or their actions deviate sharply from accepted standards, rooted in custom or hallowed by tradition, their refusal to conform should be respected, since only in such ways can fresh standards be attained which, for one purpose or another, may be found worth preserving. 'He who lets the world, or his own portion of it, choose his plan of life for him, has no need of any other faculty than the ape-like one of imitation. He who chooses his plan for himself, employs all his faculties.' In his repudiation of mediocrity Mill made a plea not only for tolerance of the original but for cultivation of the eccentric:

> 'Originality is the one thing which unoriginal minds cannot feel the use of. They cannot see what it is to do for them, how should they? If they could see what it would do for them, it would not be originality . . . In sober truth, whatever homage may be professed, or even paid, to real or supposed mental superiority, the general tendency of things throughout the world is to render mediocrity the ascendant power among mankind.
>
> 'Those whose opinions go by the name of public opinion are not always the same sort of public: in America they are the whole white population; in England, chiefly the middle class. But they are always a mass, that is to say, collective mediocrity. Their thinking is done for them by men much like themselves, addressing them or speaking in their name, on the spur of the moment, through the newspapers.'

So that, said Mill:

> 'when the opinions of the masses of merely average men are everywhere become or becoming the dominant power . . . exceptional individuals . . . should be encouraged in acting differently from the mass. . . . Precisely because the tyranny of opinion is such as to make eccentricity a reproach, it is desirable, in order to break through that tyranny, that people should be eccentric. Eccentricity has always abounded when and where strength of character has abounded: and the amount of eccentricity in a society has generally been proportional to the amount of genius, mental vigour, and moral courage it contained.'

Mill had come to the conclusion that people in a number of great civilized nations were becoming more and more like each other, that mediocrity tended to set the standards and that public opinion and legislation were increasingly leaving their mark on individuals and obstructing their natural development. Where then, he asked, lay the boundary line between what he called 'self-regarding' actions, which concern only the individual who commits them, and actions harmful to others, which society therefore has a right to condemn and protect itself against?

He made certain recommendations on this point. He admitted that actions which are directly harmful to the individual who commits them can indirectly affect other people. Mill thought that society was then justified in intervening.

'If, for example, a man, through intemperance or extravagance, becomes unable to pay his debts, or, having undertaken the moral responsibility of a family, becomes from the same cause incapable of supporting or educating them, he is deservedly reprobated and might be justly punished.'

That is, if he fails in his duty to others:

'it is no tyranny to force him to fulfil that obligation, by compulsory labour, if no other means are available. . . . The right inherent in a society to ward off crimes against itself by antecedent precautions, suggests the obvious limitations of the maxim that purely self-regarding misconduct cannot properly be meddled with in the way of prevention or punishment.'

In cases where socially undesirable behaviour becomes only indirectly harmful, causing what Mill termed 'merely contingent, or, as it may be called, constructive injury', to society, the principle of freedom should be the deciding factor. When an individual, said Mill, affects in minor degree the sympathies and interests of society at large 'by conduct which neither violates any specific duty to the public, nor occasions perceptible hurt to any assignable individual except himself, the inconvenience is one which society can afford to bear, for the sake of the greater good of human freedom'.

Mill at this point amplified his general argument concerning unrestricted development of the individual with the assumption that if society intervenes with standards and prohibitions it usually does so improperly or inappropriately. 'The acts of an individual', he said, 'may be hurtful to others, or wanting in due consideration for their welfare, without going to the length of violating any of their constituted rights'. In which case, he said, an offender may be punished by social disapproval or censure, though not by law.

'In all such cases there should be perfect freedom, legal and social, to do the action and stand the consequences. . . . Neither one person nor any number of persons, is warranted in saying to another human creature of ripe years, that he shall not do with his life for his own benefit what he chooses to do with it. . . . The interest which society has in him individually (except as to his conduct to others) is fractional, and altogether indirect. The interference of society to overrule his judgement and purposes in what only regards himself must be grounded on general presumptions: which may be altogether wrong, and even if right, are as likely as not to be misapplied to individual cases . . . All errors which he is likely to commit against advice and warning are far outweighed by the evil of allowing others to constrain him to what they deem his good.'

In judging matters of self-regarding conduct society is more likely to be wrong than right:

> 'for in these cases public opinion means, at the best, some people's opinion of what is good or bad for other people; while very often it does not even mean that; the public, with the most perfect indifference, passing over the pleasure or convenience of those whose conduct they censure, and considering only their own preference. There are many who consider as an injury to themselves any conduct which they have a distaste for, and resent it as an outrage to their feelings . . . and this standard of judgement, thinly disguised, is held up to mankind as the dictate of religion and philosophy, by nine-tenths of all moralists and speculative writers.'

For the same reasons, Mill rejected such examples of State interference in personal liberty as the legal enforcement of Sunday observance and laws to regulate or prohibit the sale and drinking of alcohol.

Mill's ideas were imbued with faith in rationalism and concepts of social harmony which were in keeping with the liberalism of his day. In his arguments concerning freedom of speech, he reasoned from an *a priori* belief in the inherent reasonableness of human beings: he took for granted partly that propagated ideas expressed certain true or false conceptions of reality, and not values or feelings; partly that truth must necessarily triumph over falsehood; and partly the usefulness of truth. However, when Mill declared that the vitality of truth depended on the unceasing struggle against delusion, he was forced to admit that even delusion could be socially desirable or expedient. When he discussed freedom of action he assumed that self-development—a mystical concept which inferred that the development of a human being was possible without any influence by his environment—should chiefly be directed toward the happiness of the individual and the welfare of society. Although Mill wrote *On Liberty* without being influenced, as far as is known, by Darwin's theories—*On Liberty* was written in 1859; Darwin's notes on natural selection and the survival of the fittest were written in 1857, read to the Linnaean Society in 1858 and his book published in 1859—Mill's approval and advocacy of free competition, was nevertheless in line with the vulgarized Darwinism of later years. From these ideas about competition all views, patterns and standards of behaviour and action valuable to the welfare of society would emanate. Mill evidently believed, broadly speaking, that the freedoms already in existence in the society of his time, were acceptable; his general views would otherwise have been put to far more radical use, either in limiting or extending the activities of government. His attempt to separate actions which solely concern the individual and actions which involve others are muddled to say the least. It is obvious that even actions which can be considered 'self-regarding' may be of the greatest social significance.

Several other typical accounts of the liberal idea of freedom are little more than variations on Mill's theme. Walter Bagehot, who was directly influenced by Darwinism and attempted to apply its theories to politics, regarded his own time as 'the age of discussion' and found in the interchange of views the essential condition of progress; by the free exchange of ideas and opinions, outworn habits could be broken, intelligence take the lead and tolerance become the natural disposition of mankind.

In his book of essays *On Compromise* (1874), Lord Morley, the outstanding and powerful theorist of liberalism in practice and in politics, was in essential agreement with Mill. However, Morley combined the principle of freedom, along lines which pointed to the reformist tendencies of the new liberalism, with the demand for reforms which would forestall the dangerous consequences of freedom. A typical argument of his dealt with Mill's reasoning about the prohibition of drinking. In a 'Note on the Doctrine of Liberty', an appendix to a new edition of his book published in 1886, Morley was critical of what he considered a primitive way of dealing with the problem of drunkenness.

> 'You pass a law (if you can) putting down drunkenness; there is a neatness in such a method very attractive to fervid and impatient natures. Would you not have done better to leave that law unpassed, and apply yourselves sedulously instead to the improvement of the dwellings of the more drunken class, to the provision of amusements that might compete with the ale-house, to the extension and elevation of instruction, and so on?'

On this point, as well as on all other forms of prohibition, he was in agreement with Mill in his rejection of this kind of interference, to which he added his own demands for positive measures which would do away with the need for restrictive legislation.

With regard to civil rights in a more specific sense, Liberalism held to its earlier viewpoint during the later phase of 'new-liberalism'. On issues which were relevant to the boundaries between civil rights and economic freedom—of which the prohibition of alcohol was the most striking example—new-liberalism was merely a transitional phase towards other theories of reform which became decisive factors in the social and political attitude to the problems of economic life.

III

EVOLUTION OF AN EMPIRE

Free Trade

Free trade between nations was one of the principal tenets of economic liberalism and it corresponded to the demand in England for freedom of contract. Pitt, a convinced Free Trader, and one of the first statesmen to adopt the teachings of Adam Smith, had already striven to secure a more flexible trade policy during his nineteen odd years as First Lord of the Treasury and Chancellor of the Exchequer, and he had, among other things, concluded a new and enlightened trading agreement with France. During the twenty-two years of warfare with France (1793–1815), economic isolation had brought new prosperity to England; high customs tariffs were considered necessary, primarily to provide the government with revenues. After the war was over, the high tariffs were retained as a protection to commerce and industry which had flourished during the war years as never before. In some areas, however, the principle of free trade was applied quite early. In the 1820s the duties on a great number of products were either abolished or lowered; and the Navigation Acts, in force since the seventeenth-century wars with Holland, were virtually abolished. These acts restricted foreign imports into England to British ships or ships of the country of origin of the goods, while trade with the colonies was forbidden to all but British ships. This policy of doing away with restrictive laws was followed during the years between 1820 and 1860 with no great opposition as far as a number of commodities were concerned. There was, however, one important exception. The heavy duties on corn remained in force. After 1828 a sliding scale was employed in order to guarantee to British farmers a fixed price very much higher as a rule than the price in the world market.

During the whole period after 1815 the question of the Corn Laws came under lively discussion and a series of proposals for their repeal was introduced. The entire Tory party was in favour of retaining them The landowners who dominated the party regarded the continued enforcement of the laws as a vital condition of the survival of their own class, of agriculture and of the nation. Opinions were for long divided inside the Whig party. Whig aristocrats like Lord Grey and Lord Melbourne were as interested as the Tories were in keeping the laws in force. Whig industrialists, however, were as a rule Free Traders —they needed no laws to protect industrial products—and they received support from intellectual groups whose mouthpieces were the *Edinburgh Review* and the *Westminster Review*. In parliamentary debate and in the newspapers both supporters and opponents of the Corn Laws nevertheless admitted the fundamental soundness of the doctrine of Free Trade. The Free Traders demanded that it should be applied immediately and generally. As early as 1819 an *Edinburgh Review* writer said that the Corn Laws were virtually a taxation of the masses in favour of the farmers and even more of the landowners. The price of corn, alike with other commodities, should be determined between buyer and seller through free bargaining, and not by the State, as was actually the case under the system of taxation. If the abolition of the Corn Laws were to lead to a situation in which some of the arable land could not be cultivated at a profit, then 'these lands *ought* to lie waste. There is no demand in the country for corn at so high a price as will admit of their cultivation.' If there were universal free trade, it would follow that every nation would produce and sell the goods it was best suited to produce. 'Capital would then everywhere be placed to the best advantage; the principle of the division of labour would be fully applied; nations as well as individuals would refrain from producing in their own countries anything that could be bought more cheaply abroad.' Even if other countries clung to their tariffs England should abolish hers, as in the long run this would lead to increased prosperity. The Protectionists replied that free trade was right in principle, but that its application in a single country could have catastrophic results. It would be necessary to allow certain industries to lapse, a course which would lead to widespread unemployment.

In its bearing on the health and morale of the nation as well as in its vital importance in time of war, agriculture was the mainstay of society. Even if the abolition of the Corn Laws were to benefit the majority they must be maintained in the interests of property. To repeal the laws would amount to the confiscation of part of a farmer's property.

The parliamentary reform of 1832 increased the prospects of success of the efforts to secure general free trade, as a result of the growing influence of industrialists and merchants at the expense of the landed gentry. In 1838 the Anti-Corn Law League was founded by seven Manchester merchants, its most prominent members being the calico-printer Richard Cobden and the Quaker cotton-spinner John Bright, who agitated for free trade all over the country. The range and activity of the Anti-Corn Law League's agitation through these two and their adherents has hardly any parallel in English political history. By means of petitions, mass meetings, electioneering and speeches and lobbying in Parliament, they sought to influence the great political parties, though they formed no party of their own. A drop in trade, combined with an exaggerated difference between the domestic price of corn and the price on the world market, created a situation favourable to the activities of the League. In 1846 the campaign precipitated a crisis and this was intensified by the Irish potato famine which made the immediate introduction of cheap corn imperative. In this situation Sir Robert Peel, heading the divided Conservative party, which was split between Free Traders and Protectionists, and with the support of Whig Radicals carried the repeal and the Corn Laws were abolished. The abolition was bitterly opposed by the majority of the Conservatives, most of them landowners, but opposition soon died away when it was found that repeal had not brought disaster, and for nearly a century afterwards England headed all other nations as the precursor and champion of free trade.

Although both Conservatives and Liberals had for long accepted the principle of free trade, as a movement it belonged primarily and in a very special way, to the Liberal Party which, so to speak, had a proprietary interest in it. The Manchester School, as Cobden's and Brights movement and doctrine were called, was incorporated with and to a certain extent signified a renewal of English liberalism. This may sound odd, since the doctrine of free trade had long been generally accepted on principle, and even before the advent of the Manchester School a considerable number of Whigs and Liberals had been in favour of abolishing the Corn Laws; but it is explained by the fact that the idea of free trade was really the core of a general attitude of optimism and belief in progress which at this time—conditioned and accompanied by a huge expansion of industry and commerce—began to pervade English and to some extent European politics in general. The pessimistic element in economic liberalism, which had made its appearance with Malthus and Ricardo, now receded; industrialism began increasingly to be regarded as a means of liberation and bringer of prosperity which, in a period of flourishing world trade, seemed to point the way to lasting peace and universal disarmament. The Manchester School doctrine became a fresh variant of liberal utopianism.

To the industrial and commercial groups who had joined forces in the struggle against protectionism, free trade seemed like a universal truth, the discovery of which must bring with it the most far-reaching and beneficial consequences. The Free Traders, in the first petition which they presented to the Commons, declared their belief that 'one of the principles of divine justice is the inalienable right of every man freely to exchange the product of his work for that which has been produced by others'. Tariffs implied 'protection for one sector of the community at the expense of all the others'. The struggle for free trade was regarded as the last phase of the struggle of the masses against a ruling and exploiting minority. The issue was one of liberating the middle classes and the working classes from the power of the aristocracy, Cobden said. The ruling class had always cared exclusively for its own interests in matters of domestic as well as foreign policy and in order to give these interests their undivided attention, it had sacrificed the welfare of the majority. Free trade, it was believed, in both its international and domestic aspects, would put an end to oppression and conflict.

According to Cobden, a system of agreements to arbitrate should supplement the proposals introduced by free trade and give a definite guarantee of friendly settlement of any differences which might still arise. Power and conquest would seem senseless, small nations would acquire the same rights as big ones, and the aim of politics everywhere would be the welfare of the individual. Free trade was in complete conformity with the principles of Christian morality. Speaking in February 1846, Cobden said:

> 'I can prove that we advocate nothing but what is agreeable to the highest behests of Christianity. To buy in the cheapest market, and sell in the dearest, what is the meaning of the maxim? It means that you take the article which you have in the highest abundance, and with it obtain from others that of which they have the most to spare; so giving to mankind the means of enjoying the fullest abundance of earth's goods, and in doing so, carrying out to the fullest extent the Christian doctrine of "Doing to all men as ye would they should do unto you".'

Seen in this light, free trade was the beginning of a spiritual and material revolution.

In a speech he made in Manchester in January 1846, shortly before the repeal of the Corn Laws, Cobden said:

> 'I believe that the physical gain will be the smallest gain to humanity from the success of this principle. I look farther; I see in the Free-trade principle that which shall act on the moral world as the principle of gravitation in the universe,—drawing men together, thrusting aside the antagonism of race, and creed, and language, and uniting us in the bonds of eternal peace . . . I believe that the effect will be to change the face of the world, so as to introduce a system of government entirely distinct from that which now prevails. I believe that the desire and the motive for large and mighty empires, for gigantic armies and great navies—for those materials which are used for the destruction of life and the desolation of the rewards of labour—will die away; I believe that such things will cease to be necessary, or to

be used, when man becomes one family and freely exchanges the fruits of his labour with his brother man. I believe that, if we could be allowed to reappear on this sublunary scene, we should see, in a far distant period, the governing systems of the world revert to something like the municipal system; and I believe that the speculative philosopher of a thousand years hence will date the greatest revolution that ever happened in the world's history from the triumph of the principle which we have met here to advocate.'

Simultaneously with this grandiose prospect for the individual man and mankind in general, Cobden viewed Britiain's imperial and foreign policy in a light which led to himself and his followers being nicknamed 'Little Englanders'. They declared colonies unnecessary and wrong. Cobden believed small nations were better than big ones because in small nations the government and politicians thought only of the welfare of the individual and not of the greatness of the nation or its expansion. England, he believed, should abstain from meddling in the affairs of other nations. He adamantly opposed the policy of intervention which led to the Crimean War and he was as strongly against Britain siding with the Poles in 1863, in their revolt against the Russians, or with the Danes against the aggression of Prussia and Austria which precipitated the Schleswig-Holstein crisis of 1864. In the event Britain's foreign policy of 'meddle and muddle' only led to big words and empty gestures which accomplished nothing either for Poles or Danes and only succeeded in lowering British prestige. Behind this isolationist attitude was the belief that England, with its policy of peace and free trade, would set an example to the rest of the world and that as a consequence the doctrine of the Manchester School through the universal rightness of its principles, would soon triumph everywhere.

According to the teachings of the Manchester School, the greatest possible freedom of contract would prevail even in England. Cobden and Bright opposed legal restriction of working hours and similar socio-political demands for reform. In the 1846 debate on the ten-hour working day both of them displayed a negative attitude in matters of principle and raised more objections than any other speaker. If Parliament, said Cobden, proposed as a fundamental principle that no interference whatever would be allowed on contracts of employment, it would be the best way to serve the interests of the working man. In the same debate Bright said that if the proposal of free trade which was on the agenda were carried, the problem of the working man would be settled by voluntary agreements without the harmful effects which adjustment by legislation always caused. State interference should be reduced not increased, among other things, by giving up government manufacture of products. In a speech in the Commons in 1846 Cobden demanded that government enterprises for the production of war materials should be discontinued:

> 'I know of nothing so calculated some day to produce a democratic revolution as for the proud and combative people of this country to find themselves in this vital matter of their defence, sacrificed through the mismanagement and neglect of a class to whom, with so much liberality, they have confided the care and future destinies of the country. You have brought this upon yourselves by undertaking to be producers and manufacturers. I advise you in future to place yourselves entirely in dependence upon the private manufacturing resources of the country. If you want gunpowder, artillery, small arms, or the hulls of ships of war, let it be known that you depend upon the private enterprise of the country, and you will get them. At all events you will absolve yourselves from the responsibility of undertaking to do things which you are not competent to do.'

Private management was considered superior in every way; government management degenerated into a careless and wasteful routine. The men of the Manchester School mingled cosmopolitanism with their *laissez-faire* beliefs, a tendency clearly shown in Cobden's advice to the English working man in a famous letter of October 1836:

> 'I would then advise the working class to make themselves free of the labour market of the world, and this they can do by accumulating twenty pounds each, which will give them the command of the only market in which labour is at a higher rate than in England—I mean the United States. If every man would save this sum, he might be as independent of his employer as the latter, with his great capital, is of his workmen.'

On one point only did the advocates of free trade demand increased State intervention. They believed in the principle of compulsory education. Education would complete the possibilities of development of the individual which came through universal freedom of contract. Every individual would be able to judge his own interest and make the contribution which his natural abilities allowed. Nothing more than this was required to ensure rapid and general progress.

The doctrine of the Manchester School obviously emanated, in its essentials, from the old economic liberalism. In whatever degree it was original this was not due to its theoretical outlook. What was to some extent new about it was its unreserved optimism, the immense expectations that it attached to the successful introduction of free trade. Above all, it may seem strange that free trade and freedom of contract should have been regarded as solutions of the social problem. The Free

Traders dissociated themselves from any thought of encroachment on the right of property or of a more equal distribution of property through government intervention; yet they still believed in the levelling-out of social inequalities. The early eighteenth-century economists had also built up a sort of structure of social harmony but this might be regarded as purely theoretical; it entailed a recognition of the inevitability, indeed, the necessity of class distinctions and poverty. For the Free Traders of the 1850s, poverty was not a necessary evil but an evil conditioned by the laws of the State and one which would shortly disappear.

The new outlook meant a liberation from the pessimistic influence of Malthus and Ricardo on the basic theories of economic liberalism. It could also be regarded as a way out of the difficulties which these two writers had emphasized by seeing the whole world, rather than just England, as the real economic unity. Whether or not the population theory of Malthus was accurate or even credible it would become meaningless in a foreseeable future if the whole world were open to immigration from a few overpopulated countries. From the same standpoint the theory of the decreasing yield of the earth and the inflexible law of supply and demand became immaterial. On the other hand, socialist demands for expropriation of capital and economic levelling could be ignored, in a general system of production operated by the community. If general prosperity could be achieved through free trade the matter of distribution became one of secondary importance. The satisfaction of basic needs for all men, which Marx predicted would take place at this time, when over-ripe capitalism had collapsed and the proletariat had taken over the bankrupt state, could be expected, according to Free Traders, quite soon and without any class struggle or cataclysm.

Similarly, the hope of peace and understanding between nations was interpreted as a consequence of the universal adoption of free trade. The network of economic connections would be so strong, the general interest in the continuance of an exchange of commodities so overwhelming, that any conflicts which arose would have to be settled by peaceful means. Just as, when business prospered and flourished and wages were high, employers and labourers ought to be able to settle unimportant differences which might arise, so governments in corresponding situations and with reasons as obvious for the continuation of peaceful coexistence would be able to come to terms by means of arbitration or special agreements. The two decisive conditions would exist in both cases: a prosperity which it was desirable not to destroy and a clear realization of mutual dependency.

The flaw in the Manchester doctrine lay, however, simply in its fantastic over-estimation of the importance of free trade. For a time, and to some extent, they were right in their prophecies. For some decades after 1846 England was certainly not governed entirely by *laissez-faire* principles; these were not applied and never could be applied. But probably no other nation, with the possible exception of the United States for a short period, has so nearly approached an ideal liberal economy as England for several decades after 1846. Free trade came very near to being completely realized; government interference in social matters was still negligible: the railways and even the telegraph system were private enterprises. Salaries increased rapidly; crises caused by unemployment were few and far between and were soon over. Shipping and huge investments overseas produced wealth without giving the working man the feeling that he was being sweated. Wars on the European continent were short-lived and in comparison with the Napoleonic Wars were relatively neither devastating nor costly—with the exception of the American Civil War, which was long-drawn-out and exacted an enormous toll in human lives. England took part in only one war, the Crimean War, and this, which is still the outstanding example of the most senseless war of the century, became in time a good argument for peace movements. The revolutionary trends of 1848 in Europe barely affected England. The state of prosperity and peace promised by the supporters of the Manchester School seemed not to be beyond reach of the nation. Besides this, a number of foreign nations had largely accepted and applied the principles of free trade, though after a few decades a protectionist reaction set in.

Increasing prosperity was followed by a relaxation of domestic policies. Free-trade agitation had been viewed with distrust by the socialist-tinged Chartist movement and was considered by the Chartists to be a deliberate attempt to side-track the working classes on to a path which could merely lead to gains of minor importance. Basically the Chartists were right in their fears, and as a result, their movement did not last long after the triumphant break-through of free trade. English socialism, which generally increased in strength during the 1830s, weakened and practically disappeared by mid-century; the Chartist movement faded out and was at length dissolved after a final flare-up in the futile demonstrations of 1848.

The writings of Karl Marx and Friedrich Engels and the conspiracies and demonstrations of the First International made little or no impression on the English working man. Very likely not one working man in a hundred was aware that a handful of German exiles living in England, fired by their experiences of the English economic, labour and industrial scene, were busily drawing up a programme for the world overthrow of capitalism by the proletariat; nor could the English working man dream that these exiles were convinced that they had started a process (which they believed to be inevitable and ordained by 'historical necessity') which would be brought to a conclusion through the organization of international communism.

England at this time became the refuge of foreign revolutionaries, but neither the government nor the English people were much interested in them; contrary to Continental ways with such folk, their activities were ignored and they were not given the publicity of police prosecution. Almost half a century was to go by before a socialist movement of any strength emerged in England and this movement was far less revolutionary than early socialism. The great reforms which had brought universal suffrage in 1867 and 1884 were carried out with no appreciable upset of the political division of power. If the suffrage of 1884 had been granted fifty years earlier, a social revolution would have seemed inevitable. The Free Traders could say, with some justification, that they had saved the existing social order.

The break-through of free trade principles was one of the causes of the growth of industrial and commercial prosperity after mid-century. The continuation of protectionism had progressively diminished the prospects of foreign nations of selling grain to England and therefore there was less prospect of a market for British industry. But in reality free trade owed its success to a coincidence. In contrast to the European countries, as well as to the United States, England already had a lead in capital, industry and marine trade which could only be fully exploited after free trade was introduced. Britain then became the investor, the exporter and the business organizer of the world, to say nothing of being its workshop. When America, Germany and other nations built up a heavy industry behind tariff barriers the situation changed. The success of free trade depended to a great extent on the fact that it went hand in hand with what was in fact a monopoly.

During the increased prosperity and peaceful economic expansion of the mid-Victorian period, the idea of progress flourished as a belief in reason, and in mankind's ability to achieve his own welfare through the rational exploitation of all that Nature had to offer. The Great Exhibition of 1851, held in the Crystal Palace, specially erected in London's Hyde Park, was the first exhibition of its kind, and a paean in praise of industry, invention, free trade, and amity among nations. A number of writers, whose books achieved both renown and a large circulation, bore witness to the improvements and advances made, and prophesied fresh and rapid progress. Buckle's *History of Civilization in England* (1856) is an outstanding example of this sort of literature and was a best-seller in its day. The recurrent theme of Buckle's masterpiece is the thought that progress is conditioned by the increasing influence of reason at the expense of emotion and unreflecting faith. He associated with this a climatic theory in which he asserted that the inhabitants of temperate zones are superior to those of torrid zones, where life is easy, no culture evolves and the dictates of the emotions gain mastery over reason. In temporate zones insight combined with a certain scepticism has triumphed over religious differences to produce tolerance and understanding. Inventions and discoveries have facilitated the rise of economy and militarism has been replaced by commerce. Above all, economic understanding has brought peace to nations; they regard each other as good customers whose good will it is desirable to retain and whom it is not in one another's interests to alienate by making war.

> 'Well may it be said of Adam Smith, and said too without fear of contradiction, that this solitary Scotchman has, by the publication of one single work, contributed more towards the happiness of man, than has been effected by the united abilities of all statesmen and legislators of whom history has preserved an authentic account.'

With the spread of knowledge, the tendency to resort to force and warfare has disappeared, though it is still in evidence among uncivilized races. In 1854, at the outbreak of the Crimean War, Buckle wrote:

> 'It is, therefore, clear that Russia is a warlike country not because the inhabitants are immoral, but because they are unintellectual. The fault is in the head, not in the heart. In Russia, the national intellect being little cultivated, the intellectual classes lack influence; the military class, therefore, is supreme.'

Buckle thought war to be a matter of weak heads and warm hearts because he believed that whatever theologians might say, the human race had more virtues than vices and that good deeds were more common than bad in every nation.

A similar belief in reason, enlightened self-interest, science and technology is to be found in Lecky's *Rationalism in Europe* (1865). In this work the Irish philosopher and historian discussed superstition, mistaken religious beliefs, and the rejection of false economic and political ideas through insight and enlightened self-interest. As an example of misguided piety Lecky cited the Crusades, one of the most popular and altruistic, yet at the same time most disastrous, periods of warfare which had plagued Europe. It was primarily mistaken ideas which had led, on the whole, to wars, internal dissension, civil war, and had obstructed progress, he said. Civilization now appeared to be heading towards the ideal of the French revolutionary philosophers. Intellectual culture tended to counteract and reduce the spirit of militarism. It had been realized that for an economy to flourish it needed enlightened self-interest, which in turn had need of peace and co-operation, and that nothing was gained by imposing protective tariffs or waging war. Unbroken peace was a possibility when industry was built up in preference to military might and when the right economic principles had come to be regarded as self-evident by the masses. Enlightened self-interest was for Lecky the *summum bonum*, the rational principle which would lead mankind towards a brighter destiny.

> 'If one observes human nature, with all its failings, it is nevertheless clear that the influence of enlightened self-interest, first of all on the actions of men, and then on their characters, is sufficient foundation for the whole of civilization; if this principle ceased to operate everything would crumble to dust.'

The liberal utopianism implied in free trade was predominant only for a couple of decades, during that brief period called by G. M. Young 'the High Noon of Victorianism'. Imperialism which, seen in a proper light, could be considered as an extension of the idea of free trade—for it entailed acquiring new, safe and unchallenged marketing areas—also became, through its active and aggressive methods, a reaction to the pacific optimism of the Manchester School. Liberalism was given a new orientation and provided with a theoretical structure in the writings of T. H. Green, which were applied in practice or proclaimed and acclaimed by the radical wing of the Liberal Party. The turning-point between the old and the new Liberalism is thought to have occurred as early as 1880, during Gladstone's second ministry. It caused the whole conception of freedom to assume a different form—as an instance of which, the debate on compulsory elementary education is highly illuminating: in 1870, when the Bill was debated, freedom meant not only freedom from government interference, but something which could also be achieved through the State, as an expansion of the prospects of the individual, by means of measures which formerly had been considered as conducive to a loss of freedom. The principle of free trade, for example, after 1880 and the subsequent transformation of liberalism, was degraded from a utopian ideal to a recourse of merely practical expediency, only to be slowly obliterated from the ideological debate in the period between the two World Wars.

Laissez-Faire and Industrialism

The principles of economic liberalism were made accessible to a wider public by means of simplified, easily understood summaries in which the explanations had been pruned of all qualifications or statements which might be open to question. This treatment freed 'the dismal science' of its drearier features, which might have proved both intellectually and morally discouraging to the lay reader. The facts could be learnt in a couple of hours from one of these little primers by anybody who could read; and the truths they expounded gave an absolute guarantee that self-regarding actions of the individual would redound to the benefit of all, and that freedom of contract would lead to social harmony and universal progress. Very likely it was not so much Adam Smith and David Ricardo or even Brougham and Macaulay who made the deepest impression on the popular mind, as a little band of popularizers, now almost completely forgotten.

Mrs Marcet, daughter of a rich Swiss merchant settled in London, and one of the best known of these popularizers in her day, tried to make the dismal science easily assimilable even by young ladies. Her *Conversations on Political Economy* (1816), 'in which the Elements of that Science are familiarly explained', was widely read on both sides of the Channel and went into fourteen editions in England. Mrs Marcet conveyed her information in a series of imaginary conversations between Caroline, a lady of good family and her governess Mrs B. In the second of the introductory question-and-answer exchanges in which Mrs B. clears the ground before really getting down to business, Caroline says: 'I find that you are constantly talking of wealth: of the causes which produce it: of the means of augmenting it. To be rich, to be very rich, richer than other people, seems to be the great aim of political economy.' She asks whether political economy, which teaches people how to get rich, is not a vulgar and dangerous science. On the contrary, Mrs B answers:

> 'Far from exciting an inordinate desire of wealth or power, it tends to moderate all unjustifiable ambition, by showing that the surest means of increasing national prosperity are peace, security, and justice; that jealously between nations is as prejudicial as between individuals; that each finds its advantage in reciprocal benefits; and that far from growing rich at each other's expense they mutually assist each other by a liberal system of commerce. Political economy is particularly inimical to the envious, jealous and malignant passions; and if ever peace and moderation should flourish in the world, it is to enlightened views of this science that we should be indebted for the miracle.'

In the conversations which follow, Mrs B. gives her reasons. Property, which is based on personal effort and division of labour, has come into existence with civilization. The possibility of increased production and heightened profit has also become a reality. The division of labour (she means, of course, work in factories) is not, as is sometimes maintained, accompanied by monotony and boredom; it gives people the opportunity of working together and living in towns and this leads to a richer life, both intellectually and socially. The rich man and the poor man have basically common interests:

'. . . the rich man exchanges with the labourer the produce or work that is already done. It is thus that he acquires a command over the labour of the poor, and increases his wealth by the profits he derives from it. . . . If the value produced by the labourer exceeds what he has consumed, the excess will constitute an income to his employer; and observe that an income can be obtained by no other means than by the employment of the poor.'

In this way, the labouring classes consume and reproduce the wealth of the rich. 'Wealth thus destined for re-production by the employment of labourers, is called capital.'

'The rich and the poor', says Mrs B., 'are necessary to each other; it is precisely the fable of the belly and the limbs; without the rich the poor would starve; without the poor the rich would be compelled to labour for their own subsistence.' The rich man, however, cannot give to the poor man the whole profit of his labour, for in that case it would be senseless to employ him. The rich man must have a share of the value produced by the work, the share that the labourer does not need for his livelihood. Nor must this profit be regarded as evil. 'So far from considering the profits which the capitalist derives from his labourers as an evil,' adds Mrs B., 'I have always thought it one of the most beneficent ordinations of Providence, that the employment of the poor should be a necessary step to the increase of the wealth of the rich.'

The rich can do no better service to the poor than by employing them as wage-earners. If the poor become too numerous, wages will drop until the balance has been restored by a rise in infant mortality. The poor should therefore be taught not to multiply beyond a certain limit. They ought also to be urged to ensure their security by thrift and through friendly societies. Poor relief is a dangerous expedient as the working man will consequently be disinclined to save and the rich, owing to the increased taxation involved will be forced to employ fewer labourers or else lower the wages of the number who are employed. 'Nature has wisely attached happiness to the gradual acquisition, rather than to the actual possession of wealth, thus rendering it an incitement to industry; and we shall hereafter see that this progressive state of prosperity is most conducive also to the happiness of the nation.'

Mrs B., in conclusion, tells Caroline that it is consequently in the best interest of society if the individual acts in his own interest, for he then invests his money in enterprises which give the greatest profit, and these are the essential conditions for the gratification of general needs.

An authoress who was to become more famous than Mrs Marcet, Harriet Martineau, was inspired by Mrs Marcet's little book to devote her own efforts to writing on economy. Miss Martineau presented economic liberalism in an even more popular way than her predecessor, by the copious production of brief didactic novels, twenty-three of them in nine volumes, under the collective title of *Illustrations of Political Economy*. The novels provided detailed commentaries on the ideas of Adam Smith, Malthus and Ricardo, interwoven with the plots of simple fictional romances. Their success was instantaneous and they were soon translated into a number of foreign languages, including Swedish (1834–36). In *Brooke and Brooke Farm* (1832), Miss Martineau made it clear, among other things, that big estates are desirable, since they render possible a complete division of labour and thus facilitate production on a large scale. However, the capitalist's own interest with regard to the land as well as other branches of the economy should be the deciding factor: 'The interference of the law is injurious; as may be seen by the tendency of the law of Succession in France to divide properties too large, and of the law of Primogeniture in England to consolidate them too extensively.'

Weal and Woe in Garveloch (1832), is concerned mainly with an explanation of the principle of population of Malthus and combines the information with Ricardo's theory of rent, in its reference to land rent. The theme of *A Manchester Strike* (1832), is the futility of trade unions and strikes. The population tends to increase more rapidly than capital; wages, therefore, tend to drop to a bare subsistence level. A maximal wage, that is 'the highest point to which wages can be permanently raised . . . which leaves to the capitalist just profit enough to make it worth his while to invest his capital', can be reached only when the supply of labour offered to the capitalist falls short of the demand and is therefore insignificant in relation to capital. Fundamentally, then, the rate of wages is mainly determined by the sellers, not the buyers of labour, because the supply of labour is regulated by the labourers themselves. The condition of labourers may best be improved, partly by inventions and discoveries which create capital, partly by husbanding instead of wasting capital: for instance, by making savings instead of supporting strikes, and above all,

> 'BY ADJUSTING THE PROPORTION OF POPULATION TO CAPITAL . . . Nothing can permanently affect the proportion of population to capital. Legislation does not affect this proportion, and is therefore useless. Strikes affect it only by wasting capital, and are therefore worse than useless.'

Her series of novels on economy, unique in literature, made Miss Martineau famous and they enjoyed an enormous circulation. Queen Victoria was taught political economy from them as a young girl, and they attracted the attention of Louis Philippe and Tsar Nicholas I of Russia, who both for a time contemplated ordering them to be used in schools. The plan, however, was shelved by both monarchs when it became known that Miss Martineau's opinions on other subjects left something to be desired. She had, for example, criticized Louis-Philippe's father, Philippe Egalité, and she had written with indignant compassion about the fate of the Polish rebels condemned to serve long terms of imprisonment in Siberia.

During the first half of the early nineteenth century the 'factory question', which was what would later be called the working men's question or simply the social question, was primarily little more than the question of industrial working hours. Social policy, with the exception of poor relief, consisted for the most part in the Factory Laws which limited working hours. As early as 1802 the first steps had been taken to shorten working hours by law to twelve hours a day for certain categories of apprentices. Subsequently, at intervals, notably in 1819, 1825 and 1833, further restrictive laws were passed which regulated the working hours of minors. In 1847 the reformists achieved their main objective, a ten-hour industrial working day for women and children. The work of adult men in the majority of industries was dependent on simultaneous work by women and children, so this meant that the ten-hour day for all workers became the rule in most factories. During the following decades the Factory Laws underwent more detailed improvements, their scope was extended and stricter regulations were laid down to control their application.

A scrutiny of the most important contributions and debates on the factory question seems to indicate that the principles of economic liberalism played a great part as a motive in the demand for these reforms. In Parliament it was always pointed out as a matter of principle that interferences in freedom of contract (in the case of child labour the parents' right of contract was the primary consideration) were to be condemned, and that therefore laws ought not to be made at all, or at least not more than was proved absolutely necessary. But the discussion of this nicety, as might be supposed, was not pursued with any doctrinary insistence. Very likely this was to some extent because the question of the factory workers, in a sense, ran parallel with the principal tenets of economic liberalism; the leading economists had seldom commented on the matter and some of them, like Malthus and McCulloch and subsequently John Stuart Mill, had expressed their agreement with the need for Factory Laws. The standing argument against the reform was: partly that it would lead to a decrease in production and thereby be instrumental in the loss to Britain of her industrial and trade supremacy; and partly that it would cause a drop in wages, particularly respecting the earnings of the children of poor working-class families. The economist Nassau William Senior was quoted to the effect that the profits of industry in England depended entirely on the last two working hours of each day. Before the abolition of the Corn Laws it was often maintained that if tariffs were abolished industry would quite easily be able to give the labourer increased advantages and that the question of working hours would then resolve itself just as the factory workers' question had done. The positive arguments for regulating working hours were mainly humanitarian and moral. The leaders of the reform, without much fear of contradiction on this point, laid great emphasis on the outrage of small children spending twelve to fifteen hours daily in the factories, mills and mines; that a whole class was growing up which lived without joy, without education and—a point often considered of paramount importance—with no opportunity or hope of any moral or religious up-bringing. The inconvenience to industry of the curtailment of working hours was denied, or reduced to its proper proportions; it was believed that a shorter working day made labourers work better and the improved health of the working man compensated, at least in the long run, for the loss of working hours.

Especially after it had been decided to impose certain restrictions, it was only exceptionally that the principal liberal arguments made their appearance in discussions of the problem. A typical instance of this was the great debate on the Ten Hours' Bill in the Commons in January 1846. Hardly a speaker rejected the Liberal theories. The most objective and fundamental statement was made by Macaulay in a violent attack on the idea that the principle of freedom of contract would prevent a stricter legislation of working hours. This principle, he said, must give way before predominant and powerful reasons such as considerations of the health and morality of the people which spoke against its application; in such cases freedom of contract even for adults could and should be restricted. Only where 'purely commercial transactions' were concerned would government interference be unjustified. The premier, Sir Robert Peel, who, in contrast to Macaulay, vigorously opposed the reform, answered that this part of Macaulay's statement closed open doors. Macaulay's criticism, he continued, affected at the utmost ten members of the House, who thought that 'the principles of Free Trade without restrictions must decide our legislation on such matters as the Health, Education and the Morals of the people'. For the majority the question of principle had been settled long ago; it was only a matter of judging how far to go in regulating working hours to suit different circumstances. The Whig leader, Lord Russell, expressed more or less the same opinions; the leader of the protectionist group, Lord George Bentinck, did the same; both of them, moreover, held the same point of view on the question as Macaulay. The retreat of the principle of *laissez-faire* on this important point was, as can be seen from what has gone before, 'not dependent on the attidude and efforts of any one party'. It has often been claimed that the Tories were the driving force in early socio-political legislation. Admittedly this party was generally critical of industrialism and a number of Conservative intellectuals and statesmen (and among the latter Disraeli stood out in a way which had no parallel among the liberals of the time) demanded social reforms on principle. It is also a fact that the man who was more active than anybody else in bringing about the regulation of working hours, Lord Ashley, later Lord Shaftesbury, was a Tory and even extremely conservative in religious and constitutional matters. Nevertheless, it is on the whole a mistake to say that the Conservatives were specially active in social legislation. Disraeli approached social problems mainly in his novels and in some of his early political writings, but his practical contribution to the solution of these problems was unimportant; he took no part before 1850 in the debates on working hours. Lord Shaftesbury was for several years a sort of deputy for the unions in questions concerning factory shifts. His successor in this capacity was nevertheless a radical Liberal, John Fielden. In the final ballots the whole party line broke down; Whigs and Tories were to be found on both sides in more or less equal proportions. Among those who were generally against the proposed reform were Conservatives like Peel and Graham, Whigs like Brougham and Melbourne, Manchester School Liberals like Cobden and Bright. After 1846 the Peelites presented a relatively united front, and in particular represented the industrial wing of the Conservative Party. It was also said that a definite line of division on the question separated landowners from industrialists. This was partly correct; the landowners readily attacked the abuses and defects of industry, while the industrialists in their social criticism and demands for reform were more inclined to make agriculture their target. Mere viewpoints, however (not necessarily conditional on class or occupation), played no great part in determining which side members were on. Shaftesbury was a landowner and landlord, Fielden an industrialist; among those who advocated restriction of working hours and wanted them enforced by law, were several industrialists who had found it impossible to achieve this by private agreement with their labourers. Finally, it must be pointed out that in a few cases temporary party-political circumstances strongly influenced the results of the ballot. Following the Conservative Party split in the spring of 1846, many of the landed gentry who had supported protective tariffs, and shortly before that had voted with the opposition or had abstained from voting, both spoke and voted for the ten-hour working day; but in all probability this was related to the fact that Peel's government, which they wanted to overthrow by all possible means, sided with the Conservatives on the issue.

John Maynard Keynes, in *Laissez-Faire and Industry* (1926), pointed out that no economist of authority had had very much to say in favour of *laissez-faire* after the time of John Stuart Mill, and even less after 1870, when John Elliot Cairnes, the Irish political economist (1823–75), 'perhaps the first orthodox economist to deliver a frontal attack upon *laissez-faire* in general', had said, in a lecture he gave at the University of London, that: 'The maxim of *laissez-faire* has no scientific basis whatsoever, but is at best a mere handy rule of practice', Keynes's observation about the reaction of economists of repute against *laissez-faire* might be stretched to cover practically all of the principal social sciences. Two exponents of economic and political philosophy who can be taken to represent variants of the new liberalism were William Stanley Jevons (1835–82), who held the Chair of Political Economy at University College, London (1876–81), and Henry Sidgwick (1838–1900), Professor of Moral Philosophy at Trinity College, Cambridge for the last seventeen of the forty-odd years he spent there.

Jevons, who achieved his fame through purely theoretical analysis, published two lectures in the early 1880s, *The State in Relation to Labour* (1882) and *Methods of Social Reform* (1883), both of which defined with precision his attitude to the social problems of his day. His general point of departure, indicated in the first of the two lectures, can be said to be utilitarian, in that he declared 'the general welfare' or 'the happiness of the people' to be the aim of government. But similar statements of Jevons, not to mention those of a number of other writers of that and later periods, must not be taken to indicate support of utilitarianism in the stricter sense of the word. Utiliarianism is remarkable partly for the fact that its devotees set utility or felicity as their aim, and thought that by so doing they could break free from older metaphysical concepts, primarily from 'natural rights', and partly because they believed that by means of these new principles they could build up a complete and universally applicable social system.

When Jevons and others talked about happiness as an aim it was really to emphasize their rejection of metaphysics based on 'natural rights', not to mention all kinds of other concepts which purported by means of *a priori* reasoning to lay down rules for the functioning of government and the community, and not least the system of utilitarianism as such. These economists did not make calculations about 'felicity' like Bentham and the two Mills; they had no thought of singling out the principle of happiness as the basic axiom from which, through a series of logical inferences, deductions and conclusions, answers to every possible social problem could be produced. The principle of happiness (or utility) became for Jevons and his followers primarily a way of expressing a general relativism. Of course this did not prevent their use of language, as it did not prevent that of the utilitarians, from being ambiguous and open to attack. What is happiness? Whose happiness? How would or could pleasurable sensations be summarized or classified? —and so on. Such criticism is somewhat meaningless, since the principle of happiness was not really used as a basic postulate, but to serve as a warning against 'systems' of all kinds; as merely a simple, though in effect vague, means of expressing a fundamental evaluation.

What is characteristic of Jevons is his attempt to judge each social problem on its own merits, without making any concessions to *a priori* reasoning. In essence, nevertheless, his attempt reveals a partiality for the established order of things; all radical reforms lay beyond his range of vision. But it also implied—and in this connection this is the important point—an independent attitude to general dogma, a refusal to be bound by them when it came to taking a stand on specific issues. Jevons was clear on this point in *The State in Relation to Labour* where he said:

> 'I venture to maintain . . . that we shall do much better in the end if we throw off the incubus of metaphysical ideas and expressions. We must resolve all these supposed principles and rights into facts and probabilities which they are found to involve when we inquire into their real meaning.'

He started out from the postulate that 'the State is justified in passing any law, or even in doing any single act which, without ulterior consequences, adds to the sum total of happiness'. He went on to say:

> 'As, then, in philosophy the first step is to begin by doubting everything, so in social philosophy, or rather in practical legislation, the first step is to throw aside all supposed rights or inflexible principles. The fact is that legislation is not a science at all. . . . It is a matter of practical work, creating human institutions.'

Having enunciated this relativistic fundamental principle, Jevons proceeded to examine the concepts of freedom and right of property. The basic theory of personal individual freedom, so frequently adduced as an argument against state interference, could not, he declared, be given much importance. Freedom was only a means to an end, not the end in itself, and as it was to some extent in conflict with general interests of society, freedom must take second place. No complete freedom of contract, he said, had ever existed; it had, for example, been prohibited for centuries, ever since the time of Edward IV, to make payment in barter, and this was because 'repeated inquiry and long experience have shown that masters abuse the liberty of making barter contracts with their workmen'. When new forms of intervention were found to be beneficial to any given portion of the community or to society as a whole, they should be put into practice without hesitation. Consequently, legislation on working hours and other working conditions, public health and domestic sanitation, ought to be planned with regard to what was suitable to each particular case. The same applied to the right of property. Unlimited right of disposal had never been inherent in ownership; taxation and the possibility of expropriation already implied considerable restrictions. The question which it was important to solve in every individual case was whether the right of property, or any given right of disposal connected with this right, was advantageous or not to society: 'Every single act ought to be judged separately as regards the balance of good and evil which it produces.' The importance of Jevons's ideas lay in his rejection of all assumptions which were in sympathy with certain old-liberal principles.

Jevons's evaluation of judgment *in casu* was linked with the emphasis he placed on the importance of the fact that in matters of legislation men allow themselves to be guided by experience; he therefore recommended thorough empirical investigation as an aid to the work of legislation. 'We cannot possibly dispense with general reasoning, but we should use it as sparingly as possible. We should choose, as it were, the lowest logical elevation within sight.' Jevons also insisted that legislation should be evolved as far as possible through experimentation. 'Before passing any great Act of Parliament which will involve the whole of an extensive trade or class in some irrevocable and costly change, we ought to try experiments, and thus obtain the most direct and pertinent evidence concerning the probable result.'

When he dealt with individual problems, however, it was evident that the social reforms he advocated were quite moderate. His views on socialization were almost without exception critical. The rights to private enterprise and private ownership were necessary, he thought, on the same grounds as those on which John Stuart Mill considered them necessary, to ensure a progressive rise in production.

State management, Jevons said, was as a rule wasteful and inefficient; as an example of this he cited the fantastic mismanagement of the dockyards, which were under the control of the Admiralty and were 'the very types of incompetent and wasteful expenditure' characteristic of State management and monopoly. He continued:

> 'It seems to me that State management possesses advantages under the following conditions. 1. Where numberless wide-spread operations can only be effectively connected, united, and co-ordinated, in a single, all-extensive Government system. 2. Where the operations possess an invariable routine-like character. 3. When they are performed under the public eye or for the service of individuals, who will immediately detect and expose any failure or laxity. 4. Where there is but little capital expenditure, so that each year's revenue and expense account shall represent, with sufficient accuracy, the real commercial conditions of the department.'

It was evident, he thought, that all these conditions were combined 'in the highest perfection' in the Post Office; while a telegraph system appeared to him to possess the characteristics which favoured unification and State management almost in as high a degree as the Post Office. Conversely, he thought that the railways should remain in private hands. The system was too complicated ('railway traffic cannot be managed by pure routine'), vast capital was required and maintenance was quite beyond the abilities of government officials. Having studied the proposals for railway reform, he advised against such a hazardous enterprise as the purchase and reorganization of the railways, and was 'inclined to think that the actual working of our railways by a Government department is altogether out of the question, while our English Government remains what it is'. Even on questions of State or communal activities other than so-called business enterprises, Jevons made very fine distinctions. He accepted the system of compulsory education regulated by the State, in consideration of the necessity of universal education. He approved of government-run public libraries, museums, parks, band concerts and such-like amenities.

'The main *raison d'être* of free public libraries, as indeed of public museums, art-galleries, parks, halls, public clocks, and many other kinds of public works, is the enormous increase of utility which is thereby acquired for the community at a trifling cost.' That such facilities could be organized and centralized for the use of the public was 'a striking case of what I propose to call *the principle of the multiplication of utility*, a principle which lies at the base of some of the most important processes of political economy, including the division of labour'. On the other hand he rejected poor relief and free medical attention. These were matters of common personal needs to which it was normal for the individual to pay due attention, without relying on outside help or guidance.

Jevons deplored widespread poverty but, contrary to economists of fifty years earlier, considered it to be a natural and inevitable condition of society. It was mainly in the deficiencies of legislation throughout centuries, both in legislative sins of omission and—even more—commission, that the reasons for the poverty of the masses must be sought. With regard to the solution of the social problem, his opinions seem to have undergone a significant change during the 1860s and 1870s. In a lecture on 'Trades Societies, their objects and policy', which he gave in Manchester, at their request, to the Trades Unionists' Political Association, in March 1868, he praised 'trade societies' which, he said 'usually combine the character of Benefit and Friendly Societies with those of strict Trades Societies'. He even conceded their ability to secure a reduction of working hours; but his praise was tempered with some reservation. 'It is impossible, in my opinion', he said, 'wholly to praise or wholly to blame a great and widespread institution like that of Trades Societies', but:

> 'So far am I from wishing that the workmen of England should cease to associate and unite together, that I believe some kind of association to be indispensible to the progress and amelioration of the largest and in some respects most important class in the population. . . . No one who looks upon the growing numbers and improving organization of the Trades Societies can doubt that they will play a considerable part in the history of the kingdom. But the greater their extent and influence become, the more essential it is that they should be well advised and really liberal in their aims and actions. It is in their power to do almost incalculable good or harm to themselves and the country of which they form so considerable a part.'

In contrast to their prospects of changing working conditions, he disputed the ability of the trades unions to influence the standard of wages of the working class. A certain labour group which could resort to organized action with relative ease could, he conceded, force up wages, but this was only because the prices of the commodities concerned were raised, which in turn lowered the standards of living of other groups of workmen. Jevons accordingly held to the traditional view that a wage increase obtained by diminishing the profits of a business was out of the question, since the employer compensated for increased wages by an increase in price. Jevons counted on the formation of co-operatives by the workmen in many branches of industry. Like other economists he recommended thrift, and a better upbringing and education.

Fourteen years later, in *The State in Relation to Labour* (1882), Jevons had adopted a more advanced viewpoint. His firm conviction of the value of socio-political legislation has already been mentioned. Even now he advocated co-operative societies, though he seemed not to believe in their importance as much as formerly; the earlier widespread belief that this form of co-operation would provide a solution to the social problem had at that time and in the light of past experience become weaker. In the same book, on the other hand, Jevons thought that the solution would be reached in the future through a sort of co-operation between employer and workman, whereby, over and above his wages, the workman would receive a share of the profits of the enterprise.

> 'I wish to see the workmen becoming by degrees their own capitalists —sharers in all the profits and all the advantages which capital confers. . . . The present doctrine is that the workman's interests are limited to those of other workmen, and the employer's interests to those of other employers. Eventually it must be seen that industrial divisions

should be perpendicular, not horizontal. The workman's interests should be bound up with those of his employer, and should be pitted in fair competition against those of other workmen and employers. There would then be no arbitrary rates of wages, no organized strikes, no long disputes rendering business uncertain and hazardous. The best workman would seek out the best master, and the best master the best workmen. Zeal to produce the best and cheapest and most abundant goods would take the place of zeal in obstructive organization.'

This statement did not exactly accord with Jevon's earlier remarks about the impossibility for trades unions in general of increasing wages except on condition that—as Jevons conceived it—part of the sum which had formerly been paid out as wages would in future assume the character of a share of the profits. In that case no real improvement in workmen's terms of employment would ever follow from a profit-sharing system. Such a system, as Jevon's line of thought indicated, could well be proposed as a means of creating in workmen a feeling of solidarity towards the enterprise, rather than as a means to direct improvement in the stanrdard of living of the working man.

The profit-sharing system, like co-operative production, contributed little of real importance to the solution of the labour question. When the third, posthumous, edition of *The State in Relation to Labour* was issued in 1894, its publisher Michael Cababé pointed out with every justification that: 'There is something pathetic in looking back and contemplating the expectations of John Stuart Mill, Thornton, Cairnes, Jevons, and many others from the spread of Co-operative Production, and the industrial transformation, surely, if slowly, to be worked all through its instrumentality.'

The fairly numerous attempts made to introduce both co-operative production and the profit-sharing system either misfired completely or were insignificant. Co-operative production as a rule, seemed to suffer from ineffectual management owing partly to a number of closely-allied management difficulties; it was impossible to form such societies because of the difficulties of obtaining capital; the workmen preferred to place their savings in 'safe' enterprises rather than risk them in ventures which they had to organize themselves. In enterprises which successfully adopted the profit-sharing system, basic wages had not exceeded the average and, generally speaking, no change in the attitude of the workmen to such enterprises was observed. As for other causes of the failure of these systems, it has been suggested that the feeling of solidarity and pursuit of a common goal which social democracy and the trades union movement evoked in the working class, turned them against all organizations of this kind.

The political and social theories of Henry Sidgwick are most concisely and lucidly expressed in his *Elements of Politics* (1891); and this work is complemented primarily by *Principles of Political Economy* (1883), and a few essays on socialist theories and their significance in the context of the national economy. Sometimes, and not without reason, Sidgwick is considered to be the last of the utilitarians. He started out generally from the basic postulates of utilitarianism and believed that from that standpoint he could draw detailed conclusions about political and social questions. His point of view, however, differed considerably, both in principle and detail, from that of his utilitarian forerunners.

In *Elements of Politics* Sidgwick said he thought a book was needed 'which would expound, within a convenient compass, and in as systematic a form as the subject-matter might admit, the chief general considerations that enter into the rational discussion of political questions in modern states'. In order to explain the scope and methods and to frame the maxims and precepts of 'Practical Politics', it was necessary, he said, to start out from a group of human beings living under particular developmental conditions:

> 'we must assume certain general characteristics of man and his circumstances—characteristics belonging not to mankind universally, but to civilized man in the most advanced stage of his development: and we must consider what laws and institutions are likely to conduce most to the well-being of an aggregate of such beings living in social relations.'

Politics, he said, must therefore be based not on history but on psychology:

> 'the fundamental assumptions in our political reasonings consist of certain propositions as to human motives and tendencies, which are derived primarily from the ordinary experience of civilized life, though they find adequate confirmation in the facts of ancient and recent history of our own and other civilized countries. These propositions, it should be observed, are not put forward as exactly or universally true, even of contemporary civilized man; but only as sufficiently near the truth for practical purposes.'

There was a duality of meaning in these basic ideas of Sidgwick's, as the quotations should show. On the one hand he seemed to wish to formulate for a civilized human society political axioms which should be objectively tenable, insofar as they were presumably accurate with respect to the nature of human beings living in such societies. On the other hand he would appear to have grafted on to this 'human nature' even the most commonly-held views on political matters. This last

6. Charles Darwin. (Photograph by Julia Margaret Cameron, 1869)

7. Thomas Huxley, *c.* 1860

8. William Ewart Gladstone. (Photography by W. E. Young)

9. Benjamin Disraeli, *c.* 1878

point proved repeatedly to be an important element in his method, inasmuch as he would formulate some particular axiom in the presumption that this or that concept actually existed. It is obvious, however, that Sidgwick did not wish to give a mere statement of prevailing opinion but that he attempted to outline a plan of action which should be appropriate in relation to the framework chosen for his investigation, even if it was not considered to be so by the standards of general opinion. The confusion present in all this gives to Sidgwick's political writings an obscurity all his own.

In a subsequent chapter, Sidgwick declared that he, like the majority of people, considered 'that the true standard and criterion by which right legislation is to be distinguished from wrong is the conduciveness to the general "good" or "welfare" '. By this he meant 'in the last analysis, the happiness of the individual human beings who compose the community; provided that we take into account not only the human beings who are actually living, but those who are to live hereafter'.

The legislative measures which he then discussed can be divided into two groups. The first comprised interference in the interests of the individual by state coercion. Such interference, wrote Sidgwick, was usually considered undesirable in civilized communities. The grounds for this were that 'men, on the average, are more likely to know what is for their own interest than government is, and to have a keener concern for promoting it . . .'. He went on to say that even if the direct effects of coercion were beneficial, 'its indirect effects in the way of weakening the self-reliance and energy of individuals, and depriving them of the salutory lessons of experience, are likely to outweigh the benefit'. Moreover, such laws were likely to be evaded, as the persons primarily concerned were not interested in observing them, and in any case, 'if any little good were done by this kind of legislation, it would not be worth the expense entailed by it both of money and the energies of statesmen need for other functions . . .'; finally, such laws would lead to a dangerous increase of 'paternalistic' power on the part of the government. These reasons were not always valid, however, but they implied all together a strong presumption that legislation of the kind indicated was undesirable. The other group of legislative measures purported to exercise compulsion on individuals in such a way as to increase the welfare of other individuals. This group comprised two kinds of measure: those which conduced to useful actions and those which prohibited harmful ones. Measures of the first kind were as a rule undesirable. As Sidgwick wrote:

> 'Most of us would generally accept . . . that the services which men have to render to others should be rendered, as far as possible, with

a genuine regard to the interests of others . . . But it is generally held that it is the business of the moralist and the preacher, not of the legislator, to aim at producing in the community this habit of thought and feeling . . .'.

Only legislation of the second type, accordingly, was in principle desirable. Both types fell inside the framework of a principle for determining the nature and limits of governmental interference, which Sidgwick called 'Individualism'. The requirement which stipulated 'that one sane adult, apart from contract or claim to reparation, shall contribute positively by money or services to the support of the others', he called 'socialistic'. The legislation of modern civilized communities, he said, was in the main framed on an individualistic basis, and his subsequent arguments were aimed at showing in part which legislative measures were desirable from the individualistic standpoint, and in part, to what extent such legislation should be modified to attain the greatest possible degree of welfare.

Having disposed of his main introductory chapters, Sidgwick went on to discuss which government interventions were desirable, or at least conceivable, from the individualistic standpoint, 'the individualistic minimum', as he put it. Only a couple of the many problems he discussed can be commented on here. Property—the exclusive and unlimited use of property—was explained from an individualistic standpoint as motivated by the fact that it was based on work, whether it arose from production or from the preservation of property, and because the work would never have been undertaken without the stimulus afforded by the exclusive right of disposal: property, moreover, stimulated the production of useful objects. Certain limitations of ownership were necessary, however, in some cases. For example, copyright in a literary work should not have unlimited duration, limits should be set to the duration of patents on inventions, and restrictions could be introduced concerning the right of a landowner to valuable minerals found on his property. Freedom of contract was, in principle, valuable. Persons of mature judgment, guided by enlightened self-interest—and it was these at which the individualistic theory was aimed—members of a civilized society, ought to regulate their rights and obligations themselves, by contract. Exceptions to the rule of the binding power of such agreement were thought to be necessary in certain cases, as when contracts were arrived at by compulsion or fraud. In the case of children, and also to a certain extent in the case of women, the State should establish limitations not usually required. Sidgwick made similar statements concerning the right of inheritance and the right of bequest. He regarded even these as means of encouraging production by giving an owner the full right of disposal of his possessions. He thought, for instance, that to limit the right of bequest to a stipulated maximum, as Mill had recommended,

> 'would dangerously diminish the motives to industry, and—what is yet more important—thrift, in the latter part of the lives of the persons who came under the restrictions. Moreover, any interference running strongly counter to the natural inclination of such persons would be likely to be extensively evaded by donation before death.'

Nevertheless, Sidgwick believed that State intervention should go far beyond the 'individualistic minimum'. Many measures regarded in a broad sense as socialistic would be justified as being devoted to the promotion of the general welfare. The individualistic principle which led to *laissez-faire* was right only in a broad sense, and ought therefore to be modified with regard to experience in different areas and circumstances. *Laissez-faire* could result in a monopoly by certain individuals or organizations. In such cases the State or the community would be justified in intervening and eventually in taking over the production concerned. 'When a whole industry in a certain district, from technical or other causes, tends to take on the character of a monopoly . . . even the weightiest economic objections to such public intervention fall away in every connection.' With this statement Sidgwick justified so-called communal socialism in particular. The State could similarly set up enterprises which, though considered of use to the community, would be difficult or impossible to realize by voluntary agreement. Postal and telegraphic services ought to be managed by the State, whereas railways could be privately owned. The State would also be entitled to establish regulations designed to be advantageous to those most closely interested in one or other enterprise but which could not be established by voluntary agreement in view of special advantages which the breach of any such agreement would bring to those who chose to ignore it—Sunday restrictions, for example, would hardly be possible except by legal enforcement. State regulation of education was legitimate, Sidgwick believed, because it encouraged ability and enterprise and was above all the means to moral and intellectual improvement. In special cases he believed that the State could step in to help certain indigent groups of the population, since this was directly related to the principle of utility or felicity.

Sidgwick also entered into the question as to what extent measures aimed at a more even distribution of income were justified. 'Human common sense', he said, accepted Bentham's axioms concerning the relation between prosperity and happiness and that increasing prosperity was followed as a rule by increasing happiness, but beyond a certain limit of prosperity happiness no longer increased in proportion to prosperity; from which it followed, that the more a society approached equality of prosperity, the greater was the individual's common happiness in that society. But this view applied only under certain conditions, which were: that the existing wealth which was to be shared was not diminished by the alteration in its distribution; that the number of persons among whom the wealth was distributed should not increase; and that the change should not diminish happiness in so far as it depended on other factors other than wealth and prosperity. Sidgwick discussed these points in detail and arrived at the conclusion that equalization of this nature involved significant risks.

Under a system of equality a decline in industry was to be expected, with a resulting decrease in wealth; and with the diminished accumulation of capital on which the progress of industry depended, inducements to industry and thrift would be diminished. There was also the possibility that the population would increase more rapidly than before equalization. Besides, wealth contributed actively to general intellectual and cultural development, both directly and by means of assistance to others, and as a result it even contributed indirectly to the happiness of each member of a society. This being so, said Sidgwick, the probability was that equalization would be the cause of a decline in culture or would at least retard its rapid growth, with a consequent diminution of average individual happiness.

In this connection Sidgwick treated socialism as an extreme means of reaching a more balanced economy. By socialization he meant, therefore, state expropriation of the means of production and the exploitation of those means in such a way as to do full justice to the demand for equality. Broadly speaking he believed that the general arguments against equality were relevant even to a socialistic organization. Salaried officials could not be expected to display the same energy and initiative as men engaged in private enterprise; this view was brought forward as the principal argument against state management. A gradual expansion of government activity, however, could be considered advantageous, though startling results, whether affecting morale or welfare, were hardly to be expected. Sidgwick advocated voluntary associations of the co-operative type for both producers and consumers, though he held out little hope that such a recourse would provide any solution to the social problem.

During the last decade of the nineteenth century, *laissez-faire* could still count on staunch supporters in England whenever social problems came under discussion. One of the foremost of them was the sociologist Herbert Spencer. In his numerous writings, from *The Proper Sphere of Government* (1843) to *The Man versus the State* (1884), Spencer consistently defended liberal principles and his criticism of government intervention progressively increased in sharpness as the Liberal party, which he had joined, modified its original policies. Even his sociological system was supported by liberal thinking; evolution, as he believed he could demonstrate, tended toward greater differentiation and simultaneously toward 'natural' harmony, independent of government activity. In political and social terms this meant first and foremost that the ancient *régime of status*, as he called it, in which people and social groups occupied long-established and unchanging positions and functions (as exemplified in feudalism) had been replaced by a *régime of contract* based on freedom of contract and the free choice of occupation; this change was a sign of the development of an agrarian and militaristic society to one which was industrial, commercial and peace-loving. A régime of contract which should give the people full freedom to develop their abilities and satisfy their needs and which, moreover, would entail a maximum of social integration, could be completely successful only if state action were limited to maintaining the judicial system and defence and leaving all the rest to private enterprise. The state should be only 'a limited liability company for mutual insurance'.

As a result of the campaigning for government intervention which was pushed forward in the 1860s and 1870s under the leadership or with the collaboration of the Liberals, Spencer wrote *The Man versus the State*, which was an indictment of his Liberal contemporaries. Formerly, he said, the Tories had represented the antiquated *régime of status*, while the Liberals were the representatives of the *régime of contract*. Now Liberalism had begun to take on the aspect of a new form of Toryism. One would have to go back again to *laissez-faire*. Spencer's reasoning displayed all the classic modes of thought typical of economic liberalism, but the most interesting thing about it was that he tried to support them by fresh viewpoints borrowed from biology and anthropology. After Darwin, biology had shown that natural selection, through survival of the fittest, was achieved through fighting and competing. If this process of selection were impeded by the care of society for the weak, then the race would deteriorate. Sociopolitical legislation, for purposes of development from lower to higher forms of life, was therefore contrary to the law of nature. But as Spencer wrote:

> 'And yet, strange to say now that the truth is recognized by most cultivated people—now that the beneficent working of the survival of the fittest has been so impressed on them that, much more than people in past times, they might be expected to hesitate before neutralizing its action—now more than ever before in the history of the world, are they doing all they can to further the survival of the unfittest!'

Only if the successful were enabled freely to enjoy their success and thus also be given the opportunity of reproducing their kind as abundantly as possible, and if those who failed were left to sink back and go under, then and only then would rapid progress be possible. By limiting or obstructing an arrangement ordained by nature, men were attempting 'to improve life by breaking down the basic conditions of life'. 'Little admiration need be felt', Spencer wrote, 'for the proffered sympathies of people who urge on a policy which breaks up progressing societies; and who then look with cynical indifference at the weltering confusion left behind, with all its entailed suffering and death.' Even in other ways and on other issues Spencer looked to 'nature' for confirmation.

He drew attention to passages in popular works on anthropology which seemed to show that liberal axioms concerning inviolability of the right of property and freedom of contract were even applicable to the existence of savages; and he inferred from this that such concepts were natural to the human race. Like so many other political ideologists, Spencer thereupon assumed that savages (in spite of their being called savages because of their inferiority in terms of civilization) would in some way act more 'naturally' and therefore more rationally than culturized peoples.

Spencer also incorporated with these views a peculiar 'law of nature' argument. The great majority had no right of making decisions other than in those areas over which society had established rules. Of course no social contract existed, but it was possible to set up boundaries to limit government action, which should be established when a society was evolved, and these limits were to be respected. Surely, Spencer observed, the members of a society would not want their right to decide what to eat or drink to be decided by the majority. He compared a society with a freely-formed organization, company or club. No question was implied of giving the majority any right of decision other than that concerned with the necessary terms of action for the members of the organization. With regard to a state, these necessary conditions could apply only to the defence of the community against external enemies and to the defence of the individual against internal enemies, that is, criminals. In this fashion Spencer came full circle to the demand, on grounds of purely 'natural' rights, for a limitation of state action. But he set a narrower limit than perhaps any earlier writer. As a consequence, his assumption appears to have been that each citizen would have to be granted a right of veto against every majority decision concerning any matter, other than defence and justice in a limited sense.

In the writings mentioned above, as well as in others, Spencer gave detailed explanations of his views on the limits of state action with reference to particular cases. Social policy, public health, public assistance, according to him, fell outside the sphere of government action, likewise all forms of education. The state should not even run the mint or the postal system, or make special arrangements, for example, for the building of lighthouses and bridges or the promotion of public communications. Every interference of the state—beyond defence and justice—was dangerous, even if the measure in itself seemed expedient. What Spencer called 'empirical utilitarianism'—in contrast to his own rational utilitarianism—meant that in each particular case 'the so-called "practical politician" ' considered only the effects which special measures would have on the actions of a particular group or groups, without taking into account the combined effect on people's lives of an aggregate of these interferences. 'No thought of such a thing as political momentum, still less a political momentum, which, instead of diminishing or remaining constant, increases', ever enters such a politician's mind. 'In this way', Spencer wrote, 'men drift unconsciously towards a more socialistic community in which the individual becomes the slave of society.' The final result of it all would be the rebirth of despotism. A disciplined army of military officials would give the highest power into the hands of its leader, after which

> 'It would need but a war with an adjacent society, or some internal discontent demanding forcible suppression, to at once transform a socialistic administration into a grinding tyranny like that of ancient Peru; under which the mass of the people, controlled by grades of officials, and leading lives that were inspected out-of-doors and in-doors, laboured for the support of the organization which regulated them, and were left with but a bare subsistence for themselves. And then would be completely revived, under a different form, that *régime of status*—that system of compulsory co-operation, the decaying tradition which is represented by the old Toryism, and towards which the new Toryism is carrying us back.'

In *A Plea for Liberty* (1891) a symposium published several years after *The Man versus the State*, a number of writers—including Spencer, who wrote an introductory essay—aimed a broadside of detailed criticism at socialism and socialistic legislation which they believed were about to become a reality. Government interference meant that the State was 'frittering away its time and energies in schemes with which it should have no concern'. The leading theme in these essays was the idea that progress in England was marching towards mass tyranny, a tyranny of the majority riddled with socialistic dogma. They felt that determined action was needed to save basic liberal principles. They explained socialism as synonymous with bureaucracy, which lays a stranglehold on all private enterprise until it ultimately undermines production and leads to general poverty. Socialism, they said, by checking natural selection, destroyed the biological foundations of progress; by levelling everything and everybody it created citizens of stereotyped mediocrity. Government and municipal commercial enterprises, such as postal services and electricity, which were very modest at that time, were regarded, on a basis of undeniable shortcomings, as wasteful and ineffectual. Free compulsory education was regarded as having helped in the destruction of English self-discipline. Free lending libraries which were introduced in some cities and towns at this time, were attacked in the same vein.

> 'That which is got for nothing is valued at nothing. Possibly the advocates of literary pauperism will see little force in the argument that if readers were left to pay for their own books, not only would books be more valued but the moral discipline involved in the small personal sacrifice incurred by saving for such a purpose, would do infinitely more good than any amount of culture obtained at the people's expense. It is true that the Free Library-party strongly repudiate the charge of dishonesty; but it is difficult to see any real difference between the man who goes boldly into his neighbour's house and carries off his neighbour's books, and the man who joins with a majority, and on the authority of the ballot box sends the tax gatherer round to carry off the value of these books.'

The system of free lending libraries really meant that those citizens who liked to read obtained privileges at the expense of others; it would be just as reasonable, or just as unreasonable, for the community to offer free theatres, free concerts, or free sports.

> 'If one man may have his hobby paid for by his neighbours, why not all? Are theatre-goers, lovers of cricket, bicyclists, amateurs of music, and others to have their earnings confiscated and their capacities for indulging in their own special hobbies curtailed, merely to satisfy gluttons of gratuitous novel-reading? A love of books is a great source of pleasure to many, but it is a crazy fancy to suppose that it should be so to all.'

Through interference of this sort, whether it concerned education, libraries or the sale of liquor, self-discipline and self-confidence were destroyed.

> 'We must insist most strongly on the injury done to the pauperized recipients of these favours. Want is the spring of human effort. Self-discipline, self-control, self-reliance, are the habits which grow

> in men who are allowed to act for themselves. The meddlesome forestalling of individual effort, which is being carried into mischievous excess, is going far to bind our poorer classes for another century of dependence.'

By such official coddling the people were deprived not only of the pleasures which came from sacrifices made for something ardently desired, but of the strength of character which is moulded by successfully conquered temptations.

> 'Can we not imagine and by determination realize an England which shall be pure without the supervision of the Vigilance Society, sober—even in the face of a thousand public-houses, open at all hours—and fond of knowledge, although—and even because—knowledge has to be won at the cost of self-denial, being the best inheritance a man can bequeath to his children as the fruit of the exertions of a lifetime?'

Some of the arguments of the essayists quoted above are of little interest today, except as curiosities, but eighty years ago they were probably typical of a considerable body of liberal opinion. These antiquated views keep good company with the references to evolution used as arguments for *laissez-faire*. At the end of the nineteenth century, Darwinism was pressed into service as a guarantee for the most disparate political theories. Militaristic nationalists maintained that wars between nations corresponded with Darwin's 'struggle for existence' and that the victory in this struggle must go to those states or nations which were most fitted to lead mankind onward. Conservative minds saw in the upper classes an *élite* which had been created by centuries of selection and on these grounds maintained that a hierarchic social structure was biologically conditioned. Socialists, using Darwin as a reference, demanded equality, which would give equal opportunity to all and thus lead to 'natural' selection. More than any of the others, the Liberals exploited Darwinian authority for their own ends. Just as human beings, they said, had evolved through free biological competition, so the best type of man would evolve through free social competition. 'The principle of the Survival of the Fittest', wrote J. M. Keynes, years later, 'could be regarded as a vast generalization of the Ricardian economics.' Certain theories which had been hit upon under the pressure of the trend toward social reform, or which expressed new viewpoints of economic liberalism with unprecedented sharpness, began to be constantly discussed.

It became usual to insist that a far-reaching social policy would weaken the energy and undermine the independence of the indigent who received public assistance, and would lead to what might be called 'a dole mentality'. With regard to this, it was claimed by the liberals that they wanted to forge social measures so as to counteract consequences of this kind. Social intervention should be carried out in such a way that the individual would be stimulated to make some positive contribution to the situation. The somewhat obscure slogan which expressed this was 'Help for self-help' and it appeared again and again, with variations, in speeches by Liberals. The expression itself was an attempt to combine the associations of social reform with the ideas of old liberalism. The idea that a social policy, and still more, socialism in its more exact sense, would lead to a general levelling and to an aesthetically as well as morally repulsive mediocrity, also played some part in later discussions of the question, especially in the wilder and more unreflecting pronouncements of demagogues. It seemed to anticipate the concept which claimed that economic differentiation was the essential basis of variation even in other spheres. But there were factors in the foregoing arguments which were felt to carry greater weight. Spencer's warning against empirical utilitarianism, which dealt individually with every problem of government intervention without any thought for the total effect of the contemplated measures, was reflected in many debates. Some or other reform was conceivably well-intentioned on the face of it, but would lead in a dangerous direction and, in combination with other reforms of a like nature, would eventually undermine the liberal social order. In particular, proposals concerning public management of a limited number of enterprises were seen as the thin end of the wedge of a more general process of socialization. Even the arguments employed were naturally not new, since the whole matter had been discussed before in detail by Bentham in his *Book of Fallacies*, but they had a special bearing on this particular question. According to Bentham it was not enough to set up presumptive objections to state intervention. It was felt that such intervention should be rejected out of hand, even if there were overwhelming reasons for permitting it. Spencer's main objections to state socialism and far-reaching government interference in general, namely that they end up in bureaucracy and total dictatorship, are part of modern liberalism's central doctrines.

The Metamorphosis of Freedom

A number of parliamentary debates on various forms of government intervention which were held during the 1860s and 1870s seem to have had certain features in common. The proposer of the Bill would set forth the particular circumstances which appeared to warrant government interference; he would demonstrate, for instance, that a great number of accidents occurred in factories and that these could be prevented by the adoption of certain laws concerning protective measures; or he would draw attention to the fact that insobriety was prejudicial in various ways and could be discouraged by more restrictive legislation of the sale of spirits. The challengers of the proposal would then try to show that the abuses or defects under consideration were less widespread or serious than had been assumed and that the recommended remedies were of doubtful effectiveness or could only be carried out at great cost or inconvenience, points which, as they took care to stress, had been ignored by the advocates of the measure. But to the opposers of the reform these objections were secondary considerations; their fundamental objection went deeper. They argued that the measure was a threat to freedom and that because of the government intervention required for its enforcement citizens would be deprived of their chances of acting and making agreements in conformity with self-interest. The measures, it was argued, though limited in themselves, implied a jettisoning of theories which were essential to life in a society. The supporters of the proposal answered their critics partly by trying to minimize the importance of the interference, partly by asserting that in fact the general freedom which all of them avowed they wished to attain was in fact furthered by government intervention and that one particular aspect of freedom was merely being exchanged for another more fundamental freedom.

Take for example the debate in the Commons, in 1870, on compulsory education. William Forster, Vice-President of the Council on Education and a Cabinet member, was the spokesman for the Government's Elementary Education Bill. He presented evidence to show that under the existing system hundreds of thousands of working-class children were deprived of any form of schooling. A change was necessary. Since the working-man had been given political power by the franchise reform of 1867 he ought to receive some form of education in order to be able to make sensible use of his right to vote. In the progressively increasing competition between nations Britain could not assert herself if the quality of her labour were not improved. Conservative critics of the Bill thought it likely that existing conditions were better than those Forster pictured and that a number of weaknesses were inherent in the details of the government proposal. Yet, although these critical voices professed to be in favour of extended education for the masses they drew attention, at the same time, to the conflict between the principle of freedom and the compulsory nature of the education bill.

In this way the word 'freedom' came to be used with growing frequency in quite a different sense from formerly. In the 1830s the prevailing meaning of freedom was freedom from government interference, and above all unlimited freedom of contract. Fifty years later the word was still used in this sense, but now it could be given an additional and quite different meaning. Freedom could now mean the protection established by the state for an individual or group in relation to other individuals or groups; that is to say, freedom could be achieved by government interference, by infringement of the freedom of contract. When the concept of freedom was invoked, for example, as a motive for legal restriction of working hours, it was either tacitly assumed or openly stated that such a measure helped to create conditions of labour which working-men would themselves demand if they were 'free' in relation to their employers, that is if they were more on terms of equality with their employers, from the point of view of contract, than was actually the case. It was considered that the exercise of State coercion compensated, or cancelled out, a lack of social freedom. But this was but a step away from using the word 'freedom' in a sense which made possible almost any kind of government interference in the name of freedom. The individual could be 'freed' from temptation, 'freed' from his own evil inclinations. He could be educated and guided in such a direction that his capacity for being and doing good and resisting evil was increased and strengthened; and from here it was an easy transition to the idea that this was a liberation, provided one supposed, to begin with, that the individual 'really' wanted to live 'a good life' and was intent on attaining 'his own highest good'. The introduction of compulsory education in line with this argument could be combined with the principle of freedom—a combination which would have been regarded as impossible a few decades earlier. In this particular case the dilemma was not so great, since compulsory education concerned children and could be regarded as a substitution of state for parental control in the matter.

The tendency to use the word freedom in this way was nothing new. It had recurred again and again throughout history in the concepts of ethics and politics. Freedom became individual development in the direction of moral excellence, and any sort of state compulsion which served to foster development toward this end therefore became a device which worked toward the ordering of things in the interest of freedom. This line of reasoning had last been pursued, with incomparable acuity, by Hegel. Among English liberals a new attitude to the principle of freedom was given definition by one of Hegel's few followers in England, the philosopher Thomas Hill Green (1836–82), who was, from 1860 onward, fellow, tutor and subsequently Professor of Moral Philosophy, at Balliol College, Oxford. His great concern for social problems expressed in his lectures and writings earned for him a reputation as an outstanding theorist of social reform which has lasted almost undiminished to the present day, while, during his lifetime, his ideas recurred with frequency in pamphlets outlining liberal political programmes.

Green expressed his opinions on this subject very clearly in a lecture he gave, in 1880, on *Liberal Legislation and Freedom of Contract*. He pointed out that a number of Bills had recently been proposed or passed which did not seem consistent with the principle of freedom of contract in the accepted meaning of the term. Earlier on, Liberalism had fought against class privilege in the name of freedom, but now it was considered by many to be doing exactly the opposite. As examples Green referred to the laws dealing with factory working hours and inspection of premises, compulsory education, housing, and various proposals to regulate the relationship between landlords and tenant farmers. It might be considered that, on all these issues, it was a question of interference in personal freedom. However, Green continued, even in cases such as these, the measures really brought about an extension of freedom. The removal of compulsion did not in itself increase real freedom, because this freedom, 'positive' freedom, consisted of 'the power or ability to so something or enjoy something worth doing or enjoying'. Progress in the form of freedom was therefore identical with 'the increased development and exercise by all, of the ability to co-operate for the general welfare, with which we regard the members of a community to be equipped'. A 'freedom' which did not fulfil this function was really no freedom at all.

From this starting point Green discussed state interference in various fields. Labour, according to the economists, was undoubtedly a commodity like any other; but it is also very much a personal matter. Accordingly, 'limitations may be established to prevent labour from being sold under conditions which make it impossible for the seller ever to contribute freely in any way to the general welfare'. Consequently, to protect the health of an individual, the State could decide how factories should be organized and in respect of women and children and minors in general, the regulation of working hours could be imposed. On the same grounds, the State had a right to prohibit certain other contracts, such as an agreement to rent insanitary housing. The State was also required to see that the young were equipped, both physically and mentally, with the necessities of their true freedom and it could therefore, among other things, make arrangements for compulsory education. Similar to labour as a commodity, the earth had special attributes in relation to other commodities. 'It is only on Earth that we can live; only over the Earth can we move from place to place.' The State, consequently, was obliged to set limitations to the ownership of land. In particular Green pleaded for abolition of entailed estate and for certain laws to safeguard tenants. Finally he was insistent in his demand for stricter temperance legislation. The English, he said 'ought to sacrifice the not very valuable freedom of buying and selling alcohol in order to be more free to exercise the abilities and foster the talents God has given them'.

With this kind of reasoning it was possible to justify all measures which could be considered socially valuable from some aspect, as motivated precisely with regard to freedom. In reality, freedom became synonymous with general welfare and in so doing lost all concrete meaning; whereas, on the contrary, the attainment of some explicit sort of freedom had been regarded formerly as a means of achieving the general welfare. It is obvious that Green's own definition of freedom contained no objective limitation and that as a result the indications he gave for one or other case, which were outside the accepted meaning of 'freedom', were purely arbitrary. In exactly the same way as he justified the motives for legislation of working hours for women and children, Green could have justified these laws for men. Why should not legislation on minimum wages, or division of land, or the socialization of production, all be regarded as aids to increasing the ability of citizens to work for the general welfare? Green's concept of freedom could also be used—as shown years later by the Fascist and Nazi régimes—in support of a régime which aimed at making the individual a complete tool of government.

Apart from special viewpoints and evaluations, assumed though not stated in the formulation of his concept of freedom, Green arrived, on all issues, at conclusions which can be regarded as typical of the Liberal compromise of his time. He started out from the assumption that freedom was beneficial, according to the old Liberal interpretation, that is, that government interference must consist of exceptions conditioned by powerful reasons; and he always regarded government interference as a means of attaining a state of affairs which, not only according to his own special terminology, but also to the spontaneous terms of common parlance, could really and reasonably be said to comprise increased individual freedom.

To give some idea of Green's political theories it is necessary to touch on some of the basic observations in one of his main works: *Principles of Political Obligation* (1895). In this, Green attempted to clarify 'the moral principles on which the State is built and which justify obedience to the laws of a government'. The State, he said at one point, 'is an institution for the promotion of the general welfare', and in another, that 'the State is an institution for the effective and harmonious preservation of the rights of its members'. Such statements could be thought to refer to 'natural rights' and in fact Green could be regarded as propounding a modernized version of 'natural rights'. Nevertheless, he did not believe that natural rights existed outside the

State, nor that the State was brought into being by social contract, or that a State was established with the aim of promoting the welfare of its members and so forth. What he meant was that the State, or at least the 'true State' was based on the general desire of its citizens to work for certain aims, foremost among them being the assurance of a sphere of freedom within which every citizen could seek 'a good life'. It could almost be said that Green regarded the essential nature of a State as a feeling of civic solidarity, based on a morality that was at once uniform and individualistic. Judging from his starting points, Green, like Hegel, must have thought that not all organizations which appear to be States are so in fact. He made no overt statement to this effect, but he implied it by saying, in one context, that Russia was called a State but that this was only a courtesy title. The whole Hegelian difference between 'the real' and 'the Absolute' could be dimly glimpsed in this remark. It was significant, too, that Green conceded the citizen the right to refuse to obey the laws of the State when these were 'incompatible with the true purpose of the State, which is to support and harmonize social relations'.

According to Green, certain personal rights, certain areas of liberty, thus became constitutional matters for the State to deal with. He himself said that such rights could be regarded as 'natural'; not in the sense that rights existed independently of society or were in any way guaranteed when a society was established, but in the sense that rights were 'necessary to the human being in order that he might fulfil his destiny as a moral being, and so that he might devote himself actively to the development and perfection of character both in himself and others'. Such rights could not exist without a conscious awareness, in the members of a society, of their mutual interests. Green's theory of the State, as shown here, developed into a closed idealistic system. He used key words in special, varying meanings, expressed in simple everyday language, as far as possible without undue loss of precision. He appeared to take for granted that such terms as 'State', 'feeling of solidarity', 'individual privileges', 'rights of individuals' and the like, were inseparable.

Like Hegel his master, Green stepped outside his ideological structure to give concrete recommendations with regard to the solutions of various social problems. He did this in the above-mentioned essay 'Freedom of Contract'. Other examples can be found in *Principles of Political Obligation* in which Green defended, among other things, the right of property as a 'natural' right. 'Every human being', he said, 'who is suited to some form of society', feels the desire for possessions and for prosperity and therefore property must be considered as included in the general welfare which society seeks to attain and which includes the striving of the individual toward self-development and the gratification of his desires. Individual property is thus an expression of the 'spiritual principle' underlying society. If only the right of property were accepted, Green wrote, differences in the distribution of property would be accepted. It was not possible, he said, to fix a definite limit to the truly legitimate desire for prosperity. His argument to justify the right of testamentary disposal of property was more involved. Among other things, Green stated that the feeling of responsibility towards the family was of great social value and that this feeling was not satisfied unless an individual possessed power over his family through the right to bequeath various sums to more or less deserving heirs. He put the further question whether the possibility of unlimited accumulation of property contributed to the rise of an unpropertied mass, the proletariat. His answer was that in principle it did not, bearing in mind the fact that skilled artisans were able, by being thrifty, to become small capitalists. On the other hand, he thought that property in land, concentrated in the hands of a few, as in former times, had been instrumental in creating a proletariat. He dismissed the idea of expropriation of land and confiscation by the State of so-called 'undeserved' profits from rising values, by invoking the principle of the right of property.

Both in his moderate recommendations for social reform and his unlimited respect for the right of private property, Green was an appropriate representative of liberalism as it had evolved by the end of the century. No full critical analysis of his general views is possible here; for this purpose a far more detailed exposition of his political theories would be necessary and before doing that one would have to give some account of his system of ethics on which his political theories are mainly founded. It is obvious that Green's line of thought was leavened by metaphysical ideas; his political doctrine was an attempt to employ the methods of German idealism in motivating English liberalism. In the main, the State in England was obviously the 'true' State, the essence of which Green attempted to clarify. It should be pointed out that in *Principles of Political Obligation*—as in the esasy on *Freedom of Contract*—there are few traces of any relationship between his general theory and his more concrete statements. When, for example, he defended the right of property and the right of bequest, he did so as if the reasons given were sheer inferences from theoretical postulates, but this was clearly not the case; Green was concerned here with ordinary common-sense reasoning, which did not necessarily have anything to do with his juridico-philosophical premises. These, it would seem, could just as well, or just as inappropriately, have been used, for instance, as grounds for equal division of property or for State expropriation of a landowner's property. Why should not the desire for the common welfare—in which each individual's desire for self-development was included—be considered, instead, to comprise aims of this kind?

Green's point of departure was quite different from that of utilitarianism. The aim for him was the 'good', not the 'happy' life. The difference between John Stuart Mill's utilitarianism and Green's moral idealism was not really of much importance. Mill modified the principle of utility or felicity to such an extent that it ended by embracing both the differentiation and the moralism: in short, the ethical self-realization which Green believed was the mission of society and of humanity. On the other hand, Green set such great store by material welfare as the basis of spiritual fulfilment, that his thinking constantly linked up with purely utilitarian lines of thought. This notwithstanding, he probably contributed more than most social philosophers of his day to the generally idealistic tinge which came to infuse English liberalism. Traces of 'the dry morale of felicity' which characterizes Benthamism and early English liberalism as a whole, are far less apparent in Green than in Mill. Practical politics of the time would seem to have developed along more or less similar lines: the somewhat pedantic rationalism of Brougham and Macaulay need only be compared with Gladstone's and Morley's passionate appeal to moral sentiments.

The Question of the Colonies

Until the advent of economic liberalism the ideas which dominated any discussion of the colonial system were concerned with the belief that colonies were primarily a means of increasing the wealth of the mother country. This idea also pervaded British thinking on the subject, even though Britain's policy, at least as far as territories populated by Europeans were concerned, was less ruled by the urge of exploitation than was that of Continental colonial powers. Britain regarded her colonies as an economic complement to the mother country. A complicated system of regulations served to secure monopolies in colonial trade and to control commerce and industry in such a way that they were unable to compete with Britain's own production. Economic liberalism criticized these aims from its own points of view and regarded a colonial system as worthless. This initiated a new phase in the English debate on colonialism. Adam Smith, the Scottish economist and professor of moral philosophy, finished his great and best-known work, *The Wealth of Nations*, just before the outbreak of the decisive dispute between Britain and her American colonies, and the book was published in 1776, the year which saw the signing of the American Declaration of Independence. With *An Enquiry into the Nature and Causes of the*

Wealth of Nations (1776–78)—to give the work its full title—Adam Smith expounded the new doctrine.

The effect of a trade monopoly, he said, was to create great disadvantages for the colonies, nor was it really of much benefit to England. Admittedly, the exclusive right to trade in certain territories gave England a relative advantage over other nations which did not enjoy this right. But if, instead, universal free trade were the rule, Britain, like other nations would profit, because colonial products would command a larger market and could accordingly be produced in greater quantity and at a lower cost. Furthermore, the monopolies caused capital to be too massively attracted to colonial trade and the great profits, in proportion to capital investment, which could be obtained through this trade, caused the question to be asked: whether British industry generally maintained profits, and hence prices, at a higher level than would have been the case had there been free trade in the colonies. The trade monopoly, therefore, which was considered essential in order to reap the greatest benefit from the colonies, was of economic value only to a small group of merchants: 'It is thus that the single advantage which the monopoly procures to a single order of men is in many different ways hurtful to the general interest of the country.' In addition to this, there was the fact that a colonial system was the cause of constant wars and thus required vast expenditure by the mother country, apart from the amounts needed for normal defence of the colonies. Nevertheless, Smith thought:

> 'To propose that Great Britain should voluntarily give up all authority over her colonies, and leave them to elect their own magistrates, to enact their own laws, and to make peace and war as they might think proper, would be to propose such a measure as never was, and never will be adopted, by any nation in the world. No nation ever voluntarily gave up the dominion of any province, how troublesome soever it might be to govern it, and how small soever the revenue which it afforded might be in proportion to the expense which it occasioned. Such sacrifices, though they might frequently be agreeable to the interest, are always mortifying to the pride of every nation, and what is perhaps of still greater consequence, they are always contrary to the private interest of the governing part of it, who would thereby be deprived of the disposal of many places of trust and profit, of many opportunities of acquiring wealth and distinction, which the possession of the most turbulent, and, to the great body of the people, the most unprofitable province seldom fails to afford.'

Nevertheless, he concluded, if Britain could resolve to take such a step, not only would she be relieved of great expense, but in all probability would be able to secure free-trade agreements with the colonies which would be more advantageous to the great masses than the existing monopolies. A relationship would evolve between Britain and her former colonies populated by the British, which would be similar to that which had existed between the ancient Greek city-states and the new communities which had sprung from them.

Adam Smith's disciples met on common ground in many variations of his theories. Malthus discussed colonization as an eventual means of counteracting the tendency to overpopulation, but his conclusions were negative. Ricardo only touched upon the question of trade with the colonies, but on this point his conclusions coincided with those of Adam Smith. Nassau Senior considered the colonial question in more detail and also from a number of aspects other than that of economy. He emphasized, among other things, that the advantages afforded by its colonies to any given nation depended mainly on the fact that most countries followed a protectionist colonial policy against their own interests; if universal free trade, which was in the interests of all, were to be adopted, the possession of colonies would produce no economic gain whatsoever. The class to profit most by the existence of colonies was the rich upper class which was able to place its sons in well-paid positions in colonial administration. On the whole, the colonies were only a burden on the mother country, particularly as a result of the huge expenditure required by administration and defence. In time the colonies would break free entirely or almost entirely. If they were governed from London, they would revolt to gain their freedom; if they had achieved partial self-government, they would demand even greater independence. And Senior concluded:

> 'In general it may be said that one of the chief causes which weakens the power and diminishes the prosperity of a great and enterprising maritime nation, is its liability to be cramped, and weighed down and exhausted, by a parasitical growth of Dependencies. It seems to be the fate of every such nation to waste her resources, first in creating them, afterwards in protecting them, and at last in vain efforts to retain them.'

Bentham, who was against all colonial policies, carried critical opposition to its farthest limits, in various contexts. He declared in his *Principles of International Law* that 'distant dependencies increase the chance of war', that 'colonies are seldom, if ever, sources of profit to the mother-country', and that colonial posts were 'the means of corruption afforded by the patronage'. In what concerned the colonies themselves, their dependency on a foreign power was a constant source of poor government. The colonial system, therefore, meant that: 'The real interests of the colony must be sacrificed to the imaginary interests of the mother-country'. England, he believed, ought to give up her colonies gradually. A few years later, in 1793, his *Emancipate Your Colonies*, 'addressed to the National Convention of France, shewing the uselessness and mischievousness of distant dependencies to an European State', made more detailed demands in this respect. In his usual tidy fashion he summarized his advice:

> 'A word of recapitulation, and I have done. You will, I say, give up your colonies—because you have no right to govern them, because they had rather not be governed by you, because it is against their interest to be governed by you, because you get nothing by governing them, because you can't keep them, because the expence of trying to keep them would be ruinous, because your constitution would suffer by your keeping them, because your principles forbid your keeping them, and because you would do good to all the world by parting with them. In all this is there a syllable not true? . . . To conclude—If hatred is your ruling passion, and the gratification of it your first object, you will still grasp your colonies. If the happiness of mankind is your object, and the declaration of rights your guide, you will set them free—the sooner the better: it costs you but a word: and by that word you cover yourself with the purest glory.'

It can be inferred from this that Bentham was even invoking the basic ideas of liberty and democracy in his demand for total and immediate emancipation of the colonies.

In one work, the *Manual of Political Economy*, written mainly after the two mentioned above, Bentham repeated economic liberalism's criticism of colonial policy. But now he emphasized other, non-economic lines of thought which favoured the colonial system, and from these he drew conclusions of quite a different nature from those of his earlier writings. Putting the question as to whether new colonies should be established, Bentham answered categorically: from an economic standpoint, certainly not, though colonies could receive the surplus population of the mother-country.

> 'When an excess of population in relation to territory exists or is foreseen, colonization is a very proper measure. As a means of increasing the general wealth of a country, or of increasing the revenue of the mother-country, it is a very improper measure. All the common ideas on this subject are founded on illusions . . . to the mother-country, the positive profit from a colony is equal to 0.'

If the surplus population of the mother-country were well governed and their progress were not impeded, colonies would gradually form new nations; and these, by language, customs, kinship and political influence, would be attached to the mother-country. Bentham's reply to the question whether colonies already established as possessions should be emancipated, was that they should, if considered solely from an economic standpoint such as the saving of the expenses of their government and the superior advantages of a free commerce, but that other factors must then be taken into account, considerations of what was due to a family which had been created and which ought not to be abandoned. The question arose, if a colony were to be abandoned, could it survive as an independent society, and whether, if that were possible, conditions of existence in such a society would not deteriorate.

> 'Is it not necessary that they should be protected and directed, in their condition of comparative weakness and ignorance? Is not their present state of dependence their safeguard against anarchy, murder, and pillage? Such are the points of view under which this question should be considered.'

Bentham finished off his observations on the colonial system by saying that the difficulty, broadly speaking, would vanish if the colonies ceased to be regarded as a means of economic gain.

> 'When we shall have ceased to consider colonies with the greedy eyes of fiscality, the greater number of these inconveniences will disappear of themselves. Set aside all false mercantile notions, and all jealousy of their subjects, and everything which renders their yoke burthensome will fall at once: there will no longer be any reason to fear hostile dispositions and wars for independence. If wisdom alone were listened to, the ordinary subject of contention would be reversed—the mother-country would desire to see her children powerful, that they might become free, and the colonies would fear the loss of that tutelary authority which gave them internal tranquillity and security against external foes.'

Consequently, from a purely negative criticism of the colonial system, Bentham arrived at a conditionally positive viewpoint. This positive attitude was nevertheless developed naturally from the negative one and included its essential features. Following a line of thought already glimpsed in Adam Smith and in Burke's celebrated speech on 'Conciliation with America' made in 1775 during the American War of Independence, Bentham concluded that the mother-country, by giving the colonies a great deal both of political and economic freedom, would bind them to her more strongly than by a policy of power and exclusive trade rights. The development of Bentham's ideas was thus, on essential points, in agreement with opinion in England and with Britain's colonial policy during the nineteenth century.

It would seem beyond doubt that the leading political circles in England during the greater part of the nineteenth century believed that the colonies, sooner or later, should be granted independence, and that according to the opinions of a great many, though not all, such a development would be to the advantage of both sides. It would be impossible, however, to extract anything very definite on this subject from the utterances of statesmen and colonial officials. A discussion of the question based on the opinions of Disraeli, Gladstone or Cobden, for example, would be unfruitful, since these parliamentarians, to say nothing of others, all laid stress on different viewpoints at different times and on the whole their opinions on the subject were neither carefully considered nor very lasting. At times one or other politician would make allusions to the ties which bound Britain to her colonies—meaning, of course, the territories populated by the British, and with this in mind they strongly emphasized the positive attitude to colonialism. At other times it was felt that the colonies ought not to be retained by force, and this was generally expressed in terms of sceptical disapproval. Common to these divergent attitudes was the view that, in one way or another, the eventual winding up of the colonial system was a foregone conclusion—an outcome regarded by some with equanimity, by others with satisfaction. The colonies came to be looked upon more as 'the white man's burden' than as an additional resource of the mother-country.

Examples of these attitudes abound. The three under-secretaries for the colonies who were most closely concerned with supervision of colonial policy from 1836 to 1871—namely Sir James Stephen, Herman Merivale, and Frederic Rogers (later Lord Blachford), all Liberals—worked to stabilize Britain's colonial empire, but believed that its eventual dissolution was inevitable. In about 1885, after the rise of modern imperialism, Rogers wrote:

> 'I had always believed—and the belief has so confirmed and consolidated itself that I can hardly realize the possibility of any one seriously thinking the contrary—that the destiny of our colonies is independence; and that, in this point of view, the function of the Colonial Office is to secure that our connexion, while it lasts, shall be as profitable to both parties, and our separation, when it comes, as amicable as possible. This opinion is founded first on the general principle that a spirited nation (and a colony becomes a nation) will not submit to be governed in its internal affairs by a distant government, and that nations geographically remote have no such common

interests as will bind them permanently together in foreign policy, with all its details and mutations.'

It is significant, though not typical of the climate in Conservative circles, that in 1833 Disraeli—who some decades later was to be a personification of the new imperialism—could write to a friend prominent in the party that, 'These wretched colonies will all be independent in a few years and are nothing but a mill-stone round our necks'. In the same year, 1833, Macaulay said in the Commons that a day might come when 'the public mind of India', having expanded under the system of British rule, would outgrow that system.

> 'It may be . . . that by good government we may educate our subjects into a capacity for better government; that having become instructed in European knowledge, they may, in some future age, demand European institutions. Whether such a day will ever come I know not. But never will I attempt to avert or retard it. Whenever it comes, it will be the proudest day in English history.'

The most extreme views came from the Manchester men. Cobden wrote to the effect that among the most beneficial results of free trade would be the loosening of the ties between England and her colonies. It was preposterous to regard the Army and Navy as items indispensable to the defence of the colonies. 'Where is the foe who would be kind enough to steal such a property? In that case we should have to prepare to defend our National Debt.'

Statements like this one of Cobden's, it must be repeated, certainly did not reflect prevailing opinion. The tone of official utterances, made by responsible statesmen like Melbourne, Derby and Palmerston, was more optimistic when they considered whether the colonies were of any value or not. Nevertheless, there was general scepticism as to the future of the colonial system.

This attitude to colonial policy, in sharp contrast to eighteenth-century mercantilism and late-nineteenth-century imperialism, was obviously conditioned by a great many different circumstances. The liberation of the former American colonies stood out as evidence that all colonies, once they have reached a certain stage of development, must desire to gain full independence. England's industry and trade at this time commanded the world market to a greater extent than either before or since, and the fact that the special trade advantages of the colonies were politically conditioned can be considered to have played a very minor role in the trade boom. Economic liberalism undermined belief in the value of the colonies. Free trade and a negative attitude to colonialism were the obverse and reverse of the coin. The workings of political liberalism operated along similar lines; partly because liberalism, linked with ideas about nationality, demanded equality of rights and independence for every developed nation. Even primitive peoples were regarded as nations in process of becoming; these would gradually reach maturity, so becoming entitled to enter into the circle of free states; and government by Britain was considered as fitted to hasten this development by an educative administration. Political liberalism also worked along other lines, which were that from the liberalist standpoint it was imperative to accept the claims of self-rule within the framework of the British Dominion, requested by some highly developed peoples. It was not possible to refuse the British population of the colonies political influence when it was possessed by the English population in England, and a rigorous limitation of the suffrage, following the pattern in England, could hardly be envisaged, because of the more egalitarian social structure of the colonies. It has been said that the English-populated colonies achieved self-government at this time precisely because of the belief that before long the colonies would become independent of the mother country. There is perhaps more justification for believing the opposite: that because it was considered just to grant the colonies self-government, their liberation from Britain could be counted upon very soon. In any case, during this period the principle of self-government was realized in those territories which later acquired dominion status. In the Canadian, Australian and South African colonies, parliamentary democracy was introduced while at the same time certain essential powers of control through the medium of British government were preserved. Meanwhile, in a number of other colonies similar arrangements were being prepared through the establishment of representative institutions.

It was only a short step from this concept of colonial policy—as Bentham's development of the theme had shown—to a fresh and positive attitude, which presaged in some respects the imperialism which could be glimpsed, though usually only vaguely and tentatively, in numerous utterances of leading statesmen. The man who first conveyed with any authority the idea that colonial self-government could strengthen instead of weakening the solidarity of the British Empire was Lord Durham, in his celebrated report of 1839, on the administration of Canada. The report suggested that, on the one hand, the Canadian colonies (which were then governed separately) should be combined into a whole, and on the other hand that the new, united colony should be granted practically complete self-government in its domestic affairs. Durham believed that the increased strength and greater independence thereby achieved by Canada would counteract any longings for separation. He hoped, once the sources of irritation with England and feelings of inferiority in relation to their independent and powerful neighbours, the United States, had been removed, that a newly-kindled national feeling would enable Canadians to become reconciled to the idea of loyalty to Great Britain. The chance for outstanding colonials to play prominent roles in their domestic administration would, Lord Durham believed, satisfy ambitions which would otherwise be directed towards separation from British rule.

This theory was soon generally accepted. More or less amplified self-government for the colonies came to be regarded as a means of holding on to the empire and not as another step towards its inevitable disintegration. It could therefore be maintained that early-nineteenth-century scepticism about the future of the colonial system was really a conditional factor in the existence of colonial domination.

The ideas, moods and impulses toward action epitomized in the word 'imperialism', began to pervade public opinion and politics in England during the 1870s and 1880s. From the point of view of practical politics it was probably all started off by one of Disraeli's speeches before the election of 1874, in which he accused the Liberals of indifference to and mismanagement of the colonies, while at the same time he proclaimed a new and active attitude to colonialism. A number of books dealing with the colonies and their solidarity with the mother country were published and were widely read, such as Sir Charles Dilke's *Greater Britain* (1868), Sir John Seeley's *The Expansion of England* (1883), and J. A. Froude's *Oceana, or England and her Colonies* (1886). They not only proved that there was a change in the way of thinking about the colonies but they helped to bring about this change. In short, the imperialist ideology can be regarded as a conscious struggle to preserve, consolidate and expand the British Empire.

The task of achieving this was carried out in two ways. First, it was a matter of strengthening the bonds uniting the Empire. From that point of view the first considerations were self-governing colonies, which were now beginning to be called dominions and were largely or almost totally populated by British emigrants. Proposals were made for an Empire federation with an imperial parliament as its highest legislative body; this idea, however, was never seriously accepted as a working programme by any government and after a few decades it was dropped as no longer having any bearing on the situation. It had proved possible to forge strong links between the mother country and the dominions, despite the loosening of old legal ties and the absence of any new ones to replace them. Dominions, of which the largest were united as federations (Canada in 1867, Australia in 1901, South Africa in 1909), acquired the status of fully-fledged nations, whose recognition, in 1931, as equal members of 'the British Commonwealth' merely confirmed a long-acknowledged fact. Time and again the dominions displayed their absolute solidarity with the mother country. A medium of debate and agreement was created in the system of imperial conferences.

The other face of imperialism was a tendency to colonial expansion. Britain did not start the race, which began toward the 1880s between the Big Powers of Europe to grab still-unoccupied territories in Africa, but she had special qualifications for out-distancing the others. Between 1884 and 1900 she acquired territories, in Africa and Asia, populated by 57 million inhabitants. This tremendous expansion was not the outcome of any systematic policy of conquest. In this respect neither Gladstone nor Salisbury were imperialists. No uniform desire or any general external cause for this expansion can really be traced after 1880. In some cases financial interest, in others military considerations, in others again, religious or humanitarian motives, were the deciding factors. Capitalists as well as missionaries were the instigators to action of the government and the organizers of popular imperialistic propaganda. The main point in this respect, is that press, parliament and government, despite differences of opinion, showed for the most part a greater willingness than they had done a few decades earlier, to accept any reasons which might be trotted out to encourage active colonial conquest. It is especially worthy of note that by all accounts the sympathies and often the enthusiasm of the great majority of the masses was aroused by talk of an active policy of conquest. Such exploits were regarded as cheap at the price, in terms both of economics and flesh and blood. Only volunteers or enlisted soldiers were used and in proportion to expense and loss of life, colonial warfare brought rewards that were rich in excitement and martial romance.

The Conservative Party was in power between 1874 and 1905, a period of nearly twenty-three years, and because of this, imperialism appears to be essentially a matter which concerned the Conservatives. It cannot be denied that both Disraeli and Salisbury pursued a far more active imperial and colonial policy than Gladstone, and that imperialistic moods were strongest in the ranks of the Conservatives. Nevertheless, there was no marked dividing line between the two parties. Several of the politicians who had espoused imperialistic ideas during the early phase of imperialism were Liberals, and some were even Liberal Radicals like W. E. Forster and Charles Dilke. Joseph Chamberlain, in company with Disraeli the most illustrious of the supporters of imperialism, formerly belonged to the radical wing of the Liberal party; the fact that Chamberlain split with Gladstone and joined the Liberal Unionists in 1886 was to a great extent due to feelings of empire unity which made him, ten years later, England's most powerful and energetic Secretary of State for the Colonies. Lord Rosebery, Foreign Secretary in Gladstone's fourth government and later Prime Minister, had already attracted attention as one of the leading exponents of imperialist doctrine. During the Boer War, it is true, the policy of aggression and annexation was criticized by a number of Liberal politicians, especially Campbell-Bannerman, but several of the principal party men besides Rosebery—such as Asquith, Grey and Haldane in particular—were, as 'Liberal imperialists', on the side of the Government. When the three last-named took their seats in the Campbell-Bannerman cabinet, it was a guarantee of the continuation of imperialistic policy. Even the socialistic Fabian Society, as regards the aspects of planning and productive efficiency, revealed imperialist and expansionist sympathies.

What is more important to establish is that the liberal and humanitarian tradition of the idea of colonialism as a civilizing influence and a preparation for future self-government, was a marked feature in the ideology of imperialism. A considerable number of writers on the subject propounded theories which were primitively nationalistic, militaristic and tinged with 'red in tooth and claw' Darwinism, the theories of a so-called power-philosophy. But it is what may be summed up as its liberalistic features that set the key-note and gave to British imperialism its distinctive character. This does not imply that English thinkers, poets or politicians gave voice to a desire to serve humanity by consolidating and expanding the British empire. A similar idea is apparent today in all ruling and conquering nations, even if at times it consists only in the thought that the superior members of the human race—in other words, themselves—ought to be enabled to become rulers. What is meant by this is that the belief of the British in their mission to serve humanity bore the stamp of liberal ideas about ends and means.

Benjamin Kidd is usually mentioned as one of the most remarkable yet most naive and extreme of all the theorists of imperialism. The two books he published in the 1890s, *Social Evolution* (1894) and *The Control of the Tropics* (1898) enjoyed a wide but brief popularity, and the first of these works was praised by such diverse admirers as the English economist Alfred Marshall (1842–1924) and the Swedish author, poet and polymath Viktor Rydberg (1828–95). Kidd is regarded nowadays as a writer of negligible intellect and his books are taken as examples of the ephemeral nature of literary and scientific acclaim. The interesting feature of Kidd's writings is their liberal and humanitarian tendency. He believed that certain nations, particularly the people of the West—by which he meant primarily the British and the Americans, and after that Europeans west of Russia—were called upon to govern the world, at least for the time being. He did not think that these peoples were superior to others in a biological or racial sense. The factor which had gone to create superior races was environment in its narrower sense of social development. Religion had played a preponderant role in this evolution, especially in creating a strong group feeling and group character. In England especially it had facilitated political and social levelling without severe conflict. Democracy, an appreciable measure of equality, a feeling of common reciprocal responsibility, a willingness to reach settlements, and social efficiency, had fitted the British (and in a lesser degree other Western peoples), to be leaders.

> 'But these qualities are not as a rule of the brilliant order, nor such as strike the imagination. Occupying a high place among them are such characteristics as strength and energy of character, humanity, probity, integrity, and simple-minded devotion to conceptions of duty in such circumstances as may arise.'

There were no aspirations to great feats or utopian goals. Results were attained by simple means: 'by the exercise of qualities which are not usually counted either brilliant or intellectual, but which nevertheless are, above all others, characteristic of peoples capable of attaining a high degree of social efficiency, and of these peoples only'. In short one could say, according to Kidd, that the essential quality which distinguished superior races was administrative activity permeated with a feeling of responsibility that was energetic, of short sight, practical and religiously-directed. A vaguely formulated, democratic and egalitarian idealism served as a background to these thoughts on superior breeds of men.

The second-mentioned of Kidd's writings, *The Control of the Tropics*, aimed more directly at the problems of imperialism. Here Kidd started out from the basic theories expounded in *Social Evolution* and applied them to the colonization of the tropics, a process which, owing to the economic importance of such regions, he regarded as inevitable, and already as good as accomplished. Kidd distinguished between two types of colonization. One entailed the exploitation of colonies as some sort of plantation, in the exclusive interest of the owner-occupier. This type of colonization—before the emancipation of the North American colonies—was of the kind employed by England and still characterized the colonial policy of other European nations. The other was England's modern type of colony, one distinguished mainly by her policy towards possessions populated by English colonists; government in these was exercised in the interests of the governed, and it was presupposed that these would gradually reach political and social maturity of a sort, following which it would be possible to grant them limited or full independence. England had wished to apply this system in the tropics, in her colonies (in the earlier sense of the word), but this was not feasible without certain modifications. Europeans could not become acclimatized to the tropics and old-type colonies could not therefore be established in such regions. It was inconceivable that a workable administration run by natives could be made to function efficiently in any reasonable lapse of time.

Therefore tropical colonies had to be run by officials sent out from England; but the administration, according to British principles, had to consider the interests of the natives and to aim at improving and educating them.

> 'The first step to the solution of the problem before us is simply to acquire the principle that in dealing with the *natural* inhabitants of the tropics we are dealing with peoples who represent the same stage in the history of the development of the race that the child does in the history of the development of the individual.'

The conclusion Kidd drew from this line of argument was that:

> 'We come therefore to a clearly defined position. If we have to meet the fact that by force of circumstances the tropics *must* be developed, and if the evidence is equally emphatic that such a development can only take place under the influence of the white man, we are confronted with a larger issue than any mere question of commercial policy or of national selfishness. The tropics in such circumstances can only be governed as a trust for civilization, and with a full sense of the responsibility which such a trust involves. . . . If [the white man] has any right there at all, he is there in the name of civilization; if our civilization has any right there at all, it is because it represents higher ideals of humanity, a higher type of social order.'

As the colonies should be administrated in the interest of the whole of humanity, the 'open door' policy must inevitably be followed; colonial tariffs must not be introduced and on the whole the colonial power must not procure trade and polical advantages over other powers.

Similar ideas, in a variety of combinations and with varying emphasis on different points of view can be detected in other writers who can be considered typical of those who proclaimed modern imperialism. During his first Slade professorship at Oxford, from 1869–79, John Ruskin, who adhered to the theories of Carlyle on this as on other issues, was active in promoting the education of young men in their responsibility to the Empire. England, he told them, should be 'for all the world a source of light, a centre of Peace . . .' which would be 'amidst the cruel and clamorous jealousies of the nations, worshipped in her strange valour, of goodwill towards men'. For this purpose England, through her 'most energetic and worthiest men' should create colonies 'as fast and far as she is able'.

Sir John Seeley, referring to 'the simple obvious fact of the extension of the English name into other countries of the globe, the foundation of Greater Britain', emphasized that this empire had been built without plan or conscious aim. 'There is something very characteristic in the indifference which we show towards this mighty phenomenon of the diffusion of our race and the expansion of our State. We seem, as it were, to have conquered and peopled half the world in a fit of absence of mind.' But he declared that England could not now shirk the responsibilities she had assumed. According to Sir Charles Dilke, the Anglo-Saxon nations should be united and strong in the interests of the whole world. 'The ultimate future of any one section of our race is, however, of little moment by the side of its triumph as a whole, but the power of English laws and English principles of government is not merely an English question—its continuance is essential to the freedom of mankind.' J. A. Froude spoke of the mission of the English nation, which could be realized only through the preservation of the empire.

> 'There is already a doubt whether we can hold for any long time our ignoble supremacy, and happily the colonies are not yet lost to us. But the holding of the empire together is of a moment to us which cannot be measured. Our material interests, rightly judged, are as deeply concerned as our moral interests, and there lies before us, if the union be once placed beyond uncertainty, a career which may eclipse even our past lustre. But, in theological language, it is the saving of our national soul, it is the saving of the souls of millions of Englishmen hereafter to be born, that is really at stake; and once more the old choice is again before us, whether we prefer immediate money advantage, supposing that to be within our reach, by letting the empire slide away, or else our spiritual salvation. We stand at the parting of the ways.'

Kipling, the canonized bard of imperialist England, expressed and proclaimed more successfully than any other, the vague ideas and sentiments which had been the emotional breeding-ground of the new imperialist policy. At the same time he helped to bring imperialism into disrepute in wide circles at home and abroad. His cynicism, his sentimental emotionalism, his vulgarity, have all been examined with critical severity. It is worth remembering that his predecessor as bard of Empire, Tennyson, was perhaps the most typical liberal of all the great Victorian poets. As early as the 1870s Tennyson was captivated by the idea of an empire federation which should have England as its centre; letters and poems of his show that he saw in the idea of such a union the beginning of a world state led by the Anglo-Saxon people: 'a warless world, a single race, a single tongue'. Even in Kipling's poems trends of thought are to be found which are typical of the liberal-humanitarian side of British imperialism. The much-derided poem, *The White Man's Burden*, is dominated by the same thoughts on Britain's educative mission as those propagated by Kidd and others.

When leading statesmen defended Britain's imperial and colonial policies, they constantly pictured them as links in the humanitarian task of fostering progress. Joseph Chamberlain declared that in modern colonial administration the feeling of obligation had replaced feelings of ownership. If British administration of the colonies did not bring peace, assurance of justice and increased prosperity to dominated territories, it was no longer justified. That such general declarations were not made solely for purposes of propaganda is evident partly from the factual expansion of colonial self-government, and partly because colonial administration was often criticized from a humanitarian point of view and this was considered important by all political groups. In any discussion of the foregoing issues differences of opinion about the actual working and results of British colonial administration were frequent, but its principles were never questioned.

A similar combination of nationalism and humanitarianism is apparent in the testimonies of the great proconsuls and empire-builders. Cecil Rhodes, the founder of the dominion of South Africa, and foremost representative of the policy of aggressive expansion favoured at the turn of the century, was influenced by Ruskin during his time at Oxford, and by the belief in evolutionary progress which was then in full bloom. Progress meant the production of 'the type of human being best fitted to give the world justice, liberty and peace', and to ensure that this type became predominant. Anglo-Saxons were the closest approach to 'God's ideal type', and the aim of empire-builders was to secure and maintain the universal predominance of this chosen race. 'Many', wrote Basil Williams in his biography *Cecil Rhodes* (1938), '. . . have vaguely held the same creed of the divinely appointed mission of the British race; but few, like Rhodes, have made it a direct spur to action throughout their lives and regarded themselves as agents of the divine purpose in so doing'.

Lord Cromer (Evelyn Baring), administrator of Egypt for more than twenty years, and the maker of modern Egypt, published an essay, *Ancient and Modern Imperialism* (1910), in which he said that the British effort to educate conquered and inferior races to be capable of self-government was something new in the history of world powers. As a result of this, he said, British policy was faced with a special dilemma, an attempt to realize two incompatible ideals: that of good government, which meant the preservation of British supremacy; and that of self-government, which implied a total or partial renunciation of that supremacy. The solution lay in education for the gradual introduction of self-government, but Cromer evidently considered that British leadership would still be needed for a long time to come. Statements by Lord Curzon, Viceroy of India (1899–1905), and Lords Milner and Selborne, High Commissioners for South Africa (1897–1905 and 1905–10 respectively), express similar ideas.

The foregoing statements about the colonies, undoubtedly typical, indicate that even in the palmy days of imperialism the colonial system was pictured as an activity which operated for the good of the colonies as well as for the whole of mankind. The principle of civilizing education with the ultimate aim of self-government was a very long-term issue. In line with this, the representative institutions which were introduced in certain dependencies were limited in the extreme when it came to active participation in government.

Nature, Darwin and Empire Builders

I

'Nature' is often used in common parlance as a word having some connotation with excellence or merit, with desirability and approval. We see ourselves and our fellow-beings in a special relationship to nature and, in one circumstance or another, talk of living according to nature, or of being in harmony with the laws of nature; of discovering and then following the laws of nature; of not transgressing the laws of nature, or not rebelling against nature. Things which are abnormal and at the same time disquieting or repulsive are often said to be against nature, offensive to nature, contrary to the laws of nature and so forth. But it is striking to notice how lightly, in conversation, the very same speaker can slip over into quite contrary meanings of the word. Then it becomes a question of overcoming nature; of mastering one's own nature; of making nature subservient to man; of using the forces of nature as tools of the human will, and so on. This ambiguous attitude is possible, on the one hand because the concept Nature, as the examples show, can be employed in a variety of quite contradictory ways; and on the other because a real difference does exist, and a diversity of attitudes toward Nature persists even when the abstraction is intended, and is understood at any given moment to express a definite meaning.

The history of ethical and political ideas can more or less be written, as at certain periods it has been written, with the Nature concept as its central theme. For St Thomas Aquinas (1225/6–74), the law of God and the law of Nature were one and the same thing. In his metaphysics what was natural was good and vice versa. Thomas Hobbes (1588–1679) conceived Nature as the dreadful state of a war of all

10. Lord Salisbury speaking at the Guildhall Banquet, 1895

11. Trial of Charles Stewart Parnell, 1889

12. The Prince of Wales (later Edward VII), with one of the wild Chillingham bulls shot during a visit to Chillingham Castle

against all, in which, like ravening wolves, 'every man is enemy to every man', and where any kind of society was better than 'the ill condition which man by mere nature is placed in'.

John Locke (1632–1704), with an optimistic faith in the Laws of Nature, believed it possible to build up a society or state according to these naturally ordained laws. Jean-Jacques Rousseau (1712–78), propounded theories in which can be detected the later concepts of liberalism, socialism, anarchism and syndicalism. According to Rousseau, the formation of a society was tantamount to the Fall of man, consequently the State would have to be destroyed or rendered as powerless as possible. Adam Smith (1723–90) also conceived Nature as some kind of divinity which, with its 'invisible hand', governed all for the best. Among the great progressive thinkers were designers of politico-economic structures of various kinds, but a dominating characteristic of all their philosophies was a belief that society or the State, either at the outset or at some later stage of its development, could be scrapped or reconciled with Nature, and so the new man would spring forth, natural, free and rational.

Darwinism changed the character of Nature. The prospect was seen to be wider than ever before, embracing as it did all living creatures; at the same time, that elusive 'something' which had been injected into the word 'nature' became more concrete, more objectively defined. 'Nature' was a struggle between all living beings; it had been going on since the beginning of time and it led, at every stage, to the survival of the fittest.

How could a political theory be evolved from such an idea, or how could this idea be fitted to an existing political doctrine? Darwin himself does not appear to have given the matter much thought. He considered himself a liberal or a radical, but supported no political views in his scientific theories. There is hardly a word of interest in this connection in his *Life and Letters* (1887), except possibly in one letter of December 1879, to a German friend, Dr Scherzer. In 1878, Socialists twice attempted to assassinate the Emperor Wilhelm I, and these attempts, by the democrats Hödel and Nobiling, were connected by a conservative newspaper, the *Kreuz-Zeitung*, with the destructive influence of Darwin's work. Darwin wrote to his friend: 'What a foolish idea seems to prevail in Germany on the connection between Socialism and Evolution through Natural Selection'.

It was evident, however, that Darwinism could be pressed into service by various theorists without too crude a misconception, or at least, no more than is customary in such cases. Particularly in Germany, but even in England and other countries, Darwin was quoted by socialists in support of socialism: if the struggle for existence led to the survival of the fittest or the supremacy of the superior, then all must start out with equal opportunities. But the enemies of socialism could also quote Darwin to their own purpose. Nations had already undergone their share of natural selection, the argument ran; the fittest people had come out on top and it was just these who were the successful and prosperous. Nationalists and militarists, on fire with racial prejudice, could also rummage about in Darwin for their arguments, and even here the Germans were in the forefront. Their argument was that in the struggle for existence, states or nations, like the species in Nature, would produce those best fitted to survive; and just as in Nature's struggle the better species had survived, so the evolutionary superiority of certain races had already been made manifest. Opponents of this view retorted that, to the contrary, the result of war was to kill off the flower of a nation's manhood; and that big nations would overcome small ones without becoming quantitatively superior.

In Victorian England, Darwinism became primarily a weapon against old-liberalism. Sir Henry Maine (1822–88), one of the most influential political thinkers of his day, spoke of 'the beneficent private war which makes one man try to climb up on the shoulders of another and remain there through the law of the survival of the fittest'. Herbert Spencer (1820–1903), even more famous and influential, defended the system of *laissez-faire*, as we have seen, against the new-liberalism which flourished at that time, which was during Gladstone's second government (1880–85). The selection of those best fitted to survive was effected through competition and struggle. If this selection were impeded, the race would degenerate. Only if the successful were allowed to enjoy their success and were given the chance of reproducing their kind to the greatest possible extent and the failures were left to perish, would rapid progress be possible.

Among the rejoinders was *Darwinism and Politics* (1889), by the Scottish economist David Ritchie, then highly esteemed, now hardly ever recalled. In his book Ritchie pointed out that Darwin was writing about the struggle between animal species, not about human beings in a civilized society. Human beings did not start out with equal opportunities and this was yet another argument against applying Darwin's reasoning. A physical condition such as a 'law of Nature' could not be reversed by Act of Parliament. Above all, Ritchie said, 'survival of the fittest' did not necessarily lead to 'survival of the best'. From the human point of view, the survival of the toughest could be detrimental and, under other conditions, could become an undesirable characteristic which would make a species, at a certain phase, multiply and survive at the expense of other potentially 'better' species. But even Ritchie, like most politically-minded Darwinists, found in the new doctrine support for a kind of traditionalism, a reverential attitude toward age-old phenomena and conditions.

> 'If we would avoid such scepticism about humanity, as would paralyse all serious effort, and make us hesitate to call anything right or wrong, we must admit the fundamental rationality of all institutions or practical beliefs that have been able to hold their ground for some considerable time, and to afford shelter and supply cohesion to considerable numbers of human beings. They must in some way have been advantageous to the society in which they prevailed, else—on the principle of natural selection—they could not have prevailed . . .'

he wrote in his book *Natural Rights* (1895). Here, then, Darwinism was the authority for an idea which had already been conveyed in other forms by Burke and Hegel.

While most socio-political writers urged people to do their bit, so to speak, in helping the laws of nature to prevail, the biologist Thomas Henry Huxley (1825–95), friend and supporter of Darwin, said in his Romanes Lecture of 1893, 'Evolution and Ethics', that instead of accepting the law of nature, people should fight against it. The word 'fit', he emphasized, had no meaning in ethics. 'Whatever difference of opinion may exist among experts, there is a general concensus that the ape and tiger methods of the struggle for existence are not reconcilable with sound ethical principles.' Social man, moral man, must not—as it was assumed he ought—take the struggle for existence as a norm. On the contrary:

> 'Let us understand, once for all, that the ethical progress of society depends not on imitating the cosmic process, still less in running away from it, but in combating it. It may seem an audacious proposal thus to pit the microcosm against the macrocosm and to set man to subdue nature to his higher ends; but, I venture to think that the great intellectual difference between the ancient times . . . and our day, lies in the solid foundation we have acquired for the hope that such an enterprise may meet with a certain measure of success.'

And Huxley went on to say:

> 'It is from neglect of these plain considerations that the fanatical individualism of our time attempts to apply the analogy of cosmic nature to society. Once more we have a misapplication of the stoical injunction to follow nature: the duties of the individual to the state are forgotten and his tendencies to self assertion are dignified by the name of rights.'

Huxley's challenge, thrown in the teeth of un-moral nature, was reminiscent of Hobbes, who considered the State and even absolute monarchy as a form of safeguard against the hostile workings of Nature. Other progressive thinkers, like Prince Peter Kropotkin (1842–1921), came by different routes to the same ethical conclusion as Huxley. Kropotkin claimed that 'mutual aid' was just as much a natural law for mankind as the 'struggle for survival'.

The effect of Darwinism on the moral and intellectual climate of the mid and late Victorian period can be widely traced in the literature of the time. It would seem possible to find in the writings of some thinkers and men of action a combination of ideas which are 'ideal types', that is, specially representative, of the thought of the age. Some of these are: belief in an inexorable process of development conditioned by specific laws, a process which had hitherto been supposed, by and large, to constitute progress: mankind had been formed through evolution; belief in the conscious ability of man to adapt himself, and to some extent to provide correctives to the 'law of nature' which, up to then, had been inscrutable and all-powerful; a critical attitude to religion, in many cases towards some specific religious ideas; belief that one or several races of mankind were superior to others, thanks to a head-start in the evolutionary climb and that this racial group or groups were called upon to lead the world. Darwinism thus became an important ingredient in what might be called humanitarian imperialism.

2

The social historian Élie Halévy, in Volume V of *A History of the English People in the Nineteenth Century* (1921–34), in which he discusses imperialism, has laid emphasis on the fact that the idea of Progress inspired by Darwinian theories was of great significance in late-nineteenth-century British imperialism. He singled out in this connection Benjamin Kidd's *Social Evolution* (referred to earlier). A number of novelists, poets and essayists are also mentioned by Halévy in the same connection, writers such as Robert Louis Stevenson, Joseph Conrad, W. E. Henley, Swinburne and of course, above all Rudyard Kipling. Though as writers they were all dissimilar, they ascribed to views by which they may be regarded as prophets and proclaimers of imperialism: 'A kind of Darwinistic philosophy expressed in the form of myths was the basis of an ethical doctrine, chaste, brutal, heroic and childlike,' wrote Halévy.

Probably the first and the most daringly original oracle of imperialism was not mentioned by Halévy and is usually almost completely ignored in any survey of the history of ideas. Winwood Reade was the author and his book *The Martyrdom of Man* appeared in 1872. It met with instant hostility. Some newspapers refused to review it; *The Athenaeum* (11 May 1872), called it 'a thoroughly worthless book, needlessly profane and indecent into the bargain'. The *Saturday Review* (12 October 1872), regarded it as 'wild and mischievous, and we should hardly be wrong if we called it blasphemous . . .'. Gladstone, to be sure, in one of his lectures, did Reade the honour of setting him on a level with David Strauss, whose book *The Old Religion and the New* (which also appeared in 1872) attempted to prove that Christianity as a system of religious belief was dead and suggested that art compounded with a scientific knowledge of nature would provide the basis for a new faith. Apart from this Gladstonian tribute, Reade was virtually ignored and though later praise came from such people as Beatrice Webb and H. G. Wells, no favourable review of the book, as far as is known, appeared until 1906. Nevertheless, despite the disapproval and the neglect of the pundits, *The Martyrdom of Man* enjoyed steady sales from the start and ran into numerous editions and impressions. The book was reprinted in 1910, the twenty-second impression was published in 1923, further impressions (more than 36,000 copies), were issued between 1924 and 1928 and it was again reissued in 1934. Conflicting opinions as to the value of the work were and are prevalent: to some it is a masterpiece, profound and prophetic; while to those unmoved by its message it is a pseudo-scientific and pretentious over-simplification of Darwinism.

Whenever Winwood Reade is mentioned it is always emphasized that he was a freethinker and he has generally been regarded as an atheist because of his denunciation of Christian dogma. This is most likely why his ideas were, so to speak, swept under the carpet from the start; and typically enough, the preface to the 1934 edition of the book was written by J. M. Robertson, a rationalist, who declared that Reade's influence had been great in spite of his lack of recognition. Reade is interesting, however, in the context of the history of ideas, not so much for his atheism or freethinking as for the Darwinistic theory of progress he expounded.

There is so far no biography of William Winwood Reade. Information about him in the *Dictionary of National Biography* is of the briefest kind. He was born in 1838 and was a nephew of the prolific and successful Victorian novelist Charles Reade of *The Cloister and the Hearth* fame. Winwood Reade broke off his studies at Oxford in 1862 to go on an expedition to Africa. His motive for the trip was an odd one: he wanted to exonerate the gorilla of the charge of being fierce and aggressive. He succeeded in proving that this anthropoid ape had indeed been maligned and was a timid, good-natured creature who only killed human beings when attacked. Reade made a second expedition to Africa in 1868 and in 1873 covered the Ashanti War as *The Times* correspondent with Wolseley's forces. In Africa he contracted various tropical diseases which undermined his constitution and undoubtedly contributed to bring about his early death. He died in 1875 at the age of thirty-six, and received an eight-line obituary notice in *The Times.* His famous uncle, in an obituary notice in the *Daily Telegraph* (27 April 1875) was quoted as saying that he believed his nephew to have been 'gifted with genius which he had no time to mature'. Had he lived he would eventually have been able to throw off 'certain questionable views' which had subjected him to 'reasonable censure'. What these views were was made quite obvious by the *Dictionary of National Biography*, which dismissed his masterpiece with the curt observation that, 'In this book the author made no attempt to conceal his atheistic ideas'.

Reade's line of thought is indicated by the four major divisions of his book: War, Religion, Freedom, Intellect. War and Religion, he said, had always been inevitable stages in the evolution of man. For the peoples which had run farthest in the race, the age of freedom had now arrived and with it, as a result, Intellect or Reason was the victor. War and Religion would soon be unnecessary after the most successful races had become world leaders; man would begin to organize himself by collective and rational effort. Something that for the time being could be called imperialistic, consisted partly in the supremacy and leadership of superior races and partly in the development of man's power. The last-named feature inspired Reade to dizzying heights of prophecy.

Among a multitude of doctrines of progress Reade's differed considerably from the generally older theories, which started out from an assumption of the inherent excellence of nature or human nature and tended to regard all known history as a series of mistakes and betrayals. Condorcet and Thomas Paine, to mention only two, saw their utopian schemes rather as a return to nature. Mankind, they claimed, had constantly been duped and defrauded by kings, priests and other swindlers greedy for power and riches; if man were given the freedom to make use of his reason, and the right to act according to it, all would be well.

Reade's thinking was not as naive as this. He advanced from the view that the bad old times had to be endured as steps to good new ones. In this respect his ideas approached those of more advanced philosophers of progress who have reasoned usually from a teleological standpoint, such as Hegel, Comte and Marx. History then becomes like mountaineering, and the philosophers of history guides who tell us how much farther it is to the summit, for every stage on the long climb is inevitable and cannot be by-passed. What was novel about Reade's theories—or, more properly, the Darwinian belief in progress—was that the milestones on the journey were not the various systems of government or forms of production or metaphysical ideas, but stages in a natural process of selection of a biological order. The muddled thinking is so obvious as to need no comment. From Reade's own premises the evolution of man cannot be placed on the same footing as the natural selection Darwin was speaking of; people, biologically speaking, are essentially the same today as they were two or ten thousand years ago.

The unique and stimulating feature of *The Martyrdom of Man* lies mainly in Reade's detailed explanations and in the vast utopian prospects he outlined. Man, he said, and the most highly developed races, had evolved because the law of the survival of the fittest had been able to operate freely. Because intelligence and not such characteristics as speed and strength had emerged victorious in the struggle for existence, a fresh stage of development, presenting new possibilities, had been reached.

There were no limits, Reade said, to the improvement of the intellect, and with a certain degree of intelligence man could choose his own path. He could gain mastery over Nature and could control development or progress.

> 'We live between two worlds; we soar in the atmosphere; we creep upon the soil; we have the aspirations of creators and the propensities of quadrupeds. There can be but one explanation of this fact. We are passing from the animal into a higher form; and the drama of this planet is in its second act.'

In this phase wars as a means of selection were still needed, though not war between the most highly developed races. Imperialism (though the word had not yet been coined) was the road to progress. 'There is a sickly school of politicians who declare that all countries belong to their inhabitants, and that to take them is a crime.' However, as primitive peoples live in ignorance and slavery they must be brought up to a higher level by forcible means.

> 'The conquest of Asia by European Powers is therefore in reality Emancipation, and is the first step towards the establishment of Oriental nationality. . . . Thus War will, for long years yet to come, be required to prepare the way for freedom and progress in the East.'

In Europe itself, Reade went on to say,

> 'it is not probable that War will ever absolutely cease until science discovers some destroying force, so simple in its administration, so horrible in its effects, that all art, all gallantry, will be at an end, and battles will be massacres which the feelings of mankind will be unable to endure.'

But in the third act of this drama of Earth, peace would be universal and everlasting.

As with War, so with Religion. It had been necessary, and it still had its uses, as a force conducive to unity and discipline. 'In Europe, Religion no longer exists as a political power, but it will probably yet render service to civilization in assisting to Europeanize the barbarous nations whom events will in time bring under our control.' When the world had been Europeanized, that is, civilized, Religion would have played its part and would die out.

Reade reasoned in a similar fashion about all the relationships of superiority and inferiority and prophesied the triumph of freedom and equality. The relationship between the sexes was set forth in terms of Victorian chastity.

> '. . . as the minds of men are gradually elevated and refined through the culture of the intellect, there rises within them a sentiment which is unknown in savage life. They conceive a contempt for those pleasures which they share with the lowest of mankind, and even with the brutes. They feel that this instinct is degrading: they strive to resist it; they endeavour to be pure. . . . But in women this new virtue is assisted by laws and customs which were established, long before, by the selfishness of men. . . . It is certainly an extraordinary fact that women should be subjected to a severe social discipline, from which men are almost entirely exempt. . . . But it is not the women who are to be pitied: it is they who alone are free; for by that discipline they are preserved from the tyranny of vice.'

It would be well for men if they were ruled as women were, Reade thought, by the moral law and severity of opinion.

> 'The passions are always foes, but it is only when they have been encouraged that they are able to become masters. . . . That men should be subjected to the same discipline as women is therefore to be wished for; and although the day is far distant, there can be no doubt that it will come: and the future historian of morals will record with surprise that in the nineteenth century society countenanced vices in men which it punished in women with banishment for life.'

Like almost all progressive thinkers of any stature Reade then proceeded from the view that he was living in an age of transition, with a new, higher, and at the same time clearly defined phase of progress in sight. His contribution was to determine in what direction progress was heading, thereby giving human beings some opportunity, by their unhindered activity, to hasten, adjust and shape this development.

In the third act of the drama, all would have reached perfection: the martyrdom of man would be over.

> 'When we have ascertained, by means of Science, the method of Nature's operations, we shall be able to take her place and to perform them for ourselves. When we understand the laws which regulate the complex phenomena of life, we shall be able to predict the future . . .'

Welfare would become universal in a united world through numerous inventions: of a new motive force, of aerial locomotion, of synthetic flesh and flour manufactured from the elements by a chemical process in the laboratory. Government would be barely necessary—science would replace politics; poetry and the fine arts would replace religion. Idleness and stupidity would be regarded with abhorrence. Women would become the companions of men and the tutors of their children. 'The whole world will be united by the same sentiment which united the primeval clan, and which made its members think, feel, and act as one.' Disease would have been eradicated, immortality invented. The new man would be more chaste than the Victorian woman. 'These bodies which we now wear belong to the lower animals; our minds have already outgrown them; already we look upon them with contempt. A time will come when Science will transform them by means which we cannot conjecture . . .'. Earth was to be like Eden before the Fall.

In such a fashion would the imperialism of united mankind have its beginnings.

> 'And then, the earth being small, mankind will migrate into space, and will cross the airless Saharas which separate planet from planet, and sun from sun. The earth will become a Holy Land which will be visited by pilgrims from all the quarters of the universe. Finally, men will master the forces of Nature; they will become themselves architects of systems, manufacturers of worlds. Man then will be perfect; he will then be a creator; he will therefore be what the vulgar worship as a god.'

3

The great British empire-builders and proconsuls were usually statesmen and civil servants who were influenced by the prevailing ideas of the age but lacked all tendencies to become obsessed or even inspired by an ideology. Lords Cromer, Curzon, Milner, Selborne and Lugard all belonged to this remarkably clever but intellectually conventional type.

Cromer, on closer scrutiny the most distinguished of this group, purported to show in his essay *Old and New Imperialism*, referred to earlier, that the British aim of educating conquered and inferior races to become capable of self-government was an innovation in the history of world powers, and created a dilemma in the attempt to realize two incompatible ideals:

> 'What would be the reply of the leading Imperialist—of the world—of the Englishman? He would be puzzled to give any definite answer, for he is in truth always striving to attain two ideals, which are apt to be mutually destructive—the ideal of good government, which connotes the continuance of his own supremacy, and the ideal of self-government, which connotes the whole or partial abdication of his supreme position.'

They all wrote like this: it was the official attitude, from Salisbury, Chamberlain and Rosebery to the British officials and civil servants in India and the newly conquered possessions in Africa. But ideal self-government was considered such a remote possibility that it was more of a decorative feature than a motive of imperialism. The goal was almost as dreamlike and distant as the land of freedom was for theorists of the dictatorship of the proletariat, and the dilemma had not yet reached the point where it gave rise to inner conflict.

Among these 'gentlemen of England' were two outsiders, Cecil Rhodes and Harry Johnston. In the minds of these two men colonialism and imperialism were a passion based on or supported by a religiously-dictated conviction that they were carrying out God's or Nature's own purpose. Both of them were inspired by Darwin and his disciple Winwood Reade. Both were active in the 'new' and so far practically uncolonized continent of Africa, and were therefore more conquerors than administrators. Rhodes was the creator of British South Africa, Johnston of British East Africa.

The two of them met for the first time at a dinner in London in May 1889, given by the Revd. John Verschoyle, editor at the time of *The Fortnightly Review*. Walter Pater and Frank Harris were also present. Rhodes was then thirty-six and Johnston thirty-nine, and they were each delighted in the mutual recognition of a kindred spirit. After their host had hinted that it was time to go home, they continued their talk in Rhodes's hotel room for the rest of the night and breakfasted together, still in full panoply of white ties and tails and still talking. They were both too self-willed and hot-tempered for the friendship to be lasting. After a few years they parted on bad terms. One of the bones of contention in the dispute about funds which ended their friendship is said to have been the question of which of them had been the first to use the expression 'From Cape to Cairo'. The idea, in fact, had come via Gladstone, Sir Rutherford Alcock, President of the Royal

Geographical Society, and a conceit of Sir Edwin Arnold the poet. Johnston, however, is believed to have propagated it as the slogan which, up to fifty years ago, was a triumphant password. Today it sounds merely ridiculous and embarrassing.

Cecil Rhodes (1853–1902) was the son of an English provincial clergyman, the vicar of Bishop's Stortford in Hertfordshire, and was sent when he was seventeen to Natal as a cure for his weak lungs. He made the beginnings of a large fortune in the Kimberley diamond rush of 1872 and in time became a sterling multi-millionaire. Unscrupulous skill in merging gold and diamond mines made him the biggest capitalist in South Africa. He returned to England, a rich young man, in 1873, to continue his education, entering Oriel College, Oxford, where he ultimately took his degree. While at Oxford he was influenced by Ruskin's vehement imperialistic pronouncements and took the Master's inaugural speech to heart:

> '. . . Will you youths of England make your country again a royal throne of kings; a sceptred isle, for all the world a source of light . . . faithful guardian of time-tried principles . . . worshipped in her strange valour, of goodwill towards men? . . . This is what England must either do, or perish; she must found colonies as fast and as far as she is able, formed of her most energetic and worthiest men; seizing every piece of fruitful waste ground she can set her foot on, and there teaching these her colonists that their chief virtue is to be fidelity to their country, and that their first aim is to be to advance the power of England by land and sea: and that, though they live on a distant plot of ground, they are no more to consider themselves therefore disfranchised from their native land than the sailors of her fleet do, because they float on distant seas . . .'

Rhodes became a financier (dealing especially through his vast British South Africa Company, which became a Chartered Company in 1889) and a politician, becoming Prime Minister of Cape Colony in 1890. In all these capacities he worked to propagate the extension of British rule in Africa, and above all he organized the conquest and acquisition of the immense territory which is called Rhodesia after him. In 1898 came the dismal and embarrassing failure of the 'Jameson Raid', an attempt to seize and occupy one of the Boer republics, the Transvaal, in connivance with Joseph Chamberlain and employing a small private army of invaders which marched ostensibly in support of the claims of downtrodden Uitlanders. As a result of the ensuing complications Rhodes was obliged to resign, in 1896, from the premiership of Cape Colony. Nevertheless, by the time of his premature death in 1902 his dreams of a British South Africa appeared to have been realized by Britain's victory in the Boer War.

There was about Rhodes a strange mingling of youthfulness and decay. Like so many other eminent Victorians, he would appear to have been sexually abnormal, or at any rate undeveloped. No erotic experience of any kind has come to light and there is no evidence of his ever having had any feeling for or attachment to a woman: his grotesque and fatal entanglement with the Princess Radziwill can be discounted in this respect. The tuberculosis of his youth had been arrested, but after thirty he was troubled by a severe heart condition which was eventually the cause of his death. He is said to have felt constantly every heartbeat as a pulse throughout his body. His obesity and his bloated and blotched face showed ever more plainly that he would not live long. He drank too much, usually a mixture of champagne and port; his biographers nevertheless insist that he was not an alcoholic, even if reports of his behaviour and conversation often give the impression of bibulous exaltation. He talked incessantly about making money, making new conquests, about the mission of Britain to lead the world. In spite of his primitive ideas and his expression of them, there was something compelling in the deep feeling underlying his enthusiasms; and his ability to persuade, to sweep all before him and dominate men and situations is too well known to need stressing. Rhodes surrounded himself from the start of his career with a group of young men who shared his ideas. They were all like himself, in their early twenties, and seemed cut out for visionary fanatics, not to say confidence tricksters, but they soon became capitalists and politicians and were looked up to by London society in wonderment and admiration as pioneers of Empire. Among Rhodes's youthful associates and accomplices were Neville Pickering, secretary of de Beers, to whom Rhodes was deeply attached and who died young; Alfred Beit, son of a Jewish merchant of Hamburg and an expert in diamonds; Charles Dunnell Rudd, his lifetime business partner; the Irishman and scholar Thomas Rochfort Maguire, whom he had known at Oxford; Charles Metcalfe, another intimate collaborator, whom he had also met at Oxford; and perhaps the most famous of them all, Leander Starr Jameson, 'Dr Jim', leader of the famous raid, Rhodes's lifelong friend who became subsequently Prime Minister of Cape Colony.

'The Doctor' is thought to have been the model for Kipling's homage to virile manhood in his poem 'If'. The cult of clean, strong, hard-living men which had Kaiser Wilhelm II and Theodore Roosevelt as its high priests and was such a striking feature of turn-of-the-century romanticism, found staunch supporters in Rhodes and his cronies. It was a cult which was to lead, thirty years later, to Nazism and all its horrors. The conversation between Rhodes and the Kaiser, in Berlin in 1899, must have been an orgy of this sort of heroics. After the conversation had ended, the Kaiser remarked to Count von Bülow his

Foreign Secretary: 'When Napoleon met Goethe at Erfurt he said: "This was a man!" I can say the same about Rhodes: "I have met a man!" '

Rhodes read *The Martyrdom of Man* when he was twenty. Darwin became his Messiah, Reade his Apostle. The analogy was apt, for the book served as his bible. Twenty years later, Rhodes himself said: 'That book has made me what I am.' The Anglo-Saxon race, preferably in collaboration with the Germans or other Teutonic races, were called upon to conquer and rule the world; natural selection had appointed the task; it remained for Rhodes and others involved to accomplish it. With this aim in mind and in the words of his youthful 'will' drawn up at the age of twenty-five, his mission was to work:

> 'To and for the establishment, promotion and development of a Secret Society, the true aim and object whereof shall be the extension of British rule throughout the world, the perfecting of a system of emigration from the United Kingdom, and of colonization by British subjects of all lands where the means of livelihood are attainable by energy, labour and enterprise, and especially the occupation by British settlers of the entire Continent of Africa, the Holy Land, the Valley of the Euphrates, the Islands of Cyprus and Candia, the whole of South America, the Islands of the Pacific not heretofore possessed by Great Britain, the whole of the Malay Archipelago, the seaboard of China and Japan, the ultimate recovery of the United States of America as an integral part of the British Empire, the inauguration of a system of Colonial representation in the Imperial Parliament which may tend to weld together the disjointed members of the Empire, and, finally, the foundation of so great a Power as hereafter to render wars impossible and promote the best interest of humanity.'

In one will and testament after another, with numerous codicils, Rhodes developed these plans, which seemed to him as feasible as the negotiations for any trust corporation in Kimberley or Johannesburg. The Rhodes Scholarships, large grants to American, German and British colonial students for a three-year period at Oxford for the study of world power, were the practical results of these dreams of a lifetime. But like Winwood Reade, Rhodes did not want colonial expansion to halt at the mere limits of the earth: 'I would annex the planets if I could. I often think of it,' he told W. T. Stead in 1901, at their last meeting.

Sir Harry Hamilton Johnston (1858–1927) could be taken, like Rhodes, as a proof of the unproven belief that physical weakness or lack of inches is a stimulus to great dreams and deeds of ambition.

Johnston was a tiny man, only five foot three, with a high-pitched voice and 'little boy' looks which he retained right into middle age; but his ambition and fund of energy impelled him to endure numerous hardships and deprivations. To some, his stature and appearance made him seem slightly ridiculous, and he tended to over-compensate for his physical handicaps. In the words of Roland Oliver his biographer, 'It was not enough for Johnston to succeed: he had to dazzle'. Unlike Rhodes, Johnston was abstemious and 'moral'; he had been strictly brought up and the carefree sexual habits of the savages amongst whom he travelled and explored always irritated him; he lived a life of blameless celibacy into middle age, marrying then for the first and only time. His marriage lasted until his death in 1927 at the age of sixty-nine.

This brilliantly clever little man, who colonized and organized vast areas of territory in British East Africa during the 1880s and 1890s, was of quite a different intellectual calibre from his famous colleague of South Africa. He became a civil servant and an empire-builder more or less by chance. He possessed brilliant gifts, no recognized qualifications, extensive knowledge and had a wide range of interests, achieving success as a talented draughtsman and painter, a philologist, plant collector and writer. His forty-odd books, mainly on political subjects, included an autobiography and even several novels, and were written during the twenty-six years which followed his premature retirement in 1901. Having aroused hostility at the Foreign Office, he found himself squeezed out; without hope of being given further office, he opted for retirement on pension at the age of forty-three and for the rest of his life devoted himself to writing and painting. His best novel, *The Gay-Dombeys* (1919), which purports to continue the story of Dickens's *Dombey and Son*, was given a eulogistic preface by H. G. Wells. This novel, much of it autobiographical like Johnston's other novels, is made to carry an imperialistic message of 'the days when the New Imperialism was brewing', but is also an entertaining story and a lively portrayal of human character which contains thumb-nail sketches of political notabilities, thinly disguised, such as Lord Salisbury and Joseph Chamberlain, not to mention others.

The influence of Darwin and Winwood Reade is evident in Johnston's ideas, as it is in Rhodes's. Johnston was an atheist to the end of his days, but Roland Oliver, in *Sir Harry Johnston and the Scramble for Africa* (1956), has pointed out that:

> 'Illogical though it might be, he believed in Evolution as in a God, and in himself as its devoted, and perhaps only intelligent servant. Moreover, though he rejected for himself its metaphysical doctrines . . . he regarded Christianity and the Christian virtues as among the highest manifestations of the evolutionary process . . .'

Like Winwood Reade the teacher, Johnston regarded religion, and above all the Christian religion, as a force for education and discipline which Anglo-Saxons, in their role of Nature's elect, should make use of, at least provisionally, for the civilizing of primitive peoples. Nor was this earth sufficient, even for Johnston, as an adequate place in the sun. He was convinced of 'the divinely-inspired mission to conquer this planet, and perhaps even more than this, as the right of that wonderful being, Man'.

Relativistic and humanitarian traits appear with particular intensity in Johnston's character and outlook. He believed in the superiority of certain races, but he also imagined simultaneously a development of 'the inferior races' which would gradually lead to equality. There was a desire for progress and improvement in his imperialism which rings with obvious sincerity. He believed that slavery should be abolished and that primitive races, freed from their capricious and cruel masters, could be raised up spiritually and materially through education and aid. In *The Black Man's Part in the War*, published during World War I, he emphasized the contribution made by negroes and other 'coloured' peoples on the side of the British during the war, and made a plea for increased efforts to civilize all these people. He condemned the 'Dutch' attitude to the natives in South Africa. In *The Gay-Dombeys* he spoke of his desire to be the parliamentary representative for 25 million negroes—but he never succeeded in getting into parliament. Before everything else, it should be placed on record that statements or suggestions glorifying harshness or cruelty occur only rarely in Johnston's writings, or for that matter in those of other imperialists. There is an obvious difference in this respect between the racial ideology of the Anglo-Saxon and that of the *Herrenvolk* which by this time was developing in Germany, to pursue its gradual course towards Nazism.

What might be described as Darwinistic imperialism reached its peak in the years round the turn of the century. It flourished in the United States during the Spanish-American war, and still more during the longer and more taxing war of conquest in the Philippines. The cry went up that it was the duty of the Anglo-Saxon race to protect and guide the underprivileged, to conquer in order to liberate (just as communist ideology insists today, though with a vastly different intellectual apparatus). Senator Beveridge, America's most brilliant ambassador of her 'manifest destiny', observed that God had made Americans expert in government so that they might take into their care the administration of primitive or senescent races. 'What alchemy', he asked, 'will change the oriental quality' of Philippine blood?

The conquest of the Sudan in 1898, and above all the Boer War of 1899, made similar demands on idealism in England. During the Boer War, the anthropologist Karl Pearson, also famous as a mathematician, wrote in *National Life from the Standpoint of Science* (1900): 'History shows me one way, and one way only, in which a high state of civilization has been produced, namely, the struggle of race with race, and the survival of the physically and mentally fitter race.' Britain would survive in this struggle, not because she was bigger or better, but because of 'a complex nervous system, the reflections of which are not merely automatic, but under the control of that classified experience which we term true wisdom'. The Boers, after Britain's victory, should be incorporated with the superior race, but the Negroes should be driven out of the State of South Africa or—Pearson suggested, with a harshness unusual for a British imperialist—they should be exterminated.

> 'The path of progress is strewn with the wreck of nations; traces are everywhere to be seen of the hecatombs of inferior races, and of victims who found not the narrow way to the greater perfection. Yet these dead peoples are, in very truth, the stepping stones on which mankind has arisen to the higher intellectual and the deeper emotional life of today.'

J. A. Cramb, a similarly well-known Professor of History in his day, declared simultaneously, in *Reflections on the Origins and Destiny of Imperial Britain* (1900), his adherence to the scientific ideas of these doctrines. The Boer War was the first imperialistic war of the modern world and it was a victory of imperialist thinking over outmoded nationalism. Cramb wrote:

> 'The higher freedom of man in the world of action, and reverie in the domain of thought are but two aspects of the idea which Imperial Britain incarnates. . . . The spaces of the past are strewn with the wrecks of dead empires, as the abysses where the stars wander are strewn with the dust of vanished systems. But the Divine presses on to even deeper realization, alike through vanished races and through vanished universes. Britain is laying the foundation of States unborn, civilizations undreamed till now . . . In those directions and towards those high endeavours amongst the subjects within her own dominion, and thence amongst the races and religions of the world, the short space that is illumined of the path in front of Britain does unmistakably lead. Every year, every month that passes is fraught with import of the high and singular destiny that awaits this realm, this empire, and this race.'

PART THREE

OF MEN AND DEEDS

I

STATESMEN AND SOCIAL LEADERS

A Political Moralist: William Ewart Gladstone

In the summer of 1884 during Gladstone's second Ministry, William E. Forster, who had been formerly, for a number of years, one of the Liberal Party leader's closest associates, rose to speak in a Commons debate on the relief of Khartoum, where for the past six months General Gordon had been besieged by the Mahdi's followers. Castigating Gladston's reluctance to send an expeditionary force to Egypt, Forster told the House that everybody but the Prime Minister was convinced that Gordon was in danger. 'And', he said, 'I attribute his not being convinced to his wonderful power of persuasion. He can persuade most people of most things, and above all he can persuade himself of almost everything.' Forster's gibe has come to be widely considered as the key to Gladstone's character.

Disraeli, to be sure, had hit upon a similarly apt witticism some years earlier, when in an after-dinner speech of 1878 he said that Gladstone was 'a sophisticated rhetorician inebriated with the exuberance of his own verbosity and gifted with an egotistical imagination that can at all times command an opponent and glorify himself'. Forster's gibe was less flippant, and more penetrating. Similar opinions can be found in numerous other summings-up of Gladstone's character, sometimes carried to the point of considering him a hypocrite. This is hardly exact: hypocrisy entails a deliberate attempt to pull the wool over other people's eyes. What Forster meant was a kind of deception that was at once more innocent and more ingrained in the very nature of the man. Gladstone was never conscious of any unworthy motives because he was invariably convinced that he was acting with the best of intentions. Persuading himself that what was expedient was also a moral duty, he did not 'practice to deceive', he deceived himself.

This is the predominant view in many works dealing with Gladstone and Disraeli, and historians in adopting it have succeeded in reversing the accepted images of these two bitterly antagonistic statesmen, the great rivals of Victorian politics. Disraeli, though avid for power, ruthless in his tactics, with 'a perfect disregard for facts', even (at least on one occasion) recklessly mendacious, knew very well what he was doing and why. He was a cynic, but because of it he was honest with himself, he was not deluded about his motives. Gladstone, a religious-minded man, a moralist and an idealist, lacked insight into the nature of his motives, and his noble phrases and lofty ideas were in reality only the implements of his inner drives. As is natural in the age of Freud, the theories of psychoanalysis have been instrumental in bringing about a revaluation of human motives and behaviour, and the idea that the outward manifestations of the subconscious are generally the opposites of their inner motivations is by now a commonplace: aggressive personalities, for instance, are often found to be timid at heart; the pushing or ambitious, outwardly self-confident, are riddled with anxieties. Judged by psychoanalytical criteria, Disraeli emerges as the moralist, Gladstone as the humbug.

This is only one of the points on which biographers of the last few decades have generally veered in favour of Disraeli. The major biography of Gladstone, John Morley's three-volume official *Life*, which appeared in 1903, was not of the first rank; its chief shortcoming was its conventional and limited delineation of Gladstone's character, omitting as it did all reference to areas of Gladstone's life, especially his private life, which later biographers considered essential to an understanding of the man. Monypenny and Buckle's six-volume *Life of Disraeli* appeared during the decade from 1910 to 1920. This work was based on much new material and was substantially as much an attack on Gladstone as a memorial to Disraeli.

Later, from 1907 to 1930, came the nine volumes of Queen Victoria's correspondence, brimming over with frantic hostility, both political and personal, in the letters to and about Gladstone. In this connection it has not always been realized that the Queen's animosity was manifested only after she had fallen under the spell of Disraeli's almost sensual personal magnetism, nor that it was the Queen's sound sense of the realistic which caused her, in her dealings with Gladstone, to treat him in a manner which often seemed irresponsible and shabby.

In popular biographies, such as *La Vie de Disraeli* (1927) by André Maurois or Hesketh Pearson's *Dizzy* (1951), Gladstone is made to appear almost a figure of fun, although as Disraeli's bitter rival he was hardly a laughing matter.

Some writers have gone even further in their eagerness to belittle Gladstone. In a novel by Knut Hamsun, *Mysteries* (1892), set in the summer of 1891, the Grand Old Man is not even allowed to be a representative of the age's naïve faith in Progress at odds with melancholy misgivings. In a couple of sarcastic diatribes spoken by Nagel, the novel's chief character, Gladstone is portrayed as a narrow-minded, vulgar and tedious bore and, for good measure, a bit of a fraud as well.

The keynote is set by the musings of Nagel over a newspaper item.

The aged Gladstone, who has been down with a cold, is up again after two days in bed. But in Nagel's view Gladstone, treading the path of righteousness, never makes a false step: 'Providence and himself will unite in protecting him. And now his cold has passed off. Gladstone will live till he dies a natural death from well-being.'

At an after-supper gathering of provincial small-town intellectuals and later at an all-night male drinking party, Nagel holds forth with his anti-Gladstone views. Seeing and hearing Gladstone speak, he says, is an amusing sight. The man is a bigot, with the certainty of his clean hands and the genuineness of his stock of goods in his look, voice, attitude, gestures. His words are simple, slow, everlasting—'Oh! how they go on and on!'

This 'Champion of the Indisputable Right' is a tireless knight-errant of right and truth, for whom the greatest truth under the sun is 'two and two make four', who 'fights tooth and nail for his convictions, straining his staunch old lungs to the utmost so that his hearers shall not lose a single one of his precious words'. In the face of this 'stark, staring rightness' it needed a deliberate effort (such as insisting that two and two made five), to escape

> 'from being crushed into banality by this man who stood so indisputably on the side of right . . . his brain stiff with universally admitted results. . . . Two and two are four, truth has conquered, to God the honour! . . . the only thing is whether one's perceptions can stand up to being pole-axed by a truth like this . . . When the act is over and the people have cheered and Gladstone has made his bow, he goes home to bed and clasps his hands and says his prayers and falls asleep without having the smallest suspicion in his soul, without the slightest shame at having filled up Birmingham and Glasgow—with what?'

Nagel's (or Hamsun's) summing up is that 'Gladstone's intellectual greatness has never made any very overpowering impression on me. . . . He was a great and serviceable force, but a force that was after all extremely ordinary in its nature—a monstrous little finger of Beaconsfield'.

There were others who wondered if Gladstone were always entirely sincere. Henry Labouchere said 'I don't object to Gladstone always having the ace of trumps up his sleeve, but merely to his belief that God Almighty put it there'. And 'Labby', a Liberal Disraeli without Disraeli's success, was one of Gladstone's admirers in spite of his extravagant lack of principle: this dig, however facetious and spiteful, was another tribute to Gladstone's rigidly moral personality and behaviour.

This touches the heart of the matter. Gladstone was dominated by general principles and moral ideas to a remarkable degree—perhaps uniquely so for a politician. There was no question—and this is vital—of his attitude being a lever for ambition and the gratification of a lust for power, or if so it was insignificant enough to be negligible. Gladstone genuinely felt himself to be an instrument of God's will, but only with that sense of the inevitable which springs from deep piety and the conviction that religious faith provides firm precepts for a man's actions. God was a reality for Gladstone, a governing and comforting force within him, not just a ministering spirit at his side. He was one of those few who would have been able to combine a brilliantly successful career in the service of God with genuine humility; here was nothing of a superman, he assumed no mantle of divinity. This genuine faith was perhaps related to the traits of insecurity and anxiety which had existed in Gladstone from his early years: as a young man he had wished to enter the Church and forsake the world. But it was also related to the active and extrovert features in him which in old age served to counteract his bouts of depression; of his sincerity, his childlike and pathetic earnestness, there could be no doubt.

But a moralistic personality such as this also has its weaknesses, though in Gladstone's case they were relatively few. He was by nature a good and sensitive man with no tendency to use moralizing as a cloak for sinfulness. On the contrary, he was a moralist down to the most trivial details of everyday life, so much so as to seem unbearable to the more worldly. The man who enlists God as his debt-collector is often tempted to send him out on painfully trivial and insignificant errands. Gladstone always had to be right by the authority of God's commands, and of ideas sent by God. Such incessant and unrelenting righteousness was extremely irritating and taken at its face value appeared even hypocritical. For Gladstone, Labouchere's 'ace of trumps' was the very word of God, but it must often have appeared to others as mere expediency, sheer arrogance, or even megalomania.

It is not surprising, therefore, that most people regard Gladstone as the epitome of humourlessness. Whereas Disraeli joked about serious matters, Gladstone took even the most trivial and insignificant things with the utmost seriousness.

At the annual Royal Academy dinner of 1876 Disraeli told Robert Browning that he thought the pictures a terrible display of painting 'destitute of all spirituality, all ideality'. In his after-dinner speech, however, Disraeli chose to comment with tongue-in-cheek irony. The feature of the exhibition which had most struck him, he said, was 'the high tone of spirituality and ideality'. Browning, who had been highly amused at this, told Gladstone, who glared and said: 'Do you call that story amusing, Browning? I call it devilish'.

Gladstone's heavy-handed earnestness is proverbial. He used to harangue the Queen 'like a public meeting'—or so she is reputed to have said, doubtless echoing Disraeli who had said to Lord Clarendon on one occasion: 'Gladstone treats the Queen like a public department; I treat her like a woman'. Yet none of this prevented him from being agreeable, entertaining, even amusing in society. Unlike Disraeli he did not play to the gallery or deliberately make epigrams for the benefit of the diarists, an activity that is often more tiresome than stimulating to those who have to listen to professional oneupmanship or the humour of after-dinner speeches; but he was nevertheless quick-witted, swift in repartee and able to discourse on almost any subject. Nor can the man be totally devoid of good humour and a sense of fun who can waltz his wife round the room in jubilation over becoming Prime Minister, as Gladstone did in 1868: or, as on festive occasions at home, when he would stand on the hearth rug with his arm round Mrs Gladstone's waist and hers round his, swaying from side to side as they sang together:

A rag-a-muffin husband and a rantipoling wife
We'll fiddle it and scrape it through the ups and downs of life.

All the biographies and memoirs of Gladstone emphasize his Christian faith, a faith that, though varying in its details, was never clouded by any shadow of doubt. It was, or at least so he regarded it, the basis of his life and activities. The reading of religious literature was not a mere duty but a sheer pleasure and he always delighted in listening to a good sermon. He kept a large Bible open on his dressing table to be read from as he dressed or undressed. Daily family prayers and church twice on Sundays was part of the household routine. Gladstone's life was exemplary in its charity and chastity, two of the major Christian virtues, as the Victorians, sincerely or not, held them to be. His political activities and their outcome which shook England were interpreted by him as the practical outcome of his faith. He was a soldier of God, whether he was supporting or opposing parliamentary reform; when he fought against the disestablishment of the Irish Church or against Home Rule, or when, in his old age, he campaigned for them as the main issues of his platform.

The most recent major biography, *Gladstone* by Sir Philip Magnus (1954), makes plain how fervent were his feelings in this respect: 'He came to repose his trust in the ability of individual men and women to hear, interpret correctly, and obey the voice of God using their private consciences to inspire and direct mankind.'

The exact nature of this faith of Gladstone's is, however, difficult to determine. He does not seem to have made any intimate confessions of the kind left by General Gordon. Innocence, lack of guile and a biblical simplicity were characteristic of the man, in spite of the idiosyncrasies of his thought and speech, the circumlocutions, the parentheses, the verbal distinctions and refinements. The core of his faith seems to have been trust in God, faith in Progress and the triumph of Good—all beliefs of an uncomplicated type, accepted without question. Such a faith can easily turn into a conviction that one is an instrument of God, and take the form of a kind of exalted self-sufficiency. This undoubtedly was a trait of Gladstone's. But it is remarkable that he preserved a certain balance; in spite of his conviction he could still distinguish between himself and God, not only feeling himself to be 'a poor, sinful creature' (a feeling which can easily turn to conceit), but that he saw in the commands of the Almighty definite demands that not even God's warrior was allowed to ignore or transgress.

Most of Gladstone's writings deal with ecclesiastical, and in a wide sense religious, matters. His attitude towards Christian churches and religious communities developed from dogmatism to tolerance. It was one of the steps in his conversion from Conservative to Liberal. Even in his forties he considered it right that the Anglican Church, to which he belonged, should be the State church in Roman Catholic Ireland; twenty years later he thought the compulsory perpetuation of such an illogicality to be an abomination. In several of his writings, notably in *Juventus Mundi: The Gods and Men of the Heroic Age* (1869), his naïvely fantastic speculations about Greek mythology, he attempted to combine Christianity with the Homeric Age which he so much admired. Ideas from the Old Testament were traced back to Homer, the Trinity foreshadowed by a combination of Zeus, Poseidon and Hades, Satan by Ate, the Virgin Mary by Latona and Christ by Apollo. In his view it was the ancient Greeks rather than the Jews who were the precursors of Christianity.

Gladstone has frequently been portrayed as a bore, a pompous authoritarian with an insufferable tendency to the relentless application of transcendent values to trivial or mundane matters. His pedantry and moralizing earnestness must at times have been trying in the extreme. In his mid-twenties he was twice rejected as a suitor because his lofty views seemed too forbidding to the two quite ordinary and normally pleasure-loving young women on whom he had successively fixed his choice. His letters, even in that day, cannot have seemed very reasonable, and indeed the harsh bigotry of his religious principles, which he expected his future wife to share, effectively frightened off the two girls he wished to marry. Then in his late twenties, he met Catherine Glynne, who eventually accepted him.

The second paragraph of his letter of proposal to the future Mrs Gladstone consisted of a single enormous sentence 141 words long, divided into eighteen clauses and sub-clauses. Though Gladstone was deeply in love it was hardly a love-letter, for instead of speaking of love he indulged in a series of lofty reflections with accompanying reservations. He ended up: 'May you live, and die, it is not less my expectation than my hope, from day to day more and more filled with the peace which passeth all understanding and of the sacredness that is its source.' Miss Glynne replied that if he wished for an immediate answer to his proposal of marriage it must be no! Her implication was that she wished to think it over and they continued to meet. Four months later, at a garden-party, she accepted him. Gladstone confided to her then that he would have preferred to become a clergyman but that he was now dedicated to making political life truly Christian.

His marriage, at thirty, to Catherine Glynne, who was as good and charming as she was beautiful, was an unqualified success. The marriage lasted until Gladstone's death in 1898 at the age of eighty-nine. He and his wife adored each other and their life together was an unbroken idyll marked by few disagreements beyond an occasional protest from her at his rigid correctitude and respectability. At times Mrs Gladstone could be impulsive, forgetful or unpunctual enough to be teased by her husband for it, but she could treat the great man with something less than reverence and tease him in return: 'What a bore you would have been if you had married someone as tidy as yourself'.

She was certainly full of fun and had a better sense of humour than her husband, yet Gladstone was not so stolidly earnest and sensible as to be entirely devoid of a sense of fun. On the few occasions when they were separated he wrote to his wife daily, sometimes two or three times in a day. His letters were full of sober exhortations but they also contained playful touches and gossip. Mrs Gladstone's were feminine, full of domestic chit-chat and affectionate endearments: my precious darling, dearest own, my own own, darling old thing; the voluminous, strongly contrasted correspondence of the couple is endearing and makes fascinating reading.

The seven Gladstone children adored their father and were always eager to tempt him away from his writing desk in 'The temple of Peace' as his library was nicknamed. But it was recognized that he was a busy man who could not always be disturbed. Gladstone was scrupulously fair, treating the children as equals, encouraging them to discuss and criticize all subjects, and to catch him out if they could. His advice on the detection and exposure of untruths sometimes backfired and to the consternation of guests, childish voices could be heard calling out 'A lie! A lie', if in telling some anecdote he enthusiastically embroidered on the truth.

Gladstone had a passion for order and economy and a detestation of waste. He justified even these traits by the belief that it was God's will that people should make the most of what they had been given. He was the sort of person who collects odd bits of string and half-sheets of note-paper and re-uses old labels from which the addresses have been erased—and Gladstone actually did all these things. But those closest to him could testify that he was nevertheless quite human.

Even the psychoanalysts seem to have been baffled by this marvel of virtue and vitality. Their Freudian conclusions hardly get any further than the usual hackneyed classifications: his belief in God, a father-complex; his economy and compulsive orderliness, anal eroticism; his forcefulness and arrogance, an underlying inferiority complex, and so on and so forth.

The only characteristic upon which opinions have been divided was Gladstone's lifelong effort to rescue and rehabilitate London's street-walkers. These activities were the cause of scandalous gossip during his lifetime and even thirty years after his death led to a lawsuit for libel (*Wright v. Gladstone*, 1927) during the course of which Gladstone's memory was officially cleared of the slanderous imputation that while publicly he had professed the highest moral sentiments, privately he had 'pursued and possessed' women of all kinds. Captain Peter Wright, the author of the slanderous statement, was unable to substantiate his allegations, and at the close of the trial, having heard the testimony of numerous witnesses, including that of Gladstone's two surviving sons, the jury declared themselves satisfied that 'the evidence placed before them has completely vindicated the high moral character of the late Mr W. E. Gladstone.'

In 1886, however, it was only natural that Gladstone's colleagues and assistants should have been worried by the ageing Prime Minister's habit of hurrying away from the House after a debate to roam the streets of an area bounded by Piccadilly, Soho and the Thames Embankment, as indeed he had done for years past. There he would accost streetwalkers or allow himself to be accosted by them, so that he could talk to them for the good of their souls and if necessary offer them practical help, food and shelter, with the assurance that they would be treated with respect by himself and Mrs Gladstone, who often accompanied him on these rescue expeditions. This work was carried on by husband and wife for nearly fifty years; they spent considerable sums of money, either as personal gifts or on the support of rescue homes, and they helped to found several homes of refuge and reclamation for 'fallen women', one of which still functions today.

Gladstone kept a record of every case he took up, but he did not demand penitence nor did he reprimand backsliders, whom he tried to rescue over and over again, even pursuing them into brothels—once even rescuing one of them right under the noses of a formidable madam and a couple of thug-like pimps. His activities were known to the police, who generally imputed the worst motives to him. It was hinted that stories of his rescue work had been presented to the Queen in an unfavourable light and that Disraeli had not neglected to instil his drop of venom in the Queen's ear, to set her mind against his rival. In after-years Gladstone was inclined to believe that this must have had much to do with the Queen's hostility towards him, although there is no proof that Disraeli ever did speak slanderously of him in this respect. Damaging gossip and rumours also spread in society, especially during periods when Gladstone championed unpopular political causes. These murmurs of scandal reached their peak between 1882 and 1886. Repeated warnings from friends, colleagues and assistants finally convinced Gladstone, in 1886, when he was over eighty, that his rescue work was too damaging to his reputation, his career and the Party, and he agreed to give it up.

The persistent rumours current both during his lifetime and after his death continued to cast doubt upon the purity of his motives. It has, however, been proved enough and to spare that Gladstone (quite apart from the fact that his wife sympathized with, and often shared, these missions of mercy), was impelled solely by a desire to rescue and reform the unfortunate women who were the object of his concern, and that in so doing he felt that he was discharging a duty to God and to mankind. Though the concentration with which he pursued this form of charity might be interpreted as an expression of repressed sexual interest, the thought need upset nobody's belief in Gladstone's moral integrity.

On 29 December 1878, his sixtieth birthday, Gladstone noted that he had been well during the past year and that his voice had withstood the vast amount of talking he had had to do. Why, he asked himself, was this?

> 'Why has my health and strength been so peculiarly sustained? All this year, and more, I think, I have not been confined to bed for a single day. In the great physical and mental effort of speaking, often to large audiences, I have been, as it were, upheld in an unusual manner; and the free and effective use of my voice has been given to me to my own astonishment. Was not all this for a purpose? And has it not all come in connexion with a process to which I have given myself?'

His answer to himself was that 'this appears to me to carry all the marks of the will of God'.

Even if Gladstone believed in principle that every issue rested with God, he did not apply this belief to the details of everyday life with the passive fatalism of General Gordon; what he wrote on his sixtieth birthday was an expression of his conviction that he himself, all unworthy though he was, acted and worked as the instrument of God's will. With advancing age the veteran statesman came to believe with ever increasing intensity that his policies were God's policies. When, having relinquished the party leadership and retired from active political life in 1875 he re-emerged the following year to grab, as some thought, at the chance of a return to power with his fierce campaign against the Bulgarian atrocities of the Turks and Disraeli's pro-Turkish policy, he did so in the name of religion and conscience. His fulminating, and some said overheated, pamphlet on *The Bulgarian Horrors and the Question of the East*, vehemently condemning Disraeli and his government, sold 40,000 copies the first week and 200,000 copies within three weeks and further swayed public opinion already aroused to moral indignation by reports about the Bulgarian atrocities, in which some 25,000 men, women and children were said to have been hideously massacred by the Turks.

Ten years later, in 1886, Gladstone was actuated by similar motives (a fervent belief in the causes of Christian civilization, justice and humanity) when he championed Home Rule for Ireland, on the strength of which cause he became, at the age of seventy-six, Prime Minister for the third time.

In both these instances and in many others besides, his policies were anathema to groups in his own party as well as to the upper class in general, with the Queen foremost in expressing her fear and dislike. When she sent for him to form his third government, she told Sir Henry Ponsonby that, 'She does not in the least care, but rather wishes it should be known, that she has the greatest possible disinclination to take this half crazy and really in many ways ridiculous old man—for the sake of the country'. Gladstone—a rich man, for years a Conservative, one of the upper-middle-class gentry by birth and of the aristocracy by marriage and social connections—became a man of the people (indeed, 'the People's William') struggling against the privileged few. The conclusion he drew was that it was only the masses who were able to feel genuinely the fundamental truths of the issues at stake. 'When did the Upper Ten Thousand ever lead the attack in the cause of humanity?' he complained. It was not what he called 'London's West End' who felt for the Christian cause, he claimed, but the simple people, and it was he, God's warrior, who voiced the feelings which inspired the unspoiled and noble populace: God, Gladstone and the masses! 'All the world over', he said at Liverpool in 1886, 'I will back the masses against the classes.'

This conviction lent to Gladstone an aura of moral grandeur which even his opponents could not fail to appreciate. He was a man who had the courage of his convictions and he pushed through his ideas without regard to the opinions of friends or party. The people became, for the moment at least, what he believed them to be. He made them feel that they were 'greater than they knew' and that in giving him their votes they were voting for divine principles, not for lower taxes. Gladstone the prophet purified and hallowed them. Through him British politics received an injection of idealism, however illusory, which proved an influence on ways of thought, speech and action with far-reaching effects in the future.

But Gladstone's sense of mission was not without its dangers. It was easy to progress from divine sanction in big issues to divine sanction in every issue, to be self-righteous and domineering on behalf of or as a result of a lofty moral stand.

Gladstone's ability to indulge in 'simple, honest self-delusion' assumed an ever greater importance for him and the sacred words 'Christian' and 'moral' became the yardstick for his opinions in big and small matters alike. He regarded his adversaries as both stupid and simple-minded—above all, simple-minded. They in turn suspected him of being simply a hypocrite and a humbug, though never a self-deceiver, since his changes of opinion were so closely linked to the tactical requirements and opportunities of the moment. The passionate yet vague appeals which Gladstone in all innocence had recourse to seemed indistinguishable from the expedients of a dishonest and calculating demagogue.

Just as it is easy to regard Gladstone as a bore in his private life, so it is easy to see in Gladstone the politician (however much one may accept his honesty and make allowances for his self-deception) an insufferably obtuse egotist in his hobnobbing with God and the masses. Nevertheless his genuine piety forced him to some degree of self-examination: it may perhaps even be said that a desire for self-mortification and thus an acceptance of critical accusations was part and parcel of his religious attitude. He sometimes made lists of the names of persons who had accused him of making offensive statements about them. His comment on one of these long lists of prominent men to who he had given offence was: 'Nothing could have united such a body of independent witnesses as this, except that what they said was the truth.' Such admissions were not, of course made in public, but there was nevertheless a trace of genuine humility in Gladstone the leader and orator; and enemies who called him a hypocrite or said variously that he was a madman, an unprincipled maniac, a criminal or a traitor, never once accused him of being puffed up with vanity.

It was as a Liberal statesman that Gladstone was esteemed and became famous. It must be remembered that from his entry into politics in 1832 (he was born in 1809) until about 1850, he was considered to be a Conservative, although he clashed with the dominating policy of the party in 1846 when he supported Peel and free trade. Gladstone was never a Liberal in a more doctrinal sense even though he became increasingly a partisan of reform and in many aspects could be regarded as a Radical. Bentham and the two Mills and other typically liberal thinkers probably influenced him more or less unconsciously, in conjunction with his constant companions, the Bible, the Greek poets and philosophers, Dante and Edmund Burke. His general ideas acquired from these sources were transformed by his temperament and experience to become Liberal in the sense that they formed the background to an unremitting struggle for tolerance, justice and progress: that is, as Gladstone, with his strong sense of tradition and his respect for established institutions, understood these ideals.

If any one concept can convey the essence of the mature Gladstone's political endeavour, it is self-government. He strove for national autonomy and this was the main trend of his foreign policy. The Colonies, according to him, should be self-governing and, as such, loosely linked with England. In 1850, in Naples he succeeded in visiting the dungeon where the patriot Carlo Poerio, sentenced to twenty-four years' imprisonment in chains, was confined, and having been convinced of the plight of some twenty thousand other political prisoners herded in King Bomba's prisons, in conditions of indescribable filth and cruelty, he became a passionate champion of the unification of Italy, and the stimulus he gave to English policy concerning this issue was perhaps decisive.

One of Gladstone's major political blunders was his statement, in a speech at Newcastle-on-Tyne on 7 October 1862, during the American Civil War, that the seccessionist southern states were about to form a nation. This was another expression of his theory of self-government and his sympathies with national independence. Again, in his *Bulgarian Atrocities* pamphlet and campaign against Disraeli's pro-Turkish foreign policy he was impelled by humanitarian reasons and a concern for the rights of nations. This attitude was evident, it appeared to many, in his feeble and indulgent policy in the years between 1880 and 1884 towards the small Boer states, as also towards Egypt and Afghanistan. It also determined his greatest cnterprise, his espousal in 1886 of the cause of Home Rule for Ireland. It was after this venture, which at the time was radical in a way which can hardly be realized today, that Gladstone—by birth, education and wealth a member of the ruling class—came to be hated by his opponents and by the majority of cultured and aristocratic Englishmen. This hatred still tends to colour the portrayal of him in biographies.

It was not solely the idea of Home Rule which changed Gladstone's outlook to a democratic one, though in practice he had been drawing year by year nearer to democracy. The outstanding proofs of this are the Franchise Reform of 1867 (actually carried through by Disraeli) and the reform of 1885. The extension of the right to vote should not be regarded as 'some Trojan horse approaching the walls of the sacred city, and filled with armed men bent upon ruin, plunder and conflagration' he said of the Reform Bill of 1867. 'Give to these persons new interests in the Constitution; new interests which by the beneficent processes of the law of nature and of Providence, shall beget in them new attachment . . .'

Gladstone's confidence in the common people constantly became more emphatic. He threw the Queen into a state of horrified alarm in 1886 by his reply to a letter of reproof she had written him:

> 'Your Majesty is pleased to regret that Mr Gladstone should repeat the cry against the wealthy and educated classes of the country. In what he has said with reference to wealth, rank and station (rather than education) he is of course open to the effective retort that in a country now somewhat fully represented he is condemned by a majority at the polls. On this he will say nothing, but he may observe that for a long series of years, on all the greater questions dependent mainly on broad considerations of humanity and justice, wealth, station and rank had been wrong, and the masses had been right.'

In spite of his radicalism Gladstone did not deflect the course of social or economic developments by any startling innovations. He could hardly be called a socialistic Liberal, and as Chancellor of the Exchequer his sense of economy always made him falter at the prospect of increasing government expenditure. Nevertheless, during his second ministry he did push through reforms to relieve the misery of the Irish smallholders and this could be regarded as a victory in the struggle of the new Liberals towards economic equality. During his later years he was, more than any other statesman, the champion of the English working man.

It is obvious that in every stage of his career Gladstone was guided to a relatively high degree by his idealistic ideas and that these were not a cloak for ambition, concealing a greed for power and office. Twice, in 1845 and in 1855, he resigned from government on what seemed very flimsy pretexts, but on both occasions it was in fact because of genuine scruples of conscience and behind his actions there was no thought of a sensational retreat in order to prepare for a brilliant return. In 1851 this devout Protestant who abhorred popery, took a strong line against the anti-papist feeling that had been aroused when the Pope divided England into dioceses, gave them territorial titles, and appointed Dr Wiseman the English Catholic leader to be Cardinal-Archbishop of Westminster. Gladstone spoke, though unavailingly, against the Ecclesiastical Titles Assumption Bill introduced by the Prime Minister, Lord Russell, and designed to invalidate the assumption of British territorial designations by Papists. Gladstone, opposing the Bill said: 'We cannot change the profound and resistless tendencies of the age towards religious liberty. It is our business to guide and control their applications.' Twenty years later, when he was in a position to do so, he repealed the Act.

This thundering and vehement orator of public meetings and the house of Commons was capable of much kindness and a sensitive concern for others. An instance of this is recounted by Sir Winston Churchill in his biography of his father, Lord Randolph Churchill. Lord Randolph, Gladstone's junior by forty years, was one of his more brutal antagonists. His address in 1886 to the electors of his constituency (South Paddington)—which his son glosses over lightly—contained some really low invective. In this diatribe against Gladstone Lord Randolph not only coined the contemptuous and damaging phrase 'an old man in a hurry', but he practically accused Gladstone of having treasonable intentions. According to Lord Randolph, the British constitution was to be torn up and the Liberal Party shivered into fragments 'to gratify the ambition of an old man in a hurry'. Here was a man, moreover, he said, who was making 'the most unparalleled claim for dictatorial power which can be conceived by free men'. He called Gladstone's project for Irish Home Rule 'this monstrous mixture of imbecility, extravagance and political hysterics', this 'farrago of superlative nonsense', and said that Gladstone, with audacious profanity 'had recommended himself to the country in the name of Almighty God'.

Gladstone, Almighty God notwithstanding, was defeated and the Conservatives returned to power with Lord Salisbury as Premier. Shortly afterwards, in December 1886, Lord Randolph, who was Chancellor of the Exchequer and leader of the House of Commons, resigned on impulse, in a tactical move to push through his views on the Defence Budget, believing that there was no one to replace him and that his resignation would not be accepted. But he had 'forgotten Goschen', as he was later reputed to have said. Salisbury called his bluff, accepted his resignation, made G. J. Goschen Chancellor of the Exchequer—and Churchill's political career came abruptly to an end. He lingered on, a gravely ill man, for several years (he died in 1895). Paralysis progressively impaired his power of speech, which became blurred, halting and incoherent. During these years of physical decline, whenever Lord Randolph rose to speak, members left the House hurriedly. Not so Gladstone, Prime Minister for the fourth time, who always remained, listened intently to his fallen adversary and gave polite and detailed answers to the painfully laboured utterances which other members fled from hearing.

Gladstone was a Member of Parliament for sixty-three years, a Cabinet member for twenty-seven, Prime Minister for twelve. His character and achievements are more remarkable than even these statistics might suggest. As a human being pure of heart he was exceptional. As a moralist-politician he was probably unique: 'a Simeon Stylites among the statesmen of his time'. He ranks with Abraham Lincoln as one of the great statesmen of the nineteenth century.

A Conservative Idol: Benjamin Disraeli

In the galaxy of Victorian statesmen Disraeli holds a special, if not unique, position as a luminary, more plainly discernible among other shining lights because of an intense and distinctive glow. He was regarded in his day by Conservative intellectuals, both at home and abroad, as the ideal fulfilment of all that a Conservative politician should be. The reason is clear: it was Dizzy's epigrammatic wit, his brilliant rhetoric, his attempt to inject life and colour into tradition through a touch of socialistic radicalism and his dazzling success in foreign affairs which made him their idol.

But the essence of his attraction was his enigmatic personality and actions. His defence of ancient and outworn institutions seems nowadays somewhat naive and over-credulous; but Disraeli managed to make this attitude subtle and intellectually beyond reproach by combining reverence for the Establishment (the monarchy, the Church, the social hierarchy) with a pervading air of scepticism. He acted like a supporter of the right, but frequently talked and wrote like a rabid revolutionary. He was not unlike a bishop who officiates with impeccable solemnity at the altar but turns out, at a dinner party, to be elegant, frivolous and a trifle profane. Quite frequently his attitude approached the most refined type of conservatism, one characterized by melancholy and pessimism: a frame of mind which dwells on a realization of the vanity and transience of all things and the childishness of wishing to make a better world.

Disraeli was one of those who are seized early in life with the fever of ambition and lust for power. Perhaps these feelings were exacerbated in him because such goals seemed, in his case, almost impossible of attainment. To begin with, he was a Jew (though baptized a Christian at the age of twelve) and although his family was well-to-do it was not rich by standards of the time; his upbringing was somewhat unconventional, his formal education having ended at sixteen, and he lacked the sort of social environment which was indispensable to a great career.

But 'Nothing succeeds like success', as Disraeli was to say in later years, and he succeeded in succeeding beyond all expectation. His father's money made it possible for him, in his early twenties, to embark on a life of extravagance, which included falling recklessly and heavily into debt; and if his marriage at the age of thirty-three to a widow of some means twelve years his senior was not a matter of cold-blooded calculation, neither was it without its practical advantages. The use of his wife's money and his improved credit afforded him a timely leg-up at one of the most difficult periods of his life. He became by degrees the dandified, inaccessible, mysterious man of the world who appears in all his novels. These novels, witty and outrageous *romans à clef*, were, in one way, the first steps to success. They made him famous, if not notorious, and eventually they even made money. Politics, his second and parallel career, brought him the greatest, if deferred, rewards: the premiership in 1868 and again in 1874–80. 'Yes', he said to friends who congratulated him the first time he became Prime Minister, 'I have climbed to the top of the greasy pole!'

The annals of nineteenth-century English Toryism include many great names which have won fresh acclaim in the light of modern research and reassessment, names such as Castlereagh, Peel, Shaftesbury, Salisbury. But in the ranks of the great there were also a number of celebrated public figures who enjoyed their share of glory in their day and yet were regarded by some of their contemporaries in the same light as present-day critics and debunkers have viewed them: that is, as political adventurers, not to say confidence tricksters. Disraeli, Lord Randolph Churchill and Joseph Chamberlain are of this brotherhood—and the greatest of them all is Disraeli.

When he died in 1881, at the age of seventy-seven, Disraeli, the first and only Earl of Beaconsfield, received an impressive tribute of national mourning, led by the Queen. Yet his old rival Gladstone avoided attending the funeral. Nothing could persuade him that Disraeli had been sincere in asking in his will for a quiet private funeral rather than the public one in Westminster Abbey which Gladstone had now offered. In his old rival's eyes, Disraeli remained what he had always been: a mountebank and a charlatan. 'As he lived so he died—all display without reality or genuineness.'

When he was old and famous, Disraeli himself provided one of the clues to his character. On a walk with Lady Derby, who was his guest at Hughenden Manor, he pointed out his father's old house, Bradenham Hall—the house where Disraeli had spent much of his early manhood. 'It was there', he told Lady Derby, 'that I passed my miserable youth.' 'Why miserable?' she asked him and he replied: 'I was devoured by ambition I did not see any means of gratifying.'

There was nothing extraordinary in the objectives of the young Disraeli's ambition—fame, riches and above all power. What made them remarkable was the almost morbid intensity of his compulsion. The explanation has often been sought in Disraeli's Jewish ancestry. Although his father, Isaac D'Israeli, was beyond doubt a highly cultured, distinguished and wealthy man, his son—with what justification it is difficult to understand—felt himself to be an outsider, a member of a despised minority group; the need to rise in triumph over this and throw it back in the teeth of society was the whiplash that drove him on. To feel equal Disraeli had to be superior—he had to become a great man.

His ways of getting on were many and varied. He wrote his novels, made every effort to get into Parliament, and, affecting a dandyism similar to Oscar Wilde's in later years, excelled in a foppish and eccentric elegance that was not without a touch of vulgarity. He made unabashed use of his friends and with considerable success courted rich and aristocratic leaders of fashionable society. But he was an old man before he attained his goal, by which time, however, he had become the leader of the Conservative Party and the personification of English nationalism.

Two episodes of Disraeli's early life, one concerning his friendship with Benjamin and Sarah Austen and the other with his love affair with Lady Henrietta Sykes, brought to light some years ago by the American scholar Professor B. R. Jerman in *The Young Disraeli* (1960)—and indispensable reading for a proper understanding of Disraeli's youthful indiscretions—reveal the striking combination of brash importunity, effrontery and dishonesty with which the young Disraeli started his climb.

In 1821 when he was almost seventeen, through the efforts of relatives he was articled as a clerk to a firm of solicitors. It was a period of feverish English speculation in South American mining and with a couple of friends—a fellow clerk and the son of a rich stockbroker—he started to speculate in the stock-market. In the course of this gamble he came into contact with a well-known financier, John Diston Powles, who employed him to write three pamphlets designed to puff worthless South American mining concerns promoted by Powles. Disraeli, who by then had left the solicitor's firm, was at the time employed by the publisher John Murray as reader and assistant and it was Murray who published the pamphlets.

Together with Powles, Disraeli then became involved in a fresh venture: an abortive attempt, in association with Murray, to start a daily paper, *The Representative*, which should rival *The Times*. Disraeli and Powles agreed to supply one-quarter each of the capital to start the newspaper—Disraeli's share to come, presumably, from his anticipated winnings on the stock-market. Both ventures proved equally disastrous. The newspaper, which made its appearance in January 1826, was doomed from the start by various factors, not least an economic depression, and lasted a bare six months. But, for reasons unknown, Disraeli had faded out even before the first issue appeared, his association with Murray having terminated mysteriously in mid-December. Almost simultaneously, the South American mining bubble burst, ruining many in the stock-market panic, among them Powles and Disraeli. Having come of age on 21 December, Disraeli now found himself in debt to the tune of several thousand pounds. It was the first of a series of financial embarrassments which were to hamper his career and plague him throughout his life.

In 1826 he made the acquaintance of Benjamin Austen, a Gray's Inn solicitor with a successful practice. Austen was a decent man, kindly, practical and methodical. He was willing to lend Disraeli money and in the ensuing years, out of friendship, helped him with one loan after another. Sara Austen, the solicitor's wife, who had been on friendly terms with Disraeli's family since the year before Disraeli had met Austen, was a clever and attractive woman, seven years younger than her husband and some eight years older than Disraeli who was then not yet twenty-two. In after years Mrs Austen's nephew, Henry Layard, remembered her as 'a woman of more than ordinary talent and of more than ordinary beauty, very ambitious of shining in society and fond of flattery and admiration'. She was appreciative of Disraeli's attentiveness and possibly not a little infatuated with the prepossessing young man who was also a precocious and self-styled genius.

Mrs Austen, who had had some dealings with the publisher Colburn, was instrumental in getting him to accept Disraeli's first novel *Vivian Grey*, which was published anonymously in 1826. She helped her young genius, advised him and even copied out the manuscript, to avoid giving any clue to the author's identity. Disraeli's friendship with the Austens lasted for a number of years, and while he was making his way as a novelist Mrs Austen continued to be his adviser, his amanuensis and, even when the need for anonymity had passed, his go-between.

Vivian Grey was a *succès de scandale* and it offended many influential people whom Disraeli lampooned in it. The secret of the author's identity was soon out and the novel did much harm to Disraeli's reputation and subsequent career. But he could never live it down, though he tried for the rest of his life to do so.

Since his early youth Disraeli's health had been a cause of anxiety to his family and until his marriage in 1839 he suffered from periodic bouts of a crippling debility, a 'mysterious illness' of the type known today as psychosomatic. (He suffered, too, in his maturity and old age from another psychosomatic ailment, bronchial asthma, from the complications of which he eventually died.)

In his youth stresses and difficulties generally brought on violent headaches which frequently obliged him to take to his bed. He was ill, on and off, in this fashion from 1826 to 1832. A tour of the Continent in 1826 with his friends the Austens did him good, and he improved somewhat in 1829 under treatment from his new London physician Dr George Buckley Bolton (who was to re-enter his life in a different and less welcome fashion some years later). But the accumulated strain of the past years—his financial setbacks and debts, the abortive and doubtless humiliating affair of *The Representative*, the terrific haste in which he wrote *Vivien Grey*—'as hot and hurried a sketch as ever yet was penned' —and its sequel, had brought him to the verge of a nervous breakdown. Convinced that warmer climates and a momentary escape from his creditors would restore his health, he determined on a tour of the East, a region in which he had developed a deep interest. So he set to work with all speed to write a pot-boiler, his third novel, *The Young Duke*. He sold the copyright to the publisher Colburn for £500 with a loan from Austen he was able to set out, in March 1830, for the Mediterranean and the Near East on a Grand Tour which was to have a vital effect not only on his future novels but, many years later, on his attitude to Britain's foreign and imperial policy.

As travelling companion Disraeli had his friend William George Meredith, who was his sister Sarah's unofficial fiancé and whose family and Disraeli's were close friends. The two young men travelled about for eighteen months, lingering in the places which most attracted them: Spain, Albania, Greece, Turkey, Egypt. When their sightseeing interests conflicted they temporarily parted company and so, while Meredith explored ruined cities in Egypt, Disraeli visited the Holy Land, which had a special interest for him as the land of his forefathers.

Tragedy cut short this Grand Tour as the two friends were in Cairo preparing to start on their homeward journey. Meredith developed small-pox and, in spite of good medical care, died after an illness of a few weeks, on 19 July 1832. Disraeli, after a month's delay in quarantine, hurried home to comfort his heart-broken sister and the two grieving families. Sarah never again contemplated marriage but dedicated herself to her family and especially to Ben, her adored eldest brother, on whom she lavished a passionate devotion for the rest of her life.

Back in London, following his tour of the East, Disraeli, who had hoped to become an instant celebrity six years previously with the publication of *Vivian Grey*, but had failed to do so, again tried to break into Society. This time he was more successful. With the help of his friend the novelist Lytton Bulwer whom he had met in 1830 and who was now at the height of his fame, Disraeli at last got a toe-hold in 'the charmed circle of Mayfair'. In this world of fashion and politics he soon found grander and more entertaining company than the Austens, whom he now virtually dropped, since they could be of little further use to him in his climb up the social ladder. Though he lived in Mayfair, a mere half-hour's walk from their house in Bloomsbury, he rarely visited the couple and confined himself to borrowing money from the solicitor by letter. Disraeli's correspondence with the Austens is a study in emotional blackmail in the course of which he used every trick of prevarication, excuse, cajolery and flattery.

In November 1833 Disraeli was beset by creditors, in love with an expensive mistress Lady Henrietta Sykes, and embarking on an ambitious new work, an epic poem no less, for which he needed peace of mind. He had recently borrowed £300 from Austen but wrote to him again to ask for a further loan, to be paid back in a year. As security he offered the copyrights (which he had bought back from Colburn) of his novels, together with the copyright of his latest, still unpublished novel, and the poem, the *Revolutionary Epick*, which he was then engaged in writing. He was, he said, 'overwhelmed with difficulties', and the worry of his debts was a hindrance in the writing of this poem, for which he had high hopes.

> 'Therefore I appeal to you, a friend often tried & never found wanting, & whom I know by long experience to be capable of great and generous actions. . . . Will you advance me the money for a year & take a formal assignment of my copyrights? . . . Assist me now, & for my future career I shall in fact be indebted to you.'

Simultaneously Disraeli received a letter from Mrs Austen, somewhat cooler than formerly, but still friendly in tone, in which she told him that she was 'always most happy to have an opportunity of being useful' to him. Disraeli wrote her in reply an enthusiastic and flattering letter, telling her about the progress of his great poem, asking her advice, complementing her on her energy in carrying out a small task of research he had requested: 'What would I give to have you always at my right hand'. As in the past he bound her to secrecy about his projects, though of course she might, he said, tell her husband.

This letter to Mrs Austen crossed with her husband's reply to Disraeli's begging letter. The solicitor, with some bluntness, refused him the loan:

> 'I am not justified in ever putting in jeopardy so large a sum as you name unless urged by the strongest & most irresistible claims upon my friendship. . . . I have asked myself have you now such claims & I am compelled to come to the conclusion that you have not. . . . You say . . . "you appeal to me as a friend often tried but never found wanting"—I am sorry to say, my dear Disraeli, that you have tried me too often & more so to add that I have felt for some time past that your recollection of it ceased with the necessity.'

Nevertheless, and perhaps to take the sting of unkindness out of his refusal, Austen signed himself 'Your most sincere friend'.

Disraeli, to whom this letter must have been quite a shock, waited for a while and then replied with a long and wounded letter. 'Rest assured', he said, 'that had I indeed supposed that I had troubled you "too often", you never would have been troubled again. I really thought you would have done anything for me, & thats the truth.'

He went on to argue that it was precisely his request for a loan that proved the depth of his friendship for Austen, since 'I ask favours, such favours, only of friends'. If he had had other friends, Disraeli added, he would not have been in the position of having 'to write this humiliating letter . . . I am sorry to be forced to say all this—but really when one's friends turn against one in this wretched world, one does not like to be deserted without a struggle . . .'.

For the grand finale he pulled out all the stops:

> 'Farewell! I am grateful for the past, & for your generous kindness which I have often experienced—It has never burthened my heart, for I thought you were delighted to assist me; it is with bitterness I at length discover my mistake . . . I accept the compliment of your signature—but I am too shrewd an observer not to feel that that is all now over, & that as far as friendship is concerned, I am now alone in the world, and always will be.'

This was the cue for Austen to be hurt in his turn, at Disraeli's disbelief in the expressions of friendship which had accompanied his refusal of the loan. He wrote back:

> 'Does it not occur to you that the more sincere the Friend, the more sensitive he is of neglect . . . I can scarcely call that a strong Friendship which holds no communication either of thoughts or actions & is in fact perfectly estranged for months tho' within ½ hours walk—I must remind you with the same pain as I mentioned it before, that you only broke thro' this estrangement on particular occasions—& this it is that I felt deeply.'

With this justification the way to reconciliation was open. A further exchange of correspondence, coupled with Mrs Austen's influence on her husband in favour of the young genius, enabled the estrangement to be patched up. The re-establishment of cordial relations, backed up by a timely Christmas call on the couple, got Disraeli the loan he wanted, and at a minimal rate of interest.

Disraeli's ruthlessness and cunning were rarely put to more effective use than in his dealings with the Austens; for, not only did he ask and receive this loan in the name of friendship, but he continued at intervals throughout the ten years of their relationship, to borrow from the solicitor on the same grounds and under pretexts of speedy repayment. He frequently postponed the repayments, finding plausible excuses for his inability to do so, coupled with protestations of gratitude and renewed avowals of friendship. But at the same time he rarely made any effort to call on the couple or go to the parties and dinners to which they invited him. Mrs Austen wrote to him in 1826 when they were working on *Vivian Grey* 'Remember that you have the entrée whenever you like to come—at all hours . . .', and in 1832 the couple gave him a standing invitation to call on them whenever he pleased. But he continued to be forgetful of them and their invitations. On one occasion the Austens, 'very irate', complained to his family that he had not turned up at one of their dinners at which he was to meet the water-colourist Samuel Prout. 'They invited you to dinner on Saturday week . . . and even waited dinner for you. . . .' Shortly afterwards he was on the verge of offending them again and was saved only by a timely reminder from Sarah that he had accepted two engagements for the same evening and that the Austens had the prior claim.

In spite of his constant excuses the couple continued to feel his neglect, and Austen, who was nothing if not straightforward, frequently wrote to tell him so; Disraeli as frequently denied that he was neglecting them. Nevertheless the neglect, the excuses and the borrowing continued. At last in 1836, Austen seemed to have had enough of this one-sided relationship. He reproached Disraeli once again for not visiting him and his wife, adding a reminder that the next payment on Disraeli's current debt was due in a few weeks time.

Disraeli's difficulties were genuine, but through ill-luck or over-optimism his affairs never seemed to pan out as he expected. What Austen did not know was that Disraeli was in the hands of the money-lenders, though the solicitor was beginning to suspect that he was not the only one from whom Disraeli was borrowing. Harried and worried by 'bills, writs, annuities, renewals, discountings, assignments . . . and all the other appurtenances of usury', Disraeli wrote Austen his usual long letter of excuses and explanations and promised to pay up. A month went by with no money forthcoming. Austen then wrote to him that he believed Disraeli's debts were greater than he had revealed, and advised him to ask the elder Disraeli for help. But this was the very last thing Disraeli wanted to do. He was anxious at all costs to keep from his father and his family the knowledge of how much he owed.

Austen peppered him with dunning letters all through 1836, complaining that his patience was exhausted, that he was being made to suffer serious inconvenience, constant disappointments, exceeding annoyance. He demanded at length that Disraeli should speak to his father and when his demand still went unheeded he threatened to sue unless he received the balance of the money due to him.

Disraeli managed to stave him off for a while longer with apologies, explanations, regrets, and more promises, while Austen's dunning letters continued in an unending stream. Finally, in February 1837, Disraeli, simultaneously hard pressed by his other creditors, consented to do as Austen insisted. He asked his father for help, though without telling the kind old man the whole truth. The elder Disraeli paid off the money-lenders and settled up all but thirty pounds of the debt to Austen. Disraeli promised to pay this off from the proceeds of his new novel *Venetia* and when the book came out in May 1837 one of the first things he did was to send Austen his thirty pounds. With this settlement Disraeli's connection with the solicitor virtually ended. 'No two people', observes Professor Jerman in his account of the episode, 'could have been more pleased to get rid of each other'. Disraeli wrote a single letter in 1839, in answer to Sara Austen, months after she had written to thank him for a copy of *Count Alarcos*, his recently published blank verse drama, and with this the Austens finally passed out of his life.

'Those who want to lead', he had written in 1834, 'must never hesitate about sacrificing their friends.' He was ruthless in discarding those who could be of no further use to him—and the Austens had ended up by being bores into the bargain. 'As the years passed by, he came to regard them as something even less pleasing,' Robert Blake observes in his major biography, 'reminders of a time when he had been raffish, struggling, debt-ridden and dependent . . .'

Disraeli appears to have conducted his love affairs with as few scruples as he did his social relationships. The motif of extortion already seen in his dealings with the Austens can be glimpsed yet again in some of the incidents and manoeuvres in his notorious affair with Henrietta Sykes, which began in 1833 and had been one of the contributory causes in his growing neglect of Benjamin and Sara Austen.

In 1832, now aged twenty-eight, the much talked-of author of a sensational novel, and a parliamentary candidate with the disarming label of 'radical tory', Disraeli had at last succeeded in gaining the entrée into smart London society. Now, rubbing shoulders with the great and near-great, on dining and party-going terms with the famous and fashionable, he could write to his sister: 'My table is literally covered with invitations, some from people I do not know.'

In these circles, for the next three years, two gentlemen, each accompanied by a lady, were often to be seen at parties, dinners, balls, routs, picnics, river parties: they were Disraeli, Sir Francis and Lady Sykes and Mrs Bolton, a lady from somewhere lower down the social scale. She was, in fact the wife of the same Dr George Buckley Bolton who had successfully treated Disraeli in 1829. They were all near neighbours: Dr Bolton and his wife lived in Park Lane, Sir Francis and Lady Sykes had their town house in Upper Grosvenor Street, while Disraeli lived in comfortable bachelor rooms in Duke Street, St. James's.

The relationship of the pleasure-going foursome was somewhat involved. Mrs Bolton had known Disraeli and his family since the late 1820s when her husband had become Disraeli's London doctor and she became a staunch supporter of the young parliamentary candidate during his

High Wycombe campaign of June 1832. Their friendship is thought to have developed that year into an affair; at all events, Mrs Bolton was commonly held by at least the male members of Disraeli's family to be his mistress. The affair with Clara Bolton lasted for a year, after which Disraeli discarded her for Lady Sykes. Some months later Mrs Bolton had found a new protector, Sir Francis Sykes. Dr. Bolton seemed content to play the role of *mari complaisant* and, as quoted in Professor Jerman's book, it was even reported in a memorandum written after Disraeli's death by Sir Philip Rose, his solicitor and friend for nearly forty years and one of his executors, that Mrs Bolton had become the mistress of Sir Francis 'with the husband's knowledge and consent, who was said to derive a pecuniary benefit from the connection'. Even Disraeli, writing to a friend, referred to Mrs Bolton as 'a decoy duck'.

Lady Sykes, Disraeli's Henrietta, a woman of striking and voluptuous beauty, headstrong, wilful, and passionate, was considered withal 'a fine and pleasant and good-natured woman'. She was also emotional, jealous, highly-sexed and entirely unmanageable by her husband who, though amiable and not unintelligent, had a character as weak as his health. When Disraeli and Henrietta began their love affair she was probably in her early thirties and the mother of four children, the eldest of whom, then eleven, had been born when Disraeli was not yet seventeen.

Disraeli had met her in the spring of 1833 and by summer they were involved in a passionate love affair which was to last for the next three years and which, in Disraeli's private estimation was harmful to his health and damaging to his career. It was certainly catastrophic to his finances. In September 1833 he wrote (in his so-called 'mutilated' Diary): 'I have passed the whole of this year (that is until the present month September) in uninterrupted lounging and pleasures . . . & one incident has indeed made this year the happiest of my life.' He added: 'How long will these feelings last? . . . Nature has given me an awful ambition and fiery passions.' Even in love he had no illusions about himself. One so determined to become a great man could never think the world well lost for love.

The reason for the appearance everywhere together of the Sykeses with Disraeli and Mrs Bolton was to conceal as far as possible the real relationship between the two couples. Sir Frances, the third baronet, whose father in his profligate youth had been involved in an appalling marital scandal, was sensitive of public opinion and insisted on the company of Disraeli and Henrietta whenever he went out with Mrs Bolton. In exchange for this he countenanced his wife's liaison with Disraeli. The two women detested each other, although Mrs Bolton made a great show of friendship to Lady Sykes. Henrietta treated Clara Bolton at best with condescension and an ill-concealed disdain; a bearing which amounted, on her own admission, to scant civility. The arrangement nevertheless worked tolerably well for the first year, during the brilliant London season of 1833.

When Sir Francis threatened to create difficulties, the existence of Mrs Bolton's husband in the background provided a useful means of bringing Henrietta's husband to heel. While Disraeli was at Bradenham, having torn himself away from Henrietta to write his *Revolutionary Epick*, he received an agitated letter from her: 'I fear me much, my Beloved, there is a storm brewing over our devoted heads.' Sir Francis was making objections to Disraeli's relations with his wife. Mrs Bolton, a discarded mistress, wounded in her self-esteem, evidently jealous and certainly hostile, had been trying to stir up trouble. She now regarded Disraeli as an arch-villain and was doing her best to turn the baronet, who was away shooting grouse, against him. Sir Francis arrived back in London from grouse-shooting apparently at the instigation of Mrs Bolton, and amid rows and arguments forbade his wife to see Disraeli again. After these scenes and when she had written and torn up several notes telling Mrs Bolton what she thought of her, Henrietta decided to go round to Park Lane and have things out face to face. When she arrived, her husband's carriage stood at the Boltons' open door. Henrietta did not wait to be ushered in but swept upstairs. A marvellously dramatic scene now took place: 'I walked in *sans* knocking, and up to the drawing room *sans* being announced,' she told Disraeli. 'Fancy their consternation. I really thought Francis would have fainted.' In full command of the situation, 'stiff as a poker and perfectly cool', Henrietta said:

> 'Mrs Bolton, I have called upon you in consequence of a scene which I am perfectly aware I owe entirely to you, and I am here to have an understanding, as from what has passed there can be no reserve between us 3. . . . It has suited all parties to be a great deal together, not certainly from the intimacy of the ladies, for I have never expressed a friendship for you. . . . I have never been even commonly ladylike in my conduct to you. . . .'

Unless Sir Francis were in town, she said, nothing would ever induce her even to set foot over the Bolton doorstep,

> '. . . but I will give Francis the sanction of my presence on the strict condition of his not violating by unjust and ungenerous threats ties which he himself has sanctioned and which both himself and yourself know have been necessary to carry on your own game.'

Mrs Bolton protested her friendship for Henrietta, whose treatment of her, she said, had caused her pain and surprise and who, she insisted, had misunderstood her intentions throughout the present imbroglio. She then proceeded to run down Disraeli: He was a heartless wretch for whom she had stuck up for years. She went on to say that Henrietta's character was gone because of Disraeli, and for good measure added that she had heard on good authority that no one would visit Henrietta next year '. . . & he will leave you, he has left you, I know him well. . . .'

Henrietta, blazing with rage, rejected Mrs Bolton's calumnies, launched out in passionate counter-attack, and at length had the satisfaction of reducing the pair to abject submission: 'Suffice for you & I that we are victorious,' she wrote to Disraeli. 'Madame cried & wrung her hands. F cried & begged me to be merciful. I did *not* cry & had apologies from both.'

At the end of August, Disraeli arrived to put things straight with Sir Francis, and Henrietta went with her husband for a few weeks tour of France. When she returned towards the end of September, Disraeli hurriedly left Bradenham, his family and his epic poem, to be with her in London.

Their idyll was now complicated by Henrietta's father, Henry Villebois, a rich Norfolk brewery magnate, who strongly disapproved of the liaisons of both his daughter and son-in-law. He intimated to Henrietta that he would have nothing further to do with her unless she broke with Disraeli, and he censured Sir Francis for consorting with Mrs Bolton who, he said, was no fit companion either for his son-in-law or Henrietta.

The two of them paid no heed to old Mr Villebois—indeed, they flouted him by both of them inviting Disraeli to stay with them at Southend. For the sake of appearances and because one good turn deserves another, Sir Francis also insisted on the Boltons staying as regular guests. Henrietta, naturally, was not pleased. 'The greatest draw-back', she wrote to Disraeli, 'will be the *damnable* Boltons.' When he returned to Bradenham at the end of November after staying with the Sykeses for a month, she chafed at the continued presence of the un-welcome couple: 'Hourly, nay every minute annoyed by the coarse vulgarity of the one, and the hypocrisy, the low cunning of the other.'

As always, Disraeli was in financial straits: the accumulated result of his early misadventure on the stock-market, the expense of his electioneering and his moving in fashionable society amid extravagant companions who now included Henrietta. In spite of his diligence as an author, the money he hoped to make out of his writings did not material-ize. Sometimes it was very much less than he had anticipated and almost invariably it was not available at the moment he needed it.

On his way back to Bradenham from Southend he broke his journey in London in order to placate Benjamin Austen and borrow £300 from him—a mere drop in the ocean of his debts. Once back at home in the country he began the correspondence, described earlier, designed to secure for him a further loan of £1,200 which he needed to cover his most pressing debts. Austen's blunt refusal called forth loyal indignation on Disraeli's behalf from Henrietta, who thought the refusal brutal and Austen's reproaches rude, 'for, after all, a man's ceasing to visit when he is in love is not an unusual occurrence, is it?' The loan, which Disraeli finally obtained in December, provided a temporary respite from his financial worries.

The course of true love seemed to run a little smoother too. In April 1834 Sir Francis went on a tour of Europe and remained abroad until late in 1836. Mrs Bolton also went abroad at this time and, as it so happened, passed out of their lives. (She was last heard of in 1835, living alone in Rotterdam and she died in France in the autumn of 1839.) For the time being there appeared to be no further obstacle to the love affair of Disraeli and Henrietta. He went to live openly with her in the Upper Grosvenor Street house and Sir Francis, writing in friendly terms to them both, sent his letters to Disraeli to that address. The pair went everywhere together, enjoying to the full 'a season of unparalleled success and gaiety'.

Lord Lyndhurst now comes on the scene. American-born, he was the only son of the painter John Singleton Copley. A clever man and a brilliant lawyer, Lyndhurst had been Tory Lord Chancellor from 1827 to 1830 and was to take seat on the wool-sack twice again, 1834–35 and 1841–46. He was known to be ribald, cynical, licentious of speech, reckless and indiscreet in conversation. His misplaced levity was thought unbecoming in a statesman and served to cast doubt on his reliability. He was also a notorious womanizer, a good-looking man whose youthful appearance belied his age. He was sixty-two when Disraeli and he first met, at the latter end of the summer of 1834, at Henrietta's. They sat next to each other at dinner and took to each other instantly, though Disraeli was less than half Lord Lyndhurst's age.

Henrietta and Lord Lyndhurst had been friendly for some time. In June she had written to Disraeli that she was going to the theatre in Lyndhurst's party and said: 'I can will in him every thing, & where women are concerned never was there a greater fool & I solemnly think not the least of a love.'

In view of Lord Lyndhurst's reputation it was commonly assumed that he and Henrietta were more than merely friends. According to the memorandum of Sir Philip Rose, quoted by both Professor Jerman and Dr Blake: 'The positive assertion at the time, that Lady Sykes was the mistress of both D. and Lord Lyndhurst was evidently true. The allegation at the time was that D. introduced her to Lord L. and made use of the influence she acquired over Lord L. to forward his own advancement.' But Disraeli's account of his first meeting with Lyndhurst would seem to settle the point of who was introduced first to whom. Nor is there concrete evidence that Henrietta was Lyndhurst's mistress. All that is certain is that he was excessively susceptible to women, that Henrietta could twist him round her little finger and that she did use her influence with him to help Disraeli's political career. Lyndhurst was, after all, an influential man, able and willing to help an ambitious younger man determined to succeed in politics, and he was well-disposed towards Disraeli from the outset. Soon after their first meeting Disraeli was invited by Lord Lyndhurst to dine with him and his family and a friendship was established which was to last until Lyndhurst's death in 1863.

In the autumn of 1834 Lyndhurst, who had been recently widowed, planned to go abroad with his daughter and sister and he invited Henrietta to accompany the party. The invitation came as a godsend, for Henrietta's father and sister were still insistent that she should leave Disraeli and were coming to London to persuade her to return to Norfolk and live with them there. She would lose her senses, she said, if she had to go to her father, and Lord Lyndhurst's offer now seemed a good way to evade the concerned interference of her relatives; besides, she believed she could be of help to Disraeli during the trip, for Lyndhurst, she told him, was anxious that he should enter Parliament. She added that she thought Lyndhurst an excellent being, though too pleasure-loving and a perfect fool where women were concerned; but she liked him, he was good-natured and she was sure she could make him do whatever she pleased.

Henrietta was very hard up, practically penniless, at the time. Sir Francis had left England without making any adequate provision for her and the children or for the upkeep of several houses, and, although Lord Lyndhurst was paying the expenses of the forthcoming tour, she needed some ready cash. The day before her departure she wrote to ask Disraeli to lend her some money:

> 'If you could conveniently send me 10£ I should be very glad. I am pennyless & what is to become of us I know not. I had to pay the washerwoman & the old coachman & the horrid house at St Leonards, & though Lord Lyndhurst pays for everything [on the trip], I may want a few pounds.'

In the autumn of 1834 Lyndhurst returned from his holiday on the Continent and Disraeli noted 'we met again with much intimacy. It was at the end of October that he first began to speak to me in confidence on political affairs.' The intimacy of the two men increased and before long Disraeli was acting as a sort of unofficial private secretary for Lyndhurst, continuing for the next two years to be his go-between and general factotum.

Henrietta was still in dire straits for money. Early in 1835 Disraeli wrote on her behalf to Sir Francis pointing out that she could not possibly keep up the position befitting a baronet's wife or educate his children on the remittance she was receiving. The baronet, who was ailing, and disinclined to face Henrietta's meddlesome family, replied that under no circumstances would he return to England; but as a result of Disraeli's intercession Sir Francis now made his wife an allowance of £1,800 a year for the upkeep of herself and their London home and authorized her to draw on his bankers for whatever sum she might require for the payment of their children's schooling.

The ill-assorted quartet of 1833 had now become an amicable threesome, composed of Disraeli, Henrietta and Lord Lyndhurst. They were frequently seen together, in the early summer of 1835, enjoying all the pleasures of the London season. Gossip followed their progress. Henrietta had made one visit to Bradenham with Disraeli in 1833, at the start of their love affair. Now she made two more, one in July and one in the autumn. This time she was accompanied by Lord Lyndhurst, and the country gentry were scandalized. From family correspondence it would seem that the visits were made more at the insistence of Disraeli's sister Sara than of himself, but the county, for whom appearances were otherwise, was incensed that Disraeli should have introduced 'his reputed mistress and her Paramour to his *Home* and made them associates of his Sister, as well as his Father & Mother'. These scandalous visits were not forgotten and did Disraeli much harm in a neighbourhood where he had hopes that the electorate would vote him into Parliament.

'Parted for ever from Henrietta', Disraeli wrote in his diary in the autumn of 1836. Whether the two lovers parted because Disraeli had tired of Henrietta's distracting and exhausting possessiveness, or whether through gossip he had discovered that he had been supplanted, is uncertain. Perhaps a combination of the two circumstances made it both expedient and possible to break off the relationship. Sir Philip Rose believed that Disraeli had broken it off of his own will. Robert Blake exploring several possibilities, has suggested that Henrietta may even have sought consolation in a fresh love affair because Disraeli had broken with her. Whatever the cause, their affair appears to have terminated abruptly, though they still exchanged some correspondence about a few details which needed settling, such as the safe-keeping of Disraeli's collection of daggers.

Disraeli had indeed been supplanted, and by his friend, David Maclise the painter, a successful, handsome, and philandering Irishman of Scottish descent, whom he had known since 1833. By the autumn of 1836 Disraeli was evidently in no doubt about Henrietta's new affair and by December all his friends knew about it and were condoling with him.

Although the 'disgraceful catastrophe' which had burst 'with triple thunder' over Disraeli's head was wounding alike to his affections and his self-esteem, he made a rapid recovery. Soon, as he phrased it in letters to a few intimate friends, his misfortune passed out of the category of 'domestic convulsions which strike one to the centre', and Henrietta could be consigned at length, among 'encumbrances' and 'malignant mistresses', to the general category of 'the plague of women'.

Sir Francis Sykes, improved in health, returned to England at the end of 1836. He apparently countenanced or feigned ignorance of his wife's new liaison. She, whether rightly or wrongly, believed he knew nothing about it, and commented, in what is believed to be her last letter to Disraeli, that her husband was tolerably kind to her, that they might go abroad and that he did not suspect that she and Disraeli had parted.

Relations between Henrietta and her husband were still amicable in the first half of 1837, when Maclise painted a family group, but later in the year, 'during the election' (as Disraeli noted in his diary), 'occurred the terrible catastrophe of Henrietta nearly one year after we had parted'. Sir Francis discovered her in bed with Maclise in the Park Lane house and was led to attempt proceedings for 'criminal conversation' against the painter. According to the report in *The Times*, this fell through because Pyne and Richards, the solicitors who handled Sir Francis's affairs, would not accept the case on the grounds that past events (his own relations with Mrs Bolton and his condonation of Henrietta's with Disraeli) might have proved damaging to him.

Sir Francis then put his affairs into the hands of another firm, who discovered that a payment of £2,000 over and above Henrietta's annual allowance had been made at some time between 1836–37. This led to another dispute and an attempted suit for recovery of the money, which also came to nothing, having been either withdrawn or settled out of court. Recent biographers have suggested that this money went to help save Disraeli from bankruptcy. At this time he had made a substantial payment to his creditors, the source of which it has been impossible to trace. The action against Maclise (*Sykes v. Maclise*, 1838) was also withdrawn and eventually no legal action was taken against Henrietta. But the tangled web of this scandal, now the object of widespread gossip, was irretrievably damaging to her and she ceased to move in society for the few remaining years of her life. She died in May 1846, three years after Sir Francis.

The election which took place at the time of Henrietta's disgrace was the General Election of July 1837. This was Disraeli's fifth election in five years and he was finally successful in getting into Parliament.

From the moment he had entered the political arena his efforts to make his way in politics had met with one setback after another. He had made his first attempt in June 1832 before the recently passed Reform Act had come into force. Now, standing for High Wycombe as a Radical, he declared that he wore the badge of no party. He had already given an inkling, in *Gallomania*, of the line he would take: 'I am neither a Whig nor a Tory. My politics are described in one word and that word is England.' Dressed in conspicuously gorgeous clothes, he harangued a tiny electorate from the portico of the Red Lion Inn on the main street of High Wycombe, but to no avail, he was defeated by twenty votes to twelve.

He had another go in December of the same year, when he stood for the first reformed Parliament. Mounting the hustings at High Wycombe once more, he was again unsuccessful, standing at the bottom of the polls when they closed on 12 December. At that time, general elections were spread over several weeks and this often enabled a defeated candidate to have another try elsewhere. Disraeli immediately put himself forward for the county of Buckinghamshire, unaware that a second Tory candidate had just been nominated. When he learned of the fact he withdrew and, nothing daunted, stood on the hustings as supporter of the second candidate. In the following year he made an attempt to stand for Marylebone and got as far as issuing his address to the electorate, but the expected vacancy did not occur.

After his second High Wycombe defeat and the disappointment of his hopes at Marylebone, he let politics slide for a while and turned his energies to getting into London society, where he made rapid headway. Simultaneously he carried on his love affair with Henrietta, wrote his epic poem and dashed off a quantity of controversial political journalism. He got to know everyone of importance and with the help of Lord Lyndhurst gained influential political friends, steadily hoisting himself, rung by rung, up the social and political ladder.

In late 1834, in readiness for the imminent General Election of 1835, he put himself forward once more as a Radical candidate for High Wycombe and returned to canvass the electorate. This time, through the good offices of Lord Lyndhurst, he had the backing of the Tories; but despite his adroit performance on the hustings he did not carry the election and found himself once more at the bottom of the polls.

His third failure convinced Disraeli that he would never succeed in entering Parliament as an independent Radical and that he must identify himself with one or other of the two great organized parties. Declaring himself henceforward a Tory he applied for membership to the Carlton Club, which, founded in 1831 by the Duke of Wellington and his friends, had become the recognized social stronghold of the Tories. He enlisted his friend Lady Blessington and others to canvass for him. His proposer and seconder were two other friends, Lords Strangford and Chandos, who in the meantime became, respectively, a member of the selection committee and its chairman. In March 1836, after considerable opposition among the committee had according to Disraeli, been overcome by his friends, he was elected; one of fifty chosen from four hundred aspirants 'all in their own opinion with equal claims'.

In April 1835 he was sent by the party to Taunton to contest the re-election of Henry Labouchere who had been obliged by the custom of those times to vacate his seat on taking up an appointment in the new Melbourne government. Disraeli conducted a grilling campaign: 'In a rage of enthusiasm; even my opponents promise to vote for me *next time*. The fatigue is awful. Two long speeches to-day, and nine hours' canvass on foot in a blaze of repartee.' His clothing and appearance were as striking as his impassioned oratory, and he won considerable popularity. He was not dissatisfied with his performance: 'I believe in point of energy, eloquence and effect I have far exceeded all my former efforts'. But in spite of them Labouchere was re-elected.

During this election Disraeli made a jibe at the Whigs, who had just entered into a parliamentary alliance with the Irish leader Daniel O'Connell. He said that they had formed an alliance with one whom they had formerly denounced as a traitor. The newspapers picked up a garbled version of Disraeli's words which made it appear that he had called O'Connell 'an incendiary and a traitor'.

From Dublin, O'Connell, riposted with a ferocious torrent of vituperation of the lowest kind, calling Disraeli, among other equally insulting names 'a vile creature', 'a living lie', a 'miscreant' and 'a reptile'. Not content with this he had a fling at Disraeli's Jewishness, calling him 'the lineal descendant of the impenitent thief of the Crucifixion'.

Disraeli responded by printing an open letter quite as offensive in tone as O'Connell's diatribe. It was known that O'Connell, having once killed a man in a duel had sworn never to duel again. O'Connell's son Morgan had recently fought a duel on his father's behalf with Lord Alvanley who had insulted the elder O'Connell, and had been called by him, in return 'a bloated buffoon'. Disraeli now challenged Morgan O'Connell to a duel. The son replied that he was not answerable for his father's words. Disraeli then published a long letter full of insulting taunts and again wrote to Morgan O'Connell to challenge him. The police intervened, however, and no duel took place. Disraeli was bound over to keep the peace. He gained a great deal of notoriety and publicity from the affair and was proud of the way he had 'squabashed' the O'Connells. The quarrel, though based on a misunderstanding, permanently impaired relations between Disraeli and the elder O'Connell. Many years later they went through the motions of a reconciliation. O'Connell sent a message of peace to Disraeli, saying that he regretted their misunderstanding and that he had long known that he had been misinformed and misled. Disraeli replied courteously but avoided any personal communication, while O'Connell, he observed, 'always made me a very reverential bow afterwards'.

After his defeat in the Taunton by-election, Disraeli bypassed the hustings for the next couple of years. During this period he wrote a good deal of political journalism and published a 200-page pamphlet, *a Vindication of the English constitution in a letter to a noble and learned Lord* by Disraeli the Younger: *The Vindication*, as it became known, in which he crystallized his ideas and gave a full exposition of his political creed. This manifesto, the most important of Disraeli's early political writings, helped to win for him a recognized position as a political thinker and writer.

Disraeli was in debt for most of his life, but it was from 1832 to 1837, during the years of his political campaigning, that his creditors, of whom Austen was the least formidable, harassed him most sorely. During these years he lived continually 'in the shade of the spongeing house', and it is little wonder that he became adept 'in all the subterfuges by which debtors commonly evade the importunity of greedy and exacting creditors', or that he 'too often caused annoyance to obliging friends by reluctant but unavoidable disappointment of their hopes'. He lived a life of squalid embarrassment which required incessant correspondence to weave the tissue of prevarications, subterfuges and half-truths he employed as delaying and time-gaining tactics. Yet such was the extraordinary resilience of his nature that amid worries and vexations that would have made nervous wrecks of lesser men, 'he managed to pursue his pleasures, his labours and his ambitions with a wonderful serenity through all'.

In 1836, at the time of his fourth attempt to enter Parliament, Disraeli's financial affairs were more complicated than ever before. He no longer had Austen to fall back on and in spite of the services of William Pyne, a solicitor whom he had met through Henrietta and who now helped him to raise the interest due on his multiple loans, the moneylenders could hardly be kept at bay. The sheriffs officers were after him, hampering his freedom of movement and obliging him to go into seclusion, even to stay indoors from dawn to dusk. His letters throughout this period, to Austen, Pyne and others give glimpses of the frustrations and humiliations he had to undergo.

King William IV died in June 1837 and the reign of Queen Victoria began. Parliament was dissolved and a General Election was set for July. It was a measure of the Tory party's recognition of Disraeli's efforts that he was now asked to stand for no less than seven constituencies. He eventually chose to accept an eighth, Maidstone, a two-candidate constituency.

The other candidate, Wyndham Lewis, was up for re-election, having represented the borough in the recently dissolved parliament, and on the strength of the first day's canvass the local Conservatives decided to nominate a second candidate. The choice fell on Disraeli. He wrote to his sister from the Carlton Club, 'In the midst of three or four hundred persons and in a scene of great excitement . . . The battle now approaches; what will be my fate I pretend not to foresee . . . all is tumult and like a camp'. On 30 June he started off with Wyndham Lewis to canvass Maidstone.

Even during this campaign there was still a danger of having writs served on him. This would have been fatal to his prospects and he begged Pyne to stave off the moneylenders, observing with wry consolation that he was glad 'to find the Sheriff's officer here among my staunch supporters . . .'.

It was Disraeli's fifth try and this time he was successful. He was elected to the first Victorian parliament in July 1837, Wyndham Lewis topping the poll with Disraeli second. He was in at last.

Queen Victoria's first Parliament assembled for its first session on 15 November 1837. Disraeli, 'conspicuous by his Jewish appearance and his highly dandified dress', took his seat, as he told his sister, 'on the second bench behind Sir Robert Peel, Stanley and Gladstone'. On leaving Bradenham to take his seat in Parliament, Disraeli had recorded the fact in a final entry of his diary, adding: I am now leaving a secure haven for an unknown sea. What will the next twelve months produce?'

They produced among other things his disastrous maiden speech in the Commons, which the Irish members greeted with an uproar composed of hostile laughter, hisses, groans, hoots, catcalls, drumming feet, loud conversation and farmyard imitations. Disraeli finally shouted at the top of his voice a prophetic defiance, which went almost unheard amid the din: 'I sit down now, but the time will come when you will hear me.'

The next twelve months also saw an event that was to be critical in his private life: the sudden death from heart failure of his parliamentary colleague Wyndham Lewis on 14 March. 'I have seen Mrs Wyndham', he wrote to his sister. 'She is, of course, at present, extremely overwhelmed. She was sitting in the room with him when he died.' Disraeli had soon become friendly with the Wyndham Lewises and they had visited him at Bradenham. He had first met Mrs Wyndham Lewis in April 1832 when he was introduced to her 'by particular desire' (hers) at a party at his friend Bulwer's. Disraeli thought her then 'a pretty little woman, a flirt and rattle; indeed, gifted with a volubility I should think unequalled!', and he is reputed to have said on another occasion when asked to take her in to dinner, 'Oh anything rather than that insufferable woman . . .'. Six years later and on closer acquantance she had apparently become less insufferable. She was his fervent supporter and champion during the Maidstone election campaign with her husband

and wrote to her brother on 30 July 1837: 'Mark what I say—mark what I prophesy: Mr Disraeli will in a very few years be one of the greatest men of his day. . . . They call him my Parliamentary *protégé*.'

Disraeli and the widowed Mrs Wyndham Lewis were drawn closer by her bereavement and her need for somebody to turn to. He advised her on her affairs and she lent him money to settle some vexing post-election trouble at Maidstone. Their correspondence had become more intimate, Disraeli began to write her love letters and at length proposed marriage, but she refused to give him an answer until the statutory year of widowhood had elapsed. An odd courtship ensued, fraught with quarrels, tiffs, scenes. Disraeli feared the ridicule of being jilted when all their friends thought they would soon marry; and he recoiled from the indignity of being thought a rich woman's paid lover. Those of Mary Anne Lewis's friends who disliked him were eager enough to convince her that he was only after her money. Disraeli went at length to her house and in a stormy scene demanded marriage. Mary Anne accused him of fortune-hunting, called him a selfish bully and showed him the door. Disraeli went back to his lodging and wrote her a long and extraordinary letter (printed in full for the first time in Robert Blake's biography) in which he declared his love to be sincere, although 'I avow, when I first made my advances to you, I was influenced by no romantic feelings'. Mary Anne's fortune, he told her, was not of a kind to make him wish to give up his cherished liberty, but though he knew that her house and money were entailed to relatives of her husband's this made no difference to him, he loved her. Finally, saying that he would make no reproaches, he reproached her bitterly for her frivolous heartlessness and bade her farewell.

Mary Anne was quite undone. Despite the melodramatic extravagance of Disraeli's *cri de coeur*, she sensed its underlying sincerity. Besides, she realized she loved him, adventurer or no. She wrote back: 'For God's sake come to me . . . I never desired you to leave the house, or implied or thought a word about money . . . I am devoted to you.' Disraeli went, she accepted him, and they were quietly married when the parliamentary session ended, on 28 August 1839, at St George's, Hanover Square. The marriage of the 33-year-old Member of Parliament to the pretty and youthful-looking 47-year-old widow of his old colleague gained for Disraeli an improved credit, the use of the interest on several thousand pounds of income, a secure social standing, and a fixed London home. It also brought him lasting domestic happiness.

Disraeli's successful marriage to Mary Anne has been written about again and again. She looked after him with a self-effacing solicitude and her devotion to his happiness and his career was entire. She helped him, believed in him and shielded him from the petty and distracting details of domesticity. Throughout the thirty years of their married life she gave him the perpetual love that, as he had told her, his nature demanded.

Disraeli for his part gave her constant amiability and affection, a courteous devotion and respect in which, on his own admission, gratitude also played a part. Mary Anne, though shrewd, was eccentric, spoke with impulsive and disconcerting candour, made ridiculous *gaffes*, dressed oddly, but Disraeli never betrayed by the flicker of an eyelid that he thought her any different from the duchesses he frequented nor did he ever permit any comment on her oddities to be made in his presence.

Separation was painful to both of them. When they were ill and confined to bed in different rooms they even wrote each other little notes. After long years of marriage, when he had become great and she odder, they still thought the world of each other. Mary Anne was so confident of Disraeli's deep attachment to her that she could confide to a friend that she knew Dizzy had married her for her money but that if he had it all to do over again he would have married her for love; but to another friend she said that she knew Dizzy was in love with her and not her money because of the affection and love he showed to her when her first husband was alive. Their consideration for each other was touching. When toward the end of her life Mary Anne became seriously ill, each sought to spare the other grief by concealing, as they thought, from each other the knowledge that her illness was mortal. While Mary Anne tried to the last ounce of her strength to lead a normal social life, as she virtually starved to death from cancer of the stomach, Disraeli witnessed her slow and suffering decline with an impassivity that barely concealed a despairing anguish. For Dizzy, Mary Anne was 'a perfect wife!' and on her death, which shattered him, he paid her a touching tribute: 'There was no care which she could not mitigate, and no difficulty which she could not face. She was the most cheerful and the most courageous woman I ever knew.' Shortly before her death Mary Anne had told a woman friend that 'her life with D. had been a long scene of happiness, owing to his love and kindness'.

But this was all thirty years in the future, together with his long and extraordinary career in the House of Commons. In 1839 he was a new Member of Parliament and a newly married man. Private fraud now being no longer necessary, public fraud could start in earnest; although, as Walter Bagehot was to observe, 'it was not fraud itself which won, but fraud in a convenient place, and with singular ability'.

Disraeli's great opportunity came during the parliamentary session of 1845. Sir Robert Peel was then Prime Minister and the autocratic leader of the Conservatives. He had come to office in the General Election of 1841 as the chosen representative of Protectionism, and he now yielded to the Anti-Corn Law factions and, in a sudden change of front, came out in favour of Free Trade. With the support of the

Liberals the measure for the repeal of the Corn Laws was eventually pushed through. The right wing's ablest and most experienced men—the Duke of Wellington, Graham, Aberdeen, Gladstone and other eminent Tories—had sided with Peel and now the Tory bloc of protectionist squires were without a spokesman. Disraeli was equal to the occasion. He attacked Peel in a series of witty and devastating speeches which harped on the theme of betrayal of the Party and the nation. Peel was acutely sensitive to ridicule and Disraeli's sarcastic barbs went home with deadly precision. As debate followed debate Peel's discomfiture became increasingly noticeable. He appeared 'stunned and stupified . . . vacillating between silence and spleen', or was seen to hang his head down 'changing colour and drawing his hat over his eyes'. The laughter which greeted Disraeli's sallies produced 'nervous twitchings' in Peel and it was evident that he was quite unable to look indifferent or conceal his mortification under the fire of Disraeli's invective.

Before long Disraeli was virtual leader of what he had dubbed 'the gentlemen of England', the embittered but woefully inarticulate landed gentry who saw, or thought they saw, their position threatened by Tariff reform. When the Peelites merged with the Liberals, Disraeli's path was clear. He became first of all leader of the Commons and subsequently the acknowledged leader of the Tories.

Disraeli's political philosophy, to judge by its development during the 1830s, on the evidence of some of his speeches and pamphlets of this period, has been called variously 'democratic toryism' and 'Conservative liberalism'. The simplest and clearest definition of this sort of label is paternalism. The trend of his thinking was that the social and economic hierarchy should be preserved, though tempered by improvements in the condition of the working classes and small farmers. The Merrie England of the good old days, the real England, would flourish again. At some time in the past it had been destroyed—by the Protector and his Commonwealth in the seventeenth century, or perhaps even as far back as the Reformation. Through such connections with and allusions to a distant and half-forgotten past, Disraeli typified Conservative thinking. Ruskin, Carlyle and Maurras preached the same socio-political hodge-podge compounded of historical romanticism, respect for the social hierarchy and vague yearnings for reform.

But when it came to putting ideology into practice Disraeli was not very effective. In all probability this was basically because reforms cost money and the governing class to which he looked for his support was unwilling to pay up. He took little part in efforts to bring about factory reforms, especially those relating to working hours. It was left to scattered groups of Conservatives and Liberals to do this and Disraeli's contribution was little more than the tenacious but unfounded belief that it was the English right wing that had introduced modern social reform. This also applies to agriculture, which was the core of his political structure.

Disraeli soon ceased to oppose Free Trade and, in contrast to one group of reformers allied with the Liberals, made no effort to check the elimination of agricultural smallholders or the concentration in a minority of the right to own land. On this point the illusory and highly opportunistic features of Disraeli's policies are most clearly apparent, as Lord Cromer pointed out in a brilliant analysis in his *Political and Literary Essays* (1908–16). Apart from the reform bill of 1867, the reforms which have been linked with Disraeli's name were as a rule forced on Parliament by public protest too vociferous to resist and Disraeli's contribution was rather one of intelligent adaptability than of originality.

Imperialism has been considered on a par with Tory-democracy as Disraeli's political legacy. This new theme appeared mainly in the closing years of his career, in speeches about England's greatness and her ties with the colonies and in successful manoeuvres such as the acquisition of the Suez Canal shares and the promotion of Queen Victoria to Empress of India; in his firm policy towards Russia before and during the Berlin Congress, and in the Afghanistan and Boer wars. In contrast to Joseph Chamberlain twenty years later, Disraeli was also not responsible in this direction for the shaping of any constructive line of action, but he figures as one of the foremost representatives of romantic colonialism and a somewhat melodramatic patriotism. It is no coincidence that the music-hall ballad which made 'by jingo' a catchword and led to the coining of the word 'jingoism' was all the rage in 1878.

'We don't want to fight, but by jingo if we do
We've got the ships, we've got the men, we've got the money too!'

The ultimate development of Disraeli's political ideas reveals flashes of great imagination, and even elements of irrationality which make it in those respects reminiscent of Hegel or Marx. He lacked the intellectual vigour to build a closed system of abstract ideas but his attempt was praiseworthy. His divided loyalty to Jewry and Christianity is apparent in his habit of labelling all institutions which were conservative, and therefore had his approval, as 'Semitic'; he called the Pope a 'Semitic' ruler and described Anglo-Saxons as a particularly 'Semitic' people. The word 'race', used in various senses, became a key-word in his evaluation of world history. He explained revolutionary movements as being due not to the dissatisfaction of the masses but to the conspiracies of mysterious 'secret societies' which wished to undermine a basically 'Semitic' and conservative Europe. Occasionally he also considered the plutocracy as an enemy—by plutocracy meaning industry and capitalistic finance as opposed to agriculture and the noble peasant. This feverish ideology is most striking in Disraeli's eulogistic biography *Lord George Bentinck* (1851), a book usually passed over in discreet silence by the majority of Disraeli's biographers, although it is the most finished product of his 'philosophy'. Not even anti-Semitism is absent from this work, in which 'wicked' Jews were supposed to play a considerable role in the 'secret societies' which, according to Disraeli were seeking to destroy 'true' Semitism. Here his confused thinking reaches a pitch unsurpassed even by certain notorious political concepts of our own times.

As a witty orator Disraeli enjoyed his greatest triumphs in the speeches he made during the debates of 1845–46, when he was attacking Free Trade and demolishing Peel. In the dreary wastes of parliamentary records these lively and impudent sallies glisten like pearls in a heap of pebbles. Disraeli found in the Commons the perfect audience for his quips, nor was this surprising: the guffaws of the world's parliaments have echoed down the ages. Disraeli had observed as early as 1831 (in *The Young Duke*) how easy it was to thrust home a taunt and raise a laugh in Parliament. A speaker needed no great powers of sarcasm. Indeed,

> 'From what I have observed there, I should think very little ones would be sufficient. Many a sneer withers, in those walls, which would scarcely, I think, blight a currant-bush out of them; and I have seen the House convulsed with raillery which in other society would infallibly settle the rallier to be a bore beyond all tolerance. Even an idiot can raise a smile. They are so good-natured, or find it so dull . . .'

A collection of Disraeli's witticisms does not, however, make attractive reading. The style is similar to Wilde's; epigramatic, full of paradoxes and playful exaggerations, most of them totally lacking in profundity, jokes with often an almost banal simplicity of contrivance. It is easy to see that many of these frequently outrageous quips and jibes must have seemed brilliant in conversation or in the keyed-up atmosphere of the House; but taken out of context and congealed in print, their feebleness is all too apparent. Disraeli is at his best in personal ridicule, fanciful exaggeration and 'grotesque images'. It was first-rate fun to call a man 'ill-bred in proportion to his intelligence' or to dismiss Darwin's theory of evolution by preferring to ignore the apes and to stand 'on the side of the Angels', to call the Conservative government 'an organized hypocrisy', or to dismiss Peel as 'a great Parliamentary middleman who bamboozles one party and plunders the other until he has obtained a position to which he is not entitled'. He could evoke delirious laughter by calling Peel 'a burglar of others' intellect' and capping this with: 'there is no statesman who has committed political larceny on so great a scale'.

Posterity can also appreciate Dizzy's witty advice to would-be parliamentary speakers:

> 'Talk to women, talk to women as much as you can. This is the best school. This is the way to gain fluency, because you need not care what you say, and had better not be sensible. They, too, will rally you on many points, and as they are women you will not be offended. Nothing is of so much use to a young man entering life as to be well criticized by women. . . .'

Disraeli took this advice himself and followed it all his life. In his old age he paid court to elderly ladies. In love with the younger of two sisters, Lady Bradford—who already had a husband—Disraeli proposed to the elder, the widowed Lady Chesterfield, so as to be always near them both; but Lady Chesterfield did not regard this as a compliment and quite understandably refused him. He corresponded with the two sisters for years in flattering and playfully amorous phrases. He lavished similar attention on his wife during her lifetime, and his romantic, mock-amorous devotion to Queen Victoria quite won his sovereign's heart. He spoke of this royal conquest, however, with his usual penetrating irony: 'You have heard me called a flatterer', he is reputed to have said to Matthew Arnold, 'and it is true. Everyone likes flattery and when you come to royalty you should lay it on with a trowel.' He explained to Lord Esher, too, some of the secret of his success in handling the Queen: 'I never refuse; I never contradict; I sometimes forget.' In spite of his irony, however, it is evident that Disraeli's feelings towards the Queen were infused with a warmth which transcended mere reverence for a sovereign. He was genuinely fond of this ageing, plump little woman who was also wise and courageous and who symbolized the aristocratic system he believed in and defended.

In his letters to Lady Bradford and Lady Chesterfield, the wistfulness that can be discerned beneath his role of perennial Cherubino is given its most significant and poignant expression. It is difficult, however, to understand how these letters of his old age can be considered important; the glory of the statesman would appear to have bathed the trivialities in a deceptive aura. Nevertheless, the letters are frequently touching. They reveal a man who has always been content to play the charmer at a fancy-dress ball, who now discovers the grinning skull behind the simpering mask and realizes at last that the only realities are old age and death.

Together with the artificiality, the theatricality, the eternal play-acting there was a streak of heartlessness in Disraeli's nature. This is not to say that he was actively cruel or vindictive, but he could be exceptionally insensitive, to say the least, to accounts of cruelty or to suffering that did not touch him personally. An instance of this is a flippant remark he made during his Grand Tour of 1830 when, a foppish and conceited young fellow of twenty-six full of attitudes and affectations, he visited the Turkish province of Albania where he spent a week in Yanina, the capital. There he was received in audience by Raschid Ali Pasha, the Turkish Grand Vizir, in his fortress-palace. Enchanted by his first glimpses of the fairy-tale East, delighted with everything in picturesque Turkish-ruled Albania, Disraeli was no less delighted, as he wrote to Benjamin Austen, 'to be made much of by a man who was daily decapitating half the province'. This extravagant piece of 'black' humour, antedated by many years the 'sick' jokes of the mid-twentieth century. It was echoed by Disraeli forty-five years after his tour of the Middle East during a Commons debate on The Eastern Question, with consequences vexatious to himself.

In 1875 the Eastern Question which, as Disraeli said, 'had haunted Europe for a century', but which he thought 'the Crimean War had adjourned for half another', again showed signs of baleful life.

The Treaty of Paris of 1856 which had imposed peace terms on Russia at the conclusion of the Crimean War had effectively stifled her influence over Turkey by annulling the rights, laid down in earlier treaties, which gave her claim to champion Christian Slavs in Turkish-ruled Balkan countries.

The Great Powers who had imposed the peace terms on Russia in 1856 not only were pledged to uphold the integrity and independence of the tottering Ottoman Empire, but found it expedient to do so, and support of Turkey became a principle of British and of European foreign policy. A conflict of interests brought Russia and Britain face to face, while the other nations involved in the crisis—France, Italy and Austria-Hungary—looked on, variously unable or unwilling to intervene.

The Ottoman Empire, under the misrule of a succession of degenerate, incompetent and spendthrift sultans, had been in decline since the eighteenth century. The corruption and oppression emanating from Constantinople throughout the Turkish provinces and colonies gave rise to frequent uprisings and their corresponding repressions.

Now, in 1875, uprisings in the Balkans brought matters to a head. Revolt in Herzegovina spread rapidly to Bosnia and by April 1876 insurrection had broken out in Bulgaria where Turkish officials had been killed and atrocities perpetrated. During the first three weeks of May the Turks in retaliation unleashed the dreaded bashi-bazouks, irregular mercenaries notorious for their cruelty, on the relatively unarmed

Bulgarian peasantry. Wholesale massacre and outrage ensued. Thousands were killed and many villages ravaged. One hill town, Batak, was burned to the ground and all its five thousand inhabitants, regardless of age or sex, were slaughtered.

In London towards the end of June, the *Daily News*, the leading Liberal organ which supported Gladstone and was hostile to Disraeli, published lurid reports of the massacres which were described in horrifying detail. Twenty-five thousand people were said to have been imprisoned or slaughtered, to the accompaniment of rape, torture and other indescribable outrages.

The reports, eventually found to have been much exaggerated, were taken up by *The Times* and partially confirmed from other sources. Disraeli however, sceptical of all such stories, as he had been twenty years earlier about similar far-fetched reports of horrors during the Indian Mutiny, believed that these Bulgarian atrocity stories were aimed at discrediting the Government. While not denying the possibility of atrocities, he played them down when questioned in the House, and in doing so made the indiscreet remark which he had occasion to regret. He hoped, he said that

> 'when we become better informed . . . of what has occurred, it will be found that the statements are scarcely warranted. . . . That there have been proceedings of an atrocious character I never for a moment doubted . . . Wars of insurrection are always atrocious . . . I cannot doubt that atrocities have been committed in Bulgaria; but that girls were sold into slavery, or that more than 10,000 persons have been imprisoned, I doubt. In fact, I doubt whether there is prison accommodation for so many, or that torture has been practised on a great scale among an Oriental people who seldom, I believe, resort to torture, but generally terminate their connection with culprits in a more expeditious manner.'

Laughter greeted this last remark, from a House always on the alert for a Disraelian quip; but as Disraeli sat down, Sir Stafford Northcote heard him mutter to himself, 'What is there to laugh at?'

Disraeli's ill-timed remark, with its unfortunate choice of words was immediately taken up. He was attacked on all sides for callous cynicism in making a public joke of the unspeakable horrors perpetrated in Bulgaria. He defended himself by saying that if the newspaper stories had been less exaggerated and his Foreign Office reports more detailed and more accurate he might have spoken differently.

Robert Blake has sifted the evidence to show that Disraeli's much censured utterance about the ways of Oriental peoples with culprits was not intentionally jocular: 'The House took this as a joke; to Disraeli's annoyance, for he was merely using one of those typically orotund phrases to which he had latterly become addicted. For years to come he was accused from platform and pulpit of having made a heartless jest about the Bulgarian massacres.'

Disraeli made matters worse by referring to the reports as 'coffee-house babble', thus giving his critics fresh ammunition for their attacks against him; but he refused ever to retract publicly. Though Disraeli denied having joked, it would, nevertheless, be equally reasonable to assume that he did in fact speak jocularly of the bloodthirsty customs of Orientals, though in doing so he was, surely, not making cynical sport of the massacre of Christian men, women and children by the Turks, but merely using his habitual sarcastic exaggeration to discredit the sensationalism of the *Daily News*.

It was second nature to Disraeli to express himself wittily. He had been at it since he was a young man and all was grist that came to his verbal mill. In his old age, with a lifetime of worldly experience behind him, the colourful imagery, the striking phrases, the clever jokes and the 'elaborately-phrased sarcasm', sprang instinctively to his lips, sometimes, as in the present instance, betraying him into indiscretion.

It therefore seems difficult to accept entirely Disraeli's own explanation of his remarks about the Bulgarian atrocities and it would seem more typical of the man that he phrased his thoughts about Orientals in a disdainful and half-jocular manner. This is not to say that his words were not ill-timed. When they provoked laughter he was vexed and he subsequently met the stereotyped moralistic reaction of pious Victorian humanitarians with distaste and obstinacy; so, in answer to their criticism and imputations of heartlessness, it was only natural that he should meet the accusations of frivolity and levity by declaring that it never had been his intention to joke about so painful a subject.

All things considered, however, it seems hardly possible to say with absolute certainty whether Disraeli did or did not intend to joke about Oriental methods of execution. Dr Blake has remarked in his biography that because of the ambivalent mixture of romance and irony in Disraeli's outlook 'one can never be sure what he was thinking about anything'.

The frivolous and superficial side of Disraeli's nature was counterbalanced by one area of feeling that remained throughout his life deep, fervent, sincere and constant: his love for England. It has nevertheless been pointed out that this devotion was not patriotism in its conventionally accepted sense, a serene almost matter-of-course glow of dutiful national pride, but a foreigner's emotion, charged with colourful romanticism, and as such tinged with an exotic, one might almost say erotic, fervour. In the presence of his beloved 'Faerie' Queen, in his attitude to the landed gentry, the prelates of the Established Church, the glamour and the prowess of Britain's valiant redcoats, he was simultaneously the lowly subject and the conqueror; in this sovereign kingdom Disraeli, the outsider, the foreign interloper, had risen to become an equal among rulers and finally the ruler. In his feelings toward England and the English can be detected that mingling of contempt with passionate tenderness which Tonio Kröger, in Thomas Mann's *novella* of that name, feels for Hans Hansen—the man of duplicity confronted with a nature that is ingenuous and open-hearted.

It may be wondered whether the words 'love' and 'patriotism' are not somewhat meaningless in such a frame of reference, and whether Disraeli's feelings were not rather those of a great actor towards a star part in a dramatically striking play. Seldom has the personality of one of history's great figures displayed so little of solid character, and Disraeli's has remained intangible. Despite the crowded incident of his career, his significant acts, his 'philosophy', the many millions of self-revealing words he wrote and spoke and the many millions more that have been said and written about him, his true personality evades analysis; it dissolves and diffuses in gesture, grandiloquence, emotional and political sleight of hand. The real Disraeli remains an enigma.

A True Tory: Lord Salisbury

Gladstone and Disraeli were undoubtedly the most remarkable of Queen Victoria's ten Prime Ministers. They personify the English parliamentary system in its classical phase as well as the breach between romantic conservatism and idealistic liberalism.

These two have overshadowed another remarkable Prime Minister, Robert Cecil, Marquis of Salisbury, whom Queen Victoria described as her most outstanding Prime Minister. Salisbury has been given much less attention by historians and has been neglected in discussions of Victorian politics. Yet he headed the government of England for a longer period than any other prime minister since 1820.

Salisbury was more an administrator than a statesman. His opinions and the measures he advocated opened up no grandiose vistas to the future. In comparison with his two more brilliant colleagues he seemed a dry, prosaic and limited man. This was in no way due to a lack of imagination or feeling, even though Salisbury himself regarded the impassioned and grandiloquent promises of Disraeli and Gladstone as excesses hardly worthy of an English gentleman. His most significant qualities were moral integrity, a keen intelligence, calm, calculating skill and a spirit of true conservatism—the antitheses of the Disraelian combination of scepticism, pose and passion.

Robert Cecil's career was typical of the English aristocracy whose last leading statesman he was. The scion of one of England's oldest and most eminent families, he was born in 1830, at Hatfield House, Hertfordshire, an Elizabethan mansion with vast surrounding lands let out to hundreds of tenant farmers. He went to Eton, which he loathed, though he subsequently sent his sons there. Then in 1849 he graduated from Oxford where he failed to display any noticeable talents save for a bent for natural science. His interest in this lasted throughout his life and found an outlet in experimental chemistry: 'he was never happy away from that damned laboratory at Hatfield'. He was one of the first to install such scientific novelties as the telephone and electric lighting, amenities which were then still in a primitive stage.

Owing to ill health Cecil was advised to cut short his stay at Oxford but he was enabled to sit for his degree after only two years, graduating with an honorary fourth. He then left England and in two years of travel, entirely in sailing ships, he visited South Africa, Australia and New Zealand, landing back in England in 1853 after a stormy voyage round Cape Horn. In the same year he was elected a Fellow of All Souls and entered Parliament as a member for Stamford, a family constituency for which he was returned unopposed. He never had to contest an election and remained M.P. for Stamford until his father's death in 1868, when he succeeded to the title. He had become Viscount Cranbourne and heir to the marquisate on the death of his elder brother in 1865. When the young Cecil entered Parliament he had neither political ambition nor knowledge, but during the ensuing decades he gave evidence of talent and an independent mind.

In 1854 he met Miss Georgina Alderson, the eldest daughter of Sir Edward Alderson, a Baron of the Court of Exchequer and a brilliant man who had left the bar and become a judge at the age of forty-three. Two years later, in the face of sustained opposition, Robert Cecil married Miss Alderson, whom his family considered neither well-born nor rich enough to become the wife of a Cecil. He began to contribute erudite historical biographical and political essays to *Oxford Essays*, various quarterlies, the *Saturday Review* and subsequently to the *Quarterly Review* for which he wrote for six years. The best of these essays were published in two volumes (1861–64) and can still be read for their perceptive irony and stylistic elegance.

When Lord Derby formed his cabinet in 1866, Cecil, now Lord Cranbourne, became Secretary for India; his prestige was in no way diminished by his resignation shortly afterwards in disapproval of Disraeli's and Derby's Reform Bill, which he stubbornly opposed. When he became third Marquis on the death of his father in 1868, Cecil left the Commons for the Lords. This move was well suited to his temperament and his feeling of contempt for rhetoric and party political tub-thumping.

The relationship between Salisbury and Disraeli was cool from the start and never developed into intimacy. Disraeli once called him 'a master of gibes and flouts and jeers', which was surely the pot calling the kettle black. The sternly reserved young aristocrat distrusted the party leader's professional glibness and had more respect for their Liberal opponent, the moralizing Gladstone. But the two Conservative leaders were nevertheless united in their political task. In Disraeli's long government of 1874–80, Salisbury was first of all Secretary for India and later Foreign Secretary. The Berlin Congress of 1878 and the 'peace with honour' which Disraeli and he brought back was a triumph for both of them. After Disraeli's death in 1881, Salisbury was the obvious leader of the Conservatives. The Liberal split over the Irish Question made him for decades the dominating force in English politics. Between June 1885 and July 1902 when he retired from public life, he was three times Prime Minister, alternating with successive short-lived Liberal administrations and over a period of fourteen years he was usually Secretary for Foreign Affairs as well.

This was a Golden Age for England as a great nation, with a tamed Ireland subdued by oppression alternating with clement reforms; an active policy of colonization; imperial conferences and 'splendid isolation'. Salisbury's wisdom and prudence became a byword at the Foreign Office, and after Bismarck's fall from power he became Europe's leading statesman.

Salisbury's outlook, like that of all staunch Conservatives, was anchored to the Church and the State. In contrast with Disraeli and other bolder and more restless thinkers, Salisbury's religious belief was not a haven of refuge for doubt and nihilism but a natural and accepted point of departure for all his actions. Salisbury wrote that according to what he had observed, 'men are not moral without a motive and a motive can only be the outcome of religious faith'. This cynical and pragmatic point of view was not a predominant feature of his thinking. Salisbury was a sincere Christian. In his youth he had read a considerable amount of theology and had meditated on the problems propounded. Later his faith crystallized into a calm acceptance of the Christian doctrine, in a faith devoid of questioning or analysis, a state of mind which was achieved by avoidance of any disturbing and dangerous speculations. Even as a young man he had jotted down in a notebook: 'The narrowness of our knowledge on these subjects serves to warn us how we bring our bounded intellects and earthly sight to bear on questions far beyond their reach.'

This belief, which sufficed to make Salisbury a church-goer and communicant, gave him the necessary inner certainty and a sufficient amount of insensitivity to earthly human suffering. Charity was a good thing, so was social improvement, within modest and reasonable limits but the essential requirement was a religious and moral life, and this was open to the poor as well as to the rich. The difference in degree between the Cecil family in its stately homes and their tenants on the farms and in the cottages was basically unimportant to Robert Cecil. This ability to mingle unassumingly with the lowly was made easier by Salisbury's lack of interest in ostentation and excessive luxury although he lived in comfort and style. His views on the unimportance of social differences were not prompted by hypocrisy.

Salisbury's nationalistic feeling caused him to accept this view even more unquestioningly. The English people appeared to him as a unity whose security and progress were the aim of politics. This was also the natural attitude of the traditional ruling class. From this vantage point the various classes and the varying interests of the population could be regarded as unimportant, almost irrelevant. He once compared the state to a limited liability company, in which every person should have a voice corresponding to his economic status, but this line of thought was not typical of his outlook; he preferred to ignore rather than defend the political, social and economic hierarchy. He gradually came to accept reforms for universal suffrage, which moreover appeared to strengthen the conservatism of his day, but when he did hesitate before, or object to attempts to introduce democratic reforms, it was because the experienced aristocracy, impartial by reason of its exalted position, seemed to him to be charged with the mission of heading the country in international rivalries and conflicts. This meant maintaining the established order of things, and this, in turn, entailed the pursuance first and foremost of a wise foreign policy. Internal reforms were unavoidable measures designed to maintain the balance which gave the nation its unity and outward strength.

In the matter of internal policy Salisbury's period of government was, in fact, relatively unproductive. The little that was accomplished, mostly during his third administration, was really the work of Joseph Chamberlain. The chief concerns of the Salisbury government were foreign and colonial policy. It was an era of negotiations, intrigues and relatively bloodless colonial activity: this applied principally to the partition of Africa. Nearly one hundred million new subjects were brought under the British crown, a record even in comparison with the colonial achievements of William Pitt the Elder. The conquest of the Sudan in 1898 and the Boer War from 1899 to 1902 marked the close of this era of colonial expansion.

The big dividends involved might give the impression that Salisbury was set on a policy of conquest, but this was not so. Like the aging Bismarck, his watchwords were security and consolidation. He detested sabre-rattling, melodramatic patriotism and grandiose imperialistic dreams. In his case it was really the occasion that made the thief, for

Britain held the best vantage ground and time after time Salisbury was forced to take action to secure positions which, had they fallen into other hands, for example those of France, Russia or Germany, would have been a potential danger to the safety of the Empire. The spirit of aggressive nationalism and imperialism which pervaded English hearts at the turn of the century was mainly due to men like Chamberlain and Cecil Rhodes.

Salisbury's essays on the statesmen he most admired, such as William Pitt (the Younger), or Castlereagh, are character studies which might well be regarded as self-portraits. Castlereagh, Salisbury said, had a mind which was utterly free from impulse and from theoretical statesmanship. In Castlereagh's eyes, as in those of the eighteenth-century rationalists, impulsiveness was synonymous with an excitability which could have no place in the concept of a nation actuated by good sense. He was not 'a man who disbelieved in the value of freedom or wished to deny its blessings permanently to any race of men'. But neither was he a theorist who 'could see no blessings to be cherished and no interests to be spared outside of his own political ideal'. As Salisbury's essay summed him up:

> 'The gradation of his mind seems to have stood thus: he cared for nationality not at all, for the theoretic perfection of political institution very little; for the realities of freedom, a great deal; and for peace, and social order and freedom from the manifold curses of disturbance, which alone can give the humbler masses of mankind any chance of tasting their scanty share of human joys—for the sake of this, he was ready to forego all the rest.'

In spite of Castlereagh's great talents and ability, fully recognized by his associates, 'they do not appear to have been drawn to him by bonds of that intense personal devotion which has united so many great statesmen with their political supporters'. His influence, therefore, died with him.

> 'His calm, cold, self-contained temperament was damaging to his fame. . . . He was the head of a powerful party in momentous times: he led the nation to the highest pinnacle of renown; he laid down landmarks of policy which have lasted through many revolutions of opinion and are respected still. But he did not found a school. His name contained no spell to bind together after his death those whom he had influenced in life: none of the tender reverence gathered round his memory with which disciples recall deeds and treasure up the sayings of a departed master.'

Those last sentences can be applied with special aptness to Salisbury. This is partly due to the fact that, except for his general adherence to

Tory policies he was practically devoid of political ideas. He was a shy man and all his life found it difficult to make small talk. His desire for solitude caused him to become a sort of *éminence grise* in his own cabinet. He immured himself at Hatfield for months on end, cabinet meetings became fewer and farther between, to the point that at times he hardly recognized some of his colleagues. Like Bismarck at Friedrichsruhe, Salisbury at Hatfield was a statesman in voluntary isolation.

Perhaps the chief distinction of Salisbury's regime is that it was the last manifestation of power in an England ruled by aristocrats. After his time social reform gradually filtered through to permeate all parties and instead of 'splendid isolation', a policy of alliances became the order of the day. Self-government or independence were now the goals for colonies and dominions. In Salisbury's day the tide of colonial expansion began to turn, and the sun, still resplendent over the vast British Empire on which it had never set, slowly but inevitably began to sink towards the horizon.

The Discrowned King: Charles Stewart Parnell

A heated argument over Parnell and politics takes place round the Christmas turkey in James Joyce's autobiographical novel *A Portrait of the Artist as a Young Man.* Mr and Mrs Daedalus—Joyce's parents—are sitting down to Christmas dinner with Aunt Dante Riordan, Uncle Charles and an old family friend, Mr Casey. They are all agreed that Parnell's overthrow was the work of the clergy but the argument round the table hinges on whether they were right or not in doing what they did.

'A damned priest-ridden race!' yells Mr Daedalus in defence of the dead patriot, goaded to fury by pious Mrs Riordan. 'We are an unfortunate priest-ridden race and always were and always will be till the end of the chapter. . . . A priest-ridden God-forsaken race!'

Mr Casey, even more exasperated, shouts hoarsely: 'Very well then, if it comes to that, no God for Ireland. . . . We have had too much God in Ireland. Away with God! Away with God, I say!'

Aunt Dante jumps up from the table, red in the face and shaking with fury. She rushes from the room but turns at the door to shriek: 'Devil out of hell! We won! We crushed him to death! Fiend!'

As the door slams behind her Mr Casey buries his face in his hands: 'with a sob of pain he cried loudly "Poor Parnell! My dead king!" ' This scene takes place in the early 1890s, some years after Parnell's death.

W. B. Yeats, in *Parnell's Funeral* and in other poems, has much the same to say about the tragedy of Parnell. It was 'The Bishops and the

Party' who ruined Parnell. Other Irish heroes—Emmet, Fitzgerald, Tone—had been murdered by 'strangers', by the English, and the Irish had 'lived like men that watch a painted stage'. Parnell, on the other hand, was the victim of his own countrymen:

> . . . But popular rage,
> Hysterica Passio dragged this quarry down.
> None shared our guilt; nor did we play a part
> Upon a painted stage when we devoured his heart.

Yeat's poem then dwells on the thoughts of how much more fortunate Ireland would have been if men like Parnell had led the movement for independence on to victory.

> 'Had de Valera eaten Parnell's heart,
> No loose-lipped demagogue had won the day,
> No civil rancour torn the land apart.'

Such reflexions are part of the legend which sprang up round Parnell, a man who was a singularly powerful force in Irish politics and subsequently in Irish literature. The legend has rarely been more effectively discussed nor its inconsistencies more sharply revealed than in *Parnell and his Party*, 1880–1890 (1957), by the Irish diplomat and writer Conor Cruise O'Brien.

Charles Stewart Parnell came from a protestant family of wealthy landowners. They were English settlers who had emigrated to Ireland from Cheshire in the seventeenth century, and had purchased an estate in Wicklow. His mother was the daughter of the American admiral, Charles Stewart, who had fought against the English in the war of 1812. The family had pro-Fenian sympathies and his ancestors had sided with the Irish cause from as far back as the rising of 1798. Parnell was educated at English private schools and studied for four years at Magdalen College, Cambridge, but took no degree. He became High Sheriff for County Wicklow in 1874 and in the same year stood unsuccessfully for County Dublin. The following year he was elected for County Meath and took his seat at Westminster. His beginnings in Parliament were inauspicious. He was nervous, unsure, inarticulate and ignorant of parliamentary procedure, but by dint of taking notice he was soon able to make himself noticed, and rose rapidly to a position of importance. He became a skilful organizer and tactician and though he was not a brilliant speaker his use of emotional appeals, his choice of telling phrases and his disdainful contempt for his opponents made him well fitted to represent a struggling minority. Among his assets must be included the fact that he was an Anglo-Irish aristocrat, to all intents and purposes an English gentleman and so not overawed by the English upper class and its conventions. He was one of those whose actions have contributed to the formulation of the dubious sociological 'law' that the struggle for freedom of a people or a group is always led by persons who stand outside or are socially superior to the people or group involved.

By 1877 Parnell, having taken good notice of the methods of the uncouth Belfast provision-merchant Joseph Gillas Biggar, had brought obstructionist tactics to a fine art. He was, like Biggar, able to enrage and frustrate the House of Commons, holding up the proceedings for hours by asking meaningless questions and making interminable speeches interlarded with long passages out of Hansard.

In 1878, during the land agitation which was intensified by the desperate plight of the Irish tenant farmers and farm labourers, Parnell worked in Ireland to foment determined resistance to rack renting and evictions by English landowners.

In 1877, with the support of the leading Fenians in England he displaced Isaac Butt from the presidency of the Home Rule Federation of Great Britain, and by October 1879 he had become president of the Land League launched by the Fenian agitator Michael Davitt. In 1880 he formulated and introduced a new tactical weapon, a system of social excommunication which came to be known as 'boycotting' after one of its first victims, Captain Boycott, the County Mayo agent for the landowner Lord Erne. The word won a permanent place, not only in the English language, but internationally in the vocabulary of agitators and revolutionaries.

Simultaneously with all these activities Parnell entered into secret negotiations with political opponents, making 'treaties' and 'combinations' in exchange for concessions in favour of the Irish cause and he attempted to play the two major English parties against each other. He had that tactical ruthlessness which is sometimes found in fundamentally honest men who believe that the cause they espouse is great and just.

By 1880 Parnell had become the chairman of the Irish parliamentary party and thus leader of the Irish nationalists. In February 1881 he opposed the government's Coercion Bill after which he was ejected from the House with thirty-four of his followers. He then refused to accept Gladstone's Land Bill as a final settlement of Irish aspirations. With other members of the Land League, he was put on trial by the Gladstone government. The jury failed to agree, but he was finally arrested and sent to Kilmainham Jail in October 1881.

During the crisis of 1885–86 he acted as the balance in English politics. The Irish vote brought about the fall of Gladstone in the summer of 1885. In the autumn elections that year, the Irish party, eighty-six men strong, held the balance. Two hundred and fifty Conservatives and 334 Liberals were returned.

With his ability, after an honest inner struggle, to reach the most tactically expedient conviction, Gladstone decided to introduce his Home Rule Bill, and at the beginning of 1886 the short-lived first Salisbury government was toppled when the Irish threw in their vote with the Liberals. Because of the split in the Liberal party the scheme to grant Home Rule to Ireland came to nothing and at the new election in July 1886 the Conservatives allied with the Liberals won a majority vote. It was considered highly probable, however, that at the following elections Gladstone's Liberals, with the support of the Irish Party, would gain power and so be able to push through Home Rule for Ireland. Parnell's party now dominated the whole of Ireland except Ulster and his popularity and power were greater than they had ever been. He was known as Ireland's 'uncrowned king', a nickname which caught on after its first use in Montreal in 1880; and the Irish saw in him already the statesman-leader of a self-governing Ireland which they believed would soon be established.

With matters at this pitch, and Parnell at the zenith of his political career, he was disgraced and his career brought down in ruins. One of his parliamentary colleagues, Captain William O'Shea, sued his wife for divorce on account of her adultery with Parnell, and though Parnell was confident of a favourable outcome, O'Shea's suit was successful. The evidence revealed that Parnell and Mrs O'Shea had been lovers for ten years and even had two children. The Irish Party dismissed Parnell from the leadership and in Ireland his supporters lost the majority. The episode has been said to have postponed the settlement of Irish Home Rule for thirty years. Parnell and Mrs O'Shea were married after the decree became absolute, but he died suddenly, only five months afterwards, in 1891, having virtually campaigned himself to death in Ireland in a foredoomed effort to regain the support of the Irish. Ireland has never since had a leader of similar stature.

It is obvious that during these years Parnell's policy, as well as that of the Irish Party, was confused and more or less deliberately ambiguous. In his fund-raising trips to America Parnell explained to the Irish immigrants who gave large sums to help finance the nationalist movement, that the aim was to break 'the last link which tied Ireland to England'. In one of his speeches in Ireland he told the men of Cork, on 21 January 1885, in words which became famous, that 'no man has a right to fix the boundary of the march of a nation. No man has a right to say "Thus far shalt thou go and no further"; and we have never attempted to fix the *ne plus ultra* to the progress of Ireland's nationalhood, and we never shall.'

In England, on the other hand, he admitted that he was prepared to regard Home Rule of the cautious Liberal kind as a final solution. He made detailed negotiations with Gladstone and other Liberal leaders and the Irish group came to be considered almost as a wing of the Liberal party. It is true that most of his more aggressive statements were made at an earlier period or in his early days of parliamentary activity and that his desire to compromise grew steadily, and it is possible that Parnell really would have been satisfied with a reform in the spirit of Gladstone's proposals. But the ambiguity was always inescapably present. Parnell and his fellow-patriots tended to be revolutionaries in Ireland and America, and reformists in England.

While his theory is perhaps a trifle too ingenious, this course of action, according to Conor Cruise O'Brien, would provide the key to much of Parnell's attitude and behaviour over the Irish question. As time went on he became more and more isolated, aloof and evasive. Sometimes not even his closest colleagues knew his address and it needed a whole apparatus of manoeuvring to arrange a meeting with him. He made very few appearances in the Commons during the last years of his career and never went to Ireland at all between 1886 and 1890. At the same time his high-handedness increased. A typical instance of his despotism is the way in which he forced the election of Captain O'Shea at a Galway by-election in 1886, despite the determined opposition of T. M. Healy and Biggar. He did this even though O'Shea had refused to take the party pledge which all national candidates were obliged to take, due to his position as a follower of Joseph Chamberlain. Furthermore, O'Shea was lacking in all obvious merits of a candidate and moreover had probably known for a long time of his wife's relationship with Parnell.

But in Conor Cruise O'Brien's view this was all to the good in terms of politics.

> 'The ambiguity of the system must be crystallized in terms of personality. The leader, in short had to become a mysterious and awe-inspiring figure. It so happened that an air of mystery was not only required by political necessity, but was congenial to Parnell's own reticent character and suited the enforced secrecy of his domestic life.'

He had to be a romantic hero, a man of destiny. One of Ireland's nationalistic newspapers wrote: 'Mr Parnell's mysterious behaviour and comings and goings contribute to his popularity and to the interest and seriousness by which all he says and does, even in Parliament, is observed.' In this respect Parnell's intrigue with Mrs O'Shea was not without its usefulness. There is no doubt that he was passionately in love with her; and her own story of the relationship gives the impression of a great mutual love. But the perpetual journeys, the secret meetings, the lies and subterfuges which the relationship made necessary for so long, for the affair started in 1880 or 1881, helped to create the legend of the unapproachable, aloof Parnell, and to give the image of a personality that was deep, devious and remote from petty mundane issues. Parnell's aura of Olympian detachment was partly the result of his withdrawal into the arms of Kitty O'Shea.

Statements by some of Parnell's colleagues lend colour to Conor Cruise O'Brien's view that this game of hide-and-seek eventually became enjoyable for its own sake. O'Brien observes that T. M. Healy gave a cynical but fairly penetrating estimate of his leader's character, seeing in him 'a splendid comedian who, reading in the Tory press descriptions of himself as a man of mystery, decided in Wilde's phrase, "to live up to the level of his blue china", and to act out his own legend'.

But when, in 1890, his position in the party came into question, he defended himself hotly and relentlessly, with no trace of the actor in his behaviour. As Conor Cruise O'Brien has said: 'In the end Parnell acted, not like the cool and rational leader of men that he had been, but like the romantic hero that he had been forced to seem. That was the tragedy.'

A number of assumptions and accusations concerning the reasons behind Parnell's overthrow have been shown by Conor Cruise O'Brien to be untrue. Gladstone demanded Parnell's resignation after the scandal of the action for divorce brought by O'Shea and he has been accused both of wishing to get rid of Parnell and of adopting a hypocritically moral attitude. In reality neither Gladstone nor the Liberal leaders, who had known for many years of Parnell's relationship with Mrs O'Shea, displayed any moral indignation and would willingly have seen Parnell, whom they regarded as a reliable ally, remain as leader of the Irish party. However, the reaction among Free Church parsons in England—the Non-Conformist conscience of the North—which was the stronghold of Liberalism, was so violent that an election was considered lost in advance if Parnell continued to be leader of the Irish nationalists. Furthermore, Parnell in his Manifesto had made attacks against Gladstone during the long debate in the Irish party over his position, which made any further collaboration between them impossible.

Parnell's supporters have also maintained that the more conservative-minded in the party and the Irish catholic clergy were responsible for his downfall. This too, is incorrect. From the Irish side, Parnell's resignation was demanded by Michael Davitt, initially his supporter and later his bitter adversary, and the Irish priesthood had hardly any influence at all. It was only after Parnell's downfall that the priests started a moralistic campaign against him.

Conor Cruise O'Brien's detailed account of the party debate over Parnell in the famous committee room No. 15, the scene of his dramatic parting, shows that there were no clear political, social or religious differences between Parnellites and the victorious majority. What mattered was the degree of loyalty toward the leader. Some remained fanatically loyal in spite of inevitably disagreeable consequences. Others, especially second-rank leaders, were impelled for the sake of the party and also perhaps out of irritation at Parnell's despotism and air of superiority, to force him to give up the leadership.

Parnell and his fate were destined to create legends and to be the cause of conflict, remorse, and bitterness. The leader who put love before duty; the nationalist wrecked by the English Liberals and the catholic priests; the party split, but for which the Irish cause would have been carried to victory; the gulf between the aristocratic leader and the masses steeped in prejudice, and between patriotism and Victorian morality—all became themes of debate and theory and an inspiration to Irish poets. 'Did this collective emotional explosion of 1890', Conor Cruise O'Brien wonders, 'help to set free the imaginative forces which, for a time in the early 1900s made Dublin—the Parnellite city—an important centre of world literature?'

At the heart of the legend, however, lies the unique personality of one of Ireland's great men, lonely, proud, passionate and disdainful.

Conor Cruise O'Brien ends his book with a quatrain from Yeats:

'And here's a final reason,
He was of such a kind
Every man that sings a song
Keeps Parnell in his mind.'

The Dilettante Statesmen: Lord Rosebery and Arthur James Balfour

The lives and careers of two of Queen Victoria's prime ministers, Lord Rosebery and Arthur James Balfour, display a number of striking parallels.

Rosebery (1847–1929) and Balfour (1848–1930), were both typical members of the British aristocracy, for whom politics was a sort of hobby which could be carried on at intervals, not interfering with their roles as capitalists and landowners, or their enjoyment of life in leisured society, nor with such occupations as travelling, reading and writing. Both men inherited great wealth when they came of age and enjoyed incomes of some £30,000 a year at a time when the pound was worth five times as much as it is today and income tax was negligible. On top of this Rosebery, on the death of his grandfather the fifth earl in 1868, succeeded to the earldom and a seat in the House of Lords, a situation which he considered adverse to a successful career in politics.

For their early and striking success both men were indebted to eminent politicians whose protégés they became. Rosebery was Gladstone's right-hand man during the Midlothian campaign which preceded the election of 1880 and finally, for a brief period (1894–95), became his successor as Prime Minister. Following this venture he remained on the sidelines of actual party politics, but for years afterwards he was regarded as a 'veiled prophet', a reputation earned for him by his cryptic though exquisitely phrased reflexions.

Balfour, who entered Parliament in 1874 as Conservative member for Hertford, followed in the footsteps of his uncle Lord Salisbury. He was his uncle's private secretary from 1878 to 1880, succeeding him as Prime Minister in 1902, when Salisbury resigned. Balfour's term of office, like Rosebery's, was fraught with intrigues and dissensions among the Tories, but after his resignation from the premiership in 1905 and from the Conservative leadership in 1911, he continued in government in a number of less important ministerial posts until shortly before his death in 1930. (He was First Lord of the Admiralty in the 1915 Coalition government, Foreign Secretary in 1916–19, and Lord President of the Council in 1919–22 and 1925–29.)

Rosebery was nominally a Liberal and Balfour a Conservative, but, politically speaking, the real difference between them was insignificant. Both men, throughout their lives, were noted for a certain elegant dilettantism in their political dealings; they regarded, or professed to regard the coarser kinds of party strife with ironic disdain. For long periods during their parliamentary activities both of them were the very embodiment of confusion and indecision. Rosebery started out a staunch supporter of the Gladstonian war-cry 'Home Rule for Ireland', but gradually veered from this position until, as a result of his 'liberal conservatism', he became more of a support to the Tories than to his own party. Balfour, during his premiership was constantly busied in planning skilful manoeuvres to avoid taking a stand in party conflicts between the pro-tariff and pro-free-trade wings.

Even the personal characteristics of the two men displayed an astonishing similarity. Both were strikingly handsome; both had impeccable manners and an air of distinction; and both displayed an elegant negligence of manner, a ready and polished wit, a suave and cool composure, which in Rosebery's case occasionally disintegrated into irritation and petulance in the face of stupidity or opposition. He was, says Robert Rhodes James in his biography of Rosebery, 'an easily impatient man, quickly disconcerted by trifles, over-sensitive to atmosphere, and extraordinarily touchy when out of humour . . .'

Rosebery and Balfour were church-goers, both of unquestioned piety; they mentioned God quite uninhibitedly, though it was apparent that neither of them was on terms of any great intimacy with the Deity. Each of them appeared to have been undersexed, and love affairs played little or no part in their lives. When he was twenty Rosebery was friendly with Mary Fox the 16-year-old adopted daughter of Lady Holland, but although he was apparently in love with the girl the friendship went no further, and their relationship terminated in mysterious circumstances which have never been explained.

In 1878, at the age of thirty-one, Rosebery married Hannah de Rothschild who was twenty-seven and the only child of Baron and Baroness Meyer de Rothschild. In 1877, her parents having died within a few years of each other, Hannah had become the heiress to a fortune of some two million pounds. The marriage was one of deep love and attachment on both sides; it also considerably multiplied Rosebery's already great wealth. His wife's early death, after only eight years of happy marriage, was a shattering blow to him from which he never fully recovered: he lived the rest of his life in great loneliness. No other romance has ever come to light. As for Balfour, it was at one time believed that he had been a chaste celibate all his life, and he lived to be eighty. Subsequently discovered letters have revealed, however, that there was at least one love affair in his life with a married society woman which was resumed from time to time over a period of decades.

Neither Rosebery nor Balfour belonged to the aristocratic set headed by the Prince of Wales, for whom drinking bouts, idiotic practical jokes and the company of *grandes cocottes*, were, it seemed, the be-all and end-all of existence. Rosebery enjoyed hunting, shooting, and racing (he ran three Derby winners, in 1894, 1895 and 1905). He was a great collector and his interests included rare books, silver, pictures and valuable trivia with historical or curious associations, such as the cushion on which Napoleon's head had rested after he had died, his travelling chair and the shutters from his bedroom. He enjoyed shooting, and there was a prodigious slaughter of game on his estates at Dalmeny, Mentmore and Rosebery. He also enjoyed constant and impulsive changes of scene among his numerous houses.

Balfour's interests were sport and music. Though he enjoyed Bach and Beethoven he idolized Handel, whom he thought 'the greatest master of choral effect the world has ever known'. He was a tireless deer-stalker, golfer and tennis player. With the invention of the safety bicycle he became a keen cyclist and with the advent of the motor car an enthusiastic motorist, though he had no gift for mechanics or understanding of machinery.

> 'His delight in mechanical advance was only equalled by his incapacity to manipulate any sort of machine. He never dreamed of learning to drive a motor car, but he did learn to ride a bicycle, as was once evidenced by his appearance on the Treasury Bench with his arm in a sling and his foot in a slipper.'

Balfour had been riding behind a hansom cab and crashed into it when the driver turned sharply in front of him to get to his place on the cab rank.

He was one of the first to own a motor-car, but his enjoyment of travel in his 1900 de Dion was fraught with uncertainties, which he sometimes recorded:

> 'On Monday, motor-car to London. It had a mild breakdown about every three miles—and finally, when we arrived within striking distance of home, we betook ourselves to hansoms, leaving the little French chauffeur in tears of mortification.'

Perhaps the most remarkable similarity between Balfour and Rosebery was their love of literature. They were both great readers, both of them wrote books, and their erudition seemed awe-inspiring to the society circles in which they moved. Their prestige as scholars and historians was enhanced by birth, wealth and political eminence.

Rosebery published four historical works: *Pitt* (1881); *Napoleon: The Last Phase* (1900); *Lord Randolph Churchill* (1906); *Chatham: His Early Life and Connections* (1910). The short study of his friend Lord Randolph Churchill, originally intended as material to assist Winston Churchill in writing his biography of his father, is beyond doubt the best of all Rosebery's writings, and is an affectionate analysis of his dead friend's stormy life, his tragic eclipse, pathetic decline and early death. In Rosebery's other books an ornate style and a somewhat conscious striving after effect serve to deck out a series of not highly original reflexions, with a result that is often tiresome. Rosebery's speeches frequently achieved a rhetorical triumph through the use of overdressed banalities, and a reading of his books suggests that this was his true style, sardonic and compressed 'and perhaps too self-consciously burnished'. He was much given to seeing 'the hand of Providence' in events, but he avoided being too rashly explicit as to what he meant by that.

Balfour was an amateur philosopher with a good reputation in academic circles, where he was much in demand as a lecturer. His works range from *A Defence of Philosophic Doubt* (1879), written when he was thirty-one, through *Essays and Addresses* (1893), with its brilliant study of Bishop Berkeley's life and writings, to *The Foundations of Belief* (1895) and *Theism and Humanism*, his Gifford Lectures of 1914, and make rather uphill reading. They all say much the same thing and might be considered in some sense a poularization of Berkeley's philosophy. Balfour's philosophic scepticism, however, led him to stress the mortality and transience of man. To give the essentials of this philosophy: we live on a tiny globe which is rushing towards its ultimate destruction; all our proud creations will crumble to dust and man will go down into the pit, and all his thoughts will perish. We know nothing about anything; thus it is not only convenient but intellectually reasonable to believe in practically anything, even in God, for example, and eternal life. This sort of metaphysical *pot pourri* was much to the taste of many at that time, as were the philosophies of William James and later of Bergson, whom Balfour greatly admired.

Both Rosebery and Balfour were brilliant speakers. Rosebery read his speeches with a mounting dramatic power; Balfour spoke with ease, using the briefest of notes and seemed in his cool detachment the very essence of the English aristocrat, able with nonchalant impartiality to take a blithe pot-shot at pheasants and philosophers alike.

Despite their many similarities, the differences between the careers and achievements of these two great amateurs were nevertheless highly revealing; Rosebery, for example was a minister for only about four years all told, Balfour for nearly thirty. Balfour often claimed that he was not, properly speaking, a politician at all and that perhaps he ought to have been a professional philosopher; but quite obviously he not only found politics entertaining, he also had a practical interest in them. During his apparently unsuccessful premiership he introduced a number of basic projects in which he was passionately interested: a law on education, defence administration reforms and the Anglo-French Agreement of 1904. Even afterwards he did valuable work: he was one of those who made possible the so-called 'Balfour Declaration' of 1917, which paved the way for the creation of the state of Israel. He was praised in various quarters for his flexibility, sound judgement and resourcefulness in cabinet meetings, and such appreciation was obviously neither given lightly nor was it mere flattery. The best of his parliamentary speeches are not just exercises in rhetoric, but lucid and penetrating analyses of situations and problems.

Sad to say, this was not the case with Rosebery. The hint of self-satisfied, deliberate dilettantism, the intellectual arrogance which could be glimpsed in Balfour was predominant in Rosebery. In addition he was irresolute, thin-skinned, touchy and given to intolerable nagging and fault-finding. When he became Secretary for Foreign Affairs in the Gladstone government of 1892, he protested that he was inexperienced and ignorant; and again in 1894, when he became Liberal premier following Gladstone's resignation, he wrote: 'I am altogether unfitted for the post, as regards capacity and knowledge.' How right he was in both cases. Yet at the same time it was evident that he was eager for power, felt that he could wield it and would not tolerate either personal or practical criticism.

English biographers have not been slow to note how fond politicians are of insisting that they loathe the exhausting labours of the rise to high office and long ardently for the peace and quiet of private life, whereas in reality they are eaten up with envy, competitive greed and ambition.

In this connection, however, it is hard to conceive of anything as repulsive as the struggle for power in which Rosebery, Harcourt and Morley were involved—to say nothing of a few others of Gladstone's heirs. Lying, flattery, rude letters, interchanges full of hostility and insolence, seem to have been almost the chief activity of this little band of statesmen who were supposed to be governing England. Early in Rosebery's career it was said of him that he 'sought the palm without the dust'.

Both Balfour and Rosebery entered politics without any vocation, and by luck and patronage rose from positions of little importance to become prime ministers. Neither was spurred on by any great ideal, not even by a great concrete aim. But whereas Balfour in the end became sufficiently experienced and interested in politics to accomplish something of importance, Rosebery remained the aristocrat out on a political picnic, and when he deliberately brought his active career in politics to an end before he was fifty, it did not seem so much a tragedy as a confirmation of foredoomed failure.

Meteor and Mountebank: Lord Randolph Churchill

It is now more than sixty years since Sir Winston Churchill's celebrated biography of Lord Randolph Churchill was written. This life of a distinguished man by his even more distinguished son ranks as a classic among English biographies, not only for its content, the fruit of an intensive study of Lord Randolph's life and thought, but for its pregnant and impassioned style. Nevertheless, as a biography the book has significant shortcomings, due partly to the fact that many documents were not available when it was written or were suppressed out of consideration for persons then still living. It also tends to gloss over defects and emphasize merits somewhat more perhaps than do most English biographies of English notables which are often, unfortunately enough, often more like pious memorials than truly objective biographies.

The participants in Lord Randolph's career are no longer alive and the restrictions upon the public and private documents concerning them have now mostly been removed by the passage of time. These circumstances have favoured the most recent biography, by Robert Rhodes James, *Lord Randolph Churchill* (1959), which contains much fresh information gleaned from documents in private collections and family archives, cabinet papers and other state documents. This biography now supplements both Sir Winston's book about his father and the admirable short study by Lord Randolph's lifelong friend Lord Rosebery.

Robert Rhodes James's book is franker and more objective than Sir Winston's and though its style lacks the sonority of Churchillian prose its admiration for Lord Randolph is almost as generous as his son's. Rosebery's, Churchill's and James's books now together provide a wider basis for an accurate character study of their subject, but a great deal in the brilliant, tragic life and career of Lord Randolph Churchill still remains unexplained and probably will always remain so.

Randolph Henry Spencer Churchill was born in 1849, the third, but second surviving, son of the Marquis of Blandford. At the age of eight, his father having succeeded to the family title as seventh Duke of Marlborough, the boy became known as Lord Randolph Churchill. In the same year he was sent to the famous school run by Mr Tabor at Cheam and in 1863 he went to Eton. He was a cheerful unruly boy, impudent and full of mischief, to say nothing of being 'bumptious, cheerfully arrogant' and exuding 'an unmistakable air of superiority'.

His conduct at Eton caused his father much concern. Lack of self-control was a noticeable feature of his personality and he was frequently taken to task by the Duke, in long letters, for his clashes with authority, the rows and scrapes he got into because of his impertinence and overbearing disposition—than which, his father scolded, 'there is nothing in the world which is so low and contemptible and makes a boy and subsequently a man so justly detestable'.

Though naturally clever, young Randolph was idle in the extreme when it came to lessons. But from an early age he had given evidence of a retentive memory and by dint of picking the brains of his schoolfellows he managed to scrape through his tasks and to keep pace without undue exertion. His parents thought, and he himself later admitted, that the money spent on his education had been wasted.

He had a passion for sport, especially riding and fox-hunting, in which connection he made many hunting friends and was a favourite with the local farmers. At home he was a charming and cheerful companion, spoiled by his mother and three sisters, who doted on him. He was reserved with strangers but open and generous with his friends, and these, throughout his life, were few but devoted.

He left Eton in 1867 and after several months of travel in Switzerland and Italy and one unsuccessful attempt to pass the entrance examination to Oxford he took up residence there, in Merton College. He was now more polished but had lost none of his old irreverence and gaiety. As an undergraduate he and his small and exclusive group of companions were full of merry pranks, constantly running foul of the proctors and their 'bull-dogs'; but in 1869 he calmed down, began to show signs of maturity and responsibility and worked hard for his final examinations in the combined school of History and Law. He narrowly missed a First but came top of the Second Class.

Lord Randolph, extrovert, extravagant and ambitious, was not attracted to cultural or intellectual pursuits; philosophy or economics were a closed book to him (as were all but a few other books) and methodical thinking was alien to his nature. Nevertheless he did read a certain amount of history as the quality of his degree indicates, and at school he underwent the traditional drilling in the classics. His favourite reading was confined to Horace, the Bible, *Jorrocks* and Gibbon's *Decline and Fall of the Roman Empire*, from all of which he could recite whole passages at a time. Gibbon's classic, with its brilliance, irony and self-confident superficiality, became his model, as it did for so many other talented amateurs. He wrote later, to his future wife:

> 'I have two old favourites. When I feel very cross and angry I read Gibbon, whose profound philosophy and easy though majestic writing soon quiets me down. . . . When I feel very low and desponding I read Horace, whose thorough epicureanism, quiet maxims and beautiful verse are most tranquillizing.'

He strongly recommended the reading of 'some great works or histories; they pass the time, and prevent you from worrying or thinking too much about the future'.

In 1873 (when he was twenty-four) during Cowes week, Lord Randolph met and instantly fell in love with the beautiful and vivacious nineteen-year-old Miss Jenny Jerome. She was one of the three lovely Jerome girls, daughters of the self-made American millionaire and Wall Street financier, Leonard Jerome. This rugged individualist had lost one fortune and made another, had once owned and edited the *New York Times* and was a racing enthusiast, supporter of the New York Turf and President of the American Jockey Club. After a courtship of three days Lord Randolph proposed and was accepted. Parental doubts about the wisdom of a match based on so short an acquaintance provoked opposition from both families. The Duke, moreover was not pleased at the idea of what he called 'an American Connection'. After a thorough investigation of the standing and circumstances of the Jerome family he was still less inclined to give his approval to the marriage and wrote to his son:

> 'From what you tell me & What I have heard this Mr J seems to be a sporting, and I should think, vulgar sort of man. I hear he owns about 6 or 8 houses in New York (one may take this as a kind of indication of what the man is.) . . . everything you say about the Mother and daughters is perfectly compatible with all that I am apprehensive of about the father & his belongings, and however great the attractions of the former they can not be set off against a connection which it so appears which no man in his senses could think respectable . . .'

For his part, Mr Jerome, who was expected to make an appropriate settlement on his daughter, was appalled by the English laws relating to the property of married women: 'I can but think your English custom of making the wife so utterly dependent upon the husband most unwise'.

At the outset of this double-barrelled parental disapproval of the proposed match, Mrs Jerome had whisked her daughter off to Paris and all communication between the young lovers was discouraged; but they were not to be put off and the parents at length agreed to a formal engagement of a year. Before eight months had elapsed, however, both sets of parents had further relented. The Duke made a trip to Paris to inspect his future daughter-in-law, was captivated, and despite a further hitch in the negotiations caused by Mr Jerome's objections to the terms of the marriage settlement, matters were finally arranged to the satisfaction of all parties. The young couple were married at the British Embassy in Paris on 15 April 1874, and after a brief honeymoon, curtailed by the reassembling of Parliament, Lord Randolph brought his bride back to Blenheim.

One of the Duke's conditions to the marriage had been that his son should first stand for Parliament as member for the family borough of Woodstock, a constituency which was practically an annex of Blenheim, the family seat. 'The Duke felt, and with reason, that unless Lord Randolph were member for Woodstock before his marriage, not only would the borough be seduced to Radicalism, but that the son in whom all the hopes and ambitions of his later life were centred might never enter Parliament at all.' The Conservative member for Woodstock at the time was unpopular and it was thought that he might lose the election. That a Radical should win the seat was a contingency that would have been 'perfectly insupportable' to the Duke and his family. Accordingly Lord Randolph canvassed the constituency, was returned by a majority of 165, and entered Parliament as a member for Woodstock. He made his maiden speech in the Commons in May 1874, a 'rather crude debating effort' which many, echoing Benjamin Jowett, thought 'the speech of a foolish young man, who will never come to any good'.

This inauspicious start of an apparently unremarkable fox-hunting aristocrat was misleading; a few years later he was a name to be conjured with in English politics, and after Disraeli's death in 1881 the Conservative party pinned their hopes on him.

Lord Rosebery, a lifelong friend of Lord Randolph from Eton days, whose brief but admirable study contains many perceptive observations aptly and elegantly phrased, believed that the transition from aristocratic playboy to ambitious politician was Lord Randolph's answer to the severe social ostracism which he incurred in 1876.

In February of that year Lady Aylesford, wife of the Earl of Aylesford, a close friend of the Prince of Wales, wrote to inform her husband that she intended to elope. She was in love with Lord Blandford, Lord Randolph's elder brother, also a close friend of the Prince of Wales. Blandford was so recklessly infatuated with Lady Aylesford that he proposed to leave his wife for her sake.

Lord Aylesford received his wife's disturbing news in India where he was a guest of the Prince of Wales who was making an official goodwill tour of Britain's vast imperial possession. Aylesford left for England without delay and the Prince, who had himself, some years before, indulged in a flirtatious friendship with Lady Aylesford, denounced Lord Blandford as 'the greatest blackguard alive', at the same time expressing his sympathy for the wronged husband. On his arrival in England Lord Aylesford announced his intention of suing for divorce and of citing Lord Blandford as co-respondent. The impending scandal provided London society with food for excited gossip.

Lord Randolph now stepped in with rash family loyalty. He begged the lovers not to elope and telegraphed the Prince in India asking him to persuade Lord Aylesford to desist from his plan of seeking divorce. The Prince, however, declined to intervene and Aylesford declined to desist.

Lady Aylesford's family, meanwhile, had persuaded her not to elope. Her husband, nevertheless, was still intent on divorcing her, so, mindful of the grim punishment of social ostracism meted out to divorced women by Victorian society, Lady Aylesford handed over to Lord Blandford a package of letters written to her by the Prince of Wales during their past flirtation. Blandford in turn handed them over to his brother. By the threat of making these letters public in the courtroom and of ensuring the Prince's presence there as a witness if there should be a divorce, Lord Randolph hoped to force the Prince of Wales to put pressure on his friend not to start divorce proceedings.

The letters, in the opinion of the Lord Chancellor, Lord Cairns, though apparently harmless enough, were 'written in a strain of undue familiarity' and contained 'many foolish and somewhat stupid expressions' which, if made public in a divorce court would cause great trouble and embarrassment to the Prince and would be injurious and lowering to the image of royalty.

In furtherance of the scheme to prevent the scandal from becoming public Lord Randolph called on the Princess of Wales to inform her of what it was proposed to do in the event of a divorce.

On receiving the news of the interview from his wife the Prince was convulsed with fury at what he considered an insult to the Princess and at the distress she had been caused by one who was supposedly his friend. He challenged Lord Randolph to a pistol duel, to be fought on the Continent on his way back from India. Lord Randolph replied with a contemptuous refusal, practically telling the Prince not to be absurd, for how could he expect Lord Randolph to raise a pistol against his future Sovereign? The Prince, through an emissary, conferred secretly with Disraeli and appealed to the Queen for help, protesting the innocence of his letters, with the result that Disraeli and members of his cabinet were detailed to help persuade Lord Aylesford to reconsider his divorce plans. For some time Aylesford was adamant but, a bare twenty-four hours after the Prince's arrival in England from his Indian tour, Aylesford yielded, as he said, in order to avoid 'great public scandal and mischief'.

Lord Randolph sent a letter of apology to the Prince (who ignored it) and left with his wife for a discreetly timed visit to his father-in-law and tour of the United States.

The Prince implemented the abrupt termination of his friendship with the Randolph Churchills by letting it be known that he would enter no house where they continued to be received. Faced with this threat of princely displeasure, London society hastened to comply and the young couple were henceforward cold-shouldered by all but a handful of the most strong-minded and courageous of their friends. Though Lord Randolph was forced to sign an abject apology worded by the Prince's advisers he did so under protest. The apology was grudgingly acknowledged, but bygones were not allowed to be bygones. The Prince's displeasure lasted for nearly nine years (until March 1884) during which time the social ostracism of Lord and Lady Randolph was rigorously enforced.

Lord Randolph's reaction to society's boycott of his wife and himself was one of embittered fury. According to Lord Rosebery it was 'the turning point of his life. The "saeva indignatio" excited in him by this social conflict, turned to politics. That was the vent for his suppressed wrath.'

Disraeli now repeated to the Duke of Marlborough a well-timed offer to become Viceroy of Ireland. The Duke accepted and in order to get Lord Randolph out of London for a time took him to Ireland as an unofficial and unpaid private secretary. The three years Lord Randolph spent in Ireland brought him into close contact with the advocates of Irish Home Rule and his travels about the country made him appreciate the desperate conditions of the peasantry of southern Ireland. His discussions with Irish friends and his first-hand knowledge of conditions in Ireland were the starting point of his political activities concerned with the Irish question—perhaps the one political subject which he thoroughly mastered and which became the springboard for his chief parliamentary activities in the future.

The election of 1880, when Disraeli's Conservative government was defeated and Gladstone formed his second cabinet, brought young Churchill his opportunity. The Government was shaky, beset as it was by internal dissension, conflicts and disturbances in Ireland and occasional trivial but troublesome incidents. Chief among these was the ludicrous but irritating controversy over the atheistic Liberal Bradlaugh's claim to take his seat in the Commons by affirming instead of taking the Oath of Allegiance. The regular Opposition was also feeble, especially after Disraeli's death in 1881, when Sir Stafford Northcote, ill and ageing, obviously no forceful leader and too respectful of Gladstone (whose private secretary he had once been), headed the Conservatives in 'dual control' with Lord Salisbury. An Opposition of elder statesmen confronted a Cabinet of elder statesmen.

This situation provided wonderful opportunities for the 'angry young men' of the day, with Parnell leading the Irish Nationalists, Dilke and Chamberlain among the Liberals, and Lord Randolph Churchill standing head and shoulders above the rest. Lord Randolph and a trio of friends who shared his views (Sir Henry Drummond Wolff, one of the Conservative members for Portsmouth; John Gorst, Conservative member for Chatham; and Arthur Balfour, member for the family borough of Hertford and nephew of Lord Salisbury) formed an obstreperous clique which one of the Irish Nationalists nicknamed 'the Fourth Party'—a nickname which stuck. The 'Fourth Party' began to attack the Government, and especially the aged Gladstone, mercilessly and without scruple, while simultaneously they treated the official Tory leader, Stafford Northcote, with unconcealed contempt.

Politics was seemingly just an extension of their pranksome young manhood, giving them an outlet for their gambling and hunting proclivities. The thrills and excitement afforded by cards and horses were replaced by the excitement of parliamentary obstruction, interruption, outrageous blows below the belt. Randolph electrified the House with his impudent sallies, as Disraeli had done forty years earlier and as F. E. Smith was to do thirty years later. At riotous dinners and lunches the four members of the Fourth Party discussed the downfall of the leader of the Opposition and of the Government and thought out the schemes and mischievous tactics with which 'Randy' would intervene, with the languid wit in which he excelled, in the nightly debates in the House. Lord Rosebery gives an inimitable picture of Randolph as a speaker:

> 'His wit, his sarcasm, his piercing personalities, his elaborate irony, and his effective delivery, gave astonishing popularity to his speeches. His slim and boyish figure, his moustache which had an emotion of its own, his round protruding eye, gave a compound interest to his speeches and his conversation.'

The 'Fourth Party' sometimes took sides with the Irish, sometimes with the discontented Radicals among the Liberals; what they tilted against was unimportant to them, so long as they could bait and taunt. As Randolph put it, 'we must harass the Government'. And they continued to do so with 'constant questions, troublesome interventions, ceaseless talk against time, filibustering obstruction'.

On one occasion Randolph compared Gladstone to Raschid Pasha, that same head-lopping executioner of Albania whose welcome to Disraeli in his youth had drawn delighted comment from the young man, in that much-quoted phrase from one of his letters home. At another time Lord Randolph paused in the middle of an important speech and sent his friend Gorst to get him a drink—'Remember, Gorst, brandy and seltzer,' he called out cheerfully after Gorst, to the astonishment of the House.

Randolph soon became as popular a speaker with the masses as he was in the House, drawing packed audiences to the biggest assembly halls of the towns he visited. His biographers emphasize the fact that his speeches are an exception to old political speeches which seem 'cold and flabby', according to Lord Rosebery, once the heat, the audience, the interruptions and the applause have disappeared. Lord Randolph's speeches still retain their freshness and interest in print, so many decades after speaker and audiences have vanished.

All this is true enough, but with one important exception which admiring biographers omit to make. While Lord Randolph's speeches continue to entertain because of a certain quality of timelessness, they achieve this quality by their irrelevance. Randolph got his best effects by a mixture of joking, irony and insolence, all verging on buffoonery. He could jeer at the young Earl of Durham, who had just come of age and into the possession of vast hereditary estates, for being one of the lilies of the field, while Randolph himself lived like a lord—with assistance from others and bedevilled by debts. 'If it is legitimate,' he said, 'and I hold that it is legitimate, to stigmatize any individual as enjoying great riches for which he has neither toiled nor spun, such a case would be the Earl of Durham', a young man 'who has studied politics about as much as Barnum's new white elephant . . .'.

One famous and typical instance of his technique was the speech in which he made fun of Gladstone's recreation of felling trees. Randolph's description of a deputation of working-men being received by the venerable and dignified statesman during one of these tree-felling sessions in the park at Hawarden, assisted by his son Herbert, is like a brilliant music-hall sketch. Lord Randolph pictured the working-men being led through the gardens into the park strewn with the rotting trunks of Mr Gladstone's chopped-down 'once umbrageous' trees. Boughs, bark and withered shoots lie all around. The deputation 'come suddenly on the Prime Minister and Master Herbert, in scanty attire and profuse perspiration, engaged in the destruction of a gigantic oak, just giving its last dying groan. They are permitted to gaze and to worship and adore and, having conducted themselves with exemplary propriety, are each of them presented with a few chips as a memorial of that memorable scene . . .'. Lord Randolph likened Mr Gladstone's politics to his recreations: they were essentially destructive. 'Every afternoon the whole world is invited to assist at the crashing fall of some beech or elm or oak. The forest laments, in order that Mr Gladstone may perspire.' All those who trusted Gladstone and hoped for something from him, said Lord Randolph, got 'chips, nothing but chips—hard dry, unnourishing, indigestible chips!'

Music-hall turns like this made Lord Randolph more popular with the working-men and with simple people than any other public speaker at that time and he was egged on to further inventive and audacious vituperation of the Liberal leaders by voices from the crowd bawling out 'Give it 'em hot, Randy!'

His self-confidence and ambition grew. In 1880 he succeeded in capturing the National Union of Conservative Organizations and was able not only to make them more effective, as Chamberlain had done earlier with the Liberals but to jockey himself into a position of control. He formed the Primrose League, which was at first ridiculed as 'another of Randy's pranks'. This Tory party association with the primrose as its emblem, its festive gatherings, badges, decorations, Dames and Knights and other grandiloquent ranks and titles, became a means of bringing together the aristocrats and the voting cattle, and proved a worthwhile investment in snobbery by speedily increasing both its membership and its influence.

Randolph himself was well fitted for the role of the people's aristocrat. His slender elegance, enormous handlebar moustaches, the bulging eyes which at Eton had won him the nickname of 'gooseberry Churchill', his exhilarating effrontery, all contributed to give him a dashing, rollicking image in which there was a touch of the burlesque which made him almost the nobleman of caricature, one which had in it just enough exaggeration to disarm any derisive or irritated disapproval.

In June 1885 Gladstone was overthrown by a chance majority of the Conservative party in conjunction with the Irish. When the result of the count was announced Randolph Churchill led the excited jubilation at the victory by leaping up on to the bench, cheering and waving his handkerchief. The Irish and most of the Tories followed suit, until the House was a pandemonium of cheers and shouting, and a flurry of waving hats, handkerchiefs and order papers. The Commons could not be dissolved, as it was necessary to draw up a new electoral register following the recently determined Franchise Reform, and Lord

Salisbury, Conservative leader in the House of Lords, formed his first cabinet, in which, after much wrangling, Lord Randolph Churchill became Secretary of State for India.

According to those who worked with him at the India Office, Lord Randolph was a conscientious and capable departmental head and administrator and got on well with his subordinates, who were devoted to him, finding him considerate, sympathetic and appreciative and above all unequalled 'in the magical art of *getting things done*'. The most notable event of his short stay at the India Office was the annexation of Upper Burma. Owing to the intrigues of the French and the hostility of King Theebaw, who had seized the throne in 1878, annexation had become a necessity if British influence and power in Lower Burma, already under British rule, were not to be threatened. A series of hostile actions by Theebaw led to an ultimatum from the Indian government, which was ignored. British troops then advanced and occupied Mandalay within three days. Theebaw was deposed (1885) and sent a prisoner to India and at Lord Randolph's insistance Upper Burma was annexed on 1 January 1886.

As Secretary for India he was already beginning to display a tendency to meddle in affairs of every kind and even to compete with Salisbury the Prime Minister. This tendency subsequently led to Lord Randolph's downfall.

But it was the state of affairs prior to the approaching General Election which was the focus of interest from all quarters. The Irish Nationalists who had brought about Gladstone's overthrow as a result of his coercive legislation for Ireland, were demanding Home Rule, and a tendency to compete for their favour made its appearance in both the big English parties. One side was actuated by the intention of making an eventual alliance with the Irish National Party; the other aimed its blandishments at the Irish settled in England, whose vote was thought to be decisive in some ten constituencies.

Randolph played an important part in this vote-getting contest. In conversations with Parnell he made statements which must be considered to imply some sort of agreement; the Right promised not to suggest a coercive legislation if Parnell would urge the Irish in England to vote Tory. Randolph gave no promise of Home Rule but neither did he make any objections to it and this must have been interpreted by the Irish as proof that at any rate he was not disposed to be inflexible on the question. Privately, in letters to Salisbury, he expressed condemnation of the hostile Scottish-Irish minority in Ulster, which was opposed to any concession to the Nationalists; only six months later he was to incite this same minority to revolt against a self-governed Ireland. As usual, it was the tactical aspect of a question which was decisive for Lord Randolph.

The results of the General Election rendered Ireland virtually the pointer on the scales. With the support of the Irish the Tories had gained as many votes as the Liberals. A series of intrigues and disagreements subsequently crystallized the situation. Gladstone, under a fire of criticism by a minority of the Liberals, changed sides to embrace the cause of Home Rule, while the Conservatives made preservation of the Union the main issue of their campaign and prepared to introduce coercive legislation. In February 1886 Salisbury was overthrown by a combination of Liberals and Irish Nationalists and Gladstone formed his third cabinet; in June the Government's proposal to give Home Rule to Ireland was rejected because a number of Liberals opposed the measure or refrained from voting; and so, in July, fresh elections were held.

Under the new dispensation Randolph Churchill became the most furious opponent of Home Rule. His election address to his constituents of South Paddington is one of the most abusive in English parliamentary history. Lord Randolph described Gladstone as 'an old man in a hurry' who was supposed to have 'reserved for his closing days a conspiracy against the honour of Britain and the welfare of Ireland more startlingly base and nefarious than any of those other numerous designs and plots which, during the last quarter of a century, have occupied his imagination . . .'. Of the claims Gladstone made for his proposed government of Ireland, Lord Randolph said: '. . . the united and concentrated genius of Bedlam and Colney Hatch would strive in vain to produce a more striking tissue of absurdities . . .'—and it was all intended, he added, to satisfy the senile ambition of 'a man who makes the most unparallelled claim for dictatorial power which can be conceived by free men'.

In a letter to his lifelong Irish friend, Lord Justice Fitzgibbon, Lord Randolph said, 'I decided some time ago that if the G.O.M. went for Home Rule, the Orange card would be the one to play.' In his public speeches he urged Ulstermen to revolt if Ireland was given Home Rule, and at the start of his triumphal speechmaking tour of Ulster in February 1886 he coined the phrase which caught the imagination of the opponents of Home Rule: 'Ulster will fight, and Ulster will be right'—a slogan which, thirty years later, was to lead Ireland to the brink of civil war, the birth-throes of independence which culminated in the Dublin Easter Week rebellion of 1919, and so led to the 'Troubles' of the twenties.

Lord Randolph soon had his reward. The Conservatives and the Liberals who had fallen away from Gladstone—the Liberal Unionists—now left the Government with a minority in the House of Commons. Gladstone resigned and Salisbury formed his second cabinet, in which Randolph, the supreme engineer of this victory, became Chancellor of the Exchequer and so second man in the Cabinet.

His reputation was now at its peak and was characterized by the vulgar ostentation of his speeches at public meetings, by his cleverness and arrogance as a parliamentary leader; he was lionized by London society and was once more on friendly terms with the Prince of Wales. 'Nothing will help Randolph so much', Disraeli had said in 1880, when the Prince's grievance against Lord Randolph had already lasted for some years, 'as success in Parliament. The Prince is always taken by success.'

Lord Randolph's triumph was short-lived. This is quite understandable, to judge by his speeches at this period and especially the correspondence with Lord Salisbury, quoted by Robert Rhodes James in his biography. Lord Randolph meddled in everything, created continual difficulties on every issue.

He demanded a new foreign policy of Anglo-German *rapprochement* and intrigued behind the Foreign Secretary's back with the German ambassador, Count Hatzfeldt, who was a close personal friend of his. He argued for hours at cabinet meetings on matters great and small, irritating and antagonizing his colleagues; with every week he became more insular and more pretentious. It was obvious that he had his eye on Salisbury's post for the near future.

He interfered incessantly in foreign affairs and his old *bête noire*, Stafford Northcote, who had been kicked upstairs into a peerage and was now Lord Iddesleigh and Foreign Secretary, came in for his full share of denigration. He was, in Churchill's esteem, vexatious almost to tears, 'such an old muff', 'an old ass full of fussy suggestions', 'a damned little Goat', and was even classified, on occasion, as '*quel crétin*'. Other members of the Cabinet fared little better—they were 'all . . . great asses'—and Churchill's habit of abusing his colleagues in this fashion in letters to his chief must have aroused the wise Salisbury's suspicions on his own behalf.

When the time came for the preparation of the Budget, Lord Randolph, who was pledged to a policy of economy, demanded reductions in defense expenditure. Lord George Hamilton was amenable about certain Navy reductions, but the Secretary for War, W. H. Smith, was adamant, and Salisbury made it clear that he sided with Smith.

On 20 December, after a final unproductive meeting with Smith, Lord Randolph went off, at the Queen's invitation, to spend the evening at Windsor. There, without revealing his intention to anyone except Lord George Hamilton, who had also been summoned to Windsor, Churchill wrote a letter of resignation to the Prime Minister. He requested 'to be allowed to give up my office and retire from the Government'. He said it, not in earnest, but as pressure to get his own way over the Defense Estimates. It was a gamble that did not come off. Salisbury called his bluff and accepted his resignation.

It was typical of Lord Randolph that, two days later, while his letter of farewell confirming Lord Salisbury's acceptance of his resignation was on its way to Hatfield, he went in the early hours of the morning to *The Times* offices, showed the editor George Buckle his correspondence with Salisbury and gave permission for the news of his resignation to be published. The story goes that in return for the scoop Lord Randolph asked Buckle for his support in a leader. Buckle refused and told him, 'You cannot bribe *The Times*.'

The sensational news of the resignation duly broke early that morning in *The Times*, where it was read with stupefaction by the Queen. Lord Salisbury's cipher telegram from Hatfield had not yet reached her and she was highly indignant to learn first from her morning paper what she later described as Lord Randolph's 'abrupt, unprecedented and disrespectful' resignation.

An account of these eventful days reveals a nightmarish situation: with Lord Randolph interfering, intriguing, alternately hectoring and uneasy, more and more unbridled in speech and behaviour, the other Cabinet members doubting, reluctant and full of gathering animosity; Salisbury irritated and bored, but patient and soothing in his efforts to keep the Cabinet together, outwardly fretting at the tiresome situation but secretly filled with inward joy at finding this troublesome colleague and rival suddenly ripe for liquidation.

Churchill thought that Salisbury would not be able to produce a successor to him, but Salisbury produced the Liberal-Unionist George Goschen, internationally renowned as economist and financier, and persuaded him, with the aid of passionate pleas by letter and telegram from the Queen, to become his new Chancellor of the Exchequer. 'I forgot Goschen' is a saying often ascribed to Churchill, though it is uncertain who first made the remark; but even if he did not say it first, the thought must surely have crossed his mind at the time and he certainly repeated it later, several times and with variations.

The explanation of Lord Randolph's resignation accepted by most historians is that it was a calculated tactical move and a direct challenge to Salisbury's leadership. Both Sir Winston Churchill and Robert Rhodes James, in their biographies, incline in their respective ways to think otherwise: that it was unpremeditated, emotional, done almost in a fit of embittered pique at not getting his own way over the Army Estimates. Lord Randolph, in this view, neither considered that he had resigned nor that he was indispensible. Robert Rhodes James believes Lord George Hamilton's comment to be the most shrewd and accurate: that Churchill's resignation was the terrible blunder of a clever man and the explanation that he had 'forgotten Goschen' merely an excuse, in the unexpected aftermath of his act, to explain away his mistake.

Churchill afterwards told his friend Rosebery that his first letter to Salisbury, written from Windsor, was not intended as a letter of resignation. Salisbury, however, took it as such and regarded it as final. Churchill's answer acknowledging Salisbury's acceptance 'on my resignation' clinched the matter once for all.

Lord Randolph certainly had no reason not to remember Goschen. When Salisbury was trying to form his second Administration in 1886 and Lord Randolph was refusing to join the Government unless Stafford Northcote went, he was asked by his longtime friend and adviser Fitzgibbon, 'Can Goschen by no means whatever be induced to take the Exchequer? Age and financial experience have immense weight in that post . . . and a middle-aged commercial Chancellor would make [the English people] easy in their minds, when you could not'. As for considering himself indispensible, Lord Randolph had said in 1885, in answer to a remark that Salisbury could not get on without him, 'He can form a Ministry if necessary with waiters from the Carlton Club.' But in December 1886 he apparently had no inkling that Salisbury would be heartily glad to get rid of him and his 'monkey tricks'.

Sir Winston Churchill maintained that far from 'forgetting Goschen', Lord Randolph had always advocated his inclusion in the Government, so much so that at the height of the Cabinet crisis, two days before his resignation, he had purposely brought Goschen and Salisbury together at a dinner. Goschen's subsequent inclusion in the Government, therefore, 'was not fatal to his schemes, for there were no schemes'.

Lord Randolph lived for another nine years after these events; but though he returned to Parliament after a couple of months of travel in the Near East he was manifestly in decline in the ensuing years and never regained power or influence. 'He has thrown himself from the top of the ladder, and will never reach it again,' Churchill's devoted private secretary A. W. Moore prophesied sorrowfully to Lady Randolph. It was commonly held that the party machine had crushed him. His Radical friends had reminded him that 'the party tie is the strongest sentiment in this country—stronger than patriotism or even self-interest'. Lord Randolph had ignored the power of the machine, which, as Lord Rosebery wrote, 'crushed him as easily as a parched pea'.

It would seem more true to say, however, that he had made himself impossible and, back in Parliament, he continued to do so. He attacked his party friends and the Liberals with equal ferocity, but succeeded more especially in antagonizing the Tories. Even more important, perhaps, was the fact that he was an ill man and was steadily growing worse. 'He is so mad and odd, and has also bad health', was Queen

Victoria's comment in July 1886. His health had never been good and in 1892 a serious illness began to manifest itself in attacks of vertigo. His statements, always extravagant, now very often contained embarrassing absurdities. At one public meeting he called on the British working man 'to unite with the aristocracy against the bourgeoisie in their common bond of sport and immorality'. Champagne and brandy, formerly in the nature of flamboyant accessories, now became compulsive needs. He experienced increasing difficulty of articulation, his speeches became rambling and incoherent, his once-phenomenal memory suffered disconcerting lapses and he became hard of hearing. Gradually as a result, the House which had once rejoiced in his sallies now began to empty as soon as he started speaking, while a handful of friends remained and tried to encourage him. Among those who stayed to the end and made a polite pretence of listening was the man he had most scorned and derided, the aged Gladstone. Lord Randolph spoke for the last time in 1893, after a tour of political meetings at which dismayed working-men witnessed him rambling incoherently and beating the table, under the delusion that he had never spoken better.

On the advice of his doctors he embarked on a world tour. His condition improved somewhat in America and China, remained reasonably stationary in Japan, Hongkong and Burma, but changed for the worse when he reached India. He was brought back to London at the end of 1894, a physical and mental wreck, and died in his home in Grosvenor Square on 24 January 1895. He was buried in Bladon churchyard, within sight of Blenheim and the surroundings of his happy childhood.

The nature of Churchill's malady has been touched on with great delicacy by his biographers, who generally mention it merely as 'paralysis' or 'a rare and ghastly disease of the brain'. They describe the symptoms of the disease as progressive paralysis accompanied by vertigo, palpitations, numbness and trembling of the hands, difficulty in articulation, deafness and loss of memory. Privately Lord Randolph's illness has usually been regarded as general paralysis of syphilitic origin. The onslaught of the disease was not noticeable until it was in an advanced stage; its effects appear to have become publicly noticed first on 17 February 1893, during Churchill's speech on the second Home Rule Bill. Historians, however, are vague about the start of the disease. Lord Rosebery in his book makes two references which do not coincide. Churchill's habitual excitability and exaggeration made it difficult to determine at what point the characteristics of his illness reached a pathological stage. The time lapse of the disease seems, however, to have been atypical, since death occurred an unusually long time after the appearance of the first symptoms, which was probably between 1886 and 1888.

The details of Lord Randolph Churchill's life and career which have been given in this brief outline coincide for the most part with the critical statements and observations of his contemporaries and in particular with the factual information conveyed in biographies about him and memoirs which refer to him. To a certain extent the outline is even in accordance with such admiring portrayals as those of Lord Rosebery, Sir Winston Churchill and Robert Rhodes James. Nevertheless, it does contrast sharply with the general opinions and conclusions of those three writers, all of whom tend to view Lord Randolph through rose-coloured spectacles which enhance and embellish, transforming blemishes and defects into beauty spots. These appreciative portrayals, especially Sir Winston Churchill's, would appear to have been the main influence in the growth of the accepted English legend concerning Lord Randolph Churchill: the legend of the politician-knight *sans peur et sans reproche;* Randolph the reformer-prophet of English politics; Randolph the Tory-Democrat.

This legend is commonly explained as having been inspired by a combination of brilliant success and complete fiasco. Lord Randolph's tragedy is one which fascinates while it disarms both envy and any spiteful feeling that it served him right. The pious saying '*De mortuis nil nisi bonum*' generally holds good until at least after the funeral, but this attitude dies somewhat harder among English biographers and their charitable judgements are accorded with particular benevolence to those whose lives have been atoned for and glorified by misfortune, ruin and early death. Men who once called Randolph Churchill a fraud and charlatan or, to quote Lord Ripon, 'a reckless and unprincipled mountebank', are all now dead; and in any case, Churchill's downfall had soon silenced their carping tongues.

Sir Winston's book is the work of a son who was able to approach his father on terms of intimacy only on a single occasion, but who grew up in the atmosphere created by this father, one compounded of the radiance, the impudence, the downfall in the grand manner. The son's likeness to the father was evident: there was the same intelligence, the gift of rhetoric, the ambition, the ruthlessness, the daring, the fluctuations of elation and depression, the sense of playing an imposing role on one of the great stages of the world and finally, the patriotism that was less love of country than was a coalition with England's destiny and greatness. What is more, the son took his father as an example and to some extent as a warning; his biography even gives the impression that, writing it as a young man, he felt himself to be his father's heir and avenger, since he subsequently deserted the Tories and went over to the victorious Liberals. In a sense Winston Churchill was writing his own biography, depicting his father, except for the tragedy, as he wished that father's son to be.

Lord Rosebery's short study and reminiscence is the portrait of a friend, written by a man who felt no rivalry or who at any rate had ceased to have any such feelings and who had never really competed with Lord Randolph. Rosebery was a Liberal and Gladstone's right-hand man, a member of the Lords since his youth; when he wrote about his lifelong friend ten years after that friend's death it was with 'all passion spent' and with political life far behind him, abandoned after the career of a brilliant amateur, first as Foreign Secretary and then as Prime Minister. What he revealed most strikingly about Lord Randolph was his gaiety and wit at smart dinner parties—a wit which acquired its tang from indiscretion and cynicism. Rosebery and Churchill spent their boyhood and young manhood together at Eton and Oxford and the magnificence of Rosebery's portrait depends a good deal upon his portrayal of Randolph as the incarnation of youth seen through a melancholy, nostalgic longing to recall the past. Notwithstanding this, Rosebery does mention Churchill's unscrupulousness as one of the prerequisites of his success. This Randolph himself acknowledged in his cynical maxim: 'Scrupulousness and generosity are the signs of a political fool'. But when Rosebery attempted to gloss over Churchill's faults by saying that 'He was human, eminently human; full of faults, as he himself well knew, but not base or unpardonable faults', he lapsed into cliché attitudes which are unworthy of so thoughtful a writer.

Attempts have been made to deck out Churchill's nature and thought with a theory of life, with an ideology. Such attempts are hardly convincing, for everything about the man leads to the conclusion that he was not only ignorant of all the so-called problems of existence, leading a life made up wholly of action, pleasure, gossip and intrigue, but that in politics he acted without premeditation, from case to case, always with an eye to the main chance. Winston Churchill, especially, attempted to make him into a reasonable Tory-Democrat, a Conservative party man with radical ideas. But this Tory-Democracy, of which Lord Randolph once said that 'Tory-Democracy is a democracy which has embraced the principles of the Tory party', would appear to have been just another springboard, an attempt to win over the working classes to the Right with a few seductive phrases *à la* Disraeli. Joseph Chamberlain, for several years between 1870 and 1880, showed true signs of political and social radicalism. He criticized the House of Lords, the established Church, the concentration of property in the hands of a few, yet he soon became a leading Conservative cabinet minister. Nothing of this kind can be found in Randolph Churchill's outlook, save possibly an aristocratic contempt for tradesmen and the middle class and a desire to link the uneducated masses with 'the gentlemen of England'.

Problem Child and Merry Monarch: King Edward VII

The flattering art of making monarchs appear larger than life is nowhere better displayed than in the biographies of King Edward VII and in the memoirs of persons who knew him initimately, which were written soon after the King's death in 1910 and have since continued to appear from time to time. A few later historians have gone to the other extreme in their attempts to demonstrate that King Edward's achievements and influence as a monarch, if not entirely negligible, hardly justified the extravagant claims hitherto made for them.

One book about the Edwardian age which found it unnecessary to give Edward VII the prominence usually accorded to him in the forefront of early-twentieth-century English history was *Edwardian Heritage: A Study of British History 1901–1906*, by William Scovell Adams. The book, which appeared in 1949, pointed out that Edward VII's influence as a monarch had often been exaggerated; but it gave, nevertheless, a more detailed character study of the King than of any other prominent figure of the period, discussing with penetration his actions and opinions, especially with regard to specific events.

That a writer of so patently Marxist an outlook as W. S. Adams should have devoted considerable space and attention to a constitutional monarch—'the second of the nine state-subsidized children of Queen Victoria' as the author calls him—shows that the character and actions of this monarch are still regarded as controversial in discussions of English history.

The element of controversy, whether consciously or unconsciously, was present from the outset. King Edward succeeded to the throne in 1901 when he was nearly sixty years old, after the longest heir-apparency in history. By that time, as Prince of Wales, he had achieved considerable notoriety as royal playboy and man-about-town, but had earned no great reputation in any other capacity. He was well known for his high living, his little trips to Paris, his love of racing, field sports and gambling; his gluttony, his obesity, his splendid cigars, and his women. He was once cited as co-respondent in a divorce case and was later involved in a resounding scandal connected with cheating at card play. Henry James was possibly not alone in deploring the exchange of 'mysterious little Victoria' for 'fat, vulgar, dreadful Edward'. The Prince's political contribution was practically non-existent for, unlike his father Prince Albert the Prince Consort, Edward had never been taken into Queen Victoria's confidence, nor was he given any official duties or training as heir to the throne. From his father onward—and

Victoria clung to Albert's belief—it was thought that 'poor Bertie' was not very bright.

The prevailing conception of the Prince of Wales as an amiable ignoramus and good-for-nothing was soon thoroughly revised when he became King Edward VII. He was presented both at home and abroad not only as a personage who acted as master of the revels in a renaissance of Merrie England, but also as an adept in that most agreeable of professions, diplomacy; indeed he was acclaimed not only as a gifted diplomatist but even as a statesman.

The reorientation of British policy from 'splendid isolation' to the Anglo-French agreement of 1904 and the Anglo-Russian agreement of 1907 was attributed to him. He was hated in Germany where he was considered as the arch-enemy who had inspired the 'policy of encirclement' and a few years later he was reviled for being, as the German people were led to believe, the instigator and originator of World War I. Historians, writing with the respect, not to say servility, which characterized biographies of him in the decades following Edward's death, frequently implied that his carefree, pleasure-seeking and sociable existence as Prince of Wales had developed his ability to get on with people of all kinds and was thus the precursor of his achievements in diplomacy.

All the expressions commonly in use when more precise judgments are not available were applied by historians to Edward VII; they singled out his practicality, his intuition, and the wisdom and common sense which compensated for his seeming lack of real intelligence.

Reaction soon set in. As early as 1912, Sir Sidney Lee, who was later to be King Edward's official biographer, wrote a somewhat critical 'Memoir' for the *Dictionary of National Biography*, of which he was Editor, in which he put forward the view that the King had played no role of any great significance either as an originator of policies or as a negotiator. Edward VII's most outstanding characteristic, according to Sir Sidney, was his total lack of any intellectual interests. These opinions were subsequently attacked sharply in a number of memoirs and biographies written by persons who had been close to the King. But Sir Sidney Lee's judgments have been confirmed on certain important points by more recent biographers. Among those who subsequently repudiated his critical opinions was Sir Sidney himself and his monumental official biography (1925–27) is full of sympathy and admiration, though even in this respect it is saved by its moderation and reserve from becoming merely an adulatory memorial. Sir Sidney Lee, as so many other writers have done, disputes both the concept of Edward VII as a man of the world and as a statesman, but indecision between these two controversial aspects of the King's personality detracts from the total effect of a balanced and lifelike

13. ' "Vice Versa"—The old Chancellor of the Exchequer and the New.' (Randolph Churchill and Gladstone, September 1886)

14. Thomas Carlyle. (By James McNeill Whistler, 1873)

15. 'Amateur navvies at Oxford. Undergraduates making a road as suggested by Mr Ruskin', 1874

portrait. The most recent major biography, *King Edward the Seventh* (1964), by Sir Philip Magnus, is laudably objective but adds little that could substantially alter the present view of Edward's life and character.

It is now quite clear that King Edward was no political leader. The policy of *ententes* which was the distinguishing feature of foreign affairs of this period was shaped by such statesmen as Arthur Balfour, Lord Lansdowne and Sir Edward Grey—not to mention their staffs of permanent civil servants—and the King merely acted on their advice or with their consent. On the other hand, there was great exaggeration in the idea once put forward somewhat crudely by the socialist Keir Hardie, maker and leader of the Labour party, who said that the King never read even the most important dispatches and hardly knew of the existence of treaties which his admirers claimed had been successfully negotiated by him. In reality the King played a definite, though very limited, role in British foreign policy, partly as a symbol of monarchy, partly as official charmer and goodwill ambassador and partly as negotiator.

It is difficult to establish the precise importance of this role of the King's in relation to specific cases. According to one frequently repeated opinion—a good example of it occurs in Lord Hastings' memoirs—Edward's five-day visit to Paris in the spring of 1903 paved the way for the Anglo-French *entente* of 1904. The French people, to whom he was familiar from his frequent earlier visits to France, were supposed to have been captivated by his genial warmth and friendliness. On the face of it this is odd reasoning. No very great number of Parisians could have come into personal contact either with the Edward, Prince of Wales who frequented restaurants, night clubs and cabarets; or with the King who visited them in 1903 when the crowds only caught fleeting glimpses of him as he drove through the main boulevards a couple of times in gala official processions, or waved to them on his way to the Opera or to the racecourse at Longchamps. Sir Sidney Lee expresses himself with more caution, but maintains that the crowds, which were cool at the start of the King's visit, became more and more enthusiastic as each day went by. Abel Combarieu, President Loubet's private secretary, gives what would seem to be a more realistic account. According to him the Parisian tradesfolk, the hand-picked audience of the social *élite* at the Opera gala performance, and the fashionable socialites in the enclosure at Longchamps, who all gave the King prolonged ovations, did so not so much from any fervent support of monarchy as from a desire to demonstrate their detestation of the Third Republic. The milling crowds which lined the streets to watch the King go by shouted out 'Long live the Boers', 'Hurrah for Russia', 'Cheers for General Marchand' (the hero of Fashoda), but they were not hostile, not even particularly ill-disposed, merely ironical, mocking and for the most part indifferent. Nevertheless with unruffled good humour, King Edward saluted and smiled to right and left as though he were being cheered to the echo.

It seems quite likely that King Edward's Paris visit of 1903 was of little real political significance, and the events which resulted in the Russian *entente* of 1907 inspire similar reflexions. Sir Sidney Lee claims that

> 'What King Edward did in France was even surpassed by the *entente* which was inaugurated with Russia . . . once more King Edward's ease of manner won the day. He smoothed away the painful memories of the past, he showed the amicable possibilities of the future, and overcame the hesitancy of Russia.'

Later memoirs have pointed out that although King Edward did influence his nephew the Tsar, his part in the actual negotiations was insignificant. To do Edward justice, he himself had no illusions (according to Sir Philip Magnus) about the extent of his control of British foreign policy, and flattering estimates of his efforts in this capacity caused him 'to chuckle in his beard'. It is obvious that it was Edward's constant round of travelling and visits—generally prompted by his craving for diversion—which gave his contemporaries the illusion of independent and successful political activity.

The King's private life and character are more difficult to assess. His perpetual search for pleasure, especially for erotic pleasures, is either taken for granted or only hinted at but never openly discussed. Put baldly, he liked women, and if they were lively, pretty and not too strait-laced, so much the better. His biographers, however, describe him as being 'appreciative of feminine charm', as being 'courteous and chivalrous to women', and so on; and Queen Alexandra is praised for her tolerant attitude to his affairs, while her husband is not criticized for his lack of consideration for her. 'King Edward had his weaknesses,' Lord Esher commented in this connection. 'But what has humanity ever gained from dwelling upon the weaknesses of great men?'

Edward's passion for gambling gave rise to similar subtle reflexions. H. E. Wortham in *The Delightful Profession: Edward VII, a study in Kingship* (1931), commented that the hypocrisy in which the attitude of a section of the English people had enveloped the subject of gambling was so noxious

> 'that one wishes the Prince might for a moment have forgotten the obligations of his position and pointed out [to the Archbishop of Canterbury and others who deplored the Prince's heavy gambling] that a people in which the gambling spirit, the spirit to take risks, is dead is itself moribund. He could have argued that the desire to

back one's luck and cunning, the belief that they will be better than that of others, is at the very root of progress and indeed of life. What is Christianity itself but a religion extolling the necessity of taking enormous risks in the hope of ultimate gain?'

And from the standpoint of ethics, the author continued, 'the Prince might have argued that the gaming table was actually a moral agent in the demand made on nerve and judgement and in the lesson it taught of bearing losses with equanimity'.

A hilarious anthology of drivel could be compiled from this and numerous other similarly ludicrous defences of the royal vices. They defeat their own purpose, however, for the fact is that such beating about the bush tends to give an exaggerated impression of the extent of Edward's dissipation, and so discretion becomes more damning than frankness.

It has been commonly claimed that King Edward was not an intellectual, indeed not even endowed with much intelligence, but that instead he was 'gifted on a higher level'. One of the royal librarians has testified to the King's interest in collections of books, but there seems, notwithstanding, to be general agreement that he was not well-read—about as much so as Louis XIV, with whom Edward VII, who was neither learned, intellectual nor artistic, has been compared. Edward's favourite reading matter is said to have been the novels of Marie Corelli (1855–1924), the late-Victorian best-selling novelist; but this can hardly be taken as proof of an excessive lack of taste, since he practically never read anything at all. From his earliest youth he had never cared for books. The Queen said as much to Gladstone: 'Newspapers, and very rarely, a novel, are all he ever reads.' In later life the Radical *Reynolds' News* was one of the newspapers King Edward was fond of reading. The paper was always favourable to him and he perused it with great thoroughness every Sunday. The King's admirers have hastened to say, however, that he preferred 'to delve into the Great Book of Life' rather than into cold print.

Edward's religious devoutness has also often been emphasized, but nobody has ever explained in what way he was devout. His attitude to religion was similar to that of most men of his age and class. He went to church and preferred the sermon to be short. He was also superstitious. Sir Philip Magnus says briefly: 'An unclouded and humble religious faith remained with him always and was an immense source of strength.' Edward himself never discussed his beliefs—it simply was 'not done' for an English gentleman to talk about religion.

Dignity and natural good breeding were also among the attributes for which Edward VII has been lauded; yet when he was nearly forty he could so far unbend as to place a donkey in a friend's bed. When he and Prince Eugène, the exiled Prince Imperial, were guests at Mrs Cust's cottage at Cowes in 1878, they hoisted the donkey into the bedroom of the son of the house, where they dressed it up and put it to bed. Like Mrs Langtry, who recorded the episode, one must wonder how they got the animal to stay in bed.

Some of the Prince's most memorable practical jokes were played on Christopher Sykes, a companion and crony of long standing. Sykes, an obsequious snob, was a tall, thin, melancholy-featured man ten years older than the Prince. His adulation and veneration of his royal friend were such that he allowed himself for years to be the butt of humiliating and ignominious pranks played on him by the Prince and his companions, usually at week-end house-parties. The story of the relationship between Sykes and Edward, both as Prince of Wales and King, is told in comic and pathetic detail by Sykes's nephew and namesake in *Four Studies in Loyalty* (1946).

On one occasion Sykes, very drunk, was put to bed with a dead seagull. The joke, which proved a huge success, was followed up the next night with a live trussed rabbit placed in the bed beside him. Hilarious fun could also be had by squirting him from soda-water siphons, dousing his bed from watering-cans, knocking his hat off, or hurling him beneath the billiard table and preventing his escape with a barrier of prodding billiard cues.

Sykes, attired in full panoply of a knight in armour, once accompanied the Prince to a huge London mansion where a fancy-dress ball was being held. He had been told that to avoid attracting attention they would use the back entrance. He was just about to follow the Prince inside when the door was slammed in his face. The front and rear entrances of the vast town house were several streets apart and it was some time before Sykes, clanking through back alleys and side streets followed by a curious and ever-growing crowd, was able to find the front door.

Some pranks, though interminably repeated, never seemed to pall on the Prince. Even when he was King he was unable to rid himself of the jocular habit of emptying a glass of brandy over Sykes's head. The first time that this happened, Sykes's nephew relates,

> 'When the brandy landed on his hair and trickled down his face to the golden beard Christopher showed a rare thing: an excess of presence of mind. Not a muscle moved. Then, after a pause, he inclined to the Prince and said without any discernable trace of annoyance or amusement: "As your Royal Highness pleases." '

This reaction caused such merriment among the company that the Prince never tired of repeating his joke. 'Moreover', Sykes's nephew records, 'the Prince's simple taste liked enlargement. In place of the glass a full bottle was substituted, and another royal discovery was that even funnier effects could be conjured by pouring the precious liquid not on to his hair, but down his friend's neck.' It would be charitable to believe that the Prince was not sober when these ceremonies were performed.

Sometimes the cigar-smoking Prince would invite Sykes to watch the smoke coming out of his eyes and while the royal countenance was obediently scrutinized, the glowing tip of the Prince's cigar would be pressed against Sykes's hand. Incredible as it may seem, this 'once only' joke was played repeatedly. According to his nephew, Sykes

> 'remained the statuesque figure he had been on the first night of the brandy glass. He never failed his audience. His hat would be knocked off, the cigar applied, the soda-water pumped over his head and he would incline and murmur: "As your Royal Highness pleases." '

Where dignity was concerned there is no doubt that Edward preserved his own. Attempts at familiarity were repulsed and nobody in his entourage was ever allowed to forget in whose presence he was. As Prince of Wales, his fondness for big meals of rich food became increasingly apparent in his corpulence, to the point that behind his back he was nicknamed 'Tum-tum'. He was sensitive about his girth and when a tipsy guest at Sandringham used the nickname to his face he gave orders that the offender was to leave next morning before breakfast. Something of the same sort happened when the Prince made a poor shot one evening at the billiard table and a misguided young man called out, 'I say, Wales, pull yourself together!' Without a word in response, the Prince turned to a servant and commanded the foolish guest's carriage to be ordered.

Edward has also been praised for his good nature, his tact and his ability to converse with all and sundry. English royalty has indeed frequently been praised for these not very extraordinary accomplishments. This can be explained by the fact that common civility undergoes a great change in values in the mind of the recipient when it comes from an exalted personage—to the extent that it is then interpreted in some degree as a flattering mark of gracious esteem. Side by side with instances of Edward's amiability, however, are others which testify to his irritability and ill-humour over losing at games, whether croquet or bridge (at which he was an enthusiastic but indifferent player), and the ease with which he lost his temper over disappointments or when his orders were not carried out to his satisfaction. According to Sir Frederick Ponsonby, his assistant private secretary, 'even his most intimate friends were all terrified of him'. His outbursts of temper could reduce members of his Household to 'a state of speechless terror', as Ponsonby himself was once reduced, and his 'angry bellow' once heard was never forgotten.

It seems practically certain, nevertheless, that Edward VII possessed genuine talents in the area of personal and social relations. When all was going well there was something genial, free-and-easy and engaging in the King's manner. He was tolerant of others as well as of himself and without being witty he had a great sense of the ridiculous. 'He was', as W. S. Adams wrote, 'aware of his own weaknesses and was not more of a hypocrite than the Royal estate inevitably compels'.

Though every one, from Queen Alexandra down, suffered at some time from his irritation and impatience, which were expressed in no uncertain manner, he was habitually generous and considerate and liked to ensure that he was surrounded by happy and smiling faces. His less endearing traits were more than offset by the palpable charm, geniality and warm-heartedness which aroused in those close to him feelings that were both warm and deep. It would be difficult otherwise to explain the affectionate warmth of the correspondence and reminiscences of his friends. When the great Lord Fisher, Admiral of the Fleet and First Sea Lord, the King's friend and Naval A.D.C., devoted a panegyrical chapter of his autobiography to his royal master he seemed to be 'laying it on with a trowel'. But when he wrote in letter after letter to Lord Esher of his grief and feeling of loss at the King's death every word quite obviously had the ring of deep and genuine feeling.

In spite of one or two periods of unpopularity during the public scandals in which he was involved as Prince of Wales, Edward enjoyed an immense popularity both as Prince and King. His winning smile, coupled with the charm, warmth and fellow-feeling which he radiated at every public appearance, seemed to bring him closer to the English people. Even before his accession he had been favourably compared with his father. 'The Prince Consort was unloved', Lord Granville remarked to von Bülow, 'because he possessed all the virtues which are sometimes lacking in Englishmen. The Prince of Wales is loved because he has all the faults of which the Englishman is accused.' After the King's death Lord Morley wrote: 'He had just the character that Englishmen at any rate thoroughly understand, thoroughly like and make any quantity of allowance for.'

Nevertheless, King Edward, the problem child, remains a problem. Since the wholesale destruction, by his command, of his private correspondence and confidential papers, carried out both in his lifetime and after his death, and the destruction of all Queen Alexandra's papers, by her wish, much about the King's complex personality and his actions can never be known. It is doubtful if a true *vie intime* can ever be written and it is difficult, today, little more than half a century after his death, to disentangle the real Edward VII from the accretions of legend.

Hypocrisy and Baccarat: The Tranby Croft Scandal

English upper-class life in some of its least edifying aspects is vividly portrayed in Elma Napier's reminiscences, *Youth Is a Blunder* (1948). Mrs Napier was born in 1892, and her book, which covers her childhood and adolescence, ends with her first marriage, in 1910, as a girl of eighteen. Her narrative, though somewhat muddled, contains many personal details which are as delightful as they are touching. The chief interest of the book, however, lies in its account of social customs and events of the transitional period of the turn of the century, an account which throws into prominence some typical features of the Victorian and Edwardian cultures.

It was a time when prudery and hypocrisy were rife. The anxiety of upper-class and middle-class society to protect young girls from learning 'the facts of life' went to the extremes of shielding them from all contact with the sexuality of animals and human beings. Mrs Napier, who was the eldest of five children, relates that she and her sister were sent away from home for their mother's confinements.

> 'It was not *convenable* that a girl should be in the house on such occasions. . . . It might smirch her reputation. A girl could envisage no career, no future, save marriage; yet she must, even at the age of nine, at all costs be kept "innocent", prevented from any scrap of knowledge that might help her to fulfil her destiny.'

Girls who believed that they would conceive if kissed—and these were no rarity—nevertheless had already secretly acquired the rudiments of knowledge about a forbidden territory: they knew that women bore children and that men had something to do with it.

As for the hypocrisy of the time, it could hardly be better illustrated than by a scandal, the great 'Baccarat Case', which convulsed Victorian society at the beginning of the 1890s.

Mrs Napier, or Elma Gordon-Cumming as she was before the first of her two marriages, came of a family that was rich and aristocratic but somewhat *déclassé*. They were continually on the move, from one of their country houses in Scotland to another; at one time they owned three, as well as a London town-house. They also went from one Continental watering-place to another, from country to country in a series of migrations which extended from Italy to Turkey—only to continue living a life of bored idleness in their fresh surroundings. Such things as books were never so much as mentioned in the Gordon-Cumming household and political opinion was confined to mild anathemizing over Winston Churchill, Lloyd George and other radical scoundrels who were leading the country to perdition.

In between travels the family occupied the ancestral mansions of Altyre (in summer) and Gordonstoun (in winter), tended by a staff of thirty servants. The pivot of this household was Elma's father, Lieutenant-Colonel (Retired) Sir William Gordon-Cumming, Bart. Sir William kept up the position of a country gentleman at the expense of his rich American wife. He was vain of his good looks and well satisfied with his good breeding, which he displayed in correct and polished behaviour on practically all occasions. The *Sporting Times* had once called him 'Possibly the handsomest man in London, and certainly the rudest'. His daughter relates that he was delighted with both superlatives. 'He never, not even when he was eighty, lost the touch of swagger in his walk, the hint of scorn for lesser mortals, the suggestion that he was irresistible.' Through fate or folly he had been condemned 'to boredom everlasting, an endless filling in of time'—and in such circumstances 'What should a gentleman do but shoot and fish and play games ?' So Sir William shot and fished, played bridge and croquet, collected postmarks, cautioned his daughters to be virtuous and as a matter of course tried to seduce every woman within arms' reach.

The year before Elma was born this imposing gentleman had been a nine-day sensation and had become for a time an internationally discussed celebrity. He was the man who had precipitated the great Tranby Croft scandal which led to the Baccarat Case, as it came to be known. This *cause célèbre* rivalled the trial of Oscar Wilde as one of the greatest sensations in the England of the 1890s, and like Wilde's *débâcle* it was highly illuminating about Victorian hypocrisy. Elma Napier's memoirs serve to throw further light on several disputed points of this old society scandal, avidly discussed in its day.

On 8 September 1890, a party of rich and fashionable people gathered for a St Leger week house-party at Tranby Croft, near Doncaster. They were the guests of a rich ship-owner, Arthur Wilson, one of the wide circle of the Prince of Wales's industrial *nouveau riche* friends. The Prince, then forty-eight, was the guest of honour and was to stay three days, accompanied by two old and intimate friends who had been invited by his desire. One of these was the forty-year-old Sir William Gordon-Cumming, a Lieutenant-Colonel in the Scots Guards, with a brilliant war record gained in action in the Zulu War and the Egyptian campaign. Gordon-Cumming had known the Prince for twenty years and for the past ten had been on terms of constant friendship and personal intimacy with him. The other friend was Christopher Sykes, the Prince's companion and crony of long standing, an amiable and harmless snob and the perpetual and long-suffering butt of His Royal Highness's tasteless practical jokes. Hitherto Sykes had usually invited the Prince to stay at his own nearby home for the Doncaster races but now, on the verge of bankruptcy as a result of his lavish entertaining for the Prince, he had to content himself with being a guest of the Wilson family.

In the evening, members of the house-party played baccarat, a game of which the Prince was extremely fond and which he had introduced into London society. During the play that evening, young Arthur Wilson, the 22-year-old son of the house, saw, or thought he saw, Sir William Gordon-Cumming cheating. Sir William, having looked at his cards to see whether they were in his favour or against him, was systematically increasing or decreasing his stakes. Under cover of his hand, in a gambler's manoeuvre known as *la poussette*, he was pushing or withdrawing counters across the chalk line drawn round the edge of the baccarat table, which had been improvised for the occasion from three whist tables. The centre table was higher than the other two, which made it difficult to see the stakes and to rake them in.

The Prince of Wales kept bank and during the two evenings of play Gordon-Cumming's winnings were mostly from the Prince, who neither saw his old friend cheating nor suspected that there was anything amiss.

On the first evening young Wilson had told his friend Berkeley Levett of his suspicions and this young man, who was a subaltern in Sir William's own regiment, was distressed to observe that Sir William did indeed appear to be cheating. Young Wilson next told his mother and, the following morning, his brother-in-law Lycett Green, and it was not long before his sister was also in the know. On the second evening, when a better table had been procured, four people were watching Sir William at the baccarat game; the fifth, Berkeley Levett, turned his head away to avoid seeing his senior officer's play. Again it appeared that Sir William was systematically cheating. The five witnesses now consulted two older guests, Lord Coventry and Lieutenant-General Sir Owen Williams, the latter a close friend of Gordon-Cumming. These two readily accepted the evidence they were given and they accordingly informed Gordon-Cumming that an accusation had been made against him.

Sir William vehemently denied that he had been cheating, but the truth of the accusation seemed to be confirmed by the fact that he made no demand to be confronted with his five accusers, merely requesting to be allowed to discuss his dilemma with the Prince of Wales.

Coventry and Williams had told the Prince meanwhile of what had occurred and had suggested that for the sake of all concerned, and for society at large the circumstances should not be allowed to go beyond those who already knew about them; and that as a condition of their silence Sir William must be made to sign an undertaking never to play cards again for the rest of his life.

Sir William repeated his denial to the Prince but was told that it was utterly useless for him to attempt any denial against the evidence of so many totally unprejudiced persons in whose interest it was that no scandal should be known to have taken place in the house. The Prince added that nobody had any wish to make things hard for Sir William.

Coventry and Williams then drew up a document which they brought to Gordon-Cummings to sign, in order, as they said, to avoid a terrible social scandal and to protect the Prince of Wales's reputation. They threatened the unfortunate Gordon-Cummings with exposure unless he signed, and told him it would be better if he left the house next morning. Sir William protested that by signing the paper he would be as good as confessing his guilt and they agreed that this was so. Nevertheless, he had no option but to sign the undertaking never to play cards again as long as he lived. The nine men who had played baccarat with him and who now all knew about the accusation, then signed the declaration and on the advice of Lord Coventry and Lieutenant-General Williams the Prince added his own signature. The document was afterwards sent by the Prince to Sir Francis Knollys, his private secretary, to be filed unopened amongst his private papers.

Sir William left next morning as stipulated, his host having promised that the affair would be safely hushed up. The Prince decided to leave too and went to watch the last day's racing from the cavalry barracks at York. None of the other guests, including Christopher Sykes, were told anything of what had occurred. Gordon-Cumming, nevertheless, feared that it would be difficult to keep a secret already known to so many and indeed it was subsequently alleged that one lady was already whispering about it at the racecourse on the last day of the Doncaster races. Sir William was also apprehensive of what his brother officers would think and say when he was obliged to refuse to play cards with them. And if in future the Prince of Wales should cut him, what of the tongues which would immediately begin to wag and start putting two and two together? In fact, by January 1891, if not before, the secret had leaked out. Gordon-Cumming received an anonymous letter from Paris which made him decide to act and the Prince of Wales soon learned with consternation, that the baronet was about to sue his five original accusers for slander, claiming £5,000 damages.

The Prince had already been involved in a court case in 1870—the

Mordaunt divorce case—in which he was subpoenaed as a witness. Lady Mordaunt, who was being sued by her husband, had made a hysterical confession naming the Prince of Wales among several men with whom she said she had been unfaithful. The Prince, who had known her since she was a girl, had written her a number of dull and innocuous letters and had made her some visits in her husband's absence. Edward successfully proved his innocence and the case was subsequently dismissed on the grounds of Lady Mordaunt's insanity. But the Prince's letters were produced in court and even published in some provincial newspapers. There was a great outcry and he received much adverse publicity.

In 1876 he had narrowly escaped becoming involved in another scandal—the threatened Aylesford divorce case—which, though it never came to court caused the Prince many anxious moments and was responsible for the breach of his friendship with Lord and Lady Randolph Churchill. He now had no mind to be involved in another scandal, especially one connected with baccarat; the very word seemed for many people to exude a whiff of gallic brimstone, and public opinion, already censorious of the way of life of the Prince and the Marlborough House set (as his circle of friends was called), was sure to be outraged.

In order to discredit Gordon-Cumming before he could bring his case to the civil courts, the Prince, with his friends and advisers, tried, in February 1891, to secure a military court enquiry into Gordon-Cumming's behaviour, and then to institute a private enquiry by the executive committee of the Guards' Club, one of the three clubs to which Gordon-Cumming belonged and from which he had already resigned pending the result of his case in the civil courts. These efforts to muzzle Gordon-Cumming proved unavailing and the trial opened in London on 1 June 1891.

Now that it was out, the scandal caused a sensation—the more so since the Prince was subpoenaed as a witness for the prosecution. The case was tried in the High Court of Justice, Queen's Bench Division, before the Lord Chief Justice, Lord Coleridge, and a special jury, and lasted seven days. The June weather was warm and the crowded courtroom grew hotter and stuffier as each day wore on. The learned judge was occasionally seen to nod during the proceedings, and he seemed incapable of understanding the rules of baccarat, in spite of painstaking explanations by the various counsels; but he gave, notwithstanding, a masterly summing up, biased and full of righteous indignation though it may have been.

The chief counsel for the plaintiff was the Salisbury government's Solicitor-General, Sir Edward Clarke, while among those defending the accused were the future Lord Chief Justice, Charles Russell and a future prime minister, Herbert Asquith (later Lord Oxford and Asquith). All fashionable London filled the public gallery. The press throughout the Empire reported the proceedings in detail with much censorious and sanctimonious comment; the Continental press, especially in France, commented with sarcastic asides and ribald cartoons. The agitated Queen, who received long telegrams each evening containing a précis of the day's court proceedings, wrote to her daughter the Empress Frederick on 8 June: 'This horrible Trial drags along, and it is a fearful humiliation to see the future King of his country dragged (and for the second time) through the dirt, just like anyone else, in a Court of Justice. . . . It is very painful and must do his prestige great harm.'

On 9 July the five defendants were acquitted and the case was dismissed with costs against Gordon-Cumming. His signature to the undertaking never to play cards again, coupled with the evidence of the five witnesses and the Prince of Wales, was considered conclusive proof of his guilt. Elma Napier claimed in her book that 'it was the Prince of Wales's hostile evidence' that had lost the case for her father. The day after the trial had ended Gordon-Cumming was dismissed from the Army, and expelled from all his clubs; and the Prince wrote of his old friend: 'Thank God!—the Army and Society are well rid of such a damned blackguard.'

On the same day Gordon-Cumming made himself an even more unspeakable cad in the eyes of his former friends by marrying his fiancée Miss Florence Garner, an American heiress who, in spite of his offer to release her, had insisted on standing by him against all the wishes and advice of her family, from whom as a result she became estranged.

The nine-day trial proceedings are of considerable interest, especially because of the brilliant performances of both defence and prosecution counsels and because of its most novel feature, the presence in court of the Prince of Wales, who attended on every day but the last. Subpoenaed like any ordinary citizen to give evidence as a witness for the prosecution, he was even called back for questioning by one of the jurymen as he was leaving the witness box. His answers to this juryman would appear to have been crucial in turning the scales against Gordon-Cumming.

'Is this jury to understand', he was asked, 'that you as banker on these two occasions saw nothing of the alleged malpractices of the plaintiff?'

Turning to the jury-box the Prince replied: 'No, it is not usual for a banker to see anything in dealing cards, especially when you are playing among friends in their house. You do not for a moment suspect anything of the sort.'

The juryman then asked the Prince what his opinion was at the time as to the charges made against Sir William Gordon-Cumming, and the Prince replied: 'The charges appeared to me to be so unanimous that it was the proper course—no other course was open to me—than to believe them.' The Prince bore himself throughout the proceedings with bland dignity but answered questions with apparent reluctance.

In his efforts to win the case for his client Sir Edward Clarke spared the Prince no embarrassment, making several very disagreeable insinuations which were later characterized by Sir Francis Knollys as public insults to the Prince. Sir Edward suggested, among other things, that Gordon-Cumming was being victimized so that the Prince could 'save face' after having made a rash conclusion from insufficient evidence concerning an illegal game which he habitually encouraged; and furthermore, that as a Field-Marshal he had ignored a military obligation by taking matters into his own hands instead of adhering to Army Regulations which required any officer to insist that the case of a brother-officer accused of dishonourable conduct be submitted to his commanding officer. He said furthermore that the law-suit should make it impossible for Gordon-Cumming's name to be removed from the Army List while those of Field Marshal the Prince of Wales and General Owen Williams remained. He suggested finally that Lord Coventry and General Williams had chosen the course they had taken at Tranby Croft because 'there is a strong influence of royalty—a personal influence—which . . . has perplexed the historian with unknightly and dishonouring deeds done by men of character, and done by them because they gave their honour as freely as they would have given their lives', and he suggested that Sir William Gordon-Cumming might be one of those men whom history records as willing to sacrifice themselves 'to save the interests of a dynasty or to conceal the foibles of a prince'. On the sixth and penultimate day of the trial, when Sir Edward finished his closing speech for the plaintiff, the crowded court room broke into cheers—to the displeasure of the judge, who called out, 'Silence! This court is not a theatre!'

Even more interesting than the trial itself was the discussion of the pros and cons of the case. These were ceaselessly debated by the newpapers, both during and after the hearing, and subsequently became the theme of a number of pamphlets and books. In defiance of the taboo on open criticism of the Prince, he and his way of life were, for a time, discussed with refreshing candour—a treatment of royalty hardly conceivable anywhere then or even nowadays, not even in a country like Sweden, with its matter-of-fact attitude to a democratized monarchy and royal family.

Nevertheless, the frankness with which the Prince of Wales was treated in 1891 had something repulsive about it, due to the self-righteous tone of his critics and the blatant insincerity of their insinuations that up to then the dissolute Prince had been considered to be a model of propriety. The severity of the criticism can be attributed to what were thought to be special and shocking circumstances—that it was by the Prince's wish that baccarat had been played at the house-party; that he took with him wherever he went his own counters marked with the Prince of Wales's feathers and motto '*Ich Dien*' (which a German cartoonist rendered as 'Ich Deal'); and that he had kept bank on both evenings at Tranby Croft and so had been the chief animator of the illegal game. The Prince's set of counters, given him by Reuben Sassoon, had proved an embarrassing gift. Years later, in his memoirs, Sir Edward Clarke related that before the trial opened a solicitor for the defendants had come to see him with a message from Marlborough House. Sir Edward was told that the Prince's box of large and brightly coloured baccarat counters marked with his crest was to be used by the defendants as evidence. Sir Edward was then asked—'because it would be unpleasant for the Prince that it should be known that he travelled about with the box'—if he would be content if the defendants produced for use at the trial other counters of the same size and colour but without the crest. Sir Edward would make no promise of concealment but consented to use the plain counters for the purpose of his opening speech.

The Times headed a chorus of condemnation from the press, in a leader which 'profoundly regretted' that the Prince should have been involved 'not only in the case, but in the social circumstance that paved the way for it'. One provincial paper proclaimed that 'the British Empire has been humiliated and the whole world is now pointing a finger at us'. The atmosphere of public censure and the wave of unpopularity which engulfed the Prince were reminiscent of the days of the dissolute George IV and his promiscuous brothers, when it was common for the press to voice the contempt in which the Royal Family were held by the masses.

In the matter of Pharisaism the Prince and his counsel were not far behind—and soon outdistanced—those who condemned him. At Tranby Croft a few hundred pounds had changed hands in a matter of moments, though this was nothing unusual; and Gordon-Cumming had won £255 during the two evenings of play. But both the judge and the prosecuting counsels vied with each other in emphasizing that they were not dealing with a game of chance as such, but with an innocent pastime indulged in within a family circle. From their soothing descriptions of the baccarat sessions at the Wilsons' one might well have thought that the party had been playing 'Snap!' or 'Happy Families'.

The trial and its incidents deeply shocked middle-class English sentiment. The novelist E. F. Benson, third of the several distinguished sons of Archbishop E. W. Benson, then the Archbishop of Canterbury, commented on the universal disgust of the English press. He said:

> 'If the Prince himself had been detected cheating he could not have been more savagely sentenced. In particular all papers of a serious or religious turn, especially church papers and Nonconformist papers, trumpeted their horror like great moral elephants running piously amok.'

In an effort to pour some oil on these troubled waters, the Prince summoned Archbishop Benson to Marlborough House to explain matters to him and the meeting led to an exchange of letters. E. F. Benson, gave an account of these manoeuvres in his book of reminiscences, *As We Were: A Victorian Peepshow* (1930).

The Prince began his interview with the Archbishop by expressing his resentment of the unjust attacks on him in the church newspapers, especially from the Low Church and the Nonconformists. He asked the Archbishop bluntly why he had instigated these attacks. The Archbishop replied that, far from inspiring attacks of any kind, he had never even spoken, much less written, a word about the scandal which, moreover, was a topic that was taboo even in his own home. He said, however, that if the Prince wished to hear his private opinion he had no objection to giving it.

Having expounded his views, the Archbishop, 'a man of unyielding middle-class morality' who hated all gambling and betting on principle, heard the Prince's explanation of two points on which he felt he had been very bitterly attacked since the Gordon-Cumming trial but was prevented by his position from answering. He had written to his sister, the Empress Frederick, after the trial (14 June 1891): 'The Press has been very severe and cruel because they know I cannot defend myself.' He now told the Archbishop, 'They say I carry about counters, as a Turk carries a prayer-carpet. But the reason why I carry counters is to check high play. High sums are easily named, but these counters range from five shillings to ten pounds.' The Prince took for granted that with counters having a maximum denomination of ten pounds 'the play would harm nobody'.

The second point the Prince wished to answer was the accusation that he had abused the hospitality of the Wilsons. He told the Archbishop that he had never been aware that Arthur Wilson disapproved of cards or forbade them in his home. In view of the abuse showered on him the Prince had made it his business to enquire into the facts, and the allegations, he said, were simply not true. The only basis for Wilson's supposed prohibition, it appeared, was that when the Wilson sons were growing boys their father had discouraged them from playing cards for high stakes. Whenever he found them playing recklessly he said to them, 'You don't understand the game. You don't play it properly, and I won't have you play it.'

Having thus disposed of the malicious and repeated slanders in the press, which he felt would put the whole country against him if they were believed, the Prince went on to say how much he deplored gambling—though he gave the Archbishop to understand that he saw little harm in rich men playing for stakes they could very well afford. Having agreed to exchange letters which should sum up the main points of their talk, they parted amicably.

The Archbishop of Canterbury was at least willing to admit that there had been misunderstandings and misrepresentations, however unconvinced he may have been by the Prince's opinion that betting was harmless and by his avowal that he loathed gambling. Full of sympathy for the Prince's point of view, the Archbishop now joined the pitched battle with a vigorous defence of the royal delinquent. He expressed in the letter he wrote to the Prince his gladness to learn the facts (the word was underlined) about which 'the utterances of various religious bodies have been so painful and ill-judged'. It would give him, he said, 'the acutest pain' to think that the Prince supposed that he sympathized with their proceedings. He went on to deplore the gambling among working-class men and women which was 'proving itself the ruin of young and old among the poorer classes'; he applauded the Prince's efforts 'for the good of the working classes and the poor', and exhorted him 'to show the people what your real mind is in respect of these thoughtless but most dangerous habits', and so 'do a world of good and evoke a world of good feeling'.

The Prince's reply formally re-stated the views he had expressed in the interview:

> 'I have a horror of gambling, and should always do my utmost to discourage others who have an inclination for it, as I consider that gambling, like intemperance, is one of the greatest curses that a country could be afflicted with. Horse-racing may produce gambling or it may not, but I have always looked upon it as a manly sport, which is popular with Englishmen of all classes and there is no reason why it should be looked on as a gambling transaction. Alas! those who gamble will gamble at everything.'

The caustic comment of W. S. Adams on this episode is that 'Edward had to use all his ingenuity to escape the censure of the Church and of the nation as a whole . . . [and] was sufficiently wily to be able to allay criticism by writing a nauseating letter to the Archbishop of Canterbury'.

Alas! those who gamble will gamble at everything. The Prince spoke from experience. He was an inveterate gambler and had played baccarat for years, and in the past he had bet considerable sums on a game of tennis or a wrestling match between two friends. Alas, too, he was unlucky at both betting and cards and he hated losing. The Queen was so distressed and alarmed by the Tranby Croft scandal that Edward at length had to refuse to visit her at Windsor unless she promised not to mention the word baccarat. But he was finally goaded by his anxious mother's nagging letters of the tiresome kind written more in sorrow than in anger, into promising to give up baccarat. Sir Sidney Lee records of this reform that

> 'He set himself to discourage, as far as he could, the vogue of gambling, which was always threatening to grow in fashionable circles. Personally, he gradually abandoned other games of cards for the newer game of bridge, in which, though he played regularly and successfully, he developed not more than a moderate skill.'

The passages in Sir Sidney Lee's biography of King Edward which deal with the baccarat scandal follow the same lines as both Edward's and Archbishop Benson's defence of the harmlessness of gambling, and his views, as well as theirs, as they expressed them, constitute as a whole a minor masterpiece of hypocrisy. The official biographer wrote:

> 'Cards formed, from the Prince's early days, a recreative solace. He was always ready from boyhood to take a hand of an evening at whist. But a love of adventure led him from time to time to experiment in card games in which chance predominated over skill. He had tried his luck on holiday at gaming in fashionable clubs—on the Riviera and in Germany—and almost all forms of card games became familiar to him in course of time. Irresponsible social gossip, which found a home in the scandalous press at home and abroad, frequently imputed to the Prince sensational gambling adventures.'

As well as being a study in hypocrisy, the Baccarat Scandal is a challenge to the detective instinct, since it is full of unresolved contradictions. Gordon-Cumming's behaviour was, to say the least, baffling. It would seem on the face of it that he did actually cheat. The evidence presented at the trial strongly pointed to the fact and was reinforced by his having signed the document in which he promised never to play cards again—this alone being virtually an indirect confession of guilt.

Yet with all this his behaviour seems beyond belief. As it transpired from evidence given, he was certainly not a rich man. In spite of owning a family seat on a country estate in Scotland (40,000 acres of poor land) and a town house, he seems to have been in need of ready cash. In any case, cheating at cards is not the sole prerogative of the hard-up. But that he should have jeopardized his whole future by cheating in a company consisting of the Prince of Wales and a number of other men of rank and influence, seems without closer investigation to have been an act of folly akin to madness.

It is equally strange that neither the Prince nor any of his habitual circle of friends had seen or had proclaimed that they had seen the cheating, although it was said to have been exceptionally persistent. Only a few members of the Wilson family had noticed it. It is also remarkable that Gordon-Cumming's counsel, Sir Edward Clarke, a man renowned for his probity, should have made the solemn declaration thirty years afterwards in his autobiography that he had always been firmly convinced of his client's innocence. During the trial there were hints from the judge as well as from the lawyers that behind the evidence as it stood a number of other significant phenomena could be discerned which had some bearing on the case. One of the counsel for the plaintiff told the jury that he hoped they would understand 'many things not on the surface'.

Gordon-Cumming was unshakeable in his denial of guilt. When asked why he had signed the document he replied that he was prepared to make any sacrifice in order to keep the Prince's name out of the affair. The judge commented on this in his summing up and direction of the jury:

> 'Here was the united testimony of five persons, all not only disinterested; all of them desirous not to believe, and all of them most anxious not to bring a scandal on the house; and all of them positively certain as to what they saw. They regarded it as surprising, and shocking. Then it is suggested that they said to themselves, "It is a sad thing for the Prince of Wales to appear to be mixed up with such a matter; it will be a bad thing for the Prince and for the Monarchy, and we must do all we can to prevent the scandal . . . But I cannot help thinking that though a man might accept almost anything, even the loss of life, he would not accept dishonour. Do you believe that an innocent man would allow himself to write his name to a dishonouring document which in effect confessed that he had cheated and filched money out of the pockets of his friends by a kind of cardsharping, simply that the world might not know that the Prince of Wales played baccarat for very moderate stakes?'

The judge having summed up the case at great length, the jury retired. They were back again in ten minutes to return a verdict against the plaintiff.

According to his daughter, Gordon-Cumming gave his wife another explanation, that he had been sordidly 'framed' by the Prince in revenge for 'having cut him out with a certain lady'. This story also claimed that 'somebody else, a nobleman known to dislike my father, had been asked to stage the game and had indignantly refused'. Another theory current at the time, says Gordon-Cumming's daughter, 'was that most of the players were "flipping counters" and that my father was made a scapegoat'.

The most probable likelihood is that some of the rumours about the case were not unfounded. These appeared to indicate certain very special reasons for suppressing the truth in the interests of the Prince's good name. For example, could most of the baccarat players have been so tipsy that they were incapable of detecting any cheating that was going on, or who, exactly, was cheating? And in that case, because of the reaction of the Wilson family, who acted in all innocence, was it not possible that the Prince's friends should have been forced to take the measures they did? Cheating in this fashion when playing with the Prince, who was notoriously unlucky in his gambling and betting, may have been common; in that case might not Gordon-Cumming have considered himself virtually blameless? Even on these assumptions the affair was bound to take on exaggerated proportions because of the attitude and intervention of the Wilson family. What is remarkable in this connection is that the Prince should stubbornly have insisted on holding the bank, in spite of the fact that this placed the other players at a decided advantage.

Again, is it not possible that the agreement which Gordon-Cumming was forced to sign at Tranby Croft arose as a result of similar incidents which had occurred elsewhere during gambling sessions, and that he was threatened and blackmailed into keeping quiet about other unsavoury secrets?

A curious hypothesis was suggested as late as 1963 by J. A. Frere in his book *The British Monarchy at Home*. In the years following the Baccarat Case, said this writer, it was rumoured that it was Gordon-Cumming who had first caught the Prince cheating and that in order to divert the attention of the other players he had then himself deliberately cheated. In support of his theory the writer claimed that attempts at some gesture of restitution to the memory of Gordon-Cumming have been made from time to time by the Crown, through offers of earldoms and honours (all of them refused) to collateral descendants of the baronet. One of these, Lord Middleton, has dismissed all Frere's presumably far-fetched claims as 'absolute poppycock, pure moonshine and sheer nonsense'

There is at present no way of substantiating any of the theories about the Baccarat Case. Most of them have sprung from private conversation, rumour, gossip and hearsay; in any case, all those who were present at the Tranby Croft house-party during Doncaster week of 1891, or who were directly connected with the affair, are presumably now dead. Perhaps at some future time a hitherto unexplored collection of letters or family papers will yield up additional facts which may throw fresh light on the mystery of the great Baccarat Scandal.

II

PROPHETS, REFORMERS AND POETS

The Valley of the Shadow of Marriage: Thomas and Jane Carlyle

Thomas Carlyle today occupies an honoured position in the ranks of the Unread Great; but little more than a hundred years ago, at the peak of an immense fame, he was widely read and discussed. Radical intellectuals revered him as a prophet of social reform, while those with conservative views held him in esteem as an English nationalist filled with laudable concern for the maintenance of tradition and hierarchy. All were unanimous in paying tribute to his erudition and to the highly original and peculiarly personal style of his writings, a style of such feverish intensity as to seem always on the verge of erupting in a great scream of anguished passion.

His popularity as a lecturer was similar to that of Bergson at the beginning of the twentieth century. Audiences from fashionable London society and the intelligentsia packed the halls where he spoke. From 1837 to 1840 he talked profitably and with evergrowing success on such subjects as literature, revolutions and heroes. The series of lectures he gave in 1839, on *Revolutions in Modern Europe*, was such a sell-out that the carriages of the appreciative upper-middle-class audiences who flocked to hear him used to block the whole street outside the lecture hall.

His books were acclaimed as literary events and were widely discussed. English and American men of letters and other notabilities visited him at his Chelsea home, 5 Great Cheyne Row, (which in 1877 became 24 Cheyne Row). The visitors lent a reverent ear to the master, who rewarded them with monologues which, if any one was rash enough to interrupt the spate of words, would turn into vehement eulogies of silence, as he raised his voice to talk down the interrupter.

At seventy-four he was one of a few distinguished intellectuals whom Queen Victoria invited, so to speak, to tea. It was in fact a five o'clock audience at the Windsor Deanery to which he was bidden, at the Queen's behest, by Dean and Lady Augusta Stanley, and at which muddy black coffee was served. Whatever the beverage, the occasion was a signal honour; but the meeting was hardly a success. To begin with, the gruff old sage of Chelsea scandalized the company by contradicting the Queen at the outset of an exchange of awkward silences. Then, to make matters worse (having had to stand for an hour), he actually pulled up a chair and sat down in her presence without being asked—in so doing, planting a chair-leg squarely on the hem of the royal skirt—while the assembled company looked on, rigid with horror. Sitting down in this august presence was something that 'would never do', indeed, was never done, or hardly ever. The Queen only very rarely invited one of her subjects to be seated; it was a favour which the aged (and disliked) Gladstone never even dared to request, and one which the Queen accorded only in private, and on terms of the strictest complicity, to her darling, gouty Dizzy, who always replaced the chair conspiratorially before quitting the presence.

Carlyle reached the pinnacle of his fame in November 1865, when he was elected Rector of Edinburgh University, in succession to Gladstone, leader of the Liberals and in opposition to Disraeli, leader of the Conservatives, whom he beat by more than double the number of votes (658 against 310). Eleven years before this, Carlyle had been nominated by some students as a candidate for the same honorary post but had been obliged to withdraw, so great were the opposition and the press vilification of such a dangerous radical as himself.

Now, at seventy, internationally acclaimed, and Scotland's most eminent living man of letters, he enjoyed an overwhelming triumph as he gave his installation address at Edinburgh's largest public hall, the Music Hall of the University. He spoke to the young men of the ideals which had guided his life since he himself had left this very university so many years ago. He stressed the importance of being diligent, advised the students to be modest, humble and attentive, extolled once again the virtue of silence and exhorted them to work: 'For work is the grand cure of all the maladies and miseries that ever beset mankind—honest work, which you intend getting done.' Carlyle's address ended on a note of optimism and a quotation from Goethe, his favourite poet, which bade his youthful listeners to 'work, despair not and to be of hope'. The silent audience broke into cheers and exultant cries as the young men surged forward with waving arms to embrace him, some of them in tears. It was Carlyle's finest hour. But this triumph was to be tinged with tragedy, immediate and personal, though he was to live for almost another fifteen years, firmly lodged in an ever-increasing prestige.

Success had come late to Carlyle and it was preceded by a life of privation fraught with external difficulties and inner conflict. He was born in the Annandale village of Ecclefechan in Dumfriesshire on 4 December 1795, the eldest son of James Carlyle, a poor Scottish stonemason later turned farmer, and Margaret Aitken, James Carlyle's second wife, daughter of a bankrupt farmer. Up to her marriage

Carlyle's mother had worked as a domestic servant; she could read with difficulty but did not learn to write until she had reached middle age. James Carlyle's only formal education had been limited to three months' schooling, but during that time he had learnt reading, fine handwriting and the rudiments of arithmetic. Husband and wife, both devoutly religious, were people of strong character from whom their seven children learned respect for authority, diligence, a sense of duty, and a strict Puritanical morality. James Carlyle was a man of independent mind, a stern authoritarian with a violent and hasty temper. He was neither loving nor kind to his children, who dreaded his anger; but he treated them with scrupulous justice. Carlyle respected and admired his father and mother and the precepts of both parents had a profound and lasting influence on his character and thought.

The family pinched and scraped to send Carlyle to school and university. He was a devoted son and, from the time he began to earn, always helped them. He supported himself for many years as a schoolteacher, living with the utmost frugality and supplementing his earnings by occasional writing, chiefly biographical and geographical articles for the *Edinburgh Encyclopedia*. He was an omnivorous reader and, though he never became a scholar or a theorist in any strict sense, he acquired in early manhood a vast and many-sided erudition.

When he was thirty Carlyle married 26-year-old Jane Baillie Welsh, an attractive young woman who came from a somewhat higher social level. She was the daughter and only child of a successful medical practitioner, Dr John Welsh of Haddington, who had died eighteen months before Carlyle met her in 1821. She lived at Haddington with her widowed mother, had a little money, and was sole heiress to the tiny moorland property and farm of Craigenputtock, near Dumfries. As a young woman she was considered beautiful, though she was no conventional beauty. Small and slight, with irregular features, she had a tip-tilted nose, a pale skin, great beautiful dark eyes and curling black hair. She was lively, intelligent, witty and well-read; something of a flirt, self-possessed and full of gay, though not always kind mockery. She was a romantic creature, passionate and ambitious, with literary aspirations and dreams of becoming the companion of a man of genius. During Carlyle's long wooing and through the copious correspondence of their courtship she was influenced and moulded by his massive intellect until he had gained complete ascendancy over her mind.

Carlyle's courtship was not propitious at the outset. Neither Jane nor her mother saw in him a prospective husband of any promise; moreover, Jane had no lack of young men of her own social level who would have liked to marry her. It was not until 1826, under Carlyle's dogged insistence in the face of Jane's repeated and often unkind rebuffs, that she gave way and they were married. With marriage to Carlyle, Jane subordinated her own captivating, independent personality to become what he considered a wife ought to be: a practical housewife and a loyal, understanding and devoted helpmate. From the outset Jane tried to become all of these things. She wrote to him on the eve of their wedding: 'I am going to be really a very meek-tempered wife. Indeed, I am begun to be meek-tempered already. . . .'

Her looks faded comparatively early, from ill-health and the stresses of a difficult and unusual marital relationship. Portraits of 1843 and 1849 show a face which became increasingly sallow, pinched and drawn. A haunting photograph taken by the painter James Tait in 1855 shows a prematurely aged, melancholy face, lined and hollow-cheeked. Its most striking features are the veiled, mournful eyes and a wide mouth which, for all the sadness of expression, seems nevertheless about to crinkle into a faint smile of ironic or malicious amusement.

Differences, difficulties and the clash of personalities notwithstanding, the couple remained throughout their marriage united in ties of the deepest intimacy although, rather than the simple tenderness of wedded love, these ties were more properly a fusion of intellectual understanding with a mutual bond of shared suffering.

The difficulties of making both ends meet obliged the couple to live for the first few years of their married life in Scotland in extreme isolation. They spent six years on the lonely farm at Craigenputtock, 'the little estate of peat bog . . . and a most dreary, untoward place to live at', where the nearest neighbours were peasant families who lived six miles away, where the mail was delivered only once a week and where, in the winter time, weeks, even months, passed without sight of a caller. Here Jane adapted herself to Carlyle's conception of a model wife, based on the womenfolk of his home. So the young woman who had never done a stroke of housework before her marriage learned to cook, bake bread, scrub floors, sew, darn Carlyle's stockings and mend his trousers and replace his lost buttons; and she even found time to read with him in the evenings.

At Craigenputtock Carlyle wrote his first major and most characteristic work, *Sartor Resartus*. This mystical 'Philosophy of Clothes', serialized in *Fraser's Magazine* (1837–8) and not liked at first, except in America, was to achieve unexpected and immense popularity—but only after *The French Revolution* and his lectures had made Carlyle famous.

Though there were inconveniences among the 'pretty extensive peat-moss' of Craigenputtock, there were few real hardships, yet, after six years of the monotony of its bleak winters and lack of society, Jane used to long for the life of Edinburgh, 'even for a sight of the peat-moss'—'anything rather than this wide waste of blinding snow!' Carlyle, too, was beginning to feel isolated, especially from literary friends—and he and Jane had made quite a few promising ones during their stay in London in the winter of 1813.

It was not until 1834, when they made their momentous decision to move to London for Carlyle to try his luck there, that their great career began. In the spring, leaving Jane in Scotland to settle up their domestic affairs and see to the packing, Carlyle went down to London, house-hunting. He found Number 5, Great Cheyne Row, in unfashionable Chelsea, a large house going for a low rental. Jane arrived, approved, and a few days later, on 10 June 1834, a hackney-coach took the Carlyles, with their smaller belongings, their maid Bessy Barnet and Chico, Jane's canary-bird, over to Chelsea. On the way, for a good omen, Chico burst out singing as they crossed Belgrave Square. At Chelsea they camped like cheerful gipsies for three days, 'amid heaped furniture', litter and carpenters, as they settled into the house where they were to live for the rest of their lives.

With such works as *The French Revolution* (1837), *Chartism* (1839) and *Past and Present* (1843), Carlyle rose to fame as a historian and social critic. It is not possible to classify these works as exclusively historical or critical, for *The French Revolution* is more in the nature of an impassioned judgement on institutions and people than it is a descriptive and analytical history of the revolution; whereas the works in which Carlyle deals with social problems are permeated with the residue of his omnivorous and indiscriminate reading of history. The essential feature of his thinking is his attack on a society transformed by the industrial revolution and on the complacent defence of that society, with its conflicting components of immense wealth and abject poverty, by the economists of *laissez-faire* liberalism.

> 'And yet I will venture to believe [he wrote in *Past and Present* of the exploited workers] that in no time, since the beginnings of Society, was the lot of these same dumb millions of toilers so entirely unbearable as it is even in the days now passing over us. It is not to die, of hunger, that makes a man wretched; many men have died; all men must die—the last exit of us all is in a Fire-Chariot of Pain. But it is to live miserable we know not why; to work sore and yet gain nothing; to be heart-worn, weary, yet isolated, unrelated, girt-in with a cold Universal Laissez-faire; it is to die slowly all our life long, imprisoned in a deaf, dead, Infinite Injustice, as in the accursed iron belly of a Phalaris' Bull! This is and forever remains intolerable to all men whom God has made.'

In another passage he castigated the idle rich and asked: 'What do these highly beneficial individuals do to society for their wages? *Kill partridges. Can* this *last?* No, by the soul that is in man it cannot, and will not, and shall not!'

The attempts of political economists, 'Respectable Professors of the Dismal Science', as he called them, to see in such conditions of social inequality the 'invisible hand' of private enterprise, like God in his Heaven making all right with the world, was branded by Carlyle as a very mockery of truth. He poured savage scorn on the 'over-production' which preoccupied Victorian captains of industry at a time when the poor of England subsisted at starvation level—'too many shirts? Well, that is a novelty, in this intemperate Earth, with its nine-hundred millions of bare backs . . .'—and he derided their much-vaunted 'progress' when it was plain that factory workers were worse off than serfs.

In these works of social criticism Carlyle made a number of specific proposals for social reform but provided no fully formulated or consistent democratic or socialistic doctrine. On the contrary, from a very early stage, ideas made their appearance which were later to dominate his thinking in what eventually became almost a conservative and authoritarian outlook. Like Disraeli in his attempts to arrive at a form of social radicalism, Carlyle dreamt of bygone days, in which he saw order, security and hierarchy. But, where Disraeli was caught up in fantasies about the Stuarts, Carlyle went back to Cromwell as Dictator and then, searching around for a subject for a new book, longingly harked back even further, to the stern and ordered rule of William the Conqueror. 'Oh, for a day of Duke William again!' he said in conversation with Tennyson, who pointed out that England was no longer the England even of Cromwell, let alone Duke William. But Carlyle obstinately repeated his longing for a day of Duke William. He eventually reached a point where nationalistic tendencies made their appearance side by side with his criticism of social evils. He praised the English as silent men of action, whereas other nations, the French in particular, were full of talk but accomplished nothing. Carlyle's reverence for instinct, custom, irrational tradition call to mind what Burke said in this connection—that ideas are only rationalizations by means of which mankind strives to make presentable, after they have been carried out, the actions prompted by dumb instinct.

Above all, it is the leaders, the heroes, Carlyle maintained, who shape humanity and lead it onward. The masses are incapable of governing. He saw democracy as something 'which means despair of finding any Heroes to govern you, and contented putting up with the want of them'.

It was obvious from the development of Carlyle's ideas in late middle and old age that his socialistic sympathies had waned, while conservatism, nationalism, anti-intellectualism and the worship of power and leadership had become the central themes of his social message. This tendency could already be discerned in *Latter Day*

Pamphlets (1850), and it became progressively more pronounced. He identified the heroes he exalted, the governing *élite* he advocated, with the existing governing class, dismissing Parliament as an assembly of inept and irresponsible chatterboxes.

In *Shooting Niagara . . . and After?* (1867), Carlyle fulminated against Disraeli's Reform Bill (which in 1867 achieved partial manhood suffrage for Englishmen), as a dangerous concession to democracy. He equated this 'leap in the dark' with 'the Niagara leap', a suicidal plunge in which Britons should find themselves 'unexpectedly (with immense surprise to most) *shooting* Niagara'. In Carlyle's ideal society the relationship between the various social groups would be characterized by what Sir Ernest Barker, the spokesman of political science, has called 'a new feudalism', in which, as Carlyle saw it, landowners and industrialists should rule and educate the employed (the 'servants'), forming with them close-knit, firmly-demarcated social units, in the relation of 'Mastership and Servantship'. The Hero would take on the characteristics of a despot or Drill Serjeant; children would be drilled from an early age in communal exercises to fit them for military training at sixteen. Carlyle uses a few favourite words over and over again: 'orderliness', 'to command and obey', 'humility', 'work'.

The mammoth *Life of Frederick the Great* (1858–65), six thick volumes over which, for thirteen years, Carlyle had agonized in his not-quite-soundproof room while Jane languished 'in the valley of the shadow of Frederick', was written to fit this theory of the Hero as Despot and Saviour.

Since writing *The French Revolution*, which had embodied his generous aspirations for man as a social animal, Carlyle's values had shifted. Now, instead of seeing historical change as ordered by social and economic forces, he veered to the view that it is the Heroes, the Supermen, who impose historical change on their age; and in worshipping the Hero as Ruler he cast aside his former humanitarian sympathies and turned a blind eye on the condition of the ruled.

His peculiar view of Frederick as Hero caused him to omit or suppress all that did not fit in with this view and to apply to Frederick standards of value which differed from those he selected in appraising his Hero's adversaries. Viewing Frederick's defects with a lenient eye, Carlyle glossed them over in picturesque euphemisms. The Hero's chicanery became a practical disregard for 'superstitious veracity'; a broken treaty was 'a kind of off-and-on Treaty'; his dissimulation was 'the art of wearing a polite cloak of darkness'. When Frederick resisted his adversaries he was heroic; when *they* resisted *him* they were obstinate sheep. Carlyle, in short, saw all Frederick's cunning and deceit as political wisdom and realism. As a point of interest, this picture is identical with a study of Frederick written sixty odd years later—Thomas Mann's essay, *Frederic the Great and The Grand Coalition* (1932).

Carlyle's *Occasional Discourse on the Nigger Question* (not, be it noted, the Negro Question) is a good example of the lengths to which he could carry his insensitive addiction to severity and sophistry. With an absurdly naïve ignorance of the true facts and conditions in the West Indies he presents a ludicrous picture of Negro slaves as idle singing and laughing pumpkin-eaters (presumably he meant water-melons), 'sitting yonder with their beautiful muzzles up to the ears in pumpkins, imbibing sweet pulps and juices . . . while the sugar crops rot round them uncut, because labour cannot be hired'.

He launches into a justification of slavery: it is the duty of the rich slave-owner to keep the blacks hard at work.

> 'The idle Black man in the West Indies had, not long since, the right, and will again under better form, if it pleases Heaven, have the right (actually the first "right of man" for an indolent person) to be *compelled* to work as he was fit, and to *do* the Maker's will who had constructed him with such and such capabilities, and prefigurements of capability. And I incessantly pray Heaven, all men, the whitest alike and the blackest, the richest and the poorest, in other regions of the world had attained precisely the same right, the divine right of being compelled (if "permitted" will not answer) to do what work they are appointed for, and not to go idle another minute, in a life which is so short, and where idleness so soon runs to putrescence.'

Behind this defence of slavery can be glimpsed a defence of total power for an *élite*, the oppression of the 'common' man by ruthless dictatorship.

Carlyle admitted that slavery was appalling and the cause of great suffering—but then all men suffer and since all suffering slaves were men, suffering men, he implied were all slaves, to be liberated only by a masterful Hero.

> 'Frightful things are continually told us of Negro Slavery, of the hardships, bodily and spiritual, suffered by slaves. Much exaggerated, and mere exceptional cases, say the opponents. Exceptional cases, I answer; yes, and universal ones! On the whole, hardships, and even oppressions and injustices are not unknown in this world; I myself have suffered such, and have not you? It is said, Man, of whatever colour, is born to such, even as the sparks fly upwards. Well, except by Mastership & Servantship, there is no conceivable deliverance from Tyranny and Slavery.'

He reverted to the 'nigger' question in *Shooting Niagara:*

> 'One always rather likes the Nigger; evidently a poor blockhead

with good dispositions, with affections, attachments—with a turn for Nigger Melodies, and the like:—he is the only savage of all the coloured races that doesn't die out on sight of the White Man; but can actually live beside him, and work and increase and be merry. The Almighty Maker has appointed him to be a Servant. Under penalty of Heaven's curse, neither party to this pre-appointment shall neglect or misdo his duties herein . . .'

Carlyle reflected sourly on the American Civil War, the abolition of slavery and the probable fate of manumitted slaves: '. . . three million absurd blacks, men and brothers (of a sort), are completely "emancipated"; launched into a career of improvement—likely to be "improved" off the face of the earth in a generation or two!'

'Mark it, my diabolic friends,' he thundered at unrepentant blacks and whites alike, 'I mean to lay leather on the backs of you, collars round the necks of you; and will teach you, after the example of the Gods, that the world is *not* your inheritance or glad to see you in it.' The voice is the voice of Carlyle but the hands are the hands of Mussolini and Hitler. No wonder Carlyle in his lifetime became a hero to the slave-owners of the American deep South, and no wonder that when he was long dead he was to be praised by some and attacked by others as one of the early prophets of Fascism and Nazism!

It is quite plain from his writings that Carlyle, especially in his maturity, was an embittered and deeply unhappy man. In this critic of social conditions there is very little love of humanity, less hope and no dreams for the future. The harshness of the reformer reveals a repellent streak of sadism. Hatred and contempt are his predominating moods and these emotions gain an ever greater ascendency in his later periods when it is individuals rather than institutions who are brought into his withering line of fire. Not even his 'heroes' are treated with affection; they are all strong, hard, men of toil without warmth or compassion; like Carlyle himself, they scourge humanity but have no love for humankind. Yet he does not give the impression of being self-righteous and arrogant, after the manner of so many other social reformers, theorists and visionaries. Undoubtedly he considered himself just as superior to the rest of the human race as did other reformers, but his hostility was also directed inwards upon himself and was as overpowering as his hatred of mankind.

The background of this bitterness has been revealed in the letters, reminiscences and memoirs of Carlyle and his wife and their correspondence with family and friends and the literary figures of their day. If Carlyle's name is destined to be saved for any length of time from the limbo of the forgotten, it will probably be more because of these personal testimonies than because of his enormous literary output. In a letter-writing age, both he and Jane Carlyle were indefatigable and copious letter writers: they kept letters that they received (though they did burn some), and their letters to others were usually kept by the recipients, so that the lives and surroundings of the couple are documented with the detail of almost total recall.

Carlyle complained constantly that he felt writing to be a torment as well as a necessity. Invitations, gatherings, social calls, visits, new acquaintances, all caused him great uneasiness and anxiety and, away from home, the physical discomfort and inconvenience of unfamiliar surroundings made him miserable. The purely physical, or at any rate the physically-manifested causes of all this are well known and have been discussed in exhaustive detail. He suffered from chronic backache; this is now known to be frequently a psychosomatic ailment, but it is equally possible that what he suffered from was a slipped disc, a complaint which has been diagnosed and for which an effective cure has been made possible only in our own time. He was morbidly sensitive to noise and suffered all his life from acute insomnia: barking watch-dogs, crowing cockerels, macaws, organ-grinders, street noises, fire-works, late-night revellers, even snoring peers of the realm, all contributed at one time or another to his sleeplessness. References to all these torments recur constantly in his and his wife's letters; and his vain attempt to have a sound-proof room built for him on top of his house, as an aid to the gigantic task of writing *Frederick the Great*, is a touching and tragi-comic episode, recounted by his many biographers.

Then, he suffered all his life from a 'nervous' stomach and from chronic constipation, for which he swallowed daily doses of the stock Victorian specific, castor oil. This crude irritant, a repulsive and violent cathartic now happily superseded as a domestic remedy, he swallowed each mid-morning in a cup of black coffee, with a devotion akin to the present-day enthusiasm for vitamin pills or antibiotics.

Some evidence seems to point to the fact that he was impotent—at any rate, partially, if not totally—though the proofs are not conclusive. This misfortune, in the light of present-day curiosity about the psycho-sexual make-up of outstanding men and women of the past, has been regarded as of primordial interest among Carlyle's peculiarities; but it is quite possible that he himself regarded it as of less importance than his other more acute or aggressive afflictions. In view of all his psycho-somatic disorders it is not surprising that his outlook should have combined the tragic view of life of a Joseph de Maistre with the pessimism and irritation of a Strindberg faced by the petty annoyances of everyday existence.

It goes without saying that a search in depth has been made into the psychological background of Carlyle's personality, into the traits underlying the more general psychic causes of his idiosyncrasies. Some years ago, in *Mr Carlyle My Patient: a psycho-somatic biography* (1949), Dr James D. Halliday attempted to follow the now customary psycho-analytical line of investigation to produce a clinical case-history in which, among other components of Carlyle's psyche, attention was drawn to its sadistic, masochistic and anal-erotic elements. But does such a stereotyped catalogue of delvings into the subconscious succeed in making Carlyle's nature any better understood? It is very much to be doubted. Julian Symons has commented on this point in an admirable and well-balanced biography *Thomas Carlyle: the Life and Ideas of a Prophet* (1952). He considers unsatisfactory such hypotheses as those of the psycho-somatic biography because, as he points out, if Carlyle was a psycho-pathological case, he was also very much more than that alone—a fact which such hypotheses disregard. Symons lays special emphasis, not without a certain relish, on Carlyle's longing to replace the faith of his childhood, inculcated in a deeply religious and moral home, with a philosophy of life which at least should enable him to retain his deeply ingrained puritanism. In discarding Christian doctrine, Carlyle clung to Christian morality.

Carlyle the man, as opposed to Carlyle the writer and reformer, nevertheless comes out of all this with our sympathies well on his side. He was not wholly or consistently the sour, churlish misanthrope he has been represented to be. Like so many who are melancholy when alone, the brusque and crusty sage was capable of being lively, almost light-hearted in company. He had a mordant wit, a great sense of the comic and his conversation held his listeners enthralled. He was capable of sensitive acts of kindness and also of generosity in the grand manner—as when, in the spring of 1835, concealing his own dismay, he sat down for several hours with John Stuart Mill to console him for the accidental destruction of the manuscript of Book I of *The French Revolution.* The book was the fruit of five months of hard work accompanied by Carlyle's usual agonies of creation. During this time Mill had been coming round every Sunday afternoon to walk with him and discuss the Revolution. When the manuscript had been completed Carlyle, 'soul and body both very *sick*', gave it to Mill to reread and make notes. Mill had taken it home, or more probably to Harriet Taylor's cottage at Walton-on-Thames where he spent his weekends. There, by some ghastly freak of negligence the manuscript was left lying about and was mistaken for wastepaper and used by the housemaid next morning to light the fire. In the afternoon Mill and Harriet arrived at 5 Great Cheyne Row, distraught in a cab.

Seeing them drive up, Jane thought they had at last eloped and exclaimed, 'Gracious Providence, he has gone off with Mrs Taylor!' Mill rushed in, pale as a ghost, almost speechless with dismay and distress. Jane went down to speak to Harriet and presently the cab drove off. The Carlyles wished the lamenting Mill had gone too, but he stayed on for three hours, while Carlyle sat consoling him.

The accident was catastrophic for the Carlyles. They needed the money the book would fetch, which was bad enough; but Carlyle had destroyed not only his notes but the rough draft. Yet his first words to Jane, after Mill had left, were, 'Well, Mill, poor fellow, is terribly cut up; we must endeavour to hide from him how very serious this business is to us.' Next day he followed up Mill's visit with a generous letter of further consolation and spoke to him almost jestingly of his preparations to start rewriting. But it was no joke. It was more like a half sentence of death, as he forced himself with much sighing and complaining to rewrite the book from memory.

Carlyle got thinner and sallower, Jane became more tart-tongued and irritable. 'My husband is anything but well,' she wrote, 'nor likely to be better till he have finished his French Revolution. I myself have been abominably all winter, though not writing, so far as I know, for the press.' They survived, and at length Book I was rewritten and gradually the whole book was finished to the great relief of both of them. 'My poor little Jeannie and me,' Carlyle mused afterwards, 'hasn't it nearly killed us both?'

The Carlyles were two beings who were fundamentally ill-matched yet indissolubly linked; their long marriage is one of the saddest examples of tragic love, if by calling it tragic we ignore the usual associations of tragedy with forced separation, external obstacles and early death. In the case of the Carlyles a different and perhaps more ghastly tragedy can be discerned in their frustrated yet close-knit relationship, which lasted for forty years.

Neither of them was easy to live with. Both were neurotic and suffered from intermittent but long-lasting ill health, about which they corresponded with each other in absorbed and absorbing detail and with unabating relish: his insomnia, his dyspepsia, his biliousness; her insomnia, her raw nerves, her crippling, black migraines; the purges, the pills, the mercury, the morphia. They were two people 'whose skins were 'much too thin for the rough purposes of human life'.

Carlyle, for all that writing was a torment, was morose when not working and moody at the best of times; but he had at least his successive books into which he could escape and, however painfully, become absorbed. Jane, who had subdued her lively mind and personality as far as she was able, to become the kind of wife Carlyle judged a wife should be, kept silent about her own frustrations, unhappiness and loneliness. She had learned to 'annihilate my I'ety', to care for Carlyle, to sympathize with him, support and air his views, fetch and carry for him, even in time to be able to hand him a glass of sherry without a word about her own troubles when he came home full of his.

16. John Stuart Mill

17. Alfred, Lord Tennyson (Photograph by Julia Margaret Cameron, 1869)

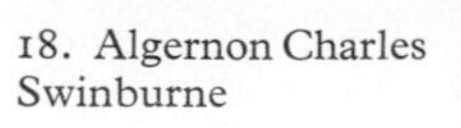

18. Algernon Charles Swinburne

19. Rudyard Kipling

She relieved her feelings in her journal and in letters full of acute and ironic observations on people, domestic events and Mr C. Though rarely explicitly stated, Jane's frustration and unhappiness, her increasing loneliness as she grew older, frailer and more ailing, can be glimpsed through her shrewd and witty correspondence; but nowhere more poignantly than in the fragments of her private journal, begun at Carlyle's instigation (much of it later destroyed by her) in which she set down self-aware philosophical musings and the complaints about the unhappiness of her married life that she had never uttered to him.

During Carlyle's long, infatuated, though quite platonic friendship with the imperious Lady Harriet Baring (afterwards Ashburton), 'a great lady who liked to have a philosopher in chains', and who completely dominated Carlyle for ten years, Jane was beset by feelings of violent jealousy. She had made sacrifices for her husband in their years of poverty and struggle—years of isolation from the congenial company, the social diversions and ceremony that she took pleasure in and Carlyle shunned and decried as 'gigmanic cant'. Having become accustomed to his bearishness, occasional rudeness and his general lack of polish, she now saw a change in his manners and behaviour which it had never occurred to him to make for her sake. What was more disconcerting, she saw him frequenting with hardly a murmur of disapproval the very society he had formerly denounced with such vehemence.

Carlyle had met Lady Harriet first in 1839, at a dinner given at Bath House, Piccadilly, by her father-in-law Lord Ashburton, for whom she acted as hostess. Carlyle impressed her and they talked for an hour, at the end of which she, in turn, had impressed him: 'one of the cleverest creatures I have met with, full of mirth and spirit—though not beautiful to look upon'. It was not until 1842, when Lady Harriet was ailing and in need of distraction, that the friendship progressed. She wrote to Carlyle that, since he was the one person she liked to talk to in preference to all others, it would be a work of charity and piety if he would go to see her. Jane did not take 'Lady Harriet's love-making to my husband' very seriously, or at least professed to be more amused than put out by it. 'When a handsome, clever, and reputedly *most haughty* woman appeals to the charity and piety of a simple man like Carlyle,' she wrote, 'you may be sure she will not appeal in vain.' When the friendship was in full swing and Carlyle was making frequent visits to Bath House to spend the evening with Lady Harriet, Jane could still shrug it off, even if a little wryly: 'For my part I am singularly inaccessible to jealousy, and am pleased rather that he has found *one* agreeable house to which he likes to go and goes regularly.'

Long afterwards, in 1855, Jane wrote bitterly in her journal:

'That eternal Bath House! I wonder how many thousand miles Mr C.

has walked between there and here, putting it all together; setting up always another milestone and another betwixt himself and me. O, good gracious! when I first noticed that heavy yellow house without knowing, or caring to know, who it belonged to, how far I was from dreaming that through years and years I should carry every stone's weight of it on my heart.'

It was not until the friendship had been in progress for some four years that Jane and Lady Harriet met. Mrs Buller, a friend of both women, insisted 'in her graceful quizzical way' that Jane should 'see a little into the thing' with her own eyes, and arranged a meeting at her house. Jane had forgotten that 'a whole bevy of Americans, male and female' had been invited to take tea at 5 Great Cheyne Row on the same evening. She tried unsuccessfully to put the Bullers off but they would not hear of it—and so great was Jane's eagerness to see Lady Harriet that she went off, 'in cold blood', leaving Carlyle, to his great annoyance, to pour out tea himself for the Americans, 'and make what excuses for me he pleased'. After all, Jane argued, it was her husband, not herself, that all these Americans were coming to stare at. The encounter with her rival took place accordingly on the appointed evening, when Jane and the 'Intellectual Circe' surveyed one another politely across tea cups—an inspection during which Lady Harriet 'took prodigious looks' at Jane from time to time. Jane's own scrutiny was characteristically more discreet, but her appraisal of Lady Harriet was none the less acute, and as there were no other strangers present and the visit lasted several hours, she had 'ample opportunity of estimating the amount of her seductions'. She found Lady Harriet likeable, immensely *large*, and only saved from being 'one of the *ugliest* women living' by the intelligence and cordiality of her expression which made her after all, Jane decided, almost beautiful.

'She is unquestionably very clever—just the wittiest woman I have ever seen—but with many aristocratic prejudices—which I wonder Carlyle should have got over so completely as he seems to have done—in a word I take her to be a very lovable spoilt child of Fortune—that a little whipping judiciously administered, would have made into a first rate woman.'

This spoilt child of Fortune was the daughter of the sixth Earl of Sandwich, and married to Bingham Baring, the shy, amiable and immensely rich son and heir of Lord Ashburton. Besides being even more well-born than her husband and full of a regal and imperturbable conviction of the superiority of her own rank and lineage, Lady Harriet was intelligent, cultured, a famous hostess and an assiduous and skilful lion-hunter. Though, as Carlyle had observed, no beauty, she was a fine figure of a woman, of stately not to say buxom proportions—and she was six years younger than slight, frail, ailing, faded Jane.

Though somewhat brusque and accustomed to dominate the conversation, Lady Harriet did not appear to Jane to display any of her reputed impertinence and hauteur: on the contrary, she was gracious, unaffected, amiable, even friendly, and Jane not only found her clever and amusing, but felt that she could have liked her very much had Lady Harriet ever given her the least encouragement. But the grand lady never showed an inclination to any intimacy and Jane was left with 'an unconquerable feeling that she does not and never can like me'.

As the wife of Lady Harriet's tame philosopher, Jane was always invited to the Barings (or the Ashburtons, as they became in May 1848, when Bingham Baring succeeded to the title). She was not slow to realize (and the thought rankled for the next ten years) that she was accepted in the brilliant circle of Lady Harriet and her friends merely as a necessary and unavoidable adjunct, wife to a man of genius—'part of your luggage, without self-responsibility', as she wrote to Carlyle in 1856, a year before the disruptive friendship was terminated by the death of Lady Harriet.

In the grand company frequented by the Carlyles from 1845–56 as guests of the Baring-Ashburtons, life was passed in elegant and luxurious idleness in which heroic feats of time-killing and over-eating were accompanied by an unceasing flow of clever, superficial talk. 'The careful avoidance of all discussion, the swift hopping from topic to topic, does not agree with me,' Carlyle told Jane, 'but the graceful skill they do it with is beyond that of minuets.' To the Carlyles, not given to minuets, such an existence seemed all the more reprehensible because these people were cultured and intelligent.

Jane did not shine and was not talkative in such dazzling company. Her terms of reference were neither smart nor sophisticated and the ironic wit which burgeoned in the domestic surroundings of unfashionable Great Cheyne Row seemed, in the grand atmosphere of Bath House and all the other Ashburton houses, homespun and provincial: it wilted unspoken. But saying little, she observed much, and passed on her impressions to her intimates, with tart comments.

She wrote to her Uncle John in the summer of 1845:

> 'I was taken to the opera . . . with Lady Harriet Baring—my debut in fashionable life—and a very fatiguing piece of pleasure it was, which left a headache and all uncomfortableness which I have not got rid of till this hour. Carlyle too was at the Opera, God help us!—went to ride in the Park at the fashionable hour then returned and dressed for the Opera!! Nobody knows what he can do till he tries! or rather till a Lady Harriet tries!!'

The Carlyles' first stay at Bay House, the Barings' seaside residence at Alverstoke, in 1845, was more trying than pleasurable and they were glad to get home to Chelsea, both of them 'worn out with "strenuous idleness" '. 'Nothing', Jane decided, 'could exceed the sumptuousity of the whole thing, nor its uselessness.' Carlyle's judgement, surprisingly, was more lenient: 'The prospect of such a thing *for life* was absolutely equal to death. Meanwhile it cannot but be said to be pleasant enough, and perhaps not useless for a season.'

In spite of the mental and physical anguish he suffered when travelling and paying visits, Carlyle could never resist invitations to stay with the Ashburtons—in Hampshire, the Highlands or France, wherever his aristocratic friend and patron happened to require his company. Nor was his infatuation for Lady Harriet his sole compulsion. The lord-loving propensity of mid-nineteenth-century Englishmen fostered a sense of obligation towards rank from which the Carlyles, for all their intellectual independence, were not immune. The deference felt to be due to an aristocrat made it difficult to refuse gracious or condescending invitations. Besides, though he disapproved of the idle rich, it was flattering to Carlyle to be sought out by the aristocracy. To the farmer's son from Ecclefechan their recognition of genius was gratifying as the homage of birth to brains.

As Carlyle's enjoyment of Lady Harriet's friendship showed no signs of waning, the great lady's domination over Carlyle caused tension and friction between husband and wife. Their disagreement came to a head in 1846 with a violent quarrel, when Carlyle, refusing what he felt was an unreasonable demand to give up the friendship, accepted an invitation to a house-party. The situation had become so intolerable to Jane that she contemplated separation from Carlyle. In her trouble she sought advice from an old friend, the exiled Italian revolutionary and patriot, Guiseppe Mazzini, who wisely counselled patience. The Carlyle's did not separate, Jane resigned herself to the situation and the friendship continued—for the next ten years, during which, in addition to his visits to Lady Harriet, Carlyle maintained a regular correspondence with her. When Lady Harriet died suddenly, in Paris in May 1857, Carlyle mourned her sincerely, and thought of her as 'the most queen-like woman I had ever known'.

But if Lady Harriet no longer came between Jane and her husband, the 'unspeakable' *Frederick* remained. Carlyle had been toiling since 1851 on volume after volume of the book, to the continuing neglect of Jane, who became sadder and more melancholy as her health declined. 'So long as I can stand on my legs,' she wrote to Jane Aitken, one of her sisters-in-law, 'he never notices that anything ails me; and I make a point of never complaining to him unless in case of absolute extremity.' The years of *Frederick* dragged by in sadness, loneliness and boredom for Jane. 'Life is too monotonous and too dreary in the shadow of the valley of Frederick the Great,' she told her sister-in-law Mary Austin in 1863.

For eleven of those dreary years she found some consolation in her little dog Nero, a present from a friend in Manchester. The shock-haired, frisky, black-and-white little 'Cuban (Maltese?) and otherwise mongrel' arrived in Great Cheyne Row in the autumn or winter of 1849 and was to Jane '. . . the pleasantest fact of my life for a good while'. Writing to her friends the Forsters, she said in a postscript:

> 'Oh, Lord! I forgot to tell you I have got a little dog, and Mr C. has accepted it with an amiability. To be sure, when he comes down gloomy in the morning, or comes in wearied from his walk, the infatuated little beast dances round him on its hind legs as I ought to do and can't; and he feels flattered and surprised by such unwonted capers to his honour and glory.'

'A most affectionate, lively little dog, otherwise of small merit, and little or no training', was Carlyle's verdict. He became gruffly fond of Nero, who was often his companion during Jane's absences and in his solitary night-time walks about the streets of Chelsea, Brompton and Kensington. Years afterwards he remembered Nero with affection: 'We had many walks together, he and I, for the next ten years; a great deal of small traffic, poor little animal, so loyal, so loving, so *naive* and true with what of dim intellect he had!' Jane lavished on the little dog all her thwarted maternal instincts and solaced in a measure her longing for companionship and some sort of demonstrative affection. Nero lived a happy life with the Carlyles and might well have existed beyond his eleven years to reach a dog's venerable old age, had not a butcher's cart run him down one day, the wheel passing over his neck. He was carried home apparently lifeless 'all crumpled together like a crushed spider'. But Jane nursed him back to some semblance of life, though never to full recovery; the accident had affected the little animal's breathing. 'My poor little dog is become a source of great sorrow, Jane wrote to a friend, 'his tendency to asthma having been dreadfully developed since the Butcher's cart went over his throat. I have made him a little red cloak, and he keeps the house with *me*.' Nero 'wheezed and suffered' all winter, struggling to go out with Jane when he saw her putting on her bonnet, coming panting to welcome her on her return; but it became apparent that Nero's days were numbered and that it would be more merciful to put an end to his sufferings. Arrangements were made with the local practitioner, Dr Barnes from the King's Road, to give the little animal a dose of strychnine. On 31 January Nero went for a last midnight walk with Carlyle—'he insisted on trying to come', Carlyle recorded. The next day, as Jane handed the little dog to the maid to be taken away, she kissed his head and he responded with a lick, 'he kissed my cheek'. Writing to thank Dr Barnes for his 'kindly done services' she said:

> 'Shall I not, as long as I live, remember that poor little dog? . . . Nobody but myself can have any idea what that little creature has been in my life. My inseparable companion during eleven years, ever doing his little best to keep me from feeling sad and lonely.'

Nero's fate dissolved the little household in tears. Carlyle though genuinely fond of the dog, soon regained his composure; Charlotte the maid wept for three days, dried her eyes on the fourth; Jane's tears were 'passionate and bitter', and she was inconsolable. She went next day for a long drive by public omnibus: 'I could not bear myself in the house where everything I looked at reminded me of yesterday. And I wouldn't be at home for visitors to criticize my swollen eyes, and smile at grief "about a dog".' Her tears gradually 'repressed themselves as was fit', but she grieved continually for Nero 'as if he had been my little human child'.

In the autumn of 1863 Jane herself was nearly run over. Returning home after a visit in Cheapside, she was about to cross the street to board the omnibus when a cab came dashing furiously towards her. Stepping hastily back on to the kerb she slipped, fell, was unable to break her fall with her 'neuralgic' right arm and tore, as Carlyle put it, 'the sinews of her thigh-bone'. In great pain, unable to stand or walk, she nevertheless managed with help from bystanders to get into a cab and reach Cheyne Row. There she was carried up to her room by Carlyle and his secretary and Dr Barnes was summoned.

This was the beginning of a mysterious illness which lasted for a year and for the first nine months she was almost continually in acute physical pain. Her suffering was increased by insomnia and an intensified neurotic state which lead her to fear that she would go mad or be tempted to commit suicide. Heavy doses of morphia prescribed for her were not always successful in deadening her pain or inducing sleep. She longed for death as a release from her torments, yet she wanted to live.

Jane was treated by a succession of doctors during her illness. Since before her accident she had been suffering from a 'neuralgia' which had rendered her right arm and hand practically useless. For this she was treated by the Ashburtons' physician, the fashionable Dr Quain (later knighted). The local Dr Barnes who had 'obliged' with Nero treated her injured leg. The niceties of medical etiquette, with perhaps a hint of deference on the part of unfashionable Dr Barnes, caused him—as Jane observed wryly—to consider her leg his patient and her arm Dr Quain's. Between the fashionable and the local doctor neither limb improved, nor did Jane's general condition. At last, having tried one ineffectual remedy after another, the doctors confessed themselves nonplussed, recommended lots of champagne, and as a drastic final resort prescribed—a change of air.

Jane dragged herself about from place to place in search of health: first to St Leonards, 'shoved into a sort of hearse', a dreary vehicle purporting to be an ambulance, which gave her grisly forebodings; back to London, though she refused to go to Great Cheyne Row with its memories of the past, pain-wracked winter and elected to stay with friends, the John Forsters, at Palace Gate; finally, up to Scotland where, after two months in the home of other friends, Dr and Mrs Russell of Thornhill, she was slowly nursed back to health on a milk diet and she even put on weight.

Meanwhile 5 Great Cheyne Row was undergoing complete re-decoration—new wallpapers, fresh paint, new chintzes—to meet Jane's desire to have 'a new colour about me' that would efface by different surroundings the bitter memories of the past year, the associations which, she said, made those rooms *terrible* for her.

Carlyle wrote her loving, encouraging letters daily throughout the whole period of her illness. Jane answered them as best she could, sometimes writing with her left hand, in letters that were sometimes like pitiful screams of pain: 'Oh my Husband! I am suffering torments! Each day I suffer more horribly. Oh, I would like you beside me!—I am *terribly* alone—But I don't want to interrupt your work . . .' With returning health her letters became more optimistic, sometimes even cheerful.

At last, in September 1864, she felt well enough to attempt the long journey down to London. She reached Great Cheyne Row on 1 October, after an absence of six months. Carlyle, who had been expecting her earlier and had been waiting impatiently for more than two hours, rushed into the street in his dressing-gown to welcome her with tears and kisses. The two maids stood on the doorstep shedding tears of joy. Jane's return to Carlyle and to their home was for him 'by far the gladdest sight that I would ever see there'. As Jane was helped in to the house, 'A faint, kind, timid smile was on her face, as if afraid to believe fully; but the despair had vanished from her looks altogether . . .' The fatigue of the journey and the excitement of homecoming produced no ill effects. She was enchanted with the wallpaper. She went to bed and, wonder of wonders, enjoyed an almost unbroken sleep till morning.

With Jane recovered from her illness, the year 1865 was perhaps one of the happiest in the lives of both husband and wife. They were no longer crushed by the burden of *Frederick;* on 5 January, as Carlyle went out to post the last of his proofs, Jane watched him 'with a silent faint and pathetic smile'. With *Frederick* out of the way, Carlyle was, companionable and affectionate. 'I cannot tell you how good Mr Carlyle is! He is as busy as ever, but he studies my comfort and peace as he never did before,' Jane wrote. They had a wide circle of friends and Jane, though more frail after her long illness, unable to bear exertion or excitement, was in reasonably good health, and her nerves, she acknowledged, were stronger than they had been for years.

She now took delight in 'a nice little Brougham, sixty pounds and brand new and handsome in a plain way . . . all glass in front . . . dark morocco and cloth inside, which won't dirty in a hurry'. It was a gift from Carlyle, and Jane was 'boundlessly proud' of it as 'her husband's testimony to her'. She believed it to be 'the very saving of her, and the source of all the health she had'. In this little vehicle, with a smart grey horse and a steady old coachman, Sylvester, up in front, dressed in 'Mr C.'s old brown surtout', she was now able to go out whenever she wished and for as long as she liked, to pay visits or take an airing, instead of having to spend six shillings for a two-hour drive in a fly or make the forays by omnibus which had so exhausted her in the past. The couple reached a peak of enjoyment and satisfaction with Carlyle's inauguration as Lord Rector of Edinburgh University in April 1866. They were now old people: he was seventy; she was sixty-seven.

Jane did not feel equal to accompanying Carlyle to Edinburgh. She 'took fright at the cold weather, the long journey and the fuss and agitation of attending my Husband thro' an operation little more agreeable to him than being hanged!' She feared, too, that, 'what with fuss, and "bad air", and confusion', he might even drop down dead. And if she were there and from emotion dropped down dead too at his side, 'what a scene that would be!'

John Tyndall the scientist, Carlyle's friend and admirer, was to take care of the old man on the long journey to Edinburgh. When he arrived on the morning of departure, Carlyle was punctually ready. Jane fussed over him, encouraged him, provided him with a tot of brandy in her own travelling flask, to drink before his speech, gave him a brandy and soda for the road. Standing with her back to the parlour door, she bade him goodbye and Carlyle returned her kiss. At the front door she exhorted Tyndall, 'For God's sake send me one line by telegraph when all is over.'

Four days later Tyndall sent his telegram: 'A perfect triumph', and Jane was so relieved that 'the sudden solution of the nervous tension with which I had been holding in my anxieties for days—nay, weeks past—threw me into as pretty a little fit of hysterics as you ever saw'.

Carlyle's speech was reported in full in many newspapers and he was generally praised as an old rebel who had finally paid his tribute to respectability. He sent Jane a copy of *The Scotsman* which did not arrive as fast as she would have liked. He was fêted in Edinburgh and after a few days of the University festivities he left for his old home at Scotsbrig to visit his family. Tyndall returned to London to delight Jane with a detailed account of the Edinburgh triumph.

On Saturday 21 April, Carlyle on his way back to London had reached Dumfries to visit his sister Jean. On that day he wrote to Jane who was expecting his return on the Monday. Jane also wrote to him that Saturday telling him that she was giving a tea-party in the afternoon to eleven friends, a function she wished to get out of the way before his return. She had neither long nor short stories to tell him, she said, before the tea-party, but after it she might have more to say, 'provided I survive it'.

Later that morning she went to lunch with her friends the John Forsters at Palace Gate. She took with her a little pug-dog, Tiny, which she had brought back with her from a visit some time previously to friends at Folkestone. She was in high spirits at the thought of Carlyle's home-coming on Monday.

She left the Forsters at about three o'clock to prepare for the tea-party and on her way home she went for her usual drive in the Park. There she put Tiny out for a run. Shortly afterwards, a carriage passing in the opposite direction bowled the little dog over. He lay for a moment yelping, then ran into some bushes. Jane stopped her carriage and was out of it almost before it had come to a halt. The ladies got out of the other carriage. Some passers-by stopped. There were explanations, apologies. Jane picked up Tiny, got back into the carriage, settled the rug over her knees and told Sylvester to drive on. He heard the little dog squeak as Jane felt a bruised toe, the dog's only injury. Then there was silence. The emotional shock had been too much for Jane. As the carriage drove on through the Park she took off her bonnet, leaned back in the corner, folded her hands in her lap, palm up, palm down, and died.

Telegrams from his brother John and the Forsters told Carlyle of Jane's death. John went next day to Scotland and fetched him, stunned with shock and grief, back to London. When he arrived at 5 Great Cheyne Row he found his last letter to Jane lying unopened on the hall table.

Jane's death shattered him. 'My poor life seems as good as over,' he wrote. 'I have no heart or strength of hope or of interest for further work.' The spirit had gone out of him. He wrote rarely after this, and nothing of importance after 1867. He lingered on until 1881, a prophet with honour, a rebel who had become an institution.

Going through Jane's papers shortly after her death the grief-stricken Carlyle was filled with deep remorse as he read of her loneliness, bitterness and boredom during the years of Lady Harriet and *Frederick*, and the unhappiness he had caused her by his irritability and unconscious lack of consideration. Often afterwards he said to Froude the historian, his close friend (and later his executor and biographer): 'Oh, if I could but see her for five minutes to assure her that I had really cared for her throughout all that! But she never knew it, she never knew it!' His grief and remorse rekindled in him, too late, something of the passion that had gone out of a marriage which, lacking 'the lineaments of gratified desire', had been deprived of the joy that is liberated by the fulfilment of happy physical union.

Art and Social Idealism: John Ruskin

Ruskin ranks with Carlyle as one of those Victorian prophets who fulminated against society, demanding a brave new world, yet were able to fit into the existing social system and achieve fame in their own lifetime.

Carlyle lived from 1795 to 1881, Ruskin from 1819 to 1900: their activity thus spans the whole Victorian age, and the numerous similarities between the two men are such that Ruskin can be regarded as the successor to Carlyle. Both of them attacked the liberal economy and its industrial exploitation of the poor with a passion as fervent as it was sincere. They helped to tear down the old *laissez-faire* liberalism which could look upon misery unmoved while it held in awe the inscrutable workings of 'the invisible hand' of supply and demand, the inflexible law governing private enterprise. Both of them had a weakness for the strong man, the Hero as Carlyle called him, and eventually both became advocates of government by the *élite* of a powerful, stable and hierarchical class structure. Their tendency to see oligarchic power personified in the aristocracy, the landed gentry, and heads of industry, enabled the two prophets—despite their criticism of the social system—to be supporters of aristocratic toryism. On the other hand, they regarded the English nation in general as an *élite* of strong, capable and enterprising people, who were thus fitted, even ordained, to rule and protect 'inferior' races, an attitude which led both Carlyle and Ruskin to become imperialists.

One can catch a glimpse of these two prophetic extremists, with their combination of poetic irrationality and passionate insight, behind the political ideas of a Disraeli or a Joseph Chamberlain, though the ideas of the two statesmen were expressed and applied within a framework of more feasible policy.

It was not surprising, when certain facts came to light concerning the pitiable sex lives of two men of such exceptionally strong character, personality and views as Carlyle and Ruskin, that the revelations should have been met with mingled glee and dismay. Recent biographers—notably Peter Quennell in *John Ruskin: The Portrait of a Prophet* (1949)—a book written after the publication of the Millais Papers—have definitely established that Ruskin was impotent, or at least that he was unable to experience a normal sexual relationship. Furthermore, his only sexual outlet would seem to have been auto-erotic in nature; a prolongation into his middle age of that adolescent phase of sexual activity dreaded and stigmatized by the Victorians as 'the sin of impurity' or 'the solitary vice'—one which, therefore, was generally accompanied, as in Ruskin's case, by acute feelings of guilt and remorse.

Ruskin was the only child of middle-aged parents who were dominating, possessive and over-protective. His father, James Ruskin, a Scot from Perth and a prosperous partner in a London firm of wine merchants, had sacrificed his young manhood to rebuild the family fortunes, brought to the verge of bankruptcy by his own father, who had then committed suicide. At twenty-three, James Ruskin had become engaged to his cousin Margaret Cox, four years his elder and housekeeper to the Ruskin household since she was twenty. Having chosen his wife 'with much the same kind of serenity and decision with which he afterwards chose his clerks', James Ruskin went to London and, while Margaret waited for him, prospered in business. They were married ten years later, in 1818, and John Ruskin was born in the following year, when his father was thirty-four and his mother thirty-eight.

Margaret Ruskin, the daughter of a widow who kept an inn at Croydon, was well-educated and ladylike. She was handsome and a capable manager, and she was also devout, puritanical and prudish. A severe but just mother, she brought up her child on the Bible, gave him his elementary education and fostered a determined ambition, which was also her husband's, that her son should become a man of distinction—preferably a bishop.

As befitted two such sober and sensible people, the marriage of James and Margaret Ruskin was harmonious and humdrum. Their household was orderly, their rule over the child strict and just. 'Nothing was ever promised me', Ruskin wrote in after years, 'that was not given, nothing threatened that was not inflicted, nothing told me that was not true.' His parents were never irritable or impatient, but children in that household were to be seen and heard only when it was required of them, and demonstrative affection, even from an only child, was not allowed—nor was it offered. The intelligent, precocious boy learnt early not to incur the severe punishments inflicted on him to make him a docile, well-behaved and orderly child. He had few toys or playmates, 'no companions to quarrel with, nobody to assist and nobody to thank', and like most only, lonely children, he became self-absorbed and self-sufficient at an early age. Ruskin's childhood, compared with those of many other children, and by the strict standards of Victorian upbringing, was not an unhappy one. Besides being rich and respectable, his parents were cultivated and he shared with them their tastes, their interests and their travels abroad. In the atmosphere of his home, in which no unseemly emotions were permitted to ruffle its chilly calm, the child was starved of the warmth and tenderness his sensitive nature craved, and this deprivation was traumatic: it left him with a deep and abiding longing for affection.

What his parents did not give they did not get. Omnipotent and omnipresent, they appeared to the child—as he wrote in old age—as some sort of 'visible powers of nature . . . no more loved than the sun and moon'. They exacted, and he gave, dutiful respect and unquestioning obedience in all things. His mother virtually never let him out of her sight—even during his three years at Oxford, when she took rooms there in term and he spent his evenings with her till lock-up. At week-ends his father came down from London to spend Sunday with them. Not until he was twenty-six did he ever make a journey without his parents. He continued to live with them until his marriage, and indeed afterwards, only finally shaking off parental authority when he was past forty and a successful and influential writer. What they had done to him bit deep; in 1860 he turned on them and reproached them, coldly and categorically, with ruining him by the terrible mistakes in his upbringing, by which they had thwarted him, he said 'in all the earnest fire and passion of life'.

The craving to give and receive the love denied him in his childhood was so great that, as he remembered towards the end of his life,'When affection did come, it came with a violence utterly rampant and unmanageable, at least by me, who never before had anything to manage'. In 1836, when he was seventeen, he fell violently in love with Adèle Clotilde Domecq, the fifteen-year-old daughter of one of his father's partners, who had come with her two younger sisters to stay with the Ruskins. Adèle was intelligent, worldly, well-bred and well dressed. Young Ruskin was shy, gauche and dazzled, and his awkward attempts to impress the sophisticated French girl made him seem to her merely naive, conceited, sentimental and ridiculous. His advances were met with 'rippling ecstasies of derision'. The frivolous and heartless Adèle, who did not know, and could not have understood, the force of his passion or its idealized nature, returned to France, uncaring of the havoc she had wrought. Ruskin pined for her and continued to pine throughout his time at Oxford. When she married, in 1840, his sense of loss caused him such acute mental distress that his health gave way and his lungs were threatened. He left Oxford, convalesced at home and travelled abroad sketching and taking notes, and returned in 1842, improved in health and spirits, to take his degree at Oxford. In 1843 he produced the first volume of *Modern Painters*, his first book, which met with instant success. After completing the second volume and making a second visit to Italy with his parents, Ruskin returned to London—only to fall in love again. This time it was with Charlotte Lockhart, the granddaughter of Sir Walter Scott. But again Ruskin's emotions were frustrated: Charlotte was in love with another man and ignored this new and tongue-tied admirer.

In the summer of 1848, when Ruskin was twenty-nine, Euphemia Gray came to stay with the Ruskins. She was the daughter of old family friends who lived in Scotland, and she had stayed with the Ruskin family from time to time on her way to and from her school in London and her home in Perth. She was now no longer a schoolgirl but, at eighteen, a nubile and pretty young woman. Charlotte was forgotten: Ruskin fell in love with Effie, as she was called. In spite of his parents' clumsy attempts to prevent the situation from developing, he persevered. Finally, with their reluctant permission, he followed Effie to Perth, proposed to her, was accepted, and they were married on 10 April 1848, in the drawing-room of Effie's home at Bowerswell.

The honeymoon, spent partly in the Lake District, was a complete and pathetic fiasco, carefully concealed by both of the young people. Ruskin's inability to reconcile an intensely idealized conception of love and the loved one with the flesh-and-blood reality of an Effie was such that either he could not or would not consummate the marriage—and indeed it was never consummated. His subsequent indifference to Effie and his neglect of her caused a gradually widening rift between the two, which Ruskin's parents, ignorant of the real cause of the young couple's differences, were not averse to widening further. By their jealous possessiveness and constant interference, the elder Ruskins helped to break up the marriage. Realizing, and being made to feel, that she was unwanted, Effie at length became obsessed by the idea that the three of them, father, mother and son, were scheming to get rid of her without discredit to themselves. She believed that they were planning her downfall by throwing her into the arms of the young and rising painter John Everett Millais, with whom Ruskin and Effie had become close friends through Ruskin's championing of the Pre-Raphaelite Brotherhood, of whom Millais was the leader.

Effie, lonely and neglected, and Millais, ardent and impulsive, were undoubtedly attracted to one another; but she behaved with the utmost circumspection and decorum, and he with the greatest restraint and chivalry.

Effie's health had broken down under the long strain of keeping up appearances, and at last, in April 1854, after seven years of this marriage in name only, she sought legal and friendly advice. Assisted by influential friends and by her parents, to whom she had finally confessed the embarrassing details of her predicament, she planned her escape. On the eve of a holiday on the Continent which the three Ruskins were preparing to take (Effie was not included), she left for Scotland, secretly aided by her father and mother who had come to take her home, ostensibly for her to regain her health in their care.

Effie was seen off at King's Cross Station by Ruskin, who had no suspicion that she intended to leave him. Her lawyer was to deliver a package with an explanatory letter to old Mrs. Ruskin, in which Effie spared no details of the causes of her departure. With her letter she returned to her mother-in-law her household account-books and keys and to Ruskin her wedding-ring, through his mother, with the message that she could have no further intercourse or dealings with the son.

Legal proceedings subsequently took their course, and in July 1854, Effie was granted a Decree of Nullity on the grounds of the non-consummation of the marriage. She resumed her maiden name and a year later, having accepted his proposal, she married Millais, to become, in due time and in the course of a long and happy wedded life, the mother of his eight children.

The Ruskins left, as planned, for their Continental holiday. Ruskin behaved with dignity and great composure in the face of this humiliating end to his marriage. He confessed himself 'neither . . . subdued nor materially changed', in spite of much gossip and considerable censure. He believed that, for him, the worst of it had been over long ago. He remained out of England for a year after Effie's flight, then returned to his parents' house to live with the old Ruskins until 1861, when he finally flung off the parental yoke.

Many years after his ill-fated marriage, when Ruskin was forty, he became infatuated with a girl even younger than Effie had been. Rose La Touche was nine in 1858 when he first saw her and became attracted to her. Because of her extreme involvement in her religion, an excessive devotion which eventually became a religious mania, and because of the opposition of her parents, to whom she was devotedly submissive, Ruskin's relationship with the girl never amounted to much more than a prolonged but intermittent correspondence, characterized on his side by passionate outpourings and whimsical sentimentality mingled with mawkish baby-talk.

Rose and her family lived in Ireland: she and Ruskin met only rarely after 1866; and though he eventually realized that there could be no hope of marrying her, his devotion to Rose La Touche persisted until her early death in 1875; she had been ailing since adolescence, with periods of physical collapse and mental confusion, and she died when she was only twenty-six. Ruskin was then fifty-six: the anguish and frustration of seventeen years of alternate hope and disappointment had worn him mentally and physically, but he sought in hard work his habitual solace from personal distress. He made no further attempts to find happiness in marriage.

Was Ruskin's case one of sublimation or compensation or any other form of relationship between what we call physical and spiritual? The question is too complicated for detailed discussion here; but it seems likely that his impotence was due not to any physical defect but to psychological causes. His rigorously puritan upbringing, while it had deprived him in childhood from the affection he craved, at the same time linked sensual pleasure indissolubly with guilt.

His first, abortive experience of love in adolescence and for a very young girl, fixed the emotional pattern of his later attachments. He was throughout his life strongly attracted to young girls, but his idealization of the purity and innocence of the immature was so intense that he was unable to reconcile his imaginative conception with reality, or dissociate sensual pleasure from its accompanying feelings of guilt and so was unable to bring courtship or love-making to any physically positive conclusion.

Ruskin's frustration and sense of deprivation resulting from his psychically-induced impotence may have been sublimated or compensated for in a marked, not to say obsessive, preoccupation with physical strength, which found outlet in admiration of the virile 'strong man', Carlyle's 'Hero', Bismarck's 'man of blood and iron'; it is only fair to mention, however, that admiration of physical strength has also been a trait of men who were themselves unquestionably virile and sexually potent; and in this connection some of Ruskin's contemporaries or near-contemporaries—notably Bismarck, Wagner, Maurice Barrès—come readily to mind. What is striking in Ruskin's emotional life is the unusual nature of his passions, his fixation on the immature body, mind and looks of extreme youth; the desperate desire for union with innocence. The paradoxical and tragic elements in this passion for purity were never more pathetically illustrated than in his abortive love affairs and the failure of his marriage.

It is probable, too, that some connection exists between Ruskin's passion for purity and the peculiarly pent-up vehemence—the 'Ruskinian fervour'—of his approach to art, the stylistic expression of his aesthetic ideas and doctrines. It must be emphasized that he expressed in a new way and with an exceptional personal conviction and sincerity the old, conventional ideas about art which he interpreted as a way of life that was truer, more 'real', profound and all-pervading. His puritan morality notwithstanding, he preached a philosophy of 'art for art's sake', or rather, of 'art for life's sake'. In *The Stones of Venice* (1851–53), there are maxims and paradoxes which have lost none of their truth and aptness even after more than a century.

Ruskin's feeling for beauty, perhaps even more than his social conscience—what he called 'social affection'—impelled him, accustomed from childhood as he was to riches and luxury, to condemn the ugliness and misery of early industrialism. His criticism of the existing order was particularly sharp in *Unto This Last* (1862), a book which greatly influenced the forerunners of the Labour Movement in England. In this book, speaking with great forthrightness and accusing severity, he took up the cudgels against the liberal economists' obsession with production as the prime essential, and demanded a more balanced economy. It was not 'merely wisely producing' that mattered, he said, so much as 'wisely distributing and consuming'. This might have seemed obvious but it was something that needed to be said at a time when political economists in general could not have cared less who consumed what, just so long as total production rose.

At this time, too, Ruskin advocated reforms which were considered so radical as to verge on the revolutionary; for example, he declared himself in favour of progressive income tax (though with qualitative and quantitative reservations), and of a super tax on incomes above a certain figure. His social affection often took the form of private acts of benevolence and bizarre enterprises which generally ended in failure. For a number of years he lectured on drawing and landscape art to semi-literate workmen at evening classes at the Working Men's College in Red Lion Square. In the winter of 1871 he tried to show Londoners that their streets could be kept clean. He engaged three crossing-sweepers to sweep the pavements of St Giles's, one of the dirtiest slum thoroughfares in London. The sweepers could not keep pace with the tide of mud swept up on the wheels and hoofs of horse traffic and the feet of pedestrians and the project was soon abandoned. In 1874 he opened a tea-shop in a Paddington slum district, to sell packages of good tea in small quantities at prices within the means of the poor of the district. Ruskin took great care to make the premises attractive and the shop window was decorated with taste; but the slum-dwellers preferred to buy from less artistic grocery stores or else to drink something stronger than tea, and this venture too, soon came to an end.

As Slade Professor of Fine Art at Oxford, Ruskin in 1874 preached his gospel of work and the joys of muscular exertion to a group of undergraduates, among whom were Alfred Milner, Arnold Toynbee and Oscar Wilde. He persuaded and encouraged the young men to spend several hours a week during the summer vacation working on a road-building scheme designed to prove that country roads could be both good and beautiful. Under the supervision of Ruskin's head-gardener, benevolently inspected from time to time by the Master himself and jeered at by Oxford sight-seers and farm yokels as 'gentlemen navvies', the undergraduates in white shirts, straw boaters and an occasional billycock, dug, shovelled, chipped flints and trundled wheelbarrows throughout the summer. When the road was at length finished even Ruskin had to admit that it was 'the most atrocious in the three kingdoms'; but the bailiff of the landowner across whose property the road had been built proffered the consoling observation that 'the young gentlemen had done no harm that could not easily be undone . . .'.

The idea of a governing *élite* became increasingly prominent in Ruskin's thinking. He envisaged a ruling class which should create order, harmony, prosperity and a solid morality. He urged the aristocracy to emulate Plato's philosopher-rulers and to make this their mission in life, on the lines of *The Republic* and *The Laws*. In Ruskin's Utopian state, a sort of medieval agricultural community, which was to be promoted by his Guild of St George, which he founded in 1871, social distinctions were to be emphasized by a special style of dress for each class of citizen; discipline was to be the guiding spirit: 'the youth of both sexes' were to be 'disciplined daily in the strictest practice of vocal music', and 'taught to speak truth with rigid care and obey orders with the precision of slaves'. In the Ruskinian Utopia, with discipline the order of the day, the emphasis was to be on obedience.

> 'The first essential point in the education given to the children will be the habit of instant, finely accurate, and totally unreasoning obedience to their fathers, mothers, and tutors; the same precise and unquestioning submission being required from heads of families to officers set over them.'

In short, everybody had to do as the Master said, with little or no allowance made for the freedom of the individual, in a community drilled into the spit-and-polish precision of so many guardsmen.

'Of course I am a Socialist of the most stern sort—but I am also a Tory of the sternest sort', said Ruskin; but at times his brand of socialism seems little more than a longing for the good old days; at other times it has points in common with the dictatorships of today. His pronouncements, similar to those of other—English and French just as much as German—anti-liberals of his time, seem to us nowadays to be fraught with sinister premonitions of Nazism and fascism.

Ruskin's various arguments concerning war, especially those in *Time and Tide* (1867) and *The Crown of Wild Olive* (1873) are recommended reading as examples of the confusion and *naiveté* which permeated his thinking. In certain passages in these works he saw war as a madness, 'insane war, founded on popular passion, whether of pride, fear, or acquisitiveness', but a madness that would disappear with the education of the masses. He added that where nations are concerned strength does not

> 'depend on extent of territory, any more than upon number of population. The strength is in the men, and in their unity and virtue, not in their standing room: a little group of wise hearts is better than a wilderness full of fools; and only that nation gains true territory, which gains itself.'

He urged women, in time of war, to dress in black so that men would be induced immediately and irresistibly to make peace so that they could see their women folk in brightly coloured clothing again. 'Let every lady in the upper class of civilized Europe simply vow that, while any cruel war proceeds, she will wear *black;* a mute's black, with no jewel, no ornament, no excuse for, or evasion into, prettiness—I tell you again, no war would last a week.'

After this, heroics abruptly got the upper hand: he extolled war as the only salvation:

> 'I found, in brief, that all great nations learned their truth of word, and strength of thought, in war; that they were nourished in war, and wasted by peace; taught by war and deceived by peace; trained by war, and betrayed by peace;—in a word, that they were born in war and expired in peace.'

He saw modern warfare, with its long-range weapons, as vulgar, unaesthetic and unchivalrous—he was writing at a time when Krupp's all-steel guns could hurl their missiles for what then seemed astonishing distances. He wrote:

> 'You must not make it a question which of the combatants has the longest gun, or which has got behind the biggest tree, or which has less wind in his face, or which has . . . the angriest mob at his back. . . . But decide your battle by pure trial which has the strongest arms and steadiest heart,—and you have gone far to decide a great many matters besides, and to decide them rightly.'

By the strongest arms and the bravest heart deciding a battle he meant that the sword and spear should once more become the accepted weapons in warfare, in the chivalrous man-to-man and weapon-to-weapon combat of the knights of old.

Ruskin's imperialism grew ever more pronounced and more grandiloquent. England, he said, must

> 'found colonies as fast and as far as she is able . . . seizing every piece of fruitful waste ground she can set her foot on, and there teaching these her colonists that their chief virtue is to be fidelity

to their country, and that their first aim is to be to advance the power of England by land and sea . . . These colonies must be fastened fleets; and every man of them must be under authority of captains and officers, whose better command is to be over fields and streets instead of ships of the line; and England in these her motionless navies . . . is to "expect every man to do his duty".'

Ruskin, it will be seen, like so many other influential philosophers of the time, offered such rich and varied fare that there was something to suit all tastes. Nor must it be forgotten that all these theories were served up with a vigorous and winning eloquence, with the kind of eagerness and personal appeal displayed by a man who knows he has got his victim into a corner. To be sure, the rhetoric is not exaggerated and is far from being, as it was with Carlyle, a sort of spiritual stuttering and stammering; but the impression of emotion on the verge of bursting the bonds of reason seems just as strong as with Carlyle.

Curiously enough, Ruskin influenced two later writers who are not usually connected with him. One was Marcel Proust, who translated Ruskin and (it is no exaggeration to say) idolized him. When Proust first read Ruskin's early critical works on art and aesthetics he wrote:

'The world was once more given an immense value in my eyes. My admiration for Ruskin gave such importance to the things he had taught me to love that they seemed to be of greater value than life itself.'

Pursuing this thought, Proust wrote:

'The beauty to which his life was dedicated was not considered by him to be an object of pleasure designed to fill life with delight, but a reality infinitely more important than life itself, and one for which he would have given his own. The whole of Ruskin's aesthetic doctrine can be seen to issue from this belief.'

What he says of Ruskin expresses Proust's own philosophy and is the motivation—insofar as it was a conscious one—of his own writing. Even on other points, not least that of style, Ruskin's influence on Proust is noticeable.

The other writer in whose work Ruskin's influence can be detected is D. H. Lawrence; and here, too, it can be fairly claimed that Lawrence's ideas owe much to Ruskin. The influence is apparent not so much with regard to the philosophy of art as a way of life, as in Lawrence's ideas about industrialism and its debasing effect on human beings; and also in the blend of tenderness and brutality in Lawrence's presentation of social conditions. His prose style bears a striking resemblance to

Ruskin's, especially when he starts to philosophize—in those turgid, confused and tortuous sentences, among which phrases of brilliant intelligence gleam and glint intermittently through the murk of the prose. The likeness to Ruskin is remarkable even in Lawrence's ability to fuse descriptive writing with a message. Ruskin and Lawrence resemble each other, Peter Quennell observed in his biography of Ruskin, 'both in their poetic brilliance and their illogicality', and he quotes as an example of this a passage from *The Queen of the Air* (1869), in which Ruskin muses on the snake as a hieratic symbol and as a natural mystery:

> 'The serpent crest of the King's crown, or of the god's, on the pillars of Egypt, is a mystery; but the serpent itself, gliding past the pillar's foot, is it less a mystery? Is there, indeed, no tongue, except the mute forked flash from its lips, in that running brook of horror on the ground? . . . that rivulet of smooth silver . . . It literally rows on the earth, with every scale for an oar . . . A wave, but without a wind! a current, but with no fall! all the body moving at the same instant . . . one soundless, causeless march of sequent rings, and spectral procession of spotted dust, with dissolution in its fangs, discoloration in its coils . . .'

Lawrence's mystical invocation in *The Plumed Serpent* (1926), inspired by the Aztec snake-cult, bears some comparison with Ruskin's musings despite its Freudian symbolism:

> 'Serpent of the earth, . . . snake that lies in the fire at the heart of the world, come! Snake of the fire of the heart of the world, coil like gold round my ankles, and rise like life around my knee, and lay your head against my thigh . . . The great Snake coils and uncoils the plasm of his folds, and stars appear, and worlds fade out . . . But dreads arise and fade in the sleep of the Snake . . . And worlds arise as dreams, and are gone as dreams . . . And man is a dream in the sleep of the Snake . . . And the dream of the body is the stillness of a flower in the dark . . . In the core of the flower, the glimmering, wakeless Snake.'

As Ruskin grew older his ideas became more disconnected, his imagery more confused, his prose more fervid and highly coloured. From 1872 onward he had become increasingly eccentric and had shown signs of mental confusion accompanied by delusions and hallucinations. The ultimate frustration, by Rose La Touche's death in May 1875, of his self-deluded hopes of a normal love relationship, affected him profoundly. He sought forgetfulness in work, filling his life with ceaseless activity, his mind seething with half-formulated ideas and projects which he dropped in varying degrees of incompletion. His manner to acquaintances and friends alternated between gentleness, with moods of effusive, sentimental affection, and bouts of vehement irascibility. Opposition made him furious; only complete obedience satisfied him. It became increasingly difficult for him to write: he suffered from dizziness and giddy spells, and the inability to assemble his ideas made him morose and irritable. His discourse was often inconsequent or extravagant and at times his friends, believing that they detected a peculiar look on his face, feared for both his mind and his bodily health. His obsessive sense of sin and guilt returned with renewed force; and all the while a torrent of uncontrollable ideas surged in bewildering confusion through his mind. Ruskin himself sensed an approaching breakdown, feeling that his mind was 'tottery', as he put it, and that he was sinking into 'dreamy scatterment and bewilderment'.

His first serious mental breakdown occurred in 1877. He recovered but, between 1881 and 1887, suffered five recurring attacks of delirium. After a year of convalescence from the last, he was able to travel, through France and Switzerland to Venice. But returning homeward he was stricken in Paris by the most severe attack up to then. Brought back to Brantwood, his home overlooking Coniston Water, he recovered sufficiently to be able to complete, in 1889, his autobiographical *Praeterita*, which he had started in 1885. The book was finished with difficulty and unsatisfactorily; having begun superbly, *Praeterita* slowly disintegrated, to become disjointed and confused and to peter out in fragmentary evocative reminiscence and in passages of decorative imagery as fitful as the fireflies he evoked in the book's famous closing phrases. He was seventy, a tired old man with an exhausted mind. After a final attack of delirium in 1889 he never again left Brantwood, where he lived on for just over another decade.

Ruskin was cared for in his last days by his cousin Joan Severn (*née* Agnew) and her husband the painter Arthur Severn, both of whom had been his inseparable companions for many years. The old man passed his days seated in his study or roaming the gardens of Brantwood in the watchful company of his valet and his dog. He had grown a beard and let his hair grow long after his first breakdown and now presented a patriarchal appearance. He led an existence of placid monotony, rarely speaking, gentle and docile in the stupor of his mental derangement. It was a brief attack, not of delirium but of influenza, that ended his life in January 1900, at the age of eighty-one.

The offered burial in Poets' Corner in Westminster Abbey was refused by his cousin, and Ruskin lies buried, as he had once said that he wished to be, at Coniston. His personal hopes and fears, his aspirations for mankind and his prophesies full of foreboding, lie buried in the thirty-nine massive volumes of his writings. As a young man, in 1848, he had written to his father from Venice: 'I seem born to conceive what I cannot execute, recommend what I cannot obtain, and mourn over what I cannot save.' Though his doctrines had a wide-reaching influence, he still believed at the end of his life that he had accomplished little or nothing, that he had, indeed, failed in his mission. He died, a deranged and mute oracle, at the dawn of a century which was to see all too few of his noblest hopes and aspirations fulfilled, but many of his most baleful prophesies come true.

A Marriage of Minds: John Stuart Mill and Harriet Taylor

In his autobiography, perhaps the most fascinating of all his writings, John Stuart Mill paid his wife Harriet a tribute of wondering admiration that is surely unique in the history of married couples.

Mill compared her 'in general spiritual characteristics, as well as in temperament and organization' to Shelley whom he believed she far surpassed, for 'in thought and intellect, Shelley, so far as his powers were developed in his short life, was but a child compared with what she ultimately became'. Harriet's gifts of feeling and imagination would, as Mill saw her, 'have fitted her to be a consummate artist'. As for public speaking, he felt that 'her fiery and tender soul and her vigorous eloquence would certainly have made her a great orator'. Nor was this all: 'Her profound knowledge of human nature and discernment and sagacity in practical life, would, in times when such a *carrière* was open to women, have made her eminent among the rulers of mankind'. As a philosopher, too, this paragon of all excellencies moved on a similar plane of intellectual superiority, in which Mill found that vigour and truth of imagination, delicacy of perception, accuracy and nicety of observation were only equalled by a 'profundity of speculative thought, and by a practical judgement and discernment next to infallible'.

In prefaces to some of his other writings, published after her death, he took further opportunities of proclaiming his appreciation of Harriet. His essay *On Liberty* was dedicated

> 'to the beloved and deplored memory of her who was the inspirer, and in part the author, of all that is best in my writings . . . Were I but capable of interpreting to the world one half of the great thoughts and noble feelings which are buried in her grave, I should be the medium of a greater benefit to it than is ever likely to arise from anything I can write, unprompted and unassisted by her all but unrivalled wisdom.'

Even Helen Taylor, Harriet's daughter, the youngest child of her first marriage, received similar praise. When Harriet died, Mill's step-daughter became his companion, helper and adviser, remaining with him and caring for him for the rest of his life. Helen Taylor altered or suppressed various passages, including the praise of herself, in Mill's autobiography which was published shortly after his death in 1873; and though she left instructions that the unexpurgated autobiography was to be published a year after her own death (which took place in 1907) it was not until 1924 that an unaltered and uncut version was published. Mill's praise of Helen could then be seen to be as glowing as his praise of Harriet. Helen, he said, had inherited much of her mother's wisdom and all of her nobleness of character and was possessed, moreover, of an ever-growing talent, original thought and soundness of practical judgement.

> 'Surely no one ever before was so fortunate, as, after such a loss as mine, to draw another prize in the lottery of life—another companion, stimulator, adviser, and instructor of the rarest quality. Whoever, either now, or hereafter, may think of me and the work I have done, must never forget that it is the product not of one intellect and conscience but of three, the least considerable of whom and above all the least original, is the one whose name is attached to it.'

Mill, though exceptionally modest, was not devoid of self-esteem. Nevertheless, he regarded himself as intellectually insignificant compared with Harriet and he told her as much: 'I am but fit to be one wheel in an engine not to be the self moving engine itself—a real majestic intellect, not to say moral nature like yours, I can only look up to and admire.' So it is not surprising that Mill, though he believed that an adequate biography and psychological history of Harriet would be impossible because there was so little material existing, beyond the facts of her birthplace, parentage and a few dates, also believed that 'were it possible in a memoir to have the formation and growth of a mind like hers portrayed, to do so would be as valuable a benefit to mankind as was ever conferred by a biography'.

The basis for such a biography was subsequently compiled and edited, with a connecting commentary, by Professor F. A. Hayek who felt that his book *John Stuart Mill and Harriet Taylor: Their Friendship and Subsequent Marriage* (1951), might be regarded as material for a book rather than the finished product. It was left to Michael St John Packe to produce the finished product, a biography, *The Life of John Stuart Mill,* which appeared in 1954, with a preface by Professor Hayek, who considered it the definitive biography which had been so long awaited.

For his own book, Professor Hayek had been fortunate in being able to bring together a great number of Mill's and Harriet's intimate letters which had come to rest in the collections of university libraries in England and America; and by his selection of the most interesting of the letters he was able to throw fresh light on the relationship of the couple with each other and with Harriet's first husband, as well as on the collaboration and achievements of Mill and Harriet before and after their marriage. Above all, the book provided a portrait of Harriet that had long been wanting.

Apart from Mill's adoring encomiums, which seemed sheer or vast delusions to a number of his friends, and which, if true, would have made Harriet the most remarkable woman who ever lived, her personality has been revealed mainly through a number of casual, critical and not always kind vignettes written by friends, acquaintances or erstwhile friends. Chief among these last was Carlyle, who wrote of her kindly enough before he began to hate her, but whose later scepticism about her genius has largely determined posterity's general impression of her mind and character. Nor was Jane Welsh Carlyle, along with other female acquaintances, behindhand in casting a critical eye over Harriet. Professor Hayek's publication of the intimate correspondence of Mill and Harriet has provided fresh grounds on which to weigh the evidence and to make a revised judgement.

Mill met Harriet in 1830, a few years after he had emerged from the first of his mental crises, which had begun to take possession of him in the autumn of 1826. At twenty, this 'manufactured man', the product of his father's and Jeremy Bentham's educational experiment, was an intellectually highly-developed but emotionally stunted 'radical reasoning machine', mentally exhausted by sustained and intensive study. During a period of deep depression and melancholia, 'the dry, heavy dejection of the winter of 1826–7', he feared that the habit of intellectual analysis had worn away his ability to feel, 'and there seemed no power in nature sufficient to begin the formation of character anew, and create in a mind now irretrievably analytic, fresh associations of pleasure with any of the objects of human desire'.

A chance reading of the *Mémoires* of Marmontel, the eighteenth-century playwright and courtier, proved a cathartic experience and the turning-point in Mill's recovery. When he came to the passage in which Marmontel tells of his father's death, his mother's despair, the poverty in which the family were left and 'the sudden inspiration by which he, a mere boy, felt and made them feel that he would be everything to them—would supply the place of all they had lost', Mill was moved to tears. This made him realize that he was still able to feel and from that time onward the dark cloud of depression began to disperse. He gradually began to enjoy life again and though he had several relapses, sometimes lasting for months, and though there were recurrences of his melancholia later in life, he was never again as utterly miserable and without hope as in that winter of 1826.

A dinner party changed the whole course of Mill's life and work. In the summer of 1830 he was invited to dine at the home of John Taylor, a prosperous junior partner in a family firm of wholesale druggists. Taylor, a Radical and a Unitarian churchgoer, was, to quote Carlyle 'an innocent, dull good man'. His wife, Harriet, who came from a family of middle-class Dissenters, was young, beautiful, intelligent, high-minded. Eleven years younger than her husband, she had been married at eighteen and was now the devoted mother of two small sons. She was competent, cultured and had literary aspirations. She moved in a circle of friends which included the preacher William Fox (on whose recommendation Mill had been invited to dinner), Harriet Martineau, the first professional woman journalist and some intelligent young men including John Arthur Roebuck and George Graham, who were close friends of Mill's.

Harriet was restless and dissatisfied. Though fond of her husband, who doted on her, she had that distaste for the physical side of marriage which was common to so many Victorian wives; besides, though Taylor was 'honourable, amiable, genial and kindly', she considered him to be her inferior in culture and refinement, and he bored her. She was in search of a kindred spirit. Mill, who had never up to that time 'looked a female creature, not even a cow, in the face'—as Carlyle was later to say—now 'found himself opposite those great dark eyes that were flashing unutterable things'.

The intense mutual interest which sprang up between the two young people soon turned to love. Yet though Mill was enchanted by Harriet's beauty, charm and grace and she was equally captivated by his looks and personality, the pair were consumed, above all, by a more austere passion, one which sprang from a common source in intellect and ideas. They met constantly, exchanged letters and manuscripts, discussed theories. Their defiance of Victorian convention caused gossip, even though they did nothing that all the world might not see. Their friendship caused considerable embarrassment to John Taylor who tried, without success, to persuade Harriet not to see Mill again.

There were several interruptions to their platonic idyll and during the first of these, about a year after she had met Mill, Harriet bore Taylor a third child, their daughter Helen. But she would not give up Mill's friendship. Eventually husband, wife and lover reached a compromise in the interests of respectability. Taylor agreed to the friendship, Harriet agreed to keep up the appearances of married life. Divorce was out of the question because of the laws and conventions of the time. Harriet decided, accordingly, that though she must sacrifice her social position because of Mill, she must also sacrifice her love for Mill for the sake of her husband and children. Henceforward her relationship with the two men would be one of platonic friendship. In the ensuing years she lived for most of the time in the country, first at Keston Heath, in Kent, and from 1839 at Walton-on-Thames, where Taylor rented a cottage for her; or she indulged her insatiable desire to travel. She and Mill met regularly, mostly at weekends, and when she travelled abroad he generally managed to spend some of the time with her. This arrangement continued for some twenty years, until Taylor's death in 1849. Two years later Mill and Harriet were married and withdrew to almost complete seclusion in a blissful but hard-working *solitude à deux* at Blackheath. Mill, and especially Harriet, for all their flouting of convention, dreaded being talked about and were highly sensitive to ridicule. During the 1840s they had withdrawn entirely from society and their seclusion in Blackheath after their marriage was prompted by the same dislike of gossip.

Their happiness in the ensuing years was clouded, though not wrecked, by ill health: their continual nervous ailments and finally the tuberculosis with which whole families infected each other in Victorian times, ignorant that the disease was contagious and believing it hereditary and incurable. Mill whose father, James Mill, had infected most of his nine children, transmitted the disease to Harriet. A year after their marriage, unmistakable signs made them realize that they were both consumptive. Thereafter ill-health dogged them constantly. In the autumn of 1868, after little more than seven years of supremely happy marriage with Mill, they were travelling to the south of France to escape the cold and damp of the English winter. There, quite suddenly, Harriet died in a hotel bedroom in Avignon.

Mill, who had believed himself doomed to early death at the beginning of 1850, outlived Harriet by fifteen years. Though devoted to her memory he gained fresh inspiration from her youngest child, Helen Taylor, who lavished on him to the end of his life a devotion and care equal to her mother's.

The letters of Mill and Harriet reveal a strange and moving love story. They lived for each other and for their work together. This was particularly true of Mill who, after he had met Harriet, gradually dropped old friends, especially those who deplored or criticized the relationship. Then, from the start of his friendship with Harriet he appears to have become indifferent to his family. After his marriage he broke with his mother and surviving brother and sisters because he believed, though apparently without grounds, that they disliked Harriet and had slighted, even slandered her. He treated them with great coldness, took offence at their letters attempting reconciliation and finally severed himself altogether from them. Harriet, on the other hand, while Taylor was alive, still reserved a great deal of her affection for her husband and children. Between Harriet and Mill there was a singular identity of affection and understanding, as their correspondence reveals in its countless expressions of love and admiration, attachment and dependence.

There was no erotic relationship between Mill and Harriet before they married and it is even doubtful if the marriage was ever consummated. Towards the end of her life Harriet stated that since the beginning of her friendship with Mill she had been no more than a *Seelenfreundin* to both him and her husband.

The platonic nature of Harriet's relationship with Mill is borne out even more conclusively by some of their letters, and in particular one of 1854, in which Harriet discussed with Mill his proposed autobiography. She emphasized that the book must make clear the implications of their relationship:

> 'strong affection, intimacy of friendship, and no impropriety. It seems to me an edifying picture for those poor wretches who cannot conceive friendship but in sex—nor believe that expediency and consideration for feelings of others can conquer sensuality.'

To judge from this it seems clear that such abstemiousness was not only a matter of coolness of temperament but also of a definite moral attitude. This may seem surprising, considering the irony and scepticism with which the two lovers regarded current ideas about religion, ethics, the conventions and even the fundamental Victorian theory of the 'purity' of women. The letters make clear, however, that all appearances to the contrary, a rigid sexual morality came naturally to them. They constantly discussed happiness as the principal aim of humanity, but Mill's ethics caused him to regard the happiness which can be achieved by self-discipline, self-denial and self-sacrifice as so much finer and more intense than the happiness which consists in the fulfilment of ordinary human wishes and desires, that with him the morale of personal happiness became all too plainly a puritanical one.

In the view of St John Packe, the attitude of Mill and Harriet to sex was, as Harriet had stated, 'that it was a question of personal inclination limited by the expediency of the circumstances. . . . In their own case inclination was sapped by intellectual prejudices.' They regarded as revolting and unjust the sexual relation sanctioned by society, in which women because they were not strong enough to resist were set aside for the satisfaction of the animal requirements of men and were denied all free share in the arrangements and decisions of even that one function. This state of affairs, in the eyes of Harriet and Mill, 'debased society to the level of a farmyard'. Therefore, although they loved one another deeply, 'each was personally disposed to stop short of physical passion, and they were sure that for example's sake they were bound to do so'.

Self-discipline must have been helped considerably by a certain emotional coolness. In one of her letters of September 1837 Harriet writes of the joy of holding hands: 'When I think that I shall not hold your hand until Tuesday the time is so long and my hand so useless. Adieu my delight'. But there is no mention in their letters of kisses or other endearments, though in the early days of their love affair they had once been seen in Paris—and the information was passed on by Carlyle —'eating grapes together off one bunch like two love birds'.

Since the end of the 1830s Harriet had been living in the cottage in Walton-on-Thames which her husband had rented for her. She rarely went to London, but Mill apparently made regular weekend visits to which she looked forward with longing: 'I am to see you on Saturday; indeed I could not get on without. . . . Adieu my only and most precious —till Saturday. Dear Saturday!'

In 1832 Harriet, at Mill's request, made several drafts of her opinions about the relationship of men and women and the position of women with regard to marriage. In the most complete of these drafts that exists she observed: 'Whether nature made a difference in the nature of men & women or not, it seems now that all men, with the exception of a few lofty minded, are sensualists more or less—women on the contrary are quite exempt from this trait, however it may appear otherwise in the cases of some.' It is obvious that Mill was one of the lofty-minded exceptions she mentioned.

The absence of lust seems, however, to have been compensated for by another of the deadly sins—a mutual revelling in pride. When, in 1853, the deteriorating health of both Mill and Harriet gave signs of approaching serious illness, he wrote to her:

> 'We must finish the best we have got to say, & not only that, but publish it while we are alive. I do not see what living depository there is likely to be of our thoughts, or who in this weak generation that is growing up will even be capable of thoroughly mastering & assimilating your ideas, much less of re-originating them—so we must write them & print them, & they can wait till there are again thinkers.'

The couple regarded friends and enemies alike with a certain contempt. Macaulay, according to Mill, was 'what all cockneys are, an intellectual dwarf . . . without a germ of principle of further growth in his whole being'. Lytton Bulwer was 'an incarnation of vanity and dishonesty'. In Harriet's eyes Toqueville was

> 'a notable specimen of the class which includes such people as the Sterlings, Romillys, Carlyles, Austins—the gentility class—weak in

> moral, narrow in intellect, timid, infinitely conceited and gossiping. There are very few men in this country who can seem other than more or less respectable puppets to us.'

Grote the historian, Auguste Comte, Miss Martineau, were written off in a few disparaging words as uninspired mediocrities. It might be thought that to sacrifice themselves with such energy for so miserable a breed would have been a dismal undertaking—but Harriet and Mill were apparently undaunted and took humanity in their stride.

Harriet was all the world to Mill, in every respect the most important being, brooking no comparison; he took second place beside her, though the tremendous fact that she loved him exalted him almost to her level. It was commonly accepted that Harriet was his helpmate, collaborator and the joint author of his works. This was his own fervent belief, proclaimed ceaselessly to her and to others. He never tired of repeating that he was Harriet's mouthpiece, a mere 'conduit for ideas'. A number of people, however, considered her a subordinate and very minor assistant. Carlyle, who said many uncharitable things about her told John Morley that 'She was full of unwise intellect, asking and reasking stupid questions'.

Harriet's share in Mill's writings and her influence on them and on him has for long been a subject of controversy. Professor Hayek sides with Mill on this point, inasmuch as he considers exact Mill's numerous statements about his indebtedness to Harriet and her influence. It might be thought that Professor Hayek overrates this influence, but possibly his study of the letters caused him to react sharply against the prevailing opinion that her overwhelming intellect, her influence and her joint authorship of most of Mill's greatest works are figments of the imagination, especially of Mill's. But no reader of the Mill-Taylor correspondence can fail to be convinced of the sharp intellect of the female partner in this marriage of minds and the extreme importance of her share in the works as they finally emerged, in particular in his greatest achievement *The Principles of Political Economy* (1848), which he altered on Harriet's demand and to which he added a chapter on the working classes written by her.

In what other ways did Harriet influence Mill? Even on this point Professor Hayek's views are opposed to those commonly held. It is his belief that

> 'her influence on his thought and outlook, whatever her capacities may have been were quite as great as Mill asserts, but that they acted in a way somewhat different from what is commonly believed. Far from it having been the sentimental, it was the rationalist element in Mill's thought which was mainly strengthened by her influence.'

This view, Professor Hayek writes, has hitherto been expressed, as far as he knows, only by one writer, the Swedish economist Knut Hagberg, in his book *Personalities and Powers* (1930). According to this writer:

> 'it is obvious that it was this woman who made him into a Radical rationalist. She has given the impress of her personality to all his greater works; to all her opinions Mill has given the form of philosophic maxims. But even in his most arid reflexions on woman's similarity with man and on the nature of Logic, Mill is really a romantic.'

Even here it might be thought that in the light of what is known about Mill and Harriet's collaboration, this is a somewhat exaggerated view. The romantic streak in Mill's character is evident from his autobiography; but is it not possible that this feature was practically as strong in Harriet's make-up? Both he and she worked systematically to become perfect rationalists—with, it may be conceded, the reservation that they would work for the good of humanity—and both of them seem to have been successful in their aim. They became progressively wiser, drier and more and more free of ordinary human weaknesses. It is hardly possible to put either of them into any fixed category of romantic-rationalist or rationalist-romantic. What, one wonders, would have been revealed if Harriet had written *her* autobiography? It seems accurate to say, as Mill did, that his passionate espousal of the emancipation of women was influenced by Harriet; but he denied that his strong convictions on the subject were adopted or learnt from her—and indeed, he emphasized that 'these convictions were among the earliest results of the application of my mind to political subjects'. But it was his and Harriet's common interest in this topic which fostered their close intimacy from the start of their friendship.

Their letters also indicate that Mill's increasing sympathy with socialism, which makes its appearance in the third edition of the *Political Economy*, was due to Harriet's influence, and in fact, numerous passages in the chapters on 'Property' and 'The Futurity of the Labouring Classes' were either dictated by Harriet or docilely altered at her behest by Mill: 'I have followed to the letter every recommendation,' he told her. Some of the changes were made against his convictions; nevertheless, he made them, but with the justification that 'they were probably only the progress we have been always making and by thinking sufficiently I should probably come to think the same—as is almost always the case, I believe always, when we think long enough'.

It is clear, in such instances, that Harriet's more robust and ruthless intelligence drove Mill to assume positions that were more daringly radical. After her death, however, he tended to revert to his former Liberalism.

An Australian scholar, H. O. Pappe, in his book *John Stuart Mill and the Harriet Taylor Myth* (1932) has made a reassessment of Harriet's influence on Mill. As the title suggests, Pappe attempts to prove that earlier works about the couple have considerably overrated Harriet's influence and, indeed, to such an extent that the influence she is supposed to have exercised over Mill and his work is virtually a myth. According to Pappe, Mill's intellectual case history shows that in all essentials he developed his ideas single handed—by following up trains of thought from initial points of departure which he had reached earlier—before he met Harriet. As a beloved and loving woman she inspired him through her interest and enthusiasm and there are some points on which her direct influence is certain, but 'Mill without Harriet would still have been Mill', whereas Harriet 'would never have made her mark in the world without Mill'. Her co-operation with him, Pappe observes, 'was in difficult circumstances, an early example of that husband-wife partnership which, thanks to the efforts of people like the Mills, has blissfully become frequent in our time'.

Pappe also explores various other avenues. He emphasizes the fact that Mill always overestimated his indebtedness to others; the lengths to which his generosity could lead him are evident in his exaggerated tribute to Helen Taylor. And while Mill, impelled by 'a masochistic feeling of guilt', generally praised Harriet's contributions, he simultaneously observed time and again in connection with one or other of his works, that his ideas on the subject had been developed independently.

Finally Pappe gives examples of several subjects upon which Mill had formed his own opinion—especially with regard to women's rights and socialism—before he could have been influenced by Harriet, even though her influence on him eventually led to more outspoken and aggressive statements on these subjects.

Pappe concludes that despite her weaknesses, such as her jealousy of Mill's friends, Harriet admirably fulfilled the role of perfect friend, united with Mill in the same likes and dislikes, capable of sharing his battles and perplexities as well as his solitude: 'But this is no reason for elevating her secondary contribution to a primary influence in our intellectual heritage'.

It would be rash to take sides in the dispute over whether Harriet's influence on Mill was a predominant factor or not; such a task would need an exhaustive study of the stages of Mill's authorship before it could lead to any definite conclusions. The general impression remains, however, that there has been considerable exaggeration of both sides of the case. On the basis of the available sources of information, Hayek's view of the extent of Harriet's contribution seems hardly justifiable, but since Pappe's view that the influence was negligible is based on the same sources a similar doubt arises.

It would be unfair not to point out the admirable sensitivity, insight and contempt for the conventional which can be found throughout Harriet's letters, which reveal, moreover, a nature of markedly feminine grace and charm. When John Taylor lay dying of cancer Harriet nursed him devotedly, rarely absent from his bedside during the two exhausting months of his last illness. She tended him in anguish, her heart wrung by deep grief and indignation at his patiently-born sufferings. 'Why should he have these torments to endure! what good to anybody is all this—he never hurt or harmed a creature on earth,' she wrote to Mill. A letter of Mill's provoked her to relieve her feelings in exasperation:

> 'You talk of my writing to you "at some odd time when a change of subject of thought may be rather a relief than otherwise"! *odd time!* indeed you must be ignorant profoundly of all that *friendship* and *anxiety* means when you can use such pitiful narrow hearted expressions. The sentence appears to have come from the pen of one of the Miss Taylors. It is the puerility of thought & feeling of any utterly headless & heartless pattern of propriety old maid.
>
> 'As to "*odd time*" I *told* you that I have not a moment unfilled by things to be done when not actually standing by the bedside or supporting the invalid—& as to "change of subject of thought a relief"! Good God should you think it a relief to think of somebody else some acquaintance or what not while *I* was dying?'

Poor Mill had only one thought when little more than seven years later Harriet, now his wife, died suddenly at Avignon.

He eventually made his home there, close to the shrine that was Harriet's grave, and for the white marble tomb he composed an adoring epitaph, florid with encomiums and capitals:

> To the Beloved Memory of Harriet Mill, The Dearly Beloved and Deeply Regretted Wife of John Stuart Mill. Her Great and Loving Heart, Her Noble Soul, Her Clear Powerful and Original Comprehensive Intellect Made Her the Guide and Support, the Instructor in Wisdom And the Example in Goodness, As she was the Sole Earthly Delight of Those who had the Happiness to Belong to Her, As Earnest for the Public Good As She was Generous and Devoted to All who Surrounded Her, Her Influence has been Felt In Many of the Greatest Improvements of the Age And will be in Those still to Come. Were There but a few Hearts and Intellects Like Hers The Earth would Already Become The Hoped-For Heaven. She Died, To the Irreparable Loss of Those who Survive her. At Avignon, Nov. 3 1858.

Fifteen years later, after an illness of three days, Mill, too, died in Avignon and was laid beside Harriet in the chaste marble tomb.

Singer, Seer and Teacher: Alfred, Lord Tennyson

Was Tennyson a poet of the first rank or merely a second-rater? The question has been put time and time again, though his critics have phrased it more subtly and their scale and methods of assessment are less crude than those used in marking up examination papers. The major poet of the Victorian age has at times come close to being dismissed as a minor poet—a class to which, according to Stephen Spender, even the mighty Shelley has been relegated now for several decades.

Tennyson's examiners, awarding him high or low marks, have employed vague, contradictory and often loosely formulated standards. Their requirements of a poet include intelligent thinking or at least ideas that are representative of the time; they look for passion and for commitment; other stipulations they make are for social awareness, or novel technical devices or simply—the vaguest requirement of all—great artistry.

Opinions tend to fall into considerable confusion, as for instance in W. H. Auden's stylish 'Introduction' to *Tennyson: A Selection from the Poems* (1946). In this appreciation, its stylishness notwithstanding, an epigrammatic jumble of half-truths makes the claim that Tennyson 'had the finest ear of any English poet; he was undoubtedly the stupidest; there was little about melancholia that he didn't know; there was little else that he did'.

However much his critics may disagree about his poetic rank, there seems to be general agreement that more than any other writer of his time Tennyson expressed the spirit of the Victorian Age. One of his many biographers, R. Brimley Johnson, in *Tennyson and his Poetry* (1913), wrote:

> 'Tennyson is perhaps the most typical genius of the Victorian era in its maturity. There is a sense in which he was pre-eminent among those greater than himself. He represents the art of his age, as Queen Victoria exemplified its domestic, and Gladstone its political, morality.'

Alfred Noyes in his *Tennyson* (1932) believed that the Laureate would be praised by posterity for the very attribute for which he was reputed at the time Noyes was writing: 'the fact that he did so completely sum up and express the great Victorian era in which he lived'; while

G. M. Young in *Victorian England: Portrait of an Age* (1936), considered Tennyson 'always the most punctual exponent of contemporary feeling'. Similar statements have continued unabated, even in appraisals made in later years. A recent biographer, Joanna Richardson, has called him 'The Pre-Eminent Victorian' and has used the phrase as the title of her study of the poet's life and work.

The critical approach to Tennyson has changed, however, in recent decades, as indeed the attitude to the Victorians has changed. Between the two World Wars the mocking and belittling appraisal of the Lytton Strachey school was dominant. It was then fashionable to regard and to present the Victorians as a collection of oddities whose peculiar habits and views possessed the merit of being amusing to the more enlightened and disillusioned. Harold Nicolson's *Tennyson: Aspects of His Life, Character and Poetry* (1923), must be placed in this category, despite its subtlety and its deliberate avoidance of the harsh judgement or the waspish comment. Like other critical studies of its time, it sets up Tennyson as 'the embodiment of the smug, materialistic Victorian ethic', and believes, moreover, that the poet pandered to this ethic, so falsifying and betraying his genius. This approach is now outdated. The Victorians are no longer ridiculed, but nowadays are taken seriously, and attempts have been made to show that they were no more stupid or peculiar than we are. Our attitude to the Victorian age is thought to have become one of nostalgic longing because the period now seems to us to have been so much more stable and secure than our own. This modified view of the Victorians, and an increasingly benevolent and respectful attitude to Tennyson, has characterized a number of studies of him written in recent times. Two such works are Joanna Richardson's *The Pre-Eminent Victorian* (1962) and Valerie Pitt's *Tennyson Laureate* (1962), a meticulous analysis of Tennyson's poetic inspiration, style and technique, and development.

The theory that Tennyson was universally considered to be the spokesman of Victorianism seems, nevertheless, to have persisted in all its original force. But what exactly does this mean? Well, for those who find the theory convincing, it means that the Victorian period was conspicious for ideas peculiar to the age, for a particular kind of morality, for a way of life which bore the unmistakable stamp of what has come to be known as Victorianism. It means, too, that Tennyson personified to a great degree these Victorian characteristics. Chronology, at least, would appear to make the theory fit. Queen Victoria was born in 1809 and reigned from 1837 to 1901. Tennyson was born in 1809 and had written much of his poetry by the time Victoria came to the throne, although it was not until after 1845, when he received his first official recognition (a pension of £200 offered to him by the Queen, on Sir Robert Peel's recommendation), that his growing prestige began to establish him in the eyes of the Victorians as a 'great' poet. He died in 1892, nine years before the Queen.

Other circumstances support the theory that Tennyson was a representative Victorian, 'the voice of a whole period and a phase of culture'.

The publication of *In Memoriam* in June 1850 established his fame and (in the opinion of Elizabeth Barrett Browning) placed him on a pedestal where he was 'recognized as a master spirit by the great public'. When Wordsworth, the existing Poet Laureate, died in 1850, a preliminary but unsuccessful search was made for a poet worthy to fill the vacancy. *In Memoriam* had appeared that year and was much admired by the Queen and the Prince Consort. Discreet enquiries about Tennyson's character and position were made and Prince Albert was informed that 'Mr Tennyson is a fit person to be Poet Laureate'. So, in November 1850 Tennyson was appointed to fill the vacancy 'in the room of William Wordsworth Esq., deceased'. It was thought that he would not diminish the lustre with which Wordsworth as Poet Laureate had invested the office; on the contrary, it was believed that he would enhance it. In some quarters this belief was held on the curious (and curiously Victorian) grounds that 'he was more a *gentleman*, in the formal British sense . . .'

Tennyson's sense of poetic mission led him to take his role of Poet Laureate very seriously. This meant that he felt it his duty to write poems for all sorts of occasions, from the deaths of great public figures to royal weddings and the nation's warlike exploits. This made him not only an official poet, but court poet as well. Accordingly, he perpetuated in verse such events as the death of the Duke of Wellington and the charge of the Light Brigade; he mourned with the Queen over sorrowful events affecting the Royal Family and rejoiced with her over happy ones. Although on such occasions he had little difficulty in thinking the appropriate thoughts, it is also evident that he tried consciously to think them and that he aspired to be simultaneously spokesman and teacher, and as such, as far as it lay in his power, to be an edifying influence on the nation.

Through this interaction between events, suitable emotions and official utterances, Tennyson undoubtedly came to be regarded by many Victorians as the High Priest of the age. In any given situation, faced with an epoch-making event, he asked himself, as it were: 'What should a Poet Laureate say in such circumstances?' And as each occasional poem appeared, the Victorians murmured to themselves: 'This time Tennyson really has expressed the feelings of the nation.'

To estimate fully the workings of this interplay of emotional currents it would be necessary to study the climate of public opinion throughout the whole country, before and after the appearance of each of Tennyson's most famous occasional poems. It would seem, nevertheless, that very probably his homage to the Light Brigade helped to crystallize national feeling during the Crimean War, just as his condemnation of mutinous sepoys as 'traitors' interpreted public feeling at the time of the Indian Mutiny. It is quite likely, too, that his poems written to celebrate Queen Victoria's two jubilees helped to strengthen the nation's loyalty to the monarchy.

The theory that Tennyson was the supreme spokesman of the Victorian Age can be supported by many more examples of a similar nature. His volumes of poems enjoyed a huge success. Not all of them were liked or approved of at first, some indeed were sharply criticized; but this did not stop them from selling like hot cakes. His popularity grew steadily, following the publication, in 1850, of *In Memoriam*, which secured his fame, and his appointment to the Laureateship in the same year, which enhanced it. By 1860 he had become the most widely read of any poet then living. Tennyson was a name even to those who could not read—and this was the condition of the greater proportion of the population when he became Poet Laureate. By the time he died, compulsory education, designed to ensure the literacy of the newly enfranchized voter, had seen to it that three generations of children were able to read and write—and of course, able to read Tennyson, if they felt so inclined.

Edition after edition of his works continued to appear. In 1853 his *Poems* went into their eighth, and *The Princess* into its fifth edition. In 1855, *Maud* sold 5,000 copies on the day of publication and in spite of, or perhaps because of, the controversy it aroused, it went on selling. The *Idylls*, published between 1859 and 1885, were bought and read by thousands as each volume appeared. In July 1864, 60,000 copies of *Enoch Arden* were subscribed, 40,000 sold very rapidly and the book was soon out of print, having to be reprinted; Tennyson made £6,000 out of it in the first year. Even today editions or selections of the poems sell some ten thousand copies yearly.

'Why am I popular?' he asked a friend, the poet William Allingham, in 1866. 'I don't write in a common language. I think it is because I am a Poet Laureate. It's like being a Lord.' He was, in the course of time, to be both.

Though Tennyson occasionally showed signs of pique when he felt that he was not getting enough attention, his conceit was tempered by timidity, his vanity offset by shyness. Despite his fondness of adulation he developed a dislike of publicity verging on the obsessive. To escape the attentions of his admirers, he fled, in 1853, to the still sparsely-inhabited Isle of Wight. There he chose to live in comfortable seclusion at Freshwater, in a beautiful eighteenth-century house, Farringford, within easy visiting distance of a near neighbour who disliked publicity as much as he did—Queen Victoria, at Osborne. In 1856 the undiminishing sales of his poetry enabled him to buy Farringford.

Even on an island it was impossible to escape his 'fans', who flocked from the mainland to stalk the poet and gawk at him over his garden gate. He told his friend Allingham that he had been chased along the road one day by two fat women and sixteen children. Once, being short-sighted, he fled from a flock of sheep which he mistook for a throng of admirers. The curiosity-seekers stared into his grounds, climbed trees for a closer look, peered into his windows, and hacked souvenirs from the walls of his summer house. In time he shied away from the very shadow of an approaching tourist. A couple of Americans who once marched to his front door demanding to see the poet got short shrift when Tennyson answered the door-bell himself and said to them, 'Well, now you have seen me will you kindly go away?'

The growing popularity of the Isle of Wight, the acceleration of building, the visitors flocking in ever greater numbers from the mainland, bringing with them what Tennyson called 'the Hero-worshippers, etc.', full of curiosity to catch even a glimpse of the Laureate, drove him away at last. He sought an even more secluded existence on top of an isolated hill in Sussex. In 1867 he bought the Greenhill estate, on Blackdown, near Haslemere, had a large, handsome and comfortable house, Aldworth, built for him on his hilltop and moved in with his family during the summer of 1869. There, in the beautiful Sussex countryside, with a magnificent view across the Downs to the Channel to inspire him, he made his home for the rest of his life.

In spite of his seclusion Tennyson continued to be an immensely well-known and popular public figure. The majestic and commanding impression he created, one eminently suited to a Poet Laureate, undoubtedly owed much to his noble, ideally 'poetic' looks, to which his stature, his fine head with its lofty brow and acquiline nose, his dark flowing locks and luxuriant beard, all contributed. His myopia lent him an air of aloofness and dignity which rendered him in appearance every inch the Victorians' conception of a Poet.

Tennyson's long friendship with Gladstone, his friendship and intimate conversations with the Queen, contributed to the respect in which he was held and to the glamour which made him a perennial target of publicity. He was the first poet to be raised to the peerage on the strength of his poetry. In January 1884 he became Baron Tennyson of Freshwater and Aldworth, a unique honour which further enhanced his great prestige. When he died in 1892 it seemed to many that, as the newspapers wrote, his passing was the end of an era. When Gladstone asked Jowett who should be made the next Laureate, the answer was: 'Don't make anyone Laureate. Nobody expects it.' The post remained unfilled until 1896.

Those critical writers who hold up Tennyson as a symbol of the age he lived in are strongly influenced by the externals of his existence: his success as a poet, the multiple editions of his works, his fame, position and riches, to say nothing of the blameless rectitude of his life, both as private person and public figure, all of which made him a legend in his lifetime and an object of national pride. What is meant is, in essence, something quite different: they mean that he was essentially Victorian in intellectual preoccupations, morals and ideas. The arguments for this view, nevertheless, would appear to be open to question.

In the view of Richard Garnett he was 'the interpreter of the Victorian era—firstly to itself, and secondly to the ages to come'. Joanna Richardson in her biography gives a similar summing-up of the qualities which in her view made Tennyson a typical Victorian:

> 'Few English poets have so identified themselves with the age in which they lived as Tennyson. He had focused into a shining point existing feeling and thought, he had reflected the common perplexities, achievements and aspirations. His influence was felt in all the arts of the Victorian era.'

Among other typically mid-Victorian features Miss Richardson emphasizes Tennyson's attitude to women, 'an attitude of worship, puritanism and condescension'. Though he believed that 'There is no superior between man and woman, each may be perfect in their own tho' different way', he also 'quite approved of woman doing all in her power to raise herself, tho' never out of her own sphere'. One keen-eyed and sharp-tongued observer, who could hardly be included among the creatures whom Tennyson classed as 'the soft and milky rabble of womankind', was Jane Carlyle. She was not slow to note of the Laureate that 'he entertains at one and the same time a feeling of almost adoration for them and an ineffable contempt! adoration I suppose for what they *might be*—contempt for what they *are*'! Tennyson himself admitted to a friend, Marian Bradley: 'I abuse women often and my wife scolds me for it, but for all that I appreciate them and would pluck my hand from a man—be he my greatest hero or dearest friend—who would wrong a woman . . .'. In his reverence for womanhood Tennyson was as chaste as his poetry and he could fittingly share 'the white flower of a blameless life' which he later ascribed to the defunct Prince Consort. The few romantic attachments or friendships with women that he had formed in his young manhood appear to have been as pure as the driven snow. In later years he told a woman friend that 'he had never kissed a woman in love, except his wife'. All the evidence points to the fact of his being 'morally pure' when, in middle age, he married Emily Sellwood, for whom he had waited for fourteen years. He had met and fallen in love with her at his brother's wedding in 1836. Their engagement had been recognized by the Sellwood family in 1838, but in 1840 Emily's father, conventional and strictly religious, opposed his daughter's marriage to a penniless poet who looked like a gipsy, was heavily addicted to pipe and cigar smoking, had broad religious views and a family background with a disturbing substratum of instability, melancholia and dipsomania. The young couple were forbidden to correspond further and the engagement was broken. But neither forgot the other, until at last, in 1850, fearing that when he died his daughter would be left alone still unmarried, Mr Sellwood withdrew his opposition. Tennyson had in the meantime become famous, which was doubtless a point in his favour. In June 1850, he and Emily, no longer a young couple, were married, at a quiet wedding, which Tennyson said was 'the nicest wedding he had ever been at'. The bride was thirty-seven, the bridegroom forty-one.

Tennyson enjoyed lifelong happiness in his marriage. In keeping with the times it was 'a perfect marriage', and Mrs Tennyson, who was gentle, wise, well-bred and well read, was the epitome of the perfect Victorian wife, self-effacing, dutiful and adoring. Throughout their long married life she not only loved, honoured and obeyed her husband, she gave him an unsparing devotion, believed in him, encouraged him, provided intellectual companionship and good food, acted as his secretary, warded off all external cares and hindrances and provided him with a happy and peaceful home in which he could recollect emotion in undisturbed tranquillity.

Their friend Jowett said of the relationship: 'She was a perfect wife, and he had the most absolute confidence in her and respect and admiration for her.' While Emily ministered to the great man's material needs and peace of mind, he reciprocated with adoring homage of womanhood, tenderness which was possibly somewhat absentminded, and not a little male condescension.

Emily's views on woman's place in a man's world coincided with her husband's. She wrote:

> 'Let women be as educated as possible but let them remember that God has created Man the Head of the Woman, not his rival. It would be hard indeed to have to obey from the beginning to the end of life were not man as a whole intellectually greater than woman as a whole. . . . Let women take care that they mate wisely with those to whom they are to be helpmates.'

Erotic, or at least sexually defined situations are not absent from Tennyson's poetry. But outbursts of passion like those in Byron or Swinburne never occur in Tennyson; even sin seems almost chaste in his poetic world, such is its air of prudence and restraint.

This pre-eminent Victorian, in Joanna Richardson's view, was Victorian in his belief in science and progress. But here, both in regard to Victorianism and to the poet himself, the theory of his representative identification with the age seems less convincing. As far as Tennyson is concerned, he undoubtedly did display in his poetry some knowledge of the new-fangled geological and biological theories of the time, but he seldom introduced scientific terminology into his poetry, nor is his imagery in any degree comparable to that of the poets of our own time who have derived inspiration and stimulus from such mysteries as relativity and the atom. It is also indisputable that Darwin's theory of the evolution of the species was the basis for Tennyson's belief that earth would in the fullness of time become a terrestrial paradise.

> 'Not in vain the distance beacons. Forward, forward let us range.
> Let the great world spin for ever down the ringing grooves of change.'

As his poetic vision saw the world,

> 'Robed in universal harvest up to either pole she smiles,
> Universal ocean softly washing all her warless isles.'

But these visions of progress are mere poetic abstractions. No vital utopianism can be detected in Tennyson's thinking, nor does he take any decided stand for or against the reforms of his time. As a rule he thought of earthly existence as a condition which it was proper to accept and endure merely as a preparation for an eternity of heavenly bliss. He believed that life would be meaningless and unbearable but for the hope of immortality. The problem of existence beyond the grave 'haunted his mind till it became a sort of cerebral nightmare', wrote Frederic Harrison in his *Autobiographic Memoirs* (1911). In a thundering rebuke to a sceptical friend who expressed doubt about the probability of an after life, Tennyson once said:

> 'If there is a God that has made the Earth and put this hope and passion in us, it must be the truth. If it be not true, then no God but a mocking fiend created us, and I'd shake my fist in his almighty face and tell him that I cursed him—I'd sink my head in a chloroformed handkerchief and have done with it all.'

In old age Tennyson expounded his views on death to Queen Victoria, during one of his intimate conversations with her at Osborne in 1883—and the Queen duly recorded in her Journal what he had said. He was by this time old and tired and half-blind; the younger of his two sons had died in early manhood and many of his lifelong friends were now dead. The Laureate 'spoke of the many friends he had lost and what it would be if he did not feel and know that there was another world where there would be no more partings, of his horror of unbelievers and philosophers, who would try to make one believe there was no other world, no immortality. . . . We agreed that were such a thing possible, God, Who is Love, would be far more cruel than a human being.'

Tennyson's belief in the immortality of the soul, the core of his religion, was frequently shaken by doubt. There are indications that his melancholy was due to, or rather, consisted in, brooding about death and the possibility of life beyond the grave. He appears to have wavered between a more robust faith, doubt, and a pragmatic attitude which considered immortality likely because people were unable to live without hope. To Tennyson, a clergyman's son, Christian dogma was a matter of indifference. 'There's something that watches over us,' he said, 'and our individuality endures. That's my faith and that's all my faith.'

He had no pronounced political opinions, but in many of his poems, as well as in letters and conversations, he touched upon contemporary problems and conditions which were the topics of party dispute and parliamentary debate. He expressed his contempt for the extreme economic liberalism of the Manchester school—a contempt probably inspired by Carlyle—in the scathing epithet 'cotton-spinners' with which he dismissed Cobden and Bright, the leaders of the Free Trade movement.

> 'Tho' niggard throats of Manchester may bawl,
> What England was, shall her true sons forget?
> We are not cotton-spinners all,
> But some love England and her honour yet . . .'

And he is said, in *Maud*, to have lampooned Bright, cotton merchant and son of a Quaker, as:

> 'This broad-brimmed hawker of holy things,
> Whose ear is stuff'd with his cotton and rings
> Even in dreams to the chink of his pence . . .'

Tennyson revered the monarchy, the House of Lords and, by and large, all forms of authority. This conservatism was combined with a vague and paternalistic desire for social reform. There is genuine indignation in passages of *Locksley Hall Sixty Years After*, in which he describes want and prostitution in big cities:

> 'Is it well that while we range with Science, glorying in the Time,
> City children soak and blacken soul and sense in city slime?
> There among the glooming alleys Progress halts on palsied feet,
> Crime and hunger cast our maidens by the thousand on the street.

There the Master scrimps his haggard sempstress of her daily bread,
There a single sordid attick holds the living and the dead.
There the smouldering fire of fever creeps across the rotted floor,
And the crowded couch of incest in the warrens of the poor.'

The combination of respect for the Establishment with pity and charitable deeds for the deserving poor is a bit hard to swallow when (in *The Princess*) he exhorts lords of the manor to fling open their gates to monthly outings of the lower orders:

'Why should not these great sirs
Give up their parks some dozen times a year
To let the people breathe?'

His long friendship with Gladstone was clouded by lack of confidence in him as Prime Minister, his distrust of Gladstone's attitude to the Irish question, his anxiety at the threat of disestablishment of the Church of England, and his outraged disagreement with the Liberal government's reduction of the Navy, which brought on a vehement, versified attack, in *The Times*:

The fleet of England is her all-in-all;
Her fleet is in your hands,
And in her fleet her Fate.

You, you, that have the ordering of her fleet,
If you should compass her disgrace,
When all men starve, the wild mob's million feet
Will kick you from your place,
But then, too late, too late.

He feared that under Gladstone the Liberals would overstep the mark with their democratic reforms and land themselves and the country in some sort of socialism. An example of his loose political reasoning can be found in Hallam Tennyson's *Memoir* of his father: 'I do not in the least mind', said the Laureate, 'if England, when the people are less ignorant and more experienced in self-government, eventually becomes a democracy. But violent, selfish, unreasoning democracy, could bring expensive bureaucracy, and the iron rule of a Cromwell.' The confusion of this statement is all the more striking considering that it was made a couple of years after the Reform Bill of 1885 had given the vote to the majority of adult Englishmen.

Even Tennyson's patriotism, which was insular and tinged with aggressive nationalism, is considered to have been typically Victorian. On the whole he distrusted foreigners and in time of war or conflict with France and Russia, in his role of Poet Laureate he turned the full force of his indignation on these nations. Nor would it be inaccurate to see him as an imperialist. When he prophesied 'the Parliament of man, the Federation of the world', when he spoke of a time 'when the world shall be one', it was an English-speaking world, led by England—'a single race, a single tongue'—that he had in mind. It was at this time that Gladstone wrote to Tennyson that on a basis of statistics it was estimated that the Anglo-Saxon race could be expected to reach a total of one thousand millions in a century, that is, by 1983.

In Tennyson' s poetry there is very little chauvinism or national glorification of Britain's mighty sway over 'inferior' races, in the style of Kipling's 'new-caught, sullen peoples'. His attitude to 'England under Indian skies', to 'those dark millions of her realm', was one of benign patronage. Safe under the motherly protection of the Great White Queen, how could Britain's dark-skinned subject races be anything but grateful and loyal? So, 'Praise to our Indian brothers, and let the dark face have his due'! On one occasion, however, in 1864, dark faces provoked him into savage Carlylean utterances. During a dinner-table discussion of the recent Negro revolt in Jamaica, ruthlessly and cruelly suppressed by Governor Ayre, Gladstone condemned Ayre, and Tennyson, his jingoism rampant, justified the governor's cruelty on the grounds that: 'We are too tender to savages; we are more tender to a black than to ourselves. Niggers are tigers, niggers are tigers.' But his nationalism was usually tempered by his inherent benevolence to all mankind—'That man's the best cosmopolite who loves his native country best'.

On the various points considered here, numerous writers have furnished, as they believe, abundant proof that Tennyson was a typical Victorian. Yet, there seems still to be some doubt that he represented any widespread or consistent body of opinion. Conscious of the difficulty, some critical writers and historians have attempted to justify the theory of his typicalness on more subtle and closely reasoned grounds. Tennyson, they conclude, personified 'the Victorian compromise'. If anything, this means that his statements concerning the problems of his time were confused and tentative and that his high-minded reassuring preachments on progress, immortality, a guiding Providence and kindred consolations, optimistic as they were, lacked certainty or true conviction.

Valerie Pitt, in *Tennyson Laureate*, gives what is possibly the most lucid explanation of the Victorian and Tennysonian dilemma, when she stresses that:

> 'Outwardly the Victorian period presents a façade of solid community belief; inwardly it displays all the symptoms of a disintegrating culture. . . . Things fall apart from age and wear, but sometimes also from the impact and pressure of internal and external forces, and the Victorian age shows both kinds of disintegration . . . Tennyson

suffered more than anyone from this shift and flow of things. He was . . . a man who would have responded eagerly to an acceptable authority. Yet he was open to every wind of the Victorian weather.'

Lacking a general and accepted sense of values, commonly held principles and a central tradition with which to confront the great moral and social upheavals of the age, the Victorian mind was rent asunder in a kind of schizoid cleavage—on the one hand, a materialistic complacency: on the other, doubt, insecurity, a longing for certainty. Because of this split, typical Victorians were odd and eccentric; consequently Tennyson, who was also odd and eccentric, was a typical Victorian.

'The Best Poet In My Dominions': Algernon Charles Swinburne

When Tennyson died in 1892 and the post of Poet Laureate fell vacant, Queen Victoria expressed her wish that Algernon Charles Swinburne should be appointed to the Laureateship. 'I am told Mr Swinburne is the best poet in my dominions,' she said to Mr Gladstone. She had certainly heard, from Tennyson himself, about Swinburne and his poetry, but it is doubtful that she had ever read any of it. Mr Gladstone, too, had almost certainly heard a few things about Swinburne, though not quite the same things, and had probably read some of his poetry. Mr Gladstone advised against the Queen's proposal, ostensibly because Mr Swinburne's politics were hardly the sort a Poet Laureate ought to profess. The Queen doubtless accepted as reasonable Mr Gladstone's objections. Mr Swinburne on second thoughts, would *not* do, and the official laurel, after much delay, finally came to rest on the brow of Alfred Austin, whose poems emerged only when he was actively inspired by 'It', as he called his poetic inspiration. With the assistance of 'It' this prolific versifier, whose chief claim to fame is his mastery of bathos, emitted, in the fullness of time, fifteen volumes of poetic works which have proved truly forgettable.

The poetry of the great defunct Laureate whom Austin replaced was a monumental expression of the 'Victorian compromise': it was religious, but enveloped in such mists of vagueness that it satisfied even moderate freethinkers; and it was patriotic, yet with dreams of a union of nations under the leadership of Britain. Swinburne's poetry, in comparison, had positively flaunted his atheism and republican sympathies. Worse still, many of the poems were full of disturbing eroticism and it was common knowledge that for several years in the past he had led a dissolute life and had been a confirmed drunkard.

Quite probably, however, Gladstone was unaware that this wild and disorderly life had indeed become a thing of the past; for Swinburne by this time—he was now fifty-five—was a reformed character and had been living for thirteen years in the care of an older man, Walter Theodore Watts (later Watts-Dunton), a persistent friend to literary men and a paragon of prudery and conventional respectability. Watts had rescued the self-destructive poet from a squalid fate in 1879. During the years that followed, at No. 2 The Pines, Putney Hill (today No. 11), under his rescuer's care, supervision and influence, Swinburne had undergone a surburban metamorphosis, to become pantheist, mild world reformer, baby-lover and jingoistic nationalist. He attacked Gladstone for the 'treachery' of his failure to send help in time to save Gordon in Khartoum:

> 'Forsaken, silent, Gordon dies and gives
> Example: loud and shameless Gladsone lives . . .'

and by the time of the Boer War he was urging his countrymen fighting in the Transvaal:

> 'To scourge these dogs, agape with jaws afoam,
> Down out of life. Strike England, and strike home!'

Swinburne's ancestry was aristocratic, his family wealthy. His father, Captain (later Admiral) Charles Swinburne, came from an old Northumbrian family with a baronetcy dating back to 1660, while his mother, Lady Jane Swinburne, was the fourth daughter of the third Earl of Ashburnham. Swinburne's childhood was a happy one, spent mainly in his home on the Isle of Wight with his four younger sisters and brother and in the companionship of some girl cousins, daughters of his mother's sister, Lady Mary Gordon, who lived near by. With his sisters and cousins Swinburne led a free open-air life, riding, rambling and swimming. In holiday time he visited Sir George Swinburne, his paternal grandfather, at Capheaton, Northumberland, and was given the run of a superb library. He went to Eton at twelve and to Balliol College, Oxford, at eighteen. With his background and education he might have been expected in due course to grow up like his forbears, who were all country gentlemen, soldiers or hunting, shooting, fishing sportsmen. How, then, did he become a poet and a rebel and seek self-destruction with such desperate intensity?

There were mysteries about Swinburne's life which early studies ignored and his first biographer, Sir Edmund Gosse, had not cared to reveal. An excellent later study of the poet, Humphrey Hare's *Swinburne: a biographical approach* (1949) bears an epigraph from Sainte Beuve: 'Those who make a study of a man of stature must dare to see everything, examine everything, and at least point out everything'. Hare suited the action to the word. His book was certainly franker and more daring than the earlier, much-read short study by Sir Harold Nicolson.

The key to the anomaly of Swinburne's life, said Hare, lay in the sexual aberration known as algolagnia—sexual excitation through pain, either inflicted or submitted to. The term, coined in 1899 by the neurologist Schrenk-Nötzing, was adopted and popularized by Havelock Ellis and is used to denote both sadism and masochism, the first being known as active and the second passive algolagnia.

Earlier writers shied away from such explanations. Harold Nicolson, writing in 1926, believed that 'There will be those, doubtless, who will one day explore the intricacies and causes of his non-existent sexual repressions, and will trace depressing and essentially erroneous analogies to Dr Masoch and the Marquis de Sade'.

The day of such explanations was indeed not far off. According to Humphrey Hare it was not possible, after the publication in 1928 of the exhaustive two-volume study *La Jeunesse de Swinburne*, by the French scholar Georges Lafourcade, to regard the poet any longer as the inexplicable phenomenon who had baffled earlier writers. It was precisely this deformation of sensuality, algolagnia, Hare believed, which was the cause not only of Swinburne's misfortunes, his unhappiness and his failure to adapt to circumstances and to society, but also of the passionate feeling which, combined with a superabundance of poetic talent and an extraordinary gift for inventive metrical structure, made him one of the most brilliant and original lyrical poets of the nineteenth century. This is doubtless correct, insofar as Swinburne's sexual activity—which from all accounts was limited to a comparatively short period of his life—was indeed characterized by this particular sexual aberration.

Nevertheless the impression remains that Hare's opinion as to the far-reaching effect of Swinburne's perversion is exaggerated. Other writers have indicated characteristics and occurrences which may have had equally far-reaching effects on the poet's psychological development and sensibility. They have drawn attention to his appearance, which invited ridicule—the tiny body, narrow, sloping shoulders, long yet thick neck and enormous head with its unruly mop of wavy, carroty hair, the weak mouth above a receding chin; the nervous mannerisms, the gesticulating arms, the twitchings and fluttering fingers when he was excited; and they also point out a tendency to what appear to have been epileptic seizures which were later brought on and exacerbated by the abuse of alcohol during the dissolute period of his life in London. Attention has also been drawn to the deep humiliation, which attended Swinburne's only known proposal of marriage, which provoked a burst of laughter. His physical aspect must have been so bizarre that he was always conscious of it, as were all those with whom he came in contact.

However this may be, it seems likely that Swinburne's earlier poems have suffered by being judged from the special viewpoint of his erotic proclivities. His supreme masterpiece *Atalanta in Calydon* (1865) has been analysed as a manifestation of his algolagnia, inspiring sadistic images of blood and cruelty. Swinburne himself felt about the sadistic and atheistic elements in *Atalanta* that it was 'de Sade with a difference'; yet the bitterness, the insistence on the transience of all things earthly, with which the poem is imbued, are echoes of what men normally feel about human mortality, and do not seem in the least strange. Such reflections, surely, are not inspired solely by a sexual obsession. Then again, many men have felt, and not a few have written, that if God really existed he would be either too ridiculous or too horrible to contemplate; and in *Atalanta* Swinburne expresses his hatred of God with undeniable intensity. The God against whom he cries out in the fourth choric ode of the poem is a treacherous, capricious and pitiless deity:

> The lord of love and loathing and of strife
> Who gives a star and takes a sun away;
> ....
> Who makes desire, and slays desire with shame;
> Who shakes the heaven as ashes in his hand;
> Who, seeing the light and shadow for the same,
> Bids day waste night as fire devours a brand,
> Smites without sword, and scourges without rod;
> The supreme evil, God.
> ....
> Thou hast kissed us, and hast smitten; thou has laid
> Upon us with thy left hand life, and said,
> Live: and again thou hast said, Yield up your breath,
> And with thy right hand laid upon us death.

Swinburne's first attempt in 1861 to win public recognition as a poet was a failure. He persuaded his father to pay for the publication of *The Queen Mother*, a five-act play in blank verse about Catherine de' Medici, and *Rosamund*, a long poem about Rosamund Clifford, the mistress of King Henry II. The book appeared in due course, but nobody bought it, nobody read it. The reviewers ignored it—all but one, who gave it an adverse review in *The Atheneum.* In two years Swinburne's first-born sold only seven copies. It was, he said 'of all still-born books, the stillest'.

With the publication of *Atalanta in Calydon* in 1865, when he was twenty-eight, Swinburne 'shot like a rocket into celebrity'. The poem is the climax of his early period of tormented and passionate lyric poetry; his second period full of his hero-worship of Mazzini and drawing fresh inspiration from the Italian struggle for unification and independence, was that of a political radical, and it culminated in *Songs Before Sunrise* (1871). The republican and revolutionary feeling which now became the leading theme of Swinburne's poetry was unfocused—he was never a consistent or a lucid thinker—and in his grandiose and vague aspirations he can be said to typify the intellectual left of his period; their heroes and his were Garibaldi, Mazzini and Victor Hugo. Napoleon III, a monster of retrograde despotism was despised and hated above all others as the 'arch-enemy', 'Napoleon the little'. The poet now saw humanity as an army of soldiers marching on the path to freedom and self-realization.

Freedom we call it, for holier
name of the soul there is none.

The link with the lyricism of his earlier poems was still apparent, but Swinburne now had found something to believe in and he became to some degree positive and optimistic. What formerly had been 'life' was now only a part of life; everything that was old and outworn, traditional and authoritarian, would be swept away by freedom and enlightenment; man's better nature, which had been stifled, would break out triumphant when his shackles had been struck off.

Here was a philosophy of progress in verse which revealed an arresting power more impressive than that of any poet since the revolutionary *avant-garde* of the early nineteenth century: it preached that the God fashioned in Man's own image, and the kings and priests, would give way before the philosophers and warriors who would rise up in the name of humanity and common sense to demand democracy and independence for oppressed peoples.

Swinburne composed very rapidly, and without difficulty. Many of his finest poems were written in two or three days in a raging fever of excitement; but his excesses during the 1870s—heavy drinking probably doing him the most harm—threatened to destroy his ability to work, to say nothing of wrecking his health.

He had left Oxford in 1860 without taking his degree, his career there, as he said, having 'culminated in total and scandalous failure'. The admiral, who regarded his son as 'an afflictive phenomenon', was deeply incensed by his academic failure, but in view of Swinburne's determination to live in London he agreed to make him an annual allowance of £400. By October 1861 Swinburne had established permanent headquarters in rooms in Grafton Street, Fitzroy Square, near the British Museum, and spent his days writing his poetry or studying in the Museum library. He renewed his relationship with his Pre-Raphaelite friends of his Oxford days—Dante Gabriel Rossetti, Edward Burne-Jones, William Morris, and found other friends in their circle. After the tragic death of Rossetti's wife by her own hand in February 1862, the painter no longer wished to live in his house at Chatham Place and invited Swinburne to share a new house with him. A suitable one was found at 16 Cheyne Walk, Chelsea, and in October they moved in; but

Swinburne subsequently spent very little time there during the two-year lease, and his friendship with Rossetti gradually cooled.

The poet had made other friends. In May 1860, shortly after his arrival in London, he was introduced to Richard Monckton Milnes (later Lord Houghton) who became his patron and friend, helping him in the publication of the poems which brought him fame and later notoriety and who was to exercise a considerable influence over the young poet for the next six or seven years. Milnes, aged fifty at the time, was a cynical, cosmopolitan man of the world who knew everybody who was anybody in all the capitals of Europe. His conversation was full of epigrams, wit and malicious gossip—in later years Swinburne referred to him as 'Baron Tattle of Scandal'. Morals did not exist for Monckton Milnes; his library of erotica was reputed to be unrivalled in Europe; he boasted of more vices than he could possibly have indulged in and once mused, with great self-satisfaction: 'Oh! How wide is the diapason of my mind, from what a height to what a depth!'

After their first meeting, Monckton Milnes and Swinburne, according to Sir Edmund Gosse, 'were soon on terms of high facetious familiarity'. Milnes, a poet *manqué* and literary critic turned bibliophile, was always actively interested in art and literature and liked to help young artists in whom he detected signs of talent; nevertheless if a friend or protégé did not become, or succeed in remaining, successful, he was dropped like a hot potato, though if his fortunes chanced to improve, Milnes as quickly picked him up again. This flair for detecting waxing or waning genius earned for him the nickname of 'The Barometer'; and in later years his friend the explorer and oriental scholar Richard Burton, who had been out of favour, was led to remark, 'Some luck must be coming my way, Houghton is so damned civil.'

Monckton Milnes was a cynical student of human nature but he was not really interested in people, only in the sensations they provided him by their reactions to one another. He found it diverting to throw incongruous or incompatible personalities together 'for kicks', just to see what would happen; and his home at Fryston, in Yorkshire, where many such experiments were conducted, became known to friends and intimates as 'The Inn of Strange Encounters'. One such encounter engineered by Milnes was that of his wispy poet-genius Swinburne with the heroic and outrageous Richard Burton, sixteen years Swinburne's senior, a man of massive physique, virile and daring, cynical, an atheist and a heavy drinker who shared his host's and Swinburne's interest in erotica and was a lively companion for carousals. These were all qualities calculated to appeal to Swinburne who, despite his puny frame, had the courage of a lion, daring to match Burton's and a blazing literary talent which the older man, who had a passionate enthusiasm for literature, envied and generously admired. Out of this strange encounter sprang a friendship which lasted for the rest of Burton's life, but Burton, whom Swinburne called 'my tempter and favourite audience', was not the best of influences on Swinburne, either physically or intellectually. Through him, however, Swinburne met Dr George Bird, an intimate friend of the explorer, who became Swinburne's physician and guardian angel, in which double capacity he saved the poet, according to Gosse, 'from many results of his wild impulsiveness' during the dissolute years between 1860 and 1867.

An important influence on Swinburne's early development was his introduction by Monckton Milnes to the works of the Marquis de Sade. It amused and stimulated the older man to become the mentor of a young one full of promise, innocent of his possible tendencies, in whom it would be diverting to encourage the development of sensibilities which Milnes was swift to detect in Swinburne's nature. At first he merely excited an aroused curiosity about the writings and philosophy of 'the divine Marquis', only later, on Swinburne's insistence, allowing him, probably in 1861 on his first visit to Fryston, to see a copy of *Justine* in his library.

Success was not good for Swinburne; it went to his head, increasing the waywardness of his life. In the years following the acclamation of *Atalanta* and the appearance of *Poems and Ballads*, which brought him notoriety as 'the libidinous laureate of a troop of satyrs', Swinburne began to frequent disreputable companions. He became involved (as did Rossetti and Ruskin) in the schemes of Charles Augustus Howell, a persuasive Anglo-Portuguese adventurer. Swinburne was fascinated by this glib-tongued charmer, who was unscrupulous, utterly untrustworthy, and an amusing, richly-inventive raconteur whose talk was 'a Niagara of lies'. For seven or eight years Howell became, according to Gosse, Swinburne's 'man of business, the partner of his amusements, the confidant of his literary projects and often his main channel of communication with the world'. But it was dangerous to become involved with such a man, and when Swinburne discovered that indiscreet and improper letters he had written to Howell were in the hands of a publisher who threatened to print them, he saw that it was time to shake off 'The pole-cat Howell; the vilest wretch I ever came across'. In 1890, some years after Swinburne had severed connections with him, Howell came to a bad end in mysterious circumstances. He was found lying in the gutter outside a Chelsea pub with his throat cut, a half-sovereign thrust between his teeth. He died in hospital some days later.

Another companion of this period was the gifted young Jewish painter Simeon Solomon, a homosexual and six years younger than Swinburne, who is believed, through the poet's example and encouragement, to have come to share his interest in flagellation. After some years of friendship Swinburne realized that Solomon's reputation was detrimental to his own and dropped him. Solomon, after serving a term of imprisonment for a homosexual offence, sank into oblivion and poverty. On his way down he incensed Swinburne by selling compromising letters written to him in the days when Swinburne and he had exchanged facetious and indecent correspondence. Solomon ended his days in complete destitution, dying in his early forties, in a workhouse hospital, of chronic alcoholism.

Swinburne's latest biographer, Jean Overton Fuller, discussing the relationship of Swinburne and Simeon Solomon in *Swinburne: A Critical Biography* (1969) makes the observation that it is as unfair to assume that Swinburne corrupted the youthful Solomon as it is to blame Monckton Milnes for corrupting Swinburne because, in each case, the younger man was neither innocent, nor averse to being instructed—on the contrary, willing and eager.

The desire to shock and outrage was part of Swinburne's instinctive passion for revolt. His painter friends were by no means puritanical, but his excesses horrified them. They have given accounts of his behaviour at parties, especially the lavish and splendid affairs given by Rossetti, at which Swinburne was one of the attractions. Drink overcame his initial shyness and he conversed brilliantly during the earlier part of the evening. But he got steadily less and less sober as the party progressed and began to talk outrageously, screaming as he became over-excited. He generally ended up reeling drunk; and it became his friends' habit before he went out to a party, to tie a label, with his address on it, to his overcoat. From time to time his father, alerted by Lord Houghton, Dr Bird or some other friend, would come up to London, pay off his debts and carry him down to the country where, at home, with rest, regular meals and the kindness of his family, he recuperated and was able to work. But it became ever more apparent, as his bouts of drinking became more frequent and prolonged, that he was threatened with chronic alcoholism.

During the poet's dissolute years a new and determined friend entered his life. Walter Theodore Watts (who added his mother's name Dunton in 1896, under the terms of a legacy and was known thereafter as Watts-Dunton), was a St Ives solicitor with literary leanings and a desire to consort with artists and men of letters. He was fascinated by the lives of gipsies and had persisted until he was successful in his attempts to strike up an acquaintanceship with George Borrow. Ruskin was his next trophy. Through Ruskin he became interested in the Pre-Raphaelites and then got to know Rossetti whom he was able to help in his chaotic business affairs. Watts soon became a friend of the Rossetti circle and was also able to be of practical service to them—they nicknamed him 'Watts the Wise'. He gave up his country business and settled in London.

Watt's first attempts, in 1873, to establish a friendship with Swinburne were not successful. He was able, however, to be of use to the poet in business matters. By autumn of that year they were writing regularly to each other and by March 1873 Swinburne was suggesting that they drop the 'Mr' from their correspondence as friends.

Many of Swinburne's old friendships, including that with Rossetti, had by now cooled. For some years he had been moving restlessly from lodging to lodging, packing, unpacking, rearranging, blaspheming, indulging in even more prolonged bouts of heavy drinking and subject to occasional epileptic seizures which caused him to injure himself—on one occasion by falling out of a hansom cab, or on another, by striking his head on the iron trestles of his British Museum desk, having to be carried out like a pale and bloodied corpse. His most severe attack of this kind occurred in July 1867 at one of Lord Houghton's large breakfast parties when, after falling, Swinburne lay in a prolonged coma. As on past occasions the Admiral came up from the country to take him home for rest and recuperation.

Swinburne was always drawn to London again after his rest cures in the country. In September 1872 he had finally alighted in rooms at 3 Great James Street, the last of the London lodging houses he was to occupy. The drinking, the bouts of elation and depression, the incessant reading, were coupled with deliberate isolation from human companionship. During 1877–88 he lived in the utmost squalor and disorder, passing his days lying supine on his bed, unable to bring himself to stir, while correspondence piled up unanswered and manuscripts were lost in the appalling litter which surrounded him.

His father having died in March 1877, he came into a little money. The drinking bouts increased and he would go for weeks lying on his bed in a drunken stupor, beset by an increasing 'torpor of mind and body'. He suffered from chronic gastro-intestinal irritation from his abuse of alcohol. He could not eat. He refused to go home or to allow any of his family to visit him. He was slowly killing himself.

Swinburne's rescue was spectacular.

His mother finally wrote to Watts, who by this time had moved to lodgings in the same street. Early one morning in September 1879, Watts found the poet utterly prostrate, starving, not having eaten for days, virtually dying. Watts carried him first to his own rooms and when he had recovered somewhat, took him to Putney to his (Watt's) sister's house. When Swinburne had recuperated there for a few days he was able to go home to the country to be cared for by his mother during a long convalescence which lasted until 1880.

It was obvious that Swinburne could never again be allowed to live alone in London. His mother agreed to make over to him immediately half of the money due to him from the sale of his father's library, on condition that he went to live in the care of Watts. The Putney villa was rented and Swinburne and his rescuer moved in, sharing the house with

Watt's sister and her family, who looked after the two men. There, in the tall, narrow, semi-detached villa of yellow brick, bay-windowed and separated from its twin by a square tower, Swinburne lived in increasingly rigid and regimented seclusion until his death in 1909.

The general attitude of biographers and writers of memoirs to the part played by Watts-Dunton in Swinburne's life, is one of contempt for a middle-aged, middle-class, respectable, retired solicitor and literary dilettante; but this is also mingled with a sneaking admiration for an incredibly generous and self-sacrificing friend. Sir Edmund Gosse saw him as 'the old horror of Putney', who exercised a rattlesnake fascination over Swinburne; nevertheless, from the available information about him, it can be inferred that Watts-Dunton was a man of particular warmth and charm. One of the chief witnesses to the quality of his attraction was Clara Jane Reich, the young woman who lived in his household for a number of years, probably as housekeeper, before becoming the first and only Mrs Watts-Dunton, when she was twenty-nine and he seventy-two. In *The Home Life of Algernon Charles Swinburne* (1922), Mrs Watts-Dunton wrote of her husband's 'magnetic presence' and of the adoring look in Swinburne's eyes when he spoke to Watts-Dunton. Most accounts, however also have something to say about Watts-Dunton's iron will and the jealous care with which he regulated Swinburne's life.

Watts-Dunton's first task in his reformation of a poet was to wean him from drink. For many years he acted as Swinburne's male nurse, not to say jailer. By slow degrees Swinburne was guided from brandy to port and from port to bordeaux; and finally, after several more years had passed by, he was content to have a mug of brown ale at the end of his obligatory morning walk to the Rose and Crown on the other side of Wimbledon Common.

Swinburne's former bohemian friends were discouraged and discarded. Only a handful of rigorously selected acquaintances was permitted to visit The Pines. Swinburne and Watts-Dunton never went abroad for their holidays. At the most they spent a few weeks every year at some English seaside resort. Little by little they withdrew from all company. Swinburne, whose passivity appears to have increased in the hands of Watts-Dunton, seemed content to have his life ordered for him. Day followed day according to a fixed timetable; a life of such monotonous regularity has probably never been led except by some inmate of a hospital or prison. In such conditions and surroundings Swinburne, the passionate poet, was slowly and inexorably obliterated and in his place a placid, and apparently contented human being emerged. For thirty years his daily routine was unvarying: he rose late, went for his two-hour morning walk to the pub, rain or shine, returned for lunch, rested in the afternoon, worked from four to six, read Dickens, or some other novelist, to the family from six to eight, dined and then worked till late at night.

Every evening the day's work was read out to Watts-Dunton, who was always encouraging and generally approving of what Swinburne had written. Swinburne came to rely more and more on Watts-Dunton's judgement. The writings poured out from The Pines; critical essays, contributions to reviews, magazines and newspapers, and twenty-four volumes of decorative poetry containing marathon historical dramas, patriotic fanfares, nature poetry, verses about children and babies, all wholesome enough to meet Watts-Dunton's strict standards of morality and good taste—or to have been the outpourings of a genuine official Poet Laureate. Five more volumes were published posthumously.

As the years passed by, the values of Swinburne's life quietly changed. The restless, tumultuous sea, which he was now permitted to contemplate once a year, replaced in some fashion the erotic passion of his unregenerate days; humanity united in brotherhood seemed to have been realized in Britain's empire. Freedom, no longer something mysterious and miraculous was represented by disciplined order maintained by British redcoats throughout the length of the empire's vast frontiers. The poet remained adamant in his refusal to accept a God—'the absurdest of human figments'—but an acknowledgement of some sort of personal existence after death provided him with something in which to trust.

By the time he died in 1909 at the age of seventy-three, carried off by influenza, Swinburne had become virtually like his father and forebears, the very model of a respectable English gentleman.

The Establishment claimed him fully in 1926 when the Putney villa, which had been acquired by the National Trust, received upon its bricks, between front door and bay window, one of the London County Council's (as it then was), Wedgwood-blue commemorative plaques. Not omitting to mention the poet's friend Watts-Dunton, given an ultimate accolade as 'poet, critic and novelist', the inscription on the plaque announces that this was the house where lived and died Algernon Charles Swinburne, poet.

Laureate of Empire: Rudyard Kipling

Take up the White Man's burden—
Send forth the best ye breed—
Go bind your sons to exile
To serve your captives' need;
To wait in heavy harness
On fluttered folk and wild—
Your new-caught, sullen peoples,
Half-devil and half-child.

Rudyard Kipling, the author of this rhymed, imperialistic platform-speech puts one in mind of an anthropologist who studies a savage tribe for a few years and then spends the rest of his life sorting, annotating and publishing his findings. Kipling's was not a life of bravery, hardship and daring. The great singer of imperial storm and stress always travelled first class on ocean liners and was seldom in the neighbourhood of front-line fire for more than a couple of hours at a time. Many of the incidents and background details of his books were derived from wide reading and information gathered from hearsay.

The chief events of Kipling's life are well known: his birth in Bombay, India in 1865 and his infancy there; the appalling time he spent between the ages of six and twelve, boarded with his younger sister in Southsea in the house of a puritanical and sadistic woman who took in the children of Anglo-Indian parents living overseas. This period was tersely and unforgettably described by Kipling in his fragmentary and unfinished autobiography *Something of Myself* (1937), and reconstructed in fictional form in *Baa, Baa, Blacksheep* (1888), and *The Light that Failed* (1891). He described in *Stalky & Co.* (1899) the brutal, though not unbearably unhappy, life of his schooldays at the United Services College, a minor public school in Devon. Founded in 1874, five years before he went there, the school provided cheap education for the sons of Army officers and was conducted on parsimonious and spartan lines. Savage discipline was enforced by the boys themselves on one another. During Kipling's first two years at the school the lives of the boys were made miserable by the school chaplain, the Rev. J. C. Campbell, a brutal and bullying assistant-master, addicted to perpetual use of the cane. His face was remembered after his departure (before which he preached an unusually unctious Sunday sermon), as being habitually set in an expression of unrelieved ferocity.

Kipling began his career as a writer at the age of seventeen with a few hectic years in India, in Lahore, on the staff of a provincial newspaper, *The Civil and Military Gazette*. He was the paper's representative in Simla, the fashionable army hill-station, a social centre and viceregal summer seat from where, at that time, the government of India was conducted for six or seven months of the year. The start of Kipling's world-wide fame was achieved in 1890, at the age of twenty-five and on the strength of a couple of volumes of ballads, some eighty short stories and a novel, which were printed or reprinted in England and America, bringing him fame and fortune and wide critical acclaim. His marriage in 1892 to Caroline Balestier, an American, initiated a long period of idyllic domestic happiness and peaceful industry. This existence was interspersed with globe-trotting or moves from one home to another in England or the United States, an existence made possible by the fame and wealth which enabled him to combine travel with the placid enjoyment of a comfortable domestic life. There was no place in his existence for spiritual or intellectual growth or development, no crises of excitement or despair could upset so orderly a life; all experiences of a more disquieting spiritual nature were cushioned off by Kipling's immense talent and imagination as a story-teller and rhymester.

Early in his career Kipling became one of the most widely read authors in the world and his books still sell steadily in great numbers. By the time of his death in 1936 his English publishers had sold seven million copies of his verses and stories and upwards of eight million had been sold in the United States. His books, translated into many languages, have been sold throughout the world and have helped to maintain his position as a best-selling author.

While a faithful public continued to buy and enjoy his books, critical opinion underwent a considerable change. At the height of Kipling's fame, in the early 1890s, his work was praised without reservation by all but one or two of the more highbrow critics. The award of the Nobel prize in 1907 was only one of many indications as to his literary position at the time.

By the advent of World War I, however, the view of Kipling as 'a case of retarded development' was already beginning to make headway. His imperialism, his paeans of hate, the peevish boy scout he so often resembled, to judge by his utterances, all helped to bring about a reversal of opinion and for a couple of decades after 1914 it was considered reactionary and naïve to admire his work. By the time of his death in 1936 his literary status had declined to vanishing point, though his popularity and sales continued undiminished. In the 1940s there was a tendency among a few intellectuals to detect some merit in the body of his writing and today his reputation seems once more to be taking an upward turn.

In his heyday Kipling was admired by contemporary writers who spoke with intellectual authority. Henry James wrote to his psychologist brother William in 1892 expressing his admiration—though he took care to emphasize the difference between genius and intelligence. 'Kipling', he wrote, 'strikes me personally as the most complete man of genius (as distinct from fine intelligence) that I have ever met.' Henry Adams, in the same year, struck up a shipboard friendship with the two Kiplings who were going to the States to live. He remembered in his autobiography *The Education of Henry Adams* (1907) that 'Rudyard Kipling . . . thanks to the mediation of Henry James, dashed over me his exuberant fountain of gaiety and wit—as though playing a garden hose on a thirsty begonia'.

The most considerable opinion of recent times was beyond doubt T. S. Eliot's, who praised Kipling and defended his ideas in an introductory essay to a selection of Kipling's verse. Though regarding the ballads in the main as 'verse but not poetry', Eliot conceded that it was 'great verse'. He added, however, that a writer can only be described as a 'great verse writer' if there is some of his work 'of which we cannot say whether it is verse or poetry'. George Orwell, criticizing Eliot's view that Kipling was 'a versifier who occasionally wrote poems', thought that while most of his verse was horribly vulgar, his best passages, though spurious were nevertheless seductive and that Kipling's rightful category was that of a 'good bad poet'. Whether verse or poetry, T. S. Eliot considered Kipling's metrical work to be that of a writer of great gifts for whom poetry seemed to have been purely an instrument. 'For Kipling the poem is something which is intended to act . . . and to elicit the same response from all readers, and only the response which they can make in common.'

In the general history of ideas, Kipling emerges as the outstanding literary representative, perhaps the foremost propagandist, of British imperialism in its task of preservation, consolidation and expansion of the Empire. Chronologically the peak of his creativity and popularity coincided with the fruition of Britain's imperialistic policy. His most famous verses, such as *The English Flag*, which contains the famous lines 'What do they know of England who only England know?', the breast-beating *Recessional; The White Man's Burden*, from which the quotation at the head of this chapter has been taken; *The Absent-Minded Beggar*; and similarly his stories of India, were jointly of immense significance as simultaneous incentives to, and symbols of, Britain's imperialistic sentiments—that mixture of patriotic pride, belief in a civilizing mission, and the romance of the picturesque and exotic. Although Kipling was frequently critical of America, it was his belief (as it was Cecil Rhodes's), that English and American Imperialism could be merged in an Anglo-Saxon doctrine of power. America's war with Spain over Cuba and her conquest of the Phillipines held the same significance for the body of opinion in the United States as did the Sudanese and Boer Wars for corresponding influential circles in England and it is also significant that Cecil Rhodes, the most committed of them all, dreamed of a combined Anglo-Saxon world-power.

Objections to imperialism are based on arguments too well known in out time to need discussion. Apart from these, imperialists have been held in contempt as inferior types of human beings who focus their aims on external and superficial ends, on aggression and lust for power, ambitions which betoken a spiritual void. Such accusations are quite understandable. From some aspects, to judge from their public utterances and their writings, Kipling, Rhodes, Theodore Roosevelt, often seem like retarded twelve-year-olds. Kipling displayed an obvious delight in the exploits of his gang of schoolboys, in *Stalky & Co.*, and 'Teddy' Roosevelt liked to call himself D'Artagnan and his chief advisers Athos, Porthos and Aramis. There is something distasteful and disquieting in this cheerful conviction of superiority, the insistence on physical fitness and efficiency, the cult of virility with its concurrent emphasis on chivalrous and chaste protectiveness towards the weak, defenceless female. Both Roosevelt and Kipling, as it happens, were undersized men who felt a compulsive need to compensate for their lack of inches by making themselves—among other things—tough and strong.

The empire, as a unity, was a loose-knit composite of distant foreign lands, civil administrators and soldiers who protected and conquered, and it was important, as an element of propaganda, to envelop the ideas of empire in an aura of romance. Attempting to justify their beliefs, apologists of imperialism could rightly draw attention to the self-critical and realistic attitudes which were mingled with the romance. Kipling exposed certain shortcomings of British rule in India. The soldiers he portrays are no glamorous heroes, but cynical, drunken womanizers, very often brutal ruffians. Nevertheless the dominant feature of his imperialism is its aura of romance. The commercial interests at stake are soft-pedalled. Officials are ready to make great personal sacrifices in the interests of the people whom they serve by governing. All his uncouth Tommy Atkinses have hearts of gold beneath their rugged exteriors. Heightened realism makes the romance more subtle. Peace, needless to say, is preferable to war—Kipling said it over and over again—but when all is said and done, how thrilling war can be! It should be emphasized that generosity of the conqueror to the conquered was a point of honour. In this respect Kipling was one of the first to advocate reconciliation after the Boer War. A proper idea of these moods could be given only through a detailed analysis of Kipling's work. His barrack-room ballad *Loot* provides a good example of the difficulties which arise in any attempt to explain his equivocal attitudes and dubious ethics. In this poem, full of jaunty rhythms and catchy rhymes, he gives what is virtually a recipe for the forciblc plunder of booty from the 'natives' in India or Burma. Edward Shanks in his biography of Kipling finds these verses atrocious and believes that in all probability *Loot* has done more harm to Kipling's reputation than anything else he wrote.

Now remember when you're 'acking round a gilded Burma God
That 'is eyes is very often precious stones;
An' if you treat a nigger to a dose o' cleanin'-rod
'E's like to show you everything 'e owns.
When 'e won't produce no more, pour some water on the floor
Where you 'ear it answer 'ollow to the boot
(Cornet: Toot! Toot!)
When the ground begins to sink, shove your baynick down the chink,
An' you're sure to touch the—
(*Chorus*) Loo! loo! Lulu! Loot! Loot! Loot! Ow the loot!

'This is wholly detestable', Shanks observes, 'and it makes the commentator on Kipling turn red when he endeavours to explain it.'

T. S. Eliot, on the other hand, made an effort to get round the difficulty by saying that of course Kipling was not defending looting just because he made one of his soldiers sing the delights of plunder. He could presumably be regarded as tacitly censuring the act by allowing the looter to condemn himself out of his own mouth. But the inescapable impression remains that by presenting the offence in such a cheerful, matter-of-fact way, the poem in a sense condones it and becomes an implicit apology for such acts.

George Orwell, challenging some of T.S. Eliot's statements in his essay *Rudyard Kipling* (1942), felt that

> 'it is no use pretending that Kipling's view of life, as a whole, can be accepted or even forgiven by any civilized person. It is no use claiming, for instance, that when Kipling describes a British soldier beating a "nigger" with a cleaning rod in order to get money out of him, he is acting merely as a reporter and does not necessarily approve what he describes.'

Orwell found no sign anywhere in Kipling's work of any disapproval of such conduct. Before looking for what to admire, he thought it better to admit right away the horrid truth that 'Kipling *is* a jingo imperialist, he *is* morally insensitive and aesthetically disgusting'.

Loot recalls one of the complacent reflexions of clever Stalky's schoolboy pals in *Stalky & Co.*: 'Just imagine Stalky let loose on the south side of Europe with a sufficiency of sikhs and a reasonable prospect of loot. Consider it quietly.'

Just what were the aims of British imperialism? Kipling's pronouncements were more or less what other spokesmen of imperialism were saying in the 1890s. The outstanding voice was perhaps that of Benjamin Kidd. What he wrote applied first of all to Anglo-Saxons in general, who represented a 'higher type of social order' vowed to the mission of civilizing 'inferior' races. The conquerors and empire builders took for granted that to do this they must have 'humanity, strength and uprightness of character and devotion to the immediate call of duty without thought of brilliant ends and ideal results'. If Kipling had attempted to formulate a systematic theory of life it would most probably have been expressed in some such terms as Kidd's. His keyword was the 'Law', by which he meant order and every man knowing his place. The 'Law' and technical progress were the gifts of conquerors to primitive races. The rulers needed to have a strong feeling of responsibility towards the peoples under their administration. Pride, boastfulness and weakness were things to be shunned and this line of thought is apparent in *Re-*

cessional. The task of empire-builders—as it was once the Romans'—was to civilize; and civilization meant, in the first instance order, coupled with solidarity, co-operative understanding between those who commanded and those who obeyed. Beyond this order stood the 'lesser breeds without the law' among whom Kipling, at one time or another, seems to have lumped all nations who were not British, even the Americans.

Anglo-Saxon imperialism could be divided into what might be called a left wing and a right wing. The left wing, which included the leading Fabians of the time, emphasized that imperialist aims must be the development, possession of full equality of rights and national autonomy of 'inferior' subject races. This policy has proved successful and the countries which have gained full independence can be said to have developed according to the left-wing pattern of imperialism. The right-wing imperialists hardly disputed these aims, which seemed to them, nevertheless, remote and unrealistic. They believed the essential requirements to be leadership, domination, law and order. Kipling evidently held these right-wing imperialistic views and his conviction of the obligation to civilize 'new-caught, sullen peoples' was mingled with the pride of the conqueror. These beliefs had bearing on his attitude to domestic policy. He was an extreme Tory and though not anti-democratic he was sceptical and almost disdainful of democracy. The 'Law' with regard to England meant social hierarchy and the upholding of tradition.

Kipling's place in the general history of ideas has been lucidly discussed by Noel Annan in an essay in *Victorian Studies* (Vol. III, 1959–60). Lord Annan points out that for decades now, Kipling has been judged less from an artistic than from a moral and political standpoint—'at the root of every assessment of Kipling lies the problem of his morality'. Kipling has been accused of being saturated with toryism and imperialism of the most vulgar kind. According to Lionel Trilling 'His toryism often had in it a lower middle class snarl of defeated gentility', and Kipling is taken to task for his cynicism and brutality, to say nothing of his rancour, callousness, caste-feeling and arrogance. 'Kipling is unloved and unlovable not by reason of his beliefs but by reason of the temperament that gave them literary expression.'

But, says Lord Annan, Kipling's attitude must be seen from a wider perspective. He was the only English writer of his time who could be compared with 'those continental sociologists—Durkheim, Weber, Pareto—who revolutionized the study of society at the beginning of the century. The same problems which forced them to invent new methods of analysing human behaviour led him to conclusions similar to theirs.' If this is not taken into account, Kipling's originality and importance cannot be appreciated. The point of departure for such a view can be found in Taine's truism: 'A human society, and particularly a modern society, is a vast and complicated thing'—a truly conservative reflection, which sums up all that has been said on the subject from Hobbes and Burke to the present. In this view, the fact that human society exists and endures is something so remarkable and important that all means are justified to secure and perpetuate the conditions of so vital a structure, and all attempts at basic alteration or reform of the established order must be regarded with mistrust.

In Lord Annan's view, 'while for most writers society is the background, or provides the interests for or is a positive threat to their characters, for Kipling the very existence of society is a problem'. This was because, he explains, Kipling had been born and brought up in India, where peace, law and order and all the elementary conditions of life in an organized society were constantly threatened; whereas his fellow-writers, on the other hand, in an England untouched for generations by civil war or revolution or economic or spiritual disaster, had started out from unchanging conditions which they took for granted as the background of political and social stability in the mother country.

That is why, the explanation continues, Kipling concentrated on a simultaneous study and defence of the bare essentials necessary to create and maintain a social structure. Included in this minimum were inflexible authority, the ability and the desire to use force to maintain authority, a pattern of behaviour which should give some sort of unity, ideas which should inspire veneration and solidarity, institutions and social strata which should lead to the formation of a hierarchy, and the fulfilment of definite social functions; that is, religion, law, custom, convention, morality—all the forces of social control imposed on individuals. This constituted—to use Kipling's favourite term—the 'Law'.

How the construction of the necessary institutions and ideas was brought about, and the nature of the resulting structure was of secondary importance to Kipling. It was enough for him that a society existed and could function. It mattered little to him if authority was harsh and arbitrary or whether 'customs or morality or religion were right or wrong', so long as the family and the school—the two most important cultural factors—were acceptable and were effective from any definite ethical or ideological viewpoint. The question he asked was 'What holds society together?' not 'Is it held together in a way which reasonably approaches the ideal?' As a consequence he naturally defended—directly or indirectly—imperialism, oppressive police force, illusionism; and he rejected enlightenment, equalization and democratic principles.

Lord Annan outlines the trend of this thinking with great analytical skill, though perhaps he tends to take it a trifle too seriously. Surely what it all amounts to is simply good old honest conservatism which by emphasizing the importance of the social minimum tries to ignore or at least reduce the need for reforms and changes. The modern sociologists he refers to—especially Malinovsky, in addition to the three already mentioned—have evolved only an incomplete theory of the nature and functioning of human society and in doing so they have often had recourse to quasi-scientific or pseudo-scientific methods. By expressing Kipling's simple creed in terms of modern sociology Lord Annan makes it seem more consciously intellectualized and subtle than it really was.

It is important to remember one thing more. Kipling's imperialism and conservatism have not been criticized or attacked solely or even mainly on the grounds of some theoretical viewpoint, but because they seemed to indicate a personal harshness and insensitivity to human suffering which characterized 'the brutally insensitive authoritarian of the middle years'—indeed, sometimes revealing what appear to be feelings of satisfaction or enjoyment in the presence of suffering.

Where de Maistre regarded the executioner as the main prop and stay of society he was right, of course, inasmuch as no society can exist without some kind of organized police force. What is so distasteful in de Maistre's thinking is the obvious relish with which he proclaims the indispensibility of the executioner. The same objection can be made to Kipling's philosophy—an aspect overlooked by Annan in his sociologist's delight at his discoveries.

Had Kipling's imperialism any basis in feelings of racial prejudice, or did he consider British or Anglo-Saxon superiority to be accidental and conditioned by environment? English critics have, by and large, exonerated him from any imputations of racial prejudice. It has not occurred to them or they choose to ignore the fact that sixty years ago, a body of learned thought accepted ideas of racial inferiority as scientifically proven. Kipling's apologists base their belief that he was free from racial prejudice on his habitual use of 'white' applied not only to persons without skin pigmentation but also to those with black or yellow skins who nevertheless merited respect. In other words 'white' in Kipling's vocabulary was only a synonym for 'decent'—so never mind the colour of Gunga Din's skin. Fichte made a similar use of such semantic subtleties when he said that 'To have character and to be a German undoubtedly mean the same thing'. But quite obviously, by pointing this out, one does not escape the belief that 'white' Gunga Dins imply a correlation of whiteness with merit; it only expresses the fact more subtly or in a more complicated way. Kipling was obviously full of primitive ideas about the 'nature' of certain races or nations—an attitude made clear in his autobiography, through casual remarks on the subject.

Are there any affinities between Kiplingesque imperialism and fascism or Nazism? Biographers have indignantly rejected such a thought. Objectively regarded, however, the English form of nationalist extremism represented by Kipling—to say nothing of Carlyle, Ruskin and others—undoubtedly has points of contact with both fascism and

Nazism. Nevertheless, this has not prevented English and American nationalism from being incomparably more humane and tolerant than the hypertrophied nationalism of Fascist Italy and Nazi Germany, nor did Kipling's espousal of imperialism lessen his whole-hearted abhorrence of the dictators of his age.

III
WARRIORS AND WARS

'Our Only General': Garnet Joseph Wolseley

'All Sir Garnet' was a catch-phrase popular in England in the 1870s and was used to mean that things were all right, all in order or, as one might say nowadays, okay. The man whose deeds prompted the expression and its meaning was Garnet Joseph Wolseley (1833–1913), the eldest son of a spendthrift Irish army captain who died when Wolseley was seven, leaving a young widow to bring up seven small children on slender means as best she might. Wolseley's mother gave him his first lessons, later sending him to a Dublin day-school where he excelled in history, mathematics and other subjects necessary or useful to a military career. At fourteen he applied for a commission without purchase, confident of reaching the standard of education required to make him eligible for appointment at the minimum age, sixteen. At seventeen, no commission being forthcoming, he wrote to the Commander-in-Chief, the octogenarian Duke of Wellington, but was ignored. He then wrote to Lord Raglan, Wellington's military secretary, but this letter, too, failed to produce any result. The following year Wolseley's mother wrote to the Duke entreating him as an act of kindness to grant her son, brought up to be a soldier like his father, the commission she could not afford to purchase. Some ten months later, a couple of months before he died the Duke granted the youth, then aged nineteen, the longed-for commission, as Ensign in the 12th Foot.

Ambitious and eager for active service, Wolseley speedily obtained a transfer, was sent to India, and thence to Burma where the Second Burma War was being waged. In his first engagement with the enemy the young ensign displayed the courage and daring for which he was to become noted. He was severely wounded, was mentioned in dispatches, and, as a result, barely out of his teens, was promoted to Lieutenant.

By the time he was twenty-six, and after several promotions, he was a Lieutenant-Colonel, priding himself on having reached all ranks without purchase. He had served with distinction in four campaigns and had been wounded four times with varying degrees of severity, losing the sight of his left eye and receiving a wound in the right leg which took away part of his shin, with crippling effects which he suffered stoically for the rest of his life. From the start he had proved to be a gallant, cool-headed leader who combined resourcefulness and initiative with the ability to implement his practical experience by a studious and intellectual approach to the problems of warfare.

He was to become, as Major-General Sir Garnet Wolseley, later Field-Marshal Lord Wolseley, the most famous and surely the most outstanding British military commander between Wellington and, one might suggest, Kitchener, Wavell, Alexander or Montgomery. 'Intellectually all other British soldiers were pygmies compared to him', wrote the biographer Julian Symons in *Buller's Campaign* (1963). Military writers have pronounced a similar verdict: 'the ablest British soldier of the past hundred years', the opinion of Major-General John Fuller, writing in the thirties, is typical. Even Wolseley's detractors had to admit his supreme talents as a military organizer, which far surpassed those of Kitchener.

Wolseley reaped his due rewards: he was knighted in 1870 after his successful suppression of the Red River rebellion in Canada; at the outbreak of the Ashanti war in 1875, now Sir Garnet Wolseley, he was appointed Commander-in-Chief with the local rank of Major-General. On his return to England, having brought the war to a successful conclusion, now a celebrated General and a national figure, he was invested by the Queen with the Grand Cross of the Order of St Michael and St George and of a Knight Commander of the Bath. He was received in the Houses of Parliament where he was given eulogies and thanks; he was also awarded a grant of £25,000, received various other honours and was appointed Major-General. He had hoped for a peerage and refused an offered baronetcy on the privately expressed grounds that it was belittling to be classed with common personages such as the Duke of Devonshire's head-gardener, who had recently been honoured in similar fashion. Wolseley was nominated member of the Indian Council in 1876 and in 1878 was appointed High Commissioner in Cyprus, the first administrator of the newly acquired island. As Governor of Natal in 1879, with supreme civil and military command in Natal and the Transvaal, he dealt briskly and briefly with unrest and challenges to Britain's authority among Zulus and Boers, returning in 1880 to England and to increased popularity as 'master of the small war', to be hailed as 'our only General', and good-naturedly caricatured by W. S. Gilbert, in *The Pirates of Penzance*, as 'the very model of a modern Major-General'.

In 1882, at the successful close of the Egyptian campaign to crush the revolt headed by Colonel Arabi, whose army was destroyed in a few hours at the battle of Tel-el-Kebir, the model Major-General was created Baron Wolseley of Cairo and of Wolseley in Staffordshire and received a large cash grant. After the unsuccessful expedition of 1885 to the Sudan to rescue Gordon, a failure considered no fault of Wolseley's, he received the thanks of the Salisbury government and was made a General and a Viscount. He was promoted to Field-Marshal in 1894, became Commander-in-Chief in Ireland, 1890–95, and, having ousted the Duke of Cambridge, Commander-in-Chief of the Army, 1895–1900.

Yet in spite of all these achievements and the multiple honours they brought him, Wolseley—except when he was on active service, engaged in some battle or 'small war'—seemed almost always to be embittered and discontented. A man in a state of constant exasperation at the inefficient organization of the War Office, he was permanently at loggerheads with the Commander-in-Chief, the Duke of Cambridge, a staunch reactionary and the Queen's first cousin, as much liked by her as Wolseley was for long disliked. Not least among his irritations was the Liberal party which was devoid of any feeling for, or sense of Empire; and then there were those dunderheads, his military colleagues, not to speak of the interminable intervals between wars, which meant the lack of the right kind of challenge for the display and recognition of his great gifts as a soldier—primarily, a talent for winning battles with the maximum of organization, economy and dispatch. Longing for a proper war, he died on the eve of the genuine article which was then looming up at long last. By that time, however, he was old and senile and virtually forgotten, practically a recluse, living in retirement with his adored wife Louisa in grace-and-favour apartments at Hampton Court or at his winter residence in the south of France, at Menton, where he died in March 1913. He received belated redress in burial in the crypt of St Paul's, close to his benefactor Wellington. The regiments escorting the gun-carriage in the funeral procession were chosen for their association with Wolseley's military career, a reminder in slow-march of his exploits in the Crimea, Burma, India, China, Canada, West Africa, South Africa and Egypt.

Numerous books about Wolseley, or about one or other of his campaigns, have appeared in recent years, one of the best and most detailed biographies being Joseph Lehmann's *All Sir Garnet* (1964). In *England's Pride* (1965), Julian Symons has given vivid and detailed treatment to the astonishing story of Wolseley's expedition to relieve Khartoum and rescue Gordon. Wolseley himself wrote a number of books between 1862 and 1904: an account of his experiences in China, *A Narrative of the War with China in 1860* (1862), a highly-successful military training manual, *The Soldiers Pocketbook for Field Service* (1869), a two-volume *Life of Marlborough* (1894), *The Decline and Fall of Napoleon* (1895), his two-volume autobiography, *The Story of a Soldier's Life* (1903–4). He even wrote (under a pseudonym) a novel, *Marley Castle* (1877), about which the less said the better. His autobiography, the second volume fragmentary and unfinished, was written in old age, when his memory had been in decay for some years, and is unfortunately unreliable.

What made Wolseley so remarkable? First and foremost, surely, that he was three persons rolled into one: the successful general, cool, clever, methodically calculating; the hero, every bit a rival to Gordon, as fearless and as eager for battle but with none of Gordon's 'half-cracked' egocentricity; the intellectual, able to associate on terms of equality not only with J. A. Froude, Sir Edmund Gosse, Andrew Lang, and Alfred Austin the Poet Laureate (remembered, if at all, as a trumpery poetaster —in any case, Wolseley had no taste for his or any other poetry), but also with the great Henry James, nowadays among the most highly esteemed of late Victorian men of letters.

Wolseley was assigned his first independent mission of importance in 1870 when he was sent to Canada to suppress a rebellion of *métis* or half-breed settlers in the Red River Valley region of the north-west. The settlers, under the leadership of the half-breed Louis Riel, had declared a provisional government at Fort Garry on the Red River, close by the village of Winnipeg, hundreds of miles distant from Toronto and the large Anglo-French settlements. After a hazardous journey westward through a wilderness of rock and forest, first by train and steamer and ultimately in a fleet of specially built boats, rowing through lakes and turbulent rivers which presented many unnavigable stretches broken by falls and rapids, round which the boats had to be dragged, the party reached Fort Garry within hours of the time predicted by Wolseley. Riel had fled at the approach of the troops and the revolt ended without a shot being fired and, in spite of accidents and sickness en route, without the loss of a single man.

Wolseley's next exploit, as Commander-in-Chief in the Ashanti War of 1873–74, was the conquest of the ferocious Ashanti, a predatory nation of slave-hunters whose fetish rites demanded the sacrifice yearly of some thousand human victims, men, women and children. The King of the Ashanti, Kofi Kalcali—'King Coffee' to the English—ruled the warrior tribes from his fine palace in a fine capital, Kumasi. Within three weeks of Wolseley's advance into Ashanti territory, King Kofi's warriors had been defeated and dispersed, Kofi had fled and Wolseley had entered the city—again without a shot being fired, and again on the day he had predicted.

For all its wide streets and well-kept houses, Kumasi was a fetid, charnel city filled with the suffocating stench of putrescence from innumerable corpses rotting in a mortuary grove where the decapitated and mutilated bodies of newly sacrificed victims were flung on to the heaped accumulations of a century. Great swarms of flies buzzed over these dreadful remains and hordes of vultures brooded, gorged but watchful, on the surrounding trees, or hovered in dark multitudes overhead.

Wolseley's peace overtures, with assurances for Kofi's safety, were answered with delaying tactics and attempted treachery. The resulting destruction of his palace by the conquerors, as they marched out of burned and looted Kumasi (taking with them King Kofi's state umbrella as a present for Queen Victoria) contributed to Kofi's decision to come to terms and he subsequently set his mark to a treaty under which he agreed to grant independence to vassal tribes, open Ashanti territory to trade, renounce human sacrifice and a pay a punitive tribute of 50,000 ounces of gold.

As civil and military Governor of Natal, Wolseley brought the Zulu War of 1879–80 to a successful conclusion after the blunders of Lord Chelmsford (whom he was to replace as Commander-in-Chief), had led to a crushing defeat of the British forces at Isandhlwana by the *impis* of Cetewayo, the Zulu king. While Wolseley was delayed by heavy seas from disembarking, the situation was further complicated by Chelmsford's hasty withdrawal after a belated victory at Ulundi, when he should have pursued the defeated Zulu army and taken Cetewayo prisoner. It was left to Wolseley to receive the submission of the principal Zulu chiefs and to organize the hunting down and capture of the now deposed and fugitive Cetewayo, a task which he set about in his usual methodical manner and accomplished in little more than a couple of weeks.

In 1882, at the battle of Tel-el-Kebir, he vanquished the forces of Colonel Ahmed Arabi the Egyptian nationalist agitator and rebel, thereby dispelling a threat to British power in Egypt which had placed in jeopardy the payment of the Egyptian national debt, the free passage of the Suez Canal and the lives and properties of thousands of Britons and other non-Egyptians.

Wolseley's final mission, in 1885, was to command the unsuccessful Gordon Relief Expedition. After a fatal two-day delay in starting out, the advance guard of a desert column commanded by Brigadier-General Sir Herbert Stewart, and after his death by Sir Redvers Buller, travelled up the Nile in two tiny steam-boats, which had been sent out by Gordon from Khartoum. The rescuers arrived two days too late: Khartoum had been stormed and Gordon was dead. This was Wolseley's first reverse and his last campaign, so that he never afterwards had an opportunity to repair the damage to his reputation caused by this single failure.

In several of his campaigns Wolseley's forces were small in the extreme, consisting for the most part of a few thousand men, only a small number of whom were British soldiers. In the action against Arabi Pasha he commanded an army of just over 40,000 men, the biggest expeditionary force sent abroad by Britian up to that time. Some of his expeditions took several months, the most celebrated of these engagements, the Arabi campaign, only three weeks. The battles he fought were as a rule simple affairs, insofar as the British troops were superior in weapons and discipline to whatever primitive adversaries they were fighting; when the enemy was engaged it was merely a matter of shooting down as many as possible in the shortest space of time. This was the golden age of colonial warfare; with small forces, great hardships; minor defeats and major victories; minimal losses and maximal gains, all neatly tied up with a glorious homecoming for the victorious troops, pictures in the penny papers and illustrated magazines, fulsome praise in *The Times* and, as the final accolade, luncheon or an audience with the Queen, who had a tender spot in her heart for her beloved Army and its glory.

If Wolseley's name had become a popular catchword and the nation looked on him as 'our only General', it was because of something more than the honours and the victories—those were taken for granted; it was because the nation's number-one trouble-shooter was unequalled as an organizer. The history of warfare, as everybody knows, is a melancholy tale of blunders and misunderstandings, of arrivals too late at the wrong destination, attacks on the wrong objective at the wrong hour, useless sacrifice, wasted bravery, hollow victories. Nothing of this kind ever happened in any of Wolseley's undertakings. Blunders were not in his book. He was a master at calculating his own or the enemy's forces, at surveying the terrain and estimating distances, at planning operational co-ordination. He used to undertake, not without a bit of swank, and even bet on it, to be at a certain place at a certain time the following day or week as the case might be; and he was as good as his word, almost invariably winning his bet. He carried out his operations with the minimum of delay, at minimum cost and with minimum losses.

In his recourse to this methodical procedure, Wolseley seems to have been almost alone among high-ranking military men between 1870–80 and probably even for some years later. The old, respectable methods of training and preparation, hallowed by tradition, relied on parades and manoeuvres; real battles were regarded as little more than full-dress field-days; there was no such thing as a general staff; the most valued stand-bys were discipline and courage. This system, or lack of it, had achieved its most catastrophic triumph in the Crimean War and at the Battle of Balaclava. Many of the older soldiers regarded Wolseley as a 'cocksure young bookworm' full of dangerous, new-fangled ideas. He particularly antagonized and irritated the peace-loving Duke of Cambridge, comfortably settled in as Commander-in-Chief of the Army since 1856, after the disaster of the Crimea, and a great lover of parades, reviews and picturesque uniforms. The Duke was an implacable opponent of all change in the Army, and believed that the only proper time ever to introduce a reform was when it could no longer be avoided. His hostility and obstructive tactics were a source of constant vexation and frustration to Wolseley and the two of them warred stubbornly for twenty-five years, each convinced that the other was a 'destroyer of the Army'. The old guard saw in Wolseley 'a low Radical', a vulgar reformer and pedant of logistics; for his part, Wolseley despised 'Royal George' and the Horse Guards clique, 'the old fogeys', the donkeys and blockheads who opposed his ideas and his enthusiastic support of Cardwell's sweeping army reforms. He surrounded himself with young, intelligent officers still eager to learn—his hand-picked, highly-competent cronies and colleagues, the 'Ashanti ring' of his earlier soldiering successes and friendships. Many of these officers in the so-called 'Wolseley gang' rose to become important military commanders; others were killed early, like Colley at Majuba; or lost confidence when they had to fight alone, without the inspiration and encouragement of the Master, like Buller at Tugela.

But Wolseley was by no means a 'civilian' or 'desk' general. Though he antagonized—and was heartily disliked by—many of his colleagues as a boastful, self-seeking upstart, all were agreed that he was an outstanding commander. His care for the fighting man, his resoluteness, tenacity and disregard of personal danger were everywhere praised. As a young officer on active service in Burma, in the Crimea, in India during the Mutiny and in China with Lord Elgin's expedition to Peking in 1860, he displayed a daring and a contempt of death unusual even in that era of ostentatious physical courage. He was wounded time and again, but whatever the severity of his condition, he fought on or at least continued to command and encourage his men until the battle had been won. His autobiography and the letters written in old age indicate—even though events may have been enhanced in the rosy glow of remembrance—that in action he was filled with, even possessed by, an excitement and exultation which most people would find abnormal. Like Ernst Jünger, the German novelist, recorder of battle scenes and interpreter of the mystique of warfare, Wolseley could well have described the repulsive smell of corpses on a battlefield as 'the Offensive perfume'. An offensive brought the young Wolseley feelings which he described as 'a heaven of ecstatic excitement', of 'unalloyed and elevating satisfaction . . . and joy':

> '. . . there can be nothing in the world like it, or that can approach its inspiration, its intense sense of pride. You are for the time being . . . lifted up from and out of all petty thoughts of self, and for the moment your whole existence, soul and body, seems to revel in a true sense of glory.'

An evening in an exposed front-line trench before Sebastopol, was 'an evening's entertainment'; picking off any enemy gunner rash enough to stick his head above the Russian trenches, was a sport which afforded him intense pleasure. 'Man-shooting' he considered the finest sport of all: 'the more you kill, the more you wish to kill'. For Wolseley and his comrades at arms the world seemed 'made for their wild amusements, of which war with its intoxicating suspense was the greatest of all'. His longing to get out to the Crimea was so great that he called it 'a sort of madness—but I was sensible enough to understand it for just what it was'. In some respects Wolseley was hypersensitive; the mere look or smell of raw meat made him queasy and to pass by a butcher's shop was an ordeal; yet he was not sickened by the ghastly mutilations of the battlefield and the sight of a dead comrade left him 'as indifferent as to a dog I had killed at home'.

This attitude pervaded even his ideas. In a way not unusual in those times, he regarded war as sublime and ennobling, an experience which induced disregard of all selfish and material considerations and enhanced the glory of dying for one's country.

> 'The ordinary, I may call it vulgar life of the English best class of society is odious to all people of thought and refinement who are not thorough-paced snobs. . . . It is horrible to say so, but I feel that a country living under our present form of Government and whose classes, that is the rich as well as the old county families, live as the Prince of Wales and all his abominable set of men and women do, can only be saved from annihilation by some such periodical upheaval as a great war.'

In his little manual for the staff officer, *The Soldier's Pocket Book for Field Service*, he made clumsy and tactless observations and advocated courses of action and conduct which seemed too much to swallow and gave offence in various quarters. Soldiers, he said, should 'be taught to despise all those of civil life' and 'should not be brought into contact with the softening influence of old men and respectable women'. He warned against newspaper war correspondents 'and all that race of drones . . . those newly invented curses to armies, who eat the rations of fighting men and do no work at all'. He took pride in classing himself, in his own words, among the 'high-souled jingoes of the purest water', in fact, 'a Jingo of the Jingoes'; he held Liberals and lovers of peace in the greatest contempt and he detested Gladstone. Summoned to Balmoral after his victory over Arabi Pasha, he and the Queen with considerable relish exchanged criticisms of Gladstone and his Egyptian policy, Wolseley agreeing whole-heartedly with the Queen's scandalized indignation at Gladstone's omission to have the rebel Arabi hanged.

Wolseley's character and attitudes do not appear to have contained any of the religious crankiness, the hatred of humanity, the possessed fanaticism that distinguished Gordon. Nevertheless he regarded Gordon as one of the two greatest men he had ever known—'and the greater of these two was General Lee.' Wolseley, had met Gordon as a young man of his own age in the Crimea: 'one of the very few friends who came up to my estimate of a Christian hero'. When he visited Robert E. Lee in 1862 at the Confederate general's headquarters near Winchester, shortly after the battle of Antietam, Lee impressed him as a man of great dignity and goodness, cheerful and serene, without a scrap of anything tense or tenebrous in his nature; the very reverse of Gordon. His liking and sympathy for two men of such diametrically opposed characters as Gordon and Robert E. Lee would seem to denote a certain complexity in his own character.

Wolseley was consciously proud not only of being intelligent but of being an 'intellectual'. He had an inherited love of books and read omnivorously, apart from his study of military manuals and books on warfare, himself wrote ambitious books, tried his hand at a novel and was eager to consort with celebrities who were eminent in fields other than his own. There was not a little of the intellectual snob in him, coupled with an arrogance which made him despise the illiterate generals who were his colleagues. When he sent home from Ashanti a George III silver coffee-pot exchanged by slave-traders for gold dust and looted from King Kofi's treasure, Wolseley wrote to his wife: 'I thought it would be a subject for conversation at breakfast whenever we might have very stupid people staying with us.'

But although he bent over backward to prove that he was not just 'a silly soldier-man', there was a less pretentious, more genuine side to his personality. He liked discussing unusual subjects and enjoyed intelligent conversation on a higher plane than is usual even in the conversation which aspires to something more than small talk.

There are several accounts of his friendship or at least acquaintanceship and meetings with Henry James, to whom he appeared 'a very handsome, well-mannered and fascinating little man—with rosy dimples and an eye of steel: an excellent specimen of the *cultivated* British soldier'. They talked animatedly—Wolseley recounting his experiences concisely and lucidly; James, as always, obscure, involved, his phrases a mesh of pauses, repetitions, reservations and qualifications. As Professor Leon Edel records in *The Untried Years, 1843–1870* (1953), the first volume of his major biography of James, the psychological novelist seems to have enjoyed talking to a distinguished fighting soldier; military history was one of Henry James's hobbies, and in the midst of his preoccupation with style he sometimes mused on the drums of Friedland and Gettysburg. When, in 1903, Wolseley sent James a copy of his autobiography, he received in return a letter which, even discounting the usual conventional courtesies and insincerities, 'the mere twaddle of graciousness', seemed to indicate that, abnormally cut off from external experience as he was, Henry James found great enjoyment in reading books of this kind—works which, as it were, hailed him from the outside world with a greeting from Action and Life:

> 'To a poor worm of peace and quiet like me—yet with some intelligence—the interest of communicating so with the military temper and type is irresistible—of getting so close (comparatively!) to the

qualities, unlike one's own that are romantic, that you have lived all your days by and with them and for them, I feel as if I had never questioned you nor sounded you enough . . . I would give all I have (including Lamb House) for an hour of your retrospective consciousness, one of your more crowded memories. . . .'

Wolseley was a figure of importance and a fascinating personality; yet one is not drawn to him with the same liking one has for the eccentric Gordon or the perennial cavalry-lieutenant 'Bobs' Roberts. Perhaps Wolseley was over-ambitious—he gives the impression of trying too hard; there is something slightly repellant not only in his intellectual conceit but in his insistence on being top-dog, on being always 'the firstest with the mostest'; surely, in a man so gifted, this was hardly necessary. He was always longing for fresh victories in other fields, to show once again that he was cleverer, abler, more efficient than the next man—perhaps driven by self-dissatisfaction, a spiritual disgust which never got as far as real self-analysis; or it may be that he was led on by illusions of salvation on some other plane.

Wolseley's professional life ended in a gentle, bemused and long-drawn-out eclipse, something like the picture he drew of Napoleon in his own book about the Emperor's decline and fall. The Commander-in-Chief, feared or admired—or both at once—by all, was becoming senile; his memory began to play him embarrassing tricks; he forgot appointments, forgot faces, denied he had written memoranda or reports he had dictated, began saying too many different things to too many different people. His disdain for others grew as he found himself ignored and slighted. And so it came about that Roberts, only a year older than himself, his despised and detested rival, was the man chosen to go to the rescue in South Africa, to restore and safeguard British prestige tarnished by victorious Boers. Created Earl Roberts of Pretoria and awarded £100,000 by the nation, he returned in triumph (even though the Boer War dragged on for another couple of years) to become and remain for many years the hero, the popular idol—while the great Wolseley, his astonishing exploits and military genius never properly recognized, was opposed, neglected, passed over, retired and finally faded into oblivion, forgetting and forgot.

A Great Christian Soldier: Charles George Gordon

The news of General Gordon's death which reached England in February 1885, a fortnight after the fall of Khartoum, aroused in the English people a mood of hysterical grief and anger almost unprecedented in the nation's history.

Overcome with sorrow and indignation, the Queen wrote to Augusta Gordon, the dead man's sister:

> 'That the promises of support were not fulfilled—which I so frequently and constantly pressed on those who asked him to go—is to me *grief inexpressable*! Indeed, it has made me ill! . . . and what I do so keenly feel, the *stain* left upon England for your dear Brother's cruel, though heroic, fate!'

A day of national mourning was declared. Memorial services were held in Westminster and St Paul's Cathedral and in parish churches all over the country. Gladstone, in his speech to the Commons, called Gordon 'a hero of heroes'—though he took care to observe that the hero had become one by ignoring government instructions which he had agreed to and, indeed, helped to draft. Gladstone and the Government were universally execrated for their failure to rescue Gordon. The Grand Old Man, stripped of his affectionate title G.O.M., now became M.O.G. —Murderer of Gordon. Eulogies of the dead man poured in from every quarter.

An unparalleled hero-cult sprang up, releasing a flood of pamphlets, sermons, books. Statues were erected to his memory, memorial windows dedicated to him in cathedrals and churches; The Gordon Boys' Homes were founded for the training of boys for the army and Gordon Boys' Clubs were established in industrial towns to perpetuate the hero's memory in Christian service to English youths, and in emulation of his charitable work twenty years earlier for the orphaned waifs of Gravesend. With such commemorative gestures the whole nation did homage to a saintly warrior-martyr.

Gordon's fame in England is undiminished. His story is enshrined in school books as an example of supreme heroism. Known in outline to every schoolboy it is probably familiar in considerable detail to most middle-aged average Englishmen today and it is not unlikely that the exploits of Gordon of Khartoum are more vivid in the nation's memory than those of any other British general, from Wellington to Montgomery.

Since the appearance of the first biographies in 1884–85, innumerable books have been written about this military hero, and about the episodes of warfare and British colonial history in which he played a part. Fresh biographies appeared in 1886, 1889, 1900, 1908 and were followed by others, in ones and twos, every few years throughout the ensuing decades. During the fifties no fewer than three biographies of Gordon were published in a single year. A major biography appeared in 1956, Lord Elton's *General Gordon*, in which gross misconceptions about Gordon's life and character, propagated by Lytton Strachey and perpetuated by subsequent biographers, were corrected. In 1965, *England's Pride* by Julian

Symons recounted with a wealth of documentation the abortive dash across the Sudan of the expedition commanded by Wolseley to save the beseiged defenders of Khartoum. In 1966, Anthony Nutting's *Gordon: Martyr and Misfit* continued the contemporary concern of re-bunking in the wake of the de-bunkers. The book, contains an appraisal in depth of Gordon's personality and offers a hitherto unconsidered hypothesis concerning his desire for death and martyrdom, the life-long obsession which, according to the author's theory, was the cause of his suicidal stand in Khartoum. A later biography *Mission to Khartoum: an apotheosis of General Gordon* (1969) by John Marlowe, combines an objective account of the hero's life and career with a lucid analysis of the political and military situation leading up to and during Gordon's last mission to the Sudan.

What are the facts behind the enduring legend of General Gordon? He took part in Britain's early nineteenth-century wars, but as a mere subaltern, barely out of his teens, first in the Crimea and then in China. Unlike other nationally acclaimed Victorian generals, such as Napier, Lawrence, Wolseley and Roberts, he never played an active part in either the consolidation or the expansion of the Empire, whether in India, Afghanistan or Africa. There were, to be sure, two earlier periods of his life, when his exploits, first in China and then in Africa, for a time made headline news.

His early career gave little hint of the lasting fame he was to achieve as the transfigured hero and martyr of Khartoum. His record at the Royal Military College at Woolwich, where he was a cadet from 1847 to 1852, was relatively undistinguished, except for rebelliousness and a hot temper. He passed out from the academy with high marks for map-making and surveying but was otherwise sadly deficient in general education. His quirks of character eventually lost for him a hoped-for vacancy in the Royal Artillery and he had to be content with what was in his estimation an inferior commission in the less popular Royal Engineers. As a junior officer, his first assignment was to assist in the construction of forts at Pembroke Dock in Wales—a task he considered useless. A similar task fell to his lot eleven years later, when he was detailed to supervise the building of an equally useless chain of forts in Gravesend.

However futile the forts, his stay in Pembroke was crucial to the development of his religious beliefs. There were no diversions in the small, dreary town, beyond the narrow social life of army folk—dinner-parties, dances, small talk and gossip—in none of which was Gordon interested. He made a friend in one of his colleagues, an earnest and pious captain. He bought a horse and gig and they drove about the countryside discussing religious matters. Gordon wrote to his sister in 1854, 'I am very lucky in having a very religious captain of the 11th of the name of Drew.' This friendship exercised a permanent influence on

Gordon's life and thought, awakening in him the mysticism which came wholly to dominate his religious faith in later years.

When war broke out with Russia early in 1854 he volunteered for the Crimea and arrived there in December. He fought in the Siege of Sebastopol and the storming of the Redan, exposing himself unnecessarily to enemy fire, and attracting attention by feats of foolhardy bravery—which, in military parlance, came under the heading of conspicuous gallantry.

In the Crimea the 21-year-old subaltern, curly-haired, blue-eyed and good-looking, with delicate, sensitive features, met an officer of his own age, Captain Wolseley. A friendship, characterized by mutual hero-worship, sprang up between them and became a lasting one. Wolseley was to say, many years later, that Gordon 'was one of the very few friends I ever had who came up to my estimate of the Christian hero!'

After the withdrawal of the Russians from Sebastopol, which they left in flames, Gordon spent four months assisting in the destruction of the port. He was decorated for his services in the Crimea, receiving the British war medal from Turkey and the *Légion d'Honneur* from the French. Needless to say, numerous other junior officers who fought in the Crimea were similarly decorated. Higher-ranking officers received even more imposing awards and adornments; Gordon waxed scornful about 'the shower of decorations and promotions which fell upon senior officers'.

In May 1865, he was sent from the Crimea to Bessarabia, on the borders of Russia and Rumania, to assist in delimiting the frontiers laid down by the Treaty of Paris; and in 1857 he was moved on to Ezerum in Turkey to establish similar peace-treaty boundaries on the Armenian border. There he spent fifteen months in the mountains of Armenia and the Caucasus, living in tents among wild and lawless Kurdish nomads, an experience which instilled in him a love for the freedom of an open air existence and a lifelong aversion to the customs and conventions of civilized society.

In 1858 Gordon returned to England where, in 1859, he was promoted to Captain and appointed as Adjutant to the Royal Engineers depot at Chatham. However, after his adventurous experiences abroad, he was reluctant to stagnate in another dreary little English town. He wrote to his parents: 'I do not feel at all inclined to settle in England and be employed in any sedentary way.' Accordingly, in 1860, he volunteered to join the British force which, under Lord Elgin, was being organized in Shanghai to send a punitive expedition against Pekin to persuade the Manchu emperor to ratify the Treaty of Tientsin. The treaty, signed in March 1858, gave to the European powers the right to trade upon the Yangtse river as far as Hankow—as soon, that is, as the Taiping rebels had been crushed and peace had been restored to China.

The fifteen-year Taiping Revolt against the Manchu dynasty had been in progress for eight years, with now the rebels, now the imperialists victorious, and with great losses on both sides. The victories of the rebels over the imperial armies had enabled them to capture and occupy many cities. Their sweeping successes in the rich Yangtse Kiang river valley and its delta threatened to split China in two.

The Manchu emperor's enforced 'friendship' with the West was, to say the least, unstable. His unwillingness to ratify the Treaty of Tientsin was accompanied by periodical aggressive acts against the Europeans.

In July 1860 a force of 12,000 British and 6,000 French troops under the command of Lord Elgin, started for Peking. The Taku forts were captured and in August the allied forces reached Tientsin. The Manchu commander offered a truce; but when Elgin's emissaries reached the arranged meeting-place they and their Sikh escorts were seized, carried off to Peking and clapped into prison. The Allied forces thereupon advanced on Peking, the emperor fled and in October, Lord Elgin, with the Anglo-French forces, occupied the city and the vast Manchu Summer Palace.

Shortly before these events took place, Lieutenant Gordon had arrived in Shanghai from England. He was able to join Elgin's punitive expedition just after the occupation of Tientsin, and entered Peking with the Allied forces. When the city was occupied, on 6 October 1860, it was discovered that four of the abducted truce emissaries, all of them English, had been tortured to death. Lord Elgin was unwilling to victimize the civilian population by taking reprisals. Accordingly, as a lesson to the Manchu emperor that Englishmen could not be barbarously done to death with impunity, Elgin ordered the destruction of the Summer Palace. This act of vandalism was considered by the British officers a fitting retaliation and a just retribution for the barbarism of the Chinese.

Lieutenant Gordon, who was detailed to carry out the destruction of the palace, found to his astonishment that it was full of priceless art treasures which impressed him as being 'as splendid as anything to be found at Windsor'. Though he was no art-lover he was distressed by the wholesale vandalism of forces of occupation especially of the French who 'smashed up everything in the most wanton way'. Concerning the destruction of the palace he wrote:

> 'We accordingly went out, and, after pillaging it, burned the whole place, destroying in a most vandal-like manner property which would not be replaced by four millions. . . . You can scarcely imagine the beauty and magnificence of the palaces we burnt. It made one's heart sore to burn them.'

When the fabulous Summer Palace was a smoking ruin, Lord Elgin demanded the ratification of the treaty and the Chinese at last complied.

Gordon returned to Tientsin where he spent a year in command of a detachment of Engineers and during this time he made explorations in surrounding areas never before traversed by Europeans. Early in 1863, with his detachment, he was dispatched with other British troops to reinforce the garrison of Shanghai, which was attacked by the Taipings.

The city, a trading centre for European commerce, had been threatened by the rebels in 1860 and in 1862 was threatened for the second time. In the face of this new menace the European traders had financed a corps of Chinese mercenaries—later given as an encouragement the grandiloquent title of 'The Ever-Victorious Army'. This band of mercenaries had been raised and trained by Frederick T. Ward, an American soldier of fortune, to supplement the city's inadequate garrison of French and Indian troops.

In September 1862 Ward was killed in a skirmish with Taipings who were retreating from Tsingpo, recently captured from them by the mercenaries. The command was assumed by Ward's deputy, H. E. Burgvine, also an American adventurer. Burgvine, though courageous, was unscrupulous and callous. One of his amusements was to have captured prisoners blown from cannon. He allowed his troops to loot but, despite his ruffianly qualifications, was unable to control the mercenaries, being devoid of administrative or military ability. He was a hot-tempered and quarrelsome man and soon fell out with the new governor of Kiangsu Province, Li Hung Chang, who commanded the imperial forces in the area. Burgvine was eventually dismissed for striking a mandarin (a bank manager from whom he was trying to get money for his troops), and the Ever-Victorious Army was once more without a leader.

Gordon seemed the only suitable commander to prevent the now commanderless mercenary army from disintegrating and going over to the Taipings. But Britain, maintaining strict neutrality in the civil war between the Manchus and the Taipings, had decreed that no British officer could serve the Manchu emperor. In view of the critical situation the British government was induced to change its policy and in January 1863 the announcement was made that British officers would be allowed to serve the Manchu emperor.

Gordon, now thirty years old and promoted to Brevet-Major, assumed command of the Ever-Victorious Army, which was then a band of some 3,500 ragged, ill-paid and undisciplined ruffians. 'You never did see such a rabble!' was Gordon's comment to a military friend on taking command. He lost no time in licking the Ever-Victorious Army into shape. He gave them uniforms, taught them discipline, forbade looting, saw that they were regularly paid by the government authorities instead of sporadically by the Shanghai merchants. He was nevertheless unable to check desertions, losing some 2,000 men before the final victory and he had to quell two mutinies, which he did with ruthless dispatch; but his authority and energy, and his personal example of reckless courage were an inspiration to the mercenaries.

The Taipings occupied some 14,000 square miles of forbidding terrain devoid of roads, dotted with rebel-occupied cities and covered with a network of interlacing canals and waterways which impeded the progress of foot soldiers. By using a flotilla of gunboats and river steamers, Gordon was able to wage rapid guerrilla warfare against the Taipings. His 'fire boats' as the Chinese called them, pursued the rebels along the river banks and were even able to drag themselves along the beds of shallow streams by sheer force of their paddle-wheels, while their wailing sirens terrorized the rebel soldiery, who fled in confusion. Gordon had told the governor, Li Hung Chang, that he would crush the rebellion in eighteen months. He was as good as his word and as one stockaded city after another was stormed and fell, the Ever-Victorious Army at last lived up to its name.

With the capture of Changchow by Gordon and his mercenaries, and of Nanking by the imperial forces, the Taiping rebellion was finally brought to an end; but though the imperial army and its commander-in-chief, Tseng-kuo Fan, rightly deserved the greater credit for having kept the rebels at bay for twelve years, forcing them to relinquish their conquests one by one, the hero-worship of Gordon in England led his countrymen to believe that it was he and his Ever-Victorious Army alone who were responsible for crushing the Taipings. He was acclaimed nation-wide as 'Chinese Gordon' and newspaper dispatches told of his exploits and his personal bravery, as exemplified in his habit of dashing, alone and unarmed at the head of his men through breaches in the stockades of the towns they were assaulting. He seemed to bear a charmed life as, cheroot in mouth, he waved them on with his rattan cane, which the mercenaries came to regard with superstitious awe and Gordon as a magical symbol, the Wand of Victory. For several years his exploits brought rejoicing to the hearts of the British nation, gripped as they were by what Gordon called 'the fiend of jingoism'.

On his return from China in January 1865, Gordon was greeted by a nation eager to acclaim him; but he dreaded the glare of publicity and fled from it. Because of his exaggerated puritanical modesty, his refusal to be lionized, to give interviews or attend social functions, he gradually and inevitably became a forgotten man. In spite of the Victorian hero-worship and the legend of 'Chinese Gordon', he was ignored and passed over for twenty years by the War Office. For reasons which have never been and perhaps never can be properly explained, he was given no opportunity of serving his country in any important capacity. He was evidently considered by many to be too eccentric, too erratic and unpredictable to take part in the great enterprise of consolidating the British Empire in India, Afghanistan, West Africa and Abyssinia. Gordon said of himself 'No man in the world is more changeable than I am'. His constant resignations and reversals of intention, his general unmanageableness, would seem to have aroused suspicion, resentment and distrust; consequently, this 'military misfit', a genius in the command of irregulars, was passed over in favour of men less gifted but who were considered more reliable.

The next six years of his life were spent either on leave of absence or in unimportant army posts. In 1865, nine months after his return from China, he was offered and accepted a post at Gravesend to direct the construction of forts for the defence of the Thames estuary. He regarded the scheme as ill-planned and its aims useless; nevertheless, he carried out the work with feverish intensity, sparing neither himself nor those who worked under him. He occupied his spare time in charitable works, teaching, feeding and clothing waifs and strays, caring for the sick and needy and cultivating an intense religious friendship with an earnest married couple, the Freeses, who were devoted to good works. His existence was spartan and frugal, with much bible-reading and meditation. At this time, too, he started to exchange letters on religious matters with his devout sister Augusta. This self-revelatory correspondence was to continue for the rest of his life and became an important source for the assessment of his character.

In 1871 he was offered the post of British representative on the eight-power Danubian Commission set up by the signatory powers to the 1856 Treaty of Paris and went to Galatz in Rumania. While on holiday in Constantinople in 1873 he met the Egyptian prime minister, who offered him on behalf of the Khedive Ismail the post of Governor of Equatoria. With official permission from the British Government he accepted it. His mission was to continue the efforts of his predecessor, Sir Samuel Baker the explorer, to stamp out the age-old slave trade and to open up the Nile communications with the Great Lakes. He was frustrated in both these undertakings and in 1876 after a disagreement with the Khedive over funds he resigned and returned to England. After several acceptances and refusals of the Khedive's renewed offer to return to his service Gordon finally agreed and was appointed Governor-General of the entire Sudan.

The myth which had clung to him since his exploits in China more than a decade ago was due more to what he was than to what he had done. Even in Equatoria and the Sudan his achievements, though more spectacular than of lasting value, gave further proof, if it were needed, of his courage and 'magnetic' personality. His remarkable feats of daring and endurance captured the imagination of his countrymen once again.

He made breakneck camel rides over the desert; and the first time he ever rode on one of these unpredictable beasts, on his way, in 1874 to take up his position as Governor of Equatoria, he made the 250-mile journey from Suakin to Berber in record time, three days less than the fastest caravan, exhausting his Egyptian escort in the process. He soon became an expert camel rider and delighted in outstripping his escort, arriving at his destination an hour or more ahead of time. In future years he made daring sorties, 'pelting along' as he put it, on his camel for hundreds of miles over the desert, often alone, quelling slave-traders and tribal chieftains with the intense, unwavering glance of his grey-blue eyes. In 1877, as newly appointed Governor-General of the Sudan, he once rode alone eighty-five miles through the burning desert to the Darfu camp of Suleiman, the young rebel son of the slave-trader Zobeir, held in Cairo in semi-captivity. Gordon's sudden appearance, his imperious manner and piercing eyes so overawed the defiant rebels that they obeyed docilely when he commanded them to disarm and disperse. Such exploits, coupled with his dogged endurance of hardship, his rigid asceticism and his fanatical Christianity, made him legendary to hero-worshipping Victorians in England.

All this was the background to Gordon's fame when he met his death in Khartoum in 1885 at the age of fifty-five; but the nation's grief and the ensuing hero-cult were conditioned mainly by his final mission and its tragic end. In 1884, the Mahdist rebellion broke out and threatened Egypt's power in the Sudan. The British government, in its ambiguous role of protector through the Anglo-French occupation and control of Egypt, decided upon the evacuation of the British garrisons. After much hesitation, Gordon was given instructions to proceed to the Sudan. What he was supposed to do there was not very clear. The instructions were conflicting. Cabinet members, Gordon and Sir Evelyn Baring, the British Agent in Cairo, all talked at cross-purposes, each believing that his intentions were clear to the others. On the one hand there were vague ideas of Gordon's evacuating the Egyptian garrisons and on the other, of his going to Suakin to report on the military situation in the Sudan, thence to return to England; but it was also hinted that perhaps he would be able to 'perform such other duties as may be entrusted to him by the Egyptian government. . . .'

In the event, having been appointed Governor-General of the Sudan by the Khedive, Gordon was surrounded in Khartoum by the Mahdi's ever-growing forces of savage Ansar tribesmen. After a ten-month siege Khartoum was stormed and during a massacre lasting six hours, in which four thousand people were killed, Gordon, the only remaining European, was speared to death on the steps of the Governor's palace—against the Mahdi's express injunction that he was to be taken alive. The corpse was beheaded according to custom and the head taken to the Mahdi's camp across the river at Omdurman. There—having been shown for identification to the captive Slatin Pasha, a former assistant of Gordon's—it was nailed to a tree on the public highway and left to hang there for three days. History does not relate what eventually happened to the head.

For almost a year before these events the British public, Parliament and the Government had been discussing Gordon's predicament. Public opinion, voiced and inflamed by vehement press campaigns led by the *Pall Mall Gazette*, built up until Gladstone was forced to act. He sent an Anglo-Egyptian expedition, under Lord Wolseley, to rescue Gordon. The relief force was hampered by innumerable obstacles, with consequent delay, which proved fatal. Khartoum fell before the Mahdist hordes on 26 February 1885. A couple of days later the two advance steam boats heading the relief column reached Khartoum under heavy fire from both banks of the Nile. A horde of dervishes menaced the rescuers from the shore. Gordon's flag had gone. The palace was a smoking ruin. The steamers turned and made their way full speed downstream again.

Gordon's earlier fame, as 'Chinese Gordon' and Governor of the Sudan, the accounts of his death, the long delay in dispatching the relief expedition, its arrival just two days too late, a burgeoning imperialism, the determination of the Conservatives to topple Gladstone and the Liberal government, all went hand in hand with the soul-searching and fear of defeat of the Liberal leaders to form the background against which the nation's grief and bitterness were expressed and a hero-cult rapidly grew up round the memory of Gordon, 'the great Christian soldier'.

Gordon Pasha remains a figure of supreme interest mainly because of the extraordinary and thrilling exploits of an adventurous life. Even in the more recent biographies, the Taiping revolt in China, the raids in the Sudan and the siege of Khartoum are all episodes which are discussed at great length and in great detail. Yet the impression remains that no writer has succeeded in making clear exactly what it was that Gordon accomplished. The accounts of his exploits seem romanticized and unreal, and in them the commanding officer and administrator is obscured by the hero who captured towns and quelled slave-traders by reckless bravery and sheer force of personality. The rhapsodic style of these biographies is perhaps due to the lack of reliable source material; and biographers have had to lean heavily on Gordon's own journals and letters, which are unconventional, contradictory and one-sided. Many of his letters were either destroyed by him or were lost. He destroyed the diaries of his years in China in a fit of anger when his mother showed them to friends and it was suggested that they should be published. Research in a more general sense has hardly been attempted, and it seems likely that such attempts are doomed to peter out in uncertainty on practically every issue. In short, the conventional estimate of Gordon's contribution to colonial history remains virtually unchanged.

A notable exception is a recent biography, Anthony Nutting's *Gordon: Martyr and Misfit* (1966), which examines the hero's life and career soberly and in painstaking detail, with exhaustive documentation based on the manuscripts of Gordon's letters, diaries and memoranda, parts of which were formerly either suppressed or ignored by previous biographers. The book propounds a plausible theory of Gordon's motivation in the crucial action which led to his death.

Interest in Gordon's life centres nowadays on the man rather than his deeds. Christian heroes abounded in the era of Victorian imperialism, with its numerous minor wars which even to those living at the time seemed almost idyllic, and the stuff of which sagas of bravery and virtue were shaped, exploits made more vivid by thrilling newspaper reports and dramatic engravings and drawings—for this was before the era of press photography and half-tone reproduction.

Lord Roberts, the contemporary and colleague of Gordon, was one of these idealized heroes. By all accounts he was more gifted, and in any case incomparably more successful, than Gordon. He was awarded the Victoria Cross during the Indian Mutiny, he led campaigns in Afghanistan and South Africa where, indeed, he was in command during the decisive phase of the Boer War. He also wrote excellent memoirs, *Forty-one Years in India* (1897). But Roberts though quite as God-fearing, noble and courageous as Gordon, was nevertheless, despite his great military talent, a very ordinary and uninteresting man. It is precisely the strange, contradictory, eccentric and half-deranged components of Gordon's character which have proved such an endless fascination to posterity.

Gordon was not a conventional Christian, nor even an ordinarily active one in the style of Roberts or Wolseley who said their prayers and placed their trust in God. He was in reality a religious crank, possessed and permeated from his young manhood by an ever-growing mystical faith and he was beset throughout his life by religious problems.

Life in its aspects of struggle, work and human relationships was irksome to Gordon. The daily round seemed to him—if not consistently, at least for long periods—something distasteful and unreal. What was real was the Bible first and foremost. He speculated and brooded on the Holy Scriptures, every word of which he believed implicitly, and he discussed them in his long correspondence with his devoutly religious sister Augusta. In many respects his religiousness was extremely primitive. After his visit to the Seychelles Islands in 1881 he pondered deeply on such matters as the Forbidden Fruit from the Garden of Eden: he believed this to be the gigantic aphrodisiac fruit of the *coco de mer* tree which he found growing on the island, and indeed, indigenous to it. Again, on his visit to Palestine in 1883, he was preoccupied to find the real sites of the hill of Golgotha, the Garden of Eden and Christ's sepulchre. During his long stay in Gravesend (1865–71) he spent his free time distributing religious tracts which he either bought or wrote and had printed. He would scatter these tracts wherever he went, pressing them on strangers or scattering them out of train windows at stations and to navvies working on the railway line.

This element of naivety in his character is linked with an unusual ignorance which his biographers mention but do not stress. Gordon would appear to have read few books other than the Bible and books of Christian devotion. Because of his purely military upbringing and education he was devoid of even the nodding acquaintance with the classical Greek and Latin writers which in those days gave the majority of 'upper-class' boys at least the semblance of some intellectual culture.

This faith based on the Bible resulted either in an ascetic morality or else it accentuated an inherent puritanism. When he was alone his meals often consisted of bread and milk, or 'a stale loaf soaked in a slop-bowl of strong tea' which he ate standing at the food cupboard. He spent the greater part of his salary on charity and the support of relatives. On his appointment to the Governorship of Equatoria one of his first acts was to reduce his salary from £10,000 a year to £2,000, to show the Khedive his disinterestedness and contempt for wordly goods. It was a tactical mistake, since the Khedive believed it was some kind of wily ruse. From this and certain other odd incidents it is not unreasonable to suspect an unconscious desire to impress—as on one occasion when Gordon, lunching with Lord Ripon, Governor-General of India, asked to have all the courses served to him on the same plate. Such demonstrations of virtue were made in all innocence, and it never entered his head that they might be construed as a parade of self-righteousness.

The faith behind such manifestations was changeable and full of contradictions but a dogmatic thread gave it consistency. Fatalism was part of it; everything that happened was God's will and any human desire to act in a contrary fashion or to attempt to alter the course of events was interpreted by Gordon as disrespect for God's omnipotent will. He regarded his own ambition, his craving for fame and influence, as a deadly sin. The very act of living was to him the greatest sin of all, the degradation before which every other human vileness paled. The mystical belief which obsessed him ever more strongly from 1873 was that before mankind inhabited the earth their souls had known the blessedness of union with God through an infinite past; after death they would again attain paradisal bliss regardless of their goodness or wickedness on earth. From this it followed that it was essentially pointless to reform, renounce, atone or even to live a righteous life, given that saint and sinner alike would enter into the same eternal bliss in the hereafter. Since Gordon's own leanings were towards asceticism and moral rectitude, these seemed to him more or less a proof of the worthlessness of mortal life rather than beneficial virtues which would serve to placate God or fill Gordon himself with a sense of becoming a better human being or more worthy of God's grace.

'All that flesh admires is doomed', he wrote to his sister in 1865. 'The flesh as a substance is as useless as the dust is and to which we must return. . . . Cursed is the man who makes flesh his aim.' Mystics of greater intellectual capacity than Gordon have been obsessed by hatred of life with its accompanying rejection of the body, but none of them has harboured this feeling with greater intensity, as can be seen again and again in his letters and journals and in recorded conversations. He believed that: 'We are born corrupt and if the devil had his way, we should be kept in ignorance of it; our permitted transgressions show us our state'. In conversation Gordon once betrayed his feeling of pride by mentioning all the countries and princes he considered 'too small' for him and hastily added: 'Yes, that is flesh, that is what I hate, and what makes me wish to die.'

Like de Maistre he saw in the executioner a symbol of justice in the wretchedness of mankind. Gordon had both killed and had had executed a number of men in his time and he said: 'I would be able to condemn a man to death without a qualm . . . and feel that I was as guilty as he. Punish, but with forgiveness and with the knowledge that we are all deserving of the same fate.' Death as a liberator was something very real to Gordon: 'every day makes us younger because it brings us nearer to the moment when He will come to set us free from our wretched bodies and weaknesses'. After a dispute with Lord Lyons, the English Ambassador in Paris, over the Egyptian question, he ended a letter with the words:

> 'I have some comfort in thinking that in ten or fifteen years' time it will matter little to either of us. A black box, six feet six by three feet wide, will then contain all that is left of Ambassador, or Cabinet Minister, or of your humble and obedient servant.'

It has been assumed, of course, that there must be some chinks in the armour of this hero, signs of the tensions and unhappiness in which he lived, reasons for them and for the contempt he felt for flawed humanity, himself first and foremost.

In his youth he had given evidence of an unruly, intractable and irascible personality. In later life he could be intolerably brusque and rude not only to his equals but to his superiors, to say nothing of subordinates or servants, and when he lost his temper he could slap faces or kick and beat his servants. He himself observed sorrowfully that some of his subordinates were so afraid of him and trembled so violently in his presence that they were unable to light a cigarette. Lytton Strachey, with the support of passages from the memoirs of the American soldier of fortune, Charles Chaillé-Long, a colleague who did not get on with Gordon and was dismissed by him, depicted him as a periodical and secret drinker. According to Strachey, Gordon sometimes shut himself up in his tent for days, alone with his Bible and the brandy bottle. Lord Elton, in his biography (1954), has refuted Strachey's calumny on the authority of various witnesses who had good grounds for knowing about Gordon's habits. In any case, the Victorians used brandy as a conventional medicinal stand-by. In some of his letters, quoted by Lord Elton, Gordon himself touches upon the matter of drink which, in Chaillé-Long's account, he delicately refers to as 'a little b. and s.' and the traditional assumption has been that Gordon periodically fought a losing battle with his craving for alcohol. This denigration, propagated by Strachey's essay, has been exposed by Lord Elton and again recently by Anthony Nutting, as without foundation.

Chaillé-Long, an American serving with the Egyptian army, had been appointed by the Khedive Ismail to guard his interests, spy on Gordon and report. The Khedive was convinced by Gordon's quixotic refusal to accept his full salary that he could not be trusted. Chaillé-Long turned out to be a thorn in Gordon's side; he was disloyal and untrustworthy and Gordon's relations with him soon deteriorated. Gordon eventually fell out with him, at last decided to get rid of him and sent him back to Khartoum. Chaillé-Long ever afterwards bore a grudge because of some disparaging remarks Gordon had written about him and in the two books he wrote he is known to have distorted the facts for purposes of his own. Gordon's friends and servants have all borne witness to his abstemious habits. Chaillé-Long's books, published in the United States, made little or no impact, especially in England, and were soon forgotten. Their denigrations of Gordon were resuscitated by Lytton Strachey, who took them at their face-value and, for his purposes of caustic debunkery passed them on without further investigation. Strachey's charges based on Chaillé-Long misread and misquoted, have been minutely examined and disposed of, point by point in Lord Elton's book.

On this point as on another basic issue, the biographies until recently have been prudishly reticent and no awkward questions have been asked. The other curious fact about Gordon that biographers have tended to side-step is that there were no women in his life. He seems indeed to have shunned them, especially the sophisticated, fashionable ones. No episodes in his life that could remotely be called erotic have ever come to light. He would almost seem to have regarded women with physical distaste. But he was fond of boys. His help and charity were given during his Gravesend period to youths and small boys, destitute and orphaned waifs whom he called his 'kings' or 'wangs' or 'scuttlers' and sometimes his 'doves'. He housed, fed, clothed and cared for great numbers of them at his own expense and got jobs for them in the navy and army. The tone of his letters about them—not, however, published uncensored—would suggest latent or repressed homosexual tendencies. This does not mean, for one moment, that he was guilty of any overt advances to any of them and it is more than likely that he was not even aware of the nature of any such inclinations if they existed. But when one of his biographers writes that Gordon 'specialized in boys because they could be treated without any fuss' and that he did it solely out of charity, it seems more embarrassing than the totally innocent approach to Gordon's desire to help young males which was expressed after his death by the opening of the Gordon Clubs for Boys and the Gordon Boys Homes.

Lord Elton and Anthony Nutting effectively dispose of Gordon's imputed overt homosexuality as a baseless slander. Lord Elton was not detained by it for more than a footnote to his edition of *Gordon's Khartoum Diary*, in which he said:

> 'This polysyllable sounds like a scientific term, but in practise it is applied to the widest variety of moral and psychological types, ranging from the addict of the grossest vice to the eminently respectable citizen who happens to be fond of boys. Gordon was certainly the latter and as certainly not the former. But the very inexactness of the label renders it serviceable to the would-be traducer.'

Anthony Nutting inclines to the view that Gordon's homosexual feelings, in whatever degree they existed, were repressed; and this raises the conjecture as to whether, if so, this was not the result of some traumatic sexual experience in early youth against which his puritanical nature and the ingrained code of the British gentleman and strict army tradition drove him to fight all his life, impelling him to take refuge from them in asceticism and his obsessive fatalistic and mystical religiousness. Nutting sees in such a trauma the probable reason for Gordon's intense death-wish which he expressed constantly throughout his life, from his expressed intention to be killed in the Crimea, to his remaining in Khartoum and his submissive acceptance of the Mahdist spear-thrusts.

The purely historical problem, and the most controversial, concerns the evacuation of the Sudan, Gordon's last assignment, the British government's attitude to the mission and its belated attempt to relieve Khartoum. The question arises in all the biographies of the 1880s and 1890s, published soon after Gordon's death. Several of these works have dealt with the matter in detail. Later on Lytton Strachey gave a brilliant, entertaining but misleading account of the affair, which he presented as a dramatic duel between Gladstone and Gordon, with Gladstone trying to force Gordon to escape from Khartoum while Gordon tried to compel Gladstone to send a relief force.

Oddly enough, no historian had attempted until recently, to disentangle the course of events objectively and in detail. Certain undisputed facts emerge, however; Gordon undoubtedly exceeded his instructions by remaining in the Sudan and allowing himself to be surrounded and besieged. He noted in his *Khartoum Journal* that he had been 'very disobedient to Her Majesty's Government'. It is equally certain that Gladstone used every pretext to postpone the dispatch of a relief force. It would have been more consistent with his policy not to send an expedition at all—after all it concerned the rescue of virtually a single Englishman—but it was irresponsible of him to delay so long before making up his mind to send the expedition.

Gordon was probably correct in his prediction that the Mahdi could be 'smashed up' as he put it, by a handful of British troops. The conquest of the Sudan by Kitchener thirteen years later cost the British Army the lives of a mere sixty soldiers. Gladstone's behaviour in the Gordon affair is perhaps the most reprehensible of his whole career. His tendency to entrench himself behind bombast and evasive, optimistic rhetoric, was never more apparent than in some of the speeches he made to the House on the question of the relief of Khartoum. He reluctantly had to admit that Khartoum really did appear to be hemmed in—'that is to say, that there are bodies of hostile troops in the neighbourhood forming more or less of a chain around it'. He went on to say, 'I draw a distinction between that and the town being surrounded, which would bear a very different meaning.' There was laughter in the House followed by jibes of 'He is hemmed in, but he is not surrounded'.

Anthony Nutting's account of Gordon as a martyred misfit ends with an assessment of Gordon's character and mentality: he propounds the theory that, whatever its traumatic origin, it was Gordon's life-long, obsessive death-wish which caused him to remain in Khartoum and to die there. With deliberate fatalism he allowed events to take their course as the agents of death which he regarded as a welcome deliverance from the flesh and the wearisome life of mortality. Death, the dark angel, would release him, he believed, to a life of eternal bliss in union with God.

Whatever the mainspring of his actions, Gordon was a God-intoxicated hero, his life subordinated to the divine will—some even regarded him as a soldier-saint. Gladstone, too, ordered his life according to the will of God—though, being a politician nobody ever thought of calling him a saint. Be that as it may, there were few among England's nineteenth-century statesmen and men of action whose lives and thoughts were as dominated by religious imperatives as those of Gladstone and Gordon. Gladstone came to be known as 'a great Christian statesman'; it seems fitting that it should have been Gladstone who called Gordon 'a great Christian soldier'.

The Chief Scout at Mafeking: Robert Baden-Powell

Mother, may I go and maffick,
Tear around and hinder traffick?

A new word was introduced into the English language in 1900, when 'Saki' (the pseudonym of H. H. Munro, a brilliant writer of witty novels and short stories) put this little couplet into the mouth of his 'Reginald', the protagonist of a series of brief, humorous sketches. To 'maffick', according to English dictionaries, is to 'exult riotously' and 'Saki' coined Reginald's verb after the unforgettable frenzy of Mafeking night, 18 May 1900, when all London, riotously exulting, went crazy with excitement.

Mafeking Night was a night when ordinarily staid and sober citizens comported themselves like inmates of Bedlam let loose; when respectable ladies and gentlemen who had not been properly introduced shook hands or even hugged one another in the streets; when members of the upper classes threw dignity to the winds in theatres and restaurants, shouting and cheering as loudly as the lower orders in pubs and music-halls; when, in the interval before the last act of *Lohengrin*, Covent Garden opera-goers were joined by the Prince and Princess of Wales who were entertaining the King of Sweden in the royal box, as the whole audience stood singing the national anthem before settling down, if this were possible, to listen with half an ear to the rest of Wagner's opera.

It was a night when the crowds came surging into the West End from all round London to throng Piccadilly Circus, where hansom cabs and horse-buses were soon wedged in by the mob; where amidst the cheer of the rejoicing thousands and the din from rattles, whistles and squeakers, soldiers and sailors were carried shoulder-high above a sea of waving Union Jacks. It was a night when toffs and swells, impeccably opera-hatted and cloaked for the evening, climbed up on the roofs of hansom cabs to fling their silk hats into the air and lead the crowd in singing *God Save the Queen*, *Rule Britannia* and *Soldiers of the Queen*; when traffic all over mafficking London was brought to a standstill in streets packed solid till daybreak with exultant crowds yelling themselves hoarse; it was a balmy night in late spring, a night when there was more immoral behaviour in London parks than in a whole month of ordinary nights.

The cause of all this pandemonium was the relief of Mafeking, news of which had been announced towards evening on London newspaper placards and had spread like wildfire as newsboys ran about the streets shouting the first editions of the evening papers.

A little South African town, besieged for 217 days by the Boers, had been relieved by a flying column of British soldiers. The whole nation joined in a delirious outburst of patriotic emotion. Of the three besieged, British-occupied towns on the borders of the Transvaal and the Orange Free State, none had held out as long as Mafeking, to become the embodiment of Britain's determination to triumph over adversity—Kimberley and Ladysmith having been relieved several weeks earlier.

The defence of Mafeking had been well covered by the newspapers. War correspondents of *The Times*, the *Morning Post*, the *Pall Mall Gazette* and Reuters had been in Mafeking throughout the siege and had managed from time to time to get reports out of the beleaguered town. For one reason or another Mafeking was always in the news—only ten days before the siege was raised there were rumours that the garrison had surrendered. A force of two or three hundred Boers had broken through the Mafeking defences to penetrate the native town, one of the defensive forts had been surrounded and occupied and twenty of the defenders manning the fort were taken prisoner. In a counter attack, the town's defenders in their turn encircled the fort, after which the Boers, sixty-eight men commanded by one of President Kruger's thirty-five grandsons, surrendered to their own prisoners inside the fort. The Boer commander, General J. P. Snijman, believing that Mafeking was as good as captured, had released a premature communiqué, with the result that continental newspapers announced in outsize headlines *Mafeking hat kapituliert*! and *Mafeking a capitulé*!

The dispatch bearing the triumphant news that not only had Mafeking not *kapituliert*, but had been relieved, reached London ten days later, on this beautiful evening in mid-May when everybody was in the mood for a celebration—and Mafeking seemed a wonderful opportunity for a spree.

The jubilation, nevertheless, could be considered somewhat misplaced. The outcome of the war in South Africa had been obvious for some time past. The British troops commanded by Lord Roberts and Lord Kitchener had defeated and captured the Boers' ablest and most trusted commander General Cronje and more than 4,000 of his men; Kimberley and Ladysmith had been relieved; the Orange Free State had been overcome and the mayor and worthies of Bloemfontein had come to hand the keys of the city to Lord Roberts as he rode in. The British troops were pushing across the Transvaal, through Johannesburg, in the advance to Pretoria. The raising of the siege of a tiny town like Mafeking, with a population of some 1,700 white men, women and children, 7,500 natives of a local tribe and a garrison of less than a thousand, was hardly a matter of much importance. Nor did the relief of Mafeking mean the end of the war, for the fighting was to drag on for another two years.

Still, there were facts behind the legendary defence of the little town which fully justified the rejoicings of Mafeking night.

The two main beliefs about the Boer War today—as far as anybody any longer gives it a thought—are surely, first: that a rapacious and predatory Britain, greedy for commercial gain, her lust for power still unsated, invaded the small Boer republics rich in gold and diamonds which formed an enclave between the British possessions of Cape Colony, Bechuanaland, Rhodesia and Natal; and second: that the outcome of the struggle between Britain and the Boers was a foregone conclusion. The first assumption though open to question, has an element of likelihood; the second may speedily be dismissed.

When the Boer Republics declared war on 11 October 1899, it was very far from a foregone conclusion that they could not possibly win. Their army of between 40,000 and 50,000 outnumbered by far the British troops, whose peace-time strength and been doubled to a mere 20,000 only a couple of days before President 'Oom' Paul Kruger had declared war and could not be increased until two months later by the arrival of an additional reinforcement of 45,000 men from England.

The Boers had the advantage of experience, knowledge of every inch of the terrain and better arms—provided by Krupp and Le Creusot. If they could rapidly defeat or capture the British garrisons they believed they could count on an uprising of the Cape Dutch and subsequent intervention by the jealous Big Powers of Europe—France, Germany and Russia—against a Britain still enveloped in her 'splendid isolation'. Accordingly, it was not unreasonable to believe, in the autumn months of 1899, that the British could be driven out of South Africa, thus enabling the Boers to establish the grim regime based on racial discrimination and concentration of power which, with the defeated and exiled Kruger as precursor and prophet, they were only to achieve many years later under Malan and Strijdom.

The Boer armies, a loose but mobile organization of 'commandos', marched simultaneously over their borders, to the east, the south and the west. For months they defeated the British troops in almost every battle. Their advance was checked mainly by three towns—Ladysmith, Kimberley and Mafeking—which the Boers, with an obstinacy they eventually had cause to regret, were intent on capturing before they pushed on. They staked everything on Mafeking, a town of some strategic importance, on the Cape Town-Bulawayo Railway, well stocked with food and forage and containing valuable railway rolling-stock and well-equipped workshops. The British garrison held out for months against almost a quarter of the whole Boer Army and even after the commander General Cronje, losing patience, had moved off southwards with six thousand of his men, leaving the remainder under General Snijman to complete the capture of Mafeking, the Boers still believed it was of particular military importance to keep the town surrounded. By containing considerable numbers of Boer troops who could otherwise have been used elsewhere to good effect, the stubborn resistance of the defenders of Mafeking—as with Kimberley and Ladysmith—quite possibly played a crucial part in deciding the outcome of the war.

The ability of the British garrison to defend Mafeking has often been attributed to the clumsy and ineffectual tractics of the besiegers. General 'Honest Piet' Cronje, who commanded the besieging forces at the start, was old, cautious and undecided. His successor General Snijman was even more deliberate and less inclined to put himself out; 'a cowardly creature who shelled the hospital, convent, the women's laager, but had not the pluck to lead an attack' was how Colonel Robert Baden-Powell, the heroic commander and governor of the besieged town, described Snijman. Matters were not made easier for the Boer generals by President Kruger who kept sending letters and telegrams from Pretoria, alternately advising caution and swift action.

The Boer troops were splendid riders and crack shots but in view of the heavy losses inflicted on their ranks they had the greatest reluctance to attack. In this respect the disciplined, drill-toughened British soldiers were far and away superior throughout the whole Boer War. During the siege the Boers made only a single attempt to take the town by assault, just a week before the relief forces arrived; even then, the attack was a dismal failure, owing to confusion among the Boers and because the attack was carried out by only a few hundred volunteers.

Early in the siege General Cronje tried to capture the town by bombardment and starvation. The Boers possessed several siege guns but the artillery of the time was fairly harmless by modern standards. By the end of October 1899 Cronje had sent to Pretoria for a big gun, a Creusot ninety-four-pounder siege gun which arrived a week later, drawn by a team of sixteen oxen, to begin the bombardment. The gun, nicknamed 'Grietje' by the Boers, was soon ridiculed by the defenders as 'Creaky'. For the next six months Mafeking was bombarded for several hours daily, Sundays excepted, but 'Creaky' did comparatively little damage. In the first place, the houses were some distance apart; then, they were made of adobe, so that instead of shattering to rubble when hit, as brick would have done, the friable sun-dried clay allowed a shell to pass through leaving merely a hole. Finally, there was the time-lag between the departure and arrival of Creaky's shells. The look-out on Cannon Kopje, Mafeking's only elevaton, could telephone to headquarters when the big gun was being loaded, when it was being aimed, when it was ready to fire and when it was fired. Then, at the alarm, beaten on the headquarters gong and echoed by bells all over the town, the population could take cover in cellars and shelters. Even after the shell had been fired there were still eight to ten seconds left before the impact, time enough for stragglers to take cover—mostly the boys, who were usually the last into and the first out of the shelters.

The British defence of Mafeking was masterly and the lion's share of the credit must go to Colonel Robert Baden-Powell, who was in later years to become the Chief Scout. Appointed Commander-in-Chief, Rhodesian Frontier Force, by Lord Wolseley, Baden-Powell with Bulawayo as his headquarters and Mafeking as his supply centre, two months before war was declared, supervised the recruiting and training of an efficient force of volunteers and recruited men in which there were very few men of the regular army. As the relations between the British and Transvaal governments deteriorated and war became imminent, it devolved upon the troops protecting the stores of supplies in Mafeking to defend the town, since no other troops were available. Baden-Powell accordingly made his preparations for the defence. He threw up a ring of sand-bag forts each manned by fifteen to twenty men and all connected by telephone, through an underground exchange, with his headquarters. The forts were spaced along a perimeter of six miles in order to keep the Boers as far off as possible and inside this ring a system of inner defences encircled the edge of the town. The telephone network and a system of signals made it possible to summon reinforcements immediately from headquarters.

Baden-Powell himself said that 'the whole thing was a matter of bluff from beginning to end'. Bluff and boldness were his strategic weapons and his Standing Orders to his men encouraged them to 'bluff the enemy with show of force as much as you like . . .' He himself proceeded to bluff the Boers in a variety of ingenious ways. He had made, in a secret 'laboratory', hundreds of little black wooden boxes which, since no bulk supply of dynamite was available, were filled with sand. To the accompaniment of proclamations and warnings of danger, an extensive 'mine' field was laid all round the town, the 'mines' connected by wires to a central observation post and the fields marked with small red flags. A few sticks of dynamite lent realism to 'testing' operations and news of the dangerous minefield surrounding the town quickly filtered to the Boer encampments through spies and Boer sympathizers inside Mafeking, where the added feeling of protection from the 'minefield' was a boost to civilian morale.

For the defenders' first daring night sortie on the Boer lines, Baden-Powell used a string of red lanterns to guide his men back after they had inflicted severe casualties on the Boers. Thereafter he kept the enemy on tenterhooks by hanging out his red lanterns at intervals at varying points round the town. The Boers, dreading further attacks, were bluffed into keeping constant night-time alerts.

Another similar ruse employed a homemade searchlight which was shone into the Boer camps after dark, obliging them to take cover hastily. The searchlight was then rushed to and fro to various parts of the town to be beamed out over the veld on to other Boer camps in turn. The ruse convinced the Boers that a ring of searchlights had been installed to discourage night attacks. Surprise raids on weak or exposed points of the Boers' advanced trenches also kept them in a state of uneasiness or compelled them to draw further back from Mafeking's defensive ring of forts.

Cannon and ammunition were improvised or knocked together out of all kinds of junk. Baden-Powell's men answered the Boers' German-made grenades with homemade ones fashioned out of tin cans filled with dynamite or gunpowder with a fuse attached. These were lobbed over into enemy trenches with the aid of a 'whip-stick'. An ancient gun used as a gatepost on a farm was unearthed by chance one day. It turned out to be an ancient Royal Navy muzzle-loader. Dug out, cleaned, refurbished and mounted, the gun proved capable of firing a ten-pound shot two thousand yards into the Boer lines. Mafeking even acquired its own big gun, which was made out of various odds and ends in the railway workshop. The gun worked well enough to hurl a homemade eighteen-pound shell four thousand yards, with impressive erruptions of flame and smoke and a thunderous bang—much to the astonishment and dismay of the Boers at suddenly being bombarded from Mafeking by an unsuspected new gun.

Wire entanglements of a very special kind were placed all round Mafeking. Baden-Powell through his field glasses, one Sunday, had observed the Boer soldiers climbing through the wire entanglements protecting their trenches. The posts were clearly distinguishable but the wires could not be seen over the distance. Baden-Powell realized that what he could not see from so far away the Boers would not be able to see either. Following his instructions, a profusion of wooden posts gathered from every available source was planted all round the town and then strung, in dumbshow, with entanglements of non-existent wire. To strengthen the illusion for the Boers, the soldiers who manned the perimeter forts were enjoined to step over or climb under the 'wires' whenever they entered or left the forts. With such imaginary devices, imaginary searchlights, imaginary night-raids and do-it-yourself artillery, Baden-Powell was able to bluff the besiegers into believing that Mafeking was protected by a multiple defence system which it would be rash to attack.

An intensive and imaginative use of anything and everything edible, combined with a common sense rationing system, kept starvation at bay, though only just. Crops of fruit and vegetables were grown in every corner. Meals were dished out at soup kitchens to avoid waste.

Baden-Powell set out to emulate the Chicago pork-packers, whose famous boast was that they used up 'everything but the squeal'. Besides oxen, calves, sheep, donkeys and mules, horses were eaten or utilized to the last shred of hide hoof or hair, even the ground-up bones serving to eke out flour—made from horse fodder. The oat husks yielded a porridge-like soup. As a treat, occasional swarms of locusts, fried or curried, were considered a rare delicacy; puddings were improvised from face powder and Baden-Powell joked that those made from violet-scented powder tasted like 'scented baby'.

The future Chief Scout was equally inventive when it came to keeping up morale. He poked fun at the enemy throughout the siege, in little messages to them or in his answers to theirs. There was a constant coming and going of messengers between Mafeking and the enemy general's camp, under protecton of the white truce flag, bearing notes from the Boer commanders and Baden-Powell's replies, usually ironic or derisive, the courtesies scrupulously observed by both sides. In answer to a request to surrender, Baden-Powell wrote back 'You will never take Mafeking by sitting and looking at it'; and when General Cronje gave notice that he was going to bombard the town with 'Creaky', Baden-Powell in his reply told the Boer general, 'I am sorry that you have to confess yourself unable to take Mafeking without bombarding it. But this course you are quite at liberty to take if you imagine it will help you. . . .'

He put out a newspaper, the *Mafeking Mail*, full of defiant mockery, jokes, patriotic verse. He organized sports, dances, amateur theatricals and variety shows, baby contests and races. His simple and conventional personality—apparent in the sort of books he wrote in later years —included an element of boyishness and a sense of fun which enabled him to throw dignity to the winds without appearing foolish. He had always been fond of amateur theatricals, in which he had displayed a talent for broad comedy, and in the 'screamingly jolly' entertainments he organized in Mafeking he impersonated Paderewski at the piano, recited monologues and sang songs in costermonger's garb. When sports were held he acted as master of ceremonies dressed up as a ring-master.

Social differences—to say nothing of racial discrimination—were maintained with an unaffected British good humour which lent an air of classlessness, however illusory, to the conditions of strict and harsh discipline demanded by life under siege. It seems reminiscent of Kipling's 'dook's son, cook's son, son of a belted earl', and the attitudes, verging on parody, of Noel Coward's *Cavalcade*.

The struggle for Mafeking was possibly a decisive episode in a war which was a basic threat to Britain as a world power. It was also a tragedy involving close on two thousand civilians and soldiers who endured the siege at a cost of great suffering, an aspect of the episode given only casual mention in accounts and memoirs.

From another aspect it was also a bit of a lark, something of a spree. Hostilities were suspended on Sundays—the devout Boers observed a strict Sabbath and Baden-Powell relaxed Victorian piety for the sake of morale with the announcement that 'Sunday would be observed up till twelve o'clock, and after that hour as Saturday'. The Boers enjoyed cartloads of good food brought from their farm houses, while the Britishers held dances, cricket and football matches and enjoyed amateur music-hall turns.

Books and newspapers of the period seem to have described the events of Mafeking in what could be regarded as a spirit of misrepresentation, since everything shocking, discreditable or distressing was, so to speak, swept under the carpet, either glossed over in laconic half-truths or hazy with the unreality of romantic warfare: 'Captain FitzClarence accounted for four of the enemy single-handed with his sword', followed by 'Captain FitzClarence was subsequently awarded the Victoria Cross for conspicuous bravery'. But apart from deliberate playing down of the facts, it can be gathered from all accounts that many of those besieged in Mafeking felt more or less what the Queen, the press and the exulting London crowds felt they ought to feel.

An immeasurable distance of time and thought and attitude separates all these people from ourselves. They seem as remote as Mars and as unreal as the Martians.

Imperial Demi-God: Horatio Herbert Kitchener

For a few years round the turn of the century British imperialism was at its peak. Ten years of a right-wing minority provided the background to England's domestic policy, with the Secretary for the Colonies, the old Liberal convert Joseph Chamberlain, acting as animator, Kipling as official bard and Benjamin Kidd as theoretician, with politicians and organizers who had been brought up on the doctrines of Disraeli, Carlyle, Ruskin and Froude. Egypt was governed by Lord Cromer, South Africa by Lord Milner, India by Lord Curzon, while Cecil Rhodes, combining capitalistic big business with greed of conquest, had created a unity which, twenty years later, was to provide Lenin with a basis for his falsified and lurid picture in *Imperialism: and Imperialist War*.

Epic events and exploits crowded fast on each other and were followed at length by the consolidation of power through numerous treaties and agreements—with Japan (1902), France (1904), Russia

20. Sir Garnet Wolseley in Egypt, 1882

21. General Gordon

22. Baden-Powell in Mafeking, 1900

23. Lord Kitchener. (Recruiting poster for World War I)

(1907), all of which paved the way for World War I and the titanic struggle to check German expansion.

A Liberal victory in the elections of 1906 made the task of domestic reform and the demand for self-rule throughout the Empire matters of major concern. The great era of British imperialism reached its climax and then came a period of winding-up, settlement and withdrawal; the slow retreat had begun.

There was much about this full-blown imperialism that was gaudy, cheap and vulgar. It brought wealth and honours to the few and offset them with excitement and adventure for the masses. Warlike patriotic ballads were popular in the tawdriest music-halls and jingoists were as numerous among clerks and domestic servants as they were at court and in society. Wars cost so little: a few pence in the pound in income tax, a few thousand fallen on the battlefields, a few more dead in army hospitals. The Education Act of 1870 had paid off; the nation was now almost totally literate and the penny papers were in full voice; skilful engravings and, later, half-tone reproduction, the forerunners of today's rapid press photography, combined with glamourous reports 'from our special correspondent in the field' to blur death and suffering into romantic unreality.

But the idea behind it all, filtering down to the masses in fiction, popular ballads and music-hall songs was noble and simple, inspired by the magical words God and Freedom. Anglo-Saxons, it was felt, had received a divine call to bring peace and order into the world, their mission was to educate under-privileged and backward races to become, in some hazy, rosy future, mature, self-governing nations who should be blessed with an English parliamentary system.

The personification of the idea of Empire, for the ordinary Englishman, was no poet or politician, not a Chamberlain or a Kipling, but a handsome, well-built general, some fifty years of age, more than six feet in height, with square-jawed, well-proportioned and mobile features adorned by outsize, bushy, handlebar moustaches—Kitchener of Khartoum. He was the 'prancing proconsul' dispatched by Britain from one territory and possession to another; sent from Egypt to South Africa, from South Africa to India, to be recalled finally to the threatened mother country only to lose first his reputation, then his life.

The biography *Kitchener* by Sir Philip Magnus (1958), bears the subtitle *Portrait of an Imperialist*. The designation is apt, for Kitchener, a tireless worker filled with burning ambition became, more than any of Britain's empire-builders, the sword of imperial conquest. But Kitchener was a professional soldier not an idealist. Like any other properly brought-up British officer he was loyal to Queen and Country but he was no dreamer and fanatic like Gordon, or teller of tales like Roberts. He appears to have read nothing except books of adventure and military history; there was apparently not a thought in his head beyond how to defeat the enemy, how to get the better of rivals and how to strengthen military power; orders, memoranda and reports were all he ever wrote. This sheer force devoid of education had no need of general ideas. He was a machine fashioned for warfare; a human machine in which there was apparently no trace of anything spiritual or intellectual, nothing imaginative, no dark secrets, nothing even mildly mysterious.

Kitchener was born in 1850, near Listowel in County Kerry, Ireland, the third child and second son of Colonel Henry Horatio Kitchener. He was christened Horatio Herbert, the first of his names being given after his father, who had been born two days before the Battle of Trafalgar and was named after Nelson. By his family, however, Horatio Herbert was always called plain Herbert. Later in life, known the world over, he received the ultimate accolade of the famous and was called plain Kitchener.

His grandfather, a London tea-merchant, had come from a family of Hampshire and East Anglia small farmers who had turned to trade, prospered and risen in the world. His father chose the army as a career, saw service in India and rose to the rank of Colonel. Returning from India he had gone on half-pay because of his young wife's ill-health (she was ten years younger than himself) and then, failing to find army employment in England, sold his commission and moved to Ireland to start a new life there.

In company with other new Irish landlords, Colonel Kitchener became wealthy by the astute purchase and improvement of property, in an Ireland decimated by the great potato famine of 1846, with a population reduced from 8 to 6½ millions by death and mass emigration and where, consequently, estates of bankrupt landlords were going cheap.

Though he was able to get the best out of the peasants who worked for him, Colonel Kitchener deplored and despised the backward Irish peasantry, who were ignorant and improvident. He was proud of his English origins and brought up his sons and daughter to share his belief that they were members of a master race set down among inferior foreigners, which was how he regarded the Irish.

The Colonel, whose truncated army career had left him disappointed and embittered, was an eccentric martinet who ran his home on the lines of a military barracks. Breakfast commenced punctually at eight, not a second earlier or later. Mrs Kitchener whose health was not good, breakfasted in bed, but she too was obliged to observe the same routine. Each morning a maid had to stand outside her bedroom door, waiting until the stroke of eight before taking in the breakfast tray.

Colonel and Mrs Kitchener slept under piles of newspapers sewn together; he believed them to be warmer than blankets, which he considered unhealthy. Warmth and cold were regulated by adding or discarding newspapers. The rustling paper kept ailing Mrs Kitchener awake until her husband hit upon the idea of tethering the newspapers to a barricade of planks erected round their bed. Her health is believed to have deteriorated because of this spartan sleeping system. In 1863 her lungs became affected and a year later, to the great grief of her family, who adored her, Mrs Kitchener died in Switzerland.

The lives of the five Kitchener children were organized and disciplined like that of a small military unit. They had few toys and no playmates and were made to work at various tasks on the estate. They were taught to fear God, honour the Queen and love their Country. Their quarrels were rare, their code of honour strict and rigid. Their father, a stern disciplinarian, gave them the right to inflict punishments on one another. They never questioned the justice of these punishments which, though often brutal, they bore with stoical submission. Kitchener's mother once rescued him from the lawn where he lay without a murmur, spreadeagled in the hot sun, crucified with the aid of ropes and croquet hoops, in expiation of some infringement of the family code.

For a few years during his young manhood Kitchener passed through a phase of religious fervour. From 1868 when, at the age of eighteen, he entered the Royal Military Academy at Woolwich, to his first service in 1871 as a subaltern of twenty-one at the School of Military Engineering at Chatham, and later at Aldershot, 1873–74, where he was posted to a mounted troop of Royal Engineers, he was attracted by High Church ritual for which he developed an ardent enthusiasm. This religious phase once over, his active interest in religion waned and for the rest of his life God hovered somewhere in the background, a sort of colonel on half-pay, out of touch with his regiment.

Kitchener's inflexible devotion to duty and to the fulfilment of any task, either demanded of him or self-imposed, to the complete disregard of comfort, affections or personalities, was a powerful element of his austere personal code. Chastity was another. As Sir Philip Magnus writes:

> 'Kitchener's sexual instincts were wholly sublimated like those of a Catholic priest . . . He was a man of rare humility and simplicity . . . and despite an increasing measure of intoxicating hero-worship to which he was continuously exposed, he lived a life of inviolable purity and self-control. He adhered inflexibly to an exalted moral code and he protected himself by constructing against the world a barricade of impenetrable aloofness.'

There was, apparently, one woman in this blameless life, but little is known about the episode, which occurred in 1883, in Cairo. Sixteen-year-old Hermione Baker (the elder of the two daughters of Valentine

Baker Pasha, in command of the Egyptian police), fell passionately in love with Kitchener, who was then in his mid-thirties. Nothing is known of the extent of his feelings for the girl and no correspondence has survived; but her family and that of her uncle, Sir Samuel Baker the explorer, believed that when she became eighteen she and Kitchener would marry. In January 1885, while Kitchener was at Korti, during the delayed attempts to rescue Gordon from besieged Khartoum, Hermione Baker died in Cairo, of typhoid fever. She was just eighteen. Kitchener is said to have worn beneath his shirt, for many years afterwards, a locket containing a miniature portrait of the dead girl, given to him by her father.

It is believed that Kitchener never had sexual relations with any woman and with one or two exceptions among the influential great ladies of his acquaintance, he detested women as gossiping intriguers. Nor did he have any friendships with men of his own age. A certain predilection for young, respectful and devoted aides-de-camp and adjutants, 'my boys', cannot be thought to suggest any form of deviant inclination. In an age which believed chastity to be as natural as unchastity is thought to be in our own age, Kitchener lived from manhood to middle-age in that frame of mind regarded by Victorians as pure and spiritual. In his case, however, the purity and spirituality consisted in thinking about troop transport and kindred matters throughout all his waking hours.

It was out of this void, unhampered by doubt or anxiety, that the great soldier came into being. His education, hopefully administered, was meagre in results; he was taught first at home by a governess, then by a succession of tutors, later, after his mother's death, at schools in France and Switzerland and finally, by a succession of crammers, to enable him to pass the entrance examination to Woolwich, which he succeeded in doing in 1868.

When he passed out of Woolwich in December 1870, and just before he was commissioned, he went with a friend to spend a holiday at Dinard with his father, who by that time had remarried and gone to live in Brittany. The Franco-Prussian War had just broken out and Kitchener and his friend, at Colonel Kitchener's suggestion, attached themselves to a field ambulance unit of the Second French Army of the Loire, to get first-hand experience of war. They took part in a bloody, three-day battle which was waged around Le Mans, and Kitchener's initiative and courage during this exploit, together with his ability to witness the slaughter of great numbers of men and horses without turning a hair, served to bring the attention of his superiors to what appeared to be the start of a promising career.

For many years, as Lieutenant, Captain and Brevet Major, Kitchener was active as cartographer, surveyer and amateur archaeologist on military expeditions to Palestine and Cyprus. He served only for very brief periods as a subaltern in regular units. His experience of the usual type of army comradeship was therefore limited in the extreme and very early in his career he developed traits of aloofness and arrogance. He spent very little time in England; during the thirty-seven years between 1874 and 1910 he did not spend a single winter in England. Like so many British army men he was fascinated, from the very start of his career, by life in the East. Not that he was drawn to any form of mysticism or became, like T. E. Lawrence, an admirer and champion of the Arab; but he liked living among foreigners inferior and subordinate to himself, in the self-assured arrogance which made the existence of British colonial officers and civil servants living in the British Raj a veritable idyll in the wilderness.

Kitchener's great opportunity came in September 1888 when he was seconded to Egypt, recently occupied by the British, where he was appointed Adjutant-General of the Egyptian Army. His diligence, his unlimited capacity for taking pains and the tireless ability to solve problems, were rewarded by a career which, in April 1892, saw him appointed Sirdar, or Commander-in-Chief of the Anglo-Egyptian army with the British army rank of Major-General. Four years later, when the Conservatives had returned to power under Lord Salisbury, he was at long last detailed—after many delays and hesitations—to avenge General Gordon's death and Britain's honour by the overthrow of the Mahdi's successor, the brutal and tyrannical Khalifa Abdullahi, and by the reconquest of the Sudan, lost ten years earlier as a result of the Mahdist uprising.

The conquest of the Sudan, a territory with an area of a million square miles and a population of two million, was virtually a feat of civil engineering; a matter of building railroads, planning marching routes of hundreds of miles, arranging transport for provisions, finding labourers, horses and camels. Kitchener's efficiency and ruthlessness triumphed over all obstacles. The two-year war, described by Sir Winston Churchill in *The River War* (1899), was mainly a series of operations enabling the troops to reach strategic positions where battles could be fought, or rather, where hordes of dervishes could be slaughtered *en masse* by machine-gun fire: for it must be admitted that when the enemy were finally engaged, the ensuing combat was less a battle than a massacre. Three thousand dead dervishes strewed the ground after the Battle of the Atbara, while Kitchener's casualties were merely 583, of which only 120 were British. At the Battle of Omdurman, the Khalifa's dervishes were shot to ribbons by British cannon and maxim-guns. In much the same way, back in England at Sandringham, the Prince of Wales and his guests could slaughter a record bag of 5,817 rabbits and 1,975 pheasants in two days' shooting. At Omdurman, against losses of 48 killed and 430 wounded, the conquerors could count more than 11,000 dervish corpses on the battlefield, to say nothing of the wounded among the 60,000 taken prisoner, many of whom died of neglect.

During the few battles of the Sudan campaign Kitchener did not distinguish himself by spectacular feats of bravery or daring; it was not his way to gamble, like the great tacticians relying on intuition, but to plan and calculate with cool precision, aiming at foreseeable results. Before the Battle of the Atbara, in April 1898, he spent days trying to make up his mind whether to attack the entrenched dervishes commanded by the young Emir Mahmoud. He discussed the situation with Major-General Gatacre, commanding the British contingent under him, and with General Sir Archibald Hunter, in charge of the Egyptian contingent. One telegram after another sped between Kitchener, Lord Cromer, the Prime Minister, Sir Francis Grenville in Cairo and the war Office, while Kitchener pondered whether he ought or ought not to attack. When finally he decided to do so, the outcome was a magnificent victory, far-reaching in its results; Britain, in competition with the French, acquired a vast new territory, beside which French conquests paled. Cecil Rhodes was already talking about a Cape to Cairo railway and Kitchener had already started construction, in January 1897 on the Sudan Military Railway across the Nubian Desert, from Wadi Halfa to Abu Hamed, which he hoped eventually to link up with Rhodes's projected railway. In after years Kitchener said he believed that it was his victory at the Atbara rather than at Omdurman which had been the turning point in his career.

Kitchener's prouddest military triumph followed some months later, on 2 September 1898, with the dawn-to-dusk battle of Omdurman, the flight of the Khalifa and the capitulation of the city. The victory had been accomplished by history's most economical war-lord, as Lord Salisbury was to say, and 'with absolute accuracy, like the answer to a scientific calculation'. Kitchener's ten-year ambition to avenge Gordon was satisfied. Two days after Omdurman he held a memorial service outside the shattered palace in Khartoum and there, moved by the singing of 'Abide With Me', Gordon's favourite hymn, Kitchener, who had a horror of all display of sentiment and emotion, wept openly, his habitual steely impassivity overcome by mingled emotions of sorrow and pride.

The slaughter at Omdurman brought great rejoicing in England. Kitchener's victory had opened the whole of the Nile valley to what he called 'the civilizing influences of commercial enterprise'. He was given a peerage for his services. He received the thanks of both houses of Parliament and a cash grant of thirty thousand pounds—and he replaced Wolseley and Roberts as the nation's war hero and idol.

The following year saw the outbreak of the Boer War, on 11 October

1899. The initial series of serious defeats inflicted, to the derision of the rest of the world, by the Boers on the British troops, impelled the Salisbury government to replace the Commander-in-Chief, Sir Redvers Buller. Field Marshal Earl Roberts was appointed—though not without some misgiving, for Roberts was sixty-nine and was much shaken by the recent death of his only son, killed at the Battle of Colenso. As a safeguard, the younger Kitchener was sent with Roberts as his Chief-of-Staff. In many quarters Roberts was regarded as a mere figurehead, with Kitchener the driving-force, but this view was inaccurate: as an orthodox military commander Roberts was Kitchener's superior. During the battle which ended in the first and only important victory for the British, the battle of Paardeberg, fought on 18 February 1900, Kitchener made grave tactical errors. Roberts had come down with fever on the day previous to the attack and was confined to his bed. The command devolved on Kitchener, who decided—too precipitately—to attack the Boer general, Cronje, and his forces, who were withdrawing towards Bloemfontein, and had taken up a defensive river position, rather than besiege, bombard and starve them into surrender. After Kitchener had surrounded Cronje, and was confident of total surrender, his troops were in their turn surrounded by Boer reinforcements and the first day's fighting ended in a stalemate, with the British troops, who had suffered heavy losses, hungry, thirsty and too exhausted to attack further.

Next day Roberts had recovered sufficiently to resume command. Against Kitchener's insistence he decided not to resume the attack but to besiege the Boers instead. After nine days of siege Cronje surrendered, and on 15 March 1900, Roberts entered Bloemfontein in triumph.

In May, with 70,000 men and 178 guns, marching northwards across the Orange Free State into the Transvaal, Roberts swept the Boers before him. Mafeking was relieved on 13 May, the troops entered Johannesburg on 31 May and on 5 June Roberts rode in triumph with Kitchener into Pretoria.

By September both Boer republics had been completely occupied. The Boer forces were scattered, British prisoners had been freed, and the leader, General Kruger, was a fugitive in Europe.

It was thought that now the Boers would be glad to make peace. Accordingly, in July, Roberts handed over the command to Kitchener and in November left for England. The Boers, however, would neither give in nor give up and hostilities were unexpectedly prolonged. The war degenerated into guerrilla fighting and Kitchener, left to face the problem of the Sudan in a new guise, was in his element.

It was no longer a question of victory for the British troops—that was a foregone conclusion—but rather of capturing the roving bands of Boers, ten to twenty thousand strong, who hoped by harassing and exasperating the British, to hold out until one or other of the Great Powers should either step in or mediate.

Five of the Boer generals were still at large, and one of them, the pint-sized Christian De Wet, by winning one minor victory after another, succeeded in making the British look thoroughly ridiculous.

Kitchener set about wearing down the Boers' will to resist by three expedients: manhunts, scorched earth and concentration camps. Between December 1900 and May 1902 he divided up the two Boer republics into a series of fenced-in areas, cooping up the guerrilla bands by means of a network of blockhouses, roughly one and a half miles apart, manned by military sentinels and joined to each other by barbed wire. He progressively reduced the distance between the blockhouses to about half a mile until, eventually, he had 8,000 blockhouses extending for 37,000 miles. The Boers trapped inside these enclosures were then hunted down like game in a series of drives in which columns of British troops, sometimes as many as sixty columns at a time, were sent out to kill or capture the guerrillas.

Kitchener created further obstacles by his scorched-earth policy, burning down farm houses, commandeering sheep, cattle and supplies; and by setting up concentration camps into which Boer women and children and old men were herded so that the hunted guerrillas could have no refuge in which to shelter and nobody to help or feed them. These tactics were ultimately successful; Boer resistance was worn down, the Boers at last lay down their arms, and the peace treaty was signed at Kitchener's headquarters in Pretoria on 31 May, 1902. Kitchener had won yet another war for Britain, and when he returned to England in July 1902 he was showered with honours. Feted by the highest in the land, he was idolized by the masses; mayors and city councilmen fell over themselves in their eagerness to make him an honorary citizen. Banquets and receptions were held in his honour. He was presented with addresses and ceremonial gifts. Having already been made a G.C.M.G. he was now created a Viscount, appointed to the Order of Merit, awarded the Grand Cross of the Bath, and promoted to the Brevet rank of General. He received a vote of thanks from Parliament and a money grant of £50,000.

In the decades that followed, Kitchener maintained his reputation without improving it. For the next seven years (1902–9) he was Commander-in-Chief in India. His aim was to reorganize the inefficient Indian Army, but he was hampered and exasperated by an obsolete system of dual control, which he shared with the Viceroy, Lord Curzon, and which prevented him from exercising his customary autocratic control of the army.

In Kitchener's view, the function of the Indian Army was not 'to hold India from the Indians' but to guard her frontiers against external attack. He believed that war with Russia was imminent. Military activities in central Asia had induced in him an obsession that an invasion of India's west frontier was being prepared and the army was in no state to defend any of India's extensive frontiers. With his usual thoroughness he set about his task of reorganization and inspection, but there was no invasion, consequently no war.

The only war he was involved in was his feud with the Viceroy over the dual control system, which had embittered their relations from the start. After endless intrigues against Curzon it was Kitchener who won. Judging by Lord Curzon's accounts of the relationship between himself and Kitchener, and from accounts by others of Lord Curzon during this prolonged duel for position, one cannot but follow the course of the conflict without a certain feeling of malicious satisfaction at the overthrow of such an insufferable snob, exaggeratedly zealous of his position and functions, as Curzon was. Curzon resigned at last and returned to England and the system which he had supported was eventually replaced by Kitchener's.

Despite his triumph over Curzon, Kitchener did not receive the Viceroyalty of India he so much coveted, and when he was passed over in favour of Sir Charles Hardinge it was the most bitter disappointment of his life. He settled for the next best thing, Egypt. Sir Eldon Gorst, British Consul-General in Egypt, had returned to England gravely ill and formally resigned a few days before his death in July 1911. Six days later Kitchener, who had for some time past been on tenterhooks regarding his future, was appointed British Agent, Consul General and Minister Plenipotentiary.

During his four years in Egypt Kitchener attempted to wean the Egyptians from their aggressive nationalist agitation and to pacify the country. He reorganized the Egyptian economy, instituted a gigantic scheme of drainage and reclamation, and established a Ministry of Agriculture. His plans to abolish the nominal suzerainty of Turkey, to annex Egypt and create a new Viceroyalty of Egypt and the Sudan were destined not to be realized by him, but in 1914 after a state of war had been declared between Britain and the Turkish Empire, Egypt was declared a British Protectorate.

The fatal year 1914 dawned. In June of that year Kitchener was created an Earl for his services to the Empire and left for England to receive his earldom. He never returned to Egypt. As he arrived in England World War I broke out. The nation called once more upon the hero, who was expected to crush the Germans as he had once crushed dervishes and Boers. He was now sixty-four years of age.

It is of interest at this point to examine the traits which had developed in Kitchener's character and had become ingrained now that he was on the threshold of old age:

Devotion to duty.

Devotion is a word we are fond of using only when it is concerned with laudable aims but it is also a quality which can just as well be directed to meaningless or evil ends. Kitchener certainly acted with the passion of one who is determined at all costs to attain a lofty goal. He could possibly have described such a goal in some confused way as 'God, Monarch and Country'. But this inspiration was not essential to his drives. In all probability his mind was seldom invaded by thoughts of any profundity. His thinking was concentrated on the day, the moment and on the practical details of immediate problems. Such devotion, lacking any conscious impulsion can seem trivial and insignificant; on the other hand, it is just this kind of blind and selfless devotion which ensures the continuance of civilized society: it motivates officials, teachers, soldiers—all those who, because of their temperaments or perhaps impelled by some obscure need for self-sacrifice, wear themselves out in causes which it never enters their heads to question and which they would have little faith in if ever they thought about them at all. In this sense Kitchener was a conscientious man, even if his conscience was merely an unreflecting compulsion towards action, prompted by a sense of duty which was devoid of any finer feelings and not even particularly virtuous.

Pride and reserve.

His aloofness and arrogance have been stressed. Kitchener had not mixed or conversed with his equals for many years of service abroad nor did he speak to any one on terms of equality except during brief visits to England. An air of pride had become as much a matter of course to him as his uniform, which was a symbol of rank and dignity as personal as it was national. His natural pride forbade him to demand flattery or accept homage and his attitude to these when offered was more one of contempt than of satisfaction. His disdain for his fellow officers was lofty to a degree, even in a profession in which contempt for colleagues is perhaps greater as a rule than in any other of the professions. He entertained lavishly and on a large scale but, except at official functions where he put himself out to be agreeable to the most exalted of the guests, he entertained without any satisfaction or visible signs of pleasure. He gave orders and asked questions and, with no aptitude for the give and take of debate, he ceased as time went on to enter into any form of discussion: it had become a practical impossibility, and he never deigned to give reasons for an opinion—that was something more suited to subordinates.

Bravery and harshness.

He risked his own life without hesitation and expected others to do the same. Other lives, inferior lives, were a matter of indifference to him. A soldier was a necessary unit of a company, regiment or army; an integral part of a disciplined group, to be inspected and sent out to the attack. He had not the slightest interest in the welfare of the common soldier. It never entered his mind to ask any of his men how they were getting on; indeed, he never spoke to one if he could avoid it. He was unpopular with the troops, but they looked up to him, nevertheless, as to a god of war.

Kitchener was a severe taskmaster with a harsh and unsympathetic manner and could not tolerate failure, weakness or even sickness. An officer who failed to carry out an assignment to his satisfaction was finished as far as he was concerned. The offender, though having done his utmost, was contemptuously dismissed without any attempt to find out the causes of his failure, for which he may have had no responsibility.

Thrift.

His obsession for economy amounted to a mania and it was linked with the one trait which has been ascribed to the 'human' side of his nature—his love of loot. His thrift and a positive greed for booty were also possibly linked with another marked trait, his taste for opulence.

From his early days as a soldier Kitchener was noted for his frugality and economy, and impressed his superiors by his monthly accounts. He believed economy to be a part of efficiency but as time went on, he tended to carry cheese-paring to extremes. Sir Evelyn Baring (later Lord Cromer) wrote to Lord Salisbury from Egypt, in 1897 about 'Kitchener's mania for economy' which, he said, 'although generally laudable, he sometimes pushes too far'.

In the Sudan, unable to obtain from the bankrupt Egyptian government all the money he required for his army, Kitchener's actions were conditioned by the need for ruthless economy. He was forced at times to adopt such drastic expedients as clothing his troops in tattered reach-me-down uniforms which barely covered their nakedness and, among other things, to pare his medical services to what seemed a heartless state of insufficiency. Consequently, at the Battle of the Atbara River, for example, the sufferings of the wounded were greatly increased as a result of the inadequate medical services. In 1898, during the first stage of the Battle of Omdurman, the dervish army was mown down by the concentrated fire of Anglo-Egyptian guns, maxims and rifles. When Kitchener's excited Egyptian troops continued to fire into the bodies of the wounded strewn over the plain, singly or in writhing heaps, an outraged Kitchener was seen riding along the front line calling out 'Cease fire! Cease fire! Cease fire!' and groaning 'Oh, what a dreadful waste of ammunition!'

During the Boer War Kitchener waged a continual battle against extravagance, and in 1915 he was still complaining about waste, objecting once again to the squandering of ammunition, this time by the armies at the front. Thrift and the love of loot were idiosyncrasies so marked and so eccentric in Kitchener that even sceptics must inevitably look for some obscure psychological basis for these traits.

After battles his aides-de-camp were ordered to keep a look out for costly swords and other war trophies which he then appropriated. He gave the Sudanese troops permission to loot after the Battle of the Atbara and reserved the best items for himself, subsequently sending to his house in Cairo a great quantity of swords, spears, chain-mail and similar trophies of the battlefield. After he had conquered the Sudan and the palace in shattered Khartoum was being rebuilt to his requirements, he gave orders 'to loot like blazes', saying that he wanted 'any quantity of marble stairs, marble pavings, iron railings, looking-glasses and fittings; doors, windows, furniture of all sorts'. In 1896–98 his brother Walter was much impressed by the furnishings of his house in Cairo: 'rooms in all directions and armour, carving, tiles and draperies from floor to ceiling'. Walter Kitchener also marvelled at the handsome furniture and the carved screens that were museum pieces: 'How he could have got all these things together seems extraordinary.'

On a couple of occasions Kitchener was obliged to relinquish some of his booty, in the face of views which plainly showed that he had overstepped the bounds of the nation's indulgence to the whims of a war hero. After the fall of Omdurman, Kitchener ordered the Mahdi's tomb, sacred in the eyes of Mahdists, to be destroyed and the Mahdi's remains dispersed. He wished to demonstrate to the fanatical Mahdist believers that their holy leader had been a mortal man and was not translated bodily to Paradise as they believed. After the tomb had been razed to the ground and the Mahdi's bones cast into the Nile, the skull, which had been placed in a box, was presented to Kitchener who for a time toyed with the suggestion that he should have the trophy mounted in gold or silver and use it as an inkstand or drinking cup. This macabre whimsicality, when the news of it got out, outraged Queen Victoria, the press and the nation. The newspapers, incensed by Kitchener's consistently unfriendly treatment of war-correspondents, whom he had classed as 'drunken swabs', mounted a vociferous campaign against him. Kitchener took heed and the skull was eventually buried secretly at night in the Moslem cemetery at Wadi Halfa. The Queen declared herself satisfied and the press vilification of Britian's idolized hero subsided as swiftly as it had been whipped up.

During the Boer War, Kitchener even carried off life-size statues of Boer statesmen and generals which he caused to be removed from the public squares of Bloemfontein and Pretoria, intending them eventually to adorn the gardens of a country seat he did not yet possess. The statues were shipped to England with a quantity of other loot, to be warehoused at the Royal Engineers' headquarters at Chatham, against the day when he should have acquired a country house in which to display them. (He was persuaded later to relinquish them and they were returned discreetly to South Africa.) When at last, in April 1911, he was able to buy an estate, Broome Park near Canterbury, and after the early-seventeenth-century house had been gutted and remodelled inside, he filled it with his treasures, many of them either loot or gifts.

In December 1898, when he was about to leave England, after his triumphal progress as Kitchener of Khartoum, he let it be known that in future, instead of jewelled caskets and ceremonial swords, he would prefer to have plate, furniture and pictures, which he could not afford to buy. Again, in 1902, at the close of the Boer War, when English towns and cities presented him with addresses and testimonials, he remarked bluntly at one stage that he would prefer to be offered gold plate, with which as Britain's official representative, he wished to impress the native princes when he went to India as Commander-in-Chief. He had a passion for gold plate and trinkets and those who wished to honour, please or placate him took care not to forget the fact. In 1903 Lady Curzon, wife of the Viceroy, after an inadvertent slight to Kitchener at a supper party, which caused him to stalk out of the residency in a huff, accompanied her apology with an olive branch in the guise of a couple of gold mustard pots. Kitchener's massive gold plate was proverbial. At a lavish dinner party given by him in Simla in 1907, one of the forty guests commented admiringly on the centre table, ablaze with gold plate, and on the five 'gorgeous' vases on the sideboard.

In 1914, Kitchener, now aged sixty-four, was appointed Secretary for War, a position for which he possessed two qualifications. The first arose from the myth of the war leader: here was a man who would represent practical affairs and victory in the midst of squabbling and intriguing politicians. Kitchener's appointment was greeted with enthusiasm by press and public and, in general, the nation's confidence in him lasted to the end. It has never been disputed that without Kitchener it would have been impossible, in the short space of eighteen months, to persuade two and a half million volunteers to enlist; and certainly not without the famous poster and its exhortation 'Your country needs YOU', from which the defender of the Empire, rejuvenated and beautified behind the imposing moustaches, gazed out with hooded, hypnotic eyes, calling the young men of England to arms against the nation's foes.

Kitchener's second qualification depended more on his military experience than on his understanding and analysis of the existing war situation. He was accustomed to regard war as an operation in which superiority in arms and troops was a necessary requirement; he did not believe and had never had cause to believe in clever strategic and tactical manoeuvres. He had little faith in the ability of the French army to stand up to the Germans, nor in the British army, too small to be able to affect the outcome of a war between France and Germany. As early as 1911 he had said that in the event of hostilities the Germans would walk through the French 'like partridges'.

Now, at a time when Europe's armies in their millions were on the march, his chief preoccupation was that the Allies should produce troops in such quantity as to be so superior in number to the enemy that all resistance could be crushed by sheer slaughter, as of dervishes—or partridges.

For a time, during the first days of the war, while the nation's hopes were pinned on a British Expeditionary Force to France, the expectation was that a peace would be concluded inside three weeks. Kitchener thought otherwise: 'We must be prepared to put armies of millions into the field, and to maintain them for several years.' He insisted that the British Army was insignificant, that the war must be expected to last for at least three years and that probably it could not be won without help from America. Events proved him right and, acting on this diagnosis, he instituted his recruiting campaign, by which he proposed to raise a new army of a million men.

But in other matters Kitchener was not so successful. L. S. Amery, who, as representative of *The Times* during the Boer War, was familiar with Kitchener's autocratic ways, refers in his memoirs, to Kitchener's 'domineering and disruptive personality', and other memoirs and biographies overflow with the sharpest criticism. In many respects Kitchener even handled his recruiting campaign clumsily. He despised the Territorial Army, regarding them as amateurs, and refused to make use of the existing machinery of the Territorial County Associations which would have been invaluable in the task of recruitment. He did not give sufficient consideration to the need for skilled civil workers. He did not get on with his military colleagues, particularly with the Commander-in-Chief of the British Expeditionary Forces, General Sir John French, who returned his contempt with hatred. As an adviser on military strategy Kitchener was often confused and misguided. When he could weigh and analyse impersonal factors, control and command men and bring his characteristic energy and drive to bear on the situation, he was in his element. But when he was confronted by a situation which demanded swift decisions based on intuition he was at a loss and blundered. He had displayed indecision at the Atbara in 1898, at Paardeberg in 1900 and now in 1915, confronted with the strategic decisions of the Gallipoli campaign, he was a prey to almost unbelievable irresolution and hesitation, changing his opinions and countermanding orders from day to day. At Cabinet meetings and at conferences with sub-committees he was either ineffectual or exasperating, sitting in silence or else uttering tedious platitudes or making opinionated and arbitrary pronouncements for which he gave no reasons. His attitude to his colleagues was one of mingled distrust and military contempt for civilians. His incapacity in discussion or debate was total and his growlings seemed puerile to the Liberal intellectuals, all experienced debaters and dialecticians, who were his colleagues in the Cabinet.

Though Kitchener remained nominally Secretary for War, he was stripped of responsibility for one department after another, beginning with munitions and ending with his role of adviser on military strategy, which was given to Sir William Robertson. The Government having finally lost confidence in Kitchener's judgement by his decisions to evacuate Loos and the Dardanelles, he became, by the summer of 1916, little more than a glorified recruiting officer. The recruiting poster with its exhortatory, or now perhaps accusing finger, was still plastered from end to end of the country, causing witty and malicious Mrs Asquith to remark that if Kitchener was not a great man at least he was a great poster.

As Sir Philip Magnus wrote in his biography:

> 'the ruling Liberal politicians, diffident of their ability to control the military caste in war, welcomed the mythical demi-god into their midst. They counted upon using the mass enthusiasm which Kitchener's name commanded, to inspire confidence, and to strengthen the Government's foundation in public opinion.'

In this respect Kitchener was still valuable to the Cabinet, and to take any action which threatened the position of this colossus and war hero would have been for the Government to court disaster. Though Kitchener was attacked from time to time by the newspapers when he blundered in his management of the war, the newspaper barons, and especially Lord Northcliffe, who started a virulent campaign against him in the *Daily Mail*, soon found that, while circulation fell, their vituperation had little effect on Kitchener's prestige with the nation. The myth was indestructible and it was a necessary myth. As time went on, Asquith, his position threatened, regarded by some of his colleagues as Kitchener's equal in incompetence, reached the conclusion that his own strongest refuge lay in the Kitchener myth, so he at least was eager to see Kitchener remain in the Cabinet. The Liberal leader, ineffectual as head of a wartime government, needed the nation's most famous general as a façade, an authoritative figure covered with military glory which should maintain intact the nation's confidence in its leaders. Asquith too, needed the talismanic magic of Kitchener's name to keep the volunteers coming in; for events were making the introduction of conscription daily more imperative and the Government was split on the issue. The premature introduction of this drastic and unprecedented measure would have entailed Asquith's resignation.

In this time of humiliation and failure hitherto unknown to Kitchener, the aging General appeared to grow in character and human feeling. He realized that the Government needed him, not because of his military abilities or judgement, but because of the nation's faith in his commanding personality and in his every act and word, even while the distrust and open hostility of his colleagues in the Cabinet grew from day to day.

'Rightly or wrongly', he wrote to Sir Douglas Haig in February 1916, 'the people believe in me. It is not, therefore, me that the politicians are afraid of, but of what the people would say to them if I were to go.'

In this mood of resignation and patriotic devotion to duty, Kitchener remained in the Cabinet as Secretary for War, although his power had been stripped away until nothing was left and he was subjected to one humiliation after another. During the last months of his life he was bitterly unhappy; the contemptuous indifference of the Cabinet, the attempt to make him the scapegoat for anything that went wrong, all preyed on his mind. His mood was one of despair, but he was also humbled and his anguish seemed to bring with it a capacity for sympathy and compassion that had hitherto been absent or resolutely repressed. He broke down and wept at his desk over letters announcing the deaths of old colleagues or younger men whom he had known and loved. He was deeply affected by the news that Lord Desborough's two sons, William and Julian Grenfell, whom he had known since they were boys, had been killed in action.

In May 1916 he accepted a personal invitation from the Tsar to visit Russia, tour the Russian fronts, offer advice and report on military co-operation and supply. The visit of the British war-hero and ally would give, it was thought, encouragement and stimulus to the war-weary Russian people, seething with unrest and threatened by revolution. Kitchener was as eager to escape for a time from his bickering colleagues and the hostile critics of his war administration, as they were to see him go: the myth was more useful than the man.

Shortly before his departure, Kitchener met his parliamentary back-bench critics and vindicated to them his administration of the War Office, answering their questions frankly and confidently. Though he acknowledged that he was no ready debater and 'had no gift for the various turns and twists of argument', his speech and answers to questions met with approval and were given one round of applause after another. This belated and unexpected personal triumph filled him with great satisfaction, giving him fresh vigour and hope. In this mood he set out for Russia.

Kitchener's life ended with a dramatic fitness worthy of classical tragedy. On 5 June 1916 he arrived at Scapa Flow to embark on the cruiser *Hampshire* which was to take him to Archangel. The official party of twelve included Colonel Oswald Fitzgerald, Kitchener's devoted personal assistant, military secretary and long-time friend; his staff, servants and personal bodyguard. After lunching with the Admiral of the Fleet, Sir John Jellicoe, on his flagship *The Iron Duke*, Kitchener boarded the *Hampshire* with his party. The cruiser sailed just before 5 p.m. in a heavy, north-easterly gale. She was escorted by two destroyers until 7 p.m., when the captain of the *Hampshire* sent them back, owing to the worsening gale. Forty minutes later, off the western coast of the Orkneys and a mile and a half off Marwick Head, the *Hampshire* struck a mine which had been laid the week before by a German submarine, in preparation for the Battle of Jutland. The exits to Scapa Flow had been mined a couple of nights before the great naval battle of 31 May, in an attempt to impede the concentration of the British Grand Fleet.

The exploding mine ripped a hole in the *Hampshire* which caused her to list to starboard; then, settling down by the head, she sank in less than fifteen minutes. There were twelve survivors, one of whom related afterwards that immediately after the explosion he had seen Kitchener, clad in a heavy military overcoat, in the gunroom flat. The body of Colonel Fitzgerald was later washed ashore, but Kitchener's was never found. In the twilight hour of his eclipse the Atlantic had claimed the war-lord; the hero who had been an unparalleled legend of Empire in his lifetime found an unknown grave in the ocean.

IV

MISTAKES AND MISCALCULATIONS

'Some One Had Blundered': The Charge of the Light Brigade

The Crimean War, waged between 1854 and 1856, was a miserable war, perhaps the most sordidly wretched engagement of any magnitude since the Napoleonic Wars which had ended forty years previously. Other conflicts of the nineteenth century could, as a rule, be regarded as a means of realizing the great concept of the age, the principle of nationalism. Independent nations had been created in the Balkans; Germany and Italy had been unified; but on what conceivable grounds of national unity, it might be asked, could Britain, France and Sardinia be sending armies to the Black Sea to help Turks fight Russians? Why, indeed, were Christian Englishmen in alliance with their late French foes, supporting Mohammedan Turks against Christian Russians? Disraeli's caustic explanation was that England was going to war to prevent the Emperor of all the Russias from protecting Christian subjects of the Sultan of Turkey. Even while the Crimean War was being waged in full ferocity or prolonged stalemate, most Englishmen considered the campaign to be utterly senseless. Posterity has continued to agree with them.

The actual warfare was as miserable and meaningless as its avowed or pretended aims. The greatest casualties among British soldiers in the Crimea were sustained not in fighting but from disease, starvation and exposure. Battles were decided through the competitive incompetence of obtuse and superannuated generals. It was an ill-conceived, ill-timed, ill-organized, inconclusive war—a war which, from all points, was what Queen Victoria, with unerring understatement, called 'an unsatisfactory war'.

Yet this was a war rich in glamour and myth, as much in the eyes of the Victorians as for generations to come. Above all it was a picturesque war, full of stirring exploits and deeds of heroism that were prompt to pass into legend—Macmahon storming the Malakov redoubt; the parade-ground discipline of weary troops in the great offensives; Florence Nightingale holding aloft her lamp to comfort the wounded and dying in the crammed, stinking wards and corridors of makeshift hospitals in Scutari and the Crimea; the Light Brigade, in a charge probably unsurpassed in the annals of war, riding to a certain doom in the 'Valley of Death' at Balaclava.

It could be claimed with some justification that both the crude realism and the romance of this war were in some way the creation of the press, which—whether to its credit or discredit is debatable—brought the horrors and heroisms of the war not only right home to English men and women, but right into their homes. It was the first time in the experience of the nation that a war had been reported at close range by a widespread free press and could be followed from dispatch to dispatch in the daily papers. For the first time, in the person of William Howard Russell, the war correspondent became an eye-witness reporter and commentator of warfare; and it was Russell (who was to be *The Times* foreign correspondent for more than half a century) whose famous letters home from the camps and battlefields of the Crimea opened the eyes of the nation to the terrible sufferings of her soldiers during the winter of 1854–55. Even those fighting the war, not to mention others present in the Crimea for one or other purpose of their own, wrote to the newspapers with criticism or praise—to say nothing of a good deal of exaggeration.

It was owing to the press that the distressing facts behind this bungled campaign were exposed, that incompetent generals and antiquated methods were brought under the searching light of publicity, their stupidities and insufficiencies stigmatized and held up to public censure. Try as they might to cover up or gloss over the facts in evasion and concealment—always, of course, 'in the interests of the nation and the British Army'—government and army authorities could not gag the press. It was the press, too, which reported and highlighted the courage and sacrifice which made the events of the war so sensational. In this way, the devotion of Florence Nightingale in the face of official obstructionism and the hitherto unsung heroism of the common soldier were made known to Britain and the whole world—thus, incidentally, paving the way for jingoism and the jingling ballads of Kipling. One result of the unwelcome publicity was that when the war was over, long-needed reforms were introduced in the training of staff, the care of the sick and wounded and in more humane treatment of the private soldier: his education, recreation, physical fitness and general welfare.

There was also a wave of adulation of the heroes of the battlefield. When Lord Cardigan arrived at Dover from the Crimea on 13 January 1855, he found to his astonishment that he was a hero. In London he was mobbed by cheering crowds; shop windows displayed his picture, the papers were full of his prowess. He was invited to stay at Windsor, where he described the Charge to the Queen and Prince Albert, and later he gave another even more picturesque account of it at a Mansion House banquet in his honour. As always, Disraeli produced a characteristic comment: 'The great hero of London at present is Lord Cardigan, who relates with sufficient modesty, but with ample details, the particulars of his fiery charge at Balaclava, to willing audiences—as often as they like.' Cardigan was made Chief Superintendent of the Cavalry, presented with a forty-foot-long testimonial, an illuminated address and a sword of honour. When he stepped off trains at railway stations he was met to the strains of 'See the Conquering Hero Comes'.

There were subsequent doubts as to how much a hero Cardigan was; but, hero or no, he had achieved one of the most durable forms of immortality—his name had been given to a garment. The cardigan, that woollen jacket which is so useful on chilly summer evenings or in brisk winter dawns is a lasting relic of the patriotic enthusiasm of a hundred years ago. Thousands of 'cardigans' were sold and they continue to be sold today in their thousands, though possibly few people associate them with the Crimean War or know that it was Lord Cardigan's use of such a jacket in the autumn chills of Crimea that popularized the garment and perpetuated its name.

Apart from setting fashions in woollen jackets and cherry-coloured cavalry pants, who and what was this Cardigan? Blackguard, fool and bungler he may have been, but there is no doubt that he did ride at the head of his cavalrymen 'into the jaws of Hell' during the ill-fated Charge.

In a masterly reconstruction and analysis of the events and contributing causes of the most publicized engagement of the Crimean War, Mrs Cecil Woodham-Smith in *The Reason Why* (1953), has given an exhaustively documented account of British military life before and during the famous battle. This skilful biographer has also placed in clear perspective the bitter personal warfare waged between the Earl of Cardigan and his brother-in-law the Earl of Lucan, the two military officers whose names, with that of Lord Raglan, are those most closely associated with Balaclava and the suicidal charge. The first half of Mrs Woodham-Smith's absorbing book explores in detail the family backgrounds, characters, lives and careers of the two men, as a prelude to an analysis of their catastrophic participation in the events of Balaclava. The tragi-comic story had never before been pieced together into a whole until Mrs Woodham-Smith did so in her book—from which the main facts in this chapter, concerning Lords Lucan and Cardigan and their part in the battle of Balaclava, have been drawn.

Both Lord Cardigan and Lord Lucan were immensely wealthy aristocrats; both were handsome, dandified, conceited and arrogant. Lord Lucan, the less unprepossessing of the two (which is not saying much) displayed signs of greater intelligence, independence of mind and military talent: Lord Cardigan was abysmally lacking in these qualities.

Lucan (Lord Bingham until he succeeded to the title in 1837 as 3rd Earl of Lucan), a professional soldier from the age of sixteen, was physically courageous and indifferent to discomfort and hardship; he was a tireless worker, who rose early, ate and drank sparingly and expected his subordinates to follow his example in all these things. In command he was a martinet, irrascible, severe, unsparing of drills, parades, inspections and, since he was almost impossible to please, more lavish with reprimands, punishments and floggings than was normally the custom under the brutal army system of the time. Having an unassailable conviction that he was always right he was also unable to distinguish what was important from what was irrelevant, and was accordingly a stickler for trivial detail; but he was undoubtedly talented, however much he lacked common sense.

An absentee landlord with vast hereditary estates in Ireland, at Castlebar, Co. Mayo, in Connaught, Lucan was harsh and pitiless in his attempts, from 1837, and through the great potato famine of 1846–47, to clear and improve the land, formerly mismanaged for years by an unscrupulous resident agent. He sought by the consolidation of infinitely divided smallholdings to bring about long-term improvements which should enable the peasantry to earn fair wages for fair work instead of living at near-starvation level from small potato plots. To do this and in face of an unprecedented population explosion, it was imperative in the view of 'consolidating' landlords such as Lucan, to reduce the numbers of the tenantry: this entailed large-scale evictions, ruthless demolition of hovels and the razing of whole villages. In pursuit of a system of cultivation from which he believed future generations of Irish peasantry would benefit, the Earl of Lucan felt no responsibility to the starving men and women doomed by eviction and famine, by whom he came to be dreaded and execrated as the 'Exterminator'.

If Lucan had few saving graces, Cardigan bore all the marks of a thoroughly repulsive and disreputable character. He was a spoilt only child, handsome, rich, recklessly courageous and utterly stupid. Because he was an only son, his ambition to become a soldier had been thwarted by his parents until he was twenty-seven, when they at last withdrew their opposition. Lord Brudenell (he became 7th Earl of Cardigan in 1837), entered the 8th Hussars as a Cornet in 1824 and through influence, and of course his money, was promoted to Lieutenant six months later and to Captain after two years' service. Like Lord Lucan he was a martinet with a fanatical obsession about drill, military etiquette and details of uniform; he was a nagging fault-finder, insulting to subordinates, abusive to them on parade, giving them humiliating reprimands before the whole regiment; he meted out punishments and floggings unsparingly to the rank and file. He was a coarse womanizer and a fancier of other men's wives—a penchant which involved him in several divorce cases. His love affairs were legendary and he was said to have fathered innumerable children in the villages on his estates; he had a megalomaniac sensitivity to fancied injury and insult, and was a vindictive and unprincipled enemy, a notoriously trigger-happy and dangerous dueller. Coarse and vain, petty and stupid, he was a grotesquely untalented man who, throughout a turbulent career, generally managed 'to get away with murder' in a lord-loving age and country in which the combination of birth, wealth and rank were accorded an almost cringing deference.

Lord Bingham and Lord Brudenell had disliked each other since they were young men. In 1829 Bingham married Brudenell's youngest sister; the marriage was not successful and when the couple separated in 1854 there was added reason for the mutual detestation of the brothers-in-law. Bingham had done brief overseas services in 1828 on the staff of Prince Vorontzov who was in charge of a brigade in the Balkans during a Russian campaign against the Turks; he had taken pains to study tactics and military history and was particularly scornful of the dull or frivolous life of peace-time soldiering, especially the round of reviews, parades and banquets in which Brudenell-Cardigan revelled and for which Bingham-Lucan sneered at him as 'the feather-bed soldier'. The two, having meanwhile inherited their earldoms, met only infrequently during the years preceding the Crimean War. While Lucan spent his time between Castlebar and the family seat at Laleham, near Chertsey in Surrey, Cardigan spent very little time with the 11th Hussars and lived a princely life on the family estate at Deene Park, in his town house in Portman Square, on his yacht *Dryad* or in Paris. Both men had long been obsessed with a desire for military glory; their compulsory collaboration in the Crimea inevitably set them at loggerheads from the outset, in a bitter personal feud that was whipped up by vanity, ambition, rancour and contempt.

When Lord Bingham and Lord Brudenell became soldiers, and right up to the reorganization of the Army in 1871 by Edward Cardwell, Secretary for War (1868–74), the Purchase System obliged officers to buy their commissions in the British Army. The system was instituted some years after the Restoration, when a standing army was formed in 1683, designed to prevent the army from ever again falling into the hands of men who might impose a military dictatorship of the Cromwellian type; and, in spite of faults and abuses, it had answered its purpose. As late as 1856 the system was defended by Lord Palmerston as a liberal guarantee against revolution and military despotism. He told the Commission on Purchase that

> 'if the connection between the Army and the higher class of society were dissolved, then the Army would present a dangerous and un-

> constitutional appearance. It was only when the Army was unconnected with those whose property gave them an interest in the country, and was commanded by unprincipled military adventurers, that it ever became formidable to the liberties of the nation.'

In short, he was defending the system as a necessary check to possible Napoleonic tendencies.

Under the purchase system a man first had to buy his commission and then pay for each subsequent step in rank. In this way a rich man could buy the command of a regiment over the heads of more experienced officers without great means. Under the system, therefore, it was inevitable that high army posts should be reserved for rich noblemen—a colonel's commission cost anything from £35,000 to £40,000—and though there was an official tariff the Government allowed and encouraged men of wealth to manipulate the system for their own ends. This meant that it was virtually impossible for a man without means, however talented or experienced, to rise in the army.

There was also a convenient short-cut to each purchased promotion. An officer could take leave of absence on half-pay for as long as he wished and still buy himself a higher rank. The service of a single day was as valid for transfer to half-pay as twenty-years of service. It was, accordingly, the custom for a young man to buy a vacant captaincy in a regiment in which he had no intention of serving; he would go on half-pay the following day, then bide his time until a vacancy in a more desirable regiment enabled him to purchase major's rank—and so on, upwards, without ever having done a day's service in any of the regiments in which he had bought his commissions. Transfer to half-pay was also a convenient way for wealthy, smart young officers in fashionable regiments to avoid tiresome service overseas—particularly in India, where added disadvantages were the discomforts of dust, heat and possibly disease. A tour of duty overseas was also damaging to prestige. Officers who did service in India were looked down upon as not quite gentlemen, for obviously it was only those without means who were unable to avoid service abroad, and how could a man without means be a gentleman? As a result, at the outbreak of the Crimean War, the despised 'Indian' officers were those with the lowest rank but with the longest military experience, and who had had experience of warfare on active service overseas.

It was by these peculiarities of the purchase system that Lords Bingham and Brudenell were able to buy their way up, as young men, to the commands of crack cavalry regiments. In 1826, when he was twenty-six, Lord Bingham became Lieutenant-Colonel in command of the 17th Lancers, one of the most famous regiments in the British Army, at a cost of £25,000—which was £20,000 more than the official tariff price. Ten years later, in May 1826, he relinquished command of the 17th Lancers, now drilled to such perfection that they were known as 'Bingham's Dandies', and went on half-pay in order to look after his Irish estates.

Lord Brudenell in 1832, at the age of thirty-two, obtained command of the 15th King's Hussars, for which it was said that he had paid between £35,000 and £40,000. Two years later, after a series of scandals and courts-martial resulting from his outrageous treatment of his officers, he was relieved of his command. In 1836, however, through Court influence, he was enabled to buy (at a price said to exceed £40,000) the command of the 11th Light Dragoons. He proceeded to drill the regiment to a spectacular pitch of precision and polish, and in February 1840 it was chosen to meet and escort Prince Albert when he arrived in England to marry Queen Victoria. The Prince became the regiment's Colonel-in-Chief and its name was changed to the 11th, Prince Albert's Own, Hussars, The men acquired new and gorgeous uniforms which featured cherry-coloured pants of incredible tightness and they were provided with magnificent horses. Much of their finery was paid for by Brundenell-Cardigan out of his own pocket. The Hussars' get-up had to be seen to be believed. Their skin-tight pants were surmounted by the shortest of royal blue jackets edged with gold braid; over these they wore fur-trimmed dolmans a-glitter with gold lace and braid and slung cape-like over one shoulder. Their tall fur hats soared even higher in great panaches of soft feathers fluttering from gold clasps. 'The brevity of their jackets, the irrationality of their headgear, the incredible tightness of their cherry coloured pants, altogether defy description', growled *The Times*.

Apart from service in India, where the army was continually engaged in minor skirmishes with hill tribes, the all-pervading preoccupation of army life was spit and polish; and the invention of new and ever more gorgeous uniforms for their troops was a hobby dear to the hearts of regimental commanders. Battles were fought in elaborate and picturesque trappings and it was in the fantastic fancy-dress of his devising, befurred and befeathered and in a blaze of gold, bright blue and cherry pink, that Lord Cardigan's 'cherry bums' rode to their deaths at Balaclava.

The British Expeditionary Army, some 25,000 strong, which disembarked at Calamita Bay, on the desolate coast of the Crimea, on 14 September 1854, was a peace-time army, rigid with military conventions and parade-ground etiquette. Its generals were all elderly men, some of whom had been on the verge of retirement, others brought back from retirement when war was declared. Lord Hardinge, Commander-in-Chief, was sixty-nine; Lord Raglan, appointed Commander-in-Chief of the Expeditionary Army to the East was sixty-seven; Lord

Lucan, appointed Brigadier-General in command of the Cavalry Division was fifty-four; Lord Cardigan, Brigadier-General in command of the Light Brigade of Cavalry was fifty-seven; and Colonel James Scarlett, appointed Brigadier-General in command of the Heavy Cavalry, at fifty-five, had been on the verge of retirement. Lord Lucan, to be sure, had seen active service in the Balkans, but that was twenty-six years ago; the other two had no experience whatever of active service. There was, of course, an extensive list of experienced cavalry officers who were much younger and had brilliant records of service in the field. Unfortunately these were the despised 'Indian' officers and the caste system which kept them down was so powerful that not a single one of them had received any appointment to a cavalry command.

Lord Raglan, the Commander-in-Chief, had served for forty years on the Iron Duke's staff. He had been Wellington's aide-de-camp in the Peninsula War which had seen the French expelled from Spain, and his military secretary from 1812 to 1815 and again from 1827 until Wellington's death in 1852. Raglan had been present at all the great actions and had lost his sword-arm in 1815 at the Battle of Waterloo; but his career had been that of a staff officer, the Duke's subordinate. He had never occupied any position of command and had never led even a platoon into battle. Now, oblivious of the passage of time, he had a disconcerting habit of referring to the enemy as 'the French', forgetting that it was the Russians who were now the enemy and that the French were his allies. Lord Raglan's little lapses were as embarrassing to his aides-de-camp as they were irritating to his French colleagues.

Commanded by these superannuated leaders the British troops fought the Battle of Balaclava, gorgeously arrayed, it is true, but stupified by drill and discipline, many of them ageing veterans of Waterloo. Discipline and courage were the chief virtues required of a soldier who was expected to behave on the battlefield exactly as if it were the parade-ground, his chief concern being not to disgrace himself or the regiment by any breach of discipline. With precision carried to this pitch of soulless perfection, it was no wonder that, to observers watching the battle from the heights above the plain of Balaclava, the fighting should seem as remote and unreal as a brightly coloured scene in a picture book, and that the men under fire, killing and dying on the battlefield, looked like a clockwork army of toy soldiers.

Lord Lucan, in his mid-fifties, was typical of these leaders who were totally unfitted for the task which lay ahead. Busied with clearing and improving his estates in Mayo, he had not seen service or handled a regiment on a parade-ground for seventeen years. During that time cavalry drill had been changed and he was ignorant of the new words of command. On his arrival at Varna in Bulgaria, prior to the invasion of the Crimea, when he came to handle the troops under his command, neither his officers nor his men understood what he wanted them to do, with the result that, at a review before the Turkish Commander-in-Chief, he got them into a complete muddle. His solution for any similar contretemps in the future was brilliantly simple—he merely ordered his troops to unlearn the new drill they had been taught and revert to the old. Unfortunately nobody knew the old drill any longer, so there was nobody to teach the men because there was nobody to teach the officers. Parade-ground manoeuvres continued to be chaotic, with Lord Lucan adamant, the troops bewildered and the officers, confronted with this state of affairs, uneasy at the prospect of battles to come.

In the Crimea matters were not improved by the feud between the noble brothers-in-law, which was intensified by Lord Ranglan's favouritism of Cardigan. Officially Cardigan was in command of the Light Brigade under Lord Lucan who commanded the Cavalry Division; but, considering that he held an independent command, Cardigan ignored and flouted his detested relative whenever possible and, with the indulgent acquiescence of Lord Raglan, went his own way. Lucan, ignored and passed over by his Commander-in-Chief, doggedly opposed the chafing Cardigan and hung grimly on to the vestiges and semblances of command with the aid of dignified but ineffectual complaints, pedantic obstructionism and the Queen's Regulations.

The siege of Sebastopol was begun at the end of September 1854. The Allied forces received their supplies and reinforcements by way of the port of Balaclava, a few miles south of Sebastopol; their navies were in control of the Black Sea. The Russians attacked at Balaclava on 25 October, and it was on this day that the famous Charge of the Light Brigade took place.

There is no point in delving into the mass of conflicting evidence contained in books, records, investigations and court inquiries, as to who was to blame for the catastrophe. Suffice it to say that four orders, scrawled hastily on tiny scraps of paper, by General Richard Airey, the Quartermaster-General, were issued by Lord Raglan at the Battle of Balaclava. The messages were obscure, contradictory and confusing. The last two were possibly intended to be read together but the final message ordering the Light Brigade to charge made no sense, taken alone as it was. To confuse the issue further, Lord Raglan shouted an added order after Captain Nolan, the aide-de-camp who galloped down from the heights to the plain bearing the final message, to tell Lord Lucan that the attack was to begin immediately. It is possible, too, that Captain Nolan misinterpreted the order. Lord Lucan, who passed it on to Lord Cardigan, displayed poor judgement. There can be no doubt, to say the least, that the action was suicidal.

It is thought that Lord Raglan wished the cavalry to attack a redoubt on the mountainside to the left of the plain, in order to recapture British naval guns in an emplacement which had been captured some time before by the Russians—who were now preparing to take away these guns.

Lord Raglan and other allied observers were posted on the Heights, a vantage point six-hundred feet up the mountainside overlooking the plain of Balaclava, which was three miles long by two miles wide and bisected into a North and a South Valley by a ridge which the British called the 'Causeway Heights'. The party of observers up on the Heights were able to see not only Lord Lucan below with the Heavy Brigade and Lord Cardigan with the Light Brigade, but also the Russians stationed on the other side of the North Valley and at the far end.

Lord Lucan, who had neglected to reconnoitre, could see no enemy on account of the hillocks between him and the Russians. Lord Raglan's message, accordingly, seemed to him quite incomprehensible. Both Lucan and Cardigan were dismayed by the final message and by Lord Raglan's verbal injunction to charge without delay. But the command had been delivered by an aide of the Commander-in-Chief and military regulations demanded that orders given by an aide-de-camp should be obeyed as implicitly as if given by the Commander himself; so, 'Theirs not to reason why, theirs but to do and die'. Accordingly Lord Lucan ordered Lord Cardigan to advance down the North Valley with the Light Brigade. The Heavy Brigade, led by himself would follow in support.

The order, on the face of it, required the cavalry to attack a Russian position defended by twelve cannon and superior cavalry units, situated at the end of the long, narrow North Valley. Both sides of this valley, the Fedioukine Heights to the left, the Causeway Heights to the right, were held by Russian infantry and artillery, with a total of forty-four cannon. The Light Brigade were required to ride through the North Valley—a thousand yards wide—under cannon and rifle fire from three directions. The brigade, which made the attack alone, consisted of 673 officers and men (not the 600 made familiar by Tennyson's poem); they were outnumbered by about ten to one by the Russian forces disposed on both sides and ahead of them. A more obvious and inescapable death trap could hardly be conceived.

The Light Brigade was drawn up in three lines, while Lord Cardigan took up a position in the front, two lengths in front of his staff, as regulations prescribed, and five lengths in advance of the front line of cavalry. Raising his sword Lord Cardigan gave the order to advance: 'Walk, march, trot'. The three lines of the Light Brigade moved off slowly, to the jingle of bits and accoutrements which could be heard in a sudden lull in the rifle fire and the booming of guns. The cavalrymen moved up the valley at a steady trot, and were followed at a short interval by the Heavy Brigade, led by Lord Lucan.

Cardigan never once looked back during the whole charge: 'a

cavalry commander about to lead a charge must keep strictly looking forward; if he looks back his men will receive an impression of uncertainty'. He tightly restrained the pace of the Light Brigade; the line was to advance with parade-ground perfection. At one point a squadron broke into a canter and their leader came abreast of Cardigan. Without lifting his gaze from the battery ahead, Cardigan checked the officer with his sword, telling him sharply not to ride level with his commanding officer; and he called out once to the quadron to check its pace: 'Steady, steady the 17th Lancers.' Beyond this he gave no further order, made no sign and did not speak again.

Captain Nolan, who had brought down from the Heights Lord Raglan's message to attack, and who had received permission to take part in the charge, at one point began to gallop diagonally from left to right across the path of the advancing ranks of cavalry. He crossed in front of Lord Cardigan, turning in his saddle to wave his sword while he shouted words that were unintelligible in the din of gun fire and the thundering of horses' hooves. It has been thought that Nolan had suddenly realized that he had misunderstood Lord Raglan's commands and wished to head off the riders into the proper direction, but what he actually intended to convey by his waving and shouting was never to be known.

At that moment a Russian shell burst ahead and to the right of Lord Cardigan and a splinter from it ripped into Nolan's heart. He dropped his sword and slumped forward, though still holding his sword arm stiffly erect, and from his throat issued a blood-curdling cry, so strange and dreadful that those who heard it afterwards described it as 'unearthly'. His horse wheeled and careered back through the ranks of advancing cavalry, the gripping knees of a consummate horseman still holding the corpse in the saddle. Cardigan was oblivious of all this, though he was conscious of Nolan's terrible shriek; nor, since he never once looked back during the whole charge, did he see the Light Brigade dwindling behind him as men and horses were mown down by rifle and gunfire from the heights on both flanks and from the battery at the end of the valley.

By a miracle Cardigan had ridden the two miles unscathed. Suddenly he was before the Russian battery from which, amid great tongues of flame and dense clouds of smoke a final salvo poured out from the twelve guns to decimate the front line of the Light Brigade.

Cardigan rode in between the guns, the first to enter the battery, and while behind him cavalrymen and Russian gunners, invisible in the blanket of smoke, slashed at each other in savage hand-to-hand combat, he rode straight through the battery and out on to the other side without striking a blow. It was, he said afterwards, 'no part of a general's duty to fight the enemy among private soldiers'.

Galloping clear of the battery and the bank of black smoke, he suddenly found himself face to face with a halted troop of Cossack cavalry who stared open-mouthed at the glittering and resplendent figure coming full tilt at them out of the murk. Cardigan checked his horse, stared disdainfully back at the Russians, then wheeled to evade a small party of the Cossacks detailed by an officer to capture him. By curious chance it was Prince Radziwill, who had met Cardigan in London and now recognized him. After a brief skirmish, during which a jab from a lance grazed his thigh and ripped his cherry-coloured pants, Cardigan rode back through the silenced guns of the battery, where the fighting had now finished. He returned as he had come, across the plain. His brigade had vanished, his *aides* had vanished. He felt no concern for them and did not dwell on their fate. 'Having led the Brigade and launched them with due impetus', as he said later, he felt that his duty had been done. But it was something of an anomaly for a general to be retreating in this solitary fashion; so, to preserve decorum and dignity he rode towards the British lines at a conspicuously unhurried pace, most of the time at a walk. Round him was a scene of havoc, the plain strewn with the dead and dying; survivors running, limping, crawling back towards their own lines, while among them 'the horses, in every position of agony, struggled to get up, then floundered back on their mutilated riders'. The Russian fire now came only from the Causeway Heights, the batteries on the Fedioukine Heights opposite having been silenced meanwhile by the French; and once again Cardigan rode miraculously unharmed.

The whole incredible episode of the Charge of the Light Brigade had been conducted by this fantastic personage as if it had been his own personal exploit. Had such a character been presented in a novel he would have been dismissed as wildly improbable. But Cardigan was all too real. He led the charge in total egotistical absorption which rendered him blind and deaf to everything but himself and his concerns, his rage at Nolan, his dignity and his idealized dream of himself as a heroic leader doing his noble duty.

The charge itself was as fantastic, but with elements of nightmare horror. The Russian batteries fired on the cavalry from three sides, men and horses fell, first one by one and then in writhing clumps increasingly more numerous. The Brigade rode on to the shouts of officers ordering them to close up so that correct military formation should not be disfigured by unsightly gaps in the ranks: and the men complied strictly with drill regulations. Riderless horses behaved as correctly as the human beings: out of long habit and training they attempted to run close beside some other horse which still bore a rider and in this way closed up the gaps in the thinning ranks which managed to reach the Russian guns.

After the charge, examining men taken prisoner during the fighting in the battery, General Liprandi the Russian commander, who spoke excellent English, suggested that they must have been primed with spirits to make an attack of such utter recklessness. The men, some of them severely, and one mortally wounded, answered indignantly and quite truthfully that they had not tasted food or drink that day and that their last rum ration had been issued and drunk the afternoon before.

When he was asked afterwards what he had thought about during the charge, Cardigan said that he had been so infuriated by Captain Nolan's flagrant breach of displine and military etiquette that he could think of nothing else. As he returned he continued to brood on Nolan's behaviour. It was his immediate intention, when he should find him, to reprimand Nolan for his breach of the Regulations which Cardigan also took as an added personal insult. Meeting General Scarlett where the Heavy Brigade had been halted by Lord Lucan out of range of the guns, Cardigan broke into furious abuse of Nolan and added a contemptuous remark about his 'screaming like a woman when he was hit'—only to be silenced by Scarlett who told him that he had just ridden over Nolan's dead body.

When the last dazed and bewildered survivors had staggered to safety, what remained of the Light Brigade was re-formed. The roll-call showed that out of 673 horsemen only 195 had returned.

After the roll-call the survivors of the Charge were kept waiting for five hours less than half a mile from their camp. They waited in silence, too dispirited to talk, and they returned in silence to the camp. Most of the men and their few surviving horses had not eaten since the evening before, but for fear of Russian attack no fires were allowed. Unable to cook food, the men had to be content with a dry biscuit and a tot of rum. They spent the night exhausted, cold, hungry, in nervous and physical shock, talking in low tones of the catastrophe and grieving for their lost comrades and their horses.

Having attended to the roll-call Lord Cardigan considered his day's work done and rode back to his yacht *Dryad* which was anchored in the congested Balaclava harbour. With special permission from Lord Raglan to dine and sleep on the yacht, he was the only officer to escape the hardships of bad food and cold nights under canvas. Aboard the *Dryad* he had a bath, his dinner with a bottle of champagne, and went to bed to enjoy a good night's rest—or so the story goes. However, in *Battles of the Crimean War* (1962), W. Baring Pemberton, on the basis of an unpublished letter of Cardigan's aide Captain H. F. B. Maxse, has declared the facts of Lord Cardigan's comings and goings after the battle to be otherwise. Whatever he may have done later in the evening, it would appear that the noble Earl, momentarily humbled by the catastrophe, his natural arrogance and hauteur supplanted for the nonce by consternation and grief, made his way after the roll-call to a camp fire where his wounded aide-de-camp was reclining, and there lay down, wrapped in his cloak, to sleep the sleep of a man 'physically, emotionally and nervously exhausted'.

Late that evening Lord Lucan had a stormy interview with Lord Raglan, who accused him of having lost the Light Brigade. Lucan defended himself hotly and after bitter recriminations, during which military etiquette was thrown aside, he left, repeating his refusal to be blamed for errors which he considered had not been his. Sitting in his tent, he passed the night in deep depression, brooding on the injustice which would make a scapegoat of him and bitterly resolved not to bear 'the smallest particle of responsibility' for the disaster.

Lord Lucan, who would not let well alone what Lord Raglan and the other generals would have preferred to forget, and smarting under a grievance against his superior officer, attempted to bring the whole bungled affair to public notice, but with no better luck. To avoid prejudice to 'the public service and the general discipline of the army', the Duke of Newcastle, Secretary for War, relieved Lucan of his command and he was recalled to England. Cardigan, preceding him by a few weeks on convenient sick-leave, had returned a hero.

The Charge of the Light Brigade was a badly bungled manoeuvre and an appalling catastrophe. Nor did it have any justification or recompense in victory: neither side having won, it was a draw. But behind all the subsequent condemnation can be glimpsed the belief that in one respect it was one of the most successful engagements in the nation's military history. As Mrs Woodham-Smith observes:

> 'The British troops, in spite of the disaster of the Light Brigade—indeed even on account of it—felt that they had a moral ascendancy. Bodies of Russian cavalry had been put to flight by handfuls of British horsemen at odds of twenty, fifty, even a hundred to one; a battery had been attacked in front by cavalry and silenced—a most extraordinary feat . . .'

Tennyson produced the appropriate versified comment on their heroism:

> 'Forward, the Light Brigade!'
> Was there a man dismayed?
> Not though the soldier knew
> Some one had blunder'd:
> Theirs not to make reply,
> Theirs not to reason why,
> Theirs but to do and die:
> Into the valley of Death
> Rode the six hundred.

When can their glory fade?
Oh the wild charge they made!
All the world wonder'd.
Honour the charge they made!
Honour the Light Brigade,
Noble six hundred!

Generations of Englishmen, reading of the exploits of Balaclava and the immortal ride of the 'noble six hundred', could feel that if fearful odds were able to call forth selfless bravery of this high order, British heroism would always be equal to whatever catastrophe, however frightful, it might be called upon to face in any future.

'My Skin is the Passport': The Indian Mutiny

I

The Indian Mutiny was sparked off in 1857, or so it is believed, by an exchange of words between a sepoy and a lascar at the great arsenal at Dum Dum near Calcutta. The sepoy, like so many Indian soldiers, was a high caste Brahmin. The arsenal labourer was the lowest of the low, an untouchable. But, as the traditional story has it, the man of lowly caste had the impudence to beg for a little water from the sepoy's *lotah*, the little brass pot used to contain water for ritual cleansing.

It was, as Major-General Richard Hilton explained in his book *The Indian Mutiny: a centenary history* (1957), as if a filthy tramp had asked a cultured European of fastidious personal habits for the loan of his toothbrush. The sepoy answered the untouchable with a haughty rebuke, only to receive the sneering retort:

> 'You and your caste! I suppose you realize that all such ideas will soon be a thing of the past. There is something brewing which will soon destroy all caste—cartridges for the new rifle, greased with the fat of pigs and cows! You will all have to bite these cartridges. It is part of the drill.'

This, the story goes, was how the rumour that the cartridges used in the new Enfield rifle were defiled (by pig fat for Mohammedans, for whom the pig was unclean, and by cow fat for Hindus, to whom the cow was sacred) began to spread in hundreds of garrisons maintained to defend the great East India Company, the symbol of Britain's might in India. Such were the preliminaries to the great Indian Mutiny.

The East India Company, the most powerful trading company in the world, relied on its Indian soldiers and trusted them. After Clive's victory over Siraj-ud-Dowlah, the Nawab of Bengal, at Plassy in 1757

24. The Earl of Cardigan

25. The march from Lucknow. (Water colour by Egron Lundgren)

26. Cecil Rhodes

27. The trial of Dr Jameson, 1896

it was mainly with the aid of the sepoys of the Bengal Army that India was conquered or subdued, inch by inch, principality by principality. Sepoys were almost as able as British soldiers. They had proved themselves well-nigh as loyal—and they were very much cheaper. Books about India all differ as to the strength of the British Indian Army and the proportion of British soldiers to sepoys at this time; but it can safely be assumed that at the outbreak of the Mutiny British troops numbered some 35,000 to 50,000 and Indian sepoys 260,000 to 310,000, in a country with a population of more than two hundred millions.

The rumour of the unclean cartridges which spread rapidly in northern India caused increasing unrest among the sepoys. During the spring of 1857 cases of insubordination which occurred were punished with great severity. Two regiments of native infantry which had displayed seditious tendencies were disarmed and disbanded. A third, preparing to revolt, was disarmed, relieved of all duties and confined to barracks. The military authorities tried to deny the rumours which undoubtedly had some truth behind them: it was necessary to bite off the greased patch on the end of a cartridge when loading the Enfield rifle and various types of fat had indeed been used to grease the cartridges. Assurances were circulated that ghee—clarified butter—would be used in future and that the defiled cartridges would be withdrawn, and this was also true, they were withdrawn and the offer was made to the sepoys to grease their own cartridges. But the damage had been done and clumsily handled counter propaganda helped to increase the mistrust of the sepoys instead of allaying it. Many of them believed that the British wished to convert them to Christianity by making it impossible for them to remain Mohammedans or Hindus, through having been forced to break caste.

The sepoys were faced with a dilemma. If they were loyal to the British they ran the risk of being considered apostates and of becoming social outcasts, rejected by their families, relatives and fellow Hindus. If they remained faithful to religious beliefs which entailed insubordination and breaking their oath of loyalty, they risked severe punishment, dismissal and poverty.

The British were faced with a different dilemma, not only before the revolt of 1857—for there had been mutinies or near-mutinies from time to time since 1806, all of them speedily and brutally suppressed—but at the outbreak of the Mutiny itself, which made the dilemma all the more fateful: should they trust, or make a pretence of trusting, the sepoys who were divided in their loyalty, or should they disband regiments which might be liable to mutiny, and thus hasten the very conflict they feared? Sir John (later Lord) Lawrence, who was successively Commissioner and Lieutenant-Governor of the recently annexed Punjab, made this difficulty clear in a letter home: 'every step we take to ensure our own safety strikes a blow at the loyal sepoy. He knows this and in turn takes a further step, and so it goes on, until we disband or suppress them, or they mutiny and kill their officers.'

After a couple of attempted revolts, in January and February 1857, which were promptly suppressed, the Mutiny proper started in Meerut, the largest station south of the Punjab, on May 10, 1857. As a result of the punishment—as always, appallingly harsh—of a number of insubordinate sepoys, the Indian garrison revolted and killed their officers and many other Europeans, men, women and children. Meerut, nevertheless, remained in the hands of the British. The rebel sepoys, cavalry and infantry, immediately set off for Delhi, once the seat of the Mogul emperors, forty miles away from Meerut. Delhi, with a population of half a million, was occupied by the sepoys without difficulty when the large Indian garrison revolted and joined the rebels. The British troops, few in number, were killed, officers were shot down right and left, their wives and children massacred, and there was a great slaughter of other Europeans, Christians and their families. The few European survivors managed to escape under cover of darkness and made their way as best they could to the nearby garrisons of Meerut and Ambala.

Meanwhile, the mutineers had declared a new Emperor of India. Inside the fortress-palace of Delhi, overrun and looted by the rebels, lived the senile, half-blind King of Delhi, the Bahadur Shah, last descendant of Timur the Lame—legendary Tamerlane—and a long line of Mogul emperors. The old man, pensioned off by the British, king by courtesy only and regarded by them with tolerant contempt, was without power or authority except in the confines of his own palace, where he held court in an atmosphere rife with every possible oriental vice and cruelty. The mutineers now proclaimed him ruler of India. The restored 'Emperor', who pretended at first that as captive of the mutineers he had accepted the title under compulsion, took heart when he saw British might crumbling before the victorious rebels and began to exercise to the full his newly conferred sovereignty.

During the days and weeks that followed, the mutiny spread, involving practically the whole of the Bengal Army, contingents of central Indian states, a great many garrisons of the north-western provinces, and Oudh and the Punjab, in a succession of revolts and massacres. Lucknow, capital of the kingdom of Oudh, which had been annexed as late as 1856, as a result of years of grotesque misrule, and which had a population of 300,000, was stormed by the sepoys and besieged when Sir Henry Lawrence retreated with a thousand Europeans and 800 loyal Indian soldiers to the Residency, which they defended for nearly four months against some 7,000 rebels.

When the Cawnpore sepoys mutinied, Dandu Panth, a descendant of the royal house of Oudh and adoptive son of the late Peshwa, declared himself Peshwa and acknowledged allegiance to the 'Emperor of Delhi'. The movement of revolt had won more adherents in Oudh than anywhere else and tens of thousands of peasant farmers flocked to join the forces of the mutineers. In recently-annexed Jhansi the sepoys forced Lakshmi Bai, the widowed Rani of Jhansi, to join the revolt and take command. The massacre of the small British garrison at Jhansi was as ruthless as the massacre at Cawnpore, and the Rani was held responsible since she had never made any secret of her hatred of the British. She, however, claimed—and her story was at first accepted by the British authorities—that she was the helpless victim of the situation and had been threatened with death unless she sided with the rebels. The Rani, a proud, handsome and energetic woman in her thirties, had remained loyal or had made a show of loyalty at the outbreak of the Mutiny, but she nursed a bitter grievance against the British because of the annexation, since when she had been engaged in fruitless legal battles with them over money. Now, riding and fighting at the head of the rebel troops, she became one of the most remarkable figures of the Indian Mutiny, of whom it was said later that 'she was the best *man* on the side of the enemy'. She died in battle, at Gwalior, in June 1858.

As the mutiny spread British rule was obliterated in an orgy of killing, burning and looting, throughout an area which must have extended over 75,000 square miles, almost the twentieth part of the vast Indian continent. This area was owned by local rulers and rich land-owning aristocracy, all important and influential Indians of high caste. The total of the Indian population which at one time or another during the Mutiny was brought under rebel rule was probably in the region of twenty-five to thirty millions.

The legendary events of the Mutiny, the tales of heroic courage and loyalty, of treachery, atrocity and suffering, were epitomized in the defence of Cawnpore, the anglicized name of Khanpur by which it became known to posterity. In June 1857, some ten days before the sepoys mutinied, Sir Hugh Wheeler the garrison commander realized that a mutiny was imminent. He was expecting reinforcements from the south and withdrew to the European cantonment with some 450 men, including loyal sepoys, Europeans and Eurasians and with more than three hundred women and children. There they occupied some disused hospital buildings which Wheeler had taken the precaution of having fortified with a ring of entrenchments and an earthwork some four feet high. The sepoys mutinied on 4 and 5 June and left the native cantonment to march for Delhi. At nearby Bithur they hoped to persuade Dandu Panth, the adopted son of Baji Rao, the deposed, pensioned, exiled and now defunct Peshwa of the Mahratta Confederation, to march to Delhi with them.

Dandu Panth, the Nana Sahib, who was afterwards as one of the leaders of the revolt to become notorious, harboured a lifelong, bitter grudge against the British; first, because of the Dalhousie 'law of lapse' by which the age-old right of an Indian ruler without natural heirs to adopt one had been abolished; secondly, because, on the death of Baji Rao, the British government had refused to continue the payment of the deposed Peshwa's pension to his adoptive heir, some 800,000 rupees a year which they insisted was in any case only a life pension to the late Peshwa. The rich young man, who had been left an immense fortune by the Peshwa, lived in state at his palace at Bithur, brooding on his wrongs and biding his time. Now he seized the opportunity for revenge. He agreed to march with the sepoys, but with the offer of gifts and the argument that they would never be given recognition by the Emperor-King of Delhi unless they had shed British blood, he persuaded them first to march back to Cawnpore to attack the garrison.

Reinforced by the Nana Sahib's private army and numerous guns, the sepoys now some thousands strong, returned with the Nana Sahib and his friend and second-in-command, Tantia Topi, a Brahmin Mahratta, to lay siege to the three-hundred defenders of Sir Hugh Wheeler's entrenchment. Hoping for the reinforcements which never came, the tiny garrison held out against heavy daily bombardment, suffering hunger, sickness and increasing exhaustion in the scorching heat of the Indian summer. Added catastrophe overtook them when gunfire with red-hot shells set light to the thatched roof of one of the buildings where to the accompaniment of the despairing cries of women and children, some forty sick and wounded perished in the flames without hope of rescue by the handful of men hard pressed to defend the entrenchment. All the medical supplies and instruments were destroyed in the blaze, so that henceforth the wounded had to die without attention. At length, as hope dwindled, the sepoys who had remained loyal were persuaded to leave the entrenchment by night and return to their homes in the neighbourhood. On 24 June, worn out by their ordeal, the remnants of the garrison surrendered on the written promise of the Nana Sahib of safe conduct for all to Allahabad by boat.

In spite of his signed assurance of freedom for the Cawnpore garrison, the Nana Sahib did not keep his word. In accordance with what was in all likelihood a preconcerted plan, the surviving defenders with the women and children were taken early one morning to the river, to a sacred bathing place, the Sati Chaura Ghat, where a flotilla of boats with thatched awnings was moored at the shallow river edge, each with its complement of boatmen aboard, waiting to take the refugees supposedly down river to Allahabad.

When at length all had embarked, Tantia Topi gave an order, and at the blast of a bugle the boatmen leapt from the boats, sepoys with muskets opened fire and two guns concealed in the undergrowth raked the boats with rounds of grapeshot at close range. The boats, grounded in the mud of the shallows, could not be pushed clear, many of them held fast by ropes and chains. The refugees then discovered that there were no oars and that the rudders had been lashed fast so that steering was impossible. Boats which managed to get into midstream merely circled back to the river bank. The thatched awnings were set alight and many of those in the boats who were not killed by gun and musket fire perished in the flames. Those who attempted to escape by scrambling overboard were hacked to death in the water by swordsmen who waded in after them. Not a man was left alive; but before the whole party had been slaughtered the Nana Sahib sent an order that no more women and children were to be killed.

A few men managed to get three boats afloat into midstream, two of them drifting to the farther bank where the occupants were hewn down by Tantia Topi's men placed there to cut off such path of escape. Of the single remaining boat which drifted downstream out of reach of musket fire, only four survivors, two officers and two soldiers, eventually escaped and lived to tell the tale. They were able to reach the advance guard of Havelock's relief force after great hardships and perils in the jungle, where they owed their lives to friendly Indians who helped and concealed them and led them to safety.

Meanwhile, on the banks of the ghat, strewn with the bodies of the slain, 125 women and children had been spared from the carnage, but with sinister intent. They were taken back to Cawnpore and imprisoned first in a large building, the Subada Koti, where they were joined by other refugees from the Fatehgarh garrison and elsewhere who had been caught in the surrounding countryside. The women were made to perform humiliating menial tasks and were subjected to every insult and indignity except sexual assault. After some days the prisoners, now numbering some 200, were herded into the Bibighar, a small, pavilion-like building of two rooms separated by a paved courtyard adjoining the hotel where the Nana Sahib had set up his headquarters. There they were confined for a week, huddled together in conditions of great suffering, half-suffocated in the overpowering heat, fed on uneatable food thrown to them as to animals, filthy, emaciated and distraught with fear and uncertainty of their fate.

While this physical and mental anguish was being endured, the expected relief force of Sir Henry Havelock was approaching, and on 16 March the Nana Sahib's army was engaged at nearby Fatehpur and put to rout. The Nana Sahib, either panicking, or furious in defeat, conferred with his friends and advisers, Azimullah Khan his confidential agent, his nephew Rao Sahib and Tantia Topi. It was decided that the prisoners of the Bibighar, sole witnesses to the massacre by the riverside, must be put out of the way. The Nana Sahib's guard detailed to carry out the order to kill the prisoners flinched at the pitiful sight of the women and children. Even the taunts of one of the Nana Sahib's concubines failed to spur them on. This woman accordingly fetched several market butchers from the city to dispatch the victims with sabres, cleavers and hatchets.

When Havelock and his Highlanders marched into Cawnpore on the morning following their victory over the Nana Sahib's army, the massacre had already been accomplished during the night and the bodies of the victims, some of them still living, had been flung down a well behind the Bibighar. From the depths of the well, somewhere among the heap of naked bodies, on top of which a pile of severed arms and legs had been thrown, faint moans reached the ears of officers and men of the relief force who had hurried to the house; but these victims, doubtless dismembered or otherwise horribly mutilated, expired before any attempt could be made to disinter them from the gruesome mass.

Both outside and inside the Bibighar horrifying traces of the slaughter could be seen. Shreds of blood-soaked clothing, intermingled with small personal belongings were strewn about everywhere. The courtyard was slippery with blood and inside the rooms the floors were covered with congealing blood which was also splashed on walls and wooden pillars. These pillars were scored deep with sabre or hatchet slashes, many low down at the height of crouching women or of small girls and boys who had left on the walls the imprints of small bloodied hands among the larger handprints of women. Severed strands and tufts of women's hair had even been embedded in the plaster from the force of sword-blows. In one room a row of women's and another of children's shoes had been found, the amputated feet still in them, and there were many other piteous evidences of the butchery. Havelock's troops and other contingents following them through Cawnpore, having inspected these horrors, were filled with the desire to be revenged on all Indians. Garnet Wolseley, a captain at the time, witnessed the dreadful sights and wrote:

> 'As for our men, revenge was in their eyes. The indignity which had been put upon a proud people by a race whom we regarded as inferior in every sense was maddening. The idea that a native should have dared to put his hands upon an Englishwoman was too much for our insular pride. An all-absorbing craving for ruthless vengeance, that most unchristian of passions, was deep in all hearts.'

In the days, the months that followed, the war cry of the British troops, as they stormed one rebel stronghold after another, was: 'Remember Cawnpore, boys!' Thousands of mutineers and even suspects were summarily hanged, with or without the pretence of trial, and the executions were frequently accompanied by punitive indignities horrible to Hindus and Mohammedans because of their faiths. No punishment was considered too cruel for the murderers of British women and children. The massacre at Cawnpore has been considered by more than one historian as indeed one of the turning points in the relationship between Britain and India.

The greater part of British-ruled India did not join in the Mutiny, which had little or no effect on the coastal regions, the Punjab, southern India and most of central India and was, in fact, confined to Bengal, the North-West provinces along the Ganges, Oudh (which provided nearly two-thirds of the Bengal Army) and the Punjab which, however, remained loyal in spite of initial unrest at Lahore and Peshawar, quelled with a firm hand by the Commander-in-Chief, Sir John Lawrence, and his subordinates. Here the warlike Pathan chieftains, impressed by this firmness with the sepoys, offered their services and those of their tribesmen in vast numbers. In Madras and Bombay the lines stood firm. Even in the regions overrun by the mutineers the population was either undecided or neutral and prepared to submit to the victors. Only a third of the sepoys mutinied: the army which crushed the rebellion consisted mainly of Indian troops. Most of the Indian princes remained loyal to Britain, though troops of Sindhia and Holkar, the two great princes of central India, joined the mutineers. Several of the Indian princes fought on the British side. The semi-independent ruler of Nepal sent large numbers of Gurkha troops to the aid of the British. The rebels never set up any government worthy of the name, nor did they make any systematic attempt to conquer fresh territories. Disputes between Hindus and Mohammedans handicapped rebel action. Even in rebel-occupied territory the great mass, mainly simple villagers, helped and fed British troops and showed great kindness to British fugitives, sheltering or hiding them, often at great risk to themselves—a proof of the divided sympathies of the Indian people.

The British quickly rallied and struck back at the mutineers. Troops arrived from England, from Burma, or were diverted from China and Persia; others were sent from the Indian provinces which had remained loyal. In this respect the Punjab played a role of special importance. The province had been annexed only eight years previously, yet it could now serve as a base and recruiting ground. The sepoys of the Punjab had been disarmed at the first signs of trouble and fresh troops recruited. The warlike Sikhs bore no grudge against the British and their rule, but many of them harboured feelings of hatred and desires of revenge against the Bengali sepoys who had helped to conquer their homeland under British leadership. The Punjabi Sikhs, Nepalese Gurkhas and Pathans from the North-West Frontier became famous during the

Mutiny for their toughness and fighting spirit—which they proved time and again in years to come in various parts of the British Empire and in Europe during World Wars I and II. But during the Mutiny Indians on both sides fought fiercely and bravely.

Events were quick to take a decisive turn. Reinforcements were soon on the march from Punjab in the west and lower Bengal in the east. As early as 8 June 1857 the troops from the Punjab were able to lay siege to Delhi and three months later, by 20 September, after days of hard fighting, the city had been cleared of the rebels and the citadel-palace stormed and recaptured.

When news of the Mutiny reached England in July 1857 the command of the forces in India was offered by Lord Palmerston to Sir Colin Campbell (afterwards Lord Clyde) a veteran of the Peninsular and Crimean Wars, a hero of both the Alma and Balaclava. Having left England for Calcutta in July, Campbell reached India in August and under his able and prudent leadership the suppression of the Mutiny proceeded apace, in the face of innumerable difficulties.

Among the adverse conditions which had to be contended with was the difficulty of communication. When the Mutiny broke out, the Commander-in-Chief, General Anson, was in Simla, the summer Army Headquarters, while the Viceroy, Lord Canning, was a thousand miles away, in Delhi. Mutinied or besieged garrisons far distant were cut off from one another. The telegraph lines had been cut, isolating the upper provinces; postal services were almost entirely interrupted and at that time there were practically no railways in India. The infantry marched or used bullock-carts. Then, the Mutiny had broken out at the height of the scorching Indian summer, when temperatures could reach anything up to 130° Fahrenheit in the shade. Forced marches were a slow, sweltering ordeal, especially for the heavily clothed and accoutred European troops, and resulted in innumerable deaths from sun-stroke, suffocation and exhaustion.

Sir Henry Havelock and Sir James Outram, on 27 September, made an attempt to relieve Lucknow with a force of some 3,000 men; but there were many casualties in the fight through the city streets to reach the Residency. Mutineer reinforcements were flocking to the city and the small force was found inadequate to cover the evacuation of 600 women and children and the handful of remaining defenders. The Commander-in-Chief then concentrated on the second relief of Lucknow and the garrison was relieved on 17 November, but the sepoys in their thousands still held most of the city, including the king's palace, the great, fortified Kaiser Bagh, and it was decided to withdraw. The evacuation, beginning on 19 November with the women and children and the sick, was carried out silently and successfully on three nights, concluding at midnight on the 22nd, when the last of the troops got safely away from the Residency under the noses of the unsuspecting enemy.

Sir Colin Campbell, having marshalled forces some 31,000 strong, returned on 2 March 1858 to commence the final siege of Lucknow. With the storming and capture of the Kaiser Bagh and other principal buildings, the siege of Lucknow was over and another turning point in the Mutiny had been reached. The rebels scattered into the countryside and there remained only the task of hunting them down and restoring law and order in Oudh. On 20 December 1858, Sir Colin Campbell, now Lord Clyde, was able to announce to the Viceroy, Lord Canning, that the Mutiny was over.

The British won nearly every major battle because of their superiority in command and weapons, not least the Enfield rifle, and the Indians produced only a single rebel leader, Tantia Topi, who displayed any outstanding military ability.

In August 1858 Queen Victoria signed the act which revoked the charter of the East India Company and transferred the government of India to the Crown. On 1 November the Viceroy, Lord Canning, published a proclamation announcing the change-over and offering full amnesty to all rebels except those who had murdered British subjects or had been leaders in the mutiny. Sixteen years later, under the benevolent eye of Disraeli, Queen Victoria assumed the title of Empress of India.

The Mutiny raised many questions to which the answers were conflicting. What were the real causes? Was it planned or spontaneous, a nationalist or a religious uprising? What were the respective roles played in it by the Indians and the British? Is it right to regard it, as it was so often considered in England at the time, as a struggle between heathen barbarism and Christian humanitarianism? What were the reactions to and the repercussions of the Mutiny: above all, what has been the attitude of succeeding generations in England and India? The controversy began not long after the outbreak of the Mutiny; it was debated in Parliament, in the newspapers, in pamphlets. Almost from the start it was reported by one of the world's finest journalists, the very first war correspondent, William Howard Russell of *The Times*, whose recollections of the Mutiny, *My Diary in India* (1858–59), were published in two volumes in 1860 and were reissued in 1958, the centenary year of the Mutiny, and again in 1960. At about the same time as Russell was touring India with the British troops, March (1858–59), Egron Lundgren, a Swedish artist domiciled in England, drew and painted events and personalities, both British and Indian, as he accompanied various contingents of the British forces from Calcutta to Lucknow. He travelled with Russell for part of the time and he subsequently provided the illustrations to Russell's diary. Mention should also be made of Felice A. Beato, a pioneer in candid-camera photography, who had recorded events of the Crimean War and who now, in 1858–59, covered the Mutiny and its aftermath, photographing scenes and sites, personalities both British and Indian and condemned rebels and their executions, with an uncompromising realism unusual for the period.

The first book about the Mutiny written with any pretensions to scholarship, Chambers' *History of the Indian Revolt*, appeared as early as 1859. Since then there has been no lack of books about the Mutiny and the historical record compiled in them is even more fascinating than the controversies about the true causes of the uprising.

English writers have put forward contrasting theories, in addition to which unmistakably pro-British or pro-Indian attitudes to the question can be discerned. In recent years, however, there appears to be no marked divergence of opinion on the matter between reputable English and Indian historians—for example in the masterly investigation by Surendra Nath Sen, published under the auspices of the Indian government for the centenary of the Mutiny under the title of *Eighteen Fifty-Seven* (May, 1957). That British and Indian historians should now have reached more or less the same conclusions is due—or so one hopes—to the objectivity with which they have sifted the evidence. But the underlying cause of their unanimity is surely the fact that peace between the two nations has been restored. It was the granting of independence to India in 1947 which made it possible in 1957 for both sides to contemplate the events of 1857 with more serenity, clarity and tolerance.

2

In the spring of 1856 Lord Dalhousie, 'the greatest of Indian proconsuls' and the youngest viceroy ever sent to India, had left for England, broken in health but with a certain feeling of pride in his achievement as viceroy. His report on the state of the country was long and detailed. He found the situation as he left it after his seven-year administration on the whole satisfactory. Many important and valuable reforms concerned with development of resources and improvement in administration had been carried out since his appointment as Governor-General of India in 1847. An enormous network of railways had been planned and started; 4,000 miles of telegraph now criss-crossed India like a spider-web; 2,000 miles of roadway had been metalled and were spanned by innumerable bridges; the Ganges canal had been constructed and opened and extensive irrigation works carried out all over India. He had made vigorous efforts to suppress suttee, thuggee, exposure of female infants and the slave trade; a Legislative Council had been organized, civil service training improved, and the service opened to all British-born subjects regardless of colour; trade, agriculture, forestry, mining and the postal service had been developed.

Under the Dalhousie administration vast areas of India had been incorporated into the territories administered by the mighty East India Company; Pegu and the Punjab had been conquered, and the principalities of Nagpur, Oudh, Satara, Jhansi and Berar had been annexed.

Sepoys, who formed the bulk of the Indian army's fighting force had for some time past been serving under improved conditions. In his report Lord Dalhousie observed that 'The native soldier's position has long been such that hardly any part of his condition demands improvement'. Border skirmishes and localized revolts against British rule were to be expected and had, of course, to be taken into account. But such matters

> 'cannot be regarded as disturbances to the general peace of India, just as the street brawls which daily come before our London courts are not regarded in England as a sign of civil war. I have therefore cause to believe, without presumption, that I leave India in external as well as internal peace.'

This glowing picture of material welfare may well have been enhanced by self-congratulatory wishful thinking; nevertheless there seems to have been little indication of widespread concern among British officers and civil servants stationed in India for the feelings of Indians, whom they generally despised as an inferior race to whom it was not even necessary to be polite. To such people the Mutiny came as a complete surprise and the real reason for it was considered by them to be the rumour of the cartridges greased with defiling cow and pig fat. Soon, however, the possibility of deeper motives underlying the revolt was under fierce discussion and many argued that the affair of the cartridges was only the spark which exploded the powder keg. As usual, the Mutiny was explained as an inevitable link in a historical process.

The search for deeper motives was obviously right and proved fruitful; nevertheless it is astonishing to find that the numerous books about the Mutiny written in this probing spirit dismiss the matter of the cartridges as of little or no consequence, simply because it seemed to the writers absurd, indeed inconceivable, that such an incident could be cause for a revolt. There is an understandable tendency among religious sects to regard the beliefs of other faiths as nonsensical superstition not to be taken seriously. The belief of Mohammedans and Hindus, respectively, in the uncleanness of the pig and the sacredness of the cow, seemed as senseless to the British as the Christian belief that under certain circumstances bread and wine become flesh and blood has seemed to the faithful of other religions. It did not appear to have penetrated those honest Victorian pates that beliefs of this kind could really have given rise to what occurred, and so other motives were sought and given prominence in the investigation. But an Indian writer such as

Surendra Nath Sen, having a more instinctively sympathetic understanding of the psychology and emotions of his own race, makes it quite clear, however much he may toy with other probable associated causes, that the affair of the cartridges could quite well have been the deciding factor which impelled the sepoys to mutiny. In the eyes of the Mohammedans or Hindus, whose religious precepts were part and parcel of their thought and behaviour in a way and to a degree which compromising Victorian Christians could hardly even begin to understand, it was a mortal sin to come into contact, however involuntarily, with substances which for Mohammedans it was a defilement and for Hindus sacrilegious, to handle or even touch. To break caste in this way meant, for both Mohammedans and Hindus, social pariahdom on earth and perdition beyond hope of redemption in the after life. Such a prospect was vividly real to the sepoys. It was the dread of eternal damnation which drove them to ask their British officers for explanations about the cartridges and the rumours of defilement and eventually to the insubordination of refusing to make use of the cartridges. Torn between two allegiances they preferred to be disloyal to their British conquerors and superiors rather than dishonour their religion—a course which, from their point of view, was plain common sense.

The inquiry into 'deeper' motives for the Mutiny brought to light many interesting facts about circumstances which may possibly have helped to provoke the uprising. But the impression one gains is that the researchers have brought forward every possible cause of discontent among the sepoys without being able to prove that any one instance really did produce widespread discontent and still less that it was a contributory cause of the actual revolt.

The paucity of reliable corroborative evidence from Indian sources essential to the documentation of the Mutiny is one of the obstacles to proof of the various theories. The rebels certainly, and Indians in general, produced few documents at this period and existing records, if any, were probably destroyed early in the Mutiny during the wholesale pillaging and burning that went on, which was not always confined to British property, nor spared that of Indians. It can well be understood, therefore, that research has perforce been based on British records. Even Surendra Nath Sen has had to rely for evidence almost entirely on British documentary sources: state papers, memoirs and correspondence.

One English writer has called the Indian Mutiny 'a purely military affair'; another has seen it as 'a religious war'; to a third it was 'a rebellion of reactionary vested interests against a regime which tried to reform ancient institutions too fast and in a rough-shod way'. All of these opinions have one thing in common: they dissociate themselves from the idea that there was an Indian nationalist revolt against British rule.

The 'purely military affair' interpretation was the one which lasted longest. It was usual to speak of 'the sepoy mutiny', so justifying the specialized aspect of the events. It was emphasized that for various reasons the sepoys for some time before the Mutiny had been discontented with and mistrustful of conditions under British rule. Indian soldiers could not rise higher than the rank of lieutenant or captain and this rank applied only in relation to native soldiers, thus creating the anomalous situation in which a British sergeant was the superior of a native officer. Sepoys were paid much less than the British rank and file. New regulations concerning uniforms, types of headdress and hair styles aroused resentment. Indian regiments, contrary both to custom and agreement, were detailed for duty to territories outside India or—and this was considered an abomination by Hindus—'across the water' to Burma. British reverses and failures in a number of wars, notably in Persia and Afghanistan, had undermined Indian faith in the unconquerable British. These and other similar circumstances are thought to have contributed to the disaffection which precipitated the uprising.

It has been assumed that there were also a number of religious reasons. In some cases the British failed to respect the sacred pattern of ritual observance both of Mohammedans and Hindus. Christian missionaries in India at the time were more active than they had ever been, proselytizing in schools, hospitals, prisons and the market place; and there were even a number of fanatically pious British officers who tried to convert their sepoys to Christianity. Many Indian soldiers, however mistakenly, saw in the various reforms and new regulations, such as the introduction of the more efficient Enfield rifle, attempts to prepare the ground for the introduction of the religion of the foreign conquerors.

The East India Company had in the main followed a policy regarded as generally consistent with Britain's customary colonial policy: that is, to interfere as little as possible in the habits and customs of the conquered races. But under the influence of utilitarian and liberal doctrines which were gaining influence in England at this period, a number of reforms were nevertheless instituted which to the Indians seemed like insults to sacred traditions, however natural such changes may have appeared from the point of view of the British, to whom the barbaric habits and customs of heathen natives seemed equally senseless or repugnant. Among these changes were certain not very drastic land-reforms on liberal lines; attempts to establish legal equality for all Indians; the prohibition of suttee—the ritual suicide of Indian widows on the funeral pyres of their husbands; and a law setting aside the immemorial ban on the remarriage of widows; and such is the force of time-honoured custom that even the women regarded these changes as sacrilegious. Great resentment was aroused by the policy of annexation which brought directly under British rule Indian principalities whose rulers had no natural heirs (thereby abolishing the immemorial Indian custom of adopting an heir) or whose reigning princes were notoriously incapable or undesirable, as in the case of the Nawab of Oudh, whose principality was annexed in 1856. Even though both Indian and European historians are agreed that the misrule of the Kingdom of Oudh was a scandalous case of corruption, extravagance and licentiousness, the population, nevertheless, reacted violently against the annexation.

It is hardly possible to establish exactly how much these and other measures contributed to the conditions which provoked the uprising. Later English historians, it is true, have laid increasing emphasis on the view that a growing solidarity and national feeling among Indians may have played a significant part in the causes of the Mutiny. The concept of a communally united India has been regarded as merely the wishful thinking of a few intellectuals; yet, in a few regions, especially in Oudh, a sort of local nationalism did become apparent. Moreover, British rule created anti-British feeling among Indians because it conferred a privileged position on the white man, whose superiority, as a member of the white race, was more or less openly taken for granted. Indians were given only inferior appointments with low wages. They could not associate with the whites on any terms of equality. Segregation was strictly maintained: in clubs, hotels and on the railways. A few observations by William Howard Russell of *The Times* in his Indian Mutiny diary, though not devoid of exaggeration, hit the nail on the head: 'My skin is the passport—it is a guarantee of my rank. In India I am at once of the governing class—an aristocrat in virtue of birth—a peer of the realm; a being specially privileged and exempted from the ordinary laws of the State.' Russell never ceased to complain of British rudeness to Indians: 'The insufferably rude and insolent behaviour of some of our fellow-countrymen, which here I witnessed for the first time, does, in my mind, go far to create dislike to us.' He went on to remark:

> 'In no instance is a friendly glance directed to the white man's carriage. Oh, that language of the eye! Who can doubt? who can fail to misunderstand it? It is by it alone that I have learned our race is not even feared at times by many, and that by all it is disliked.'

Indian historians seem to have developed their interpretation of the underlying causes of the Mutiny in contradiction to the theories which deny any nationalistic basis to it. In doing so they emerge from the circumscribed area of theory to take a broader but more obscure viewpoint. A couple of decades ago, during the Indian struggle for independence, they declared in a number of books, in passages censored by the British government, that the Indian Mutiny was 'a war of independence', 'a war of liberation'.

In *The Discovery of India* (1946), written during World War II, Jawaharlal Nehru's interpretation was less extreme. His chapter on the Indian Mutiny displays a noticeable hesitation between a nationalistic and a more critical view. The Mutiny, Nehru wrote, was essentially

> 'a feudal outburst headed by feudal chiefs and their followers and aided by the widespread anti-foreign sentiment ... It is clear, however, that there was a lack of nationalist feeling which might have bound the people of India together. Nationalism of the modern type was yet to come. India still had to go through much sorrow and travail before she learnt the lesson which would give her real freedom. Not by fighting for a lost cause, the feudal order, would freedom come.'

But Nehru's account is marked by a simultaneous sympathy for the Mutiny as a potentially nationalistic movement, and by the view that the Indian princes who helped on the side of the British were, so to speak, 'quislings' before their time.

Nehru's Minister of Education, A. K. Azad, in his preface to Surendra Nath Sen's centenary book about the Mutiny, was more emphatic than Sen in his belief that nationalistic feeling existed among Indians at the time, but he laid emphasis on the great significance of religious motives and on the fact that the leaders of the rebellion were as a rule governed by purely selfish interests. According to Azad all this shows that the division between Mohammedans and Hindus was not as wide as it was later to become, and this made it possible for them to collaborate during the first phase of the Mutiny.

This view, which, in connection with the Indian 'national unity' interpretation, would lay the blame on Britain for the partition of India from Pakistan, is far too arbitrary. Sen makes it clear that disputes between Mohammedans and Hindus played an important role during the Mutiny, besides which, the majority of the co-religionists of both groups were either indifferent or took sides with the British.

Surendra Nath Sen points out, as indeed do some British historians, that a minority was involved in the uprising and that the masses remained neutral. When an indisputable majority, however passive, sympathizes with the aims of a rebellion, such a movement can be called nationalistic; but this was not the situation in India.

> 'Outside Oudh and Shahabad there is no evidence of that general sympathy which would invest the Mutiny with the dignity of a national war. At the same time it would be wrong to dismiss it as a mere military uprising. The Mutiny became a revolt and assumed a political character when the mutineers of Meerut placed themselves

under the King of Delhi and a section of the landed aristocracy and civil population declared in his favour. What began as a fight for religion ended in a war of independence—for there is not the slightest doubt that the rebels wanted to get rid of the alien government and restore the old order of which the King of Delhi was the rightful representative.'

No impulse towards political or personal freedom lay behind the uprising. On the contrary:

'The Mutiny leaders would have set the clock back to the good old days when a commoner could not expect equal justice with the noble, when the tenants were at the mercy of the *talukdars* and when theft was punished with mutilation. In short they wanted a counter revolution. Whether military success would have secured it is another question.'

Earlier writers stated categorically that the mutiny was planned, that the revolt broke out simultaneously in various places because there was a concerted master plan. One proof of this was supposed to be the passing round of *chapatis* in the spring of 1857 as a signal for the uprising. Early in March 1857 a mysterious passing round of *chapatis* (unleavened maize cakes, the 'bread' of Indian households) was observed. They were thought to originate from Cawnpore but no one appeared to know, or would not say, why or from where the *chapatis* came. A *chowkidar* (village watchman) would appear at a village and would hand four *chapatis* to the *chowkidar* of the village, saying 'To the north, the south, the east and the west', with instructions to make four more *chapatis* and hand them on to watchmen of four other villages. The *chapatis* multiplied and spread with astonishing speed, in the fashion of a 'chain-letter'.

It was also claimed that foreign agents—Russian, Persian and Afghan—in conspiracy with the Nana Sahib and other Indian princes had prepared the ground for the mutinies. Surendra Nath Sen's research has made a clean sweep of all these hypotheses. According to him the mysterious *chapatis* could have had no connection with the uprising; inasmuch as they were passed round, the fact was given different interpretations: they were traditional warnings against illness or they were used as a means of causing illness. The foreign agents who were supposed to have instigated the Mutiny also seem to have been figments of somebody's imagination. Everything points to the fact of the mutinies having broken out spontaneously, even though, of course, rumours of mutinies and the disbanding of regiments were fuel for the outbreak of fresh mutinies elsewhere. These circumstances support the opinion that the affair of the greased cartridges was indeed the deciding factor.

3

The reports of atrocities committed by Indians during the Mutiny and versions given sensational treatment for home consumption, did more damage than practically any other feature of the Mutiny. In newspaper reports which laid claim to impartiality and in novels and stories read by all classes, the Indians were depicted as rebellious devils who had burned, pillaged, looted and plundered, raped British women and tortured and murdered men, women and children alike. This was what Indians, these brown-skinned oriental heathens were like; the picture was forcibly impressed on the minds of British newspaper and novel readers, arousing feelings of mingled hatred and contempt directed towards an alien race and faiths that were not Christian. The Mutiny was proof positive of Britain's right to rule, it proved the superiority of the white man. British military commanders were glorified as crusaders and heroes. Legends grew up round the exploits of dead generals such as Sir John Nicholson, the conqueror of Delhi; Sir Henry Lawrence who fell at Lucknow, Sir Henry Havelock, who recaptured Cawnpore. In recent years it has become customary to highlight the exploits of both sides in the fighting, but the tendency to contrast Indian cruelty with British courage is still apparent.

There is no possible doubt that in many cases Indians did perpetrate mass murders, they did kill women and children and they did torture their victims. But with time there has been a tendency not to dwell on these deeds and an even greater tendency to paint a less inflammatory picture of the events. The view that there is much to be forgiven on both sides has become the accepted one, replacing former more emotional versions. The worst cruelties were committed, it is now believed, not by sepoys and their leaders but by the mob and by criminals and thugs who took advantage of the confusion and the breakdown of law and order to indulge in all kinds of excesses. Instances of rape, an outrage which tended particularly to inflame passions in England, were either unconfirmed or untrue. There appear to have been very few cases of sexual outrage committed by Indians against English women.

It cannot be denied that the garrison of Cawnpore was massacred in spite of promise of safe-conduct. But in several books published a decade or so after the Mutiny it was clearly established that neither the Nana Sahib nor the sepoys were directly responsible for the slaughter of the two hundred women and children whose bodies were found at the bottom of the Bibi-ghar well by the troops who relieved Cawnpore. On the contrary, the sepoys, refused to do the killing when a subordinate of the Nana Sahib, without his knowledge, gave the order for the massacre and this moreover, was carried out by professional butchers. 'It is both unfair and wrong to accuse a nation of this cruel deed', Sir G. W.

Forrest wrote in his copiously-documented *History of the Indian Mutiny* (1904). He also emphasized in this investigation that white women were not 'violated or dishonoured' before they were killed. The sense of outrage over Cawnpore was intensified when it was believed that despairing messages from the murdered women had been found scrawled on the walls of the Bibi-ghar. It was discovered afterwards that these messages had been written by the troops who had gone to the Bibi-ghar to view the traces of the killing. Cawnpore, therefore, is no longer considered, as it was earlier, an overwhelming proof of the cruelty and treachery of Indians in general.

Even during the Mutiny, reports reached England that the British themselves were guilty of cruelty or at any rate of excessively harsh and vindictive punishment of the rebels. William Howard Russell in particular repeated this again and again. The painter Egron Lundgren, who travelled with Russell for a time, tried, however, to ignore 'blood-curdling stories' and has hardly anything to say in his memoirs about this aspect of the Mutiny. Russell tells of cases where great numbers of Indians were hanged merely on suspicion of having taken part in the mutiny and how English officers took obvious satisfaction in organizing and attending executions and how in some circumstances the British soldiers found amusement in inventing ingenious ways of hanging rebels, in groups or in positions of agonizing torture. Russell's evidence and that of others showed that in capturing a rebel stronghold, whether fortress, building or house, everybody in it was killed, that in some cases troops on the British side tortured prisoners and even burned them alive—Howard Russell saw a party of sikhs roasting a sepoy alive over a small fire—and that British officers were capable of beating their Indian servants for an insignificant offence until they bled. When reports and orders connected with the Mutiny were afterwards collected and published it was evident that the reconquest of India after the Mutiny had been accomplished by methods of terrorism.

This was the mid-Victorian era, when both 'civilization' and religion were the fashion. Britain's victorious generals were often pious men and they acted harshly in the name of God. When Sir John Lawrence, Governor of the Punjab, crushed the attempt at mutiny in Peshawar in June 1857, he pondered whether he ought to execute all 120 sepoys. 'I do not think we are justified in the eyes of the Almighty in doing this.' Only about forty, he decided, deserved to be executed, those of bad character, those known to have participated actively in the mutiny or to have insulted their officers. 'If this is not enough I will take the old soldiers. All these will be shot or blown from cannon, whichever is more suitable.'

The deeply religious General Nicholson thought it 'outrageous' to punish those who had murdered women and children merely by hanging them. They ought, he considered 'to be flayed alive, broken on the wheel or burned to death'. Colonel James Neill's hangings were so numerous and so indiscriminate that his officers had to remind him that essential labour must be spared. It was his belief that 'No one who has witnessed the scenes of murder, mutilation and massacre, can ever listen to the word "mercy", as applied to these fiends'. In Cawnpore he decided that the ring-leaders should wipe and even lick up the blood from the floor of the Bibi-ghar before they were executed. Sir Colin Campbell, however, put a stop to this practice.

Even Colonel Neill prayed, before sentencing, for power to act with justice. Any Indian found with a weapon on him was executed out of hand during the reconquest. The largely innocent population of Delhi suffered greatly from these indiscriminate reprisals. The problem was how far to go with regard to suspects and sympathizers. Hanging and being blown from cannon were in many cases combined with treatment which according to the religion of the victim would, in his eyes, condemn him inevitably to eternal damnation. Mohammedans, for example, were covered with pig fat and sewn up in pig-skins, and the mental agony of those executed in this fashion can be imagined.

In this era of puritanical piety and prudery, an assault on a woman was an almost unmentionable crime, one which filled Victorian breasts with unparalleled horror and hostility. It was emotions of this kind which led the otherwise kindly Captain Roberts (later Field-Marshal Earl Roberts of Kandahar and Pretoria) to write to his sister in August 1867, that the tragedy had excited in his mind 'such feelings of horror that I would cheerfully undergo any privation, any amount of work, living in hopes of *revenge* on these cruel murderers. This feeling is shared by every European in the Camp'. When the Mutiny was debated in Parliament in 1857 the Prime Minister, Lord Derby, who recommended a policy of leniency, said:

> 'For every man captured with a weapon in his hand a just punishment will be meted out and this punishment is death. For the evildoers who have committed unmentionable and unimaginable atrocities towards women death is too merciful a punishment. They ought to be condemned to a more severe sentence, to corporal punishment or to the most degrading slavery.'

According to the *Cambridge History of India* the rigid morality of the period had an important effect in an unexpected quarter: British officers ceased to have relationships with Indian women and thus were no longer able to know what the Indian masses were thinking.

The cruel severity of the British is to some degree explained by the harshness of the Penal Code at the time, especially in England—at least before the penal reforms or later decades—when capital punishment was imposed for many lesser crimes than murder.

Another explanation involving both British and Indians was that rumours of British cruelties and harshness incited the Indians to fresh atrocities. Long before the massacre at Cawnpore Indians had heard of the rampagings of Colonel Neill at Allahabad; the British believed implicitly every piece of information about the terrible deeds of the Indians. But as far as the behaviour of the British is concerned, the prevailing emotion which prompted their acts of retaliation, that a superior race had been affronted, undoubtedly influenced them greatly.

William Howard Russell wrote: 'In fact the peculiar aggravation of the Cawnpore massacre was this, that the deed was done by a subject race—by black men who dared to shed the blood of their masters, and that of poor helpless ladies and children.'

What were the consequences of the Mutiny? On a few specific points it is possible to give definite answers. One major result was that the rule of the East India Company was transferred to the British Crown. The number of British troops in India was increased. Indian troops were more systematically separated into regiments of Mohammedans and Hindus. The warrior races, Sikhs and Ghurkas held a major position and distinctive place in recruiting.

The artillery, in which sepoys were no longer allowed to serve, was composed exclusively of white British troops. Certain administrative reforms were a direct consequence of the Mutiny.

With regard to long-term consequences, as with the 'deeper' 'more profound' causes of the Mutiny, only tentative speculation is possible. The Mutiny, it is believed, strengthened Britain's belief that it was right and necessary to keep this 'unreliable race' under British rule. As a consequence, the mutiny stimulated doctrinaire imperialism which, during the 1870s and 1880s had thrust aside earlier tendencies in England to regard the colonies as the white man's burden, or as objects of education towards self-government. Another result was the feeling of superiority towards Indians, especially Hindus, which grew in England. Preconceived notions of Indian incompetence and guile became more pronounced than formerly and one historian of the period has even claimed that the ideas and behaviour of the well-known characters in E. M. Forster's novel *A Passage to India* (1924), can be traced to events, experiences, and concepts of 1857 which resulted in a generally accepted attitude to the Mutiny. It is also believed, however, that the fear of a fresh and bigger mutiny of sepoys was one of the decisive motives of British policy in India and one which in some degree contributed to the decisions which in 1947 resulted in Britain's dignified withdrawal from the country.

In his preface to Surendra Nath Sen's book, mentioned earlier, A. K.

Azad wrote that British tactics of 'dividing to rule' became more marked after the Mutiny and he seemed to think that the partition of India and Pakistan was a result of this policy and thus indirectly a consequence of the Indian Mutiny. It has also been supposed that the idea of having recourse to another armed revolt had been discredited by Indians because of the failure of the Mutiny and that therefore the modern method of passive resistance as a means to the achievement of independence could also be traced indirectly back to 1857. These and many other attempts to reconstruct and relate cause and effect may contain germs of the truth but whether generalizations of this sort are right or wrong is beyond proof. The general view in India, in contrast perhaps to that held in Pakistan, would appear to be one which was emphasized in an issue of *The Hindu Weekly Review*. The magazine was of the opinion that the Mutiny helped to develop a sense of national identity which a few decades later was expressed by the formation of the Congress Party, and which after many years more led to an India freed at last from British rule.

Imperialism and Conspiracy: Jameson's Raid

'I beg to direct your attention to Africa . . .', the Reverend David Livingstone told his hearers in the Senate house of Cambridge University in 1857. 'I go back to Africa to try to make an open path for commerce and Christianity; do you carry out the work which I have begun. I leave it to you!'

Not many decades later, a bare forty years, it looked as though Britain's cash-and-Christianity mission in Africa was nearing a successful completion—at least in the matter of the cash if not the Christianity. The small Boer republics, the Orange Free State and the Transvaal, which had been formed in 1835 by the Great Trek of the Boers from Cape Colony across the Vaal and Orange rivers, were almost completely surrounded by British possessions: Cape Colony to the south, Natal to the east, Rhodesia to the north, and bordering only to the north-east on a non-British possession, the Portuguese colony of Mozambique. This constellation of possessions was complete by the beginning of 1890. Expansion to the north and east had been for the most part privately organized through Rhode's Chartered Company of South Africa, which had obtained vast concessions from the British government. This whole period of South African policy was marked either by co-operation or conflict between governments and capitalists.

Simultaneously with this the struggle for power was concentrated in the Transvaal, more precisely in the towns of Pretoria and Johannesburg.

Britain had recognized the independence of the Transvaal in 1881, with the proviso that the republic would make no treaties without consent of the British government. But after huge deposits of gold were discovered in 1886 at Witwatersrand and hordes of gold-seeking Uitlanders had flocked into the area, the suspicious and mistrustful Boers began to exercise repressive discrimination, which led to tension between Britain and the Transvaal government.

The Boers continued to live according to their pastoralist traditions, big landowning farmers employing native workers in conditions somewhere between those of farm labourers and slaves. They were not tempted by the gold finds. The mines were owned and worked by the so-called Uitlanders—outsiders, the motley throng of European whites who were not Boers, but came from every conceivable quarter of Europe, the vast majority of them, however, being British. The government of the Republic was quite satisfied to tax the huge profits from the Rand gold mines—twelve million pounds in 1897. In the 1890s more than seventy-five per cent of the Republic's revenue came from the Uitlanders, and these, eighty per cent of them British, were backed up by Britain in their demands for civil rights and in their protests against excessively heavy taxation. The Boers retorted that nobody obliged the Uitlanders to stay in the country, that they earned huge profits in spite of heavy taxation and that if they were granted equal rights with the Boers then, in the words of President Kruger, 'the freedom of the republic would not exist any longer'.

A few figures from books of reference of the period (probably not entirely accurate) will serve to demonstrate the peculiarity of the situation. In 1896 the white population of the Transvaal was estimated at 150,000, of which 63,000 were Boers and 83,000 Uitlanders. But the black population of 600,000 was not taken into account: when the newspapers talked about racial conflict they meant conflict between Boers and Uitlanders. Pretoria, three miles north of the mining area, was a town of 12,000 inhabitants and the mining town of Johannesburg, with a population of more than 100,000, was inhabited predominantly by Uitlanders.

The Boer government spent a great part of its revenue on armaments —£1 million in 1897—especially on the purchase of cannon from Krupp and Le Creusot. The taxes paid by the Uitlanders therefore, were in essence being used to acquire defensive weapons intended to protect the Boers against the Uitlanders.

The Uitlanders made a 'humble petition' to the Queen to intervene. The Boers looked to Germany and France for support.

The principal actors in the drama suited their parts to perfection. The powerful president of the Transvaal, Paul Kruger, was an elderly farmer and hunter whose habit it was to receive visitors and deputations seated on the stoep of his unpretentious house, thoughtfully puffing at his pipe and with a Bible ready to hand in which he claimed he found the answers to difficult problems. In looks, dress and manners Kruger was so very much the peasant that at times it all seemed a pose, but there was no doubt of his sincerity in championing a nation of simple Boer farmers whose pastoral, innocently primitive lives, guided by the Old Testament, were threatened by 'civilization', capitalism and, in their eyes, all the vices and iniquities of modernity.

Cecil Rhodes, a guiding spirit in British imperialistic expansion, held three key positions in the 'scramble for Africa'. He was founder and principal shareholder in Consolidated Goldfields of South Africa, the huge gold trust which dominated the management of Witwatersrand—'the Rand'—just outside Johannesburg; he was managing director of the Chartered Company of South Africa and as such was the conqueror of the territories which combined Matabeleland and Mashonaland, an area of 75,000 square miles. These were informally named after him and officially became Rhodesia in 1895. Rhodes had been Prime Minister of the Cape Colony since 1890. He was filled with a lust for power spiced with a belief in progress, the schoolboy heroics of a sort of boy-scout mystique. He talked endlessly of the mission of the Anglo-Saxon race to conquer and improve the world and his grandiose dreams of annexation and exploitation soared beyond ambitions for a federation of South African states under the British flag. Sighing for fresh worlds to conquer, he cast a longing eye even at outer space: 'I would annex the planets if I could'. His idea of improvement was a world where everything could be done faster and more efficiently. He had no intellectual interests and women left him cold. Severe illness at nineteen had permanently affected his heart. When he was barely over forty his health broke down, he became obese, suffered increasingly from his heart complaint and his face became blotched and puffy, his complexion 'livid with a purplish tinge'. Fearing that he would soon die, he was continually haunted by the dread of not being able to accomplish all he had intended. The zeal with which he planned, persuaded and managed, hastened his end. He did not live to see fifty. 'So little time and so much left to do!' he murmured repeatedly as he was dying.

Was there a third actor in the drama of Jameson's Raid? This has always been a controversial point in the historical and political disputes over the ill-advised and ill-fated venture, a vexed question for the past sixty years. Nowadays the question can be considered solved and the answer is Yes. The third man was Joseph Chamberlain, former town councillor and Mayor of Birmingham, first a Radical Liberal and then a Liberal Unionist, President of the Board of Trade with a seat in the Gladstone government of 1880 and, in the summer of 1895, when he was nearly sixty, Secretary of State for the Colonies in the Salisbury Coalition government of Liberal Unionists and Conservatives. In contrast to the Premier, who was happiest in sceptical inactivity, Chamberlain was an impetuous man filled with pent-up passion and ambition—they called him 'Pushful Joe'—a skilled and experienced debator who had been in political exile for many years after his resignation in 1886 over the issue of Home Rule, which he bitterly opposed and which split the party and toppled Gladstone. 'Chamberlain is like those wives who ruin their husbands and Salisbury like the men who are ruined by their wives', was how John Butler Yeats, the painter-father of Yeats the poet, saw the difference between the two men.

Chamberlain became an imperialist with the same urge to manage and persuade that he employed in getting to be town councillor and Mayor of Birmingham. Nobody could prevaricate and mislead with greater elegance and sang-froid than this middle-class businessman who affected a manner and dress that made him almost a caricature of an aristocrat, a monocle glittering in one eye, a white orchid in his button-hole, youthfully clean-shaven among the whiskers and beards of the day, and with the help of a touch of camouflage masquerading as a sort of political 'portrait of Dorian Gray'. In the numerous negotiations connected with Jameson's Raid he scored some of the greatest triumphs of his career—a fact which has only come to light some sixty years afterwards.

During the late autumn of 1895, Rhodes and his closest associates in the South Africa Company and Consolidated Goldfields in Johannesberg hatched a plot to crush Kruger's republic. Under the leadership of a so-called 'Reform Committee' composed of sixty-four Uitlanders of a dozen nationalities, with occupations from mine-owners to stockbrokers and including a sanitary inspector, the Uitlanders were to start an armed revolt and take over the government. Thousands of rifles were smuggled into the country and passed round, and a para-military organization was formed.

Simultaneously with the uprising in Johannesburg, to help the rebels and ensure the success of the *coup*, a troop of police and volunteers were supposed to invade the Transvaal across the border from Bechuanaland where a newly acquired railway strip was administered by the Chartered Company.

The leadership of this action was entrusted to Dr Leander Starr Jameson, formerly a practising physician, a friend and hero-worshipper of Rhodes and now his most devoted right-hand man. Under the pretext of unrest among the natives Jameson gathered a force of some 5,000 volunteers in and around Pitsani, a village on the strip near the Transvaal border, some thirty miles from Johannesburg, where he had been appointed Resident Commissioner. To justify this manoeuvre a number of prominent Uitlanders sent a letter in advance to Jameson at Pitsani, with trumped up and completely fictitious information about unrest in Johannesburg which would be a threat to the lives and property of the Uitlanders. 'Thousands of unarmed men, women and children of our race', the letter said, 'will be at the mercy of well-armed Boers, while property of enormous value will be at the greatest peril. . . .' The committee virtually invited Doctor Jim to come to their aid. 'The circumstances are so anxious that we cannot but believe that you and the men under you will not fail to come to the rescue of people who will be so situated.'

The letter was dated 28 December, the day before the revolt was supposed to start. What was supposed to happen after the victory of the insurgents had not been settled in detail. It was intended that Britain's Governor of Cape Colony and High Commissioner of South Africa, Sir Hercules Robinson (afterwards Lord Rosmead), should intervene as mediator and advisor. The Transvaal was subsequently to be incorporated in some way or other into British South Africa.

The plans were all laid, but gradually it became apparent that there was no valid reason for an uprising in Johannesburg at the time appointed for the rescue raid. There was something illogical in the notion of a sudden uprising in the name of freedom and justice in a country at peace and with a flourishing economy. The miners, who were predominantly Uitlanders at this time, showed little enthusiasm. Their wages were good; so good indeed that the mine-owners frequently complained that they were being squeezed by both the miners and Kruger. A revolt solely of capitalists and their clients—lawyers, journalists, engineers and office employees, people in the catering business—would have been an absurdity: on the one hand they were too small a group and, on the other, millionaires make unconvincing revolutionaries. Letter after letter was sent to Jameson from Johannesburg urging him to postpone the whole business.

But Jameson stood firm. Rhodes had not told him to wait. He believed that the uprising would start at the news of the raid, or at least when he and his men reached Johannesburg. So, on 29 December, Jameson, at the head of his band of almost 500 horsemen, rode over the border of the Transvaal. Their departure was impressive. The Chartered Company had provided 400 bottles of champagne; most of the raiders were decidedly merry and a good many of them quite tipsy. 'God Save the Queen' was sung and Jameson assured his men that the raid had the full approval of the British government. The raiders were all young men, numbers of them barely in their twenties, many of them former British officers; the pay was good, the rations generous, abundant stores had been concentrated at strategic points along their proposed route, they were to be joined at Mafeking by a contingent of tough experienced ex-troopers of the disbanded Bechuanaland Border Police, and inside four days, they confidently believed, they would be entering Johannesburg as heroes of the Empire.

Abysmal disaster lay in wait for them. Kruger had cunningly and cleverly obtained a list of the sixty-four members of the Reform Committee and had reinforced the police. As soon as information had been received that the raid was under way, mass arrests which included the whole Reform Committee, were made in Johannesburg. Kruger who, in his wife's words, had not been 'across a horse' for many years, kept his old white horse ready saddled in the stable and slept with a loaded rifle at his bedside. Simultaneously with all this, commandos were organized and on the third day of Jameson's ride, on New Year's day 1896, he and his troops were surrounded. As usual the Boers refrained from attacking. They let Jameson and his band continue on their way, meanwhile engaging them in continual skirmishes until they reached Doornkop, only a few miles from Johannesburg. There the invaders were lured into an impossible position before a steep kopje held by the Boers, and ambushed in a *cul-de-sac* from which there was no escape. After a last-stand fight 'surrounded on all sides by the Boers, men and horses wearied out, outnumbered by at least six to one', the raiders surrendered with an improvised white flag, said to have been an apron borrowed from an old black farm woman. There were no Boer casualties. Seventeen of Jameson's men were killed, thirty-five were missing and there were fifty-five wounded. Jameson and the rest of the raiders were led off to Pretoria jail. Three weeks later he and his officers were handed over to the British government and shipped back to England, where eventually Jameson and a few of the others were tried and given short prison sentences. The conspirators in the Transvaal were sentenced on the spot; after some cat-and-mouse play with death sentences by Kruger, the penalties were few and slight, but wily 'Oom Paul' received huge sums of money which went to swell the treasury—fines of up to £25,000 each from the rich and prominent Johannesburgers who were the leaders of the Reformers and the intended revolt.

Chamberlain condemned the Raid immediately he got word of it and while it was still in progress. By doing so and by emphasizing its 'purely private' nature, he was able to shrug off all responsibility for it, both then and for a long time afterwards. Rhodes also regretted the Raid, quite as much and as genuinely as Chamberlain, for without a simultaneous uprising in Johannesburg Jameson's action was meaningless—but Rhodes made no statement until a few days after the Raid had ended in failure and never made any denial of his responsibility in the planning and financing of the adventure. This difference of attitudes was one of the grounds for the numerous discussions and settlements during the years following the Raid.

Reaction in Britain was complex. The newspapers and the politicians dissociated themselves from the affair as a matter of course, even if their disclaimers were at times couched in terms so discreet as to be almost apologetic. A feeling of disgrace rather than the prickings of a guilty conscience seemed to be the prevailing mood of public opinion. Many statements gave the impression that the failure caused more uneasiness than the crime.

Alfred Austin, the Poet Laureate, elevated by *Punch* to the rank of 'Monarch of Minor Poets', probably expressed the feelings of the British masses in a poem as trumpery as it was hypocritical. In the numerous stanzas of his *Jameson's Raid*, his first official effusion as Poet Laureate printed characteristically enough in *The Times*, he gave vent alternately to regret, praise and sobs and it is obvious that the Laureate had been much impressed by the Uitlanders' trumped-up 'women and children' letters of invitation to Jameson.

There are girls in the gold-reef city
There are mothers and children too
And they cry, 'Hurry up! for pity!
So what can a brave man do?
If even we win, they'll blame us
If we fail, they will howl and hiss.
But there's many a man lives famous
For daring a wrong like this!

On the continent a frantic campaign against 'perfidious Albion' broke out; it was the beginning of a glorification of the Boers which was to reach its culmination four years later during the Boer War. The reason for this ill-feeling was partly the fact that Britain was more isolated at this period than ever before or since. Her relations with France were strained owing to disputes about the Colonies, and relations with Germany were frayed by the rearming of the German navy. But feelings of indignation against Britain were doubtless genuine in many quarters: agressivity and deception in the rivalry for colonies was nothing rare, but obdurate and systematic brigandage was something which civilized Europe was not and did not become accustomed to until the advent of communism and fascism. Britain's critics were in general agreement that the Raid was a machination of the British government and that Chamberlain was as guilty as Rhodes.

The biggest shock of all was undoubtedly the German Kaiser's telegram of congratulation to Kruger on 3 January, the day after Jameson's surrender. Kaiser Wilhelm said:

> 'I express to you my sincere congratulations that without calling on the aid of friendly Powers you and your people, by your own energy against the armed bands which have broken into your country as

disturbers of the peace, have succeeded in re-establishing peace, and defending the independence of the country against attacks from without.'

The telegram implied that the Transvaal, in spite of the Pretoria and London Conventions of 1881 and 1884 was a wholly independent state, and it contained a veiled promise of assistance from Germany in any similar situation. The German Emperor could not have done the British government a greater service by sending his telegram which, however, according to Otto Hamman's account of the episode was sent in consultation with his official advisers. With obvious relief the British press turned from frequently hypocritical censure of Rhodes and Jameson to violent attacks on the Kaiser for daring to meddle in Britain's South African affairs. In the ensuing years the so-called 'Kaiser's telegram' was a constant source of anti-German propaganda and also provided a defence for Chamberlain and the leading imperialists. It rallied the nation, fostering the feeling that the country must stand together and that accusations from abroad must either be refuted or ignored in the national interest, and this frame of mind pervaded even the Liberal opposition leadership. Consequently a moral basis was achieved for the conspiracy of silence concerning the underlying facts of the Raid—facts which have only come to light and have been clarified in the past few years.

Very little concerning the preparations for the attempted revolt was revealed during the trial in London, 20–29 July 1896, of Jameson and his officers, or at that of the Reformers in Johannesburg earlier, in April; the aim of those proceedings was to establish the defendants' complicity in the affair. This was why a Parliamentary investigation was considered necessary, and for the purpose a Committee of Inquiry was set up. For purely technical reasons, however, hearings did not commence until 5 February 1897. The Select Committee chosen 'To inquire into the origin and circumstances of the Incursion into the South African Republic by an Armed Force. . .', was composed of fifteen members, as was customary in such cases. The Chairman, W. L. Jackson (afterwards Lord Alveston), a former Irish Chief Secretary, had the leader of the Opposition, Sir William Harcourt sitting on his right, and on his left the Colonial Secretary, Joseph Chamberlain, whose inclusion on the Committee was a kind of foregone assumption of his innocence. There were two other Conservative ministers, Sir Richard Webster, the Attorney General, and Sir Michael Hicks Beach, Chancellor of the Exchequer, and the Committee was completed by five conservative back-benchers and five Liberal M.P.s. The work of the Commission consisted mainly in the public hearing of evidence in the Grand Committee Room, neither grand nor very large, behind the great adjoining Westminster

Hall. Some hundred witnesses were heard during the five months of twice-weekly sessions, among them Chamberlain, Rhodes, members of the management of the Chartered Company and officials of the Colonial Office.

From the start there was something unreal about an investigation which, had it been conducted with any vigour or determination, could have wrecked the Salisbury government, discredited several of Britain's most distinguished leaders, and brought English politics into disrepute in world opinion. It was characteristic that at the first session of the public hearing the Prince of Wales, a friend of several of the most implicated capitalists, arrived with the Duke of Abercorn, one of several noblemen on the Board of the Chartered Company, and Lord Selborne, Under-Secretary for the Colonies.

The interrogations were frequently searching and occasionally questions were asked, especially by the Liberal firebrand Labouchere, which came uncomfortably close to the facts in the background. On the whole, however, the Committee avoided asking awkward questions about the complicity of members of the British government. Assertions that important telegrams between London and Capetown had gone astray were accepted without further question—they had been lost, possibly destroyed, but in any case were not forthcoming.

Chamberlain was treated with great respect and—as in previous as well as subsequent debates in Parliament—he answered indiscreet questions with a supercilious assurance that made any overt or even implied suspicion seem insolent and caddish. He explained things away, misled and lied with such nonchalance that it would hardly be too far-fetched to suspect in him some almost pathological inner conviction of blamelessness—the feelings of innocence which less distinguished wrongdoers sometimes succeed in summoning up in similar situations. Another witness as clever at dissimulation as Chamberlain was Miss Flora Shaw (who later became Lady Lugard). She was a brilliant woman journalist, *The Times*'s colonial expert, and was called to answer allegations that *The Times* was implicated in the Raid and had had some sort of communication with the conspirators. The Committee as well as the public, with traditional Victorian chivalry, appeared to take for granted that 'a minister of the Crown' and a 'lady' would not dream of lying.

On 13 July 1897, after five months of intermittent hearings, the Committee published its report, condemning the Raid. Rhodes was blamed for his active assistance to the raiders and to the Reformist conspirators in Johannesburg. But British officialdom was exonerated: 'Neither the Secretary of State for the Colonies nor any of the officers of the Colonial Office received any information which should have made them or any of them, aware of the plot during its development.'

The Committee's pronouncement was a dignified, one might almost say necessary, accompaniment to Queen Victoria's Diamond Jubilee, with its theme of Empire, which was celebrated on 22 June with a spectacular display of homage to the 78-year-old Queen-Empress as the South Africa Committee was holding its final sessions. During the fortnight of Jubilee celebrations, prime ministers from the Colonies were honoured and took precedence before princes of the blood, white and dark-skinned colonial troops paraded amid the delirious acclamations of the crowds and Britain's naval might was displayed at the Spithead review—all of it calling forth an emotional outpouring of the pride of Empire which was to be hymned afterwards (though with glimmerings of misgiving) in the solemn grandiosity of Kipling's *Recessional.*

The British press in general accepted the Committee's verdict of Not Guilty. A few newspapers, however, made ironical remarks, and several politicians observed privately that the inquiry was meant to whitewash things, not to clean them up. The wits got to work and the Committee became 'The Worshipful Company of Whitewashers', its proceedings 'The Lying in State at Westminster' or 'The Committee of No Enquiry'. The French press was particularly acid, attacking the inquiry as a well-concocted fraud; *Le Temps* said that it was 'the apotheosis of the Birmingham Statesman', but that it was also 'the abdication of the conscience of Great Britain'.

During the years that followed, with the culmination of British imperialism in the Sudan and Boer wars, and the formation of a new power-bloc in Europe, the matter of Jameson's Raid was overshadowed, though it was occasionally brought up in Parliament by embittered idealists and abroad by Anglophobes.

In a number of books written between 1920 and 1950 Chamberlain and the Colonial Office were generally given the benefit of the doubt. It was considered possible, though not certain, and by some not even probable, that there had been any official British complicity in the plot. This benevolent view received strong support when J. L. Garvin's biography of Chamberlain appeared in 1932–34, and by bringing into the open documents which could have proved awkward for Chamberlain and which Garvin energetically explained to his advantage, gave the effect of careful and scrupulously fair examination.

After World War II fresh and conclusive investigation into the Jameson Raid resulted in several books. The massive volumes of *The History of 'The Times'* contain remarkably frank appraisals of the episode, especially in the final volumes. The third volume in particular, with its account of the Raid and its origins, includes information which points to the fact that both Chamberlain and *The Times* itself were more deeply involved in the preparations than had previously been admitted. In 1951 the South African historian Dr Jean van der Poel produced a highly charged, well-written and passionate book, *The Jameson Raid,* based mainly on the

Bower Papers, including the unpublished hundred-page *Apologia* left by Sir Graham Bower, secretary at the time of the Raid, to Sir Hercules Robinson, High Commissioner in the Cape, and one of the two men who admitted guilt at the inquiry. Dr van der Poel's book, which quoted extensively from the Bower Papers, revealed that Chamberlain, Robinson and other British statesmen and officials were deeply implicated in the plot. Another historian, Elizabeth Pakenham (now Lady Longford), in her copiously documented book which contains further new material, agreed with Dr van der Poel's conclusions, while having reservations about some of the South African writer's more extreme statements in condemnation of the British government's part in the affair.

The most recent edition of *The Cambridge History of the British Empire* accepts the latest findings in essence. It has by now been fairly well established that Chamberlain was indeed implicated, and that 'he wished the uprising to take place so that Britain would be able to intervene'. This was made clear in his so-called 'hurry-up' letter to Sir Richard Meade, Permanent Secretary to the Colonial Office, in which he said:

> 'Now as to the Transvaal. Might it not come off just at the critical time if it is postponed now? The longer it is delayed the more chance there is of foreign intervention.
>
> It seems to me that either it should come *at once* or be postponed for a year or two at least. Can we ensure this? If not we had better not interfere, for we may bring about the very thing we want to avoid. . . . I cannot say that any time would be a good one, but can the difficulty be indefinitely postponed?'

He was undoubtedly involved in the preparations both of Jameson's Raid and the intended uprising in Johannesburg and it is certain that the South Africa Committee in 1897 was a party to the conspiracy of silence which characterized the handling of the events preceding the Raid.

The historians mentioned earlier have unearthed a great deal of richly complicated and sensational material connected with this episode of Britain's colonial history, in which certain facts can be pinpointed. Their information clearly shows that the Colonial Secretary, the High Commissioner and prominent personalities connected with *The Times* were aware of the plans for a revolt in South Africa and sympathized with the conspirators. Chamberlain was informed at an early stage of what was intended and took an active part in the preparations. He urged the prospective rebels to hurry things up, asked for information as to whether their motive was annexation to Britain and connived in granting to the Chartered Company concessions which made it possible to station Jameson on the Transvaal border.

Nevertheless Chamberlain was sincere in his alarm when the raid actually did take place, alarmed at the idea that without an uprising in Johannesburg it was doomed to fail and so have disastrous consequences for himself, the Government and England. Sir Hercules Robinson was as deeply involved and had promised to go to the Transvaal after the uprising to 'mediate'.

The Times, perhaps like a number of other institutions and individuals who escaped exposure, was deeply implicated in the plot, the prime movers on its staff being Charles Moberley Bell, the newspaper's Managing Director, and Flora Shaw its first woman special correspondent and its expert on Colonial affairs, while the Editor-in-Chief, George Buckle, was kept in the dark about their activities.

Moberley Bell's determination to be first with the news of the revolt, or at least not to be out-scooped by a rival newspaper, is an early example of high-powered journalism. Having heard that the uprising had been provisionally fixed for Saturday 28 December, he gave a *Times* special correspondent, Captain Francis Younghusband, an urgent message to pass on to Rhodes: 'I want to impress upon Rhodes that we hope the *New Company* will not *commence business* on a Saturday. P.S. Because of Sunday papers.' Since 'The Thunderer' only thundered six days a week it was important to have the revolt make its headline news in time for the Monday papers.

To ensure against leakages the plotters generally sent telegrams using a simple code-jargon of substituted words, in which a 'company' was 'floated' or 'commenced business'. The telegram which broke the news of Jameson's ride to the Johannesburg Reform Committee said: 'The contractor has started on the earthworks with seven hundred boys; hopes to reach terminus on Wednesday.' During the South Africa Committee's inquiry, when pressed as to whether he remembered sending a certain cable, or if it was a letter, Rhodes snapped back, 'I never write letters.' Communications from Chamberlain never went direct to Rhodes or other leaders in South Africa, but were given orally to Chartered Company officials. In some cases an alibi of a kind was provided—particularly in the case of Sir Hercules Robinson—by saying during intimate conversations, 'I think I know this privately, but not officially.' This reservation was held to justify and even to render morally necessary public denial of any knowledge of the matter.

Another conspiracy came to light during the hearings of the South Africa Committee. Chamberlain and Rhodes, though not friends, were accomplices. Chamberlain considered it necessary for Rhodes publicly to shoulder the blame for the Raid and was afraid that Rhodes would be revenged by telling the truth. According to both Dr van der Poel and Elizabeth Pakenham, the two men reached a private agreement. Chamberlain promised to renew Chartered Company concessions while

Rhodes promised to withhold the most compromising telegrams. Before this agreement was reached, according to Dr van der Poel, Chamberlain was prepared to start a war with the Transvaal to cover up his culpability, In the event, Rhodes saw to it that the telegrams disappeared. Some of them were found later among Chamberlain's papers, others were probably destroyed and their fragmentary reconstruction has only been possible from other sources.

Mention should be made of the latest theory about the missing telegrams, put forward by Brian Roberts in *Cecil Rhodes and the Princess* (1969). This writer suggests that the highly compromising telegrams found their way into the hands of an eccentric Polish adventuress, the Princess Radziwill, a determined friend of Rhodes, who pursued him, first with infatuation and then with hatred, and had a hold over him because of the incriminating documents—they may or may not have been the telegrams—which she claimed to have in her possession.

Both Dr van der Poel and Elizabeth Pakenham agree that the South Africa Committee, or at least quite a few of its members, must have guessed how matters stood and consciously avoided exposure of the truth. Why did they do this and why did the Liberals not try to take political advantage of the opportunity? Numerous motives have been suggested. Perhaps the Liberal leaders feared, or were even quite certain, that their own government, prior to June 1895, had made equivocal promises or negotiated shady deals in South Africa. However, this is hardly probable since the former Premier and Foreign Secretary Lord Rosebery whose colonial policy, in contrast to Lord Salisbury's, was particularly active, was highly censorious of the Committee's report. Another explanation is that, from the party political point of view, an impeachment of the Colonial Secretary would have been too dangerous a path to tread: it would not have been exactly pleasant to come before the British electorate as friends of Kruger and the Kaiser and enemies of the Empire. Perhaps the most important motive was the sort of patriotic feeling which had caused so many Frenchmen to choose either the lie or silence in the Dreyfus case of all too recent memory—Dreyfus was convicted and sentenced in 1894. The members of the Committee dreaded and loathed the possibility of disclosures and exposures which would cast shame on England, increase European hostility and perhaps—as it was whispered both now and at the time of the Dreyfus case—even make a major war inevitable.

There has been much speculation on the influence of Jameson's Raid on the subsequent course of colonial and foreign affairs. Some say that the deterioration of Anglo-German relations gave a sharper tilt to the Gadarene slope which led to World War I. The Raid has also been blamed for the Boer War; if it had not aggravated the antagonism between Boers and Britons and if the Kaiser had not sent his notorious telegram to raise the Boers' hopes of outside aid, a peaceful settlement of the South African dilemma would have been quite possible at the time. General public opinion as to the consequences of the Raid is hardly worth discussing, but there is little doubt that Jameson's ill-fated filibustering venture and the subsequent attitude of Britain contributed and continue to contribute to the tension between the two great white peoples of South Africa.

PART FOUR

EPILOGUE

THE VICTORIANS AND OURSELVES

Our generation has fallen on evil times. God, as we used to know him, has vanished and with him everything that the name signified; but the old feelings of sin, remorse and anxiety remain. Carefree paganism has proved to be of little help. We can no longer find any comfort in the thought that man's nature is essentially good or that a glorious future still beckons: this age has witnessed the triumph of evil, and we live in the shadow of a mushroom cloud. We have lost all our illusions: there are no longer even any myths to compensate for our vanished happiness.

Life, it would seem, dealt more kindly with the Victorians, as indeed it did with their contemporaries of Sweden's 'Age of the Oskars'. They were able to reconcile God and Mammon; for them earthly progress was to be followed, or so it seemed, by its prolongation in a heavenly hereafter—the notion of Hell was already beginning to be regarded as somewhat old-fashioned. Technology was still a liberating force; permanent peace could be glimpsed through the smoke of military skirmishes and 'small wars' around the globe. There was still much that remained to be altered and improved, and the shortcomings inspired and kept alive a reforming zeal; but nowadays the desire for improvement which inspired the Victorians is a stimulus we no longer react to. The five-day working week will never seem as dazzling a goal to us as the restriction of child-labour to an eight-hour day did to the Victorians.

Because of this lack of inspiring goals our generation is filled with weariness and despondency and is anxiety-ridden as never before. We envy our Victorian ancestors their staunch faith, their moral fibre, their vigour and strength of will. At any rate these are the qualities which cling with persistence to the obstinately enduring myth of Victorianism. The vitality of the myth is apparent not only in the jubilation of the conservative-minded at the decay of the belief in progress, but in the disgruntled, grudging admission of the other side that the belief really has died out.

The cult of Victorianism which has sprung up in recent years to become such a feature in the contemporary exchange of ideas, is often used not only as a pretext for grousing about our own times, but also to blossom out into a eulogistic recreation of the past. Professor Basil Willey—to hark back to the early pages of this book—pointed this out in his 1948 radio talk when he said that first we debunked the nineteenth century and now we long to return to it. Books about every phase of the Victorian period are much in demand and new ones are continually appearing. 'In our unpleasant century', said Professor Willey, 'we are mostly displaced persons and many feel tempted to take flight into the nineteenth as into a promised land, and settle there like illegal immigrants for the rest of our lives.'

The whole question, of course, is clearly one which concerns only the comparatively well-to-do and cultivated, particularly intellectuals. For a man of the working class in his right mind to dream of going back to the days of low wages, long working hours and general insecurity would be too ridiculous to take seriously.

G. M. Young's *Victorian England: Portrait of an Age* is a handy manual to the cult of Victorianism. In this short and concise essay, written in 1936 as an introduction to a series of monographs on the period, the ideas which have been explored in the earlier pages of this book are introduced with a brilliance, wit and single-mindedness worthy of the great French historians of culture. If the work is studied at all critically it can be observed that, in common with many other writers of stylish introductory essays, Young is merely, as it were, taking us on a conducted tour of a museum, pointing out as he goes constellations of fixed stars on old maps of the heavens.

The early years of the Victorian age, he tells us, were not as wonderful as they were claimed to be and he goes on to say that as early as 1850 a decline had set in which was unmistakable by 1880. Although Victoria came to the throne in 1837 and died in 1901, only a fraction of her reign can truly be called Victorian: on close examination the period would seem to fall between the introduction of free trade and the Crimean War—a bare decade.

Humphrey House, in his posthumous collection of essays *All in Due Time* (1955), discussed the cult of Victorianism as well as the ideas prevalent when he wrote. Underlying the cult he found reactionary tendencies to anti-intellectualism, harshness in the upbringing of the young, prudery and sentimentality. But only a few Victorians were like the conventional picture of them, House said; one of the few authentic Victorians he mentioned was Trollope, whose return to popularity in recent years (although apparently already on the wane) is symptomatic of the attraction of the Victorian age for our times.

House said of the early and mid-Victorians—the period found most typical by G. M. Young: 'The more I read of the early and mid-Victorians, the more I see anxiety and worry as a leading clue to understanding them. They were not complacent compromisers. They were trying to hold together incompatible opposites, and they worried because they failed.' In short, there was really no such thing as a 'Victorian compromise' to bring them the rewards of tranquility and security. The Victorians were faced with unexpected problems, in religion, politics, economy and many other fields, with which they were unable to cope;

they tried, not very successfully, to manage by linking such incompatibles as dogma and free thought, immortality and a hell-less after-life, *laissez-faire* liberalism and humanitarianism, marriage and the right to free love. They worried and were unhappy because they found that none of these things would work. The gradual withdrawal of God was as terrifying to them as the atom bomb and other horrors of modern technological warfare are to us.

When historians disagree so emphatically, whose idea of the Victorians can be taken as the right one? Of course there is no final answer, though the question arouses interesting speculations. One thing is clear, however: the great influential Victorian thinkers and writers have been stripped of their traditionally-accepted sincerity, simplicity and self-assurance by the curiosity and frankness of today. Tennyson is the great figure who perhaps best stands up to close scrutiny; as far as is known, no skeletons have yet been found in his cupboard. But his anxiety and his efforts, consequently both comical and touching, to hold on to some belief in God, progress and 'the Parliament of man, the Federation of the world' is plain for all to see. It is open to question whether even Trollope can be classified as a solid Victorian; to be sure, there is something incredibly naïve about him, yet even his attempt to reconcile opposites—such as the Manchester school of liberalism and indignation at ruthless businessmen—is pathetic. The former idea of Dickens as a jovial family-man has turned into one of an anguished, covetous and tormented creature, greedy for riches and adulation, broken in health and with a broken marriage, who killed himself by continuing to make the exhausting but lucrative lecture-tours he could not resist. Thackeray's melancholy is not hidden by his outward gaiety and wit over a few glasses of port at the end of a good dinner. Nor did philosophers of the time present a happier or more contented picture. Mill's personal tragedy was more profound than the one he revealed in his autobiography. Carlyle and Ruskin can also be seen, in the light of present-day interest in sex, as a couple of maladjusted, more or less abnormal beings whose grandiose visions were painfully wrested from obsession and suffering.

There has been a change in the general attitude towards these personalities in recent decades. Lytton Strachey started a trend characterized by a kind of ironic debunking which, though inflected with malice, was not entirely unkind and was done with entertaining finesse. Under the thrusts of his pen the Victorians were made to seem somewhat ridiculous, slightly unreal, like performing dogs, to be patted on the head for their engaging tricks, but not to be taken seriously. The Prince Consort and his devotion to duty, Manning's religious difficulties, Florence Nightingale's masterful goodness, Gordon's reckless bravery and (as we have seen) his almost certainly apocryphal alcoholism—all of them were made to appear at once amusing, odd and irrelevant, as if they had been so many animals in a zoo, observed by a dispassionate, even unfeeling bystander. Later biographers, though not less critical in their revelations of flaws of character, mistaken ideas and the complicated pattern of human emotions, have shown more sympathy in their presentation of eminent Victorians.

History is the essence of innumerable biographies, Carlyle said; yet an age is something more than the sum of its great personalities, and caution is required, as Kitson Clark warned, in assessing the testimony of 'that self-conscious, self-confident minority who seem to have made history and certainly have normally written it, whose voices, unless we are careful, are the only ones we are likely to hear from the past'. Humphrey House has reminded us in this connection that many Victorians 'were lonely and isolated, and many others were stupid, vulgar, unhappy and unsuccessful'. To get some idea of what Victorians (in the time-honoured and more agreeable sense of the word) were really like, we should also have to go further down—and this is essential—into the lives of ordinary, average men and women. Such people, however, seldom or never write autobiographies and are unfortunately not as a rule interesting enough to become the subject of a good biography, or even to warrant one at all, for that matter. As for the statesmen and generals, even they have ceased to seem genuine or trustworthy representatives and witnesses of their age—and this is a pity.

The question remains: was the Victorian Age a great or merely a monumental age? It was, at all events, one which produced many men of stature and even a few women, fighting fearful odds, whose lives, actions, goals and achievements are continually fascinating to our generation. They strove for improvement and believed in progress as a natural and universal law—which had special application to the English: 'The history of England is emphatically the history of progress'. The achievements of the Victorians in social and legislative reforms, in intellectual and material advancement, which have played so great a part in shaping the democratized society of today, have left their mark not only on England, but in some degree on Western and Westernized civilization everywhere. The Victorian Age, wrote Christopher Dawson, 'was a great revolutionary age—an age in which Britain did more to change the world than she has ever done before or since'.

Victorian aspirations were generous, far-reaching, idealistic, noble; but, paradoxically, Victorians often did the right things for the wrong reasons and the wrong things for the right reasons. They made their mistakes, foolish or terrible, and with their successes they left to succeeding generations a legacy of many social and spiritual problems which they had found too baffling to be able to solve. They have been called 'giants with a limp', and lame giants the Victorians may well have been, but, limp and all, their strides were still the strides of giants.

SELECTED BIBLIOGRAPHY

It was thought convenient to divide the bibliography into sections corresponding to the various sections of the book; hence the repetition of certain works which were quoted from or consulted in varying contexts. The bibliography lists the principal works which have been consulted, but for reasons of space many works from which information has been gleaned have been omitted.

Other material consulted but not listed in detail includes: *The Dictionary of National Biography**, *Hansard**, *The Times**, *The Daily Telegraph*, *The Illustrated London News*, the *Illustrated Weekly News*, the *Sphere* and other newspapers and periodicals for the period, including *The Athenaeum**, *The Edinburgh Review**, the *Fortnightly Review**, the *Quarterly Review**, the *Westminster Review**, the *Spectator* and a number of medical publications, for the years appropriate to the various sections of the book.

An asterisk against a title indicates that the work or publication is the source of a quotation used in the main text.

PART ONE: VICTORIA AND HER TIMES

I Victorianism

ACTON, William, Dr
Prostitution, considered in its Moral, Social Aspects, in London and other large Garrison Towns. J. Churchill, 1857; 2nd edn. 1870.
Functions and disorders of the reproductive organs. J. Churchill, 1857.

ARNOLD, Thomas, Dr
Sermons. 1829–34, 1844–45.

BANKS, Joseph A. and Olive
Feminism and Family Planning in Victorian England. Liverpool University Press, 1964.

BEALES, H. L.
Ideas and Beliefs of the Victorians (Victorian Ideas of Sex). Sylvan Press, 1948.

BLACKWELL, Elizabeth, Dr
Counsel to Parents on the Moral Education of the Children. Hurst Smyth & Son, 1878.
The Moral Education of the Young in relation to Sex. Hatchards, 1879.
The Human Element in Sex. J. & A. Churchill, 1884.

BRIGGS, Asa
The Age of Improvement. (*The History of England*, Vol. 8). Longmans, 1959.

BROWN, Horatio F.
Life of John Addington Symonds (compiled from his papers and correspondence, quoting passages from unpublished autobiography), 2 vols. J. C. Nimmo, 1895.

CECIL, Lady Gwendolyn (Gascoyne)
Life of Robert, Third Marquis of Salisbury, 3 vols. Hodder & Stoughton, 1931–2

CHESTERTON, Gilbert Keith
Essays. See Pearson, Hesketh.

CLARK, G. Kitson
The Making of Victorian England (Ford Lectures, 1962). Methuen, 1962.

CLOUGH, Arthur Hugh
Poems and Prose Remains. Macmillan, 1869.

DUNN, Waldo Hilary
James Anthony Froude: A Biography. Clarendon Press, 1961.

ELLIS, Sarah, Mrs
The Daughters of England. 1845.

FROUDE, James Anthony
**Shadows of the Clouds* (Tales by Zeta [pseudon.]). 1847.
**The Nemesis of Fate*. J. Chapman, 1849.
**Autobiography*. See Dunn, Waldo H.

GLOVER, Edward
**Ideas and Beliefs of the Victorians* (Victorian Ideas of Sex). Sylvan Press, 1948.

GOSSE, Edmund
**Father and Son*. Heinemann, 1907.

GROSSKURTH, Phyllis
**John Addington Symonds: a biography*. Longmans, 1964.

HALEVY, Elie
**History of the English People in the Nineteenth Century, 1815–1895*, 6 vols. Ernest Benn, 1929–51.

HAMMOND, J. L. and Barbara
The Village Labourer. Longmans, 1912.
The Town Labourer. Longmans, 1913.
The Age of the Chartists. Longmans, 1930.

HARE, Augustus
**The Story of My Life*. Geo. Allen, 1896.

HOOD, Edwin Paxton
**The Age and its Architects: Ten Chapters on the English People in Relation to the Time*. 1852.

HOUGHTON, Walter, E.
**The Victorian Frame of Mind 1830–70*. Yale University Press, 1957.

HOUSE, Arthur Humphrey
**All in Due Time*. Rupert Hart-Davis, 1955.

HUGHES, Thomas
**Tom Brown's School Days*. 1856.

HUXLEY, Thomas Henry
**Collected Essays* ('Agnosticism'). 1889.

INGLIS, C. K.
**Churches and the Working Classes in Victorian England*. Heinemann, 1963.

JOWETT, Benjamin
**Essays and Reviews* ('On the Interpretation of Scripture'). 1860.

KINGSLEY, Charles, Revd.
Alton Locke, Tailor and Poet: an autobiography. 1850.
**Westminster Sermons* (No. 26; 'God and Mammon', 1874). Macmillan, 1890.
Charles Kingsley: His Letters and Memories of his Life, edited by his wife, 2 vols. H. S. King, 1877.

KIPLING, Rudyard
**Stalky and Co.* Macmillan 1899; (sixteenth reprint 1947).
**Something of Myself.* Macmillan, 1937.
**Recessional*
*The Times, 1897: in *The Five Nations*, Methuen, 1903.

KNOWLTON, Charles
Fruits of Philosophy. 1841. Reprinted from the American edition by F. Watson, London.

MACAULAY, Thomas Babington, Lord
*'Sir James Mackintosh' (1835), in *Critical and Historical Essays Contributed to the Edinburgh Review*, 3 vols. Longmans, 1843.

MAYHEW, Henry
**London Labour and the London Poor*, 4 vols. 1851–62.

MILL, John Stuart
The Subjection of Women (1869). Longmans, 1906.

MILLER, Joseph Hillis
The Disappearance of God: Five Nineteenth-century Writers. Belknap Press of Harvard University Press, 1963.

MOORE, Theophilus
**Marriage Customs and Modes of Courtship.* 1814, 1820.

PALMERSTON, Lord (Henry John Temple, Viscount)
*Speeches (1847–64). To be found in *Hansard.*

PETRIE, Charles Alexander, Sir
The Victorians. Eyre & Spottiswoode, 1940.

PLACE, Francis
Illustration and Proofs of the Principles of Population. 1822. (New edition by Norman E. Hines, with letters on birth control, critical and textual notes. G. Allen & Unwin, 1930.

PORTER, George Richardson
**Progress of the Nation* (Preface). C. Knight, 1851.

RELIGIOUS TRACT SOCIETY
**Domestic Life, or Hints for Daily Use.* 1841.

RUSKIN, John
**Sesame and Lilies: 'Of Queens and Gardens'.* Smith Elder, 1865.

RUSSELL, Bertrand
Ideas and Beliefs of the Victorians. (Introduction). Sylvan Press, 1949.

SEWELL, Sarah Ann, Mrs
**Woman and the times we live in.* 2nd edn., 1869.

SMITH, Adam
The Wealth of Nations (*An Inquiry into the Nature and Causes of . . .*) 1776.

SMYTH, Charles, Canon
*'The Evangelical Discipline' in *Ideas and Beliefs of the Victorians.* Sylvan Press, 1949.

SOMERVELL, D. C.
English Thought in the Nineteenth Century. Methuen, 1929.

STEAD, William Thomas
'A Maiden Tribute in Modern Babylon', in the *Pall Mall Gazette*, 1885.
The Armstrong Case. H. Vickers, 1885.
My First Imprisonment. E. Marlborough, 1886.

STRACHEY, Lytton
**Eminent Victorians.* Chatto & Windus, 1918.
Queen Victoria. Chatto & Windus, 1921.

SYMONDS, John Addington (the younger)
**Autobiography* (see Brown, Grosskurth)

TENNYSON, Alfred, Lord
**In Memoriam* (1850)
**Idylls of the King* (1859–85)

THACKERAY, William Makepeace
Vanity Fair (1847–48)
**Letters and Private Papers.* Edited by Gordon N. Ray. Vol. II: 1841–51. Oxford University Press, 1945.

TREVELYAN, George Macaulay
**Ideas and Beliefs of the Victorians* (Introduction). Sylvan Press, 1949.

TROLLOPE, Anthony
An Autobiography, 2 vols. Blackwood, 1883.

VIZETELLY, Ernest Alfred
Emile Zola, Novelist and Reformer. John Lane, 1904.

WALKER, Alexander.
**Woman Physiologically considered as to Mind, Morals, Marriage, Matrimonial Slavery and Divorce.* 2nd edn., 1840.

WEBB, Beatrice
**My Apprenticeship.* Longmans, 1926.

WEBER, Max

Die protestantische Ethik und der Geist des Kapitalismus. 1904–5. Translated by Talcott Parsons, as *The Protestant Ethic and the Spirit of Capitalism.* G. Allen & Unwin, 1930.

WILBERFORCE, William

A Practical View of Christianity. 1797.

WILLEY, Basil

**Nineteenth Century Studies.* Chatto & Windus, 1949.

YOUNG, G. M.

**Victorian England: Portrait of an Age.* 2nd edn., Oxford U.P., 1953.

II Victoria

ANDREN, Georg

Parlamentarism och partier in England 1846–52. Uppsala University, 1929.

BAGEHOT, Walter

**The English Constitution.* H. S. King, 1872.

BOLITHO, Hector

Albert the Good (with correspondence of the Prince Consort). Cobden Sanderson, 1932.

Albert, Prince Consort. Max Parrish, 1964.

BOLITHO, Hector (ed.)

The Prince Consort and His Brother: 200 new letters. Cobden Sanderson, 1934.

**Further Letters of Queen Victoria.* Macmillan, 1938.

BROWNING, Robert

Poetical Works. Edited by the author. Chapman & Hall, 1863; new edition, reprinted, John Murray, 1951.

COMBE, Andrew, Dr

The Management of Infancy, physiological and moral. 10th edn., revised, edited, and with preface, by Sir James Clark; Maclachlan & Stewart, 1860.

CORTI, Egon Caesar, Count

The English Empress. Cassell, 1957.

CREEVEY, Thomas

**The Creevey Papers: a selection from the correspondence and diaries.* Edited by the Rt Hon. Sir Herbert Maxwell, Bart. John Murray, 1903.

CRESTON, Dormer

**The Youthful Queen Victoria.* Macmillan, 1952.

DICEY, Albert Venn

Lectures on the Relation between Law and Public Opinion in England in the 19th Century. Macmillan, 1905.

FREDERICK, EMPRESS (Victoria, Princess Royal and Crown Princess of Prussia, German Empress).

Letters of the Empress Frederick. Edited by Sir Frederick Ponsonby. Macmillan, 1928

FULFORD, Roger

The Prince Consort. Macmillan 1949.

**Queen Victoria*. W. Collins, 1951.

GLADSTONE, William

A Chapter of Autobiography. John Murray, 1868.

Gleanings of Past Years, 8 vols. John Murray, 1878–97.

GREVILLE, Charles Cavendish Fulke

**The Greville Memoirs, 1817–60*. Edited by Henry Reeve, 8 vols. (1875–87).

Edited by Lytton Strachey and Roger Fulford, 8 vols. (1938).

Edited by Roger Fulford (Macmillan, 1963).

GUEDALLA, Sir Philip,

**The Queen and Mr Gladstone: a selection from their correspondence*. Edited, with commentary. Hodder & Stoughton, 1933.

HAGBERG, Knut Hjalmar

Victoria Drottning av England. Stockholm, 1947.

HARDIE, Frank M.

**The Political Influence of Queen Victoria*. Oxford U.P., 1935; reprint, Frank Cass, 1962.

LEE, Sir Sidney,

**Queen Victoria: a biography*. Smith Elder, 1902.

**King Edward VII: a biography*, 2 vols. Macmillan, 1925–27.

LONGFORD, Elizabeth

**Victoria R. I.* Weidenfeld & Nicholson, 1964.

MAGNUS, Sir Philip,

**Gladstone: a biography*. John Murray, 1963.

**King Edward VII: a biography*. John Murray, 1964.

MARTIN, Sir Theodore,

Life of H.R.H. the Prince Consort, 5 vols. Smith Elder, 1876–80.

**Queen Victoria as I Knew Her*. Blackwood, 1908.

PONSONBY, Arthur (Lord Ponsonby of Shulbrede)

**Henry Ponsonby: his life from his letters*. Macmillan 1942.

PONSONBY, Sir Frederick, (ed.) (later Lord Sysonby)
Letters of the Empress Frederick. Macmillan 1928.

PONSONBY, Frederick (Lord Sysonby)
Recollections of Three Reigns. Eyre & Spottiswoode, 1951.

STRACHEY, Lytton
**Eminent Victorians*. Chatto & Windus, 1918.
**Queen Victoria*. Chatto & Windus, 1921.

VICTORIA, Queen
**The Letters of Queen Victoria: A Selection from Her Majesty's Correspondence*: First Series 1837–61, edited by A. C. Benson and Viscount Esher, 3 vols. (1907). Second Series, 1862–85, edited by G. E. Buckle, 3 vols. (1926). Third Series, 1886–1901, edited by G. E. Buckle, 3 vols. (1930). Published by John Murray.
**The Girlhood of Queen Victoria: A Selection from Her Majesty's Diaries between the years 1832 and 1840*. Edited by Viscount Esher. John Murray, 1912.
**Queen Victoria's Early Letters 1821–61*. Edited by John Raymond. First published 1907; Batsford, 1963.
**Leaves from a Journal: A Record of the Visit of the Emperor of the French to the Queen and of the Visit of The Queen and H.R.H. The Prince Consort to The Emperor of the French, 1856* (privately circulated, 1880). Edited by Raymond Mortimer: Andrè Deutsch, 1961.
**Leaves from a Journal of Our Life in the Highlands*. Edited by A. Helps. Smith Elder, 1868.
More Leaves from a Journal of Our Life in the Highlands. Smith Elder, 1884.
*Further Letters of Queen Victoria from the Archives of the House of *Brandenburg-Prussia*. Edited by Hector Bolitho. Thornton Butterworth, 1938.
**Dearest Child, Letters between Queen Victoria and the Princess Royal, 1858–61, a selection from the Kronberg Archives*. Evans Bros, 1964.
Dearest Mama, Letters between Queen Victoria and the Crown Princess of Prussia, 1861–1864. Evans Bros, 1968.

PART II: THE TREND OF IDEAS

I: The Basis of Utilitarianism

BENTHAM, Jeremy
**Works*, 11 vols. Published under the superintendence of his executor John Bowring, 1838–43. Vols I, II, III, IV, IX, XI.

DICEY, Albert Venn
**Lectures on the Relation between Law and Public Opinion in England during the Nineteenth Century*. Macmillan, 1905.

MILL, James
Elements of Political Economy. 1821–2.
Essays on: Government, Jurisprudence, Liberty of the Press, Education, Prison and Prison Discipline, Colonies, Law of Nations. Reprinted from the Supplement to the Fifth Edition of the *Encyclopedia Britannica* 1816–23 (reprinted 1828).

MILL, John Stuart
Autobiography. Edited by Helen Taylor, 1873.

MYRDAL, Gunnar
The Political Element in the Development of Economic Theory. Routledge & Kegan Paul, 1953.

II: *Questions of Government*

BAGEHOT, Walter
Biographical Studies. Longmans, 1881.

BARKER, Sir Ernest
Political Thought in England from 1848 to 1914. 2nd edn, Thornton Butterworth, 1930.

BARNES, Donald Grove
George III and William Pitt, 1783–1806. Stanford University Press, 1939; Oxford U.P.

BRIGHT, John
Speeches on Questions of Public Policy. Macmillan, 1868.

BROUGHAM, Henry Peter, Baron Brougham and Vaux
Speeches of Lord Brougham upon questions relating to Public Rights, Duties and Interests. A. & C. Black, 1938.

BUTLER, Sir James Ramsay Montagu
The Passing of the Great Reform Bill. Longmans, 1914; reprint, Frank Cass, 1964.

CHEVRILLON, André
Sydney Smith et la renaissance des idées liberales en Angleterre au XIXe siècle. Paris, 1894.

COBBETT, William
Rural Rides. William Cobbett, 1830; new edition, Reeves & Turner, 1885.

COBDEN, Richard
England, Ireland and America. 1865.
Speeches on Questions of Public Policy. Edited by John Bright and Thorold Rogers. Macmillan, 1870.

DARWIN, Charles
The Life and Letters of Charles Darwin, with an autobiographical chapter, 3 vols. Edited by his son, Francis Darwin. John Murray, 1887.

GLADSTONE, William Ewart
**Speeches and Public Addresses 1886–1891*, 2 vols. John Murray, 1892–94.
**The Irish Question*. John Murray, 1886.

GROTE, George
**The Minor Works of George Grote*. Edited by Professor Alexander Bain. John Murray, 1873.

LOWE, Robert, Viscount Sherbrooke
**Speeches and Letters on Reform*. 1867.

MACAULAY, Thomas Babington, Lord
**Critical and Historical Essays*, 3 vols. Longmans, 1843.

MILL, John Stuart
**Principles of Political Economy*, 2 vols. 1848.
**Utilitarianism* (1861). Reprinted from *Frazer's Magazine*.
**Representative Government*. 1861.
**On Liberty*, 1859.

MORLEY, John, Viscount
**On Compromise*. Chapman & Hall, 1874. (Edition of 1886 has note on the Doctrine of Liberty.)

SMITH, Sydney, Revd.
**Sermons, 1830–1857. The New Reign: The Duties of Queen Victoria: A Sermon Preached at the Cathedral of St Paul's by the Revd. Sydney Smith*. 1837.
**Essays, Social and Political: The Ballot*. Ward Lock, 1877.

TREVELYAN, George Macaulay
Lord Grey of the Reform Bill: being the life of Charles, the second Earl Grey. Longmans, 1920; reprint 1952.

WELLINGTON, Arthur Wellesley, Duke of
**Speech on the second reading of the Reform Bill* (1831). In *Hansard*.

III: Evolution of an Empire

BARING, Evelyn (Lord Cromer)
**Ancient and Modern Imperialism*. John Murray, 1910.

BEVERIDGE, Albert Jeremiah, Senator
**The Meaning of the Times and other speeches* (1908). The Bobbs-Merill Company, Indianapolis, 1908.

BLACHFORD, Lord (Frederic Rogers)
Letters. 1896.

BUCKLE, Henry Thomas
History of Civilization in England, 2 vols. J. W. Parker, 1857, 1861.

BURKE, Edmund, Rt. Hon.
**Speech on Conciliation with America*. J. Dodsley, 1775.

CABABE, Michael (ed.)
*'Introduction' to third posthumous edition of Jevons's *The State in Relation to Labour*. Macmillan, 1894.

COBDEN, Richard
**Speeches on Questions of Public Policy*. Edited by John Bright and Thorold Rogers. Macmillan, 1870.

COLE, George Douglas Howard
British Working Class Politics 1832–1914. Routledge & Kegan Paul, 1941.

CRAMB, J. A.
**Reflections on the Origins and Destiny of Imperial Britain*. Macmillan, 1900.

DARWIN, Charles
The Origin of Species by means of Natural Selection. John Murray, 1859.
The Descent of Man. John Murray, 1871.
**Life and Letters*. Edited by Francis Darwin. John Murray, 1887.

DILKE, Sir Charles
**Greater Britain*. Macmillan, 1868.

ENGELS, Friedrich
The Condition of the Working Classes in England in 1884, with preface written in 1892. Translated by F. K. Wischnewetzky. Sonnenschein, 1892.

FROUDE, James Anthony
**Oceana, or England and her Colonies*. Longmans, 1886.

GREEN, Thomas Hill
**Liberal Legislation and Freedom of Contract* (Lecture, 1880). Slatter & Rose, Oxford, 1881.
**Principles of Political Obligation*. Longmans, 1895.

HALEVY, Elie
**A History of the English People in the Nineteenth Century*, 5 vols. T. Fisher Unwin, Ernest Benn, 1921–34.

HEADLAM, Cecil
The Milner Papers. Cassell, 1931–33.

HEKSCHER, Gunnar Edvard
Parlamentarism och Demokrati i England. Stockholm, 1937.
Brittiska Imperiet. Stockholm, 1939.

HOBBES, Thomas
Leviathan. Andrew Crooke, London, 1651.

HOBHOUSE, Leonard Trelawny
Democracy and Reaction. T. Fisher Unwin, 1904.

HUXLEY, Thomas Henry
**Evolution and Ethics* (Romanes Lecture, 1893). Macmillan.

JEVONS, William Stanley
**Trades Societies, their objects and policy.* 1868.
**Methods of Social Reform.* Edited by H. A. Jevons. Macmillan, 1883.
**The State in Relation to Labour.* Macmillan; 1st edn 1881; 2nd edn 1882; 3rd (posthumous) edn 1894.

JOHNSTON, Alix (ed.)
The Life and Letters of Sir Harry Hamilton Johnston. Jonathan Cape, 1929.

JOHNSTON, Sir Harry Hamilton
**The Black Man's Part in the War.* Simpkin Marshall, 1917.
The Gay-Dombeys, a novel, with preface by H. G. Wells. Chatto & Windus, 1919.
**The Backward Peoples and our relations with them.* 1920.
**The Story of My Life.* Chatto & Windus, 1923.

KEYNES, John Maynard (Lord Keynes)
**The End of Laissez-Faire.* Hogarth Press, 1926.

KIDD, Benjamin
**Social Evolution.* Macmillan, 1894.
**The Control of the Tropics.* Macmillan, 1898.

KIPLING, Rudyard
**The Seven Seas.* Methuen, 1896.
**The Five Nations.* Methuen, 1903.

KNAPLUND,
The British Empire 1815–1839. Hamish Hamilton, 1942.
Gladstone and Britain's Imperial Policy. G. Allen & Unwin, 1927.

KROPOTKIN, Prince Peter
Mutual Aid: A Factor of Evolution. Heinemann, 1900.

LAMBTON, John George (Earl of Durham)
**Report and Despatches on British North America.* 1839.

LECKY, William Edward Hartpole, Rt. Hon.
**Rationalism in Europe,* 2 vols. Watts, 1910.

LENIN, Vladimir Ilitch Ulianov
**Imperialism as the Highest State of Capitalism,* V: Imperialist War (1917). Foreign Languages Publishing House, Moscow, 1947.

LOCKE, John
Works of John Locke: 'Two Treatises on Government' (1689–90). J. Churchill and S. Manship, London, 1714.

LUGARD, Lord (Frederick John Dealtry, 1st Baron Lugard)
The Dual Mandate in British Tropical Africa. Blackwood, 1922; 4th edn 1929.

MACAULAY, Thomas Babington, Lord
**Miscellaneous Writings and Speeches.* Longmans, 1871.
**Reviews and Essays.* Longmans, 1874, 1875.

MACKAY, Thomas (ed.)
**A Plea for Liberty.* John Murray, 1891.

MAINE, Sir Henry James Sumner
**Popular Government: Four Essays.* John Murray, 1885.

MALLOCK, William Hurrell
The New Republic. Chatto & Windus, 1877; new edn 1899.

MALTHUS, Thomas Robert
Essay on the Principle of Population. J. Johnson, London, 1798; 2nd edn, enlarged and altered, 1803.

MARCET, Jane, Mrs (*née* Haldimand)
**Conversations on Political Economy.* Longman, Hurst, 1816.

MARSHALL, Alfred
Principles of Economics. Macmillan, 1890.

MARTINEAU, Harriet
Autobiography, 3 vols. 1877.
**Illustrations of Political Economy*, 9 vols. Charles Fox, London, 1832–34.

MARX, Karl
Das Kapital (1867–94). Translation from 3rd German edn by S. Moore and E. Aveling, and edited by Friedrich Engels; published by Swann, Sonnenschein, London, 1896.

MILL, John Stuart
**On Liberty.* 1859.
**The Subjection of Women.* 1869.

MILLIN, Sarah Gertrude
**Cecil Rhodes, a biography.* Chatto & Windus, 1933.

MILNER, Alfred, Lord
**England in Egypt.* Edward Arnold, 1892; 12th edn 1915. (See Headlarn).

MURRAY, Robert Henry
Studies in the English Social and Political Thinkers. Robert Heffer & Sons, Cambridge, 1929.

NEHRU, Jawāhir-lal
Toward Freedom. 1941.
**The Discovery of India.* Meridian Books, 1946, 1951, 1956.

OLIVER, Roland
The Missionary Factor in East Africa. Longmans, 1952.
**Sir Harry Johnston and the Scramble for Africa.* Chatto & Windus, 1956.

PEARSON, Karl
**National Life from the Viewpoint of Science.* 1900.

READE, William Winwood
**Savage Africa.* Smith Elder, 1863.
**The Maryrdom of Man.* 1872. Trübner, 4th edn, 1877. Watts, 1934.

RICARDO, David
**Principles of Political Economy and Taxation.* 1817; new edn 1871.
The Works of David Ricardo. John Murray, 1852.

RITCHIE, David George
Darwinism and Politics. Swann, Sonnenschein, 1869.
**Natural Rights.* Muirhead Library of Philosophy, Sonnenschein, 1895.

RONALDSHAY, Earl of
The Life of Lord Curzon. 1928.

SEELEY, Sir John Robert
**The Expansion of England.* Macmillan, 1883.

SENIOR, Nassau William
**Historical and Philosophical Essays.* 1865.

SHRIDHARANI, Krishnalal
**My India.* Gollancz, 1942.

SIDGWICK, Henry
**Principles of Political Economy.* Macmillan, 1883.
**The Elements of Politics.* Macmillan, 1891.

SMITH, Adam
**An Enquiry into the Nature and Cause of the Wealth of Nations* (1776–1778). A. Strahan and T. Cadell, 5th edn, 1879.

SMITH, Sydney, Revd
Works, 4 vols. Longmans, 1839–40
**Sermon, The New Reign: Duties of Queen Victoria.* 1837.

SOMERVELL, David Churchill
English Thought in the Nineteenth Century. Methuen, 1929.

SPENCER, Herbert
**The Proper Sphere of Government*. W. Brittain, 1843.
**The Man versus the State*. Williams and Norgate, 1884; reprint by Watts (Thinkers Library), 1940.

TENNYSON, Hallam
**Alfred, Lord Tennyson: a memoir by his son*. Macmillan, 1897.

TOCQUEVILLE, Alexis Charles Henri Clérel de
**De la Démocratie en Amérique*. 1835 (English translation, *Democracy in America*, 1835).

WELLINGTON, Arthur Wellesley, Duke of
**Speeches*, 2 vols. 1854.

WILLIAMS, Basil
**Cecil Rhodes*. Constable, 1938.
The Selborne Memorandum (Introduction). Humphrey Milford, Oxford, 1925.

PART III: OF MEN AND DEEDS

I: *Statesmen and Social Leaders*

ADAMS, William Wheen Scovell
**Edwardian Heritage: a study in British History 1901–1906*. F Muller, 1949.
**Edwardian Portraits*. F. Muller, 1957.

BALFOUR, Arthur James, Earl of
**A Defence of Philosophic Doubt*. 1879.
**Chapters of Autobiography*. Edited by Mrs Blanche Dugdale. Cassell, 1930.

BASSET, Tilney
Gladstone to His Wife. Methuen, 1936.

BATTISCOMBE, Georgina
Mrs Gladstone: The Portrait of a Marriage. Constable, 1956.

BENSON, E. F.
**As We Were: A Victorian Peep-Show*. Longmans, 1930.

BLAKE, Robert (Lord Blake)
**Disraeli*. Eyre & Spottiswoode, 1966.

BLUNT, Wilfrid Scawen
My Diaries, 1888–1914, being a personal narrative of events. M. Secker, 1919–20.

BRIGGS, Asa
Victorian People. Odhams, 1954; Penguin, 1965.

CECIL, Gwendolyn, Lady (Gascoigne)
**The Life of Robert, Marquis of Salisbury*, 4 vols. Hodder & Stoughton, 1921–32.

CECIL, Robert (Marquis of Salisbury)
**Historical and Biographical Essays*, 2 vols. (Reprinted from the *Quarterly Review*) John Murray, 1905. (Essay on Castlereagh, in Vol. II.)

CHILSTON, Viscount
W. H. Smith. Routledge & Kegan Paul, 1965.

CHURCHILL, Sir Winston Spencer
**Lord Randolph Churchill*. Macmillan, 1906; Odhams, 1952.

CLARKE, Sir Edward George
**Gordon-Cumming vs. Wilson and others: Speeches for the plaintiff*. John Murray, 1891.
**The Story of My Life*. John Murray, 1918.

COMBARIEU, Abel
**Sept ans à l'Elysée avec le président Emile Loubet*. Hachette, Paris, 1932.

CORNWALLIS-WEST, Mrs (Lady Randolph Churchill)
The Reminiscences of Lady Randolph Churchill. Edward Arnold, 1908.

CUST, Lionel, Sir
King Edward VII and His Court: Some Recollections. John Murray, 1930.

DEACON, Richard
**The Private Life of Mr Gladstone*. F. Muller, 1965.

DISRAELI, Benjamin (Earl of Beaconsfield)
Vivian Grey. Published anonymously. Colbourn, 1826–27.
The Young Duke, 3 vols. Geburn & Bentley, 1831.
Vindication of the English Constitution in a letter to a noble and learned Lord. Saunders and Otley, 1835.
Henrietta Temple, 2 vols. Colburn, 1837.
Sybil, or The Two Nations, 3 vols. Colburn, 1845.
The Revolutionary Epick, 2 vols. Moxon, 1834.
Lord George Bentinck: A Political Biography. Colburn, 1852; Longmans, 8th edn, revised, 1872.
Mr Disraeli to Colonel Rathborne (Letters on the annexation of Oudh etc.). 1858.
**Lord Beaconfield's Letters, 1830–1852*. Cassell, 1887, reprinted 1928.
**The Letters of Disraeli to Lady Bradford and Lady Chesterfield*, 2 vols. Edited by the Marquis of Zetland. Ernest Benn, 1929.

Letters from Benjamin Disraeli to Frances Anne, Marchioness of Londonderry, 1837–1861. Edited with an introduction by the Marchioness of Londonderry. Macmillan, 1938.

DUGDALE, Blanche E. C., Mrs
Arthur James Balfour: First Earl of Balfour, K.G., O.M., F.R.S. Cassel, 1936.

ERVINE, St John
Parnell. Ernest Benn, 1925

ESHER, Reginald Brett, Viscount
**Letters and Journals*, 4 vols. Nicholas & Watson, 1939.

FRERE, J. A.
The British Monarchy at Home. Anthony Gibbs & Phillips, 1963.

GLADSTONE, Herbert, Viscount
**Thirty Years After*. Macmillan, 1928.

GLADSTONE, William Ewart
A Chapter of Autobiography. John Murray, 1868.
Juventus Mundi: The Gods and Men of the Heroic Age. Macmillan, 1869.
The Bulgarian Horrors and the Question of the East. John Murray, 1876.
Gleanings of Past Years, 8 vols. John Murray, 1879–97.
The Irish Question. John Murray, 1886.
**Speeches and Public Addresses, 1886–91*, 2 vols. John Murray, 1892–94.

GUEDALLA, Sir Philip
Bonnet and Shawl. Hodder & Stoughton, 1928.
**The Queen and Mr Gladstone*. Hodder & Stoughton, 1933.

HAMILTON, George, Lord
Parliamentary Reminiscences and Reflections, 2 vols. John Murray, 1916–22.

HAMSUN, Knut
**Mysterier* (1892). (English translation by Arthur B. Chater: Knopf, New York, 1927)

HARDIE, Frank
**The Political Influence of Queen Victoria*. Oxford U.P. 1933; reprint, Frank Cass, 1963.

HARRISON, Henry
Parnell Vindicated: The Lifting of the Veil. Constable, 1931.

JAMES, Robert Rhodes
**Lord Randolph Churchill*. Weidenfeld & Nicholson, 1959.
**Lord Rosebery*. Weidenfeld & Nicholson, 1963.

JENKINS, Roy
Sir Charles Dilke: A Victorian Tragedy. W. Collins, 1958.

JERMAN, B. R.
**The Young Disraeli*. Oxford U.P., 1960.

JOYCE, James
**A Portrait of the Artist as a Young Man*. 1915.

KEPPEL, Sonia
Edwardian Daughter. Hamish Hamilton, 1958.

LANGTRY, Lillie Emilie Charlotte (Lady de Bathe)
The Days I Knew. Hutchinson, 1925.

LEE, Sir Sidney
**Life of King Edward VII*, 2 vols. Macmillan, (1925, 1927).

LESLIE, Anita
**The Fabulous Leonard Jerome*. Hutchinson, 1961.

LAYARD, Sir Austen Henry
**Autobiography and Letters*. John Murray, 1903.

MAGNUS, Sir Philip
**Gladstone*. John Murray, 1954.
**Edward VII*. John Murray, 1964.

MANN, Thomas
**Tonio Kröger*. Translated by H. T. Lowe-Porter. M. Secker, 1928.

MARTIN, Sir Theodore
Life of H.R.H. The Prince Consort, 5 vols. John Murray, 1879.
A Life of Lord Lyndhurst. John Murray, 1883.

MAURICE, M. A. J., General, and ARTHUR, George, Sir
The Life of Lord Wolseley.

MAUROIS, André
La Vie de Disraeli. Paris, 1927.

MINNEY, R. J.
**The Edwardian Age*. Cassell, 1964.

MONYPENNY, W. F. and BUCKLE, G. E.
**The Life of Benjamin Disraeli, Earl of Beaconsfield*, 6 vols. John Murray, 1910–20.

MORLEY, John
**Life of W. E. Gladstone*, 3 vols. Macmillan, 1903.

NAPIER, Elma
**Youth is a Blunder*. Jonathan Cape, 1948.

O'BRIEN, R. Barry
**Life of Charles Stewart Parnell*, 2 vols. Smith Elder, 1899.

O'BRIEN, Donat Conor Cruise
Parnell and his Party, 1880–1890. Clarendon Press, 1957.

O'SHEA, Katherine (later Parnell)
**Charles Stewart Parnell: his love story and political life*, 2 vols. Cassell, 1914.

PEARSON, Hesketh
Labby: The Life of Henry Labouchere. Hamish Hamilton, 1936.
**Dizzy*. Methuen, 1951.

PONSONBY, Arthur (Lord Ponsonby of Shulbrede)
**Henry Ponsonby: his life from his letters*. Macmillan, 1952.

PONSONBY, Sir Frederick (Lord Sysonby)
**Recollections of Three Reigns*. Eyre & Spottiswoode, 1951.

RAYMOND, E. T.
**Mr Balfour*. W. Collins, 1920.
The Man of Promise: Lord Rosebery. T. Fisher Unwin, 1923.

ROSEBERY, Archibald Philip Primrose, Earl of
**Lord Randolph Churchill*. A. L. Humphreys, 1906.

STEAD, William T.
The Discrowned King of Ireland (C. S. Parnell) with some opinions of the press on the O'Shea Divorce Case (1899). Office of Review of Reviews.

SYKES, Christopher
**Four Studies in Loyalty*. W. Collins, 1946.

THE TIMES
*The Baccarat Scandal Trial Proceedings (May-June 1891).

WATSON, Alfred E. T.
**King Edward as a Sportsman*. Longmans, 1911.

WORTHAM, Hugh Evelyn
**The Delightful Profession: Edward VII, a study in Kingship*. Jonathan Cape, 1931.

YEATS, William Butler
*'Parnell's Funeral', in *Collected Poems*. Macmillan, 1963.
*'Gather Round Me, Parnellites' in *Last Poems*, 1936–39, Macmillan, 1963.

YOUNG, Kenneth
**Arthur James Balfour*. G. Bell & Sons, 1963.

II: *Prophets, Reformers and Poets*

ADAMS, Henry
**The Education of Henry Adams*. Houghton Mifflin, New York, 1918; Constable, London, 1919.

ALLINGHAM, Helen (*née* Paterson) (ed.)
William Allingham: A Diary. Macmillan, 1907.
Letters to William Allingham. Longmans, 1911.

ANGELI, Helen Rossetti
Pre-Raphaelite Twilight: the story of George Augustus Howell. Richards Press, 1954.

ANNAN, Noël (Lord Annan)
*'Kipling's Place in the History of Ideas', *Victorian Studies*, Vol. III. 1959–60. (Reprinted in *Kipling's Mind and Art*, ed. Andrew Rutherford. Oliver & Boyd, 1964).

AUDEN, Wystan Hugh (ed.)
**Tennyson: An Introduction and a Selection*. Phoenix House, 1946.

AUSTIN, Alfred
Autobiography. Macmillan, 1911.

BENSON, E. F.
**As We Were: A Victorian Peep-Show*. Longmans, 1930.

BLISS, Trudy (ed.)
Jane Welsh Carlyle: a new selection of her letters. Gollancz, 1950.
Thomas Carlyle: Letters to his wife. Selected by Trudy Bliss. Gollancz, 1953.

BODELSEN, Carl A. G.
Aspects of Kipling's Art. Manchester U.P., 1964.

BORCHARD, Ruth
John Stuart Mill, the Man. Watts, 1957.

BRIGGS, Asa
**The Age of Improvement*. Longmans, 1960.

CARLYLE, Jane Welsh
**Letters and Memorials of Jane Welsh Carlyle*. Prepared for the press by Thomas Carlyle. Edited by J. A. Froude. Longmans, 1883.
New Letters and Memorials of Jane Welsh Carlyle. Annotated by Thomas Carlyle and edited by Alexander Carlyle. John Lane, 1903.
**Letters to Her Family*. Edited by Leonard Huxley. John Murray, 1924.
**Early Letters*. Edited by D. G. Ritchie. Longmans, 1889.
Jane Welsh Carlyle: a new selection of her letters. Selected by Trudy Bliss. Gollancz, 1950.

CARLYLE, Thomas
The French Revolution. James Fraser, 1837.
Sartor Resartus. 1833–34, 1838. 2nd edn, James Fraser, 1841.
Heroes and Hero Worship. James Fraser, 1841.
**Past and Present*. Chapman & Hall, 1843.

Latter Day Pamphlets. Chapman & Hall, 1850.
Occasional Discourse on the Nigger Question. Thomas Bosworth, 1853.
The History of Friedrich II, commonly called Frederick the Great, 6 vols. Chapman & Hall, 1858–65.
Inaugural Address at Edinburgh University, 1866. Edmonston & Douglas, London, 1866.
Shooting Niagara. Chapman & Hall, 1867.
Letters of Thomas Carlyle. Edited by C. E. Norton. Macmillan, 1886.
Reminiscences. Edited by Charles Eliot Norton. 2 vols. Macmillan, 1887.
Letters of Thomas Carlyle to His Youngest Sister. Edited by Charles Townsend Copeland. Chapman & Hall, 1899.
New Letters of Thomas Carlyle. Edited by Alexander Carlyle. John Lane, 1904.
Love Letters of Thomas Carlyle and Jane Welsh. Edited by Alexander Carlyle. John Lane, 1909.
Thomas Carlyle: Letters to his Wife. Selected by Trudy Bliss. Gollancz, 1950.

CARRINGTON, Charles
Rudyard Kipling: His Life and Work. Macmillan, 1955.

ELIOT, Thomas Stearns
*Introductory essay to *A Choice of Kipling's Verse*. Faber & Faber, 1944.

ELLIS, Havelock
Studies in the Psychology of Sex, Vol. I, III: *Love* and *Pain*. 3rd revised edn, 1910.

FICHTE, Johann Gottlieb
Addresses to the German Nation. 1807–8.

FROUDE, James Anthony
Thomas Carlyle: a history of his life in London. 1885.
My Relations with Carlyle. Longmans, 1903.

FULLER, Jean Overton
Swinburne: a critical biography. Chatto & Windus, 1968.

GAUNT, William
The Pre-Raphaelite Tragedy. Jonathan Cape, 1942. (Published by the Reprint Society, 1943, as *The Pre-Raphaelite Dream*.)

GOSSE, Sir Edmund
The Life of Algernon Charles Swinburne. Macmillan. 1917.
The Letters of Algernon Charles Swinburne, 2 vols. (With Thomas J. Wise.) Macmillan, 1918.

HAGBERG, Knut Hjalmar
**Personalities and Powers*. Translated by Elizabeth Sprigge and Claude Napier. John Lane, 1930.

HAKE, Thomas, and RICKETT, A. Compton
The Life of Watts-Dunton. 1961.

HALLIDAY, James L.
Mr Carlyle My Patient: a psychosomatic biography. Heinemann Medical, 1949.

HARE, Humphrey
**Swinburne: a biographical approach*. H. F. & G. Witherby, 1949.

HAYEK
**John Stuart Mill and Harriet Taylor: Their Friendship and Subsequent Marriage*. University of Chicago Press, 1951.

HOLME, Thea
The Carlyles at Home. Oxford U.P., 1965.

JACKSON, Holbrook
The Eighteen Nineties. Grant Richards, 1913.
Dreamers of Dreams. Faber & Faber, 1948.

JAMES, William, Admiral Sir
**The Order of Release*. John Murray, 1947.

JOHNSON, R. Brimley
**Tennyson and His Poetry*. Harrap, 1913.

KIPLING, Rudyard
Stalky and Co.

LAFOURCADE, Georges
**La Jeunesse de Swinburne*, 2 vols. Oxford U.P., 1928.
**Swinburne: a literary biography*. Oxford U.P., 1932.

LAWRENCE, David Herbert
**The Plumed Serpent*. 1926. Penguin, 1950.

LEITH, Mary C. J.
The Boyhood of Algernon Charles Swinburne. Chatto & Windus, 1917.

LEON, Derrick
Ruskin, the Great Victorian. Routledge & Kegan Paul, 1949.

MANN, Thomas
Three Essays ('Frederick the Great' and 'The Grand Coalition'). 1932.

MAUROIS, André
**Proust and Ruskin* (Essays and Studies by Members of the English Association). 1932.

MAYFIELD, John S.
**Swinburne's Boo*. Goetz, Washington, 1954.

MILL, John Stuart
Autobiography (without alterations or omissions). Columbia U.P., 1924.
The Subjection of Women. 1869.

NICOLSON, Sir Harold
**Tennyson: Aspects of His Life, Character and Poetry*. Constable, 1923.
Swinburne. Macmillan, 1926.

NOYES, Alfred
**Tennyson* (1932)

ORWELL, George
**Rudyard Kipling* (essay, 1942, reprinted in *Dickens, Dali and Others*, 1946; and in *Kipling's Mind and Art*, essays by various authors, edited by Andrew Rutherford. Oliver & Boyd, 1964.)

PACKE, St John
**The Life of John Stuart Mill*. Secker & Warburg, 1954.

PAPPE, Helmut Otto
**John Stuart Mill and the Harriet Taylor Myth*. Melbourne U.P., 1960.

PITT, Valerie
**Tennyson Laureate*. Barrie & Rockliff, 1962.

POPE-HENNESSY, James
**Monkton Milnes: The Years of Promise*. Constable, 1951.

PRAZ, Mario
The Romantic Agony. Translated by Angus Davidson. Oxford U.P., 1933.

QUENNELL, Peter
John Ruskin: Portrait of a Prophet. W. Collins, 1949.

RICHARDSON, Joanna
**The Pre-Eminent Victorian: a study of Tennyson*. Jonathan Cape, 1962.

RUSKIN, John
Lectures on the Political Economy of Art. 1858.
**Unto This Last*. Smith Elder, 1862.
**Sesame and Lilies*. Smith Elder, 1865.
**Ethics of the Dust*. Smith Elder, 1866.
**Time and Tide*. Smith Elder, 1867.
**The Queen of the Air*. Smith Elder, 1869.
**Fors Clavigera*, 4 vols. G. Allen, 1871–87.
**Munera Pulveris*. 1872.
**The Crown of Wild Olive*. Smith Elder, 1873.

*General Statement explaining the nature and purposes of St George's Guild. 1882.
*Praeterita, 6 vols. G. Allen, 1887–89.

SHANKS, Edward B.
*Introduction to *Selected Poems of Swinburne*. Macmillan, 1950.
**Rudyard Kipling: a study in literature and political ideas*. Macmillan, 1940.

SITWELL, Edith
Introduction to *Swinburne: A Selection*. Weidenfeld & Nicholson, 1960.

SPENDER, Stephen
**Tennyson: An Introduction and a Selection*. 1946.

SWINBURNE, Algernon Charles
**Collected Poems*, 5 vols. Chatto & Windus, 1917.

SYMONS, Julian
**Thomas Carlyle: The Life and Ideas of a Prophet*. Hamish Hamilton, 1952.

TENNYSON, Alfred, Lord
**Complete Works*, 9 vols. Edited by Hallam Tennyson. 1907–8.
**Poems*. Oxford Standard Authors, Oxford U.P., 1953.

TENNYSON, Hallam, 2nd Lord
**Alfred, Lord Tennyson: A Memoir*. Macmillan, 1897.
Tennyson and His Friends. Macmillan, 1911.

THOMAS, Edward
Algernon Charles Swinburne: A Critical Study. M. Secker, 1912.

TRILLING, Lionel
**The Liberal Imagination: Essays on Literature and Society*. 1951. (Reprinted in *Kipling's Mind and Art*, edited by Andrew Rutherford. Oliver & Boyd, 1964.)

WATTS-DUNTON, Clara
**The Home Life of Algernon Charles Swinburne*. Philpot, 1922.

YOUNG, G. M.
**Victorian England: Portrait of an Age*. 1936; Oxford U.P. 1953, 1957.

III: *Warriors and Wars*

AMERY, Leopold S. (ed.)
The Times History of the War (in South Africa), 6 vols. 1900–9.

BADEN-POWELL, Olave, Lady (with Hillcourt, William)
**Baden-Powell: The Two Lives of a Hero*. Heinemann, 1964.

BLUNT, Wilfrid Scawen
My Diaries, 1888–1914. S. Swift.

BRACKENBURY, Sir Henry
The Ashanti War. Blackwood, 1874.

CHAILLÉ-LONG, Charles
**My Life in Four Continents*, 2 vols. Hutchinson, 1912.
**The Three Prophets: Chinese Gordon, Mohammed-Ahmed-El Mahdi, Arabi Pasha*. D. Appleton, New York, 1884.

CHURCHILL, Sir Winston S.
**The River War*. Longmans, 1899.
Great Contemporaries. Thornton Butterworth, 1937.

CROMER, Evelyn Baring, Earl
Modern Egypt. Macmillan, 1908.
Political and Literary Essays. 1908–11.
**Ancient and Modern Imperialism*. John Murray, 1910.

EDEL, Leon
**Henry James: a biography*. Vol. I: *The Untried Years* (1953); Vol. II: *The Conquest of London*. (1962) Rupert Hart-Davis.

ELTON, Godfrey, Lord
**General Gordon*. W. Collins, 1954.

GARDNER, Brian
Mafeking: A Victorian Legend. Cassell, 1969.

GARVIN, J. L.
Life of Joseph Chamberlain. Macmillan, 1932–34.

GORDON, Charles George, General
**Gordon's Letters from the Crimea, the Danube and Armenia 1854–88*. Edited by D. C. Boulger. 1884.
**Reflections in Palestine*. 1884.
**General Gordon's Private Diary of His Exploits in China*. Amplified by S. Mossman. 1885.
**Last Journals*. Edited by Augusta M. Gordon. 1885.
**Letters of General Charles George Gordon to His Sister Augusta, Edited by the latter*. 1888.
**General Gordon's Khartoum Diary*. Edited by Godfrey Elton. 1961.

HEADLAM, Cecil (ed.)
The Milner Papers: South Africa 1897–1899, 1899–1905. Edited by C. Headlam. Cassell, 1931, 1933.

JAMES, David
Lord Roberts. Foreword by the Rt Hon. L. S. Amery. Hollis & Carter, 1954.

JÜNGER, Ernst
In Stahlgewittern. Berlin, 1922. English translation, *The Storm of Steel*, by Basil Creighton. Chatto & Windus, 1929.

LEHMANN, Joseph
All Sir Garnet. Jonathan Cape, 1964.

MAGNUS, Sir Philip
Kitchener: Portrait of an Imperialist. John Murray, 1958.

MARLOWE, John
Mission to Khartoum: The Apotheosis of General Gordon. Gollancz, 1969.

MAURICE, F., Maj.-Gen. Sir and ARTHUR, George, Sir
Life of Lord Wolseley. 1924.

MILNER, Alfred, Viscount (see Headlam)

MORLEY, John
Life of W. E. Gladstone, 3 vols. Macmillan, 1903.

NUTTING, Anthony
Gordon, Martyr and Misfit. Constable, 1966.

READE, Winwood
The Story of the Ashantee Campaign. Smith Elder, 1874.

RONALDSHAY, Earl of
The Life of Lord Curzon. Hodder & Stoughton, 1928.

SAKI (H. J. Munro)
The Complete Short Stories of Saki (Reginald's Peace Poem). John Lane, The Bodley Head, 1930.

SLATIN, Rudolf Karl von (Slatin Pasha)
Fire and Sword in the Sudan 1879–1895. 1896.

STRACHEY, Lytton
Eminent Victorians ('The End of General Gordon'). Chatto & Windus, 1918.

SYMONS, Julian
Buller Campaign. Cresset Press, 1963.
England's Pride: The Story of the Gordon Relief Expedition. Hamish Hamilton, 1965.

WOLSELEY, Garnet Joseph, Field-Marshal Viscount
A Narrative of the War with China in 1860. 1862.
The Soldier's Pocket Book: Field Manoeuvres. 1872.
Marley Castle, a novel (published as edited by Sir Garnet Wolseley). 1877.

*_The Story of a Soldier's Life_, 2 vols. Constable, 1903–4.
*_The Letters of Lord and Lady Wolseley_. Edited by Sir George Arthur. 1922.

IV: _Mistakes and Miscalculations_

ADYE, General Sir John Miller
A Review of the Crimean War. 1860.
Recollections of a Military Life. Smith Elder, 1895.

AMERY, Leopold S. (see The Times)

AZAD, Maulana Abul Kalam (see Sen, Surendra Nath).

BALL, Charles
History of the Indian Mutiny, 2 vols. 1858–59.

BLUNT, Wilfrid Scawen
My Diaries 1888–1914. M. Secker, 1919.

CLOETE, Stuart
African Portraits: Kruger, Rhodes, Lobengula. W. Collins, 1946.

DOUGLAS, Sir George, and RAMSAY, Sir George Dalhousie, (eds.)
The Panmure Papers. 1908.

DUBERLY, Frances Isabella (Mrs Henry Duberly)
Journal kept during the Russian War: from the departure of the army from England in April 1854 to the fall of Sebastopol. Longmans, 1855.
Campaigning Experiences in Rajpootana and Central India, during the suppression of the Mutiny 1857–1858. Longmans, 1859.

EDWARDES, Michael
British India 1772–1947. Sidgwick & Jackson, 1967.

FORREST, George Sir William
*_History of the Indian Mutiny_, 3 vols. Blackwood, 1904–12.

FORSTER, E. M.
A passage to India. Edward Arnold, 1924.

GARVIN, J. L.
Life of Joseph Chamberlain. Macmillan, 1932–34.

GREVILLE, Charles Cavendish Fulke
*_The Greville Memoirs 1814–1860_, 8 vols. Edited by Roger Fulford and Lytton Strachey. Macmillan, 1938.

GROSS, Felix
Rhodes of Africa. Cassell, 1956.

HAMMANN, Otto
*_Um den Kaiser: Erinnerungen 1906–9_. Berlin, 1919.

HEADLAM, Cecil (ed.)
The Milner Papers. 1931, 1933.

HIBBERT, Christopher
The Destruction of Lord Raglan: A Tragedy of the Crimean War 1854–55. Longmans, 1961.

HILTON, Major-General, Richard
**The Indian Mutiny: a centenary history*. Hollis & Carter, 1957.

KAYE, Sir William, and Colonel G. B., MALLESON
A History of the Sepoy War in India, 6 vols. 1864–80.

KINGLAKE, Alexander William
**The Invasion of the Crimea*, 9 vols. Blackwood, 1877–88.

LUNDGREN, Egron Sellif
**En Målares Anteckningar*, Vol. II. Stockholm, 1873, 1874.

MAULE, Fox (Lord Panmure, later Earl of Dalhousie)
The Panmure Papers, 2 vols. Edited by Sir George Douglas and Sir George Dalhousie Ramsay. Hodder & Stoughton.

MAUROIS, André
La vie de Cecil Rhodes. Paris, 1953.

NEHRU, Jawāhir-lal
**The Discovery of India*. Meridian Books, 1956.

PAGET, George, General Lord
**The Light Cavalry Brigade in the Crimea*. John Murray, 1881.

PAKENHAM, Elizabeth
Jameson's Raid. Weidenfeld & Nicholson, 1960.

PEMBERTON, Baring W.
**Battles of the Crimean War*. B. T. Batsford, 1962.

RHODES, Cecil
Political Speeches and Addresses. Edited by Vindex. Chapman & Hall, 1900.
**Last Will and Testament of Cecil Rhodes*. Edited by William T. Stead. 1902.

ROBERTS, Brian
**Cecil Rhodes and the Princess*. Hamish Hamilton, 1969.

ROBERTS, Frederick Sleigh, Earl
**Letters written during the Indian Mutiny*. Macmillan, 1924.
**Forty-one Years in India*, 2 vols. Bentley & Son, 1897.

RUSSELL, William Howard
The War in the Crimea. Routledge, 1855.
The British Expedition to the Crimea. Routledge, 1858.

My Diary in India in the year 1858–59 (with illustrations by Egron Lundgren), 2 vols. Routledge, 1860.
My Indian Mutiny Diary. Edited by Michael Edwardes. (Re-issue 1959.)
The Great War with Russia. Routledge, 1895.

SELBORNE, Roundell Palmer, Earl of
Memorials, 4 vols. Macmillan, 1896–98.

SEN, Surendra Nath
Eighteen Fifty Seven. With a Foreword by Maulana Abul Kalam Azad, on the Indian Mutiny. Delhi, 1957.

VAN DER POEL, Jean
The Jameson Raid. Oxford U.P., Capetown, 1951.

WILLIAMS, Basil
Cecil Rhodes. Constable, 1968

WOODHAM-SMITH, Cecil
Florence Nightingale. Constable, 1950.
The Reason Why. Constable, 1953.

ADDENDA

Part Three, I

MARTIN, Ralph G.
Lady Randolph Churchill: A Biography 1854–1895. Cassell, 1969.

Part Three, II

Effie in Venice. John Murray, 1965.
Millais and the Ruskins. John Murray, 1967.

Part Three, III
WOLSELEY, Lord—PRESTON, Adrian (Ed)
In Relief of Gordon: Lord Wolseley's Campaign Journal of the Khartoum Relief Expedition 1884–1885, Edited by Adrian Preston. Hutchinson, 1967.

INDEX

Works mentioned in the text and listed in the bibliography have been omitted from the index. The corresponding text and bibliography page numbers, which follow index entries of authors' names, are marked with an asterisk.

ERRATA and CORRIGENDA

P. 38, paragraphs 3, 5, line 1, for Maurice read: Hare—see Index, Hare
P. 268, para. 1, 1.31, for Thomas read: James—see Index, Maguire
P. 290, para. 4, 1.2 for whe read: who
P. 293, para. 1, 1.7, read: £500, and with a loan . . .
P. 303, para. 2, 1.10, for Sara read: Sarah—see Index, Disraeli
P. 319, para. 2, 1.10, para. 4, 1.2, for Cranbourne read: Cranborne; para. 3, 1.1, for Georgina read: Georgiana—see Index, Salisbury
P. 383, para. 1, 1.1, for James D. read: James L.—see Index, Halliday
P. 455, para. 5, 1.5, read: Wolseley had met; para. 5, 1.8, read: Winchester, Va.
P. 510, para. 3, 1.9, for Captain H. F. B. Maxse read: Captain H. B. F. Maxse—see Index, Maxse
P. 540, para. 2, 1.12, for Alveston read: Allerton—see Index, Jackson